Delinquency and Social Policy

DELINQUENCY
AND SOCIAL
POLICY

EDITED BY
PAUL LERMAN

PRAEGER PUBLISHERS
New York · Washington · London

PRAEGER PUBLISHERS
111 Fourth Avenue, New York, N.Y. 10003, U.S.A.
5, Cromwell Place, London S.W.7, England

Published in the United States of America in 1970
by Praeger Publishers, Inc.

© 1970 by Paul Lerman

Library of Congress Catalog Card Number: 72–101667

Printed in the United States of America

To
Carla, Nina, and Joshua

Contents

Part Six   Social Planning and the Prevention and
                Control of Delinquency

Preface

There are three important rationales for creating this book: educational, practical, and theoretical. Educationally, there is a need at both the undergraduate and the graduate level for a collection of papers dealing extensively with major policy issues of the prevention and control of delinquency, including: the sociolegal boundaries of delinquency definitions, the control and guidance of police discretion in interpreting and enforcing the definitional boundaries, fairness and justice in the administration of juvenile justice, the search for humane and effective correctional practices, and the limits on agency cooperation and social planning in controlling and preventing youthful misbehavior.

Although many books have dealt with some of these issues, they have done so in only fragmentary fashion. Furthermore, policy issues have been treated as a matter of less importance than theories of the genesis and handling of delinquency. This is a dubious educational practice, for theories must be tested in the arena of social affairs to determine their power to describe and explain. Educating students to think critically and creatively about the implications and potential consequences of operationalizing ideas is certainly a worthwhile goal. To accomplish it, there have to be new materials, and perhaps redesigned courses, that focus on the consequences of making real and hypothetical decisions.

In pursuing this perspective, it is not necessary to downgrade the traditional emphasis on theories. Policy and theory are potentially of equal importance. If the theory is valid and the policy implications can be put into practice, then the two can stand roughly in the same relationship as science and technology, or basic and applied research.

This book, we have said, also reflects a practical perspective, related to the increasing public concern with "law and order." For the first time in America's history, federal funds are flowing to localities to support ongoing programs of social control; in the past, only "demonstration" projects were supported. If this money is to be used wisely—not just politically—then the best thinking of social scientists and interested professional groups should play some part in the disposition of funds. In a democratic society, where citizen participation is at least tolerated if not appreciated, source material should exist that will help citizens to fill the roles of critics and advocates. The recent publications of the President's Commission on Law Enforcement

and the Administration of Justice contain useful policy material and discussions, but these are scattered throughout a number of Task Force reports,
and it is unreasonable to expect the nonspecialist to read all of them. This
book, therefore, includes sizable excerpts from the Task Force reports on
juvenile delinquency, the police, corrections, the courts, crime assessment, and
science and technology. But social scientists, professionals, citizens, and students also need an intellectual framework to guide their policy-oriented readings, and the Commission's reports by themselves are too uneven to supply it.
This book attempts to fill that need—not just for the Commission selections,
but for other readings as well.

The third reason for creating this book is theoretical, but it is not unrelated
to academic and practical interests. For many years, our efforts to deal with
the problem of delinquency have been governed by an ideology that places
primary emphasis on changing the offender, the offender's family, or the offender's community. There has been a reluctance to ask whether the existing
societal mechanisms for responding to youthful deviance have also contributed
to the problem. For example, if we merely narrowed our traditional legal
definitions of delinquency, it is possible that police-youth relations would be
less strained in ghetto communities, that fewer boys would have police records
to follow them for their rest of their lives, that court dockets would be
reduced, and that fewer correctional facilities would have to be built to
accommodate population growth. Obviously, this approach would not solve
the problem, but it could yield many benefits that might outweigh our current
costs—and perhaps make the problem more manageable in the process. If
paying attention to the societal response to youthful deviance can have these
rewards, then it seems wise—as well as useful and educationally sound—to
pursue this line of theoretical analysis.

Our intellectual frame of reference involves a number of assumptions. First,
since the ways in which society responds to deviant activities can influence
the effectiveness of control efforts, it appears quite plausible that societal
responses are part of the delinquency problem. As a corollary assumption, it
is evident that a society could choose among a variety of organized responses
to the problem of youthful misconduct, but that some of the choices might
exacerbate the problem rather than alleviate it. Unfair enforcement of statutes,
for example, could call into question the moral legitimacy of the laws as well
as of the enforcement authority, thereby making it likely that statute violations would occur more frequently. In brief, there are always social options
open to define and deal with social problems, and the ones we choose become
part of the problem.

This theoretical perspective is not entirely new, as many readers will
recognize. However, it has rarely been pursued in a systematic fashion for all
the major decisional responses to delinquency. Some of the readings utilize
this framework (often implicitly), but their analyses usually refer to just the
laws, or the police, or the courts, or corrections, rather than to all of these
decisional units. If we can understand the kinds of decisions that are made
by these critical subsystems of the institution of social control, then we can
discern the interrelationship of consequences—whether unintended or intended. Becoming aware of outcomes that do not appear to be socially beneficial may sensitize critics to search for new guidelines for social policy. These
new options, of course, would also have to be examined for their impact on
youth and on related subsystems of the institution of social control.

Some readers may disapprove of our application of the term "social policy" to the decisional directions of the current societal responses to juvenile delinquency. They might argue that many decisions are not the product of rational deliberation—that many decisions do not consider alternatives with respect to goal attainment, and that decisions are not usually based on an assessment of the costs and benefits that might accrue with existing or projected resources. Technically, these criticisms might be right, but they are unreasonable. At the level of everyday practice, there are preferred styles or orientations toward making decisions concerning juveniles. It is our contention that the current operating criteria for decision-making in local communities and on the state and federal levels constitute the policy guidelines of today's efforts at delinquency control and prevention. Whether we can theoretically understand the existence and social impact of these operational guidelines is of crucial importance, for we shall make little progress in improving our ability to deal with this social problem unless we can make sense out of what we are now doing and accomplishing.

In general, then, this is a book with a distinct purpose, focus, and theoretical orientation. Most of the selections were chosen because they distinguish and describe current decision-making criteria and processes, as well as the influences on and consequences of those decisions. Few of them are included in other readers, in part because of the unique focus of this collection. Wherever possible, the selections reflect empirical studies and so impart the flavor of policy-oriented research.

It is possible that readers will approach the selections quite differently from the way in which the editor intended, but if their attention has been directed toward examining the decisions of societal agents and organizations, a communality of interests will have been attained. There may be broader dividends as well: We might learn more about the hidden values of dominant sectors of our society. Further, we might learn that a useful way to study *any* social problem is to focus on shared definitions and on our practices regarding that which is bothersome. Striving for multiple rewards is an attractive policy—in designing a collection of readings as in other pursuits.

PAUL LERMAN

Teaneck, New Jersey
September, 1970

PART ONE

THE MEANING AND SCOPE
OF DELINQUENCY

Introduction

Definitions of delinquency usually make reference to legal statutes that proscribe certain types of behavior for specific age ranges of boys and girls. Although this strictly legalistic approach is a useful starting point, it can mask the social processes and nonlegal standards that accompany the application of legal categories. In practice, delinquency is a socio-legal label symbolizing the application of many standards in a decision-making process that transforms youthful misbehavior into a legal category. It is exceedingly difficult to know what the label means unless the standards and the process of social transformation are adequately understood.

The first three readings in this section provide historical perspective on the types and range of standards that have been utilized in defining the misconduct of American youth. Three points in time have been selected: the paper by Powers (#1) describes the handling of youth by the criminal courts of early Massachusetts (1620-92); the excerpts from documents of the House of Refuge of New York (#2) indicate the standards of the early 1800's; the selection by Platt (#3) discusses the social invention of the legal category "delinquency" at the turn of the twentieth century.

These historical readings plus selection 4, which summarizes current legal criteria for proscribing youth behavior, make it evident that we are descendants of the Puritans, the refuge managers, and the child-savers. Depending on one's own standards, the parallels may be gratifying or disquieting. A close reading of these selections indicates that modern delinquency statutes and official practices are closely linked to earlier societal reactions to youthful misconduct. Throughout our history, we have tried, through the language of criminal law, to translate our moral likes and dislikes regarding youth into statutory proscriptions. Some of the specific items of disliked behavior have changed, but the willingness to impose a dominant group's conception of morality through coercive mechanisms has not changed appreciably in three hundred years.

There has also been a continuing tendency to classify as "criminal" or "delinquent" behavior that is peculiar to youth. Growing up in idleness or truanting from school are legal offenses of which only the young can be accused; only youth can be charged with acting "incorrigible" or ungovernable; only youth can be accused of displaying a "tendency" to be delinquent.

Even the rationale for labeling youthful misbehavior as illegal is not new. The managers of the House of Refuge praised themselves and their supporters for their beneficence in saving children; our generation relies on the expression of benign intentions to treat and rehabilitate.

There are similarities, too, in the fact that we use the law not only to define violations *per se,* but also as a socially legitimate excuse to accomplish other purposes. The eager reformers described by Platt were unabashedly frank in their use of the law to further their ends. Today, officials may agree on a common legal classification in order to obtain treatment of a child, and some legal scholars argue for maintaining broad legal statutes to ensure adequate protective and child-welfare services.

These historical continuities indicate that critical value dilemmas have been associated with our use of the delinquency label. On the one hand, there is a desire to protect the child from future harm; on the other hand, we are willing to expand our conception of criminality in order to extend that protection. A second dilemma involves our appreciation and toleration of differences versus the strong Puritan-oriented striving to enforce a specific ideal code of child-rearing or behavior. A third dilemma involves a desire to offer voluntary services to children and their families as opposed to a willingness to employ a coercive apparatus to deliver services that are not sought or accepted. These dilemmas are implicit in 3, 10, and 5, by Platt, Sheridan, and the President's Task Force on Juvenile Delinquency and Youth Crime.

If the American approach to a legal definition of misconduct has tended toward broadness, intolerance, and morality legislation, it has also been tempered by administrative discretion on the part of police, judges, and even citizens. Even in Puritan times, the courts took a youngster's age and circumstances into account in an attempt to soften the impact of the law on youth. This combination of virtually limitless scope and benevolent discretion persists today in every American community and is a central characteristic of the American meaning of delinquency.

Selection 5 describes the operation of discretionary decision-making as "pre-judicial dispositions" by the police and the courts. Although the police and the court intake workers are certainly involved in dispositional decisions concerning youth, it is important to realize that this quasi-judicial responsibility also entails other kinds of decision. For any given suspected infraction, decisions are made concerning whether and how official intervention should occur, and what the basis of the intervention ought to be. Deciding *whether* to intervene involves deciding whether an observed infraction is worth "noticing" or a complaint about an infraction worth considering. *How* to intervene involves the decision to act formally or informally by recording or not recording the youth's name and the infraction. *What* basis of intervention to use involves a determination concerning the legal charge used to classify the infraction and legitimate the intervention.

It is evident that these decisions sort youngsters into—or out of—the juvenile court system. By engaging in screening decisions as well as pre-judicial dispositions, police and court intake workers become the principal operational interpreters and definers of the laws pertaining to youth. It is their definitions that constitute the most important meaning of delinquency in a community. The critical importance of their labeling power can be readily understood by considering the facts disclosed in selection 5: about half of recorded police-youth encounters do not result in court appearances, and about half of the cases that reach the intake personnel of juvenile courts are not brought before a judge. This means that for every 100 suspected youth offenders, only 50 will be defined by the police as "delinquents," and of these only 25 will be defined in a court petition as "delinquents."

Of the two major defining groups, the police are more important. By their exercise of discretion they serve as the central gatekeepers for the juvenile court system. The studies cited by the President's Task Force provide evidence that whether policemen will exercise discretion in a benevolent manner may depend not only on their interpretation of the relative seriousness of the youth's behavior but also on how well the youngster can handle relationships with adult authority figures. Youngsters who fail this test may be defined as delinquents; those who possess adequate social skills may avoid becoming so labeled.

Another means of avoiding a delinquency definition is to enlist the aid of groups in providing an alternative definition for the same behavior. Currently a psychiatric label often serves as an acceptable alternative. While this aspect of the labeling process involves the cooperation of psychiatrists, social workers, and psychologists, selection 6, by Miller and Kenney, demonstrates that some professionals question this practice. The use of mental hospitals rather than courtrooms as a setting in which to decide moral questions concerning behavior is, of course, an issue in its own right; the conflict between mental health and legal values is discussed in Part III. Here we wish to demonstrate that police and court workers are not the only groups that shape the meaning and scope of delinquency definitions. The behavior of professionals and even of suspected offenders can influence the labeling process.

The idea that the process of assigning legal labels can be influenced by interest groups that advocate the application of their social standards has profound implications. For the youngster who is a candidate for a delinquency label, it means that his actions can be classified according to non-legal criteria; he can avoid the sanctions and social consequences associated with the legal categorization. On a theoretical level, it means that the balance of power among competing interest groups underlies the successful imposition of a special social definition; a variety of groups may agree that behavior is in a deviant direction, but they may offer competing social classifications to indicate how it should be treated. In a pluralistic society, the same action might be typed as "delinquent," "acting out," "sinful," "experimental identity-seeking," "precocious," or "a mistake." Acceptance of the legitimacy of a given legal or social classification indicates that the definition favored by one or a coalition of competing interest groups has been successfully imposed. In the case of youth assigned to mental hospitals for deviant actions, for example, it means that psychiatrically oriented interest groups have been successful in imposing *their* social definition of the behavioral situation. For social policy, the idea that legal definitions are subject to influence indicates that this is a potential target of change. This strategy and the associated readings are discussed later in this introduction.

Thus far three levels of meaning have been discussed in relation to the readings in this Part: legal criteria, competing social standards, and discretionary decision-making. A fourth level also warrants attention—the statistical meaning of delinquency. We have grown accustomed to accepting official counts of police arrests, or of recorded contacts, as the major indices of youth misbehavior. The readings raise serious doubts that this assumption is warranted for either social-policy or research purposes.

Selection 7, on the factors affecting the reporting of crime, indicates that official records refer to police behavior and victim behavior as well as to youthful behavior. To the extent that victims complain to the police, the statistical meaning of delinquency will refer to official rates that are subject to the victim's cooperativeness. If there are more cooperative victims, this may be reflected in a rise of official delinquency rates—with or without an increase in youthful misbehavior. The President's Commission suggests that there is more victim complaining now than in the past.

Police behavior is involved in delinquency statistics in two ways: by discretionary decisions and by reporting practices. Regarding the latter, selection 7 provides evidence that the increasing professionalization and upgrading of the police forces have led to more efficient and honest record-keeping. Better records can result in an apparent increase in the scope and volume of delinquency even when discretionary behavior *and* youth behavior have remained stable.

Wilson's study of eight communities (selection 9) indicates that the official rates of delinquency provide better indices of police decisions to record and arrest than of youthful misconduct. The differences recorded between the official rates of Albany, New York, and Oakland, California, are too great to support the contention that youth activity is being measured. Evidently statistics in the two communities vary largely because the operational definition of delinquency varies. What is tolerated or deemed inconsequential in Albany is defined as worthy of notice and illegal in Oakland. If the police of Albany began to act like the police of Oakland, there would be a tenfold increase or more in the rate of delinquency; the meaning as well as the recording could shift dramatically without a corresponding increase in actual misbehavior.

It is disturbing to realize that the definition of delinquency varies by time and place—that it is relative to community tolerance, official practices, bookkeeping efficiency and honesty, and victim cooperativeness. It is disturbing because it means that we do not have a reliable and valid basis for assessing incidence, prevalence, or shifts in the magnitude of the problem. The President's Task Force on Assessment attempted to cope with this issue, and their discussion and conclusions are included as selection 8. Evidently, the most satisfying recommendation that can be provided for stabilizing our statistical image of delinquency is to concentrate on the most serious offenses. The Task Force staff estimates that offenses that would be felonies if performed by adults are least likely to be overlooked by victims and the police and therefore most likely to be reported accurately. This is probably true, but the recommendation pertains to only a small fraction of the offenses that bring youth into contact with the police and courts. From a technical point of view, we are advised to discount—even be skeptical of—official reports dealing with juvenile status and petty offenses. This involves, of course, a restricted definition of delinquency.

Besides this technical argument for redefining delinquency, there are other reasons for changing the meaning and scope of the term. The President's Task Force on Delinquency, in a discussion of legislative standards, not included here, contends that juvenile-status offenses should not be defined as cause for juvenile-court jurisdiction and police arrest. The report argues that current treatment and protection efforts are relatively ineffective; therefore it might be wise to restrict the population of children that society must contend with to those who commit actual crimes. A similar recommendation is offered by Sheridan in selection 10. However, he proposes other grounds: the possibility that treatment efforts in institutions may criminalize youngsters who are not yet criminally inclined.

The redefinition of juvenile-status offenses as child-welfare problems could, of course, have important consequences for all subsystems dealing with children—the police, the courts, detention facilities, correctional institutions, public and private child-care-agencies, and even schools. For example, according to Sheridan, such a redefinition of official delinquency would eliminate 50 per cent of the children from detention facilities and about 40 per cent from state juvenile reformatories.

If local communities wished to provide assistance to youngsters with family problems (as evidenced by charges of "incorrigibility," "runaway," and "beyond the control of parents") and school problems (as evidenced by "truancy"), they would have to re-examine the entire network of services to children and families. Even relatively wealthy states such as New York appear to be unwilling to do this but, rather, play at reform by inventing a new category for delinquency without crime—"persons in need of supervision" (PINS)—and then treating these youngsters in the same detention facilities and institutions as "delinquents." In the absence of improved child-welfare services and innovative school programs, it may be more humane for states to cease their efforts to coercively "help" youth in need of supervision by stigmatizing their difficulties with parents and teachers as acts of "delinquency."

However persuasive the arguments for changing the American approach to legally defining delinquency may be to many, meaningful legislative proposals to narrow the scope of youthful illegal behavior have a dim prospect of gaining widespread acceptance in the near future. As the readings indicate, there is a lengthy historical tradition associated with broad and diffuse statutes. Legislative change would have to occur at a statewide level, where all the varied interest groups (secular and nonsecular) would contend in a highly visible manner. A more viable strategy might be to take advantage of the competing social standards associated with interest groups, as well as the long-cherished practice of exercising discretion in law enforcement and the administration of justice. It is conceivable that by expanding the rationale and alternatives for "pre-judicial" dispositions, the operational meaning and scope of delinquency could be administratively redefined. This approach is less visible and rather undramatic, but its potential for inducing social change should not be underestimated. Part II continues this line of reasoning in the discussion of the control and guidance of police discretion.

1. *Crime and Punishment in Early Massachusetts, 1620–1692* *

EDWIN POWERS

. . . THERE WAS NO AGE limitation on criminal responsibility excepting as specifically set forth in the laws. There is no evidence that the common-law rule exempting children under seven from punishment by the courts was ever adopted by the Bay Colony. We have mentioned the rule that children would receive "such allowances and dispensations . . . as religion and reason require," and our examination of available court records reveals no case where young children were harshly treated by the courts. In 1668 the General Court ordered that "in all criminal cases every person, younger as well as elders, shall be liable to answer to their owne persons, for such misdemeanours as they shall be accused of," although in civil cases all under twenty-one years of age had to be represented by "parents, masters, or guardians." We have also previously referred to the rule that all children had to be taught the capital laws. But as for the violation of certain specific criminal laws the General Court preferred to set a minimum age of responsibility in each case.

For example, for sodomy, a capital crime, children under fourteen were to be "severely punished" but not executed; for cursing and smiting parents, a capital crime, only those "above sixteen years old, and of sufficient understanding" could be put to death; for being stubborn or rebellious sons, a capital crime likewise, only those "of sufficient years and understanding (*viz.*) sixteen years of age" were liable; for arson, a capital crime, the law also applied only to those "of the age of sixteen years and upward"; for "denying the Scriptures to be the infallible word of God," again the minimum age was sixteen for those who were liable to the death penalty.

For all other capital laws, it might be reasonably assumed that there was no intent to hold young children criminally responsible. Although children under

* From *Crime and Punishment in Early Massachusetts,* by Edwin Powers, Boston, Mass.: Beacon Press, 1966, pp. 442–46, 528–29. Reprinted by permission of the Beacon Press, copyright © 1966 by Edwin Powers.

fifteen or sixteen might be accused of such crimes (as indeed some were accused of witchcraft), there is no evidence that anyone under the age of fifteen was executed in the Bay Colony.

No child under the age of discretion, which in this case was fourteen, could be punished by the constable for telling lies that were "pernicious to the Publick-weal," but their parents or masters were directed to "give them due correction . . . in the presence of some officer."

For profaning the Sabbath, the law applied only to those over the age of fourteen. Great responsibility was placed upon parents to see that their children conformed to the rigid Puritan code of conduct on the Sabbath. For example, if a child "above seaven years old (not that we approve younger Children in evil)" violated the Sabbath laws by playing or "uncivily walking in the Streets and Fields, travelling from Town to Town, going on Shipboard, frequenting Common Houses and other places to Drink, Sport or otherwise to mispend that precious time," the parents were liable to admonishment for the first offense, a fine for the second, and for the third the County Court could "augment punishment according to the merit of the Fact."

There were other laws, too, designed to keep children's behavior in line with Puritan standards, that did not set down any age limitation but presumably in such cases the intent was to govern all who were under the age of twenty-one.

Children and servants who became "rude, stubborn, and unruly" could be taken from their parents, after due warning, and placed for some years with Masters who would "force them to submit unto Government" until they were twenty-one, if boys, eighteen, if girls.

Magistrates could order that children and servants who behaved "disobediently and disorderly towards their Parents, Masters and Governours" be whipped but not by more than ten stripes for each offense, or they could bind them over to the next County Court.

The child or servant who stole fruit from another's orchard or took wood, clothes, or other objects from one's yard could be openly whipped if his parents or guardians would not pay the owners' treble damages. Public whipping of children under the age of fourteen was probably rare or possibly never occurred. Usually in the case of small children the parents were ordered to whip them privately in the home but in the presence of a court officer. A law of 1668 provided for the commitment of stubborn children or servants to a House of Correction.

Children born in New England, sons and daughters of the original planters and settlers, were frequently found lacking in those sterling qualities of godliness and devotion so characteristic of their parents. And when they were found remiss in their duties or delinquent in behavior, the blame usually could be attributed to the lack of proper religious training in the home. When the Indians struck in 1675 and devastated the Colony in the series of attacks, religious leaders immediately sought for reasons for God's anger.

What were these evils that provoked the Lord to such length? The General Court set down twelve "provoking evils" and provided appropriate remedies in each case.[1] Only three of the "evils" specifically concerned children and youths.

1. Many young people evidently found it difficult to sit quietly through the long, tedious Sabbath service, the General Court reporting that there was "much Disorder and Rudeness in Youth in many Congregations in time of the

worship of God, whereby Sin and Prophaneness is greatly increased." It was thereupon ordered that children and youth must sit together "in publick view" and that "some Grave and Sober Purson" be appointed to watch them and present the names of those found "Delinquent" to the next Magistrate or Court. For the first offense an admonition was in order, for the second a fine of five shillings, to be paid by their parents or governours, or a whipping by them or, if found "Incorrigible," they were to be whipt with ten stripes or sent to the House of Correction for three days.

2. There was existing at that time "a woful Breach of the Fifth Commandment . . . in Contempt of Authority, Civil, Ecclesiastical, and Domestical," an evil attributed chiefly to youths and servants who went out at night without permission "meeting with Corrupt Company," a practice "of a very perilous Nature, and the Root of much Disorder." First offenders were to be subject only to an admonition, but for all subsequent convictions one could have been fined (up to ten shillings) or whipped (not exceeding five stripes).

3. A practice had grown up, "a loose and sinful Custom," among the youths who, like youths today, wished to get away from the dull routine of family life and ride out into the country for a few drinks and a little fun now and then. The General Court found that "oft times Men and Women together" would ride from town to town "upon pretence of going to Lectures" but would instead "Drink and Revil in Ordinaries and Taverns, which is in itself Scandalous, and it is to be feared a notable means to debauch our Youth, and hazard the Chastity of such as are drawn forth thereunto." Unmarried persons who took such journeys "merely for their pleasure" would be considered "Riotous and Unsober persons, and of ill Behavior." Upon conviction they would be required to give sureties for good behavior in the sum of twenty pounds. Upon refusal to do so, they faced a prison sentence of ten days or a fine of forty shillings.

In the seventeenth century there was, of course, no delinquency-prevention program, but the authorities kept a vigilant eye on youth and placed heavy responsibilities on parents. They were required at least once a week to "Catechise their children and servants in the Grounds and Principles of Religion" and if they were unable to do so they were to teach them "some short Orthodox Catechisme without book" so that they would be able to pass a test to be given by the parents or any of the Selectmen.[2] Parents were also charged with the responsibility for bringing up their children "in some lawfull Calling, Labour or imployment, either in husbandry or some other trade, profitable for themselves and the Common-wealth, if they will not or cannot train them up in learning, to fit them to higher imployments."[3]

Parents could chastise their children for disobedience but a child "shall have free libertie to complaine to Authoritie for redresse" if parents "wilfullie and unreasonably deny any childe timely or convenient mariage, or shall exercise any unnaturall severitie towards them."[4] Parents could not with impunity neglect their children, for "neglectors of their families" were deemed to be "idle persons" by a 1668 law and were thus subject to commitment to the House of Correction.[5] Although the term "baby-sitter" is of modern origin, it was probably not customary to leave children alone at night, as the Urselton family of Ipswich discovered: "Frances Urselton and his wife were admonished for leaving their children alone in the night in a lonely house, far from neighbors, after having been warned of it. He was to be punished, if any danger came from it."[6]

. . . The Bay Colony did not adopt any crucial "test" of criminal responsibility, such as the so-called right-and-wrong test of modern times. It did, however, suggest "special allowances and dispensations" to children, idiots, and the mentally disturbed (or the "distracted persons," as they were called). It did not follow the common-law rule of exercising all children from criminal liability under the age of seven, nor did it propose any definition of "idiot." Nevertheless, in dealing with children, the courts exhibited a surprising degree of humane and kindly treatment toward the very young, usually referring the willful, unruly, or disobedient child to his parents for correction. Young children were not publicly whipped and, so far as available records reveal the judgments of the courts, probably no child under fifteen was executed. Great care was taken to see that children were properly brought up, knew the capital laws, learned their catechism, received an education and some vocational training, and did not "mispend" their time and their money in taverns where liquor was sold or violate the Sabbath laws in traveling about or engaging in sports or frivolous activities. Many of the criminal laws set a minimum age limit, usually fourteen or sixteen, excusing from punishment offenders below such limits. . . .

NOTES

ABBREVIATIONS USED IN NOTES

Col. Laws (1648): *The Book of the General Lawes and Libertyes Concerning the Inhabitants of the Massachusets,* printed according to order of the General Court, Cambridge, 1648, reprinted from the copy in the Henry E. Huntington Library, with an Introduction by Max Farrand (Cambridge: Harvard University Press, 1929).

Col. Laws (1660): *The Book of the General Lawes and Libertyes Concerning the Inhabitants of the Massachusets,* printed according to order of the General Court, Cambridge, 1660, reprinted, with supplements to 1672 and with the Body of Liberties of 1641, with introduction by William H. Whitmore, by order of the City Council (Boston, 1889).

Col. Laws (1672): *The General Laws and Liberties of the Massachusets Colony,* printed by order of the General Court, Cambridge, 1672, reprinted with supplements through 1686 with an introduction by William H. Whitmore, by order of the City Council (Boston, 1887).

Essex County Court: *Records and Files of the Quarterly Courts of Essex County, Massachusetts (1636–1683)* (published by The Essex Institute, Salem, Mass., 1911–1912, 8 volumes, George F. Dow, editor).

MCR: Massachusetts Colonial Records. *Records of the Governor and Company of the Massachusetts Bay in New England,* 6 volumes, (1628–1686), Dr. Nathaniel B. Shurtleff, editor (published by order of the General Court): from the Press of William White, Printer to the Commonwealth, Boston, 1853–1854.

[1] MCR, v. 5, pp. 59–63 (1675); Col. Laws (1672) pp. 233–37 (1675). The other nine "provoking evils" were: (1) neglect by the church to catechize the children and to inquire into "their Spiritual States"; (2) the "manifest Pride openly appearing amongst us in that long Hair like Womens Hair is worn by some men either their own, or others Hair made into Perewigs: And by some Women wearing Borders of Hair, and their Cutting, Curling, and Immodest laying out their Hair, which practice doth prevail and increase especially among the younger sort"; (3) "the evil or pride in Apparrel, both for Costliness in the poorer sort, and vain, new strange Fashions both in poor and rich, with naked Breasts and Arms . . . Superfluous Ribbons," etc.; (4) ". . . the open meetings of Quakers, whose Damnable Heresies, Abominable Idolatries, are hereby Promoted, Embraced and Practised to the Scandal of Re-

ligion, Hazard of Souls, and Provocation of Divine Jealusie against his People" (including evidently King Philip's war); (5) "much Prophaneness amongst us in persons turning their Backs upon the publick Worship before it is finished, and the Blessing pronounced"; (6) "the shameful and Scandalous Sin of Excessive drinking Tipling, and Company keeping in Taverns and Ordinaries"; (7) common swearing and cursing "in ordinary Communication, which is a Sin that grows amongst us"; (8) "the sin of Idleness (which is a Sin of Sodom) doth greatly increase"; (9) shopkeepers and merchants charging too much for their goods and "Mechanicks and Day Labourers" also guilty of that evil, a crime the Colonial people called "oppression."

[2] Col. Laws (1648) p. 11; (1660) p. 136; (1672) p. 26.
[3] *Ibid.*
[4] Body of Liberties (1641), Art. 83; Col. Laws (1648) p. 12; (1660) p. 137; (1672) p. 28.
[5] MCR, v. 4, pt. 2, p. 395 (1668).
[6] Essex County Court, v. 2, p. 247 (1660).

2. *The Founding of the New York House of Refuge**

SOCIETY FOR THE REFORMATION OF JUVENILE DELINQUENTS

FIFTH ANNUAL REPORT, &C. 1830

THE SOCIETY for the Reformation of Juvenile Delinquents, has now been in operation five years. Previously to its organization much pains were taken to explain to the public the necessity for such an institution, the principles upon which it was to be established, and the benefits it was expected to afford.

At each anniversary, the execution of the original design, and its favorable results, have been fully disclosed. In compliance with the expectations of the public, and the duty of the Managers, another report is now to be presented.

After having exhibited the usual financial and statistical accounts for the past year, and given assurances of the general prosperity and augmented usefulness of the establishment, it will be impossible to add any thing very new to former expositions. But as these may be forgotten, or unknown to many, it will not be improper, it is presumed, to notice, generally, with as little repetition as possible, the objects of the institution, its operation, and its effects. Such remarks will be offered as are suggested by the experience we have now had, or as grow out of circumstances connected with the institution.

There is a disposition in human nature, while present advantages are enjoyed, to forget the past.

* *Documents Relative to the House of Refuge,* Instituted by the Society for the Reformation of Juvenile Delinquents in the City of New York, in 1824, New York, N. Y.: Mahlon Day, 1832, pp. 184–87.

We shall not appreciate the usefulness of this establishment unless we remember what was the condition before this asylum was opened, of that class of the community which is its object.

In New York, as in every large city, there were a number of forsaken children, many of them orphans, and many who derived no protection from parents, who received no instruction from them but in wickedness and profanity, and no example but in the practice of vice and immorality. These destitute beings began life by resorting to dishonest means to maintain it and became criminal in their infancy. The law made no distinction between the minor, after a very immature age, and the adult offender; much less did it consider the education, the wants, or the temptations of the criminal. The nature of the punishment for the old and hardened sinner, and for the helpless, ignorant, starving child, was the same.—Not only was there no difference in the nature of the punishment inflicted on the old and the young, but the treatment of all while under accusation, or detained for trial, was similar. All were secluded in the same apartments. The inexperienced child was associated with the aged, and hardened criminal, under circumstances calculated to impart the contamination of bad society.

It often happened that young persons who were brought into this situation, were not accused of any crime, but were committed for no other reason than that they were vagrants; and they were vagrants only because they were houseless orphans, or were driven from their unprovided homes, by the cruelty or vices of their parents.

When the same walls enclosed old and young offenders, the consequences were such as must have been expected. From the moment a child was obnoxious to a criminal proceeding, he was lost. There could be no hope of saving him from destruction, if he were innocent, or of reforming him if he were guilty. His life was one of incessant transitions from crime to punishment, each offence more aggravated in its character, till he became a hardened villain, and ended in being a capital felon.

Benevolent men who had an opportunity of witnessing this deplorable condition of things, devised the House of Refuge as a means of alleviating, if not remedying, evils so disgraceful to humanity, and with which the savage might have reproached the boasted refinements of civilization. . . . We should not suffer the active zeal of such men in the organization of this charity to be forgotten, not only because the world owes them a large debt of gratitude, but because a remembrance of their zealous co-operation in its establishment, should subdue the hostility of some, who have endeavored to make it be believed that its principal means of support are diverted from a more legitimate appropriation of them. But the institution never has touched a cent to which there is any more lawful, more appropriate, or more conscientious claim. No one could be unfriendly to such a charity, or could desire to take from it the favor of the public or of the legislature, if he were acquainted with the great benefits it is daily affording to the community. Let the person who would question its utility, or benevolence, so far subdue his prejudices as to be induced to visit the House of Refuge. Let him see for himself within its walls, two hundred children enjoying health, comfort, and education. Let him turn to our records and learn what was the condition of these young persons before they were consigned to our care. Let him also learn how many have been redeemed and regenerated. Let him turn his thoughts back to the time when there was no refuge for the parentless, or the deserted, or [the] seduced child of poverty. Let him imagine these brought to the bars of our criminal courts, and tried, and condemned. Let him reflect on what was their subsequent treatment. Let his imagination follow them to their prison, and keep them in view till they were again turned into the streets to starve, or to steal.— But let him further imagine that the doors of the House of Refuge are opened, and the children he sees before him left to wander without protection or home: and if he has any thing of humanity in his composition, it could not but recoil from the consequences which he must see would ensue.

While we are adverting to the founders of this merciful charity, it is just to claim for them the credit of having been the first to establish an institution on the principles we have adopted. This, because we have called our building the House of Refuge, a name which has long been applied in Europe, is often denied. But the Society for the reformation of Juvenile Delinquents, is very different in its powers, and indeed in its objects, from any institution that existed previously to its incorporation, in this or any other country.

It is true that before our society was thought of, Houses of Refuge existed in England, and probably elsewhere. But these were either pure charities to receive and comfort destitute children, so long as they should be in want of mere penitentiaries for the punishment of such as were convicted of crime. There was no authority to detain a child who was not criminal, and all the power and control over one who was so, was prescribed by his sentence, and ceased when that expired, and he quitted the walls of the prison. No provision could be made for his protection during his non-age.

The legislature has very much enlarged the objects of our institution, and entrusted to its managers powers that have not heretofore been delegated. These are essential to its beneficient action, and mark the great difference between it and other institutions that previously existed, however similar they may be in name. If a child be found destitute—if abandoned by its parents— or suffered to lead a vicious or vagrant life; or if convicted of any crime, it may be sent to the House of Refuge. There is in no case any other sentence than that it shall "there be dealt with according to law." That is, it may if not released by some legal process, be there detained, if the managers should think it unfit to be sooner dischaged, until it arrives at age. Parents or guardians, from the time it is legally sentenced to the Refuge, lose all control of its person. When it is believed that a child is reformed, the managers have power, with its consent, to bind it as an apprentice, till the age of eighteen years, if a female, and if a boy till the age of twenty-one. It is these important features that mark the difference between our institution and all others that previously existed; and it is in this sense that we may say with truth, that the New York House of Refuge was the first of its kind ever established.

3. The Rise of the Child-Saving Movement *

ANTHONY M. PLATT

MATERNAL JUSTICE

. . . THE 1880's AND 1890's represented for many middle-class intellectuals and professionals a period of discovery of the "dim attics and damp cellars in poverty-stricken sections of populous towns" and of "innumerable haunts of misery throughout the land." [1] The city was suddenly discovered to be a place of scarcity, disease, neglect, ignorance, and "dangerous influences." Its slums were the "last resorts of the penniless and the criminal"; here humanity reached its lowest level of degradation and despair. [2]

The discovery of problems by "delinquent" youth was greatly influenced by the role of feminist reformers in the child-saving movement. It was widely agreed that it was a woman's business to be involved in regulating the welfare of children, for women were considered the "natural caretakers" of wayward children. Women's claim to the public care of children had some historical justification during the nineteenth century, and their role in child-rearing was considered paramount. Women were regarded as better teachers than men and were also more influential in child-training at home. The fact that public education also came more under the direction of women teachers in the schools increased the predominance of women in the raising of children. [3]

Child-saving was a predominantly feminist movement, and it was regarded even by antifeminists as female domain. The social circumstances behind this appreciation of maternalism were women's emancipation and the accompanying changes in the character of traditional family life. Educated middle-class women now had more leisure time but a limited choice of careers. Child-saving was a reputable task for women who were allowed to extend their housekeeping functions into the community without denying antifeminist stereotypes of woman's nature and place. "It is an added irony," writes Christopher Lasch in his study of American intellectualism,

> that the ideas about woman's nature to which some feminists still clung, in spite of their opposition to the enslavement of woman in the home, were these very clichés wihch had so long been used to keep her there. The assumption that women were morally purer than men, better capable of altruism and self-sacrifice, was the core of the myth of domesticity against which the feminists were in revolt. . . . [F]eminist and anti-feminist assumptions seemed curiously to coincide. [4]

Child-saving may be understood as a crusade that served symbolic and

* From Anthony M. Platt, "The Rise of the Child Saving Movement: A Study in Social Policy and Correctional Reform," *The Annals*, Vol. 381 (January, 1969), pp. 21–38. Reprinted by permission of the author.

status functions for native, middle-class Americans, particularly feminist groups. Middle-class women at the turn of the century experienced a complex and far-reaching status revolution. Their traditional functions were dramatically threatened by the weakening of domestic roles and the specialized rearrangement of family life.[5] One of the main forces behind the child-saving movement was a concern for the structure of family life and the proper socialization of young persons, since it was these concerns that had traditionally given purpose to a woman's life. Professional organizations—such as settlement houses, women's clubs, bar associations, and penal organizations—regarded child-saving as a problem of women's rights, whereas their opponents seized upon it as an opportunity to keep women in their proper place. Child-saving organizations had little or nothing to do with militant supporters of the suffragette movement. In fact, the new role of social worker was created by deference to antifeminist stereotypes of a "woman's place."

A Woman's Place

Feminist involvement in child-saving was endorsed by a variety of penal and professional organizations. Their participation was usually justified as an extension of their housekeeping functions so that they did not view themselves, nor were they regarded by others, as competitors for jobs usually performed by men. Proponents of the "new penology" insisted that reformatories should resemble home life, for institutions without women were likely to do more harm than good to inmates. According to G. E. Howe, the reformatory system provided "the most ample opportunities for women's transcendant influence." [6]

Female delegates to philanthropic and correctional conferences also realized that correctional work suggested the possibility of useful careers. Mrs. W. P. Lynde told the National Conference of Charities and Correction in 1879 that children's institutions offered the "truest and noblest scope for the public activities of women in the time which they can spare from their primary domestic duties." [7] Women were exhorted by other delegates to make their lives meaningful by participating in welfare programs, volunteering their time and services, and getting acquainted with less privileged groups. They were told to seek jobs in institutions where "the woman-element shall pervade . . . and soften its social atmosphere with motherly tenderness." [8]

Although the child-savers were responsible for some minor reforms in jails and reformatories, they were more particularly concerned with extending governmental control over a whole range of youthful activities that had previously been handled on an informal basis. The main aim of the child-savers was to impose sanctions on conduct unbecoming youth and to disqualify youth from enjoying adult privileges. As Bennett Berger has commented, "Adolescents are not made by nature but by being excluded from responsible participation in adult affairs, by being rewarded for dependency, and penalized for precocity." [9]

The child-saving movement was not so much a break with the past as an affirmation of faith in traditional institutions. Parental authority, education at home, and the virtues of rural life were emphasized because they were in decline at this time. The child-saving movement was, in part, a crusade which, through emphasizing the dependence of the social order on the proper socialization of children, implicitly elevated the nuclear family and, more especially, the role of women as stalwarts of the family. The child-savers were prohibitionists, in a general sense, who believed that social progress depended on efficient law enforcement, strict supervision of children's leisure and recreation, and the regulation of illicit pleasures. What seemingly began as a movement to humanize the lives of adolescents soon developed into a program of moral absolutism through which youth was to be saved from movies, pornography, cigarettes, alcohol, and anything else that might possibly rob them of their innocence.

Although child-saving had important symbolic functions for preserving the social prestige of a declining elite, it also had considerable practical significance for legitimizing new career openings for women. The new role of social worker combined elements of an old and partly fictitious role—defender of family life—and elements of a new role—social servant. Social work was thus both an affirmation of cherished American values and an instrumentality for women's emancipation.

JUVENILE COURT

The essential preoccupation of the child-saving movement was the recognition and control of youthful deviance. It brought attention to, and thus "invented," new categories of youthful misbehavior which had been hitherto unappreciated. The efforts of the child-savers were institutionally expressed in the juvenile court, which, despite recent legislative and constitutional reforms, is generally acknowledged as their most significant contribution to progressive penology.

The juvenile court system was part of a general movement directed toward removing adolescents from the criminal-law process and creating special programs for delinquent, dependent, and neglected children. Regarded widely as "one of the greatest advances in child welfare that has ever occurred," the juvenile court was considered "an integral part of total welfare planning." [10] Charles Chute, an enthusiastic supporter of the child-saving movement, claimed, "No single event has contributed more to the welfare of children and their families. It revolutionized the treatment of delinquent and neglected children and led to the passage of similar laws throughout the world." [11]

The juvenile court was a special tribunal created by statute to determine the legal status of children and adolescents. Underlying the juvenile court movement was the concept of *parens patriae,* by which the courts were authorized to handle with wide discretion the problems of "its least fortunate junior citizens." [12] The administration of juvenile justice differed in many important respects from the criminal court processes. A child was not accused of a crime but offered assistance and guidance; intervention in his life was not supposed to carry the stigma of criminal guilt. Judicial records were not generally available to the press or public, and juvenile court hearings were conducted in relative privacy. Juvenile court procedures were typically informal and inquisitorial. Specific criminal safeguards of due process were not applicable because juvenile proceedings were defined by statute as civil in character.[13]

The original statutes enabled the courts to investigate a wide variety of youthful needs and misbehavior. As Joel Handler has observed, "The critical philosophical position of the reform movement was that no formal legal distinctions should be made between the delinquent and the dependent or neglected." [14] Statutory definitions of "delinquency" encompassed (1) acts that would be criminal if committed by adults; (2) acts that violated county, town, or municipal ordinances; and (3) violations of vaguely defined catch-alls—such as "vicious or immoral behavior," "incorrigibility," and "truancy"—which "seem to express the notion that the adolescent, if allowed to continue, will engage in more serious conduct." [15]

The juvenile court movement went far beyond a concern for special treatment of adolescent offenders. It brought within the ambit of governmental control a set of youthful activities that had been previously ignored or dealt with on an informal basis. It was not by accident that the behavior selected for penalizing by the child-savers—sexual license, drinking, roaming the streets, begging, frequenting dance halls and movies, fighting, and being seen in public late at night—was most directly relevant to the children of lower-class migrant and immigrant families.

The juvenile court was not perceived by its supporters as a revolutionary experiment but rather as a culmination of traditionally valued practices. [16] The child-saving movement was "antilegal" in the sense that it derogated civil rights and procedural formalities while relying heavily on extralegal techniques. The judges of the new court were empowered to investigate the character and social life of predelinquent as well as delinquent children; they examined motivation rather than intent, seeking to identify the moral reputation of problematic children. The requirements of preventive penology and child-saving further justified the court's intervention in cases where no offense had actually been committed but where, for example, a child was posing problems for some person in authority, such as a parent or teacher or social worker.

The Personal Touch

Judges were expected to show the same professional competence as doctors and therapists. The sociologist Charles Henderson wrote:

> A careful study of individuals is an essential element in wise procedure. The study must include the physical, mental and moral peculiarities and defects of the children who come under the notice of the courts. Indeed we are likely to follow the lead of those cities which provide for a careful examination of all school children whose physical or psychical condition is in any way or degree abnormal, in order to prevent disease, correct deformity and vice, and select the proper course of study and discipline demanded by the individual need. [17]

Juvenile court judges had to be carefully selected for their skills as expert diagnosticians and for their appreciation of the "helping" professions. Miriam Van Waters, for example, regarded the juvenile court as a "laboratory of human behavior" and its judges as "experts with scientific training and specialists in the art of human relations." It was the judge's task to "get the whole truth about a child" in the same way that a "physician searches for every detail that bears on the condition of a patient." [18]

The child-savers' interest in preventive strategies and treatment programs was based on the premise that delinquents possess innate or acquired characteristics which predispose them to crime and distinguish them from law-abiding youths. Delinquents were regarded as constrained by a variety of biological and environmental forces, so that their proper treatment involved discovery of the "cause of the aberration" and application of "the appropriate corrective or antidote." [19] "What the trouble is with the offender," noted William Healy, "making him what he is, socially undesirable, can only be known by getting at his mental life, as it is an affair of reactive mechanisms." [20]

The use of terms like "unsocialized," "maladjusted," and "pathological" to describe the behavior of delinquents implied that "socialized" and "adjusted" children conform to middle-class morality and participate in respectable institutions.[21] The failure empirically to demonstrate psychological differences between delinquents and nondelinquents did not discourage the child-savers from believing that rural and middle-class values constitute "normality." The unique character of the child-saving movement was its concern for predelinquent offenders—"children who occupy the debatable ground between criminality and innocence"—and its claim that it could transform potential criminals into respectable citizens by training them in "habits of industry, self-control and obedience to law." [22] This policy justified the diminishing of traditional procedures in juvenile court. If children were to be rescued, it was important that the rescuers be free to provide their services without legal hindrance. Delinquents had to be saved, transformed, and reconstituted. "There is no essential difference," said Frederick Wines, "between a criminal and any other sinner. The means and methods of restoration are the same for both." [23] . . .

NOTES

[1] William P. Letchworth, "Children of the State," National Conference of Charities and Correction, *Proceedings* (St. Paul, Minn., 1886), p. 138. The idea that intellectuals discovered poverty as a result of their own alienation from the centers of power has been fully treated by Richard Hofstadter, *The Age of Reform* (New York: Vintage Books, 1955); and Christopher Lasch, *The New Radicalism in America, 1889–1963: The Intellectual as a Social Type* (New York: Alfred A. Knopf, 1965).

[2] R. W. Hill, "The Children of Shinbone Alley," National Conference of Charities and Correction, *Proceedings* (Omaha, Neb., 1887), p. 231.

[3] Robert Sunley, "Early Nineteenth Century American Literature on Child-Rearing," in Margaret Mead and Martha Wolfenstein (eds.), *Childhood in Contemporary Cultures* (Chicago: University of Chicago Press, 1955), p. 152; see also, Orville G. Brim, *Education for Child-Rearing* (New York: The Free Press, 1965), pp. 321–49.

[4] Lasch, *op. cit.*, pp. 53–54.

[5] Talcott Parsons and Robert F. Bales, *Family, Socialization, and Interaction Process* (New York: The Free Press, 1955), pp. 3–33.

[6] G. E. Howe, "The Family System," National Conference of Charities and Correction, *Proceedings* (Cleveland, 1880), pp. 212–13.

[7] W. P. Lynde, "Prevention in Some of Its Aspects," Annual Conference of Charities, *Proceedings* (Chicago, 1879), p. 167.

[8] Clara T. Leonard, "Family Homes for Pauper and Dependent Children," *ibid.*, p. 175.

[9] Bennett Berger, review of Frank Musgrove's *Youth and the Social Order*, in *American Sociological Review*, 32 (1927), 1021.

[10] Charles I. Chute, "The Juvenile Court in Retrospect," *Federal Probation*, 13 (Sept. 1949), 7; Harrison A. Dobbs, "In Defense of Juvenile Courts," *ibid.*, p. 29.

[11] Chute, "Fifty Years of the Juvenile Court," *National Probation and Parole Association Yearbook* (1949), p. 1.

[12] Gustav L. Schramm, "The Juvenile Court Idea," *Federal Probation, op. cit.*, p. 21.

[13] Monrad G. Paulsen, "Fairness to the Juvenile Offender," 41 *Minnesota Law Review*, 547–67 (1957). Note: "Rights and Rehabilitation in the Juvenile Courts," 67 *Columbia Law Rev.*, 281–341 (1967).

[14] Joel F. Handler, "The Juvenile Court and the Adversary System: Problems of Function and Form," *Wisconsin Law Review*, 9 (1965).

[15] Handler and Margaret K. Rosenheim, "Privacy and Welfare: Public Assistance and Juvenile Justice," *Law and Contemporary Problems*, 31 (1966), 377–412.

[16] A reform movement, according to Herbert Blumer, is differentiated from a revolution by its inherent respectability and acceptance of an existing social order: "The primary function of the reform movement is probably not so much the bringing about of social change, as it is to reaffirm the ideal values in a given society." Blumer, "Collective Behavior," in Alfred McClung Lee (ed.), *Principles of Sociology* (New York: Barnes & Noble, 1963), pp. 212–13.

[17] Charles R. Henderson, "Theory and Practice of Juvenile Courts," National Conference of Charities and Correction, *Proceedings* (Portland, Ore., 1904), pp. 358–59.

[18] Miriam Van Waters, "The Socialization of Juvenile Court Procedure," *Journal of Criminal Law and Criminology*, 12 (1922), 61, 69.

[19] Illinois Board of State Commissioners of Public Charities, *First Biennial Report* (Springfield: Illinois Journal Printing Office, 1871), p. 180.

[20] William Healy, "The Psychology of the Situation: A Fundamental for Understanding and Treatment of Delinquency and Crime," in Jane Addams (ed.), *The Child, the Clinic, and the Court* (New York: New Republic, 1925), p. 40.

[21] C. Wright Mills, "The Professional Ideology of Social Pathologists," in Bernard Rosenberg, Israel Gerver, and F. William Howton (eds.), *Mass Society in Crisis* (New York: Macmillan, 1964), pp. 92–111.

[22] Illinois Board *Sixth Biennial Report* (Springfield: H. W. Rokker, 1880), p. 104.

[23] Frederick H. Wines, "Reformation as an End in Prison Discipline," National Conference of Charities and Correction, *Proceedings* (Buffalo, 1888), p. 198.

4. *The Legal Basis of Delinquency* *

THORSTEN SELLIN AND MARVIN E. WOLFGANG

A CLEAR DEFINITION of fundamental concepts is a prime requisite for all research. Therefore, any study of delinquency must first establish the meaning of this term. This task has often been neglected by criminologists who have spent more time on examining the terms and concepts of the independent variables than of the dependent one—delinquency—which they have hoped to explain. As Mack has written: "It is impossible to undertake any such [etiological] research without having to decide first of all what you mean by delinquency. This is a condition which most textbooks and research papers acknowledge in their first paragraph and then go on to ignore." [1] The need for a definition of delinquency is equally stressed by Tappan, who states:

> Certainly there is no more central question in this study and probably none more difficult to answer. Yet it is important to see the nature of delinquency

* Thorsten Sellin and Marvin E. Wolfgang, *The Measurement of Delinquency*. New York: John Wiley & Sons, 1964, pp. 71–86.

as clearly as possible and to understand the problems that have impeded efforts at definition . . . , because on the interpretation of the term depend all those vital differences which set off the juvenile delinquent from the adult criminal at the one extreme and from the non-offender at the other.[2]

These quotations may appear strange in view of the fact that definitions of delinquency exist in laws that provide the basis for dealing with juvenile offenders. It is these definitions that have been used in the compilation of official statistics about delinquency and delinquents, on which so many studies have relied, or in classifying delinquents, when the researcher has had access to the original records of public agencies. Indeed, innumerable variables have been statistically correlated with the events covered by the legal terms "crime" and "delinquency" and provocative theories about these phenomena have been formulated, but even in the most sophisticated researches little or no account has been taken of the great diversity of conduct represented, not only by the inclusive designation of "delinquency," but even by such legal categories as "offenses against the person," "offenses against property," criminal homicide, rape, robbery, burglary, larceny, and others. This, we think, is a cogent reason for the dissatisfaction with present definitions of juvenile delinquency and for the demand that something be done about it. But first, let us look at what the law calls delinquency.

This involves not only an examination of the specific statutes, which in creating juvenile courts also prescribed the scope of their jurisdiction in terms of the kinds of conduct and classes of juveniles affected, but also of the criminal law, since all juvenile court statutes in the United States provide that a child is a juvenile delinquent if he commits any act that would be a crime if done by an adult. Were delinquency limited to such conduct, our task would be simpler, but all jurisdictions except the federal label a variety of other forms of conduct as delinquency. Sussmann has listed all of them in the order of their frequency and has shown, for each state, which ones are specified.[3] They number thirty-four, varying from truancy, incorrigibility, and running away from home to using tobacco in any form. No state has adopted all of them, but Indiana leads with seventeen; Maine, at the other extreme, names but one—"growing up in idleness and crime." Some of them could equally well come under the heading of dependency or neglect because the distinctions are often difficult to draw. As a matter of fact, some states classify as delinquency a condition that other states define as dependency or neglect.

The problem is not limited to the United States, as is seen from the following statement:

In many countries the meaning of juvenile delinquency is so broad that it embraces practically all manifestations of juvenile behavior. Under the influence of certain theories, juvenile delinquency is identified either with maladjustment or with forms of juvenile behavior which actually are more a reflection of poor living conditions or inadequate laws and regulations than a delinquent inclination. Thus, disobedience, stubbornness, lack of respect, being incorrigible, smoking without permission, collecting cigarette butts, hawking and the like are considered juvenile delinquency. Very often these "forms of delinquency" are hidden in statistical data under the vague term "other offenses." More often than would be desirable, these "offenders" are lumped together with real ones not only because services and institutions for them are not available but also because, according to some policies and practices, all of them are considered "maladjusted" and sent to the same institutions. The result is an artificial inflation of the juvenile delinquency problem and its "forms." [4]

Confusion results from these legal definitions of delinquency.

It is reasonable to believe [says Tappan] that all, or at least a vast majority of, normal children sometimes indulge in forms of behavior that might come within the purview of the juvenile court. Whether a given child will get into trouble depends largely on the interpretation that is attached to his conduct and the willingness or ability of the parent to deal with it. Considering the broad scope of legal provisions on insubordination, "questionable behavior," "injuring or endangering the morals or health of himself or others," truancy, running away, trespassing, and petty theft, it would be difficult to find any paragons of virtue who would be wholly exonerated of delinquency, save through parental understanding and leniency.[5]

The lack of uniformity among jurisdictions makes comparative studies especially difficult. Although violations of criminal laws and ordinances are generally considered "delinquency" when committed by a juvenile, many states give exclusive jurisdiction to the criminal court if the violation is of a certain kind. This holds true for capital crimes in the federal code and in the laws of eleven states (Colorado, Georgia, Iowa, Maryland, Massachusetts, Minnesota, South Carolina, Tennessee, Delaware, Vermont, and West Virginia) and for crimes punishable by life imprisonment in the first eight of these mentioned; for murder in five states (Kansas, Louisiana, Montana, New Jersey, and Pennsylvania); for homicide (Texas); for manslaughter (Montana); for rape (Louisiana, Tennessee); for attempted rape (Louisiana); for crimes of violence (Illinois); for crimes punishable by more than ten years imprisonment (North Carolina); for infamous crimes (Maine); for traffic law (Indiana, New Jersey) or motor vehicle law offenses (Rhode Island); and for "any crime" (Florida).[6] Juveniles prosecuted for these offenses in the jurisdictions just mentioned fall outside of "delinquency" properly speaking. In studies of the illegal conduct of juveniles, they would, of course, have to be included, but if they have not been processed by juvenile courts they do not figure in the records of these courts which have so often been the chief source of data for delinquency studies.

Comparative analysis of such studies is complicated by still another problem, namely the lack of a standard definition of who is capable of engaging in "delinquency," both as to age and sex. Considering the fifty-two jurisdictions—constituted of fifty states, the District of Columbia, and the federal government—anyone under twenty-one years of age can commit a "delinquency" and therefore be adjudged a juvenile delinquent in four of the jurisdictions; under nineteen in two; under eighteen in twenty-eight; under seventeen in ten; and under sixteen in eight. This is true for both sexes, but in one state that has a maximum limit of nineteen for males, the limit is twenty-one for females; in two states these maxima are respectively sixteen and eighteen, and in five states, seventeen and eighteen. The effect of these diverse age limits on interstate research is easy to imagine, unless comparable age and sex groups have been used.

Except for the jurisdictions mentioned earlier, no state has given criminal courts exclusive jurisdiction over juveniles, but most have given them concurrent jurisdiction, which means that a juvenile in these states may, under certain circumstances, be adjudged a criminal rather than a delinquent. The scope of this power varies greatly among the jurisdictions, as may be seen from Table 1, which takes only juvenile males into consideration.[7]

Although it can be seen that more than half of the jurisdictions (28) limit delinquency to illegal conduct by those under eighteen years of age, there could be substantial errors made, for instance, in comparing the results of studies made in the eleven states, in which any juvenile may be prosecuted for crime, with those made in the two states (New Hampshire and Virginia) where criminal courts have no jurisdiction at all over those under eighteen.

In most states there is no lower age limit set for the adjudication of a child

TABLE 1. CRIMINAL COURT JURISDICTION

Where the original jurisdiction of the Juvenile Court extends to age	The Criminal Court has overlapping or concurrent jurisdiction over juveniles	
	Above the age of ___	In _____ jurisdictions
21	11	1
	17	3
19	all ages	1
	14	1
18	all ages	11
	19–21	1
	11–21	1
	13	5
	15	8
	none	2
17	all ages	2
	9	1
	11	1
	15	1
	16	1
	none	4
16	all ages	2
	14	1
	none	5

as delinquent; Mississippi and Texas place that limit at ten and New York at seven.[8]

Our brief discussion of how diversely "delinquency" and "delinquents" are defined in American statutes and how judicial administration may affect the assignment of an offense or an offender to the criminal or the delinquency area has been pursued to indicate one aspect of the difficulties involved in securing uniform and reliable data for the measurement of delinquency. Although these difficulties are especially great when data from different jurisdictions are involved, they are not absent in studies dealing with a single state or community. So long as the definition of delinquency in law in any jurisdiction includes so many ill-defined kinds of conduct and admits of the exercise of wide administrative discretion at all levels in handling juvenile offenders, the problem of standardization of data needed for measurement purposes will always face the student. Indeed, it has forced us, in the present research, to develop a system of classifying delinquent acts that is in a sense independent of the labels attached to them by the law.

THE PENNSYLVANIA JUVENILE COURT ACT

The source documents used in our study are records of various kinds, compiled by the police of Philadelphia in connection with their routine enforcement of the law. So far as juveniles are concerned, such enforcement is circumscribed by what is considered to be delinquent conduct by the legislature of the Commonwealth of Pennsylvania and recorded in an act of June 2, 1933, Public Law 1433, with amendments of 1937, 1939, 1953. Section I, Subsection 2 and 4, contains the following definitions:

> (2) The word "child," as used in this act, means a minor under the age of eighteen years.
> (4) The words "delinquent child" include:
>   (a) A child who has violated any law of the Commonwealth or ordinance of any city, borough or township;
>   (b) A child who, by reason of being wayward or habitually disobedient, is uncontrolled by his or her parent, guardian, custodian, or legal representative;
>   (c) A child who is habitually truant from school or home;
>   (d) A child who habitually so deports himself or herself as to injure or endanger the morals or health of himself, herself, or others.

As can be seen, Section 1, Subsection 4a, defines delinquency as any act that, if committed by an adult, would be a crime; and Subsections 4b, c, and d define delinquency in terms of an age status and constituting acts or conditions that could not be attributed to an adult.

THE STANDARD JUVENILE COURT ACT

The definition of delinquency . . . used in the Pennsylvania statute is no longer supported by leading authorities. It is challenged, in particular, by the drafters of the Standard Juvenile Court Act. The first edition of this act was published by the National Probation Association in 1925. It was revised and reissued in 1928, 1933, 1943, 1949, and 1959. Prepared by the Committee on Standard Juvenile Court Act of the National Probation and Parole Association, in cooperation with the National Council of Juvenile Court Judges and the U.S. Children's Bureau, the new act emphasizes the basic concept in *parens patriae*. Under the act, Article 1, Sections 2e and 2f, a "child" is defined as a person under eighteen years of age and a "minor" as any person under twenty-one years of age. As in the 1943 and 1949 editions of the act, the terms "delinquency" and "neglect" are avoided. Article 2, Section 8, Subsection 1 reads:

> [Except as otherwise provided herein, the court shall have exclusive original jurisdiction in proceedings]
>   1. Concerning any child who is alleged to have violated any federal, state, or local law or municipal ordinance, regardless of where the violation occurred; or any minor alleged to have violated any federal, state, or local law

or municipal ordinance prior to having become 18 years of age. Such minor shall be dealt with under the provisions of this act relating to children. Jurisdiction may be taken by the court of the district where the minor is living or found, or where the offense is alleged to have occurred. When a minor 18 years of age or over already under the jurisdiction of the court is alleged to have violated any federal, state, or local law or municipal ordinance, the juvenile court shall have concurrent jurisdiction with the criminal court.[9]

This delimitation of the scope of juvenile delinquency has received recent support from two sources. The Second United Nations Congress on the Prevention of Crime and the Treatment of Offenders, London 1960, passed a resolution that stated: "The Congress considers that the scope of the problem of juvenile delinquency should not be unnecessarily inflated . . . it recommends that the meaning of the term juvenile delinquency should be restricted as far as possible to violations of the criminal law." [10]

The New York Joint Legislative Committee on Court Reorganization, in its draft of a Family Court Act, has taken a similar stand:

"Juvenile delinquent" is defined in the proposed legislation as "a person over seven and less than sixteen years of age who does any act which, if done by an adult, would constitute a crime, and requires supervision, treatment or confinement." This definition, considerably narrower than the current definition, accords with the common understanding.[11]

We believe that statistical collections and analyses in terms of the definitions of delinquency must adopt this delimitation if they are to provide a useful measurement or index of the volume, character, or trend of delinquency.

Although the present research has had to depend on the definition of delinquency found in the Juvenile Court Act of Pennsylvania in selecting an appropriate sample of delinquent acts for analysis, we decided that it would be impossible to utilize the data on the "juvenile status" offenses in the construction of an index to delinquency. Such offenses are viewed by most writers only as predelinquent behavior or symptomatic of potential delinquent behavior. That is why it is often argued that they should not be labeled delinquency, and that is the chief reason behind the recommendations of the Standard Juvenile Court Act.

Truancy, for example, is a violation of a regulation requiring compulsory school attendance, but the explanation for truancy involves parental influence or lack of it or the failure of educational facilities and authorities to solve purely educational problems. To call the absence from classes delinquency places the truant in the same category with more serious violators of substantive legal codes. Shulman suggests: "Since chronic truancy often antedates serious delinquency by several years and may serve as a valuable warning signal of impending serious behavior disorder, we may raise the question of whether its formal handling as an aspect of juvenile delinquency is a proper one." [12]

The law presumes that children belong at home, and consequently a child who runs away from home is considered delinquent. But as in the case of incorrigibility and ungovernable behavior, the problems of family neglect are the important issues to be considered by the juvenile court in handling these children rather than behavior that constitutes serious and injurious threats to other members of the community

Excluding these and similar acts from use in the measurement of delinquency and concentrating only on violations by juveniles of the law and ordinances that, were they committed by adults, would be considered crimes reduce but do not eliminate the problem of legal definitions and classifications. The substantive content of the definitions of these offenses in the criminal law therefore has to be considered since it is common practice in official statistics of delinquency, especially in police statistics, to classify delinquents and their conduct in categories designated by labels derived from the criminal law.

The Labels of the Criminal Law

Since police agencies are entrusted with the enforcement of the criminal law, it is both obvious and natural that, in the investigation of offenses, they think in terms of the specific definitions of crime contained in the law. When a complaint is made and they investigate the incident, or when they observe an offense being committed, its objective characteristics lead them to call it burglary, robbery, larceny, and so on. And when they prepare reports on the incidents on some standard forms, these labels are recorded and furnish the basis for later periodic tabulations of the number of different offenses the police have dealt with whether or not an offender is taken into custody. The result is that when juveniles are apprehended by the police, their offenses are not labeled "delinquency" but are given appropriate criminal designations or, in the case of juvenile status offenses, a specific designation supplied by the juvenile court law, such as truancy, runaway, incorrigibility, and so on.

No police department, to our knowledge, publishes any statistics of juvenile offenses. Since most offenses are committed by unknown persons, those committed by juveniles can be segregated only when an apprehension is made. Even then, however, the practice is to publish only statistics of juvenile delinquents without reference to the number of offenses of different legal categories that have been "cleared" by their apprehension. In any event, such statistics are commonly relied on today as indicators of the movement and character of juvenile delinquency. Therefore, it becomes necessary to ask if (a) the criminal law labels best characterize delinquency and (b) if customary practices of statistical classification of juvenile offenses present the best picture of such delinquency.

Answers to these questions are complicated by the fact that the problems they involve are not independent of one another. The criminal law of a state may contain a very large number of distinctive crime designations, several hundreds of them, but when police departments record offenses with a view to their later inclusion in statistics, they are accustomed to use relatively few such designations and give the same label to a variety of offenses that resemble one another in some way. This practice has become more and more common and has been greatly stimulated by the formulation of the Uniform Classification of Offenses in the early 1930's. This classification is used in national statistics of offenses known to the police and of persons charged with offenses and published in *Uniform Crime Reports* issued by the FBI and based on reports now submitted by most civil police agencies in the United States. The classification, as slightly revised in 1958, contains twenty-six offense categories. Police agencies periodically submit reports to the FBI on standard forms containing these categories; and to facilitate the preparation of these reports the police now tend to label offenses not according to the more specific designations in the criminal law but by the the the code numbers and titles use in the Uniform Classification.

UNIFORM CLASSIFICATION OF OFFENSES

Part 1
   1. Criminal homicide
      a. Murder and non-negligent manslaughter
      b. Manslaughter by negligence
   2. Forcible rape
   3. Robbery
   4. Aggravated assault
   5. Burglary—breaking or entering
   6. Larceny-theft (except auto theft)
      a. $50 and over in value
      b. Under $50 in value
   7. Auto theft

Part 2
   8. Other assaults
   9. Forgery and counterfeiting
   10. Embezzlement and fraud
   11. Stolen property: buying, receiving, possessing
   12. Weapons: carrying, possessing, etc.
   13. Prostitution and commercialized vice
   14. Sex offenses (except forcible rape, prostitution, and commercialized vice)
   15. Offenses against the family and children
   16. Narcotic drug laws
   17. Liquor laws (except drunkenness)
   18. Drunkenness
   19. Disorderly conduct
   20. Vagrancy
   21. Gambling
   22. Driving while intoxicated
   23. Violation of road and driving laws
   24. Parking violations
   25. Other violations of traffic and motor vehicle laws
   26. All other offenses

Each of the titles in the above classification is derived from the criminal law but of necessity each covers a considerable variety of illegal conduct. When juvenile delinquency that violates the criminal laws is subsumed under them, the result is a highly simplified and considerably distorted picture of that delinquency. A few illustrations will suffice. They will be limited largely to some of the titles of offenses that in Uniform Crime Reports are considered as "index crimes"—that is, susceptible of use as a measurement of criminality. These are murder and non-negligent manslaughter, forcible rape, robbery, aggravated assault, burglary–breaking and entering, larceny or theft of property valued at $50 or more, and auto theft (motor vehicle theft). It should be recalled that so far as juveniles are concerned these titles are applicable only in descriptions of *offenses* attributable to juveniles or to *apprehended juveniles* charged with their commission.

Robbery

This title implies to most people that there is only one kind of robbery, that it is terrible, and that it connotes taking something of value from a person, usually with violence. Yet evidence points to significant differences in the quality of these acts.[13] As Beattie points out,

> . . . There is no knowledge of the variation that has occurred in different types of robbery. Such increases or decreases as have been observed may be due to variations in armed robbery or in strong-arm robbery, which in some instances amounts to no more than drunk rolls. Reports are often received today that children have been engaged in highjacking coins from each other. These incidents have been reported as robberies.[14]

The victim-offender relationship is also important, by sex, age, and other variables. There is certainly a vast difference between a 16-year-old boy's forcing a gas station attendant at the point of a gun to give up money from the cash register and an eight-year-old boy's twisting the arm of another eight-year-old boy in the school corridor in order to take his lunch money. Both acts are classified legally and statistically as robbery. This same kind of situation was referred to in the 1956 Annual Report of the Crime Prevention Association of Philadelphia:

> And again, what is "highway robbery"? In the thinking of the American people, this indeed is a serious offense. Yet we know of a case last year in which a 14-year-old approached another boy of similar age and demanded 15 cents; the boy accosted stated he had only a quarter. The "highway robber" took the quarter, had it changed and returned to the other boy 10 cents. *This offense is listed as highway robbery.* Another instance involved two boys who extorted 20 cents daily for a week from another boy as he went to and from school. This youthful highjacking was reported by the victim's parents to the police; charge against the two offenders—highway robbery. Now we must admit that such extortion and highjacking is nasty behavior but to call this highway robbery and still keep a straight face is naive.[15]

Burglary

Burglary is another example of the need for subclassifications, for while it is an offense that has shown a steady increase over the past years, we are never sure what kind of burglary has been increasing. The California Report has raised this same question: "Is the increase in safe burglary, large-scale residential and commercial burglary, or in just small-scale pilferings that are technically burglary? A large part of the latter could be the result of juvenile behavior. Under present classification methods, this question cannot be answered."[16] There are wide variations in the state statutes that define burglary. Although breaking into a locked car is defined as burglary in California and is reported thus in many instances, it is an offense that is often reported by many law-enforcement agencies as petty theft and classified as larceny.

Some of these problems were raised in papers presented in 1960 before the Social Statistics Section of the American Statistical Association. It was pointed out, for example, that broad crime groupings are used to tally major offenses that differ according to some element in definition. The following cases were given as illustrations:

(a) Two juveniles while on school vacation break into a neighbor's barn, steal some nails, a hammer, and a saw in order to build a treehouse nearby; (b) a prowler sneaks into an unoccupied bedroom and rummages for money or jewelry while the occupants are having dinner downstairs; (c) a team of thugs, armed and with heavy burglar tools force entrance into an office and attack a safe. Each of these cases is classified ordinarily as a "burglary" according to police statistical practices.[17]

Both from the viewpoint of police protective services and of threats of danger to life or property, these acts are clearly distinguishable, but the differential variables are hidden in formal statistical tabulations that use legal categories. Such factors as the presence or absence of violence to obtain entry, the legal or illegal presence of the offender at the scene of the crime, and the amount of property loss or damage are totally neglected.

Assaults

The legal definitions of aggravated assaults, sexual assaults, rape, and similar offenses against the person each cover a variety of forms of conduct. The 1958 California report again suggests

. . . because of the relationship of the parties or the conditions under which the assaults occurred, many altercations, largely domestic quarrels, characterized in reports as aggravated assault, do not seem to fall in the general area of felonious assault. There is need to subclassify this type of offense in order to arrive at a true picture of assault.[18]

A New Jersey analysis of juvenile-court cases a decade ago alluded to the same problem: "Personal injury, while having a higher percentage of dismissals as malicious mischief, does not carry comparable value under analysis. A majority of personal injury complaints were not assault cases per se—proper classification would be street fighting." [19] Moreover, the differences between a simple assault and battery and aggravated assault and battery are such that not only police variations but statutory provisions as well lend confusion rather than clarity to the classification problems. The legal nomenclature often distorts the true character of an attack on the person because of the difficulties of determining "grievous bodily harm" or extent of the injury and because suspects are often willing to confess to a simple assault or the police and courts are willing to accept a plea of guilty to a simple assault in order to obtain a conviction even when the more serious aggravated assault occurred.[20]

Rape

The categories of rape—even forcible rape—assault with attempt to ravish, sexual license, and sexual offenses generally fail to provide qualitative information on the broad range of activities and on the dimensions of seriousness or injury that may be involved in these acts. Forcible rape can range from violent and unprovoked attacks on women by strangers to a common pick-up in a barroom that ends in greater sexual intimacy than the woman intended. The lines between forcible rape, statutory rape, fornication, and contributing to the delinquency of a minor are never clear from statistical tabulations which merely use these legal terms. Without examination of the detailed descriptions in police reports, the compilations of data in tabular form usually fail to represent important distinctions in the facts. As the United Nations Congress in 1960 reported on an attempt to collect international data on sex offenses: " 'Sexual license' was too vague. The replies do not always make clear what kind of offenses are referred to: Full sexual relations or sexual games between children? Relations between lovers, sexual promiscuity, dissolute behavior, prostitution?" [21]

Certainly there are vast differences in the types of offenses that are listed as "assault with intent to ravish." The conduct of a sixteen-year-old boy who attacks a thirty-year-old woman and drags her into a dark alley to assault her sexually but is thwarted by screams and the appearance of a police officer is surely different from that of a nine-year-old boy's exploratory sexual curiosity with a neighbor girl aged eight. When she innocently tells her mother about the afternoon's adventure, and when the mother imagines horrendous things, calls the police, and has the boy arrested, this case, like the previous one, is listed as "assault with intent to ravish." Once again, Beattie has remarked:

> Much has been said in recent years of the apparent growth of viciousness in certain types of crime. There is no basis upon which to determine whether or not there has been such a growth. There have been many cases that have received a great deal of publicity, but without careful classification, it cannot be known whether the impression of increase is backed by fact.[22]

We believe that these illustrations suffice to show that the use of the broad titles of offenses derived from the Uniform Classification of Offenses for a description of delinquency chargeable to juveniles would be an unsatisfactory procedure that cannot provide sensitive measures of delinquency.

A second problem arises out of certain arbitrary practices of classifying and ordering offenses in official statistics of delinquency. These practices are directly attributable to the manner in which the Uniform Classification is applied in accord with the instructions governing its use. There are, of course, many ways of presenting offense statistics. The offenses involved could be listed alphabetically, or grouped in broad classes—for instance, offenses against the person, offenses against property—with appropriate subclasses, or grouped according to the Uniform Classification, to mention but a few patterns. For reasons already stated, the last mentioned method is the most common one in American police statistics.

There are two built-in features of the use of this classification that reduce its value. First, an implicit hypothesis underlies it, namely that its twenty-six classes are arranged in decreasing order of seriousness. This hypothesis is not completely invalid. Certainly most offenses in Part 1 of the classification are more injurious than most of those in Part 2, but arson, kidnapping, abortion, blackmail and extortion, and malicious mischief now falling into the last class of "all other offenses," and simple assault and battery (item 8) and embezzlement and fraud (item 10) may in fact involve personal injury or loss of property, for instance, than many of the offenses listed among the "index crimes" under rape, aggravated assault, burglary and larceny. Therefore, the present grouping of the offenses by the broad legal labels employed does not provide the best typology of offenses based on an hypothesis of degree of seriousness, not to mention the fact that it does not provide for different weighting of the classes, nor of the great number of variants among the offenses included in any single class. One theft of $50 is given as much weight as one homicide, and one such theft as much weight as one of $5,000.[23]

Second, the manner in which the classification is used conceals a great deal of delinquency known to the police because it offers no possibility of counting all the *components* of a delinquent event. The problem does not arise in the case of uncomplicated events. A mere breaking and entering can be classified as burglary, but suppose that in committing this offense a juvenile also steals property of great value and, on being surprised, assaults and wounds the owner with a dangerous weapon. The instructions for classifying this total event require that only the offense highest in the order of the Uniform Classification be counted—in this instance, the aggravated assault and battery. This conceals both the burglary and the theft. If a juvenile holds up the occupants of an automobile, kills the driver, rapes his female companion, and steals her pocketbook, jewelry, and the car, this complex event must be counted as one non-negligent criminal homicide (item 1) and the rape and the thefts will be concealed. All kinds of other complex events could be cited to show that the manner in which offenses are commonly tabulated for statistical presentation results in an incomplete picture even of the delinquency known to the police.

The conclusion seems inescapable that when an offense is given, in official police statistics, a broad legal label which does not allow for adequate discriminatory separation and weighting of the variants covered by it, and when all but the hypothetically most serious component of a delinquency event are concealed by the procedure followed in scoring offenses, the resulting statistics are not adequate for the measurement of delinquency. . . .

NOTES

[1] J. A. Mack, "Juvenile delinquency research: A criticism," *Social Rev.*, 3 (July 1955), 56.

[2] Paul W. Tappan, *Juvenile Delinquency* (New York: McGraw-Hill, 1949), p. 3.

[3] Frederick B. Sussmann, *Law of Juvenile Delinquency* (New York: Oceana, 1959), pp. 21–22.

[4] The Second United Nations Congress on the Prevention of Crime and the Treatment of Offenders (London, Aug. 8–20, 1960). *New Forms of Juvenile Delinquency: Their Origin, Prevention, and Treatment*. Report prepared by the Secretariat, A/Conf. 17/7.

[5] Tappan, *op. cit.*, p. 32.

[6] Based on Sussmann, *op. cit.*, pp. 65–77, as adapted from Tappan, "Children and youth in the criminal court," *Ann. Amer. Acad. polit. and soc. Sci.*, 261 (Jan. 1949), 129–30.

[7] Compiled from Sussmann, *ibid.*

[8] Sol Rubin, "The legal character of juvenile delinquency," *Ann. Amer. Acad. polit. and soc. Sci.*, 261 (Jan. 1949), 6.

[9] "Standard Juvenile Court Act," *National Probation and Parole Assoc. J.*, 5 (Oct. 1959), 344.

[10] See *Report Prepared by the Secretariat*, 4 (New York: United Nations, 1961), 61.

[11] Joint Legislative Committee on Court Reorganization, II, "The Family Court Act," New York State, Daniel G. Albert, Chairman (Albany, 1962), p. 6.

[12] Harry M. Shulman, *Juvenile Delinquency in American Society* (New York: Harper & Row, 1961), p. 33.

[13] These differences in adult robberies have recently been examined in some detail by F. H. McClintock and Evelyn Gibson, *Robbery in London* (London: Macmillan, 1961).

[14] *Crime in California 1958*, p. 18. See also, Nochem S. Winnet, *Twenty-Five Years of Crime Prevention* (Philadelphia: Philadelphia Crime Association), *Annual Report, 1956*, p. 1: "Hundreds of robberies were reported. An analysis showed many of them involved petty sums, one as low as ten cents, a tribute exacted by one school child from another."

[15] Winnet, *Ibid.*, p. 11.

[16] *Crime in California 1958*, p. 18.

[17] Edward V. Comber, "Discussion," *Proc. Social Statistics Section 1960*, 8 (Washington, D.C.: American Statistical Association, n.d., mimeo), 36–37.

[18] *Crime in California 1958*, p. 18.

[19] *Children in New Jersey Courts 1953*, p. 24.

[20] See Donald J. Newman, "Pleading guilty for considerations: A study of bargain justice," *J. Crim. Law, Criminol., and Police Sci.*, 46 (March–April 1956), 780–90.

[21] United Nations Congress, London, Aug. 8–20, 1960, A/Conf. 17/6, p. 64.

[22] *Crime in California 1958*, p. 19.

[23] For a more detailed discussion of these and related problems, see Marvin E. Wolfgang, "Uniform crime reports: A critical appraisal," *University of Pennsylvania Law Rev.*, 111 (April 1963), 708–38.

5. *The Processes of Pre-judicial Handling* *

TASK FORCE ON JUVENILE DELINQUENCY
AND YOUTH CRIME

LOOK TO PG. 194

. . . ANY GROUP OR INDIVIDUAL ATTEMPTING to formulate a plan of action toward an alleged delinquent must make a number of decisions: (1) identification of an act as delinquency; (2) screening for appropriate action; (3) planning and implementing service.[1]

Ascertainment of the fact of delinquency is a duty of all official agencies trying to bring a delinquent minor under their authority. The standard of proof may vary according to the stage in the law-enforcement process; the facts that justify the police in taking a minor into custody will not necessarily satisfy the juvenile court as a basis for adjudication.[2] In some instances, the reasonable grounds for official action toward juveniles at various stages of delinquency control have been legislatively articulated.[3]

Identification of delinquency is also a necessary step for agencies and individuals seeking to control lawlessness through informal means. Social agencies, for example, must determine at intake whether an individual is a delinquent and, therefore, a suitable client. Since the unofficial agencies of the delinquency-control system can impose sanctions by referring clients for formal action, the fact-finding procedures they employ assume considerable importance. The same is true of fact-finding by official agencies bent on ap-

* Task Force on Juvenile Delinquency and Youth Crime of the President's Commission on Law Enforcement and Administration of Justice, *Juvenile Delinquency and Youth Crime*, Washington, D.C.: Government Printing Office, 1967, pp. 11–16.

plying informal measures; attaching the tag of delinquency without scrupulous attention to the facts raises the same kinds of question about fairness when done unauthoritatively—usually, nonetheless, well publicized—as it does in formal action.

At the screening stage any unit of delinquency control, official or otherwise, has several options. They include outright dismissal, acceptance for service, or referral (the last an effort to direct a youngster to community services that he needs but is unfamiliar with or resists).[4] Screening decisions depend on the evaluator's judgment of what he or his agency can offer, what is available elsewhere, and what limitations are imposed by the known priorities for service.

Both planning and carrying out service are functions performed by every unit that accepts a case. For adjudicated delinquents, the framework of service (disposition) is set by the law; with few exceptions, however, the law is silent about permissible action toward nonadjudicated delinquents.[5] Treatment programs may include those of voluntary or ad hoc associations, of public or private delinquency-prevention agencies, of welfare agencies, of the newly created poverty program units, or of other institutions that have expanded beyond their originally stated functions to reach nonadjudicated delinquents.[6]

Any individual or community group that initiates work with delinquents may properly be regarded as part of the delinquency-control system. To see the system in its entirety, and to identify existing alternatives to adjudication for those classified as delinquent, it is necessary to recognize the formal and informal dimensions of the system and the stages of decision-making common to both. An official agency may deal with nonadjudicated as well as adjudicated delinquents; it may perform unofficial functions as well as official ones, perhaps acquiring from its formal authority leverage to operate informally.

PRESENT PRACTICES

At the outset, a broad disclaimer is essential: Information on prejudicial handling is not sufficiently reliable to offer firm generalizations, nor can an accurate description be given of particular phases of this dispositional process. Some delinquent acts apparently are adjusted so unsystematically and informally that the process is invisible. A storeowner's intervention to adjust theft, a victim's compromise of assault, a schoolteacher's mediation in an act of vandalism are instances of unrecorded informal handling. They are known to exist, but no useful generalizations can be made about their rate of occurrence or the circumstances of adjustment.

There are reasons for that ignorance. Widespread indifference to informal aspects of bureaucratic operations explains it in part, for not until recently has research in criminal law been directed beyond the stated official functions of social institutions. The current interest is the result of heightened curiosity about the latent functions of bureaucracy. In part, too, the lack of knowledge is a product of the discreet silence that cloaks ancillary activities about which an organization feels uncomfortable. A school, for instance, may in fact adjust many situations involving delinquency. It has an interest in offenses occurring in or harmful to the school, and it has an interest in its pupils.

For children who inspire the compassionate attention of their teachers, the school may bend its efforts to secure adjustments even of wholly extraschool offenses. But the school may feel it cannot afford publicly to acknowledge these actions of its staff for fear of creating anxiety among parents and risking criticism for allocating time to nonacademic concerns.

In addition, adjustments by individuals may well be beyond the reach of systematic research. Where a satisfactory resolution is privately reached, the personal nature of the confrontation between a suspected juvenile and his accuser is an effective shield to recording.

Within the official agencies of delinquency control, alternatives to adjudication of delinquents have tended to emerge haphazardly, as unplanned and unofficial aspects of a community's system. At least one juvenile court law acknowledges the likelihood of screening by police [7] as well as court staff, though typically the function is implicit in other duties imposed by law, and the laws of over half the states authorize screening at the point of intake.[8] But, predictably, the emphasis in juvenile court legislation is on the law enforcement and judicial process as it applies to juveniles who are officially handled—taken into custody, formally alleged to be delinquent, adjudicated, and declared to be wards of the court subject to sanctions set forth in orders of disposition. The laws do not provide affirmative guidelines for screening out of the delinquency-control system or for selecting measures of restraint or rehabilitation to apply to those so channeled.

Statistical data concerning the pre-judicial handling process are even less available than data concerning the formal processes and, as is true of data collection generally, what are available are less than systematic.[9] With few exceptions, information on pre-judicial handling is restricted to the aspects officials acknowledged. While the account that follows is therefore necessarily inadequate, it bears out impressions of the magnitude and unplanned character of the process.

Police

Statistics reveal how many juvenile offenders come into official contact with the police; they do not reveal the number of unofficial contacts on the street or in the stationhouse. In cases of more than brief or casual contact, a trip to the stationhouse for questioning by the arresting officer or juvenile specialist [10] is usually required. The dispositions available to the police range from outright release, usually to the parents, to referral to the juvenile court. Court referral may mean citation, filing of a complaint, or physical removal of the child to detention awaiting formal action. Between those extremes are referral to community resources selected by the officer and station adjustment, by which is meant the juvenile's release on one or more conditions. The term station adjustment, as used here, implies an effort by the police to control and change the juvenile's behavior. Both national [11] and local [12] data indicate great variation in the use of these alternatives. Differences, expectably, are more marked among the many jurisdictions than within a jurisdiction's pattern of handling from year to year. Across the country, it is clear, discretionary action by the police in screening juvenile offenders accounts for the removal of significant numbers from the formal juvenile justice system.

It is likely, moreover, that reliance on police discretion is especially marked in some of the major urban centers.[13] In one midwestern city in 1965, for instance, 66.1 per cent of all official police contacts with juveniles were adjusted, a proportion that has stayed remarkably constant in recent years.[14] In a small eastern city, however, the proportion of offenders referred to court rose between 1963 and 1965 from 56 to 70 per cent, reflecting, in the words of a report, "either a more serious nature of offense or a stricter attitude on the part of the police." [15] In either event, discretionary judgment to refer or to retain for police handling was exercised in a wide variety of offenses, from the serious to the minor.[16] However sharply specific communities depart from this norm, for the nation the tendency to use pre-judicial handling is pronounced. In the past five years, intradepartmental handling by police has been reported to occur nationally in between 45 and 50 per cent of all juvenile contacts.[17] Each option, moreover, can be and often is used for almost every type of offense. Involuntary manslaughter, rape, serious assault and battery, armed robbery, burglary, and many other felonies are adjusted by the police, frequently at significantly high rates.[18]

But what action do the police initiate for those screened out? National data do not provide a breakdown; referrals to court (juvenile and adult), referrals to welfare and other agencies, and interdepartmental handling or release are the usual categories of action reported. Analyses of individual departmental reports are somewhat more helpful. So, too, are inquiries into practices in specific localities. According to a recent law review account, hearings are scheduled in some police departments whenever station adjustment is under consideration.[19] The outcome can be release with reprimand, imposition of direct sanction, referral to a social service or similar community resource, or referral to the court.[20]

Written standards for adjustment or referral to the juvenile courts are not uncommon. The manual of the youth division of the Chicago Police Department contains such standards.[21] The youth officer's attention is directed to the type of offense, the juvenile's past experiences and personal background, and the attitudes of parents as well as offenders. Existence of community resources is listed as another factor. How these and similar guides [22] are used in practice, however, is less clear.

By all accounts the type of offense is important. Court or departmental policy requires that some offenses be handled by the court, though this policy may not always be followed by the police. More serious offenses, if adjusted at all, seem to be adjusted relatively less often than minor ones. A past offense or the status of the juvenile as probationer or parolee makes certain juveniles ineligible for the pre-judicial process.

Data on the impact of race on policy determinations are somewhat contradictory and difficult to assess. Several commentators have asserted that race is weighed in the scale; one study supports this.[23] But other data reflect remarkably similar court referral rates for whites and Negroes.[24]

Another imponderable is demeanor—the juvenile's behavior and apparent attitude toward the police. By policy, a denial of involvement requires a court referral in some jurisdictions. Some police officers seem to feel that a denial of guilt or a defiant attitude indicates an uncooperative youth, one who will not be amenable to treatment.[25] Such a youth is considered a greater risk to the community if released, and police prefer to have that judgment made by the court. A similar rationale may account for referrals of juveniles whose parents are defensive about their misbehavior or resent police intrusions.[26] Some experienced juvenile specialists, in fact, regard the parents' attitude as more significant than the child's.

When adjustment is the course of action, typically the police issue a warning or make a referral to a nonjudicial agency. One reported practice is as follows:

> In Kansas City, for example, the police administer a stringent though informal discipline program called grounding. A typical grounded youth must attend school unless a doctor's explanation is obtained for his absence. At all other times he may leave the house only if accompanied by a parent, and then not for any activity that is primarily engaged in for pleasure. He must dress conventionally and have his hair cut in a reasonable manner; and he must study at home for a minimum prescribed period each day. After this schedule is enforced for a month, lesser conditions will be imposed for the duration of the school year. A high degree of success in preventing future offenses is claimed to result from this program.[27]

In the many neighborhoods where juvenile specialists and patrolmen are acquainted with the juveniles whose cases have been adjusted at the station, closer supervision on the street may result. In any event, the police themselves see the screening mechanism, with its adjustment possibility, as a way of assisting parents in their efforts to control a problem child, of reassuring the community, and of providing a fertile ground for friendship between the youth and the police. The net result, they claim, is an "association [that] assists in reorienting the child, gives him a new set of values, helps him to break away from undesirable associates and habits, and frequently is all that is needed to stop his wayward behavior." [28]

The discretionary options that have been considered up to this point are dismissal, community referral, station adjustment, and referral to court. Another crucial determination is whether to refer to court officials for detention. In theory, court officials control decisions to detain, but in processing juveniles brought to the detention home by the police, these officials appear to be influenced significantly by the prior police determination of the need for secure custody.[29] Some surveys have indicated that in a large proportion of the cases that the police bring to detention homes an initial period of detention follows.[30] That is, relatively few of the detention referrals are released at the point of intake to the detention unit. Many, of course, are released within a twenty-four- to forty-eight-hour period. Moreover, some of the juveniles initially detained are not thereafter made the subjects of petitions in the juvenile court, and of those who are, many are released after adjudication to live in the community.

It appears that the police place substantial dependence on overnight detention. Overuse of detention represents not only the problem, general to the criminal justice system as a whole, of overreliance on incarceration in lieu of release on bail or recognizance, but also a particularly vexing problem in juvenile justice. Admittedly, the police face a dilemma. They are often looked to as the only public agency available twenty-four hours a day. By virtue of the breadth of legislative standards for intervention in the lives of children, they possess broad discretionary powers. It is hard to say how many cases of juveniles detained briefly might have been handled otherwise, had alternative resources been available. But studies have repeatedly pointed to detention rates that are high in spite of the lack of facilities throughout the country and that could be markedly reduced. More diligent search for parents or other responsible adults might in some instances have produced satisfactory alternatives. Thus the conclusion emerges that detention has sometimes been employed not so much for protection of the juvenile or the community as for its shock effect on an alleged offender.

In sum, the range of police dispositions is considerable, and the criteria for selection of disposition are seldom set forth explicitly, ordered in priority, or regularly reviewed for administrative purposes. In-service training designed to assist police in exercising their discretionary functions is unusual; the few examples deserve further investigation, for improvement of the police discretionary process holds promise of more discriminating judgments between offenders who should be retained in the system and those who need, if anything, service rather than adjudication.

Agencies Outside the Formal Juvenile Justice System

Many kinds of organizations can play a significant role in nonjudicial handling of delinquents. Mental health agencies, social agencies, school guidance units may offer highly relevant services. Some programs have been specifically tailored for controlling and redirecting acting-out youth; street gang work is one notable example.[31] Groups that sponsor programs designed to reduce delinquency commonly reach into high-risk areas and attempt to identify, screen, and extend service to nonadjudicated delinquents. In dealing with adjudicated delinquents, their activities parallel those of the police, judge, probation, and parole officers. Yet rarely are they closely coordinated.

In a few communities, quasi-official organizations have been developed to handle certain types of juvenile offenders instead of sending them through the juvenile justice system. An obvious practical advantage of such units is relief for the overburdened official agencies by diversion of cases into new channels. From a theoretical point of view, the most compelling argument in favor of this development is the imperative need to find new techniques to modify the behavior of juvenile criminals and those who appear to be crime prone.

A few juvenile court jurisdictions have experimented with informal disposition and service arrangements in local communities, rural, suburban, and densely urban. These experiments range from the institutionalized use of conference committees appointed under rule of court [32] to cooperative service agreements among juvenile court, police, and social agencies.[33] A standard feature of such innovations is case selection from the categories of relatively minor offenses and troublesome noncriminal behavior. Characteristically, the cases include vandalism, petty theft, defiance of parental authority, and truancy.

Arrangements of this type are now in effect in such disparate places as Essex County, New Jersey (Newark); King County, Washington (in towns on the perimeter of seattle); Oakland County, Michigan (Pontiac and environs); and a rural county in Illinois. One motivation for experimentation seems to be dissatisfaction with police handling, whether because of lack of juvenile specialists or paucity of police (as in the rural areas) or volume of delinquents (as in the cities), or for lack of confidence in police methods. These specialized programs, moreover, have been decentralized, thus affording timely guidance close to home to help change a juvenile pattern of misconduct.

Typically, these experiments have firm structural ties with the juvenile court, which sets the ambit of authority for the local group or office. Depending on the type of community program, court probation officers may supply the service or work closely with participants from local areas. Where the local plan demands that laymen not formally attached to the juvenile court decide on disposition, probation officers sometimes provide guidance.

In a number of urban areas, local comprehensive centers for social service and related types of care are being formed. These centers, which engage neighborhood residents both as staff and as advisory board members, provide previously unavailable resources to official delinquency-control agencies and thereby offer new and augmented alternatives to adjudication to the hard-pressed officialdom. Wholly extrastatutory, these and similar social structures can enhance significantly the system's pre-judicial operations. Their contribution depends on financial capacity and other factors, none more significant than the expectations of police and juvenile court. Lacking a stated role in the formal system, these centers exist at the sufferance, if not encouragement, of officials in law enforcement and juvenile administration agencies.[34]

The Juvenile Court

Published data from juvenile courts clearly indicate the significance of the screening and informal disposition functions. Although there are vast variations in practice from state to state and within each state, persistent reliance on pre-judicial dispositions is a striking fact of life in the juvenile court, viewed nationally and over a span of years. Of the delinquency cases referred to courts in 1957, the year in which the present system of reporting was instituted, 52 per cent were disposed of pre-judicially. Nine years later, in 1964, the latest year for which published statistics were available at this writing, the proportion was substantially the same.

A close look at the pre-judicial aspects of the juvenile court process reveals that a number of options have been identified and put into use. Some are prevalent in all courts, some in only a few. Some are unique to juvenile justice, others common in the criminal courts as well. On examination, it appears that the special status of informal dispositions in the juvenile court is a product of the intake process, itself inherited from the social work tradition that has given the court its administrative character. Juvenile court intake, though unique among the processes of the judicial system, is taken directly from the social agency, where it is regarded as commonplace and necessary.[35]

Intake Generally

Intake is "essentially a screening process to determine whether the court should take action and if so what action or whether the matter should be referred elsewhere." [36] Intake is set apart from the screening process used in adult criminal courts by the pervasive attempt to individualize each case and the nature of the personnel administering the discretionary process. In criminal justice, at the postarrest stage, decisions to screen out are entrusted to the grand jury, the judge, or, usually, to the prosecutor. The objective is screening, as an end in itself; attempts to deliver service to those screened out are rare.

At intake in the juvenile court, screening is an important objective. But referral to, if not insistence upon, service and imposition of controls are additional goals. Thus, the express function of intake is likely to be more ambitious than that of its criminal-law counterpart.[37] And the function is performed chiefly by persons who are neither legally trained nor significantly restricted, in the exercise of their discretionary authority, by procedural requirements comparable to those of the criminal law.

Thus, intake is a broadly conceived screening and helping process conducted within a judicial tribunal by probation officers or by the judge as *pater patriae*. The supporting cast usual in criminal dramas is missing from most juvenile courts. Neither defense attorney nor prosecutor regularly appears. Even states with recently enacted right-to-counsel provisions in their juvenile court laws have not generally experienced significant increase in the number of attorneys appearing on behalf of delinquent juveniles; New York State is a striking exception.[38] Nor does the prosecutor [39] usually participate in the pre-judicial stages of juvenile cases, except as he may review petitions, routinely or on request, to ascertain their legal sufficiency. Indeed, in metropolitan courts that task often falls to a legal assistant to the judge, not to the lawyer who represents the state's interests.

In the juvenile court intake process there is nothing comparable to the key role played by the prosecutor in criminal cases during bargaining for dismissal or lesser charges. Instead, the agreement—to adjust, for example, or to file for neglect or supervision rather than delinquency—is made between the probation officer and the juvenile and his parents. In some places the judge is directly engaged in the process, as when he actively participates in informal hearings that culminate in informal dispositions. In other places he is general supervisor of the staff's execution of informal adjustments and consultant on difficult cases.

Intake and Dispositional Choice

The options at intake include outright dismissal, referral to another community agency for service, informal supervision by the probation staff, detention, and filing of a petition. Selection among them turns in part on what is available, in part on the facts. Unless a *prima facie* case of jurisdiction is established, the only defensible recourses at intake are immediate dismissal or voluntary referral to a social agency or other source of assistance.[40] Giving the juvenile and his parents information and advice is, of course, not only permissible but desirable. The line should be clearly drawn, however, between facts potentially establishing jurisdiction and those that do not, no matter how urgent the underlying human needs. Juvenile courts that are alert to the signal importance of this distinction provide all probation officers, through ready access to the judge or to a legal assistant, with consultation on interpretation of the law.

The jurisdictional grounds, however, are broad, and at intake most cases are potential subjects of the juvenile justice process—if not for specific delinquent acts, then as incorrigibility or neglect. Most commonly, therefore, the major task at this point is to determine which cases to handle formally rather than whether a case for intervention exists. The choice is generally among dismissal (with or without referral to community service resources), unofficial handling by the court, and filing of petitions. Making that choice may call for exploration of the facts of the offense, the juvenile's background, and other facets of the case.

Preliminary conferences, explicitly provided by the most recently enacted statutes, supply a forum for deliberation and negotiation. Checks on conduct and consequences of these conferences have been included, to maximize their usefulness and guard against abuse. The Illinois Juvenile Court Act illustrates the new approach:

> Section 3–8. Preliminary conferences. (1) The court may authorize the probation officer to confer in a preliminary conference with any person seeking to file a petition under section 4–1, the prospective respondents and other interested persons concerning the advisability of filing the petition, with a view to adjusting suitable cases without the filing of a petition.
>
> (2) In any case of a minor who is in temporary custody, the holding of preliminary conferences does not operate to prolong temporary custody beyond the period permitted by section 3–5.
>
> (3) The probation officer may not prevent the filing of a petition by any person who wishes to file a petition under this act.
>
> (4) This section does not authorize any probation officer to compel any person to appear at any conference, produce any papers, or visit any place.
>
> (5) No statement made during a preliminary conference may be admitted into evidence at an adjudicatory hearing or at any proceeding against the minor under the criminal laws of this State prior to his conviction thereunder.
>
> (6) Efforts at adjustment pursuant to rules or orders of court under this section may not extend for a period of more than 3 months.[41]

The basic choice is between adjudication and the various nonjudicial alternatives. The selection is signified by filing a petition or deciding not to do so. Children's Bureau information[42] reveals that roughly half of all delinquency cases are disposed of without petition.[43] In some courts they outnumber the cases petitioned and heard. But the kinds of dispositional choices made in the course of pre-judicial handling by court staff are similar to those rendered in formally adjudicated cases. Institutional commitment is one conspicuous exception; apparently it is used only in adjudicated cases. The same proportion of cases, both pre-judicial and judicial, is screened out without further action: 8.2 per cent. Probation, used in 49 per cent of the adjudicated delinquency cases, has a counterpart in so-called informal supervision, which is applied to nearly 20 per cent of the pre-judicial cases. The picture changes, however, for dismissals following investigation: only 11 per cent of the adjudicated cases but almost half of the pre-judicial dispositions are so handled. Informal dispositions are used in many different circumstances—for a wide range of offenses, for first offenders and repeaters, for older as well as younger delinquents, and for both boys and girls (though far less often for girls).

It is noteworthy that the proportion of pre-judicial cases in a jurisdiction varies according to its demographic characteristics. The Children's Bureau division of courts into rural, semiurban, and urban jurisdictions reveals a tendency of semiurban juvenile courts to rely especially on unofficial handling: 57 per cent of delinquency cases in these areas, 50 and 47 per cent, respectively, in urban and rural areas. Among the factors that may contribute to that differential use of unofficial handling are differences in composition of populations, in types of offenses committed, in police practices, and in availability of alternatives.

Some limits have been set on pre-judicial handling. Time limits have been established by statute or policy in some states. In others, complainants and child or parents have the right to have a petition filed.[44] It is sometimes said that juveniles committing certain acts, such as sex offenses, arson, and burglary, must go directly to the formal hearing stage, but that statement is apparently open to qualification.[45]

Clearly certain offenses are adjusted less often and with more difficulty than others,[46] perhaps because greater circumspection is required when dealing informally with certain types of offenses. Extenuating circumstances must be carefully documented, consultation with the judge is essential, a plan of service must be worked out and agreed to by the parents. But it is difficult to isolate the precise elements that determine whether a case will be disposed of informally or by adjudication. Even the administrative guides available to the probation staff may be silent on this aspect of case determination. In many juvenile courts that have written instructions to staff, the guidelines for pre-judicial adjustment are couched in terms of case processing —where to seek what service—rather than in terms of the crucial elements that are supposed to govern pre-judicial case selection. Again, the influence of social work tradition is partly responsible, in its emphasis on the desirability of individualizing each case.

Discretionary decisions to dismiss or otherwise adjust are, however, by no means completely ad hoc and idiosyncratic. In some courts, supervisory systems and in-service training attempt to promote uniformity among probation officers assigned to common tasks. Further, the experience, knowledge, and self-discipline of officers with professional training aid their efforts to articulate case selection criteria and attempt consistent application in a conscious effort to promote specific goals.[47] . . .

NOTES

[1] The classification is derived from that found in A. Kahn, "Court and Community," in Rosenheim, ed., *Justice for the Child* (1962), p. 217. For a book-length statement of his approach to the treatment and control of delinquent and neglected children, see Kahn, *Planning Community Services for Children in Trouble* (1963).

[2] Remington, "The Law Relating to 'On the Street' Detention, Questioning and Frisking of Suspected Persons and Police Arrest Privileges in General," in Sowle, ed., *Police Power and Individual Freedom* (1962), pp. 11, 18–19.

[3] See, e.g., the specification of grounds for taking juveniles into custody in N.Y. Family Ct. Act 721, 722 (1963).

[4] The difficulties of securing effective referrals, especially in work with delinquents, have generally been understated. Some of them are elaborated in Spergel, *Street Gang Work: Theory and Practice* (1966), pp. 136–44.

[5] But see the provisions for adjustment efforts in N.Y. Family Ct. Act 734 (1963) and Ill. Juvenile Ct. Act 703–8 (1966). See also *Standards for Juvenile and Family Courts.*

[6] For an indication of the range of police attempts to affect the conduct of non-adjudicated delinquents, see Note, "Juvenile Delinquents: The Police, State Courts, and Individualized Justice," *Harv L. Rev.*, 79, (1966), p. 775 [hereinafter cited as *Juvenile Delinquents*].

[7] Ill. Juvenile Ct. Act 703–2 (1) (1966): "A law enforcement officer . . . shall . . .

take the minor to the nearest juvenile police officer. . . . The minor, *if not released*, shall be delivered without unnecessary delay to the court or to the place designated by rule or order of court for the reception of minors." (Italics added.)

[8] *Standards for Juvenile and Family Courts,* 53–60; see also Sheridan, "Juvenile Court Intake," *J. Family L.,* 2 (1962), 139.

[9] Thus, for example, little or nothing is known about police decisions not to arrest or not to take juveniles into custody. See Barrett, *Police Practice and the Law— From Arrest to Release or Charge, Calif. L. Rev.,* 50 (1962), pp. 11, 25–35; Goldstein, "Police Discretion Not to Invoke the Criminal Process," *Yale Law Journal,* 69, p. 543. But see Skolnick, *Justice Without Trial* (1966), for an enlightening account of police practices in two jurisdictions.

[10] E.g., Ill. Juvenile Ct. Act 703–2 (1966).

[11] The classifications used in the Uniform Crime Reports and the percentages for each in 1965 are: handled within department and released (46.7 per cent), referred to juvenile-court jurisdiction (46.1 per cent), referred to welfare agency (2.9 per cent), referred to other police agency (2.7 per cent), and referred to criminal or adult court (1.7 per cent). [1965 FBI Uniform Crime Reports 104 (Table 13).] Figures are national totals for reporting agencies. FBI data do not differentiate among types of intradepartmental handling; some departments, however, distinguish between referrals to juvenile court in which the juvenile is detained and referrals to court with concomitant release to parents or other adults. See note 12 *infra.*

FBI data are reported for eight categories: six groups of cities, divided according to population, and suburban and rural areas. Data reveal intradepartmental handling and release in 38.5 per cent of the juvenile offense cases reported by Group I (cities over 250,000); 48.9 per cent in reporting cities of Group II (100,000– 250,000; 5 per cent or more in all remaining city groups (50,000–100,000, 25,000– 50,000, 10,000–25,000, under 10,000) and in suburban areas; and 29.6 per cent in rural areas. Referral to juvenile-court jurisdiction occurred in more than 50 per cent of all cases only in Group I cities and in rural areas, and the percentage of referrals to welfare agencies was larger in Group I (6.1 per cent) than in any other category (between 1.0 and 2.1 per cent).

[12] In one large midwestern city, for example, data show the following pattern of police disposition in 1965: Out of a total of 38,531 offenses recorded in 1965, 25,455 cases were adjusted (11,573 released to parents and 13,882 referred to community agencies); 5,652 cases were referred to the juvenile court; and 7,424 cases were referred for detention. Chicago Police Dep't, Youth Div., 1965 Ann. Offense/ Offender Data Sheet. These data are routinely collected but not published.

[13] But see *Juvenile Delinquents,* 776.

[14] Chicago Police Dep't, Youth Div., 1965 Ann. Offense/Offender Data Sheet.

[15] Stanford Research Institute, A Description of Active Juvenile Offenders and Convicted Adult Felons in the District of Columbia, Juvenile Offenders 44 (prepared for Office of Law Enforcement Assistance, U.S. Dep't of Justice, 1966).

[16] *Ibid.* at 47, 48 (Tables 60, 61).

[17] The Uniform Crime Reports for 1961 through 1965 show that informal police handling of juvenile offenses during that period occurred in no less than 45 per cent and no more than 50 per cent of all the cases.

[18] Special data analysis of the Chicago Youth Division reports shows adjustment rates for Part I offenses (homicide, rape, serious assault and battery, robbery, burglary, and theft) ranging from 8.9 per cent of offenders' cases adjusted (auto theft) to 93 per cent (shoplifting). There were some adjusted cases in every offense category except murder: e.g., rape (9.3 per cent), armed robbery (30.5 per cent), attempted burglary (66.1 per cent), bicycle theft (85.6 per cent). Adjustment of Part II offenses was generally higher: e.g. drinking (80.6 per cent), disorderly conduct (92.6 per cent), simple assault (55.6 per cent), trespassing (94.1 per cent); but compare incorrigibles (19.5 per cent). Chicago Police Dep't, Youth Div., 1965 Ann. Offense/Offender Data Sheet.

See Stanford Research Institute, *op. cit., supra* note 15; Terry, "The Screening of Juvenile Offenders" (Ph.D. dissertation, University of Wisconsin, 1965).

[19] *Juvenile Delinquents,* pp. 779–85.

[20] *Ibid.*

[21] Chicago Police Department, Youth Div., Manual of Procedure (1965).

[22] *Juvenile Delinquents,* p. 778, and Tappan, *Juvenile Delinquency* (1949), p. 173.

[23] Piliavin and Briar, "Police Encounters with Juveniles," *Am. J. Sociology,* 70 (1964), p. 206. See Goldman, *The Differential Selection of Juvenile Offenders for Court Appearance,* pp. 42–44 (NCCD ed. 1963).

[24] Terry, *supra* note 18; Stanford Research Institute, *op. cit.,* note 15.

[25] *Juvenile Delinquents,* p. 781.

[26] *Ibid.,* p. 784.

[27] Wilson, *Police Planning,* pp. 135–36 (2d ed., 1957), quoted in *Juvenile Delinquents,* pp. 785–86, note 40.

[28] *Ibid.*

[29] Freed and Wald, *Bail in the United States: 1964* (1964) pp. 97–98; NCCD, *The Cook County Family (Juvenile) Court and Arthur J. Audy Home* (1963), pp. 137, 138–39. For discussion of the detention decision as an aspect of the intake function, see Sheridan, *op. cit.,* pp. 152–53.

[30] Sheridan, *op. cit.,* and studies cited in Freed & Wald, *op. cit.,* pp. 98–100.

[31] There is a useful analysis of these efforts in Gold and Winter, *A Selective Review of Community-based Programs for Preventing Delinquency* (1961). Also see the variety of programs reported in Children's Bureau, U.S. Dep't HEW, *Research Relating to Juvenile Delinquents* (1962).

[32] See, e.g., Rubin, "Volunteers Serve the Court," *Juv. Ct. Judges J.,* 15 (1964), p. 19; see also Elson and Rosenheim, "Justice for the Child at the Grassroots," *American Bar Association Journal* (1965), 51, p. 341. Arguments against this approach are set forth in Woodson, "Lay Panels in Juvenile Court Proceedings," *A.B.A.J.,* 51 (1965), p. 1141.

[33] See, e.g., Juvenile Protective Ass'n., Report on the Englewood Project (1958); New York City Youth Board, Monograph No. 2, *How They Were Reached* (1954); Silver, "Retooling for Delinquency Prevention and Rehabilitation in Juvenile Courts," *Fed. Prob.,* 30 (1966), p. 29.

[34] See the evaluation offered in Wheeler, Cotrell, and Romasco, *Juvenile Delinquency: Its Prevention and Control* (Russell Sage Foundation, 1966), pp. 5–10.

[35] See generally Sheridan, *op. cit.*

[36] *Standards for Juvenile and Family Courts,* p. 46.

[37] Indeed, the very emphasis on helpfulness to the child has given rise to—or provided a useful rationalization for—extended interferences in juveniles' lives. See Tappan, "Unofficial Delinquency," *Neb. L. Rev.,* 29 (1950), p. 547; *Juvenile Delinquents, passim.*

[38] Skoler and Tenney, "Attorney Representation in Juvenile Court," *J. Family L.,* 4 (1964), pp. 31, 77, 80, 96.

[39] *Standards for Juvenile and Family Courts,* 73, recognizes the need for "an attorney to represent the State, especially in contested cases," but does not take a position on the controversial question of what public office should supply him—district attorney's office, corporation counsel's office, police department, or other.

[40] Cf. *id.,* p. 59, urging that casework services be supplied through the court in communities where no other resources are available.

[41] Ill. Juvenile Ct. Act 703–8 (1966); cf. *Standards for Juvenile and Family Courts,* pp. 59–60.

[42] Those familiar with the Children's Bureau Statistical Series reports on juvenile courts will recognize that the terminology used in the text differs from that in the reports. The change has been made to maintain a consistent vocabulary in the text.

[43] Children's Bureau, U.S. Dep't HEW, Stat. SER. No. 83, Juvenile Court Statistics—1964, p. 11 (Table 6).

[44] E.g., N.Y. Family Ct. Act 734 (b) (1963); cf. Sheridan, "Juvenile Court Intake," *Journal of Family Law* 2 (1962), pp. 139, 143–44.

[45] *Statistical Report,* Circuit Court of Cook County, Juvenile Division, table 4, Jan. 1, 1965–Dec. 31, 1965, shows 252 cases of burglary adjusted out of a total of 711; no breakdown on arson, rape, homicide, or armed assault is available, however.

[46] Terry, *op. cit.*

[47] This is not to suggest, however, that increased professionalization of staff would result in a high proportion of pre-judicial dispositions. On the contrary, there is evidence to suggest that the more sophisticated the juvenile-court judge and staff members are about behavioral science, the greater is the tendency to channel juveniles into the stream of official processing (Wheeler, Cottrell, and Romasco, *op. cit.*). This underscores the necessity for clear policies of commitment to non-adjudicatory tracks of handling and for continuous administrative monitoring of their implementation.

6. *Adolescent Delinquency and the Myth of Hospital Treatment* *

ROBERT B. MILLER AND EMMET KENNEY, M.D.

IN THE LAST TEN YEARS the configuration of the patient census in mental hospitals has undergone profound changes, changes that are not confined to annual increases in rates of admissions. The story is many-sided and includes more than the mathematics of multiplied admissions. We are seeing not only more patients but also changes in philosophies, attitudes, and community expectations, changes that place increased demands and responsibilities on the psychiatric hospital.

The demand for mental health services has increased every year since World War II, but the patients going into hospitals now are not the same as those who entered a few years ago. The admission rate of psychotics has declined each year while the intake of personality disorders has doubled in the last ten years. People want more from psychiatric facilities than symptomatic relief. Whereas once the request might have been to cure alcoholism —a rather large order even now—the current insistence is to clear up adultery, wife-beating, and bad-check-writing. In the psychiatric world view that grew up in the forties and fifties, crime and delinquency were "seen mainly as reflections of family instability and personality maladjustments," and "psychiatric categories functioned as both cause and effect, as independent variable and dependent variable alike." [1] The tendency for twenty years has been to psychologize problems of living in our society, to assign psychological causes to many of the ills of our culture.

It is not surprising, then, that there is a generally accepted need for ever-increasing psychiatric facilities. It behooves us, however, who make psychiatric referrals in correction to look critically at specific services for specific people and to assess how these services are used, what is offered, and which needs are met. One service in great demand these days, and the one with which this paper is concerned, is inpatient treatment of adolescents.

A three-year study of the admissions of adolescent patients to the inpatient service of a psychiatric hospital [2] was conducted, and the relevance of psychiatric services to these patients and their problems was explored. The study consisted of two parts: (1) a review of all patients between the ages of twelve and nineteen who were admitted to the hospital from July 1, 1961, to June 30, 1964, with regard to official and unofficial reasons for referral, the expectations of the referral source, and the eventual diagnoses made; and (2) a follow-up study begun six months after the survey period to determine to what extent treatment recommendations had been carried out and whether there might be a definable relationship between treatment and improved social functioning.

During the three-year survey period, we admitted 140 male and 107 female patients between the ages of twelve and nineteen, and were unable to admit an additional fifty-one male and twenty female adolescents because of the lack of bed space or the failure of referring agencies and families to follow through.

WHY PATIENTS WERE REFERRED

We soon discovered, as have others,[3] that the real or unofficial reasons for referral were often at variance with the official ones. Since the policy of our inpatient service is to advise referral sources of progress in each case and to keep them involved in discharge planning as much as possible, the real purposes of referral soon show up. Almost no referrers gave the complete reason or motive for referring a patient—not because of deception but rather because of a feeling of urgency or a lack of knowledge regarding the nature and limits of psychiatric services. Many professional persons, including physicians and social workers, referred adolescent patients for a "psychiatric evaluation," the most common official reason for referral; they described these patients as confused, emotionally disturbed, getting into trouble for no reason, and not realizing the consequences of their actions. More often than not, such descriptions applied to delinquent or acting-up behavior; either before or at the time of admission we found that the unstated reason for referral was to get the patient out of trouble or out of jail, and to remove the problem from the community in the hope of finding a magical solution through a psychiatric examination. As one might expect, parents were less sophisticated than professionals in requesting help for their sons and daughters. Beatrice Freeman speaks of those parents who "beg for quick hospitalization as a way of shielding a boy from serious trouble with law-enforcement agencies. All feel a desperate need to do something." [4] We found this description to be true of parents of youths in trouble. On the other hand, families of frankly psychotic adolescents were usually more ambivalent in regard to hospitalization.

TYPES OF PATIENTS

Before proceeding further we might summarize in broad diagnostic categories the types of patients referred. Table 1 indicates the final psychiatric diagnoses, as well as the official requests for evaluation and treatment, of the 247 adolescents (twelve to nineteen years old) in the study; Table 2, an index of the unofficial, often unstated, but far more real reasons for referral, enumerates the percentages of patients in each category who were referred because of major problems associated with antisocial behavior; Table 3 shows the referral sources.

The Community-conflicted Patient

Over half the patients were placed in the "personality disorders" diagnostic category. The staff felt this group responded least well to inpatient treatment because, on the whole, these patients were the least disturbed and the most puzzled over the reasons for admission. At the same time, they presented the most acute problems in the community. The greatest disparity between official

TABLE 1. General Diagnoses and Official Reasons for Referrals

| Diagnostic Category | Category Totals | | Official Reasons for Referral | | | | | |
| | | | Evaluation | | Treatment | | Evaluation and Treatment | |
	Male	Female	Male	Female	Male	Female	Male	Female
Chronic brain disorders	18	13	9	6	5	4	4	3
Psychotic disorders	22	18	4	3	2	1	16	14
Mental deficiencies	14	13	11	9	1	1	2	3
Psychoneurotic disorders	3	11	2	7	1	3		1
Personality disorders *	81	50	53	30	13	6	15	14
Undiagnosed	2	2	1			1	1	1
Totals	140	107	80	55	22	16	38	36

* Mostly transient situational personality disorders.

TABLE 2. Referrals Because of Major Behavior Problems

| Diagnostic Category | Category Totals | | Immediate Legal Conflict | | Antisocial Behavior * | | Percentage of Category Total |
	Male	Female	Male	Female	Male	Female	
Chronic brain disorders	18	13	3	1	4	2	32.2
Psychotic disorders	22	18	1		2	1	10.0
Mental deficiencies	14	13	2	1	8	7	66.6
Psychoneurotic disorders	3	11	1	3	2	5	78.6
Personality disorders	81	50	51	25	29	23	97.7
Undiagnosed	2	2	1		1	2	100.0
Totals	140	107	59	30	46	40	70.9

* The cases in this column were not in conflict with the law at the time of referral, although some had been previously; all were demonstrating behavior unacceptable to the family, school, or community at large.

TABLE 3. Sources of Referral

Diagnostic Category	Court	County Attorney	Police or Sheriff	Social Agency	Private Attorney	Family	Physician	Total
Chronic brain disorders	4			5		10	12	31
Psychotic disorders	1	1		4		9	25	40
Mental deficiencies	2			4		6	15	27
Psychoneurotic disorders	2	2		3	1	2	4	14
Personality disorders	36	29	11	17	5	11	22	131
Undiagnosed	2			1		1		4
Totals	47	32	11	34	6	39	78	247

and unofficial reasons for referral occurred in this group. Of these eighty-one male and fifty female patients, seventy-six were referred by court workers, county attorneys, and law officers officially for either evaluation or treatment or both but really because the youths were in some immediate legal conflict. Another fifty-five referrals came from families, physicians, social agencies, and private attorneys who requested immediate admission for evaluation or treatment because of the patient's acting-up behavior, which was about to require authoritative intervention. In only three cases was there no problem of extra-legal behavior. In nearly every case in the personality disorder group, then, the referring person made a point of the patient's seeming illness, as evidenced by his resistance to community pressures to conform. In twenty-four of the cases the court required psychiatric evaluations before making legal dispositions; in these instances the official and actual reasons for referral came closest to being the same. However, in 128 of the 131 personality disorder cases, 97.7 per cent, the actual and urgently felt reasons for referral were to remove the adolescent from his community, to have the hospital take the problem and solve it, to avoid an otherwise inevitable legal disposition, and, in short, to let the cup pass.

The statistics in our study are generally supported by unpublished figures from the National Institute of Mental Health, which indicate that, from 1955 to 1963, the first admissions of patients with neuroses and personality disorders to county and state mental hospitals increased 100 per cent, while the admissions of brain disorders decreased nearly 8 per cent, functional psychoses decreased over 5 per cent, and mental deficiencies decreased 0.3 per cent.

The Nondelinquent Patient

With the exception of the psychoneurotic and undiagnosed groups, which accounted for eighteen cases and which were similar to the personality disorder group as far as reasons for and sources of referral were concerned, the other groups (i.e., cases of brain damage, psychosis, and mental deficiency) were referred on a markedly different basis, with specific descriptions of symptoms and usually without a sense of urgency on the part of the source.

Of these ninety-eight patients, seventy-seven were referred by families and physicians, thirteen by social agencies, and eight by legal sources. In these cases the official reasons were the real ones and included assurances of co-operation, a willingness on the part of the referring agent to become involved, and a desire to share responsibility for treatment. The family's, physician's, or court's request was really something like, "This boy cannot help himself. His problem is medical, not legal. What can *you* do?"

COMMUNITY EXPECTATIONS

We often were not certain just what the community agency or family really expected in a case until we began mentioning disposition. For instance, we routinely told the person who requested a psychiatric evaluation that the procedure would require about two weeks of hospitalization, and this statement was never questioned. However—and particularly in the personality-disorder and psychoneurotic groups—the referrer frequently objected to the patient's discharge when the date for it rolled around. In fact, of the 145 patients in these two groups, ninety-two were referred officially for evaluation, and seventy-six of these remained in the hospital longer than two weeks because no one was prepared to take them at the end of the evaluation period. It was true that sixteen of these seventy-six patients appeared able to benefit from a longer hospital stay, and they remained for that reason, and also because of our inability to move them out. The official requests for evaluation in all groups of patients implied the following expectations: (1) "We want to be advised what to do," (2) "Give us your opinion of the illness," (3) "Tell us whether the patient is competent" (in the case of a minor this is a rather puzzling request), and (4) "We want to know whether the patient can benefit from psychiatric treatment." The underlying reason in most cases, of course, was to make the patient behave.

Regardless of the reasons for referral and the expectations from treatment, a mandate runs through the statistics insisting that the mental health disciplines construct answers to the social ills of our times. Dr. Thomas Szasz has commented strongly on the unreality of this demand made by "those who regard it [psychiatry] as a panacea for crime, unhappiness, political fanaticism, promiscuity, juvenile delinquency—and virtually every other moral, personal, and social ill of our time."[5] These problems have always been present in society and have been dealt with in various ways; the current trend, at least in the case of our adolescents, is to look toward mental health facilities for solutions.

Table 4 shows the percentage of posthospital recommendations accepted by the referral sources in the dispositions of all the patients. In 175 of our cases (Group A), the real reason behind the requests for psychiatric help was antisocial behavior in some form,[6] including truancy, vandalism, robbery, sexual offenses, and other violations of law and social moral codes. The other seventy-two cases (Group B) involve none or relatively little of this behavior; these, however, were definitely the more incapacitated patients; for example, the schizophrenic and the organically and mentally deficient. Only thirty-two of the 175 patients in Group A were diagnosed in the latter categories, and most of these were mentally retarded. Using these figures, one might draw several conclusions, not the least obvious of which would be that, for nearly

71 per cent of the adolescents admitted (175 out of 247), the primary symptom of mental illness—and the major concern of the community—was socially deviant behavior.

TABLE 4. Aftercare Recommendations Accepted by Referral Sources
Disposition of 247 Adolescents

| | Number and Per Cent of Recommendations Accepted | | | | | |
	Outpatient Treatment or Other Supervision		Transfer to Other Hospital or Institution		Total	
	N	%	N	%	N	%
Group A—Patients with behavior problems	97	68	4	12.5	175	59
Group B—Patients with serious mental disabilities	52	91	15	100	72	93

Benefits of Hospitalization

When we considered the results of hospitalization and treatment, we found that we were on rather uncertain ground. Our facility had been designed and programed for the treatment of mentally ill adults, but we were admitting many emotionally upset adolescents whose problems seemed more appropriately the concern of the community's social and legal institutions than of the hospital. At the time of referral, 116 of the patients, or 47 per cent of the total 247, were tentatively described by the referrers as schizophrenic or psychotic, but we found only 71 of them to be psychotic or brain-damaged. The remaining 53 per cent were described upon admission as emotionally disturbed, upset, or retarded; in nearly all of these the most remarkable symptom of illness was an acting-up behavioral disturbance of some kind. Therefore, we measured results or progress in terms of clinically observed remission of antisocial behavior in the hospital—by whatever means this was accomplished. Of course, the results within the small group without behavioral problems, mainly the schizophrenic patients, were measured according to the remission of the primary signs of their illness. These methods may not have been the best criteria, but they seemed practical. It should be remembered that of the 175 cases in which misbehavior, not primary symptomatology, was a major reason for hospitalization, only 32 (or 18 per cent) showed significant evidence of organicity, psychosis, or retardation.

In Group A we noted predictable forms of antisocial or asocial behavior—that is, predictable to the extent that minimal stress or frustration and the emotional demands of interpersonal relationships would precipitate such reactions as tantrums, rebellion, rejection of authority, and withdrawal, as well as the ordinary defenses of denial and projection. Such behavior was difficult to mitigate within the hospital setting because there was no consistent attitude on the part of staff toward limit-setting and program structure. Workers in the various disciplines of psychiatry, psychology, nursing, occupational therapy, education, groupwork, and casework treated each adolescent in a partialized, parochial manner, according to the part of his personality or problem they identified. No amount of team effort was wholly effective in formulating an integrated, consistent approach to the patient. Furthermore, in this kind of environment, where the focus is on illness, there is an allegiance to permissiveness, the most conducive fertilizer in the cultivation of behavior disorders.

DISPOSITIONS AND RECOMMENDATIONS

About 82 per cent (143) of the cases in Group A did not appear to need prolonged or intensive psychiatric intervention. In fact, continued hospitalization of these patients beyond a two-week evaluation period seemed to encourage manipulative and acting-up behavior. They were discharged with recommendations for follow-up service on an outpatient, court-probation, or casework basis; 97 of the 143 followed through on our recommendations. In nearly all of these cases we were able to work with the families to some limited extent during hospitalization, which ranged from not less than two weeks to not more than five months, and to emphasize the need for consistent discipline and continued help outside the hospital.

The other 18 per cent (32 out of 175 cases) demonstrated so little internal control that we recommended further hospitalization or institutionalization for each. However, in only four instances were our recommendations accepted by families and responsible agencies. For the most part these patients returned to the same living situations from which they had come into the hospital.

Of the 72 cases in Group B with diagnoses of psychosis, brain disease, and retardation, in which behavior was not a primary concern, we discharged 57 to their homes with plans for outpatient or day patient supervision and transferred 15 to state hospitals or institutions for long-term care. These recommendations met with over 90 per cent acceptance by the referrers.

FOLLOW-UP STUDY

We did a follow-up study six months after the survey period to determine how our patients were faring. We secured minimal information on every patient, and although we learned the current status of only 149 (or 85 per cent) of Group A and 66 (or 92 per cent) of Group B, the percentages were high enough to justify our making observations and comparisons.

Table 5 summarizes the treatment or supervision status of the two groups in January 1965. We found in the larger, less disabled group that, of the 101 patients who had accepted aftercare recommendations, fifty-one were still under some kind of agency, court, medical, or clinic supervision, apparently doing well enough to keep out of training schools and other institutions; twenty-five had continued under supervision or treatment until termination by reason of improvement; four had been discharged from other state hospitals because of improvement; seven had moved from their communities and may or may not have concluded supervision; four had been admitted to state hospitals; six had been committed to training schools; and four had been sent to other public and private institutions. The remaining seventy-four patients,

TABLE 5. Aftercare Treatment, Supervision, or Institutional Status Six Months After the Three-year Study

	Group A (Antisocial Referrals)			Group B (Disability Referrals)		
	Patients who accepted aftercare recommendations	Patients who did not accept recommendations	Totals	Patients who accepted aftercare recommendations	Patients who did not accept recommendations	Totals
Agency, court, medical, or clinic supervision	51	9	60	44*	1	45
Supervision terminated— improved	25		25	3		3
Discharged from state hospitals, institutions— improved	4		4	2		2
Moved away from community	7	9	16	2		2
Admitted to state hospitals	4	1	5	16	1	17
Committed to training schools	6	4	10			
Sent to other public and private institutions	4	3	7			
No known supervision past or present		48	48		3	3
	101	74	175	67	5	72

* Includes 12 mentally deficient youngsters, 4 of whom were awaiting admission to a state school.

those who had declined follow-up care, were, on the whole, doing as well as their peers, the 101 who had accepted our recommendations. Five of them had become involved in further trouble in their communities and were therefore on court probation; four eventually had gone into outpatient treatment; nine had moved but were presumed to be getting along acceptably; one had been admitted to a state hospital; four had been committed to training schools; three were in other public or private institutions; and forty-eight had not received formal supervision at all outside their families. The information we gathered concerning these unsupervised adolescents was inadequate to describe their current social functioning, but at least it indicated they were not institutionalized and were not in serious trouble in their communities.

We were unable to conclude that Group A received direct or indirect benefit from hospitalization, but the referring agencies and families were not so cautious in their judgments. We were generally praised regardless of the outcome. If the patient made a better adjustment following hospitalization we were given full credit; if his problems persisted we were told that at least we had done more than anyone else had been able to do. We were never certain what we had done. We had seen nothing of any significance happen to these patients in the hospital; our recommendations for aftercare were not, to say the least, assiduously followed; and some of us had the unsettling thought that these youngsters would have fared as well without hospitalization. However, our follow-up study showed that families and community agencies, even the 42 per cent who had rejected our recommendations, believed that hospitalization had benefited the patients.

As to the seventy-two more psychiatrically disabled and retarded patients in Group B, we learned that three were apparently not yet under any sort of aftercare supervision but that the others had generally followed our treatment suggestions. None was in or had been in a training school. We had recommended originally that fifteen of these patients be transferred to other state hospitals or institutions, and nineteen had eventually gone into such facilities. Four others, all retardates, were awaiting admission to the state school for the mentally retarded. In all of these cases, of course, the need for evaluation had been clear. We felt when they left that they had benefited from treatment and that they would continue to benefit from the aftercare procedures we suggested.

SUMMARY AND CONCLUSIONS

The data of this study were not conclusive enough to justify an authoritative or definitive statement regarding the treatment of adolescent patients in a psychiatric hospital. We tried to evaluate our services to the community in terms of the kinds of problems referred to us, the expectations of the agencies and families who sent us patients, and the possible effects of treatment upon social functioning. Our statistics indicated, as we had long suspected, that the major demand of the community was for the care and treatment of youths with behavior disorders. Most of the adolescents referred to the Institute over a three-year period were described as ill; certainly illness was of concern to the referral sources. The question, however, came to be: What do you mean by illness? When we began looking at them closely, our referrals seemed to point toward an extremely broad interpretation of mental illness, which, as Dr. Szasz says, consists more and more of problems of living, not necessarily disease.[7]

Is there a difference between social-moral and medical-psychiatric problems? No statistics anywhere answer this question. In practice, there appears to be no distinction, and perhaps there should be none. Perhaps the psychiatric hospital is becoming more sociological than medical in its therapeutic approach. Nevertheless, the treatment of behavior disorders, particularly those of adolescents, remains an elusive problem. After all, how does a hospital treat delinquency and other deviations from social norms? To date, there is nothing in the literature or practice to tell us how and no one has ever demonstrated that problems of delinquency can be successfully treated on a large scale in a psychiatric facility. We cannot treat misbehavior. Certainly our goal is to find the underlying reasons for the behavior and to remove them. But what about the behavior in the meantime? It keeps getting in the way. How is it mitigated and controlled? The hospital has no answer to these questions.

There was comparatively little disagreement among staff concerning the benefits of hospitalization for the obviously ill adolescents. Even though the outlook for some of them was not good, and our follow-up study indicated that therapeutic failure ran fairly high, we knew that hospitalization was necessary, that there was a reasonable chance of helping each of them to some degree, and that recommendations for disposition and aftercare could be made authoritatively with some assurance they would be carried out. By contrast, a psychiatrist, a social worker, or a psychologist in a hospital cannot, or should not, presume to tell a court how to deal with a delinquent, even if he knows what to recommend.

As for the patients with behavior problems, we were a little disconcerted to find that, in the eyes of the community, hospitalization had benefited those who were currently doing well—that is, behaving themselves. We had not anticipated that many of these patients would make an early, satisfactory adjustment. Still others who we had thought would be able to cope with their problems could not do so. In any event, we had no way of determining the effect of inpatient care on the subsequent adjustment of any patient. We had recommended some form of aftercare supervision as desirable in every case, but a significantly large group received no posthospital supervision and yet, according to our limited data, were doing as well as the supervised group. Such results caused us to speculate that most of our adolescent patients could have benefited equally well from a stay in a closed institution or an open facility with a psychiatric consultation service. Very few of these youths had received anything approaching definitive psychiatric treatment in our institute—not because it was unavailable but because they could not accept the purpose or meaning of it.

Our role became that of disciplinarian, limit-setter, authoritative counselor, and, in some cases, jailer. We attempted, fairly successfully, to help each adolescent establish at least one meaningful relationship with a staff person. Traditional psychotherapy, however, was not possible in the majority of cases, because adolescents generally reject this approach and because the use of drugs and electric shock, of course, was not warranted. In other words, we used no techniques in treatment that would not have been available in any adequate juvenile institutional setting. Furthermore, the policy of admitting relatively healthy patients, however unacceptable their behavior may be, to psychiatric hospitals not only serves to establish the notion of illness but also delays the inevitable confrontation of the patient with his behavioral difficulties.

Implicit in the expectations of most referral agents and families was the faith or hope or even prayer that the hospital would, through some mystique, separate the youth from his unacceptable behavior. Perhaps because of this faith the community generally believed we had succeeded when we considered we had failed.

NOTES

[1] Frank Riessman and S. M. Miller, "Social Change Versus the Psychiatric World View," *American Journal of Orthopsychiatry* (Jan. 1964), pp. 30–31.

[2] Of the four state mental hospitals in Nebraska, three serve the state on a regional basis; the fourth, the one in which this study took place, is a teaching and research facility, and, as such, accepts referrals from every county.

[3] See Jane H. Pfouts, Martin S. Wallach, and Joan W. Jenkins, "An Outcome Study of Referrals to a Psychiatric Clinic," *Social Work* (July 1963), pp. 79–86, for a good discussion, together with an extensive bibliography, of the variables in referrals.

[4] Beatrice Freeman, "Helping the Disturbed Adolescent Accept Hospitalization," *Social Work* (Oct. 1961), p. 70.

[5] Thomas S. Szasz, "What Psychiatry Can and Cannot Do," *Harper's* (Feb. 1964), p. 50. Dr. Szasz explores this subject at length in his *Law, Liberty, and Psychiatry— An Inquiry into the Social Uses of Mental Health Practices* (New York: Macmillan, 1963 and *The Myth of Mental Illness—Foundations of a Theory of Personal Conduct* (New York: Hoeber-Harper, 1961).

[6] After working with the patients, families, and agencies long enough to evaluate their underlying concerns and expectations, we determined behavior to be the real precipitating factor in referral and admission.

[7] Szasz, "What Psychiatry Can and Cannot Do," *supra* note 5, pp. 50–51.

7. *Factors Affecting the Reporting of Crime* *

PRESIDENT'S COMMISSION ON LAW ENFORCEMENT AND ADMINISTRATION OF JUSTICE

. . . FROM THE TIME THAT police statistics first began to be maintained in France, in the 1820's, it has been recognized that the validity of calculations of changes in crime rates was dependent on a constant relationship between reported and unreported crime. Until the Commission surveys of unreported crime, however, no systematic effort of wide scale had ever been made to determine what the relationship between reported and unreported crime was. . . . These surveys have now indicated that the actual amount of crime is several times that reported to the police, even in some of the precincts with the highest reported crime rates. This margin of unreported crime raises the possibility that even small changes in the way that crime is reported by the public to the police, or classified and recorded by the police, could have significant effects on the trend of reported crime. There is strong reason to believe that a number of such changes have taken place within recent years.

CHANGING EXPECTATIONS

One change of importance in the amount of crime that is reported in our society is the change in the expectations of the poor and members of minority

* President's Commission on Law Enforcement and Administration of Justice, *The Challenge of Crime in a Free Society,* Washington, D.C.: Government Printing Office, 1967, pp. 25–27.

groups about civil rights and social protection. Not long ago there was a tendency to dismiss reports of all but the most serious offenses in slum areas and segregated minority-group districts. The poor and the segregated minority groups were left to take care of their own problems. Commission studies indicate that whatever the past pattern was, these areas now have a strong feeling of need for adequate police protection. Crimes that were once unknown to the police, or ignored when complaints were received, are now much more likely to be reported and recorded as part of the regular statistical procedure.

The situation seems similar to that found in England. The university of Cambridge's Institute of Criminology, which in 1963 conducted an exhaustive study of the sharp rise in crimes of violence, concluded in its report that:

> One of the main causes for an increase in the recording of violent crime appears to be a decrease in the toleration of aggressive and violent behavior, even in those slum and poor tenement areas where violence has always been regarded as a normal and accepted way of settling quarrels, jealousies, or even quite trivial arguments.

POLICE PRACTICE

Perhaps the most important change for reporting purposes that has taken place in the last twenty-five years is the change in the police. Notable progress has been made during this period in the professionalization of police forces. With this change, Commission studies indicate, there is a strong trend toward more formal actions, more formal records, and less informal disposition of individual cases. This trend is particularly apparent in the way the police handle juveniles, where the greatest increases are reported, but seems to apply to other cases as well. It seems likely that professionalization also results in greater police efficiency in looking for crime. Increases in the number of clerks and statistical personnel, better methods of recording information, and the use of more intensive patrolling practices also tend to increase the amount of re-

TABLE 1. REPORTING SYSTEM CHANGES—UCR INDEX
(Figures Not Comparable with Prior Years)

Name of City	Years of Increase	Amount of Increase (Index Offenses)		
		From	To	Per cent Increase
Baltimore	1964–65	18,637	26,193	40.5
Buffalo	1961–63	4,779	9,305	94.7
Chicago	1959–60	56,570	97,253	71.9
Cleveland	1963–64	10,584	17,254	63.0
Indianapolis	1961–62	7,416	10,926	47.3
Kansas City, Mo.	1959–61*	4,344	13,121	202.0
Memphis	1963–64	8,781	11,533	31.3
Miami	1963–64	10,750	13,610	26.6
Nashville	1962–63	6,595	9,343	41.7
Shreveport	1962–63	1,898	2,784	46.7
Syracuse	1963–64	3,365	4,527	34.5

* No report was published for Kansas City, Mo., for 1960.
SOURCE: "Uniform Crime Reports, 1959–1965."

corded crime. Because this process of professionalization has taken place over a period of time and because it is most often a gradual rather than an abrupt change, it is difficult to estimate what its cumulative effect has been.

Wholly different kinds of changes have occurred in a number of cities. In 1953 Philadelphia reported 28,560 Index crimes plus negligent manslaughter and larceny under $50, an increase of more than 70 per cent over 1951. This sudden jump in crime, however, was not due to an invasion by criminals but to the discovery by a new administration that crime records had for years minimized the amount of crime in the city. One district had actually handled 5,000 complaints more than it had recorded.

The Commission could not attempt an exhaustive study of such changes in reporting procedures. It has noted (in Table 1) a number of instances in which the UCR indicated changes in reporting procedures for major cities during 1959–65. All of these changes have resulted in an increase in the level of reporting for all subsequent years. It has also noted that changes of this sort are still taking place, being indicated in 1966 for Detroit, Chattanooga, Worcester, Massachusetts, and New York City, among others.

Perhaps the clearest illustration of the impact that changes in reporting systems can have is that shown by the history of such changes in New York City and Chicago. These cities are two of the nation's largest police jurisdictions, accounting in 1965 for 20 per cent of all reported robberies and 7 per cent of all reported burglaries. Changes in their reporting systems have several times

FIG. 1. Robbery and Burglary Trends for Chicago and New York, 1935–1966

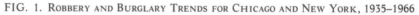
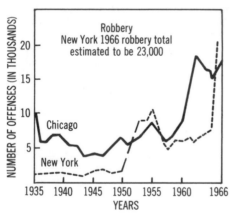
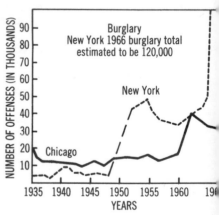

* UCR did not report any data for New York, 1949–1951.

    source: "Uniform Crime Reports, 1936–1966." 1966 figures estimated from eleven months' report.

produced large paper increases in crime. Figure 1 illustrates the pattern dramatically.

Although Chicago, with about three million people, has remained a little less than half the size of New York City, with seven and a half million throughout the period covered in Figure 1, it was reporting in 1935 about eight times as many robberies. It continued to report several times as many robberies as New York City until 1949, when the FBI discontinued publication of New York reports because it no longer believed them. In 1950 New York discontinued its prior practice of allowing precincts to handle complaints directly and installed a central reporting system, through which citizens had to route all calls.

In the first year, robberies rose 400 per cent and burglaries 1,300 per cent, passing Chicago in volume for both offenses. In 1959 Chicago installed a central complaint bureau of its own, reporting thereafter several times more robberies than New York. In 1966 New York, which appeared to have had a sharp decline in robberies in the late fifties, again tightened its central controls and found a much higher number of offenses. Based on preliminary reports for 1966, it is now reporting about 25 per cent more robberies than Chicago.

The existence of the UCR system has been one of the strongest forces pushing toward the adoption of better and more complete reporting. The FBI has been alert both to the need to encourage better reporting and to the problem that sizable changes in reporting present to the national statistical system. Through a careful system of checks, the FBI is able to identify the units that are reporting on a different basis than the previous year. It then restricts its computations of trends from one year to the next to those police agencies that have had comparable records and reporting practices. In 1965, for example, computation of changes from 1964 were limited to agencies representing 82 per cent of the U.S. population; 147 reporting agencies representing about 10 per cent of the population were eliminated because of changes in reporting practices.

In order to make comparisons for periods greater than one year, the UCR assumes that the city that underwent the change in reporting practices has had the same experience as other cities of its size and state throughout the period and re-estimates the amount of crime for all prior years back to its base period of the 1937–40 average. In the 1960–65 period, use of this system reduces the 36 per cent increase in Index crimes against the person based on published rates to a 25 per cent increase, and the 39 per cent increase in crimes against property to 36 per cent. Cities are returned to the trend computation after they have had two years of comparable experience under the new system.

This system is perhaps as good as can be devised. It is obviously very hard, however, to estimate how much crime would have been reported in a major city in the year prior to that in which the system of reporting was changed, and even harder to say what the crime rate was five years earlier. It seems unlikely that the level of robbery in New York today is thirteen times what it was in 1940 or triple what it was in 1960, but how does one decide for the purpose of long-term comparisons? The cities that have significantly changed their reporting systems since 1959 account for nearly 25 per cent of all reported Index crimes against the person and about 16 per cent of all reported Index property crimes. The real question is not the method of estimation, but whether the yardstick at the present time is too changeable to allow significant trend comparisons to be made at the national level.

A further problem is raised by the fact that a number of other large cities have not yet adopted the central complaint bureaus and strong staff controls necessary for an effective reporting program. In one of these cities, commission staff members were informed of a precinct file 13, where citizen complaints not forwarded to the central statistical office were filed for the purpose of answering insurance inquiries. The President's Commission on Crime in the District of Columbia recently criticized Washington's failure to record all offenses reported to the police. It is not clear how large this group of cities is, but disparities between cities of the same size for each of the Index offenses are so great that they seem most unlikely in the absence of some variation in reporting practice.

The reporting problem arises at least in part from the tendency of some cities, noted in 1931 by the Wickersham Commission, to "use these reports in order to advertise their freedom from crime as compared with other municipalities." This tendency has apparently not yet been fully overcome. It sometimes arises from political pressure outside the police department and sometimes from the desire of the police to appear to be doing a good job of keeping the crime rate down. Defective or inefficient recording practices may also prevent crimes reported by citizens from becoming a part of the record.

The commission believes that each city administration and each agency of justice has a duty to insure that its citizens are being fully informed of the full rate of reported crime in the community. Not to do so means that the community is being misled and that it has no benchmark to measure the effectiveness of its prevention and control program. It may also mean that the community is unaware of an increasing problem. In the case of large cities, not to report crime accurately also penalizes those administrations and police departments that are honest with their citizens by causing them to suffer unjust comparisons with other cities.

The Commission recommends that those cities that have not already done so should adopt centralized procedures for handling the receipt of reports of crime from citizens and institute the staff controls necessary to make those procedures effective.

INSURANCE

Another factor that probably increases the amount of reporting for some crimes is the sizable increase in insurance coverage against theft. It is difficult to evaluate this factor. However, because many persons believe that they must report a criminal event to the police in order to collect insurance, more reporting seems likely. . . . One indication that this may be the case is the high rate of reporting for auto theft noted by the NORC survey. Insurance is usually involved in auto theft. . . .

8. *The Distribution of Juvenile Offenses* *

TASK FORCE ON ASSESSMENT

. . . MOST OF THE STUDIES dealing with juvenile delinquents show spatial distributions in the city only according to the total delinquency rate or occasionally the rate of truancy. A recent study in Madison, Wisconsin, however, divides the city into three relatively distinct areas and provides information on the types of acts by juveniles which resulted in a contact with the police.[1] A police contact in this study meant any interaction between a Madison police officer and a juvenile that resulted in a report being filed with the Crime Prevention Bureau of the police department.

The distribution of different types of acts by juveniles resulting in a police contact are shown . . . in Table 1 according to the place of residence of the offenders. The rates are for the period 1950–55 and are based on school estimates of the juvenile population age six to eighteen. They reflect the results of a sample of 1,876 juveniles whose records showed a total of 4,554 acts or police contacts, an average of 2.47 acts per person. The West district in Table 1 is an area of high-income, middle- and upper-class residents, the East district is composed of laboring and middle-class residents of moderate income, and the Central zone has residents of the working class and lower working class with generally low incomes.

The variation in police contact with juveniles in these districts is quite large. The rate is only 66 per 1,000 juveniles for those living in the West zone, but for those in the East zone it is more than twice as great (138), and for those in the Central zone it is nearly three times as great (193). It is clear from Table 1 that a considerable amount of police contact with juveniles is not for acts that would be criminal for an adult. Furthermore, these types of contact are experienced proportionately much more often by those residing in the Central and East districts. This is particularly true of contacts involving suspicion, investigation, or information. The West district juvenile rates come closest to the other districts in connection with acts involving vehicles. The relative likelihood that a juvenile will be involved in a serious criminal act shows quite sharp gradations from one district to another with the exception of burglary, where the entral rate (5) is very close to the East rate (4) but greatly different from the West rate (1).

The trustworthiness of such findings on the geographical distribution of delinquent acts depends . . . on how well the agency statistics reflect the distribution of all serious acts of delinquency or crime that actually happen. This will clearly vary in relation to the seriousness of the offense, whether the act is reported to the police or not, whether it can be detected by the police or not, whether the record system is accurate or not, and a number of other factors. However, for the purpose of comparing different areas of a city, it is not necessary to know about every act that occurs. Official information would still

* Task Force on Assessment of the President's Commission on Law Enforcement and the Administration of Justice, *Crime and Its Impact—An Assessment*, Washington, D.C.: Government Printing Office, 1967, pp. 64–65.

TABLE 1. Delinquent Acts Resulting in Police-Juvenile Contacts by
Zone of City: Madison, Wisconsin, 1950–55*

	Average acts per 1,000 juveniles per year			
Acts	Central District	West District	East District	Total City
Incorrigible, runaway	34.10	13.55	29.97	26.65
Disorderly conduct	31.82	14.05	22.40	23.65
Contact—suspicion, investigation, information	25.92	6.47	17.80	17.61
Theft	23.35	4.37	13.30	14.61
Traffic (operation)	16.45	11.45	12.37	13.73
Vagrancy	19.77	4.27	12.90	13.03
Liquor	9.17	1.65	7.77	6.49
Burglary	4.77	.67	4.17	3.36
Auto theft	4.15	1.77	2.85	3.06
Sex offenses	2.13	.20	1.23	1.27
Traffic (parking)	1.27	.87	.90	1.06
Truancy	1.12	.47	1.00	.91
Assault	.75	.00	.40	.42
Other delinquent acts	10.08	3.04	6.02	6.76
Total delinquent acts	185.05	63.13	133.08	132.65

* Sample of City of Madison juveniles from files of Crime Prevention Bureau, 1950–55.
SOURCE: Lyle W. Shannon, "Types and Patterns of Delinquency in a Middle-sized City," *The Journal of Research in Crime and Delinquency,* 1 (Jan. 1964), 60–62.

be adequate for most crimes to show the *relative* variation in crime rates be-tween different city areas, provided that the offenses and the offenders in these areas have roughly the same chance of coming to official notice and action. There is increasing evidence from studies of police handling of juvenile of-fenses that this assumption is probably true, especially for the more serious offenses which are not confined within the family context, as in the case of domestic assaults.[2] These studies show that relatively little discrimination based on race, social class, or income appears to operate for the more serious offenses. In both recording and disposing of juvenile offenses, the arrest his-tory of the offender, the type of offense, and the age of the offender appear to have the most effect in deciding what action to take.[3]

In disposing of minor offenses, however, such criteria as race, family status, and income level may enter into the official decision sufficiently to bias the statistics against the lower-income areas of residence. Recent studies also in-dicate that this type of bias in the delinquency statistics, produced by a greater likelihood that official action resulting in a record will take place in the poorer areas, varies from one city to another depending on the type of police depart-ment and the standards of the police officer. Two recent comparative studies of a "professional" police department and an old-time "fraternal" police de-partment indicate important differences in police recording and disposition of juvenile offenses.[4] The professional department arrested a larger proportion of the juveniles with whom they came in contact and released fewer of them. The fraternal department was more reluctant to arrest and refer to the court. However, the professional department was more likely to ignore such factors as race, family status, and economic status. The fraternal department was more likely to take these criteria into account in the recording and disposition of offenses, but even when these were taken into account, they affected primarily the way minor offenses were handled. Evidence on this point is also available from a study of communities in the area of Pittsburgh which found that the rate of referral of Negro juvenile offenders to court for serious offenses was 87.5 per cent of those arrested and the rate for white children was 79.3 per cent. However, for minor offenses, the rate of referral for Negro children was 53.2 per cent and the white rate 22.6 per cent.[5] This type of bias would over-represent the Negro areas of residence as compared to white areas in juvenile statistics on court referrals by place of residence.

Apparently, the biasing effect of public attitudes, economic and social status, and police criteria for decisions do affect significantly the recording and disposition of offenses and offenders and consequently the rates for different areas of the city. Several studies, for example, have now shown that police reactions to the attitudes of the juvenile toward the authority of the police make a great deal of difference in the decision to arrest and record a contact, and it may be that persons of a racial minority group and low economic status in a slum area will be more likely to be defined as having a defiant and hostile attitude.[6] Nevertheless, the available studies and findings do encourage the belief that, if only the more serious offenses are counted, a reasonable amount of confidence may be placed in the picture they present of the relative variation in the delinquency rates between different city areas. . . .

NOTES

[1] Lyle W. Shannon, "Types and Patterns of Delinquency in a Middle-sized City," *The Journal of Research in Crime and Delinquency*, 5 (Jan. 1964), 53–66.

[2] Nathan Goldman, *The Differential Selection of Offenders for Court Appearance* (Washington, D.C.: National Research and Information Center and National Council on Crime and Delinquency, 1963), and A. W. McEachern and Riva Bauzer, "Factors Related to Disposition in Juvenile Police Contacts," in Malcolm W. Klein (ed.), *Juvenile Gangs in Context* (Englewood Cliffs, N.J.: Prentice-Hall, 1967), pp. 148–60. For additional references and a useful review, see David J. Bordus, "Recent Trends: Deviant Behavior and Social Control," *The Annals of the American Academy of Political and Social Science*, 369 (Jan. 1967), 149–63.

[3] Goldman, *ibid.*, at. pp. 125–32.

[4] James Q. Wilson, "The Police and the Delinquent in Two Cities," in Stanton Wheeler (ed.), *Controlling Delinquents* (New York: Wiley, 1967); and Aaron Cicourel, *The Social Organization of Juvenile Justice* (New York: Wiley, 1967).

[5] Goldman, *op. cit.*, p. 127.

[6] Irving Piliavin and Scott Briar, "Police Encounters with Juveniles," *American Journal of Sociology*, 70 (Sept. 1964), 206–14; Carl Werthman, "The Function of Social Definitions in the Development of Delinquent Careers," in *Task Force Report: Juvenile Delinquency*, President's Commission on Law Enforcement and Administration of Justice, Appendix J, (Washington, D.C.: Government Printing Office, 1967); and Werthman and Piliavin, "Gang Members and the Police," in David J. Bordua (ed.), *The Police: Six Sociological Essays* (New York: Wiley, forthcoming).

9. Police Discretion in Eight Communities *

JAMES Q. WILSON

FIVE OF THE COMMUNITIES in this study are industrial, working-class cities with a median family income that is below the state average, a declining downtown business district, and a population that is at least one fourth of foreign stock; four of the five (Albany, Newburgh, Oakland, and Syracuse) have, in addition, a large and growing Negro population. The fifth, Amsterdam, was bypassed by the northward migration of Negroes and, because the city has lost much of its industrial base and thus many of its low-skill jobs, Negroes are not likely to start arriving. The other three communities are well-to-do suburban areas; Brighton is a town near Rochester; Highland Park is a city near Chicago; and Nassau is an urbanized county adjacent to New York City. These suburbs have all experienced rapid population growth in the last decade or two. There are virtually no Negroes in Brighton or Highland Park; only about 4 per cent of the Nassau population is nonwhite. . . .

[There are] many important differences, of course. In New York State, "foreign stock" means primarily white European Catholics; in Oakland, the same term refers mainly to Mexican-Americans. And the foreign stock of the industrial cities of New York tend to live in old, fairly stable, ethnically homogeneous neighborhoods; though such neighborhoods have existed in Oakland, they are not conspicuous today. Rapid population movements, the heavy influx of Negroes (and Indians and Mexicans), and the weakness of institutional (for example, church) ties to a particular place have made Oakland's white population rather heterogeneous or, perhaps, "assimilated." The economic base of the communities differs as well. Albany, besides being industrial, is also a capital city where the three largest employers are the city and county of Albany and the state of New York. One fourth [of] the work force of 1960 was employed in public administration, public utilities, and public education. Employment is thus more stable and, in addition, the city is flooded with politicians and lobbyists when the legislature is in session. In all three suburban communities, a large fraction of the work force is employed in the nearby central city, but in Nassau there is also a good deal of indigenous economic activity—an aircraft plant, several very large shopping centers, and an assortment of industrial and commercial enterprises. Albany, Amsterdam, and Newburgh are all river cities and Syracuse is on the site of the old Erie Canal, but shipping to or through these places is no longer substantial. Oakland, by contrast, is a bustling port city where sailors from both merchant and naval vessels regularly come ashore seeking entertainment. (Not finding much, most of them promptly cross the bay to San Francisco.)

All eight places have their own police departments. Though Nassau is a county, its department is not a sheriff's office but a large agency supplying

* Reprinted by permission of the author and the Publisher from James Q. Wilson, *Varieties of Police Behavior*, Cambridge, Mass.: Harvard University Press, pp. 89–95, 111–18. Copyright 1968 by the President and Fellows of Harvard College.

regular municipal police services to about 80 per cent of the county's population (the remainder is served by twenty-odd city and village departments). Obviously, the magnitude and character of the problems confronting the police vary a good deal among the eight communities. In this analysis I shall from time to time speak of "high crime" and "low crime" cities. Table 1 indicates how this distinction is made. Albany, Newburgh, Oakland, and Syracuse all have reported rates of murder and auto theft, the two crimes about which police reports are generally most accurate,[1] one or both of which are

TABLE 1. RATES OF MURDER AND AUTO THEFT REPORTED BY THE POLICE IN
EIGHT COMMUNITIES, 1965, BY POPULATION SIZE
(RATES PER 100,000 POPULATION)

Community by Population	Murder and Non-negligent Manslaughter Rate	Auto Theft Rate
Over 1,000,000		
National average	9.6	585.6
Nassau County *	1.5	205.2
250,000 to 500,000		
National average	7.2	468.2
Oakland	8.7	615.8
100,000 to 250,000		
National average	6.4	353.1
Albany	2.5	565.0
Syracuse	2.8	325.1
25,000 to 50,000		
National average	3.1	212.4
Amsterdam	0	57.1
Brighton	0	63.3
Highland Park	0	121.3
Newburgh	10.0	220.0

* Crimes and crime rates for Nassau County are only for those sections of the county served by the Nassau County Police Department; the rates are based on population estimates for 1965 for NCPD-served areas.

SOURCE: For communities, reports of local police departments to the FBI, 1965; for national averages, FBI *Uniform Crime Reports,* 1965, pp. 94–95. Rates for communities based on 1965 population estimate by local planning agency; rates for national averages based on 1965 population estimated by the U.S. Bureau of the Census.

at or near the national average for cities of their size and much higher than the rates for the other four communities. Oakland has the highest rates, followed by Albany, Newburgh, and Syracuse; Amsterdam and Brighton have the lowest, followed by Nassau and Highland Park. The reported rates for many crimes have risen in all four high-crime cities—spectacularly in the case of Syracuse, partly because that police department was reorganized in 1963–64 in a way that led to more accurate, and thus more numerous, reports of offenses known to the police.

There are three reasons for making this distinction. First, a high rate of serious crime many incline the police to devote their resources to preventing, insofar as they can, such offenses and apprehending the perpetrators, to the neglect of such "minor" offenses as traffic violations, juvenile misconduct, and various adult misdemeanors. And even where there is no such emphasis, the police might claim there is in order to justify a lax attitude toward "small stuff." Second, a higher-than-normal crime rate is often associated with the presence of a larger-than-normal Negro population in the city. The four high-crime cities have the highest proportions of Negroes. Some studies have found that the nonwhite percentage of a city's population is strongly correlated with rates of murder and assault.[2] The extent to which this is true—and if true, the reasons for it—are questions that need not concern us here.[3]

What does concern us is the fact that the presence of large numbers of Negroes raises in especially acute form the potential problem of unequal police treatment of citizens. Though the police in a community with no Negroes might treat the rich or politically powerful one way and everybody else another, it would be very hard to prove—the rich and powerful are not likely to admit it and everybody else may be unaware of their different treatment or, if aware of it, lacking in a sense of group identity or the organizational capacity with which to express their feelings in the matter. Negroes, on the other hand, being marked by color, are perhaps more likely to be singled out for special treatment if the police have any such tendency, are more likely to *believe* they get special treatment because they are Negroes, and are likely to have organizations and leaders ready to express such views. Third, in cities with higher-than-average crime rates, crime is more likely to become a political issue. This has been the case in every one of the four high-crime cities here described. By contrast, the low-crime cities—except for Nassau, where there has been some political concern over juvenile delinquency, narcotics, and residential burglaries—have not had a public debate over "crime in the streets."

*   *   *

When a victim of a crime calls the police, the latter have little discretion *whether* to intervene (not answering a citizen call is easily made the subject of a complaint) but they may have considerable discretion regarding *how* to intervene. In the routine case, of course, there is little for the patrolman to do but fill out a report on the offense and file it at headquarters. If a suspect has been caught by a citizen or a store guard, however, the patrolman can choose whether to make an arrest, ask the victim to make a citizen's arrest and allow the officer to take the suspect into custody on the citizen's behalf, or do nothing. Doing nothing can be risky but, if the offense is a misdemeanor and the officer did not see it commited, doing something is also risky.

That risk is greatly reduced, and accordingly the officer's discretion is considerably broadened, when the suspect is a juvenile. The law restricting the power of the police to make arrests in misdemeanors does not apply to juveniles in some states. Under California law, for example, a patrolman may "take into temporary custody" without a warrant a person under the age of eighteen if the officer "has reasonable cause for believing" that the juvenile has, among other things, violated "any law."[4] Once in custody, the juvenile may be taken before a probation officer to determine whether further detention is necessary or the police may release him, with or without some form of reprimand, or order him to appear before the probation officer at a later date.[5] Under New York law, the police have somewhat less authority. They may take into custody without a warrant a person under the age of sixteen who commits or attempts in the officer's presence a crime, who has committed a felony but not in his presence, or who the officer has reasonable cause to believe has committed a felony.[6] The police, once they have taken a child into custody, must immediately notify the parents and either release the child to them without bond or take the child directly to the local family court or to a reception center designated by the family court.[7]

Most citizen-invoked law enforcement deals with theft (larceny, burglary, and auto theft). If a suspect has been caught, the police will have some discretion if he is an adult and considerable discretion if he is a juvenile. The police administrator can constrain this discretion, but not, as with traffic tickets, by setting production norms or, as with vice, deciding how much crime he will tolerate. Rather, he will create, or fail to create, various procedures or specialized units for handling suspects. A detective squad is one such specialized unit used for following up on "cold" cases—that is, those in which no suspect was on the scene at the time the patrolman arrived. Not every administrator specializes even to this degree—in Highland Park, for example, there was not until fairly recently a detective squad and thus there was no organized follow-up on burglary reports. But the chief's greatest opportunity for shaping, intentionally or unintentionally, the discretion exercised by his men in this area lies in the decision to create a juvenile unit and to determine its strategy.

Of the eight communities studied, three (Nassau, Oakland, and Syracuse) had specialized juvenile divisions, three (Albany, Amsterdam, and Newburgh) had no juvenile specialists, and two (Brighton and Highland Park) had at least one officer who spent more or less full time on juveniles. The consequence of specialization is that juveniles are "taken seriously"—there are officers who devote their energies to deciding how to handle them, who follow up leads on suspected juvenile offenders, and who keep records on delinquents and suspected delinquents.

The police department in the four high-crime cities differ substantially in the rate at which they arrest persons on charges of larceny, the most common victim-producing crime. As Table 2 shows, the arrest rate in 1965 in Albany

TABLE 2. ARREST RATES FOR LARCENY, BY AGE GROUP, IN FOUR HIGH-CRIME CITIES, 1965 *

City	Arrest Rates for Larceny per 100,000 Population		
	All Persons	Adults †	Juveniles ‡
Albany	92.5	96.6	80.6
Newburgh	163.3	186.4	105.9
Oakland	894.0	416.7	1,201.8
Syracuse	203.3	138.5	374.6

* All rates are calculated on the basis of estimates of the number of persons living in the city in 1965 whose ages corresponded to the age group of those arrested.

† Persons sixteen years of age or over in the New York cities and eighteen years of age or over in Oakland.

‡ Persons under the age of sixteen in the New York cities and under the age of eighteen in Oakland.

was only half that in Syracuse and one ninth that in Oakland. The rate in Newburgh was also lower than that in Syracuse and only one fifth that in Oakland. A major reason for this difference is the fact that in Albany and Newburgh very few juveniles are arrested on this charge, but in Oakland and Syracuse many are. Persons under the age of sixteen accounted for about

23 per cent of the larceny arrests in Albany and 18 per cent of those in New-burgh, but 48 per cent of those in Oakland and 51 per cent of those in Syra-cuse. In fact, because a person in California is a juvenile until he reaches the age of eighteen, an even larger proportion—over 62 per cent—of the Oakland larceny arrests that year were made under the procedures governing the han-dling of juveniles. If we compare only the adult arrest rates in the four cities, much of the difference disappears. As Table 2 shows, the adult arrest rate in Albany is about the same as in Syracuse and the rate in Newburgh is even higher than that in Syracuse. The Oakland rate is still high but not nearly as high as when all larceny arrests are treated together—the difference between Oakland and Albany falls from nearly ten to one to about four to one and the difference between Oakland and Newburgh drops from over five to one to a little over two to one.

If the crime committed by a juvenile is serious enough, he will be arrested in any city. To a patrolman, a felony arrest is a "good pinch" even if the felon turns out to be fifteen years old. Thus, such juvenile arrests as occur in Albany and Newburgh are primarily for major crimes. Of the 167 arrested in Albany in 1965, 114 (68 per cent) were held for robbery, aggravated assault, burglary, and auto theft. In Newburgh the same year, 74 per cent of the 31 juveniles arrested were held for these major offenses. The one juvenile ar-rested in Amsterdam was held for robbery. By contrast, in Syracuse, and to an even greater extent in Oakland, police officers arrest many juveniles for misdemeanors as well as felonies. In Syracuse only 31 per cent and in Oak-land only 14 per cent of those formally processed by the department were charged with what, if committed by an adult, would be a felony; the rest were held for misdemeanors and offenses.

Over time the differences are even more striking. Despite a good deal of talk among patrolmen about the rising lawlessness of youth, juvenile arrests between 1960 and 1965 decreased by 20 per cent in Albany and by 22 per cent in Newburgh. In Oakland and Syracuse, by contrast, they increased by 55 and 54 per cent, respectively.[8]

The fact that juvenile arrest rates are substantially influenced by depart-mental policies and that such arrests account for a large part of all arrests for petty larceny may explain why arrest rates for this offense are not significantly associated with the population characteristics of cities. It is quite another story with major thefts, however. Because they are felonies, arrests can occur on the basis of probable cause; because they represent large losses or frighten-ing events, there is likely to be a victim who takes the matter seriously; be-cause (judging from arrest statistics) major thefts are more likely than petty ones to be committed by adults, the discretion afforded by the laws govern-ing juveniles does not apply. As a result, arrests for these crimes—grand lar-ceny and robbery—tend to vary with community characteristics, while arrests for petty larceny seem to be independent of such characteristics (see Table 3) but, as argued above, quite dependent on police policies.

This finding casts doubt on the view that the police in middle-class suburbs are "soft" on the kids, presumably out of regard for the political influence of their parents, whereas the police in working-class communities are "tough," perhaps because such parents are lacking in influence. There is, of course, no way to know how much juvenile crime occurs in any community and there-fore no way of knowing what proportion goes unreported and what propor-tion, though reported, is ignored by the police. But the strong impression of

TABLE 3. CORRELATION BETWEEN ARREST RATE FOR VARIOUS THEFTS AND
COMMUNITY CHARACTERISTICS IN 41 NEW YORK COMMUNITIES, 1962

Community Characteristic	Petty Larceny	Grand Larceny	Robbery
Median family income	—.03	+.43	+.22
Percentage of families earning over $10,000 a year	+.03	+.51	+.34
Percentage of population nonwhite	—.01	+.36	+.47

interviewers is that suburban police officers are intimately familiar with what is going on—in great part because, lacking much serious crime to attend to, they have the time and the inclination to keep track of minor matters. Furthermore, there are highly developed informal communications in a small town: teachers, parents, and little old ladies keeping watch on flower gardens are apt to notice any strange or objectionable behavior and they will want to "do something" about perceived threats to property.[9]

When the suburban police learn of a juvenile incident, they tend to take it seriously—again perhaps because they have little else to do or perhaps because the community wants it so. Nathan Goldman, in a study of police-juvenile contacts in four small Pennsylvania communities, found that the police were more likely to detain a juvenile in a high-status residential suburb he called Manor Heights than in a small working-class town ("Steel City") in the same county—37.3 children per thousand (between the ages of 10 and 17) were detained in Steel City but 49.7 per thousand in Manor Heights. However, a larger proportion of the Steel City arrests were for the more serious offenses—26.9 per cent of the Steel City juvenile arrests but only 6.7 per cent of those in Manor Heights were on charges more serious than larceny. Accordingly, a much higher percentage of the Steel City juveniles were referred to court—46.1 per cent as compared to 8.6 per cent in Manor Heights. The Manor Heights police were thus not letting the sons of the affluent off easy—they were picking them up at a higher rate than the Steel City police were detaining the sons of blue-collar workers, and for less serious offenses. And when the Manor Heights police found a child who had committed a serious offense, they were even more likely to send him to court than the Steel City police—96.0 per cent of all arrests on "serious" charges went to court in Manor Heights, only 80.1 per cent in Steel City. [10]

There are, in short, as many reasons to believe that a middle-class community is tough on juveniles as to believe that it is soft on them. In this study, Goldman's general findings are confirmed with the important qualification that there are significant differences among police departments in upper-middle-class suburbs. Table 4 shows the number of juveniles in the low-crime communities processed by the police for all offenses in 1965 and, of those processed, the number arrested—that is, turned over to the court for a formal hearing on delinquency charges. There is no record on how many juveniles were handled informally in Amsterdam, but it is striking that despite the working-class character of the city only *one* juvenile was formally arrested, and in that case the charge was very serious—robbery. Brighton and Highland Park, about the same size as Amsterdam but much higher in socioeconomic status, had 133 and 135 juveniles, respectively, processed by the police and of these, 9 from Brighton and about 30 from

TABLE 4. JUVENILES PROCESSED AND ARRESTED IN FOUR LOW-CRIME
COMMUNITIES, 1965

City	Number of Juveniles Processed *	Number of Juveniles Arrested †	Juvenile Arrest Rate	Per Cent of Those Processed Arrested
Amsterdam	—‡	1	13.4	—
Brighton	133	9	93.8	6.8
Highland Park	135	30	312.5	22.2
Nassau County §	—	440	110.6	—

* By "processed" is meant that the police brought the juvenile to police head-quarters for questioning on a criminal charge and completed a formal record on him.

† By "arrested" is meant that the police have taken the juvenile to the local juvenile or family court for formal disposition on delinquency charges.

The juvenile arrest rate is based on the number of persons estimated to be living in the community in 1965 under the age of sixteen. In Highland Park, a person is a juvenile until he reaches the age of eighteen, but for purposes of comparison only those who were under the age of sixteen are included here.

‡ Not available.

§ The Nassau County arrest and population figures apply only to those parts of the county patrolled by the NCPD.

Highland Park were taken to court.[11] Nassau County police took 440 juveniles to court, for an arrest rate about the same as Brighton's. Of all the persons picked up by the police on charges of larceny, *none* in Amsterdam was a juvenile but 32 per cent were in Brighton and 90 per cent were in Highland Park.

No doubt there are cases of the police protecting the children of the rich, but on the whole theft in suburbia is not treated lightly. That Brighton and Highland Park have specialized juvenile officers while Amsterdam does not may account for some of the difference. But specialization alone does not necessarily lead the police to make more arrests. The administrator can through specialization achieve the opposite effect, as the case of Nassau County shows. Since 1963 the police there have had a Juvenile Aid Bureau, expanded in 1967 to a Youth Division, but the number of juveniles arrested has *declined* as a result. Between 1963 and 1964, they dropped by 10 per cent and between 1964 and 1965 by another 23 per cent. This change was in accordance with the intentions of the police administrators. The commissioner later told an interviewer that he had instructed the lieutenant in charge of the juvenile bureau to try to cut arrests: "I told [him] that if he didn't cut juvenile arrests by 30 per cent in two years, I would consider the JAB a failure. We're a semi-social agency. I think it's a great mistake to feel that you're dealing with the problem solely by making more arrests." By contrast, the police in neighboring Suffolk County, which also created a juvenile bureau (in 1961), decided to operate it on the opposite philosophy —to stop delinquency by increasing the number of arrests. Accordingly, between 1963 and 1964 such arrests increased by over 30 per cent.[12] . . .

NOTES

[1] See President's Commission on Law Enforcement and Administration of Justice, *The Challenge of Crime in a Free Society* (Washington, D.C.: Government Printing Office, 1967), p. 21. There is no pejorative implication in the term "high-crime

city"; it is simply a convenient label to distinguish one group of cities from the other. There are, in fact, many American cities with far higher crime rates than those discussed in this study.

2 See Karl Schuessler, "Components of Variation in City Crime Rates," *Social Problems,* 9 (Nov. 1962), 314–23. The Schuessler study is marred by a too uncritical acceptance of the validity of reported crime rates, but his finding of an association between the murder rate—the most reliable statistic—and the proportion nonwhite is probably valid. . . .

3 There is some evidence that the primary factor is economic. See Belton M. Fleisher, "The Effect of Income on Delinquency," *American Economic Review,* LVI (March 1966), 118–37. Using as data the number of juveniles arrested or appearing in court (somewhat suspect because it leaves out of account the much larger number of juveniles handled informally by the police) for 101 American cities over 25,000 and for 45 Chicago suburbs, Fleisher concludes that "a 1 per cent increase in incomes may well cause a 2.5 per cent decrease in the rate of delinquency" (p. 134) and that "the addition of a racial variable adds almost nothing to the explanatory power of the regression model in any of the samples" (p. 133).

4 California, *Welfare and Institutions Code,* Secs. 602, 625.

5 *Ibid.,* Secs. 626, 628.

6 New York, *Family Court Act,* Sec. 721; *Code of Criminal Procedure,* Sec. 177.

7 New York, *Family Court Act,* Sec. 724.

8 Here and elsewhere, the Oakland arrest figures for juveniles exclude persons charged with loitering because no similar charge is available to the police in the New York cities studied.

9 Though there is a good deal of talk about "suburban delinquency" or "middle-class delinquency" and even some speculation that if the *true* rates of delinquency in the suburbs were known they would not be much better than those in the central cities, there is surprisingly little systematic evidence on the matter. The best study thus far made is that by Walter Miller, who concludes that, far from there being a great and rising amount of middle-class, suburban delinquency, the rate of offenses in these outlying areas is vastly lower than in the central cities and rather stable. . . .

10 Nathan Goldman, *The Differential Selection of Juvenile Offenders for Court Appearances* (New York: National Council on Crime and Delinquency, 1963), p. 86. See also James Q. Wilson, "The Police and the Delinquent in Two Cities," in Stanton Wheeler (ed.), *Controlling Delinquents* (New York: Wiley, 1968), pp. 9–30.

11 The Highland Park figure is an estimate. Fifty-one persons under the age of eighteen were taken to court. There is no record as to how many of these were under sixteen, but applying age-specific arrest rates for juveniles from national figures for cities of that size, thirty seems a conservative guess.

10. *Delinquents Without Crimes* *

WILLIAM H. SHERIDAN

THE PROBLEM

. . . RISING CONCERN ABOUT THE increasing rate of juvenile delinquency has stimulated activity by many professional groups. One of these, the legal

* William H. Sheridan, "Juveniles Who Commit Noncriminal Acts—Why Treat in a Correctional System?" *Federal Probation,* Vol. 31, No. 1 (March, 1967), pp. 26–30.

profession, has been most lethargic about the courts and the law in this field, but nevertheless has criticized the courts for nonconformance with the requirements of due process of law. Other groups have accused them of both mollycoddling and being punitive. Still others charge the courts with being autocratic, of empire-building, and of operating independently outside the community's social-service structure. Much of this criticism was well founded so far as many courts were concerned. This was particularly true of those courts that interpreted their role to the public as being the primary preventive and correctional agency in the community.

The courts, however, should not be made the sole scapegoat. The responsibility for the present state of affairs in the field of juvenile delinquency must also be shared by others. Among them are those who fail to revise outdated legislation which governs the courts; there are budget-scared public officials who fail to provide funds for adequate services; there are administrators of public and private programs upon whom the courts depend who spend most of their energy bemoaning the deficiency of the courts rather than improving their own programs; there are the learned groups who find it so easy to theorize but so difficult to come up with effective remedies for delinquency; there is the general public which, on the one hand, demands greater protection while, on the other, refusing to support preventive and correctional programs to provide greater protection at less cost in the long run.

But there is also reason to believe that the correctional system itself contributes to the very problem it was established to correct.

The Children

Generally speaking, children coming under the jurisdiction of juvenile courts for delinquent conduct may be classified into two categories. First, there are those who have committed acts that would be crimes if committed by adults; and second, there are those who have not committed such offenses. The latter group may be further divided into two subcategories composed of youngsters who have violated specific ordinances only applicable to children, such as curfew, truancy, alcohol, or tobacco ordinances, and those who have broken no law but who are designated "beyond control," "ungovernable," "incorrigible," "runaway," "minors in need of supervision" (MINS), or "persons in need of supervision" (PINS). With few exceptions, the same dispositions are permitted in the case of these children that are authorized for youngsters who have committed acts that would be crimes if committed by an adult. In other words, children who have not indulged in criminal conduct find themselves thrown into the correctional system.

The number of children in the second group coming before the courts is considerable. A conservative estimate indicates that this group comprises about 26 per cent (approximately 184,000) of the total number of children's cases coming before the courts.[1]

For example, a summary review of between fifteen and twenty correctional institutions for delinquent children shows that about 30 per cent of their inmates were children convicted of conduct that would not have been judged criminal had they been adults. A review of ten studies made by the Children's

Bureau on state and local detention programs showed that 48 per cent of the 9,500 children studied had not committed adult criminal acts. Of the 1,300 children in this study who were actually in jail pending hearings, about 40 per cent fell into the noncriminal category. Of the remainder of the children, who were in detention homes, 50 per cent were in this category. One state even reported that in 1965 39 per cent of the children appearing before its juvenile courts were there for noncriminal conduct—truancy, incorrigibility, and running away.

Finally, looking at the populations of public and private institutions for delinquent children in 1960, I found that in the United States there were 476 children under ten years of age; one in every six of these was under seven!

There is evidence that a somewhat different practice applies in girls' cases. The Children's Bureau has found that more girls than boys fall into the category of children who have been tried for acts that would not have been criminal for adults. Fifty-two per cent of all girls' delinquency cases were in the second category outlined above. This figure for boys was only 21 per cent. This situation can be partially explained by the common practice of filing a petition for "incorrigibility" or "beyond control" for girls, when in fact their conduct would fall into the "criminal" category if committed by adults. This practice probably results from either a tendency to protect girls or the inability to prove a criminal act. It may also reflect the fact that we have permitted freer conduct for boys than for girls.

NEGATIVE IMPACTS

There is a considerable body of opinion that holds that the label of "delinquent" sets a youngster apart from his peers—in his own estimation and in that of the community in general. Through forced association with others similarly labeled, this feeling is reinforced. He begins to think of himself as a delinquent and acts accordingly.[2]

Placing such children in correctional institutions exposes them to association with more sophisticated delinquents who have committed serious offenses and developed a pattern of delinquent conduct. Even more to be condemned is the fact that they come in contact with hardened adult criminals in jail detention and in adult penal institutions to which some are committed or transferred as being incorrigible.[3]

Juvenile correctional institutions are constantly plagued with the problem of overpopulation.[4] The paucity of adequate staff in correctional programs, both in terms of training and temperament, is also common knowledge. Despite all measures, statutory or otherwise, to protect from stigma the youngster who is a product of the correctional system, it is well known that such stigma exists to almost as great a degree as in the adult field. It may act as a bar to employment or enlistment in the armed services. It may even continue to be a handicap for years. There is, for example, the case of the family whose application for public housing was turned down partly on the basis that the husband committed minor offenses as a juvenile.[5]

In the light of the present inadequacy of our correctional systems and of their negative impact on youthful offenders, placement in the system should be used only as a last resort. Furthermore, it should not be used for children who have indulged in conduct that would not be a crime if committed by an adult. No doubt many children in this category *are* in need of better supervision, care, and treatment, even including removal from home, but their needs should *not* be met by subjecting them to a correctional process designed for persons involved in criminal conduct.

One Solution

As a means of preventing this subjection of children to the correctional process, the suggestion has been made that the jurisdiction of the court in delinquency cases be limited to children who have broken laws that are applicable to all ages and that children alleged to be delinquent for other reasons be referred to public and private social agencies, clinics, and schools.[6] Although this proposal has promise, it also may be an oversimplification of the problem.

Even in stable families there is a certain amount of child-parent conflict, particularly in relation to the older adolescent group. This conflict is a normal part of growing up and is generally a painful period for the adolescent. Many parents will readily agree that it is an equally difficult experience for them. Fortunately, in all but a small percentage of families, the storm is weathered through the use of common sense and skillful handling or through the gradual process of maturation, which appears to be a major curative factor even in serious cases of delinquency.

In a number of families, because of physical, emotional, or other social or cultural pressure, conflict reaches a point where the parents are unable to cope with it. A situation can develop where a sixteen- or seventeen-year-old decides to leave home and go out on his own without any supervision whatsoever. Is society willing to permit this kind of a situation? Probably not. To do so would appear to be unfair to the adolescent as well as to the parents, who still may be held responsible for his care, supervision, and conduct. It is also unfair to the community, since in such situations the adolescent's conduct may indicate a drift toward criminal acts. Furthermore, in such conflict situations experience has shown that it cannot be assumed that parents are always acting in the best interest of the child. The parents may be equally arbitrary and unreasonable in their demands. In these situations the courts have recognized that the youngster is entitled to an advocate in his own right.[7]

Where parent-child relations reach an impasse, there must be some constituted authority which can intervene . . . with or without the consent of the parties. Such intervention obviously involves some curtailment of basic personal rights and should conform to due process of law. In this country, we have traditionally looked to the courts to determine when, under what conditions, and to what extent the state may intervene in the private lives of its citizens. For these reasons, I believe that a court should continue to have jurisdiction over these types of situations. But other remedies are worthy of exploration.

OTHER REMEDIES

Intervening Service Between Complainant and Court

In the first place, every possible step should be taken to reduce the need for intervention by the courts. This means that help must be available in the community to which police and court-intake staff can refer cases. In many communities, the only agencies that might provide such services are the welfare department and the school. Often they are not equipped to do so. Even in larger communities where a variety of public and private agencies have been established, corrections personnel have generally had little success in securing services: Rigid intake policies and already established waiting lists have effectively screened out the delinquent and his family; and established agencies have been extremely reluctant to accept referrals from police or court, particularly where these involve troublesome and rebellious adolescents.

For this reason, we need a new program that would operate as an intervening service between complainants and the court by taking responsibility for working with community agencies to secure services for youngsters referred to it. Where these services are not available, it should be equipped to provide the service or care directly. There have been a few demonstration programs of a somewhat similar nature. For one reason or another, some have been terminated and to date we have no effective evaluation.[8]

It would receive referrals from a variety of sources: police, juvenile courts, schools, public and private social agencies, and the parents of runaways or incorrigibles.

The new program should be required to accept all referrals from police and courts since this would represent a particularly vulnerable group. The same should apply to complaints of parents as to runaways or incorrigibles. A fixed but not unduly lengthy period, perhaps thirty days, would be permitted for evaluation. The case might then be closed as not needing further service, or an agreement might be concluded between the agency and family for continuing service or care. If the need for care was indicated and the family refused, then the situation would be referred back to the originating source for referral to court on the original complaint. Or where the original referral was the family, and resolution is not possible without official action, the agency would refer the matter directly to court. But the family would always have freedom of choice and could have the matter brought to the court.

Whether information secured through this process should be admissible in court and the adjudication hearing needs careful consideration. It should not be used where the original complaint involved an act that would be an adult crime or a specific offense applicable to children only, such as a curfew violation. In cases such as incorrigibility and running away, a liberal use of such information may well be necessary.

Often children will be referred to court who are in need of counseling but not court action. The establishment of such service would provide police and court with an instrument of correction for all children not needing official action.[9] Similarly, schools could avail themselves of the services pending establishment of such a program within their own area.

The above procedure would, of course, require some change in the process of court referral. Many statutes, as well as the *Standard Family Court Act* and the *Standard Juvenile Court Act*,[10] now provide that *any* person may file a petition if the court deems such action necessary to protect the child or the community.

I recommend that the filing of petitions alleging "incorrigibility," "beyond control," "runaway," or "truancy" be restricted to school officials or representatives of public or private agencies providing services for children and families. This would deny access to court to police, parents, and relatives, who now account for most of these types of referrals. And there should be an absolute bar to anyone to file a delinquency petition on any child under seven.

Juvenile Court Intake

Another checkpoint in the gateway to the correctional system is juvenile court intake. This process is essentially a screening device to determine whether court action is needed in the interests of the child or the community.[11] Effective operating intake, of course, is necessary to curtail the number of youngsters being drawn into the correctional system. Some evidence indicates, however, that in many courts the process is either nonexistent or operates to speed up the flow of cases into the court rather than to act as a screening mechanism. Since this is a specialized procedure, it should be discharged in larger courts by a separate unit and in smaller courts by an individual.

In a recent study, however, 82 per cent of 1,200 . . . courts [studied] reported they had no separate intake unit or worker to discharge this function.[12] About one fourth of these reported that the judge discharged this function, while others said it was performed by field probation officers, prosecuting attorneys, court clerks, or public social agencies.

Determining the interests of the public or the child in requiring further action is probably one of the most crucial decisions in the entire correctional process. Since, in effect, it is "case control," it has an impact on court operations as well as on programs of agencies that receive the individual for care after court disposition.

Although some common criteria are used in intake decision-making, great diversity exists in practice.[13] Also, there has been little research to assess their reliability or the weight to be given each. In a sense, the nature of the decisions depends on the philosophy or orientation of those responsible for them. These, in turn, are influenced by other factors affecting personal bias, such as professional background, training, experience, concepts of the role and function of the court, and community attitudes. And although studies show a large percentage of probation officers to be college graduates, only a small number of these specialized in social sciences. Smaller still was the group with any graduate training. Also, in-service training programs are lacking and salaries are low.[14]

Decision-making at intake is complicated by the rather broad (and often imprecise) nature of the jurisdiction conferred upon juvenile courts. Unless proved criteria, uniform policy, and proper staffing and organization are established, children will still be drawn into the correctional system on a haphazard basis—the highly subjective value judgments of a variety of individuals. For children who have not committed adult crimes, certain limitations need to be imposed upon court dispositions and agency action. Decisions of judges and of other personnel responsible for the care and treatment of children in the correctional and child welfare fields are *presumably* based on the traditional concept of "the best interests of the child." However, we all know this calls for almost unlimited freedom in decision-making. This achievement would be possible only under ideal conditions— for example, envisioning that all that needs to be known about human behavior is known; having all the necessary facilities and services of high-caliber staff available; and possessing infallibility in decisions, from the judge down to the custodial supervisor.

Limitation on Placements

Obviously, such conditions are not attainable. Therefore, certain limitations must be imposed on both judicial and executive decision-making to minimize error and insure protection against abuse.

Two such limitations are discussed here since they have particular reference to the group of children under discussion, namely, those children who have committed acts that would not be criminal if committed by an adult.

In order to keep these children out of the correctional system, disposition in these cases should be limited to placement in a noncorrectional setting. Vesting such legal custody in agencies or institutions designed for children who have committed crimes *should be prohibited*. Some of these children may have committed minor violations even though they were brought to court as being "incorrigible" or "beyond control," and a tendency might arise to file more petitions alleging criminal conduct merely to get them placed in institutions. To counteract this, the court should be required to make not only jurisdictional findings but also additional findings as to the specific charges in the petition.

I further recommend that when legal custody of such children *is* vested in an agency, the agency should be prohibited from transferring them to a facility designed primarily for children who have committed criminal acts. The present Standard Family and Juvenile Court Acts [15] prohibit the placement of neglected and incorrigible children in such institutions.[16] They do not limit, however, the placement of children who have violated laws applicable only to children.

These limitations are admittedly stringent; however, if we are in earnest about reducing crime and delinquency and if we believe in differential treatment, these steps are necessary. These limitations, furthermore, demand greater efforts by public and private social agencies. Their services will have to be strengthened to provide counseling and a variety of facilities if the needs of this particularly vulnerable group of children are to be met.

NOTES

[1] U.S. Department of Health, Education, and Welfare, *Juvenile Court Statistics, 1965*, Children's Bureau Statistical Series 85 (Washington, D.C.: Government Printing Office, 1966).

[2] See Stanton Wheeler and Leonard S. Cottrell, Jr., *Juvenile Delinquency—Its Prevention and Control* (New York: Russell Sage Foundation, 1966), pp. 22–27.

[3] U.S. Department of Health, Education, and Welfare, *Delinquent Children in Penal Institutions*, Children's Bureau Publication 415 (Washington, D.C.: Government Printing Office, 1964).

[4] U.S. Department of Health, Education, and Welfare, *Statistics on Public Institutions for Delinquent Children, 1964*, Children's Bureau Statistical Series 81 (Washington, D.C.: Government Printing Office, 1965), p. 8.

[5] In Manigo v. New York City Housing Authority, 273 NYS 2d 1003 (1966). The court indicated that although a juvenile record standing alone could not be considered as a reason, nevertheless, such offenses could be considered in showing a pattern of conduct. Also see, Aiden R. Gough, "The Expungement of Adjudication Records of Juvenile and Adult Offenders: A Problem of Status," in *Washington University Law Quarterly*, 1966 (April 1966), 147–90.

[6] See Sid Ross and William Kilpatrick, "Crimes for Kids Only," in *Parade Magazine* (Dec. 5, 1965). Also see, Sol Rubin, "Legal Definition of Offenses by Children and Youths," in University of Illinois Law Forum, *Current Problems in Criminal Law*, 1960 (Winter 1960), 512–23.

[7] See In re Sippy, 97 A.2d 455 (D.C. 1953); Selby v. Jacobucci, 349 P2d 567 (Colo. 1960).

[8] Demonstration Projects: (a) Enfield Police Department, Thompsonville, Connecticut; (b) Active Community Teams, Inc., City of Detroit; (c) Collegefields, United Community Fund and Council of Essex and West Hudson Counties, Newark, New Jersey; (d) Parkland Non-Residential Group Center, Kentucky Child Welfare Research Foundation, Inc., Frankfort, Kentucky; (e) Youth Opportunities Board of Greater Los Angeles, Los Angeles, California.

[9] The volume of cases handled by courts unofficially indicates that this is a large portion.

[10] Published by the National Council on Crime and Delinquency, 44 East 23 Street, New York, New York 10010.

[11] For detailed discussion of the process, see John A. Wallace and Marion M. Brennan, "Intake and the Family Court," 12 Buffalo L. Rev. 442 (1963); William H. Sheridan, "Juvenile Court Intake," 2 J. Fam. L., U. Louisville 139 (Fall 1962); Wallace Waalkes, "Juvenile Intake—A Unique and Valuable Tool," *Crime and Delinquency*, X (April 1964), 117–23.

[12] *Survey of Juvenile Courts and Probation Services*, developed by the Children's Bureau in cooperation with the President's Commission on Law Enforcement and the Administration of Justice, 1966.

[13] See Herbert A. Bloch and Frank T. Flynn, *Delinquency: The Juvenile Offender in America Today* (New York: Random House, 1956).

[14] The Children's Bureau-Commission survey, *op. cit.*, indicates that about 75 per cent of the courts reported no in-service training and the same percentage reported a maximum annual salary of less than $5,000.

[15] See Sec. 24 "Decree," *op. cit., supra* note 10.

[16] *Standards for Juvenile and Family Courts* (Washington, D.C.: U.S. Government Printing Office, 1966, p. 87) has a similar limitation applicable to neglected children only.

PART TWO
THE POLICE

Introduction

As the chief enforcers of "law and order," police are generally expected to see that laws are obeyed and social order maintained. The laws they are expected to enforce relate primarily to statutes that define crime and delinquency. Some of these statutes refer to classical crimes—i.e., crimes in which there is a clear victim and offender, the offense involves a "social harm" that the community recognizes as such, and law enforcers can legitimately use coercion to discourage infractions. Other statutes depart markedly from this conception. Disorderly conduct, drunkenness, vagrancy, loitering, malicious mischief, and similar offenses may disturb the peace, but it is often unclear whether anybody has been victimized, whether there has been any social harm, and whether coercion ought to be employed. But these offenses are actually the object of police attention much more frequently than offenses that comprise the FBI's Index of Major Crimes. They tend to merge with the peacekeeping and order functions of the police and bear minimal relation to classical criminal-law enforcement. It is probably accurate, therefore, to conceive of the police as engaging most frequently in order enforcement, and only secondarily in law enforcement. Reports compiled by the police as well as studies of police calls from citizens support this contention.

But order maintenance and law enforcement are not the only important tasks performed by today's policemen. They are also expected to find lost and runaway children, take expectant mothers to the hospital, direct street traffic, provide first aid, and be on call for a range of community requests for emergency services. Wilson (selection 2), in analyzing a sample of citizens' complaints radioed to police cars in Syracuse, New York, estimated that over 37 per cent involved "service" calls, 30 per cent "order maintenance," only 10 per cent direct "law enforcement," and the remainder "information gathering." In decreasing order of frequency, the police are called on to be service officers, order officers, and law officers.

Implementation of these multiple tasks requires many complex decisions, particularly in situations that involve youth. As noted earlier, the police exercise discretion regarding *whether* and *how* to intervene, as well as *what* disposition shall be made of the specific situation that they confront. In a very real sense, they act as pre-judicial policy-makers. They actually administer more justice on the sidewalks than do formal judges sitting in courtrooms. It is important for us to understand the reasons for the existence of this quasi-judicial power if we are to evolve policies that are effective as well as just.

The exercise of discretion is not a new phenomenon, as the first three readings of Part I demonstrate. These accounts all relate attempts to mitigate the harshness of the law on behalf of a special class of offenders—youth. However, this argument in defense of discretion has also been put forward on behalf of adults. If the application of the law is sometimes too severe for adults, there is even more reason for applying it cautiously when dealing with young offenders.

In addition, American legislatures have overcriminalized the penal code in an attempt to control behavior that might disturb the public order. The crimes dealing with disliked behavior—gambling, extramarital exploits, loitering, drunkenness, and similar offenses—can be technically violated by a majority of citizens. Discretionary judgment permits these statutes to be *underenforced,* thereby permitting greater freedom in personal behavior. Again, the case for discretion in reference to juvenile-status offenses is even stronger. The restrictions on youth behavior would be too onerous if the laws pertaining to school attendance, obedience to parents, curfew, boyhood scrapes, and other order offenses were meticulously enforced.

The third argument in defense of police discretion is a practical one, for both adults and youth. There are just too many laws and too many cases to handle all known violators within the official criminal-justice system. In order not to be swamped by sheer volume, we must employ screening mechanisms. The police are a logical starting point, since they are the most frequent petitioners to juvenile courts.

These three arguments indicate that mere enforcement of law and order is not always the primary concern of policemen. Other values constantly compete with the values embodied in formal statutes. The police adhere to humanitarian values when they exercise discretion to mitigate the severity of the law's application in a specific infraction event. Where the offense is not a classical crime they can interject their own moral values to neutralize the statutes. And in the interests of the value of efficiency, they can decide to help courts and correctional agencies keep from becoming overloaded. The arguments that rely on the values of humanitarianism and efficiency do not question the moral legitimacy of the laws police are entrusted to enforce; the underenforcement of order and juvenile-status offenses, however, directly questions legislative judgments about what shall constitute a criminal or delinquent act.

These kinds of value conflict are not produced by the police, but they are the group that must confront competing values and operationally attempt to forge a version of law and order acceptable to diverse elements in a community. In practice this may mean that the versions of law and order vary by individual policeman, precinct, city, and state. While the exercise of discretion may be founded on reasonable premises, in practice it may also give rise to inconsistencies and unfairness in the enforcement of statutes. The problems of police fairness, justice, and effectiveness are as germane to social policy as are the operations of the juvenile court. Examination of the problem of discretion within the context of the policeman's multiple functions, therefore, forms the core of the selections in this part.

Selection 1 focuses on the management and exercise of discretion on the streets of ghetto communities and implicitly questions existing urban practices. The studies cited by the Task Force are unclear regarding the administrative control over police discretion in a police organization. If police are persistently found to use seriousness of offense, sex, age, and number of previous contacts as the bases for judgments concerning juveniles, are these decisions guided by a police chief's verbal order, a set of administrative guidelines, the officers' personal views, the peer standards of fellow-officers? The same question can be asked about the criteria of ethnicity, class, or youthful attitude toward authority.

Wilson's *Varieties of Police Behavior* is the first major attempt to investigate this problem on a juvenile (as well as adult) level of administrative practice. His findings, excerpted in selection 2, indicate that police administrators play a central role in defining the organization's handling of all types of law and order offense. While they are responsive, in varying degrees, to community and political influences, they can function quite autonomously in areas where little pressure is brought to bear by dominant segments in their jurisdiction. According to Wilson, the police chief is a central social actor; he can define in practice what law and order actually mean in an urban community. This finding may not be applicable to large metropolitan centers, since New York, Chicago, and Los Angeles were not included in Wilson's sample of eight communities.

Wilson categorizes administrative attempts to guide discretion into three ideal types, organizational styles: watchman, legalistic, and service. In a department governed by a watchman style, serious offenses are attended to, but otherwise police act as if order maintenance rather than law enforcement were their primary concern. Many juvenile offenses are glossed over since youth are expected to misbehave, and this is permissible as long as the policeman can handle his beat without "rocking the boat." Informal dispositions and an attempt to work out complaints on a personal level are encouraged. This broad exercise of discretion (in the direction of not handling minor and status offenses as occasions for arrest) accounts for the extremely low juvenile-delinquency rate in such departments. Watchman-style departments keep as few records as possible, so it is difficult to "make a record" out of the way infractions are handled.

In contrast, a legalistic department is guided by the ideal that all laws should be enforced equally. Differences between order and status offenses and classical crimes tend to be minimized although not completely obliterated. Every official contact with a juvenile tends to be recorded even if a formal charge of delinquency is not to be pursued. This leads, of course, to very high rates of juvenile delinquency, as in Oakland, California.

The service-style department is concerned with all aspects of policing, but it is less likely than the legalistic department to process juveniles by making an arrest. Police are expected to regulate juvenile behavior on behalf of the community's mandate to maintain order and decorum, but they are expected to do this as a service for the community, rather than by filing arrest charges as law-enforcement officers. While smaller middle-class suburban communities are particularly likely to have this orientation toward public order, a large area, like middle-income Nassau County, can also function in this manner. Because Nassau officially contacts juveniles much more frequently than Albany (a watchman department), its rates of delinquency are higher. However, Nassau also adjusts more complaints by exercising discretion than does Oakland, California; therefore its rates are not so high as those of a legalistic department. The result is an official rate between those of the watchman and legalistic styles.

While many readers might be inclined to favor a service-style department, it is evident that this is a difficult organizational type to initiate and administer in heterogeneous urban areas. The operation of this sophisticated discretion, in which surveillance of the police is as persistent as surveillance of juveniles, requires a degree of professionalization and training that few police organizations possess. It is also not clear how a police department can be persuaded to change organizational style without changing the top leadership of the department. In addition, it is conceivable that closer scrutiny of a service-style department would disclose that too many juveniles were still being processed formally, and that unfair criteria are sometimes used in arriving at an official disposition.

The problem of guiding police discretion is explored further in selection 3, which proposes a strategy of written guidelines and in-service training within a philosophy of "emphasizing nonjudicial avenues of disposition"; in addition, a community youth service bureau is proposed to deal with these nonjudicial dispositions as an alternative to court referral. Myren and Swanson (selection 4) propose a more legalistic strategy, with emphasis on administrative controls, written guidelines, and frequent conferences between police and court intake workers to work out differences over decisions. Their proposals represent the ideal strategy of organized police groups, since their report was carefully scrutinized and discussed prior to publication by an array of these organizations. Reading 5, by Skolnick, raises some questions about the assumption that professional training will automatically lead to enlightened and fair police decisions.

Selection 6 focuses on the problem of having a juvenile record of arrest. Hess and LePoole discuss the practice of circulating records to nonpolice sources so that juveniles are stigmatized for life, even if arrest did not lead to conviction. Their report of the widespread abuse of confidentiality of records highlights once again the profound importance of police decisions regarding juveniles. Not only are youth affected by police decisions as youth; they are also affected years later, as adults. How to keep and use police records is an intrinsic part of the broader issue of how to guide and control police discretion.

1. *Police Contacts with Citizens on the Street** *

TASK FORCE ON THE POLICE

IT IS EXTREMELY DIFFICULT for a policeman to maintain his composure in all street situations even though this is expected and demanded of him in nearly all police departments. For example, the Law Enforcement Code of Ethics, which has been adopted by nearly all departments and police associations, requires the following:

> I will . . . maintain courageous calm in the face of danger, scorn, or ridicule; develop self-restraint; and be constantly mindful of the welfare of others.
> I will never act officiously or permit personal feelings, prejudices, animosities or friendships to influence my decisions. . . . I will enforce the law courteously and appropriately without fear or favor, malice or ill will, never employing unnecessary force or violence. . . .[1]

But the capability of a policeman, and particularly one who works in a high-crime-rate or slum neighborhood, to act in a restrained manner is constantly tested. There are countless pressures which increase the difficulty of performing police work calmly and with restraint. Typically, an officer is expected to maintain order on the street, to keep "a clean beat," and to disperse mobs, to remove "undesirables," whether or not legal tools for accomplishing these results are available. A policeman's authority is daily challenged by unruly juveniles anxious to detect any weakness or fear. In dangerous neighborhoods, he may be mocked, threatened, or even spat upon. Police work requires that policemen continually see the tragedy of victimized citizens and the sordid lives of the reprehensible and unfortunate elements of the community. And a policeman must always live with the prospect that he may be subject to attack without warning.

Even if an officer is of the highest quality, his work and the people with whom he must deal may cause him to become disillusioned or angry. If he is not of the highest quality or if he has not been properly trained, if he is prejudiced or hotheaded, he may succumb to his anger or resentment and physically or verbally abuse someone who offends him.

The problems of police-citizen contacts are multiplied and exacerbated when the citizens involved are youths. Youths commit a large and increasing proportion of crimes. They are out and around, noticeable to the patrolling officer. They travel in groups, which may make them appear more suspicious and at least potentially harder to control. They spend time in such local gathering places as pool halls, recreation centers, record shops, and street corners, and they often acquire information useful to the police. The antipathy toward the police that they might have at any age by virtue of race, neighborhood, or experience is heightened by youth's natural dislike for authority.

* Task Force on the Police of the President's Commission on Law Enforcement and Administration of Justice, *The Police,* Washington, D.C.: Government Printing Office, 1967, pp. 179–83.

It is hardly surprising that youths and policemen are not always on the best of terms. Various factors influence their reactions to and relations with each other. Informal street contacts are rarely recorded, and little factual information is available about their real extent and nature. Several recent studies and field research projects, however, have begun to explore the causes of friction between police and juveniles.

In one study, a series of interviews was conducted with San Francisco gang boys—white, Mexican, and Negro—over a two-year period.[2] While the survey was limited to gang members, it has broader significance both because its observations and analyses deal with activities of the boys independent of their gangs and because gangs and their members probably have greater contact than other youths with the police.

As the San Francisco observers point out, besides needing to obtain information from youths and to apprehend them when they have violated the law, the police also feel an obligation to receive respectful behavior from them, both to symbolize their law-abiding attitude and to attest their acceptance of the particular police officer's authority. The youths in question, however, feel an equal need to establish and maintain their autonomy—a need that, in the case of many lower-class gang boys, has been a way of life since they were children and successfully asserted their independence of overworked, ineffectual, or absent parents. One of the most tangible ways in which gang boys assert autonomy is their claim to control of a street corner, city block, or other geographical area as the inviolable site of their activities. But the gang's private hangout is also the policeman's beat, and "although the boys attempt either subtly or violently to convince outsiders that their behavior at the hangout is a strictly private affair, the police tend to insist with equal conviction that all behavior on public property is their legitimate concern."[3] According to one sociologist, the Chicago police illustrate the conflict by saying, when displeased by a gang's hangout behavior, "Give me that corner!"[4]

The struggle for street-corner control may be the backdrop for encounters between police and juveniles, but it is the more pointed, circumscribed encounters—stops, searches, trips to the stationhouse—that shape their views of each other. As the San Francisco sociologists point out, when policemen are suspicious of youths in a strange neighborhood, or their furtive actions, or their gathering together in groups, they are often supported in their suspicions by common sense and experience, as well as by want of alternative means to solve crimes and preserve public order. But feeling themselves both demeaned and challenged, the youths may react with more or less open defiance and hostility, slouching or smirking or answering the officers in an offhand or uncooperative manner, thereby challenging the policemen, in turn, to "put-up-or-shut-up." In that situation, the officers, fearful of losing face and sacrificing authority on future occasions, may feel virtually forced either to arrest the juveniles for a vague or minor offense (suspicion of robbery, loitering, disturbing the peace, violating curfew regulations) or to make it appear that they are being let go out of the goodness of the officer's heart. The San Francisco study concludes that "this is why criminal records of many gang boys are often heavily laced with such charges as 'suspicion of robbery' and 'suspicion of rape.'"[5] Similarly, a study of disorderly conduct arrests of both adults and juveniles in the District of Columbia found that in almost a quarter of them the arrest had been made only for loud and boisterous talking or obscene remarks to the police.[6]

The San Francisco gang study, in taped interviews of youths, found that the appearances of authority thereby gained is more than offset by the resentment and disrespect created:

> One day we were standing on the corner about three blocks from school and this juvenile officer comes up. He say, "Hey you boys! Come here!" So everybody else walked over there. But this one stud made like he didn't hear him. So the cop say, "Hey punk! Come here!" So the stud sorta look up like he hear him and start walking over. But he walking over real slow. So the cop walk over there and grab him by the collar and throw him down and put the handcuffs on him, saying, "When I call you next time come see what I want!" So everybody was standing by the car, and he say, "All right you black ———! Get your ——— home!" Just like that. And he handcuffed the stud and took him to juvenile hall for nothing. Just for standing there looking at him.[7]

Demeanor appears to affect police disposition after arrest as well as arrest in the first instance. Juvenile officers and patrolmen interviewed in the San Francisco study estimated that demeanor is the major factor in 50 or 60 per cent of juvenile dispositions.[8] Another study of juvenile offenders reports police officials in agreement that "defiance on the part of a boy will lead to juvenile court quicker than anything else."[9] The more general significance of demeanor is illustrated by a study of a western police department in which it was found that charges against speeders, prostitutes, and other offenders depended in large part on the suspect's demeanor.[10]

Not all policemen equate unusual attire or surroundings with actual or potential lawlessness, and not all interpret defiance as need or justification for custody. This distinction is not lost on youth:

> Those two studs out in Lakeview wouldn't always be on our back for play-ing neither. We'd be standing on the corner pulling some kinda phoney (!) ———, and they pull up to find out if we was up to something. But they talked to us nice. They wouldn't let us get away with nothing, and, I mean, them cats would bust you if they had to. But they talked to us nice.[11]

Such officers—as the gang boy himself points out—are not necessarily softer, more lenient, or less effective. But by avoiding ethnic slurs, by recognizing and making allowance for the exuberance and the naturally combative and non-conforming attitudes of adolescents, these policemen allow adolescents to escape the uncomfortable spotlight of constant suspicion. Such a spotlight is not only frequently undeserved but it may encourage the youths to act as their audience, the police officers, appear to expect.

VERBAL ABUSE AND DISCOURTESY

Commission studies reveal that there are abuses in some cities that range from simple discourtesy to clearly unwarranted and excessive use of force against persons of all ages. In focusing on such abuses, it is important to bear in mind that in the large majority of instances officers were observed to handle themselves with courage and often with restraint. Therefore, it is important that the following material be read not as a general description of the conduct of all police officers but rather as a description of certain conduct that cannot be tolerated regardless of how frequent or infrequent it may be.

No matter is more important to police-community relations than the manner in which police officers talk to people on the street. The Michigan State survey found that while allegations of excessive physical force receive the most attention, verbal abuse and discourtesy were probably greater irritants to community relations.[12] If officers are abusive, insulting, or condescending, the most insignificant contact can become an occasion that arouses hostility against the police. On the other hand, if police officers are polite, forthright, respectful, and, where appropriate, friendly, a field interrogation, a traffic ticket, or even an arrest can actually increase the respect of the citizen, as well as others who see the incident, for the police.

Commission surveys revealed that a number of officers treat citizens in a demeaning manner. In one Commission study, observations were made in several cities of several hundred routine contacts between police and citizens, usually in a home or on the street. Most of the persons interviewed were witnesses, bystanders, and victims, rather than suspects. The study showed 9 per cent of the persons received a polite request from the officers; 5 per cent received an impersonal summons which was neither polite nor nasty; 66 per cent were interrogated without introduction; and 15 per cent of the interrogations began with a brusque or nasty command like "Come 'ere, punk" or "Get your ———— over here, pork chop." [13]

Discriminatory statements in particular produce both anger and strong counterprejudice among minority groups.[14] The use of racial epithets, such as "nigger," "coon," "boy," and "Pancho," appears to be widespread, even though their use is condemned by responsible police administrators. The President's Commission on Crime in the District of Columbia found that "offensive terms such as 'boy' or 'nigger' are too often used by officers of the Department" and that "in most cases, the language is chosen deliberately to demean the citizen and demonstrate the superiority of the officer." [15] And a study of police handling of juveniles in two police departments stated that, while the observer never heard derogatory remarks made to Negroes by officers on the professionalized force, he heard dozens of insults and derogatory remarks by officers in the less professionalized department.[16] It is precisely this type of language that solidifies the conflict between minority groups and the police.

Many police departments have regulations that require that citizens be treated with courtesy and respect and train their officers accordingly. One of the most far-reaching is that of the San Diego Police Department:

> *We should treat all juveniles as we would want our own children treated, even the "hard core young hoodlum,"* for our job is to help juveniles toward good citizenship and build respect for the police and not to create "cop-haters" and criminals. *Always be fair, impartial, honest, and constructive.* [Emphasis in original.] [17]

A similar rule might properly be applied to adults as well.[18]

But the general instructions of most departments are neither sufficiently forceful nor specific as to the manner in which police officers should conduct themselves with regard to citizens. General police statements concerning the need for courtesy are not enough. All departments, for example, should formulate clear policies that prohibit the use of racial epithets. A similar recommendation was made by the President's Commission on Crime in the District of Columbia:

> The chief of police should issue a directive concerning verbal abuse of citizens by police officers, which identifies and prohibits the use of trigger words such as "boy" or "nigger." The Metropolitan Police Department should make it clear that violation of its order will be cause for disciplinary procedures. Current department statements on the subject, which urge that "undue familiarity with the use of such terms as 'bud,' 'Junior,' 'Mac,' be avoided," are neither sufficently forceful nor directly related to the problems of the community.[19]

Shortly after that report, the chief of police issued a more specific directive than had previously existed.

Other police departments also prohibit certain forms of address. For example, the Chicago Police Department has the following policy:

> At all times Departmental personnel will:
> 1. Never show any bias or prejudice against race, religion, or any other group or individual.
> 2. Act, speak, and conduct themselves in such a manner as to treat all persons with complete courtesy and with that respect due to every person as a human being.
> 3. Never "talk down" to any group or individual or engage in the use of derogatory terms such as "nigger," "boy," "wop," "kike," "chink," "shine," "burrhead," "dago," "polack," "bohunk," and the like.[20]

Some departments, such as Baltimore, require that their officers address persons as Mr. _____, Mrs. _____, Sir, or Madam.[21] Such forms of address should be used as a matter of common courtesy.

Of course, it is often difficult for officers to be respectful when dealing with citizens who are abusive or disrespectful. But, as was expressed by the President's Commission on Crime in the District of Columbia after it deplored the use of abusive language both by police and citizens: "Officers must be held to a higher standard of conduct in performing their official duties."[22] This view was also expressed by O. W. Wilson, the superintendent of police in Chicago:

> The officer . . . must remember that there is no law against making a policeman angry and that he cannot charge a man with offending him. Until the citizen acts overtly in violation of the law, he should take no action against him, least of all lower himself to the level of the citizen by berating and demeaning him in a loud and angry voice. The officer who withstands angry verbal assaults builds his own character and raises the standard of the department.[23]

Consequently, if citizens show disrespect for an officer, such conduct, alone, while reprehensible, does not justify making an arrest or taking other action.

Finally, police officers should be encouraged to talk to citizens about non-police matters while on duty, as they are in New York, rather than prohibited from conducting such conversations with citizens.[24] The BSSR survey of three Washington, D.C., precincts shows that hostility in Negro males declines as informal contacts with the police increase.[25] These contacts allow the police to establish friendships rather than having solely the role of making arrests and interrogations.

PHYSICAL MISCONDUCT

Unjustified use of force, like verbal abuse, cannot be tolerated in law enforcement. Many persons, and particularly those from minority groups, believe that police officers sometimes or even frequently engage in excessive or unnecessary physical force. The Commission was not able to determine the extent of physical abuse by policemen in this country since recent studies have generally not been systematic. Earlier studies, however, found that police brutality was a significant problem. For example, the National Commission on Law Observance and Enforcement (the Wickersham Commission), which reported to President Hoover in 1931, found considerable evidence of police brutality.[26] The President's Commission on Civil Rights, appointed by President Truman, made a similar finding in 1947.[27] And in 1961, the U.S. Civil Rights Commission concluded that "police brutality is still a serious problem throughout the United States." [28]

The Commission believes that physical abuse is not as serious a problem as it was in the past. The few statistics which do exist suggest small numbers of cases involving excessive use of force.[29] Although the relatively small number of reported complaints cannot be considered an accurate measure of the total problem, most persons, including civil rights leaders, believe that verbal abuse and harassment, not excessive use of force, is the major police-community relations problem today.[30] It is clear, however, that excessive force remains a serious problem in parts of the South. There are too many well-documented instances of brutality against Negroes and civil rights workers in the recent past to doubt that it still occurs today. For example, during the Mississippi march in the summer of 1966, state, county, and local law-enforcement officers on several occasions struck demonstrators.[31] On numerous other occasions, law-enforcement officers have watched white citizens attack civil rights demonstrators or have otherwise failed to prevent or halt private violence.[32]

Moreover, one study undertaken by the Commission also determined that excessive use of force remains a significant problem outside the South as well. During the study, Commission observers systematically accompanied police officers on regular patrol in a number of major cities—primarily in high-crime and slum precincts—for periods ranging from five to eight weeks. During the survey, observers witnessed, during 850 eight-hour patrols, 5,339 police-citizen encounters—encounters that included police contacts with suspects, witnesses, victims, and bystanders. While watching these encounters, Commission observers reported that there were twenty instances where officers used force where none was clearly required or where its use was plainly excessive. Of the incidents observed, most did not appear to be based on racial prejudice. More than half of those subjected to excessive force were white. Almost all of the victims appeared to be poor. They included drunks, sexual deviates, or juveniles who were regarded by the police as hoodlums, and most appeared to contest verbally the police officer's authority.[33] . . .

*   *   *

While this limited study gave the Commission no basis for stating the extent to which police officers use force, it did confirm that such conduct still exists in the cities where observations were made.

One other study conducted in a large city revealed that when juveniles show disrespect to officers, many of the officers prefer to settle the challenge to their authority by physical means. This study indicated that certain officers would justify their use of force by deliberately provoking the juvenile until he could be considered to be resisting arrest. This technique is described in the statements of one police officer and one juvenile taken during interviews in this city:

> For example, when you stop a fellow for a routine questioning—say, a wise guy—and he starts talking back to you and telling you that you are no good and that sort of thing. You know you can take a man in on a disorderly conduct charge, but you can practically never make it stick. So what you do in a case like this is to egg the guy on until he makes a remark where you can justifiably slap him, and then if he fights back, you can call it resisting arrest.[34]

*   *   *

> Another reason why they beat up on you is because they always have the advantage over you. The cop might say, "Don't talk back to me or I'll go upside your head!" You know, and then they say they had a right to hit you or arrest you because you were talking back to an officer or resisting arrest, and you were merely trying to explain or tell him that you hadn't done what he said you'd done. One of those kinds of things. Well, that means you in the wrong when you get downtown anyway. You're always in the wrong.[35]

A survey of policemen in one midwestern city in 1951 also indicated that many officers had misconceptions about when they were justified in using force. Officers were asked to respond to this question: "When do you think a policeman is justified in roughing a man up?" They gave the following responses: [36]

Reason	*Percentage*
Disrespect for police	37
To obtain information	19
For the hardened criminal	7
When you know the man is guilty	3
For sex criminals	3
When impossible to avoid	23
To make an arrest	8

The interviews provided considerable detail concerning the officers' rationale. They believed that the use of force to obtain evidence that would justify an arrest in a felony case was acceptable—"to rough him up a little, up to a point. . . . You feel that the end justifies the means." [37] Force was seen to be permissible with sex criminals when the officer knew that a person was guilty, did not have enough evidence, and considered it necessary to ensure that the criminal was punished. The officers said that force was justified in cases involving disrespect such as:

> I was on the beat, and I was taking [a man] down to the station. There were people following us. He kept saying that I wasn't in the army. Well,

he kept going on like that, and I finally had to bust him one. I had to do it. The people would have thought I was afraid otherwise.[38]

The officers believed that the only way to treat certain groups of people, including Negroes and the poor, is to treat them roughly.[39] On the other hand, this study did conclude that illegal force was not used as frequently and with as little provocation as the officers' statements would suggest.

To prevent physical abuse by police officers requires that all police departments take great care in selecting personnel, formulate strong policies on permissible conduct, dismiss officers who engage in physical misconduct, regularly review personnel practices, comprehensively investigate all complaints made against individual officers, and strongly discipline those officers who misbehave. . . . Policies should be formulated not only to bar unnecessary force but to describe, to the extent possible, the amount of force permissible for making arrests and carrying out other police activities. Such policies can best be enforced if all officers who use physical force for any reason are required to report in writing the circumstances under which the force was used.[40]

DISCRIMINATION

The University of California study found that members of minority groups in Philadelphia and San Diego generally believed that discrimination is practiced against both middle-class and poor persons from minority groups.[41] Polls of minority groups show similar results.[42] It is extremely difficult to establish the extent to which such allegations are accurate since discrimination is likely to be only one of several factors affecting an officer's decision in any particular situation. Negroes, other minority groups, and the poor are arrested and probably stopped in disproportion to their numbers. However, these groups frequently live in high-crime areas. Consequently, normal, completely fair police work would doubtless produce the arrest or stopping of larger numbers of these groups.

Two studies of referrals to juvenile courts in several cities found that the police referred significantly more Negro than white juveniles for the same types of offenses, particularly for minor offenses.[43] Another study of police handling of juveniles in two large cities found that the eastern, nonprofessional police force referred three times as many Negro juveniles to court as whites. On the other hand, the western, more professional police force tended to treat similar types of offenders alike.[44] And, the Commission's study, based on observation of routine police work in several northern cities, found that the police did not discriminate between whites and Negroes of the same economic class; instead, police conduct seemed to depend on economic status and on whether the person was a drunk, a homosexual, or otherwise an outcast.[45]

. . . A high percentage of Negroes believe that the police provide inadequate protection in minority communities.[46] Lack of protection can take the form of police being slow to respond to calls, having inadequate personnel, or tending to ignore offenses by one minority person against another in contrast to those by members of minority groups against whites or whites against whites. While the lack of attention paid to investigating violations against others of the same race is probably decreasing, it still exists in many localities.[47] For example, the American Bar Foundation study undertaken in the mid-1950's found that it exists especially in large cities and particularly as to serious offenses such as aggravated assault.[48]

Police officers should not base decisions to arrest, stop, use force, or the like, in whole or in part, on race, poverty, or civil rights activity. All decisions must be based on objective evidence that creates suspicion, proof of guilt, or threat of danger to the officer or public, as the law requires.

NOTES

[1] Law Enforcement Code of Ethics; see Ch. 7, "Police Integrity."

[2] Carl Werthman and Irving Piliavin, "Gang Members and the Police," in David Bordua, ed., *The Police* (New York: Wiley, 1967), pp. 56–98.

[3] *Ibid.*, p. 62.

[4] *Ibid.*

[5] *Ibid.*, p. 91.

[6] Patricia M. Wald and Joel E. Hoffman, "Report on the Disorderly Conduct Status of the District of Columbia" (unpublished manuscript, 1966), p. 25.

[7] Werthman and Piliavin, *op. cit.*

[8] *Ibid.*, p. 74.

[9] Nathan Goldman, *The Differential Selection of Juvenile Offenders for Court Appearances* (Washington, D.C.: National Council on Crime and Delinquency, 1963), p. 106.

[10] Jerome H. Skolnick, *Justice Without Trial* (New York: Wiley, 1966) pp. 90, 94, 95, 108, 111. See also the similar accounts of Philadelphia police officers in Joseph D. Lottman and Gordon E. Misner, "The Police and the Community" (Berkeley: University of California School of Criminology, 1966), Vol. 1, pp. 112; Vol. II, pp. 145, 156, 168, 169.

[11] Werthman and Piliavin, *op. cit.*, p. 68.

[12] Raymond Galvin and Louis Radeley, "A National Survey of Police and Community Relations" (East Lansing: Michigan State University, 1967), p. 17.

[13] Donald J. Black and Albert J. Reiss, Jr., *Police and Citizen Behavior in Field Encounters: Some Comparisons According to the Race and Social Class Status of Citizens* (Ann Arbor: University of Michigan, 1966), p. 10.

[14] Robin M. Williams, Jr., *Strangers Next Door: Ethnic Relations in American Communities* (Englewood Cliffs: Prentice-Hall, 1964), pp. 46–48, 253, 257–58, 283, 301.

[15] President's Commission on Crime in the District of Columbia, Report on the Metropolitan Police Department (Washington: U.S. Government Printing Office, 1966), pp. 66–67.

[16] James Q. Wilson, "The Police and the Delinquent in Two Cities" (unpublished report), p. 30.

[17] J. R. Laffoon, *Field Interrogation* (San Diego, Calif.: San Diego Police Department, July, 1965), p. 38.

[18] *Ibid.*, pp. 41–44.

[19] *Supra* note 15, p. 74.

[20] Galvin and Radeley, *op. cit.*, p. 187.

[21] Richard Severo, "Strong Police Command Vital to Avert More City Violence," *Washington Post*, June 30, 1966, p. 6.

[22] *Supra* note 15, p. 74.

[23] O. W. Wilson, *Police Administration* (New York: McGraw Hill, 1963, 2nd Ed.), p. 188.

[24] Thomas A. Johnson, "New Police Plan Used on Crowds," *New York Times*, July 25, 1966, p. 16.

[25] For a similar result, see Donald Lowell Johns, "A Study of Some Factors Related to the Formation of Attitudes Toward the Police" (Master's thesis, Berkeley, University of California School of Criminology, 1966), pp. 122, 144.

[26] National Commission on Law Observance and Enforcement, *Report on Lawlessness in Law Enforcement* (Washington, D.C.: Government Printing Office, 1931).

[27] President's Commission on Civil Rights, *To Secure These Rights* (New York: Simon & Schuster, 1947), pp. 25–27.

[28] *The 50 States Report* submitted to the Commission on Civil Rights by the State Advisory Committees, 1961 (Washington, D.C.: Government Printing Office, 1961). p. 687.

[29] In fiscal year 1965, FBI statistics show that there were only nine convictions out of 1,787 cases of excessive force investigated, and in fiscal 1966 there were 1,671 excessive-force complaints investigated and only three resulted in convictions. These data were provided by Jerome Daunt, Chief, Uniform Crime Reporting Section, FBI, March 7, 1967.

[30] Galvin and Radeley, *op. cit.,* p. 66; Walter Gellhorn, *When Americans Complain* (Cambridge, Mass.: Harvard University Press, 1966), pp. 176–77; William Raspberry, "Physical Violence May Be Gone, But Police Brutality Still Exists," *Washington Post,* May 27, 1966, p. 1.

[31] Gene Roberts, "Police Seize 11 in Rights March," *New York Times,* June 24, 1966; "175 Negroes Are Pursued and Clubbed," *Washington Post,* July 11, 1966; See *supra* note 28, p. 1.

[32] U.S. Commission on Civil Rights, *Law Enforcement: A Report on Equal Protection in the South* (Washington, D.C.: Government Printing Office, 1965), pp. 174–75; "Court Told How Police Ignored Negro Beatings," *Washington Post,* Sept. 16, 1966; see also *supra* note 28, pp. 29–44, 105–09.

[33] Albert J. Reiss, Jr., "The Use of Physical Force in Police Work" (Ann Arbor: University of Michigan, 1966), pp. 16–17; report prepared for the President's Commission on Law Enforcement and the Administration of Justice.

[34] William A. Westley, "Violence and the Police," *American Journal of Sociology,* 59, pp. 34–41, as quoted in Werthman and Piliavin, *op. cit.,* pp. 92–93.

[35] Werthman and Piliavin, *op. cit.,* p. 93.

[36] Westley, *op. cit.,* p. 38. Only one reason was counted—either that first mentioned or that given most heatedly or at greatest length—for each officer. Dr. Westley believed that the officers were cautious with him because of recent criticism by the chief of police and the community about the use of violence.

[37] *Ibid.,* p. 36.

[38] *Ibid.,* p. 9.

[39] *Ibid.,* p. 40.

[40] This was also recommended by Chief Stanley R. Schrotel in "Supervising the Use of Police Authority," *Journal of Criminal Law, Criminology and Police Science,* 47, pp. 590–91.

[41] Lottman and Misner, *op. cit.,* Vol. I, p. 78, 107; Vol. II, pp. 105, 153.

[42] Bureau of Social Science Research, "Salient Findings on Crime and Attitudes Toward Law Enforcement in the District of Columbia (a preliminary technical report submitted to the U.S. Department of Justice, Office of Law Enforcement Assistance, 1966), p. 13B.

[43] Goldman, *op. cit.,* pp. 42–44, 57–58, 65–67, 73–75, 88–89; Irving Piliavin and Scott Briar, "Police Encounters with Juveniles," *American Journal of Sociology,* 70, p. 212.

[44] Wilson, *op. cit.,* pp. 9–10, 29–30.

[45] Werthman and Piliavin, *op. cit.;* William M. Kiphart, *Racial Factors and Urban Law Enforcement* (Philadelphia: University of Pennsylvania Press, 1957), pp. 9–10, 11–17.

[46] Lottman and Misner, *op. cit.,* Vol. I, p. 139.

[47] Law Enforcement Code of Ethics, Ch. 7, "Police Integrity," p. 172; *The 50 States Report,* p. 92; George F. Simpson and J. Milton Yinger, *Racial and Cultural Minorities* (rev. ed.; New York: Harper & Row, 1958), pp. 511–12.

[48] Wayne R. LaFave, *Arrest: The Decision to Take a Suspect into Custody* (Boston: Little, Brown, 1965), pp. 110–14.

2. *Varieties of Police Behavior* *

JAMES Q. WILSON

IN SOME COMMUNITIES, the police in dealing with situations that do not involve "serious" crime act as if order maintenance rather than law enforcement were their principal function. What is the defining characteristic of the patrolman's role thus becomes the style or strategy of the department as a whole because it is reinforced by the attitudes and policies of the police administrator. I shall call this the "watchman" style, employing here for analytical purposes a term that was once—in the early nineteenth century—descriptive generally of the mission of the American municipal police.[1]

In every city, of course, all patrolmen display a watchman style,—that is, a concern for the order-maintenance aspect of their function—some of the time, but in a few places this style becomes the operating code of the department. To the extent the administrator can influence the discretion of his men, he does so by allowing them to ignore many common minor violations, especially traffic and juvenile offenses, to tolerate, though gradually less so, a certain amount of vice and gambling, to use the law more as a means of maintaining order than of regulating conduct, and to judge the requirements of order differently depending on the character of the group in which the infraction occurs. Juveniles are "expected" to misbehave, and thus infractions among this group—unless they are serious or committed by a "wise guy"—are best ignored or treated informally. Negroes are thought to want, and to deserve, less law enforcement because to the police their conduct suggests a low level of public and private morality, an unwillingness to cooperate with the police or offer information, and widespread criminality. Serious crimes, of course, should be dealt with seriously; further, when Negroes offend whites, who, in the eyes of the police, have a different standard of public order, then an arrest must be made. Motorists, unless a departmental administrator wants to "make a record" by giving a few men the job of writing tickets, will often be left alone if their driving does not endanger or annoy others and if they do not resist or insult police authority. Vice and gambling are crimes only because the law says they are; they become problems only when the currently accepted standards of public order are violated (how accurately the political process measures those standards is another question). Private disputes—assaults among friends or family—are treated informally or ignored, unless the circumstances (a serious infraction, a violent person, a flouting of police authority) require an arrest. And disputes that are a normal business risk, such as getting a bad check, should be handled by civil procedures if possible. With exceptions to be noted, the watchman style is displayed in Albany, Amsterdam, and Newburgh [N.Y.]. . . .

* Reprinted by permission of the author and the Publisher from James Q. Wilson, *Varieties of Police Behavior*, Cambridge, Mass.: Harvard University Press, pp. 140–41, 144–46, 154–55, 172–83, 188–91, 200–5, 210–11. Copyright 1968 by the President and Fellows of Harvard College.

The police style in these cities is watchmanlike because, with certain exceptions dictated by the chief's policies or the city's expectations, the patrolman is allowed—and even encouraged—to follow the path of least resistance in carrying out his daily, routine assignments. His desire "to keep his nose clean" is reinforced by the department's desire "not to rock the boat." The police handle the problem of an adversary relationship with the public by withdrawing from as many such relationships as possible. As in all cities, these departments are highly sensitive to complaints from the public, though they differ in their handling of them. There is no formal complaint procedure nor any internal review or inspection system; instead, the chief handles such matters personally. Depending on the kind of political system of which he is a part, he may defend the department vocally, or hush the matter up quietly, or, if an influential person or segment of opinion has been offended, "throw the man to the wolves" by suspending or discharging him. (There were cases of officers dismissed in all three cities.) The chief tries to avoid such difficulties, however, by tightly restricting the discretionary authority of his patrolmen ("don't stick your neck out" unless you can make a "good pinch") and by having them refer all doubtful matters to the sergeants, the lieutenant, or even the chief himself.

In none of the three cities did even the critics of the police allege that serious crime was overlooked, nor did anyone deny that police tolerance of vice and gambling had declined somewhat over the years. All three communities were once a good deal gaudier, and there is still a lot of life left in Albany and Newburgh. But all have become, at least publicly, more decorous, and this was accomplished without any significant change in the police—it was simply understood that the politicians and the community and church leaders wanted things a bit quieter, a process aided in Albany by the fact that the governor tore down the wooliest part of the city. (As in all land-clearance programs, a large proportion of small businessmen, illegitimate as well as legitimate, never survive the relocation process.)

To a watchmanlike department, the penal law is a device empowering the police to maintain order and protect others when a serious infraction has occurred; the exact charge brought against the person is not so important—or rather, it is important mostly in terms of the extent to which that particular section of the law facilitates the uncomplicated exercise of police power and increases the probability of the court sustaining the action. The charges of public intoxication and disorderly conduct are useful, and thus frequently used, in this regard—they are general, they are difficult to dispute, they carry relatively light penalties and thus are not likely to be resisted, and they are not technically, in New York, "crimes" that might hurt a man's record.

In these cities, the patrolman is expected to ignore the "little stuff" but to "be tough" where it is important. For example, the police have essentially a "familial" rather than law-enforcement view of juvenile offenders. Their policy is to ignore most infractions ("kids will be kids") and to act *in loco parentis* with respect to those that cannot be ignored: administer a swift kick or a verbal rebuke, have the boy do some chores ("Tom Sawyer justice"), or turn him over to his parents for discipline. An Albany probation officer who handles many young people told an interviewer that "sometimes a cop has to do things that aren't strictly legal, like taking a kid into the back room. . . . The parents should do it but don't."

The Amsterdam police recall fondly the days when such elaborate procedures were not necessary. The officer who caught the window smasher or bicycle thief meted out curbstone justice that would instill, if not the fear of God, then at least the fear of cops. "You used to be able to take care of the whole thing yourself," one officer told an interviewer, "but if you hit a kid today, you would really get clobbered." Whatever was once the case, it is clear that the police still rely largely on informal means for controlling juveniles—lecturing them on the street corner, taking them home to their parents, or telling them to "break it up" or "move along." Such informal methods have even been institutionalized in what one department calls "Saturday morning probation." Juveniles who commit more serious, or more frequent, offenses are told to come to police headquarters every Saturday morning for a few weeks or months to report on their behavior. The parents are informed and told the alternative could be an arrest. The chief conceded to an interviewer, "It's probably not kosher," but the family court judge is aware of the system and cooperates. If the offense is not, in the eyes of the police, a "real" crime at all—as, for example, drinking under age—nothing is done. If it is a "real" crime—such as auto theft or a burglary—then an arrest is made.

*   *   *

In *any* police department, accurate case records are very important. . . . By case records are meant records of crimes, criminals, and police actions, not *statistical* records, which are of little value to anybody in most instances. But in a watchmanlike department, records are skimpy and often incomplete —except for detectives preparing a case, producing written documents is not highly rewarded. A patrolman answering a call in these three cities rarely fills out any forms unless something very serious has happened.

How the patrolman behaves at all depends very much on who, if anyone, is supervising him. "I don't care who the police chief is," said one, "I only care who my sergeant is." Standardized procedures are neither the practice nor the ideal. A senior Albany officer explained why: "Never write things down. The written word is always there, like in a newspaper. . . . If you print it, it's always there and people can look it up. I think it's a mistake to have too many things written down in a department. Anyway, you can never go by the book out in the streets. It won't work."

Related to the absence of written rules is the lack of specialization. Specialization is another way to produce what written rules tend to produce: uniform behavior. An officer given the task of handling all juveniles, for example, will develop an operating procedure, whether formal or informal, that will produce more consistent, which is not to say identical, police behavior toward juveniles than if each patrolman or detective handles the juveniles he meets on his own. The merits of specialization are not at issue here; the point is that the three departments have few specialized personnel. None has a juvenile officer, and for several reasons. It would take a man off the streets (or require hiring a new man, which the department cannot afford); it would require new procedures to coordinate patrolmen and juvenile officers involved with the same juvenile, and these would cause "headaches"; it would constrict the generalized role of the patrolman who is supposed to "handle his beat" and anything that comes up on it; and—perhaps most important—it would create an organizational pressure to "get involved" in matters beyond strict police work and thus in matters with uncertain and possibly threatening repercussions. A senior Albany officer explained his objections in these words:

"I don't believe in it [assigning juvenile officers]. . . . Seems to me the police-man shouldn't try to be the parent. . . . You get into the homes and start tell-ing people how to run their families and that causes bitterness against the police. I'm in favor of staying out of those situations."

Having a minimum of specialized or special-duty squads has an important implication for organizational behavior: *There will be few places to which one can be transferred in the department and few incentives to seek transfer there.* Most men will spend most of their police lives on patrol; unless they make detective, they will be in uniform driving a car or walking a beat—even after making sergeant, in most cases. In Albany, a patrolman could get as-signed to the traffic division, but that means riding a motorcycle or standing at a traffic intersection during long icy winters. *If there are few rewards to be sought outside the patrol force, there is little incentive to work hard to get out.* If there were a number of "cushy" jobs for patrolmen in the force—desk jobs, investigative jobs, staff jobs—patrolmen might become "producers" (writing tickets, making arrests) to attract attention and get those jobs. But there are not, and so they don't. Thus, an unspecialized department tends to be a watchmanlike department that in turn tends to resist specialization.

*   *   *

THE LEGALISTIC STYLE

In some departments, the police administrator uses such controls as he has over the patrolmen's behavior to induce them to handle commonplace situa-tions as if they were matters of law enforcement rather than order mainte-nance. He realizes, of course, that the officer cannot always act as if his duty were merely to compare observed behavior with a legal standard and make an arrest if that standard has been violated—the law itself, especially that gov-erning misdemeanor arrests, does not always permit the application of its sanctions. But whenever he acts on his own initiative, or to the extent he can influence the outcome of disorderly situations in which he acts on the initia-tive of the citizen, the patrolman is expected to take a law-enforcement view of his role. Such a police style will be called "legalistic," and it can be found in varying degrees in Oakland [Calif.] and Highland Park [Ill.] and to a growing extent in Syracuse [N.Y.].

A legalistic department will issue traffic tickets at a high rate, detain and arrest a high proportion of juvenile offenders, act vigorously against illicit en-terprises, and make a large number of misdemeanor arrests even when, as with petty larceny, the public order has not been breached. The police will act, on the whole, as if there were a single standard of community conduct—that which the law prescribes—rather than different standards for juveniles, Negroes, drunks, and the like. Indeed, because such persons are more likely than certain others to commit crimes, the law will fall heavily on them and be experienced as "harassment."

The Oakland and Highland Park police departments began functioning this way in about the mid-1950's; Oakland continues to do so, and Highland Park has modified its policies only slightly since the appointment of a new chief in 1965. Syracuse began moving in this direction in 1963, with the ar-rival of a "reform" police chief and deputy chief; it is too early to tell how far it will proceed. For now, it has only some of the earmarks of a legalistic department—and these primarily in the field of traffic enforcement.

The concept "legalistic" does not necessarily imply that the police regard all laws as equally important or that they love the law for its own sake. In all the cities here discussed, officers distinguish between major and minor crimes, feel that private disputes are usually less important than public disorders, and are willing to overlook some offenses and accept some excuses. Indeed, because the "normal" tendency of police officers . . . is to underenforce the law, a legalistic police style is necessarily the result of rather strenuous administrative efforts to get patrolmen to do what they might not otherwise do; as such, it is never completely successful. Though there may be a few zealots in a watchmanlike department, they will be few indeed and will probably concentrate their efforts more on making "good pinches," which in any department are rewarded, than on "pushing paper" (that is, writing tickets or citing juveniles). In a legalistic department, there is likely to be a sizable number of patrolmen with comparatively little zeal—typically older officers, or officers "left over" from a previous and different administration, or officers of any age who do not regard the benefits (in terms of promotions, official recognition, or good duty assignments) of zealousness as worth the costs in effort and possibly adverse citizen relations.

The legalistic style does mean that, on the whole, the department will produce many arrests and citations, especially with respect to those matters in which the police and not the public invoke the law; even when the police are called by the public to intervene, they are likely to intervene formally, by making an arrest or urging the signing of a complaint, rather than informally, as through conciliation or by delaying an arrest in hopes that the situation will take care of itself.

Though in many cases they are required by law to rely on citizen arrests, the police in following the legalistic style do not try to privatize the handling of disputes and minor offenses. Citizen arrests are facilitated, prosecution of shoplifters is encouraged, juveniles are handled formally, and drunks are arrested "for their own protection." Prostitutes are arrested (but drugstore pornography, because the law affords few grounds for an arrest, is pretty much left alone). Even in Highland Park, a small town, drunks and juveniles have been handled more formally since the mid-1950's and bad-check passers are often prosecuted even when the merchant is willing to drop charges. As the chief told an interviewer, "Once we get that check, we'll sign a complaint and we'll prosecute. We've got the check with their name on it and the date, and it's marked 'insufficient funds,' so we've got all the evidence we need. A lot of the stores would just as soon not prosecute, I suppose, but . . . we're not a collection agency." At the same time, since Highland Park *is* a small and affluent town, the police are hardly eager to intervene in domestic disputes—to be precise, wife beatings—which, unlike the barroom brawls of the big city, are rich in opportunities for an officer to get himself in trouble. The police once handled such dilemmas occasionally by calling the local magistrate (until recently, an elected magistrate handled all local cases) and asking him to try informally to reach a settlement and, of course, to take responsibility. This is no longer the case; now, the victim would be asked to sign a complaint ticket.

Though the legalistic department will issue a large number of traffic tickets, not every department with a high-ticketing rate can be called legalistic. Because he has an unambiguous performance measure, the police administrator can obtain almost any level of ticketing he wishes without necessarily altering the way the police conceive their function, as when ticketing is delegated to a specialized traffic-enforcement unit. A legalistic department will typically go beyond this, however, and put *all* patrolmen, not just traffic specialists, under some pressure to "produce." To the extent this policy is followed, some change in the patrolman's conception of his function ensues. Sometimes, however, the opposite occurs. In Highland Park, the chief responsible for the heavy emphasis on traffic enforcement was replaced, in 1965, by a chief who shifted the department's strategy without greatly affecting its ticket productivity and without abandoning its general law-enforcement orientation. He did this by substituting specialization for quotas—easing somewhat the pressure to produce on the force as a whole and giving the task to one or two officers who would do little else.[2]

A better test for the existence of the legalistic style can be found in those situations where the administrator's control of his subordinates' conduct is less certain and where therefore greater and more systematic efforts must be made to achieve the desired behavior. The handling of juvenile offenders is just such a case. In Oakland and Highland Park, and perhaps to a growing extent in Syracuse, the police take a law-enforcement rather than familial view of their responsibilities in delinquency cases. Perhaps "institutional" view would be more correct, because the police in none of these cities feel their task is simply to make an arrest whenever possible. Indeed, the officers are keenly aware of the importance of the family and spend considerable time talking to parents, but the relationship between officer and juvenile or officer and parent is formal and institutional—the officer seeks to invoke specialized, professional services (probation officers, judges, child-guidance clinics) rather than to apply his own form of discipline or to resort to appeals to clergymen or others presumed to wield "moral" influence. Of course, to take advantage of the professional services the community provides, the juvenile must be brought into these institutions—and that, typically, requires an arrest.

In Oakland, for example, the police do not arrest a large number of juveniles because they want to have the boys punished by the juvenile court (in 1965 only 11 per cent of the 6,772 boys referred by various police agencies to the juvenile division of the Alameda County [Oakland] probation department were sent on to court, and of these only a fraction were placed in any correctional institution). Indeed, large numbers of juveniles are arrested *despite* the nine-to-one odds against the youth's having to experience much more than a conversation with a probation officer. An arrest is made because, being official, it is thought to be the right way to do things and because experiencing an arrest, getting a record, and even talking to the probation officer may do some good. Nor do the police stop there. In recent years the Oakland police have operated a "Good Citizenship School" for children between the ages of eleven and fourteen, usually first offenders, who come with a parent to headquarters for a two-hour class every week for four weeks. During 1966 about a thousand juveniles attended, and a version of the program has been incorporated into the curriculum of the public schools. The Oakland officers approve of such institutional programs; they are much less likely than officers from New York communities to approve of more informal methods of dealing with delinquency.[3]

The Oakland police also encourage citizens, such as store security guards, to handle by arrest persons caught perpetrating minor crimes, such as shoplifting. The police frown on stores that seek only restitution rather than prosecution. A sergeant assigned to the shoplifting detail regularly meets with security guards to discuss procedures for handling such cases. Partly as a result of this, of the 155 shoplifters processed by the police in December 1965, not one had the charges dismissed because the complainant failed to prosecute. (Not all were arrested, either. Some of the juveniles were reprimanded and released and some adults were given a "district attorney citation" which, perhaps extralegally, requests the offender to appear before a prosecutor for what is in effect a lecture and warning.) As one Oakland officer told an interviewer: "We insist that the citizen come in and sign the complaint; most of them, of course, we know, since they are store security guards. And if occasionally the citizen won't sign, we [that is, the police] will sign 'on information and belief' if we are sure of the facts."

The zealous police chief who served in Highland Park between 1956 and 1965 instilled a law-enforcement orientation to juvenile offenses. "Laws," he told an interviewer as well as his own men, "are on the books to be enforced." The practice of dealing informally with juveniles "on the street" was to be discontinued. A sergeant explained the new philosophy:

It's Chief X's philosophy that the case is either unfounded or you had better have charged them with the offense which they are suspected of having committed. When we come across a group of kids scuffling after a basketball game, there's no such thing as "messing around" in his eyes. Either there's no trouble and no reason to stop them or else you had better bring them in.

The results of these new directives were dramatic. Between 1958 and 1959 the number of juveniles brought into the station increased from 77 to 507.[4] That more kids were detained does not mean more were punished—there was no great increase in the number going to court, largely because the additional juveniles brought to the station had committed only minor offenses.[5] But the chief was determined to see that those sent to court were punished. The judge who handled juvenile cases in the county reported that when the new chief first came to town, "he would come to court himself with every juvenile offender and would invariably complain that too many were being granted probation." But probation was granted anyway, and eventually the chief gave up. According to the judge, "He didn't come here anymore."

When the chief resigned in 1965, his successor, though a local man with a quite different personality, did not change fundamentally the policy on juveniles or, for that matter, on most other offenders. In 1963 the city had adopted a curfew ordinance that made it illegal for a person under the age of eighteen to be on the streets after 11 P.M. between Sunday and Thursday and after midnight on Friday and Saturday. The police enforced it, and from May 1964 to September 1966 they brought twenty-one cases charging curfew violation before the local court. When asked why, a sergeant explained: "The curfew law was passed so we would have a way of locking up kids who gather in gangs downtown looking for trouble. If you leave them there alone at night . . . they'll look for some way to prove what smart guys they are, such as by kicking in a plate-glass window." The chief confirmed this:

We used to be able to get a boy on a juvenile-delinquency charge for almost anything. We never had trouble finding some grounds for bringing the boy in. The new [state] juvenile code makes it a lot tougher to arrest him, so we adopted the curfew law. It's in conformity with the state statute. . . . We still have to bring him into the station, but at least we've got a charge on him that we can use to get him off the streets.

In Syracuse, also, the police have changed somewhat the manner of handling juveniles, though not as drastically as in Highland Park. Between 1961 and 1965, the number of juveniles disposed of by the police increased from 1,132 to 1,398, an increase that might reflect the growing number of young lower-income Negroes in the population. In the same period, the proportion who were referred to family court increased from 44 to 58 per cent; by contrast, the proportion referred to religious or church-connected welfare organizations for informal guidance decreased from 3.2 to 1.1 per cent. This greater reliance on formal, court-centered proceedings as opposed to informal, church-centered ones occurred simultaneously with the advent of the new police leadership and its emphasis on police professionalism. It is not clear that the "reform" caused a significant change in police treatment of juveniles —the available data are too skimpy and the officers involved deny it—but such data as exist are not inconsistent with that possibility.

The police in these cities, however, do not arrest because they like making arrests, or hate teen-agers and Negroes, or love the penal code. Almost every officer interviewed in these departments said in one way or another, "We're not out to make arrests" or "We don't believe an arrest is always the answer." Such statements are quite sincere and not at all inconsistent with the fact that these men *do* make arrests and issue tickets at rates much higher than those found in other departments.

One reason the statement and the behavior can coexist is that the officers know that they see many offenses, usually minor, that they "let go" without an arrest or ticket; they are not especially aware—there is no way that they could be—that the police in other cities let many more go. Moreover, the average patrolman knows that most of his time is spent on things he does not regard as "real police work," much less on things that result in arrests. If anyone should suggest that he is "zealous" about making arrests, he would deny and perhaps resent it.

The fact that so many arrests are made, and that they are made as much as possible on the basis of a fixed, not a variable, standard of behavior, is primarily the result of departmental policies. It is the administrators who devise these policies, manipulate the rewards and sanctions that get them carried out, and reflect on their justification. The patrolmen are primarily "doing their job"—making runs, stopping cars, filling out forms, and putting up with citizen behavior that is tedious, bizarre, or even dangerous. When he thinks of his role, it is usually with a mixture of irritation that the "brass" in the offices "don't know what it's like out here on the street," disgust that the so-called good citizens and the courts are not supporting the police, and anger that the people who misbehave show so little respect for the police and provide so little cooperation. These views are about the same whether one is in a legalistic or a watchman department. The police administrators effect the difference between these police styles in part intentionally and in part unintentionally.

To some degree they demand that their officers enforce the laws because they believe it is right that all laws be enforced. In November 1966 the Highland Park chief sent out a letter to local businessmen expressing concern that some were allowing persons under the age of eighteen to buy cigarettes and also "openly smoke them in their place of business." The chief reminded them that this was a violation of an Illinois law that the police intended to enforce. The Oakland Police Department announced in January 1967 that because of the number of stolen bicycles and the difficulty in tracing and recovering unlicensed bicycles, it would intensify the enforcement of bicycle-licensing ordinances by issuing juvenile citations to owners of unlicensed bikes. Parents were warned that disregarding this citation could result in a juvenile-court appearance. Such policies would be followed in a watchman department only if they were required by a public hue and cry, and that would be most unlikely. Moreover, the police in a legalistic city obey the law themselves. In Oakland, the police parking lot is across the street from headquarters. The direct route to take to and from the building is to cross in the middle of the block. Routinely, interviewers watching the shifts change saw officers leave the building, walk to the corner, wait for the light, cross, and walk back to their cars. "Once or twice, maybe, I'll dash across the street," a patrolman told an interviewer, "but you get used to not jaywalking, and that's the way it is all the time."

The administrators of these departments want high arrest and ticketing rates not only because it is right but also to reduce the prospect (or the suspicion) of corruption, to protect themselves against criticism that they are not doing their job or are deciding for themselves what laws are good or bad, and to achieve, by means of the law, certain larger social objectives. Almost invariably a legalistic department was once a corrupt or favor-doing department. In Oakland, the police had been accused of tolerating gambling, conniving with insurance companies, and rolling drunks in the city jail. In Syracuse they had been accused of consorting with and accepting favors from gamblers and the political friends of gamblers. In Highland Park, they had been regarded as "sloppy," "ineffective," and interested in "looking out for themselves and their friends." Because police chiefs are broken by scandal, not crime, a new chief, hired to put an end to scandal, will seek to put an end to the officers' discretion concerning what laws will and will not be enforced. *All* laws will be enforced. Discretion, except under carefully defined circumstances, creates opportunities for officers to use that discretion out of improper or corrupt motives or, what is almost as bad, to *appear* to do so out of such motives. Police departments are judged by the public to a great extent in terms of appearances and rumors; the best way to stifle rumors of corruption or favoritism is to make sure that everybody gets a traffic ticket, every bookie is put out of business, and every glue-sniffing teen-ager is hauled in for questioning.

A police chief may also, for reasons to be developed in a later chapter, want to take the police "out of politics," at least formally. The most obvious way to achieve this is to assert that there is a clear difference between law-givers and law-enforcers or, more generally, between policy and administration. Every police officer likes to remark, "We don't make the laws"; in dealing with an angry housewife who has received a ticket or whose son has been arrested, it is a conventional observation intended, obviously, to reduce interpersonal conflict by representing the police officer as the impersonal, and slightly sympathetic, agent of a remote "Law." In a legalistic department, that view becomes the position of the chief as well as the patrolman, and partly for the same reason—to dissociate the department from the lawmaking process, which is essentially a political process, thereby making it clear that so long as the department "does its job" the responsibility is on others to decide what it shall do, and thus no one can accuse the department of being "political" by making its own decisions as to what laws to enforce. It is harder to keep the department out of politics if it appears to be making political judgments, and it may appear in just that light if it does less than enforce all the laws all the time.

The chief also knows that the law is a device to achieve certain social objectives—order, peace, security, certainty, and liberty. He is aware that by enforcing certain laws he can achieve the purposes of other laws, and this gives him and his department a reason to enforce laws that otherwise might appear trivial and thus be ignored. Enforcing traffic laws is desirable not simply because it is their duty and because such enforcement is one way to prevent automobile accidents. (The police know it is not the only way and agree that it is hard to prove conclusively that it is even one way, but it is, in their view, the only way open to them, and they feel they must do something.) Furthermore, stopping cars for traffic infractions affords an opportunity to check the identity of the driver and the registration of the car; from time to time, the police discover fugitives, stolen merchandise, illegal weapons, and stolen cars this way. This, in turn, leads to even more arrests. This screening process is a kind of positive feedback system that helps explain why high-arrest departments are so *much* higher than low-arrest departments: the more traffic tickets you issue, the better the chance of catching a real criminal; if you catch a real criminal, you make yourself look good; thus rewarded, you have even greater incentive to make more car stops.

The same instrumental view of the law extends into other areas where the police act on their own initiative. A drunk becomes the victim of a strong-arm robber; arrest him and you prevent a robbery. Juvenile vandalism can, the police believe, lead to a career in crime; better to investigate now and take it seriously now. Teen-agers loitering on a street corner late at night might cause mischief later on; thus, in Oakland and Highland Park, the police enforce an antiloitering or curfew law. Besides being illegal, vice also leads to muggings and the rolling of drunks; arrest prostitutes and you reduce the number of rollings.

In watchmanlike departments, account is also taken of the consequences of a law violation, but the consequences considered are limited, for the most part, to those that are immediate, personal, and direct. Will *this* drunk hurt *himself* or some nearby person *soon* if I let him go? Is *this* car driving so recklessly as to endanger others on *this road?* Are *these* kids getting into mischief *right now?* Legalistic departments, by contrast, additionally take into account consequences that are general, remote, and impersonal. For the patrolman from a working-class background, the pattern found in watchman-style departments may be, in some sense, "natural." In the management of violence generally, working-class persons are likely to take into account primarily the immediate consequences of actions, while middle-class persons are more inclined to take into account motives and long-term consequences. For example, working-class parents are apt to resort to physical punishment "when the direct and immediate consequences of their children's disobedient acts are most extreme, and to refrain from punishing when this might provoke an even

greater disturbance." Middle-class parents, on the other hand, seem "to punish or refrain from punishing on the basis of their interpretation of the child's
intent in acting as he does"; thus, a furious outburst will be punished if it
represents a "loss of self-control" but not if it is merely an "emotional release." [6]

*   *   *

Some Consequences

Because the legalistic police style encourages patrolmen to take a law-enforcement view of the situations they encounter, it also encourages them to
take as their standard of justice one that assumes that the function of the law
is to punish, on the basis of individual culpability, those who depart from
the behavior required by the law. Justice consists generally of equals being
treated equally, but in the legalistic style equality does not depend on attributes of person but only on attributes of behavior. "All men are equal before
the law" means that the only just distinctions that may be made among them
are on the basis of their behavior in areas defined by the law. This criterion is,
of course, rather different from the standard of distributive justice employed in
the maintenance of order or the resolving of family disputes and thus rather
different from the standard that the patrolman regards as somewhat "natural."

Because what is expected of him is somewhat at odds with his inclination,
the standard the patrolman actually employs will rarely be fully in accord
with the standard required by the legalistic department. Just as no administrator can control perfectly the patrolman's behavior in order-maintenance
situations, so also it cannot determine perfectly the standard of justice he will
employ in those situations. Nonetheless, such departments do have an effect
on police behavior. In another study, I compared the way in which two big-
city departments—one on the east coast, the other on the west—handled
juvenile offenders. The western department displayed what I here call the
legalistic style, the eastern department the watchman style. By examining
juvenile records, it was possible to determine by race the proportion of juveniles coming in contact with the police who were arrested as opposed to being
reprimanded and released. In the legalistic western city, the proportion arrested for eight major offenses was almost identical for the two races—whites
were arrested in 46.5 per cent of the cases, Negroes in 50.9 per cent. Only
for one common offense was there a significant difference—a higher proportion of Negroes than whites were arrested for loitering. In the watchmanlike
eastern city, however, Negroes were three times as likely as whites to be arrested—42.9 per cent of the Negroes but only 15.7 per cent of the whites were
taken to court.[7]

An explanation can be only speculative. Perhaps, as with the Albany drunk
arrests, the watchmanlike department regards the Negro as less constrained
by community and familial norms; thus, an arrest will accomplish for the
Negro what in the case of a white can be achieved by admonition or informal
penalties. Indeed, given the importance of family considerations for juvenile
behavior [8] the choice between arrest and warning may be especially important.

In Oakland at the time of my research, there was no significant difference
in the arrest prospects of white and Negro juveniles once they had become

involved with the police. (I could obtain no comparable data for watchman departments.) But the legalism that apparently produces equitable dispositions also produces frequent dispositions. Compared to a watchman-style department such as Albany, the Oakland police are over *four times* as likely to arrest a Negro (or a white, for that matter) for larceny and driving while intoxicated and almost *fifty* times as likely to arrest one for gambling. In 1965, over 15,000 Negroes were arrested by the Oakland police and perhaps another 27,000 were given tickets for moving traffic violations. If each arrest or ticket involved a different Oakland Negro (and, of course, they did not because some were picked up more than once and some were from out of town), then over 38 per cent of all Oakland Negroes had a formal involvement with the police that year. Syracuse, primarily because of its intensive traffic enforcement, produced a figure almost as high: 29 per cent. The comparable figures for Albany and Newburgh were much lower: 12 per cent and 9 per cent, respectively.[9]

This police style has two important consequences: first, any group that experiences such a high level of police activity and is self-conscious about these matters may feel that it is being "harassed"; and, second, even though the proportion of improper police actions may be much smaller than in most other cities, the absolute number of such incidents may be significant because of the high volume of police-citizen interactions. Exacerbating such feelings may be police policies designed to prevent crime, such as aggressive preventive patrol and the preparation of field-contact reports on "suspicious" street activities. Taken together, these elements of the legalistic style, even though wholly within the law, based on sound empirical generalizations as to the areas in which crime is most likely to occur, and as nondiscriminatory as organizational leadership can make them, may be experienced as "harassment." Every Negro interviewed for this study made this charge.

The police, in turn, are angered by these accusations. They know that their department is honest and that it enforces all laws strictly, tolerates no illegal enterprises, and employs the most modern police technology. Only such an organization, they believe, can give police protection to law-abiding Negroes and whites alike. To the police, the Negro leaders who charge harassment are competing for followings by creating issues where none in fact exist and complaining of police procedures essential to a proper enforcement of the law. By denouncing "harassment," they are promoting public resistance to police work; instead, they should be urging citizens to cooperate more fully with the police.

*   *   *

THE SERVICE STYLE

In some communities, the police take seriously all requests for either law enforcement or order maintenance (unlike police with a watchman style) but are less likely to respond by making an arrest or otherwise imposing formal sanctions (unlike police with a legalistic style). The police intervene frequently but not formally. This style is often found in homogeneous, middle-class communities in which there is a high level of apparent agreement among citizens on the need for and definition of public order but in which there is no administrative demand for a legalistic style. In these places, the police see their chief responsibility as protecting a common definition of public order against the minor and occasional threats posed by unruly teen-agers and "outsiders" (tramps, derelicts, visiting college boys). Though there will be family quarrels, they will be few in number, private in nature, and constrained by general understandings requiring seemly conduct. The middle-class character of such communities makes the suppression of illegal enterprises both easy (they are more visible) and necessary (public opinion will not tolerate them) and reduces the rate of serious crime committed by residents; thus, the police will be freer to concentrate on managing traffic, regulating juveniles, and providing services.

Such a police policy will be called the "service" style, and it can be found especially in Brighton and Nassau County. In such communities, which are not deeply divided along class or racial lines, the police can act as if their task were to estimate the "market" for police services and to produce a "product" that meets the demands. For patrolmen especially, the pace of police work is more leisurely (there are fewer radio messages per tour of duty than in a community with a substantial lower class) [10] and the community is normally peaceful; thus apparent threats to order are more easily detected. Furthermore, the citizenry expects its police officers to display the same qualities as its department-store salesmen, local merchants, and public officials—courtesy, a neat appearance, and a deferential manner. Serious matters—burglaries, robberies, assaults—are of course taken seriously, and thus "suspicious" persons are carefully watched or questioned. But with regard to minor infractions of the law, arrests are avoided when possible (the rates at which traffic tickets are issued and juveniles referred to Family Court will be much lower than in legalistic departments) but there will be frequent use of informal, nonarrest sanctions (warnings issued to motorists, juveniles taken to headquarters or visited in their homes for lectures).

Because the two departments that most clearly—and, to some extent, by their own admission—display the "service" style are Nassau and Brighton, one might suppose that they are merely watchman-style police departments with a different, less divided, or more demanding clientele: prosperous suburbanites want to be left alone with respect to their own minor indiscretions, to have "undesirables" kept away and the peace maintained. To some extent this is true, but it is not the whole story. The Albany Police Department, if transplanted to Nassau, probably would not—and certainly, without major internal changes, could not—begin to serve this new and different constituency in accordance with its demands. Those matters about which the Nassau police believe, no doubt rightly, that Nassau residents feel strongly—residential burglaries, teen-age narcotics, juvenile misconduct, personal and courteous "service"—are best dealt with by specialized police units and a certain type of officer. Creating these units and recruiting and training these officers would alter fundamentally the character of the Albany force in ways described below.

The Organizational Context

It is more relevant to ask why or in what ways the Nassau and Brighton departments, which are composed of honest and well-trained men, do not behave like their counterparts in Oakland and Highland Park. With respect to some matters—maintaining good records, insisting on good police behavior—

they do, but for them to have the same style as their western counterparts they would have to intensify traffic enforcement, use more formal and, from the point of view of the young person, more punitive means in handling juveniles, arrest drunks on sight, and neglect no laws on grounds that they are too trivial to be enforced. This would not require, as would the Albany to Nassau transplantation, a change in manpower—the Brighton officers could easily function in the Highland Park department and the Nassau officers in the Oakland department. It would require, however, a change in administrative policies. And, if the Nassau police had to face the Oakland problems—very high crime rates, a large lower-class population, conflict with organized Negroes—they might very likely adopt many, if not all, of the latter department's policies. The important point is that the Nassau department could adopt many of those policies now, especially with respect to traffic and juveniles, but it does not.

The fact that Nassau maintains a service style is all the more striking considering its size. With 3,200 members, one might expect that it would necessarily have many bureaucratic characteristics and that the administrative policies necessary to manage a large bureaucracy—a multiplication of reports, well-defined chains of command, the development of statistical measures of performance—would lead to emphasis at the patrol level on producing large numbers of whatever can be measured (arrests, tickets, and so on), "looking good on paper," handling situations uniformly "by the book," and keeping costs down. Though this sort of thing exists, it is less than one might expect.

The reason is that the Nassau department, especially in recent years, has deliberately adopted many practices that would institutionalize the service rather than the legalistic style. The ultimate motivation for this is political, not in the partisan sense, but in the sense of having regard for the opinion of the community. More immediately, however, these practices aim at keeping the department "small" and close to the people, emphasizing community and public relations, maintaining the best and the shiniest of buildings and equipment, and developing various control procedures that make service a major concern to officers at every rank. And community concerns over some specific law-enforcement problem are met, and often anticipated, by the department by creating a specialized unit to deal with it.

Nassau's patrol force and all its detectives except those in specialized squads operate out of eight precinct stations scattered about the county. Specialized investigative units, plus all staff services, operate in the main headquarters building at the county seat. The eight precincts are not simply administrative conveniences, however; they are designed in part to keep the patrol force "local." When a citizen calls for police services, he calls his precinct; if a patrol car is required, the precinct calls the central radio dispatcher at headquarters. If the citizen calls headquarters directly, by mistake, he is referred back to his precinct. Patrolmen work out of their precinct stations and, although the county is heavily residential, consisting mostly of low-density buildings, nearly 40 per cent of the precinct posts are manned by patrolmen walking foot beats. "Professional" police doctrine—and certainly the doctrine operative in Oakland—calls for motor patrols in all but the most congested areas, such as business centers and large apartment projects. When asked about the reliance on foot patrols, a senior officer explained that "the villages expect these foot posts. . . . The villages would complain if we removed the foot men." [11]

Nearly every precinct station is of recent construction and all are immaculately maintained. A citizen entering is confronted by a desk where a lieutenant, sergeant, and patrolman are on duty (when a citizen enters the Oakland or Syracuse police headquarters, he faces a bank of automatic elevators). The room is air conditioned; no other room, including that of the precinct commander, is similarly equipped. One precinct commander told an interviewer, "The air conditioning is to keep the citizen happy and the desk-officer cool-headed." The commander meets once a month with the local village leaders to discuss any local police problems. The needs of these groups are taken very much into account. One village, thinking of asking the NCPD to patrol its area and abandoning its own police force, told the NCPD, as reported by a senior officer who spoke to the local officials, that "They wanted to be sure they had as policemen men who understood the special problems of a rich community." The NCPD, according to one official, assured them that it would "give them well-screened men who would understand their special needs."

Though understanding the "special needs" of a group may lead to leniency in such police-invoked actions as drunk arrests, it also leads, at least in principle, to strictness in handling citizen complaints, such as those about the increase in residential burglaries. The problem is that burglary is one of the most difficult crimes to solve, no matter how efficient and determined the police department—there are usually no witnesses, few clues, and often not even a good estimate of when the crime occurred. The department does what it can—detectives follow up on every case, there is a specialized burglary detail which sometimes organizes stake-outs (that is, places a property or a suspect under surveillance), and in addition there is a "burglary patrol." During 1965 this patrol, operating in high-risk areas of the county, stopped and searched over 12,000 vehicles and questioned over 14,000 "suspicious persons." Eighty-six arrests resulted, but only nine were for burglary.

On matters that are not serious crimes—that is, on most matters the patrolman deals with—the service orientation of the department is clear. At the time of this research, serious juvenile crimes (felonies if committed by adults) were handled by the detectives; other matters were turned over to the Juvenile Aid Bureau for, in most cases, nonarrest treatment. In 1965 the JAB handled 2,711 such cases, and less than 5 per cent were taken to Family Court. Most were handled through family interviews. Likewise with drunks—though there are 2,869 liquor licenses in effect in the county, only 107 arrests on public intoxication charges were made in 1965 for a rate one sixth that of bone-dry Highland Park. And there is no traffic-ticket quota. Though an "Enforcement Index" is used to plan the traffic-enforcement strategy by selecting high accident-rate areas for special attention, there is no general pressure to produce tickets like that found in Syracuse or Oakland. Perhaps more important, providing service to motorists is an important part of traffic work— of the three highway-patrol vehicles regularly assigned to the busy Long Island Expressway, for example, two are specially equipped as "assistance vehicles," and in 1965 they provided services to 5,367 motorists who experienced engine trouble, ran out of gas, or the like.[12]

In Nassau, "public education" is an integral part of law enforcement. The NCPD increased the size of its narcotics squad from two in 1962 to forty-eight in 1966. Narcotics arrests increased correspondingly, from 70 in 1962 to 174 in 1965. Knowing that not every user can be detected or every pusher arrested, the commissioner assigned twenty-six of the forty-eight men to "public information" work—giving lectures, organizing displays, and the like. This serves two purposes: it alerts the public to the symptoms of narcotics use and thus produces some investigative leads, and it makes the community more aware of what the police are doing about a matter of deep community concern.

The "community relations orientation" is a central feature of the department's training, evaluation, and leadership. The commissioner put it frankly to an interviewer: "I believe very strongly that you have to sell modern police practices to the community. You have to have community support. . . . I think it's important to have outside teachers and speakers come in. . . . We want the civilian point of view. . . . You have to sell police services to the public at large."

*   *   *

The Brighton chief is concerned about traffic but, although he maintains a "norm" for ticket issuing, he has not induced his men to produce tickets at more than two thirds the rate of the legalistic department in Highland Park. Partly, the reason is politics—it is possible in Brighton but almost impossible in Highland Park to bring influence on the police regarding "overly zealous" traffic enforcement. But partly it is the attitude of the police themselves. As the chief wrote in a letter to the author, "It is a good idea to have a norm, but the norm should not be too high." And special circumstances should be taken into account. For minor infractions, such as faulty equipment on the car, a warning ticket is issued, which is forgotten if the defect is corrected. When police felt obliged to lower the speed limit on a straight, thinly populated road after a car hit a cow, they realized that the new limit (35 miles per hour) would be regarded as unreasonable by motorists accustomed to driving at the old limit (50 miles per hour). Accordingly, the officers were instructed to arrest only those driving over 50 and simply to warn those driving between 35 and 50.

In handling juveniles, a similar policy operates—unlike watchman-style departments, the police do not overlook violations of the law but, unlike legalistic departments, they are less likely to handle those infractions by taking the person to court. A Brighton detective explained the department's approach: "If we can possibly do it, we try to avoid an arrest. We don't want to send [them] into the courts. We try to handle it right here in the department. We bring the parents in here, and usually they're cooperative once we bring the situation to them."

Serious cases will be taken to court, but otherwise such action is seen as of little value—the court is "too busy" and anyway the juvenile will probably receive probation, which, in the eyes of many officers, is "nothing—you're supposed to come in, at first, maybe every two weeks and tell the probation officer what you've been doing, what your grades are like." A typical youthful offense in Brighton is larceny. In 1965 there were over three hundred larcenies reported; 63 arrests resulted, 20 of which were of juveniles, almost all of whom were released with no court action.

This informality and apparent leniency do not indicate that the police in a town like Brighton ignore such matters; on the contrary, owing to the greater visibility of misconduct in a "quiet" town and the lower tolerance for disorder among its residents, the police become involved in many situations—especially involving juveniles—that would be ignored in a larger or more heterogeneous community. For example, four boys who followed a girl into her driveway and "rocked her car" and made indecent gestures were picked up by the police on disorderly conduct charges. Though they signed confessions no charges were filed. Another group of teen-agers were picked up because they had "stayed out all night" (a girl was with them); they were released to their parents. That same year four boys were arrested for annoying a resident by "ringing his doorbell"; they, too, were released without a court appearance. It is hard to imagine any of these matters leading to police involvement in larger cities. It should be noted that all of these incidents were counted as cases of "disorderly conduct" on the police records. They are obviously not comparable with similarly labeled big-city events in which, typically, an officer has been assaulted or a serious street fight has occurred. Of the seventy-two disorderly conduct bookings in Brighton during one year (May 1965–July 1966), only seven involved a fight; fifty-eight involved primarily annoying others by language, manner, or action; the remainder involved miscellaneous offenses.

These considerations suggest that community size may be an important variable in police behavior. That it is not a controlling variable is evident from the great differences among Amsterdam, Brighton, Highland Park, and Newburgh. However, even though the Nassau County police display, and speak of themselves as having, a service orientation, they are nevertheless a large bureaucratic organization serving over a million persons spread over a far-flung county. . . .

NOTES

1 A social scientist reading this [article] will understand that any typology is an abstraction from reality that is employed, not to describe a particular phenomenon, but to communicate its essential or "ideal" form—in this case, the "flavor" or "style" of the organization. The lay reader should bear this in mind and guard against assuming that because two or three police departments are grouped together they are identical in all respects. They are not. Furthermore, a typology can only suggest, it cannot prove, that a particular operating style is associated with certain organizational characteristics. Finally, merely because it was found convenient in this study to group these departments together into three styles, no one should assume that these are the only police styles or that every police department in the country displays one or the other of them. I assume if enough departments were studied that one would probably learn of other styles in addition to these and that one would certainly learn that many, if not most, departments display a combination of two or more styles.

2 When the specialized enforcement strategy replaced the quota system, the morale of the Highland Park patrolmen improved. But the new methods did not substantially reduce the chance that a motorist would be ticketed. In 1965, though the new chief was in office for about nine months, the number of moving violation tickets issued was about the same as the average for the preceding three years when the former chief, and thus the quota system, prevailed.

3 A survey of the attitudes of police officers of all ranks and specialties from 316 police departments across the country revealed that officers from the Middle Atlantic states, including New York, were significantly more likely than officers from the Pacific states, including California, to believe that the police should try to find jobs for older juveniles who come to their attention, that they should operate Boy's Clubs and Little League baseball teams, and that in minor cases the offending juvenile ought simply to report periodically to the police for informal

probation. George W. O'Connor and Nelson A. Watson, *Juvenile Delinquency and Youth Crime: The Police Role* (Washington, D.C.: International Association of Chiefs of Police, 1964), pp. 115–26.

[4] This figure includes all persons under the age of eighteen. . . .

[5] One anecdote makes the point. An officer patrolling a busy street in Highland Park saw a boy walking alone after the curfew hour. The officer recognized him and knew that he returned every evening at about this time on his way home from his girlfriend's house. The officer decided to give him a ride. He radioed the station to tell them what he was doing but the chief, who overheard the communication, cut in to tell him, "We're not running a taxi service," and ordered the boy brought to the station and his parents summoned to pick him up. (From an interview.)

[6] Melvin L. Kohn, "Social Class and Parent-Child Relationships: An Interpretation," *American Journal of Sociology,* 67 (1963), p. 478; italics added. See also Kohn, "Social Class and Exercise of Parental Authority," *American Sociological Review,* 24 (1959), pp. 312–66.

[7] James Q. Wilson, "The Police and the Delinquent in Two Cities," in Stanton Wheeler (ed.), *Controlling Delinquents* (New York: Wiley, 1968), pp. 13–14. Supporting evidence from another California police agency can be found in A. W. McEachern and Riva Bauzer, "Factors related to Disposition in Juvenile Police Contacts," in Malcolm Klein (ed.), *Juvenile Gangs in Context* (Englewood Cliffs, N.J.: Prentice-Hall, 1967), pp. 148–60. But on court dispositions, compare Sidney Axelrad, "Negro and White Male Institutionalized Delinquents," *American Journal of Sociology,* 57 (1957), 569–74.

[8] See, for example, Thomas P. Monahan, "Family Status and the Delinquent Child; A Reappraisal and Some New Findings," *Social Forces,* 35 (March 1957), 251–58, and Ray A. Tennyson, "Family Structure and Delinquent Behavior," in Klein, *op. cit.,* pp. 57–69.

[9] Arrests are tabulated by race, but traffic tickets are not. The figure for Negro ticketing was estimated by assuming that Negroes receive tickets in proportion to their percentage in the population. If in fact Negroes are ticketed excessively, the totals given above should be higher; if, because of lower automobile ownership rates, they are ticketed less than whites, the totals should be lower.

[10] During the first week of June 1965, the Brighton police sent 124 nonadministrative radio messages to patrol cars and the Newburgh police sent 173; the towns are approximately equal in population, but the median income in Brighton is twice that in Newburgh. Furthermore, a substantially higher fraction of the Newburgh calls (8.9 per cent) were for "crimes in progress" than of the Brighton calls (3.2 per cent).

[11] Some foot patrolmen are being shifted to scooters.

[12] There are in addition six patrol cars assigned to precincts, which work the Expressway.

3. Pre-Judicial Dispositions: Critique and Recommendations *

TASK FORCE ON JUVENILE DELINQUENCY AND YOUTH CRIME

. . . EVALUATION OF PREPETITION DISPOSITION of juveniles must of necessity proceed in considerable ignorance, in view of the lack of systematic, uniform information. Certain criteria can, however, be isolated, by which to measure informal handling procedures and to indicate what appear to be some of the major evils of present arrangements. The following comments, while largely speculative, are grounded on the observations and informed opinions of many experienced officials and scholars.

What should be the goals of the pre-judicial process? First, a great deal of juvenile misbehavior should be dealt with through alternatives to adjudication, in accordance with an explicit policy to divert juvenile offenders away from formal adjudication and authoritative disposition and to nonjudicial institutions for guidance and other services. Employment agencies, schools, welfare agencies, and groups with programs for acting-out youth all are examples of the resources that should be used. The preference for nonjudicial disposition should be enunciated, publicized, and consistenily espoused by the several social institutions responsible for controlling and preventing delinquency.

Such a policy would avoid for many the long-lasting consequences of adjudication: curtailment of employment opportunity, quasi-criminal record, harm to personal reputation in the eyes of family and friends and public, reinforcement of antisocial tendencies. The case for using alternatives to the criminal process has been elaborated in other portions of this report. The same arguments apply—perhaps even more persuasively—to the juvenile justice system. The juvenile will wear the label longer, while he is likely to outgrow the conduct that brought him the badge; one who acquires the status of a deviant in his youth faces the prospect of lifelong stigmatization. For a certain proportion of juvenile offenders the consequences appear to be cumulative. And in some cases the stigma is for behavior that does not carry the risk of formal disabilities for adults. His future is at stake and so is society's.

At the same time that marginal offenders ought to be screened out of the formal fact-finding and dispositional stages of the juvenile justice system, there should be a greater emphasis on official handling of the more serious and intractable offenders. Improvements in the several stages of the predispositional process would result in more selective and discriminating judg-

* Task Force on Juvenile Delinquency of the President's Commission on Law Enforcement and Administration of Justice, *Juvenile Delinquency and Youth Crime,* Washington, D.C.: Government Printing Office, 1967, pp. 16–21.

ments as to those who should be subjected to formal and authoritative surveillance in the interest of community protection.

MISUSES OF THE PRE-JUDICIAL DISPOSITION PROCESS

The rationale for pre-judicial handling rests on the greater flexibility, efficiency, and humanity it brings to a formal system operating within legislative and other definitive policies. But pre-judicial methods that seek to place the juvenile under substantial control in his pattern of living without genuine consent are not permissible. The difficult task is to discriminate between the undesirable uses of informality, benevolent as well as punitive, and the tolerable, desirable modes of guidance.

Modes of social aid and intervention occur along a spectrum from coercion to consent, with many intermediate shades lying in the range of mild control or persuasive request. The outer reaches of the spectrum are easiest to state. A friendly word of advice, which the juvenile feels free to reject, lies at one end. At the opposite end are authoritative dispositions that send the juvenile to a penal institution. Here the intervention of the state contravenes the will of the child and abridges his parents' rights if accomplished without due observance of the prescribed formalities of juvenile justice.

The punitive uses of informality are improper and dangerous. Substantial interference with parental judgment and curtailment of the juvenile's activities must be preceded by adjudication or the intervention is extralegal. The well-known practice of informal probation is vulnerable to attack on this ground; by measuring a juvenile's conduct according to conditions informally laid down by officials of the state, it constitutes an interference with choices of parents and juvenile that is legitimate, under our legal traditions, only when the basis for intervention has been established in accordance with procedural rules.

Likewise improper is referral to detention purely for purposes of deterrence, particularly where a *prima facie* case of jurisdiction does not exist. This is not to say that detention has necessarily been used punitively if the case is later dismissed without petition. Neither would pretrial confinement of a criminal suspect be attacked solely because his case was subsequently dismissed in court. When many cases in which detention was used are later dismissed without petition, however, there is reason for inquiry, especially if there are at the same time official expressions favoring the shock value of detention.[1]

Other possibilities for misuse of discretionary judgment are less blatant than detention or informal probation. Coercive measures that are part of treatment regimens intended and believed to be beneficient also afford opportunities for misuse of discretion. At police, community-agency, and court-intake stages, leverage exists by virtue of the power to file a delinquency petition. Dispositional methods prescribed at any of these stages may therefore be subject to attack as forms of coercion without adjudication.

Examples of adjustment used at those points include police programs of "grounding" or performing tasks such as carwashing on Saturday for police in exchange for the release to parents; quasi-compulsory conference committee dispositions directing regular visits to a counselor or production of essays on a topic selected for its wholesomeness. The line between helpful or irrelevant but harmless duties and painful or even destructive burdens is very difficult to draw. In any event, however, officials should have no further authority to refer to the court after a voluntary agreement has been worked out with the child or his parents. Once the power of referral ends, continuation in a plan of reparation or rehabilitation should rest on consent rather than authority.

Questionable Factors in Pre-Judicial Disposition

Controlling discretionary judgment at the point of screening requires greater knowledge about its exercise than now exists. At this point we know little more than that a multitude of factors governs discretionary judgment. One source of difficulty in evaluating pre-judicial disposition is the vast range of pertinent considerations. If, for example, a policeman has as a guide to disposition a list of six major factors,[2] all of them subject to various interpretations, who is to say his judgment is wrong, and on what grounds?

One unstated factor in decisions to retain or release may be flatly condemned—race. And there are other factors, such as place of residence (in a high-crime neighborhood, for instance) or family characteristics, which may bear an indirect association with the avowedly irrelevant factor of race. It is difficult to keep these factors separate in a decision made under stress and often without knowledge of important facts.

Even more troubling is the question of the significance of a juvenile's demeanor. Is his attitude, remorseful or defiant, a sound measure of his suitability for pre-judicial handling? Can the police, or anyone else for that matter, accurately detect the difference between feigned and genuine resolve to mend one's ways, or between genuine indifference to the law's commands and fear-engendered defiance? Attaching weight to attitude also implies presupposing the child's involvement, a presupposition reflected in some referral policies that mandate court referral whenever the juvenile denies commission of an offense. If the act or conduct is minor and would otherwise be disposed of by referral, the more defensible policy would seem to be the use of pre-judicial disposition.

The Impact of Screening on Juvenile Behavior and on Bureaucracy

There are two bases for concern about present prejudicial dispositions. On the one hand, serious offenders may be released in the course of the pre-judicial process when, for the sake of public safety, they should be retained and their cases adjudicated. On the other hand, juveniles who are not risks to the community but demonstrate a need for redirection may not be directed to appropriate sources of assistance either because the resources are not present or because transfer to other social institutions is not made. Both are grave indictments of the present pre-judicial dispositional system.

Statistical evidence for these assertions is scarce. Support for them abounds, however, not only in the common-sense observations of laymen well acquainted with child behavior problems within their own communities but also in an impressive accumulation of informed expert opinion. Data reveal the inadequacy of present pre-judicial screening to protect the community. Screening that leads to numerous adjustments for a juvenile within a relatively short time provokes questions about its effectiveness. While the primitiveness of the available data may preclude isolation in any given case of the facts of the offense, the legal issues, and the goals intended to be served, it is reasonable to speculate that sequential adjustments of serious offenses by the same individual reflect great pressures on the administering officials to reduce a heavy caseload. The exercise of discretion, moreover, to relieve the load of cases may be affected by nondiscretionary policies. If a police department, for example, is expected to refer to court all instances of certain crimes, and consequently feels the weight of paperwork and court appearance that this directive produces, it may be unable to assign the proportion of its efforts to the discretionary type of case that it otherwise would. In the case of discretionary judgment that is officially allowed, the officer who makes the judgment must make a record.[3] The time that is taken by justifying decisions in relatively trivial matters is lost from investigation and deliberation in more serious ones.

It seems likely that the stresses on the crucial screening institutions—police and court intake—result chiefly from insufficient staff. Screening consequently suffers from mass production. The deficiencies that inhere in using automatic processing techniques to make highly discriminating judgments are reinforced by an almost total lack of feedback. The decisions are not regularly reviewed for internal agency consistency or, perhaps more important, for the subsequent validity of the screening judgment. Operating agencies are best located to tackle such research; yet it is almost nonexistent either within them or under outside auspices.

The absence of follow-through also has ramifications with respect to juveniles referred for nonjudicial handling. Typically, the official agency gets in touch with a clinic, social agency, youth board, or similar organization. But the time to explain a referral to the juvenile or a member of his family is short, and in the impersonal, populous districts of an urban area the referral case is often lost. The juvenile may not arrive at the selected place of service, or he may be refused service [4] without the referring official's finding out in time to take other steps. Even where there is a well-articulated referral system with smoothly operating procedures, sheer numbers of cases may substantially lessen its effectiveness. If the time lapse between apprehension and referral is a matter of days, the subsequent follow-up by a selected community resource may occur at a point when the juvenile and his family have surmounted their initial fear, anger, or regret and concern, and the contact is regarded as an unwelcome reminder of past unpleasantness instead of an avenue of help in time of crisis.

Bureaucratic Considerations

Several kinds of agencies may play a part in the informal dispositional process. Who should play the major or exclusive role has been the subject of debate. The police and the probation staff will have a screening function as long as the juvenile court maintains its essential structure. But there is disagreement as to whether their screening responsibilities should be reduced and their informal control efforts altogether eliminated.

With respect to the pre-judicial function of the police, it can be argued that discretionary power increases their influence over the behavior of juveniles. Deployed about the city and county, the police have frequent contacts with juveniles and stand a better chance to identify the serious crime risks than do officials more removed; it follows that they may judge more wisely which juveniles to leave alone and which to divert to nonjudicial tracks. This line of reasoning suggests that police discretion should be enlarged in cities where existing policy requires automatic court referral for many crimes and other types of misbehavior.[5]

Opponents of substantial discretionary police powers argue that informal dispositional duties divert police from primary law-enforcement tasks. The authoritative mantle of the police, moreover, is said to make them appear to the public as figures of control, hence unlikely agents of help. Internal bureaucratic pressures may produce a predominantly punitive ethic. The subtle character of screening judgments calls for different personalities and preparation and for administrative checks of a sort that can be monitored more efficiently within the juvenile court.

The case for and against discretionary judgment at the intake stage turns on similar considerations. The intake officer's distance from the neighborhood and his lack of knowledge of the child and his environs may suggest curtailing his discretionary power. But by training and through internal supervision the intake staff may be able to reach consistent decisions based on articulated policy with less difficulty than the police.

Inserting agencies outside the juvenile justice system into the channels of pre-judicial dispositions further complicates the picture. As indicated previously, the tenure of decentralized units of delinquency adjustment outside the formal system of juvenile justice depends in large measure on the tolerance of the juvenile court judge, and their functions depend on the rules and practices governing direct court referral. To be effective, the work of such local units must be geared to the operations of both police and court. Active participation by youth board workers, social agencies assuming major responsibility for neighborhood work with predelinquent and delinquent youth, and other agencies—public or voluntary—would complicate the screening process and the monitoring of referrals, and enormous efforts would be required to achieve some degree of evenhandedness. Such efforts are both warranted and necessary, however, to make effective nonjudicial disposition a reality.

RECOMMENDATIONS FOR STRENGTHENING THE PRE-JUDICIAL PROCESS

In general, the following principles should guide pre-judicial dispositions:

1. Pre-judicial dispositions should be made as early as possible in the stages of official agency contact;

2. They should be based on stated criteria that are shared with and regularly reviewed by all delinquency control authorities within the community; and

3. Whenever attempts are undertaken to render guidance or exert control (as distinct from screening without further action), the pre-judicial handling agency should be alert to coercive possibilities and the dispositions it can render should be effectively restricted.

This approach seeks to accommodate the aims of the pre-judicial dispositional process to the widely differing practices that now exist. Accordingly, it is inappropriate to specify here the preferred agencies or to limit the possible forms of pre-judicial disposition. Details are less important than insuring inclusion in a given system of all the necessary basic aspects of the pre-judicial disposition process. One possible screening referral and service scheme is outlined, however, at a later point.

Police

The police should promptly determine which cases are suitable for pre-judicial disposition. Where there are juvenile specialists, they should be present at the stationhouse for as many hours of the day as possible and available on call when absent, to facilitate speedy pre-judicial decisions. The police should have written standards for release, for referral to nonjudicial sources, and for referral to the juvenile court. They should not be precluded from making nonjudicial referrals in juvenile cases involving minor criminal acts, noncriminal delinquent behavior, and violations of probation and parole. While policies for probation and parole violators require close coordination between the police and other authorities, an automatic bar to adjustment seems unnecessary.[6] Rather, there should be an area of discretion and a clear understanding that adjustments must immediately be reported by the police to the court or correctional agents concerned.

The standards for release and adjustment should be sent to all agencies of delinquency control and should be reviewed and appraised jointly at periodic intervals. They should be made the basis for in-service training that would consider, besides the decision-making duties of the police, materials pertinent to increasing understanding of juvenile behavior and making more effective use of nonjudicial community resources.

In cases where information on the child is needed, it should be sought through home visits as well as from official records,[7] and the police should be aided, or replaced, by paid case aides drawn from the neighborhood within the police district and selected for their knowledge of the community and their ability to communicate easily with juveniles and their families.

In addition to outright release and referral to nonjudicial agencies with or without a warning, the police should have the option to refer directly to the juvenile court specified classes of cases, including those of more serious offenders, repeated offenders for whom other and persistent redirecting efforts have failed, and certain parole and probation violators.[8]

The police should not undertake to redirect juveniles by such means as conducting quasi-judicial hearings or imposing special duties or personal obligations.[9]

These recommendations call for the use of discretion by the police, subject to administrative control and with some outside restriction on its exercise, in accordance with articulated standards, and emphasizing nonjudicial avenues of disposition. They also posit the existence of auxiliary staff to provide the police with more information than they now acquire and to follow up referrals to community agencies. These are measures that can be adopted immediately. They require coordination with other delinquency-control agencies, particularly the court; efficient deployment of juvenile specialists; and better training for both specialists and regular patrolmen. They also offer a means of adding manpower in order to improve screening and referral. That objective will be achieved not only through greater professionalization of the police but also through use of subprofessional aides. Funds from the Office of Economic Opportunity and other organizations, administered directly by the police or through cooperative arrangement with a welfare center or youth-serving agency, are potential resources to accomplish these ends.

Police practices following custody should thus continue as at present but with two significant changes: Cases deemed suitable for adjustment would be referred to a mandatory-intake youth-serving agency within a neighborhood service center (the youth services bureau proposed and described in detail below), and the categories of cases that could be referred by the police directly to juvenile court would be restricted. Exercise of discretion to release outright would continue to be permitted in those cases where, in the judgment of the police, there was no immediate threat to public safety. There would no longer be direct referral to court of minor delinquents (violators of ordinances and of many misdemeanors) or of noncriminal-law-violating juveniles. Those limitations are consonant with the fundamental preference for nonjudicial handling. For that handling to be effective, however, the alternatives to adjudication must expand sufficiently so that the police and other members of the community have some assurance that meaningful action will be taken for juveniles diverted to a nonjudicial track.

Community Agencies; Youth Services Bureau

There should be expanded use of community agencies for dealing with delinquents nonjudicially and close to where they live. Use of community agencies has several advantages. It avoids the stigma of being processed by an official agency regarded by the public as an arm of crime control. It substitutes for official agencies organizations better suited for redirecting conduct. The use of locally sponsored or operated organizations heightens the community's awareness of the need for recreational, employment, tutoring, and other youth development services. Involvement of local residents brings greater appreciation of the complexity of delinquents' problems, thereby engendering the sense of public responsibility that financial support of programs requires.[10]

The variety of programs already existing testifies to the abundance of creative ideas and the range of possible operational forms. A criterion essential for guiding community efforts is that services be local.[11] The farther removed from place and time of the juvenile's conduct the decision on disposition takes place, the more likely that the result will be unhelpful or have stigmatizing consequences.

The informal disposition process provides opportunities to engage laymen, as volunteers or paid part-time or full-time staff, to augment the ranks of full-time professional staff in the official agencies. One approach to use of laymen as case aides is outlined below.

There are, of course, hazards in encouraging pre-judicial dispositions by community agencies. One is the danger of misguided benevolence. Decentralizing and deformalizing juvenile handling do not preclude unwarranted stigma. Concerned citizens, by definition strongly motivated and possessed of firm opinions, can interpose obstacles to the smooth-flowing application of professional judgment and can themselves contribute to creation of a hostile environment for juvenile miscreants. But services should not be avoided because they may be abused. Rather, ways should be sought to minimize the dangers. The same safeguards that can be introduced in the pre-judicial disposition function of the court and the police offer protection against overreaching or arbitrary recommendations of local unofficial agencies.

Referrals by police, school officials, and others to local community agencies should be on a voluntary basis. If the request to seek available help is ignored, the police or, in certain communities, another organized group may refer the case to court. But to protect against abuse of that power, the option of court referral should terminate when the juvenile or his family and the community agency agree upon an appropriate disposition.[12]

It is also essential that the dispositions available to such local organizations be restricted. The purpose of using community institutions in this way is to help without coercion, and accordingly it is inappropriate to confer on them a power to order treatment or alter custody or impose sanctions for deviation from the suggested program.

These measures could be put into effect in the near future, with existing institutions and without major alteration of policy. Even where institutionalized community methods of encouraging pre-judicial dispositions are used, as in those areas with citizens' committees to hear and dispose of cases, amendment of the juvenile-court law has not been required. The determinative factor is the interest of local officials and laymen.

Long-term recommendations for enhanced use of community service agencies, however, require creation of new social institutions. The neighborhood centers supported by the Office of Economic Opportunity and associated agencies, which now offer social welfare, legal aid, and medical care, among other services, do not appear presently to be making a sufficient impact on delinquency control [13] but could serve as the basis for the necessary institutions.

One recent proposal for nonjudicial handling is contained in the British White Paper of August 1965 entitled "The Child, the Family, and the Young Offender." [14] It recommends new arrangements for determining and providing treatment for offenders under the age of twenty-one. Any child under sixteen who is in need of care, protection, or control would be brought before a local family council appointed to function in local authority areas. The council would attempt in all cases to reach agreement on treatment with the parents of the child. Where the facts are in dispute or where council and parents cannot agree on treatment, the matter would be referred to a magistrate's court for determination.[15] Children over sixteen and under twenty-one would automatically be referred to a special magistrate's court that would also sit as a young offender's court for the older age group.

The British proposal is more far-reaching than any of the adjudication alternatives being considered in the United States.[16] It closely resembles the approach of the Scandinavian countries, which rely heavily on child welfare committees instead of courts for delinquency control. Thought in the United States has concentrated on creating *alternatives* to adjudication in an expanding number of cases rather than on providing substitutes for adjudication.

An essential objective in a community's delinquency-control-and-prevention plan should therefore be an agency that might be called a youth services bureau, with a broad range of services and certain mandatory functions. Such an agency ideally would be located in a comprehensive community center and would serve both delinquent and nondelinquent youths. While some of its cases would normally originate with parents, schools, and other sources, the bulk of the referrals could be expected to come from the police and the juvenile court intake staff, and police and court referrals should have special status in that the youth services bureau would be required to accept them all. If, after study, certain youths are deemed unlikely to benefit from its services, the bureau should be obliged to transmit notice of the decision and supporting reasons to the referral source. A mandate for service seems necessary to insure efforts to control and redirect acting-out youth and to minimize the substantial risk that this group, denied service by traditional social agencies, would inevitably be shunted to a law-enforcement agency.

A primary function of the youth services bureau thus would be individually tailored work with troublemaking youths. The work might include group and individual counseling, placement in group and foster homes, work and recreational programs, employment counseling, and special education (remedial, vocational). It would be under the bureau's direct control either through purchase or by voluntary agreement with other community organizations. The key to the bureau's success would be voluntary participation by the juvenile and his family in working out and following a plan of service or rehabilitation.

In this respect, the bureau would function as do the traditional public and voluntary child welfare agencies, rendering service on request of parents or with their consent. In the absence of appointment as guardians or custodians, these agencies lack power of compulsion; their services are by administrative arrangement and depend upon parental consent. The bureau would attempt to act in the same manner, with the difference that its clientele would be less tractable (and probably somewhat older) than the child population served by most child welfare agencies. Thus, the significant feature of the bureau's function would be its mandatory responsibility to develop and monitor a plan of service for a group now handled, for the most part, either inappropriately or not at all except in time of crisis. Through application of differential formulas or earmarked grants, funding of the bureau should take into account the special difficulty of serving this youth group and provide financial resources adequate to its responsibility.

The youth services bureau should also accept juveniles on probation or parole, through prearrangement with other public agencies or purchase of care for individual cases negotiated by the probation or parole officer. It should accept "walk-ins" and parental requests for voluntary service. It should respond to requests for aid from other organizations and individuals. But the compelling priority would be youth who have already demonstrated their inability to conform to minimal standards of behavior at home or in the community. The financial and legal leverage provided under this proposal is intended to insure intervention in those cases.

It is essential that acceptance of the bureau's services be voluntary; otherwise the dangers and disadvantages of coercive power would merely be transferred from the juvenile court to it. Nonetheless, it may be necessary to vest the youth services bureau with authority to refer to court within a brief time—not more than sixty and preferably not more than thirty days—those with whom it cannot deal effectively. In accordance with its basically voluntary character, the youth services bureau should be required to comply with a parent's request that a case be referred to the juvenile court.

In many communities there may already exist the ingredients of a youth services bureau in the form of community or neighborhood centers and programs for juveniles. All communities should explore the availability of federal funds both for establishing the coordinating mechanisms basic to the youth services bureau's operations and for instituting the programs that the community needs.

NOTES

[1] Cf. Cal. Report, Pt. 2 at 81.

[2] See, e.g., the factors listed in *Chicago Police Department Youth Division Manual of Procedure* (*1965*) as guidelines for the three possible dispositions of community adjustment, adjustment and referral, and filing a petition in juvenile court:
1) type and seriousness of the offense
2) the previous behavioral history of the juvenile
3) environmental factors including the disposition and capacity of the juvenile
4) the attitude of the parents and "their ability to provide the necessary supervision and guidance"
5) the attitude of the complainant
6) community resources

[3] For an illuminating exposition of the impact of bureaucratic pressures on police practices in general, see Skolnick, *Justice Without Trial* (1966).

[4] See, e.g., comment in 1963 Juvenile Court, Cuyahoga County, Ohio, Ann. Rep. 10: "Less than on (*sic*) half of those cases referred to local private agencies were accepted for service." See also Kahn, *Planning Community Service for Children in Trouble,* 14–15, 214 (1963).

[5] See, e.g., the recommendation to that effect by the President's Commission on Crime in the District of Columbia, Rept. 659 (1966).

[6] Thus curfew violation—though technically a new delinquency in many jurisdictions —should not require automatic referral to the juvenile court but rather should be susceptible of police adjustment. Police adjustment should not foreclose subsequent action by the correctional authority, however.

[7] Necessary information includes data on place of residence, family composition, school or employment status, and other information useful in screening and referral. These data—unlike those related to previous offenses—may not be fully recorded by the police nor readily secured by them if they are understaffed or if the juvenile's parents are either unavailable for questioning or unable to supply the desired information. See the list of pertinent considerations listed in the *Chicago Police Department Manual, op. cit.* Some of this information will be hard to obtain unless the police are well acquainted with the child's neighborhood or have the time to make a thorough investigation of his home and surroundings, and demands on law-enforcement officers will sometimes preclude their undertaking these indispensable independent investigations.

[8] It is contemplated that juveniles on probation or parole who commit serious violations of law will generally be referred to the court; as to minor infractions or violations of the juvenile code that do not contravene criminal law, see *supra* note 7.

[9] Note, "Juvenile Delinquents: The Police, State Courts, and Individualized Justice," 79 *Harvard Law Review* (1966), pp. 805–06.

[10] See generally Elson & Rosenheim, *Justice for the Child at the Grassroots,* 51 A.B.A. 341 (1965).

[11] Services could be developed under the guidance or within the direct administrative ambit of state agencies, as long as they are accessibly located.

[12] An appropriate analogy is the time limitation imposed on court intake staffs seeking nonjudicial adjustments in preliminary conferences. Both New York and Illinois impose such a time limitation. Similarly, officially approved neighborhood groups

that attempt to handle minor cases of delinquency should be precluded from using authority to refer to court to procure the show, if not the substance, of compliance. Inevitably, the risk of failure of compliance is present, but it is slight in comparison to the dangers of overreaching inherent in the combination of official power and protracted guidance. Therefore, the option of court referral should be foreclosed altogether. Insistence on the adoption of one alternative at the loss of another serves to emphasize the importance of improving present criteria for screening and referral.

13 Cf. Wheeler, Cottrell and Romasco, "Juvenile Delinquency: Its Prevention and Control" (Russell Sage Foundation, 1966), reprinted in Part VI, selection 2.

14 CMD. No. 2742.

15 With one exception: Family councils would have power, "even in a case in which the parents disagee, to refer a child to an observation centre for a limited period for assessment and for a report on the type of treatment that is likely to prove beneficial in his case." *Ibid.*, at 7.

16 The White Paper proposals are critically analyzed in a special number of the *British Journal of Criminology,* 6 (1966) 101–69.

4. *Police Work with Children* *

RICHARD A. MYREN AND LYNN D. SWANSON

USE OF POLICE DISCRETION not to invoke the criminal process has been characterized as resulting in low-visibility decisions in the administration of justice.[1] The term "low-visibility decision" is used to refer to decisions by public officials about which information is not readily available to the public for consideration and criticism. This characterization does not result in an argument that police should exercise no discretion, but in an assertion that police discretion should be guided by written policy statements of the police administrator, the public prosecutor, or the legislature, as recorded in public documents, and that the exercise of discretion should be reported in a systematic way. Only in this manner, it is argued, can the public evaluate the effectiveness of its criminal laws.

This is equally true of the use of police discretion in cases of juvenile delinquency. Exercise of such discretion is necessary to effectuate individualized handling based on the principle that, in the usual case, the home is the best place for the rearing of a child. As in the case of criminal-law enforcement, guidelines for the police in these cases can be established by the police administrator or by the legislature. Since there is usually no prosecutor because of the nature of juvenile court proceedings, the court intake workers or the judge himself might assist the police command in the formulation of criteria for the decision not to invoke juvenile court jurisdiction even though there is a basis for it.

In addition to the naked legal question of a basis for the exercise of discretion by the police in juvenile cases and the legislative-administrative ques-

* From Richard A. Myren and Lynn D. Swanson, *Police Work with Children,* U.S. Department of Health, Education and Welfare, Children's Bureau Publication No. 399 (Washington, D.C.: U.S. Government Printing Office, 1962), pp. 27–38.

tion of establishing flexible criteria to guide its exercise, there are additional problems raised by this need for police discretion. If the judgment is to be made, there must be a basis for it. This has led to police agencies' attempting to take detailed social histories and actually to hold hearings in an attempt to get information on which to base a decision. These are nonpolice functions. It would seem better to limit the exercise of discretion by the police to those cases in which the answer to whether to refer to juvenile court would be apparent from the facts obtained in a normal police investigation. If social history or a hearing proves necessary, the case should go to court. The rule for the police to follow would seem to be: When in doubt, refer the case to court.

REFERRAL TO JUVENILE COURT

There is no magic formula applicable in all situations that will automatically decide for the police officer whether a given case should go to court. If the police and court workers do not agree on the criteria to be used for deciding whether a given case should go to court, some of the police referrals may be rejected by the court intake workers and the police will also be criticized for withholding other cases that, in the opinion of the intake personnel, should have been referred. When this happens, police-court relationships become tense.

The remedy for this lies in a four-point plan of police-court cooperation:

1. Appointment of liaison officers by the police to the juvenile court and by the court to the police;
2. Joint establishment of referral criteria by the police and the court;
3. Training of both police and court workers in the use of these criteria; and
4. Continuous review and evaluation of referred cases by both police and court intake supervisors to assure that:
   a. The criteria which have been established are understood and applied, and
   b. These criteria will be revised in the light of experience as necessary.

Police review for this purpose should concentrate on those police cases in which there was no referral and the juvenile later again violated the law, and on those in which there was referral and the case was either refused by the court or dismissed without further action. Court intake review for this purpose should concentrate on those court cases that were accepted by intake and later dismissed by the court without further action, and on those cases referred by the police and rejected by court intake in which the juvenile later again violated the law. Joint analysis of these cases by a police-court committee should yield information useful in refining referral criteria, in estimating the extent to which the existing criteria are understood and applied, and in assembling case materials for training which would be useful for both police and court intake workers in developing an ability to assess need for court referral through vicarious rather than through direct experience.

Criteria for court referral will vary from community to community even when the communities are operating under the same juvenile court law. They will depend upon a number of variables, among which are the following:

1. Sociological nature of the community in which the work is being done—for example, whether it is the industrial core city of a metropolitan area or one of its bedroom suburbs;

2. The social, educational, and welfare services available in the community on a voluntary basis as opposed to those in a larger area available through utilization of the authority of the court; and

3. The education, training and experience of the police officers making the referrals.

Because no two communities will be alike in these respects, the criteria must be established for each community through cooperative planning with the particular needs of that community in mind.

It is sometimes suggested that problems arising from differences of opinion about the kinds of cases that should go to the juvenile court can be met by requiring that all police referrals to the court be made by the juvenile specialist unit. This is an unnecessary restriction. The decisions which are necessary in these referrals are no more difficult than many other decisions that must be made by line officers. With the guidance of well-written criteria as explained in well-planned training sessions, with the continuing help of their supervisors, and, when needed, with consultation from the police juvenile specialist, police line officers can make and are making meaningful juvenile court referrals. Although liaison with the court should be a juvenile specialist responsibility, requiring all referrals to be made by the specialist will place such a burden on the specialist unit that its other equally important functions cannot be performed satisfactorily. The presence of a well-operating specialist unit which has the confidence and cooperation of the court should make it unnecessary for all referrals to be made by that unit.

ALTERNATIVES TO COURT REFERRAL

In considering whether a case that might be referred to juvenile court should be referred, the police officer must be aware of the available alternatives. There are two. One is to leave the juvenile with or release him to his family. The other is to make a referral to a community social or welfare agency. The first alternative would be used if the officer decided that the family was strong enough, and the problem small enough, so that the family, once aware that it had a problem, could handle the matter itself without outside help. The more strength found in the family, the greater the problem that can safely be left with it. This decision by the officer presumes some knowledge of the family. This may exist because of previous contact or may be derived from discussions with the juvenile and his family. This is a final police disposition and should be reported as such.

If the officer believes that there is a local social-service or welfare agency, whether public or private, that might help the family meet its problem, and if he further believes that the family would appreciate and accept the help of the agency, he may refer the case to such an agency. This is a process that requires intimate knowledge of the social and welfare agencies of the community. If the officer does not have this knowledge, he should consult with the juvenile specialist in his department or refer the case to him.

There are two primary problems in making referrals to social agencies. One is that an element of coercion might be introduced that would make it difficult for a fruitful family-agency relationship to be established. The other is that some community agencies may refuse to accept referrals from the police. It is true that it is much easier to establish a satisfactory family-agency relationship when the family voluntarily seeks the services of the agency. In many police referrals, the coercive element is plainly stated. The family is told that if it doesn't resort to the agency, the case will be sent to court. If this kind of government authority is needed, the case should go to court initially. Even where this statement is not made, the family will all too often get the impression that such a condition is implied. Both situations are unfortunate.

This danger can be overcome by training the police officer in referral techniques. . . . He should be taught to make it clear that the referral is a final police disposition and that he has faith in the ability of the family to solve its problem with the help of the agency. He should also be taught the other skills and knowledge necessary to make good referrals.

In the past, many agencies have not followed through on police referrals. Either no action at all would be taken or only a perfunctory effort would be made on the part of the agency to establish contact. One reason for this attitude is the belief that police contact with the family, prior to and as a part of the referral, introduces an authoritative element which makes it necessary for the agency to expend much more time and effort to achieve any recognizable results than is necessary in cases where the relationship does not involve the element of authority.

This is an attitude that progressive social-service and welfare agencies have abandoned. Many agencies have found that some of their most gratifying results have come in cases originally referred by police. It is true that these cases present a special challenge, but meeting this challenge has frequently resulted in an agency's being able to obtain budget increases from the community united fund on the basis of this increased service. Lack of staff has also been cited by agencies as a reason for failure to follow on police referrals. If an agency does not have sufficient staff to accept the referral in the first place, the situation should be made clear to the police at that time. Where the police have difficulty in working with community agencies, the problems should be aired through the community body responsible for planning services for children and youth. Referral to a social-service or welfare agency is also a final police disposition and should be recorded as such.

In some of the larger cities, new agencies have been established or old ones reoriented to actively seek out police referrals. One direction that this effort has taken has been for local social agencies to provide group-work services to street clubs of aggressive youths. The services are provided by young men and women, called youth workers, who associate themselves with these clubs. This effort has resulted in a new awareness of the importance of collaboration between police and social-agency personnel and of the interdependence of their functions. The youth workers have found that their qualifications must include a working knowledge of pertinent state laws and· city ordinances, such as the criminal law and the juvenile court code. They have also discovered the necessity for developing skill in defining their objectives, the nature of their services, and the need for close cooperation with the police. The police, on their part, have come to recognize the youth workers as a previously untapped resource to which they can refer individuals or groups of youths whose behavior has disturbed community life and demands the kind of attention that they, as police, should not give. Many unresolved problems in this police-youth-worker relationship require continuing attention and mutual effort. But this relatively new approach points to improvement in the ability of some social agencies to accept and carry through on referrals from police and to an increased recognition by the police that social agencies can and will accept referrals from them.[2]

Another incidental problem arises in those cases in which the police decide not to refer the case to court but yet, because of the hour and the place, do not think that they can just turn the juveniles loose. This frequently results in the police transporting the juveniles to their homes. It is not clear just what the status of the juveniles is during such transportation and what the possible liabilities of the police officer and the city might be. A statute authorizing such a procedure and making it clear that the young persons so transported are not "in custody" or "under arrest" might be desirable. Where no such statute existed in analogous cases, civil suits have been brought against the police officers and the city.[3]

LEGAL COMPLICATIONS IN CASES INVOLVING JUVENILES

Police officers rely heavily on the cooperation of the citizenry in their work toward the solution of crimes. In many instances, it is possible to proceed in an investigation without obtaining a search warrant or without making an arrest because the citizens involved consent to waive their constitutional right to these procedures. When asked by police to assist in clearing up a reasonable suspicion which has arisen about their possible connection with an offense, most citizens will agree to cooperate. They may even allow the police to search their homes, offices, or automobiles without search warrants and often agree to accompany the police to the station to talk over an apparently incriminating situation. When voluntary consent is thus given, the police do not need court process or other legal authority because these have been waived by the citizen in giving his consent. These informal procedures result in great saving of time for both the police and the citizens involved, and are certainly to be encouraged.

The reason behind the legality of these procedures with adults is that the constitutional safeguards regarding arrest and search-and-seizure are being waived by a mature person who understands what he is doing. This is also true with some young persons, but probably not with all. In considering whether consent of a young person of juvenile court age in such a situation is truly a voluntary consent, the courts have considered the immaturity of the child as one of the factors to be weighed. For example, in discussing whether statements made by a child are voluntary, the courts have said that the age of the child along with the hour at which he was questioned, the duration of the questioning, whether he was given food and allowed enough rest during the period of questioning, whether he was allowed to seek the advice of his parents or of a lawyer, and the apparent overall attitude of the police toward his rights were all important factors to be considered.[4] In view of the immaturity of many young persons of juvenile-court age, serious consideration should be given to allowing the parents to be present during the questioning. The overall test is whether the young person has been treated with fundamental fairness.

This means that police officers must decide in each case whether a child is sufficiently mature and sophisticated to really know what he is doing when he gives consent to be taken to the police station to be questioned, or to be searched without being "taken into custody" or "arrested" on the basis of probable cause. Factors to be considered by the police in making this decision in addition to the age of the child are his apparent intelligence and all around maturity, his experience or lack of experience in such situations involving the police, the seriousness of the violation that he is suspected of having committed, and the extent of the continuing danger to society in the situation. Even when the police decide that the child is mature enough to make these decisions for himself, every effort should be made to notify his parents at the earliest possible moment so that they can furnish their support and advice to him. The basic test of the legality of such procedures with children of juvenile court age is whether the proceeding shows fundamental fairness to the child and due consideration for his rights along with the right of society to be free of violations of law.[5]

Because this concept of fundamental fairness is given somewhat different substance in different jurisdictions, every police administrator should seek the counsel of his legal advisor as to what the law probably is in his jurisdiction before he sets policy as to questioning, searching, and taking juveniles to the police station with or without "taking them into custody" or "arresting" them.

Because of a belief that the problem of a child is also a problem of his family and that a child should have the right to the advice and support of his family when he is in trouble, the Children's Bureau has recommended that children who are going to be questioned about alleged violations of law be approached through their families if at all possible.[6] . . . This would not affect routine questioning of juveniles in the neighborhood when all persons found there, both adults and juveniles, are being interviewed, not as possible suspects but on the chance that they may have some information that may be helpful to the police. It would not affect unsolicited admissions and confessions made to police officers by juveniles. It would affect the questioning of juveniles suspected of violations of law, whether before or after the evidence amounted to probable cause, in cases in which the police had not yet decided to refer the case to court. Whenever possible, juveniles should be interviewed in such cases in their homes after a discussion of the case with their parents. If the parents prefer, the questioning could occur at some other suitable place. In any case, the child should have the significance of his statement explained to him, he should be told of his right to remain silent if he so desires, and that he may contact his parents and have counsel. The child and his parent should also be told whether his contact with the police amounts to an arrest or taking into custody.

Admissibility of Juvenile Confessions

When investigating the kind of alleged violation of law by a juvenile that may be waived to criminal court if this is allowed by the law of the jurisdiction, police officers should keep in mind that the law as to admissibility of confessions and admissions is stiffer in the criminal courts than it generally is in juvenile courts. A recent case in the U.S. Court of Appeals for the District of Columbia held that statements made to police by a juvenile during a period when the juvenile court was considering whether to waive jurisdiction could not be admitted in the district court after waiver had in fact occurred.[7] The court held that "It would offend these principles [of fundamental fairness] to allow admissions made by the child in the noncriminal and nonpunitive setting of juvenile court procedures to be used later for the purpose of securing his criminal conviction and punishment." It has also been held that such statements, when later repudiated by the juvenile, will not be considered trustworthy even in the juvenile court.[8] These court decisions emphasize that police should not rely too much on statements of juveniles for establishing jurisdiction of the juvenile court or for conviction after waiver to criminal court.

Taking Juveniles into Custody

Regardless of the desirability of leaving a juvenile with his parents, there will be occasions on which he must be taken into physical custody. This is another police operation that has been affected in different ways in different jurisdictions by the different statutes passed along with the juvenile court laws. The result in many jurisdictions has been ambiguity in the law, which makes it unclear just what the duties and responsibilities of the police are. There are twenty-nine jurisdictions that apparently seek to avoid the "arrest" of juveniles.[9] Most of these jurisdictions refer to the apprehension process as a "taking into custody." Ten of these jurisdictions expressly state that the process is not an arrest.[10] Despite these provisions, several of the ten have other statutes that refer to "arrested" children. The real problem is what effect this change in terminology has on the rights and responsibilities of the police officer who makes the apprehension. Because this is not an arrest, the police officer justifiably asks whether the law of arrest applies or whether some new set of rules governs his actions. Only three[11] of the twenty-nine jurisdictions that provide that the apprehension shall not be an arrest face this question. All of these three state that the same rights and responsibilities evolve as in a case of arrest. Based on these statutes and on the logical demands of the situation, this should be assumed in all jurisdictions until specific laws are passed to clarify the situation. This would mean that the police would have the same right to secure and search a juvenile taken into custody as they have with an arrested adult. The right to question has been discussed above. It also means that the police have the same responsibilities to inform the juvenile about his legal rights, to allow him to contact friends, relatives, or counsel, to ensure that he be allowed to appear before some judicial officer within a specified period of time, and to abide by the general standards of fair treatment. This ambiguity in the law is unfortunate: "Whatever the difficulties, existing legislation can certainly be made more adequate. Police agencies deserve clearer guidance in the discharge of their law enforcement responsibility than is afforded by law today."[12]

When a police officer has decided that there is a basis for juvenile court jurisdiction over a child, . . . that circumstances indicate that the child is in need of the help of the court, and . . . that the child should immediately be taken into custody for transfer to the court, he then must carry out the procedures necessary to accomplish this result. Since the primary reason for taking the child into custody is to obtain the help of the court for the child, he should then be taken to the court as soon as possible. The term court here is used to include the probation office and the detention facility of the court. The exact place where transfer of control over the child will take place, whether in the court room, at the probation office, or at the detention home, should be established by court policy. This is the duty of every juvenile court judge.

Burden of Proof

Another difference of significance to police between proceedings against adults and those on behalf of juveniles is the nature of the case that police must be able to prove when they get the juvenile to court. The generally recognized burden of proof beyond a reasonable doubt that must be met in adult criminal cases is not applicable in juvenile court cases. The issues there need generally be proved only by a preponderance of the evidence, the same standard as is usually applied in civil cases.[13] However, if the case is being referred to juvenile court on an allegation that the juvenile has committed an act that would be criminal if committed by an adult, there still must be proof of every element of the offense involved.[14] This is sometimes overlooked. In some cases, there is also the possibility of waiver to criminal court, where the adult standard of proof beyond a reasonable doubt does apply. This means that investigation of any case in which there is a possibility of such transfer should continue until proof beyond a reasonable doubt is available. . . .

NOTES

[1] Goldstein, *Police Discretion Not to Invoke the Criminal Process; Low-Visibility Decisions in the Administration of Justice,* 69 Yale L. J. 544 (1960); see generally LaFave, *The Police and Nonenforcement of the Law* (Pts. 1, 2), 1962 Wis. L. Rev. 104, 179. Evolution of the British police practice of screening juvenile cases can be traced through the following articles: Note, *The Police and Child Offenders,* 100 Just. P. 468 (1936); Note, *Police Cautions for Juveniles,* 109, JZ:9. P. 374 (1945); Note, *The Policeman's Warning,* 118 Just. P. 229 (1954); Note, *Liverpool's Juvenile Liaison Officers,* 120 Just. P. 328 (1956); Elmes, *Police and Liberty,* 122 Just. P. 480 (1958); and Hargrove, *Police Discretion,* 25 Sol. 337 (1958). For a sociological discussion of this police practice, see Goldman, The Differential Selection of Juvenile Offenders for Court Appearance, Dec. 1950 (unpublished sociology disertation in University of Chicago Library).

[2] Blake, *Youth Workers and the Police,* 8 Children 170 (1961).

[3] See MacDonald, *The Police and the Mentally Ill,* 1 Crim. L. Q. 400 (1959); Note, *The Police and Lunatics,* 113, L. T. 137 (1902); Tiedeman, *Police Control of Dangerous Classes Other Than by Criminal Prosecutions,* 19 Am. L. R. 547 (1885); Szasz, *Civil Liberties and the Mentally Ill,* 9 Cleve. Mar. L. Rev. 399 (1960).

[4] Haley v. Ohio, 332 U.S. 596 (1948); Perrygo v. United States, 2 F. 2d 181 (1924).

[5] In addition to this basic test of fundamental fairness, the law might someday focus its attention on the capacity of children to give a voluntary consent in these situations. Public policy might well dictate that such capacity is vested in the parents or other legal guardian of children of tender age rather than in the children themselves. This would mean that the police would have to get the consent of the parents or guardian as well as the consent of the child. (See McBride

v. Jacobs, 247 F. 2d 595 [1957].) This would be true when the child is at school or in a detention facility as well as when he is under the nominal control of his parents.

A concomitant question then would be whether or not that capacity would shift at some time from the parent or guardian to the child. Several answers suggest themselves. For example, it might be reasoned that the capacity vested in the young person when he passed the age at which he would be beyond the jurisdiction of the juvenile court. Or it might be held that it be vested in him when he reached the age at which his case could be waived to criminal court, if the juvenile court law of the jurisdiction had a waiver provision. A court might also hold that the capacity shifted from parent or guardian to the child when he reached the age of fourteen, an age with common law significance in the law of criminal responsibility. Another possibility would be that the time of vesting in the child would be different in each case depending on a number of factors such as those listed above. Sound legal arguments can be made in favor of each of these possible positions.

6 U.S. CHILDREN'S BUREAU, DEP'T OF HEALTH, EDUCATION, AND WELFARE, STANDARDS FOR SPECIALIZED COURTS DEALING WITH CHILDREN 38 (C.B. Pub. No. 346–1954).

7 Harling v. United States, 295 F. 2d 161 (1961).

8 In re Four Youths, Nos. 28-776-J, 28-778-J, 28-783-J, 28-859-J, D.C. Juv. Ct., April 7, 1961, as reproduced in 7 *Crime and Delinquency* 280 (1961). However, if the juvenile later takes the stand and testifies in contradiction to his confession, his statement to the police may be introduced on cross examination in order to challenge the credibility and veracity of the juvenile witness.

9 Alaska, District of Columbia, Florida, Guam, Idaho, Indiana, Kansas, Kentucky, Maryland, Michigan, Minnesota, Missouri, Montana, Nevada, New Hampshire, New Jersey, New Mexico, Ohio, Oklahoma, Oregon, Puerto Rico, Rhode Island, Texas, Utah, Virgin Islands, Washington, Wisconsin, and Wyoming.

10 Georgia, Guam, Kentucky, Minnesota, Missouri, New Mexico, Oregon, Virgin Islands, Wisconsin, and Wyoming.

11 Georgia, Kentucky, and Oregon.

12 Remington, *The Law Relating to "On the Street" Detention, Questioning, and Frisking of Suspected Persons and Police Arrest Privileges in General*, 51 J. CRIM. L., C., & P. S. 386, 394 (1960).

13 Advisory Council of Judges, National Council on Crime and Delinquency, Guides to Judges on Evidence and Procedure in Juvenile Courts 78–81 (second draft for discussion at annual meeting, May 1961).

14 For a suggestion that the burden of proof should be the same in establishing juvenile court jurisdiction as it is in criminal trials, see Goldberg and Sheridan, *Family Courts—An Urgent Need* 12 (U.S. Children's Bureau, Dep't of Health, Education, and Welfare, Juvenile Delinquency: Facts and Facets Series No. 6, 1960).

5. Police "Professionalism" and the Rule of Law *

JEROME H. SKOLNICK

. . . THE IDEA OF PROFESSIONALISM is often invoked as the solution to the conflict between the policeman's task of maintaining order and his accountability to the rule of law. The meaning of this idea, however, is by no means clear. In sociology, there have been two main traditions, one emphasizing professional ideals and values, the other stressing technical competence. In Durkheim's view, what is distinctive about the idea of "professional" groups is not merely that such groups have high status, or high skill, or a politically supported monopoly over certain kinds of work, or a distinctive structure of control over work—most important is an infusion of work and collective organization with moral values, plus the use of sanctions to insure that these moral values are upheld. Arguing against the laissez-faire doctrines of the classical economists, for example, Durkheim pleaded for the introduction of morality into economic life:

> [W]hen we wish to see the guilds reorganized on a pattern we will presently try to define, it is not simply to have new codes superimposed on those existing; it is mainly so that economic activity should be permeated by ideas and needs other than individual ideas and needs . . . with the aim that the professions should become so many moral *milieu* and that these (comprising always the various organs of industrial and commercial life) should constantly foster the morality of the professions. As to the rules, although necessary and inevitable, they are but the outward expression of these fundamental principles. It is not a matter of coordinating any changes outwardly and mechanically, but of bringing men's minds into mutual understanding.[1]

An alternative concept of "professionalism" is associated with a managerial view emphasizing rationality, efficiency, and universalism. This view envisages the professional as a bureaucrat, almost as a machine calculating alternative courses of action by a stated program of rules, and possessing the technical ability to carry out decisions irrespective of personal feelings. As Weber says:

> Above all, bureaucratization offers the optimal possibility for the realization of the principle of division of labor in administration according to purely technical considerations, allocating individual tasks to functionaries who are trained as specialists and who continuously add to their experience by constant practice. "Professional" execution in this case means primarily execution "without regard to person" in accordance with calculable rules.[2]

In the effort to introduce fairness, calculability, and impersonality into an American administration of criminal justice that was often riddled with

* Jerome H. Skolnick, *Justice Without Trial*, New York: John Wiley & Sons (Science Edition), 1967, pp. 235–43.

corruption and political favoritism, most writers who have seriously examined police have also tended to subscribe to reforms based upon the managerial conception of "professional." Reviewing the works of such police reformers as O. W. Wilson or William Parker, we find that the conception of "professional" emphasizes managerial efficiency based upon a body of "expert" knowledge. A recently completed volume by law professor Wayne LaFave contains a similar point of view. In his concluding chapter, LaFave advocates a conception of the police as an administrative agency, with, presumably, the presumptions of regulation associated with such "expertise." He writes:

> The development of police expertness should be encouraged, and its existence should be recognized when appropriate. . . . There is need, and ample precedent in other fields, for the development of methods of communicating the existence of police expertness to trial or appellate courts which are called upon to decide arrest issues. The relationship between the court and the economic regulatory agency might serve as a model in the absence of a more highly developed proposal.[3]

There are, however, costs in developing a professional code based on the model of administrative efficiency. Such a conception of professionalism not only fails to bridge the gap between the maintenance of order and the rule of law; in addition, it comes to serve as an ideology undermining the capacity of police to be accountable to the rule of law. The idea of organization based on principles of administrative efficiency is often misunderstood by officials who are themselves responsible for administering such organizations. In practice, standardized rules and procedures are frequently molded to facilitate the tasks of acting officials. The materials of this study have clearly demonstrated that the policeman is an especially "nonmechanical" official. As Bruce Smith says:

> The policeman's art . . . consists in applying and enforcing a multitude of laws and ordinances in such degree or proportion and in such manner that the greatest degree of protection will be secured. The degree of enforcement and the method of application will vary with each neighborhood and community. There are no set rules, nor even general principles, to the policy to be applied. Each policeman must, in a sense, determine the standard to be set in the area for which he is responsible. Immediate superiors may be able to impress upon him some of the lessons of experience, but for the most part such experience must be his own. . . . Thus he is a policy-forming police administrator in miniature, who operates beyond the scope of the usual devices for control. . . .[4]

Smith may be making his point too strongly. Nevertheless, as a system of organization, bureaucracy can hope to achieve efficiency only by allowing officials to initiate their own means for solving specific problems that interfere with their capacity to achieve productive results. Some of these procedures may arise out of personal feelings—for example, relations between police and traffic violators—while others may become a routine part of the organizational structure. Examination of a procedural code, for example, would disclose no reference to the systematic use of informants. Given the task of enforcing crimes without citizen complainants, however, it becomes necessary for police to develop alternative methods to those used to apprehend violators in "standard" or "victimizing" crimes. These techniques of apprehension may demand considerable organization and skill on the part of the individual official, skill not so much in a formal administrative sense as in the sense of knowledge and ability to work within the effective limits of formal organization. As described, for example, the informer system requires so much ability that an aesthetic of execution has come to be associated with its use; it has become such an intrinsic component of police work that the abilities of the "professional" detective have come to be defined in terms of capacity to utilize this system.

As a bureaucratic organization, however, the police and governmental institutions, increasingly and generally, have a distinctive relationship to the development of the rule of law. The rule of law develops in response to the innovations introduced by officials to achieve organizational goals. It is certainly true, as Bendix asserts, that "a belief in legality means first and foremost that certain formal procedures must be obeyed if the enactment or execution of a law is to be considered legal." [5] At the same time, while legality may be seen as comprising a set of unchanging ideals, it may also be seen as a working normative system that develops in response to official conduct. The structure of authoritative regulations is such that legal superiors are not part of the same organization as officials and are expected to be "insensitive" to "productive capacity" as contrasted with legality. Thus, for example, a body of case law has been emerging that attempts to define the conditions and limits of the use of informants. Legality, therefore, develops as the other side of the coin of official innovation. As such, it is both a variable and an achievement. To the extent that police organizations operate mainly on grounds of administrative efficiency, the development of the rule of law is frustrated. Therefore, a conception of professionalism based mainly on satisfying the demands of administrative efficiency also hampers the capacity of the rule of law to develop.

The police are increasingly articulating a conception of professionalism based on a narrow view of managerial efficiency and organizational interest. A sociologist is not surprised at such a development. Under the rule of law it is not up to the agency of enforcement to generate the limitations governing its actions, and bureaucrats typically and understandably try to conceal the knowledge of their operations so that they may regulate themselves unless they are forced to make disclosures. But the police in a democracy are not merely bureaucrats. They are also, or can be conceived of as, legal officials—that is, men belonging to an institution charged with strengthening the rule of law in society. If professionalism is ever to resolve some of the strains between order and legality, it must be a professionalism based upon a deeper set of values than currently prevails in police literature and the "professional" police department studied, whose operations are ordered on this literature.

The needed philosophy of professionalism must rest on a set of values conveying the idea that the police are as much an institution dedicated to the achievement of legality in society as they are an official social organization designed to control misconduct through the invocation of punitive sanctions. The problem of police in a democratic society is not merely a matter of obtaining newer police cars, a higher order technical equipment, or of recruiting men who have to their credit more years of education. What must occur is a significant alteration in the ideology of police, so that police "professionalization" rests on the values of a democratic legal order, rather than on technological proficiency.

No thoughtful person can believe that such a transformation is easily achieved. In an article estimating the prospects for the rule of law in the Soviet Union, Leonard Schapiro has written, "It is perhaps difficult for dictators to get accustomed to the idea that the main purpose of law is, in fact, to make their task more difficult." [6] It is also hard for police officials in a democracy to accept this idea. In the same article, Schapiro reports the case of two professors who were criticized for urging thc desirability of adopting certain principles of bourgeois law and criminal procedure, arguing that observance of legal norms must prevail over expediency in government legislation and administration. They were officially criticized for incorrectly understanding "the role of legal science in the solution of the practical tasks of government," [7] a criticism not too different from the sort often leveled by "professional" police administrators in the United States against those who, for example, insist that the police must act legally for their evidence against the accused to be admitted. The argument is always essentially the same: that the efficient administration of criminal law will be hampered by the adoption of procedures designed to protect individual liberties. The police administrators on the whole are correct. They have been given wide and direct responsibility for the existence of crime in the community, and it is intrinsically difficult for them to accustom themselves to the basic idea of the rule of law: "that the main purpose of law is, in fact, to make their task more difficult."

THE COMMUNITY AND POLICE CONDUCT

If the police are ever to develop a conception of *legal* as opposed to *managerial* profcssionalism, they will do so only if the surrounding community demands compliance with the rule of law by rewarding police for such compliance, instead of looking to the police as an institution solely responsible for controlling criminality. In practice, however, the reverse has been true. The police function in a milieu tending to support, normatively and substantively, the idea of administrative efficiency that has become the hallmark of police professionalism. Legality, as expressed by both the criminal courts community with which the police have direct contact, and the political community responsible for the working conditions and prerogatives of police, is a weak ideal. This concluding section will attempt to locate the main sources of support for the managerial concept of police professionalism.

A posthumously published article by Professor Edmond Cahn distinguishes between "the imperial or official perspective" on law and "the consumer perspective." [8] The official perspective, according to the author, is so called "because it has been largely determined by the dominant interests of rulers, governors, and other officials." [9] In contrast, the "consumer" perspective reflects the interests and opinions of those on the receiving end of law. In the "consumer" view, therefore, constraints on the decision-making powers of officials are given more importance than the requirements of the processing system and those who carry out its administration. Cahn adds that "a free and open society calls on its official processors to perform their functions according to the perspective of consumers." [10] At the same time that he argues against it, however, Cahn demonstrates in his own article the empirical strength of the presumption of correctness in official conduct. So in large part do the materials in this study.

The "official perspective" is most persuasive because it operates as the "established" mode of law enforcement, in the broadest sense of that term. The administration of criminal justice has become a major industry in modern urban society. FBI data show that during 1963 there were 4,437,786 arrests reported by 3,988 police agencies covering areas totaling 127 million in population. In California alone during 1963 there were 98,535 adult felony arrests and 595,992 adult misdemeanor arrests. There were in addition 244,312 arrests of juveniles.[11] During 1962 to 1963, the District Attorney of Los Angeles County had a staff of 546 (with 180 lawyers) and a budget of just over $4,800,000.[12]

Under these circumstances of mass administration of criminal justice, presumptions necessarily run to regularity and administrative efficiency. The negation of the presumption of innocence permeates the entire system of justice without trial. All involved in the system, the defense attorneys and judges, as well as the prosecutors and policemen, operate according to a working presumption of the guilt of persons accused of crime. As accused after accused is processed through the system, participants are prone to develop a routinized callousness, akin to the absence of emotional involvement characterizing the physician's attitude toward illness and disease. That the accused is entitled to counsel is an accepted part of the system, but this guarantee implies no specific affirmation of "adversariness" in an interactional sense. Indeed, the most respected attorneys, prosecuting and defense alike, are those who can "reasonably" see eye-to-eye in a system where most defendants are guilty of some crime.

The overwhelming presence of the "official" system of justice without trial provides normative support for the policeman's own attachment to principles of administrative regularity in opposition to due process of law. Under such circumstances, it should not be surprising to find the policeman adopting the "official" perspective too, since his role is to make the initial decision as to whether a charge has been warranted. Having made the charge, he of all people can hardly be expected to presume the innocence of the defendant. He has, in practice, listened to the defendant's story and assured himself of the latter's culpability. In his own mind, there are numerous guilty parties whom he has not arrested because he does not feel their cases will hold up in court, even though he is personally convinced of their guilt to a moral certainty. Police may feel most strongly about the "irrationality" of due process, but in fact other role players in the system of criminal justice may also be observed to be more concerned with efficiency than legality. If the policeman is the strongest advocate of a "rational bureaucratic" system emphasizing factual over legal guilt, he may well be simply because it is the definition of his ability as a worker that is most affected by the application of the rule of law.

An "order" perspective based on managerial efficiency also tends to be supported by the civic community. The so-called power structure of the community, for example, often stresses to the police the importance of "keeping the streets clear of crime." The La Loma County Grand Jury, composed of "prominent" citizens—mainly businessmen and bankers—typically expresses concern not over violations of due process of law but over a seemingly ever rising crime rate and the inability of police to cope with it. Similarly, the

Westville *Courier,* the city's only newspaper, makes much of crime news, exaggerating criminality and deploring its existence. The police, quite sensitive to press criticism, find little support for the rule of law from that quarter. Indeed, when a newspaper runs an editorial, or a political figure emphasizes the importance of "making the streets safe for decent people," the statements are rarely qualified to warn law-enforcement officials that they should proceed according to the rule of law. On the contrary, such injunctions are typically phrased as calls for zealous law enforcement or strict law enforcement. James Q. Wilson has described this as the "problem of the crusade." As he says:

> Even if the force has but one set of consistent ends specified for it by the commissioner or superintendent, and even if adherence to those ends is enforced as far as possible, it is almost inevitable that there will come a time when the commissioner will decide that something must be done "at all costs"—that some civic goal justifies any police means. This might be the case when a commissioner is hard-pressed by the newspapers to solve some particularly heinous crime (say, the rape and murder of a little girl). A "crusade" is launched. Policemen who have been trained to act in accord with one set of rules ("Use no violence." "Respect civil liberties." "Avoid becoming involved with criminal informants.") are suddenly told to act in accord with another rule—"catch the murderer"—no matter what it costs in terms of the normal rules.[13]

The emphasis on the maintenance of order is also typically expressed by the political community controlling the significant rewards for the police—money, promotions, vacations. Mayors, city councilmen, city managers draw up police budgets, hire and fire chiefs of police, and call for "shakeups" within the department. Even the so-called liberal politician is inclined to urge police to disregard the rule of law when he perceives circumstances as exceedingly threatening. Thus, Wilson adds:

> When Fiorello La Guardia became mayor of New York City he is said to have instructed his police force to adopt a "muss 'em up" policy toward racketeers, to the considerable consternation of groups interested in protecting civil liberties. The effort to instill one set of procedural rules in the force was at cross-purposes with the effort to attain a certain substantive end.[14]

In contrast to that of political authority, the power of appellate courts over the police is limited. In practice, the greatest authority of judges is to deny the merit of the prosecution. Thus, by comparison to the direct sanctions held by political authority, the judiciary has highly restricted *power* to modify police behavior. Not only do appellate courts lack direct sanctions over the police but there are also powerful political forces that, by their open opposition to the judiciary, suggest an alternative frame of reference to the police. By this time, however, the police have themselves become so much a part of this same frame of reference that it is often difficult to determine whether it is the political figure who urges "stricter law enforcement" on the policeman, or the law-enforcement spokesman who urges the press and the politician to support his demands against laws "coddling criminals," by which he typically means rulings of appellate courts upholding constitutional guarantees, usually under the Fourth, Fifth, Sixth, and Fourteenth Amendments. Whether the policeman is the "man in the middle," as Wilson portrays him, and as police prefer to present themselves, or whether police have by this time come to be the tail wagging the press and the politician, is the subject for another study. Beyond doubt, however, there are enough forces within the community, perhaps by now including the police themselves, to provide the working policeman with a normative framework praising managerial efficiency and opposing due process of law.

CONCLUSION

This chapter has indicated how the police respond to the pressures of the dilemma of having two sets of ideals thrust upon them. As workers in a democratic society, the police seek the opportunity to introduce the means necessary to carry out "production demands." The means used to achieve these ends, however, may frequently conflict with the conduct required of them as legal actors. In response to this dilemma, police "experts" have increasingly adopted a philosophy of professionalism based on managerial efficiency, with the implied hope that advancing technology will somehow resolve their dilemma. As indicated, it has not, and by its very assumptions cannot. First of all, in those areas where violations of the rule of law occur, advanced technology often results in greater violation. Technological advances in the form of wiretaps, polygraphs, stronger binoculars, and so forth only make the police more competent to interfere with individual liberty. Secondly, the model of efficiency based on bureaucracy simply does not work out in practice. Warren Bennis has catalogued the limitations of bureaucracy in general, and such limits are certainly applicable to large urban police forces. The following is a sample:

1. Bureaucracy does not adequately allow for personal growth and development of mature personalities.
2. It develops conformity and "group-think."
3. It does not take into account the "informal organization" and the emergent and unanticipated problems.
4. Its systems of control and authority are hopelessly outdated.
5. It has no adequate juridical process.
6. It does not possess adequate means for resolving differences and conflicts between ranks and, most particularly, between functional groups.
7. Communication and innovative ideas are thwarted or distorted owing to hierarchical division.[15]

The working policeman is well aware of the limitations of "scientific" advances in police work and organization. He realizes that his work consists mostly of dealing with human beings, and that these skills are his main achievement. The strictures of the rule of law often clash with the policeman's ability to carry out this sort of work, but he is satisfied to have the argument presented in terms of technological achievement rather than human interaction, since he rightly fears that the public "will not understand" the human devices he uses, such as paying off informers, allowing "fences" to operate, and reducing charges, to achieve the enforcement ends demanded of him.

Police are generally under no illusions about the capacity of elected officials and the general public to make contradictory demands upon them. A certain amount of lip service may be paid to the need for lawful enforcement of substantive criminal law, but the police are rarely, if ever, rewarded for complying with or expanding the area of due process of law. On the contrary, they are rewarded primarily for apprehension of so-called notorious criminals, for breaking "dope rings," and the like. As a matter of fact, police are often much more sophisticated about their practices than the politicians who reward them. Police, for example, generally recognize the complexities of the meaning of such a term as "hardened criminal" and of the difficulties involved in carrying out a system of enforcement in line with the strictures of due process of law. The working detective who has used an individual as an informant for years, who has developed a relationship with the man in which each can depend on the word of the other, is not taken in by newspaper exaggerations of the man's "criminal" character.

Finally, the dilemma can never be resolved since it contains a built-in dialectic. Appellate decisions upholding the integrity of procedural requirements may well move large segments of the community to a greater concern for the security of the substantive ends of criminal law. Especially when the police are burdened with the responsibility of enforcing unenforceable laws, thereby raising the specter of a "crime-ridden" community,[16] decisions that specifically protect individual liberty may increase the pressure from an anxious community to soften these, and thus contain the seeds of a more "order-oriented" redefinition of procedural requirements. Over the past twenty years, courts have been increasingly indulgent of the rights of the accused. Whether this trend will continue, or whether the courts will redefine "due process of law" to offer legitimacy to what is presently considered unlawful official behavior may well be contingent on the disposition of the civic community.

If this analysis is correct in placing ultimate responsibility for the quality of "law and order" in American society on the citizenry, then the prospects for the infusion of the rule of law into the police institution may be bleak indeed. As an institution dependent on rewards from the civic community, police can hardly be expected to be much better or worse than the political context in which they operate. When the political community is itself corrupt, the police will also be corrupt. If the popular notion of justice reaches no greater sophistication than that "the guilty should not go free," then the police will respond to this conception of justice. When prominent members of the community become far more aroused over an apparent rise in criminality than over the fact that Negroes are frequently subjected to unwarranted police interrogation, detention, and invasions of privacy, the police will continue to engage in such practices. Without widespread support for the rule of law, it is hardly to be expected that the courts will be able to continue advancing individual rights, or that the police will themselves develop a professional orientation as *legal* actors, rather than as efficient administrators of criminal law.

NOTES

[1] Emile Durkheim, *Profession Ethics and Civic Morals,* trans. Cornelia Brookfield (New York: The Free Press, 1958), p. 29.

[2] Max Rheinstein, *Max Weber on Law in Economy and Society,* trans. Max Rheinstein and Edward Shils (Cambridge: Harvard University Press, 1954), p. 350.

[3] Wayne R. LaFave, *Arrest: The Decision to Take a Suspect into Custody* (Boston: Little, Brown, 1965), pp. 512–13.

[4] Bruce Smith, *Police Systems in the United States* (New York: Harper & Row, 1960), p. 19.

[5] J. R. Bendix, *Work and Authority in Industry* (New York: Harper Torchbook, 1963), p. 112.

[6] Leonard Schapiro, "Prospects for the Rule of Law," p. 112. *Problems of Communism*, 14 (March–April 1965), 2.

[7] *Ibid.*, p. 7.

[8] "Law in the Consumer Perspective," *University of Pennsylvania Law Review*, 112 (Nov. 1963), 1–21.

[9] *Ibid.*, p. 4.

[10] *Ibid.*, p. 9.

[11] Edward L. Barrett, "Criminal Justice and the Problem of Mass Production," in Harry W. Jones (ed.), *The Courts, and the Public, and the Law Explosion* (Englewood Cliffs, N.J.: Prentice-Hall, 1965), p. 95.

[12] *Ibid.*, p. 98.

[13] James Q. Wilson, "The Police and Their Problems: A Theory," *Public Policy*, 12 (1963), 199.

[14] *Ibid.*

[15] Warren Bennis, "Beyond Bureaucracy," *Trans-action*, 2 (July–Aug. 1965), 32.

[16] Police statistics also contribute to this perception. See Gilbert Geis, "Statistics Concerning Race and Crime," *Crime and Delinquency* (April 1965), pp. 142–50.

6. *Abuse of Juvenile Records* *

ALBERT G. HESS AND FRÉ LE POOLE

ACCORDING TO THE FBI, there were 5,031,393 arrests of adults in the United States in 1965.[1] The FBI does not receive complete data from all parts of the country; the reported figure covers only 69 per cent of the population. Prorata computation for the total population indicates a total arrest figure of over 7,200,000 in 1965.[2] This is a count of *arrests, not persons;* obviously, since a number (unknown) of persons are arrested more than once during a year, the number of persons arrested is smaller than the number of arrests.[3] Exactly how much smaller it is is not known, but the number of Americans who have arrest records must amount to many millions. An estimate characterized as "conservative" indicated that there is one new offender in every eight arrests and that "about 40 per cent of the male children living in the United States today will be arrested for a nontraffic offense sometime in their lives."[4]

ARREST RECORDS IN THE UNITED STATES

Pre-sentence investigation reports commonly include, in addition to previous convictions, a listing of arrests not followed by conviction.[5]

A person applying for acceptance by the Armed Forces, for a position in the civil service or in a private firm, for a license, for membership in a professional or labor organization, for apprenticeship training, or for a scholarship is often required to answer a question worded approximately as follows:

* Albert G. Hess and Fré Le Poole, "Abuse of the Record of Arrest Not Leading to Conviction," *Crime and Delinquency*, October, 1967, pp. 494–505. Reprinted by permission of the authors.

"Have you ever been arrested, taken into custody, held for investigation or questioning, or charged by any enforcement authority?" [6]

An affirmative answer often produces an unwarranted conclusion. Those who have to decide about the application frequently disqualify the applicant immediately when he admits having been arrested.

According to a study of New York City area employment agencies by the New York Civil Liberties Union, 75 per cent of the agencies sampled do not make a referral when the applicant has an arrest record. The refusal to refer is automatic and unqualified; the fact that the applicant was not convicted of the offense for which he had been arrested has no effect on the refusal.[7] According to another investigation, sixty-six of seventy-five employers would not consider hiring anyone who had been charged with assault and had been acquitted.[8] Even if an employer does not want to exclude such a person automatically he might be required to do so by surety companies that will not approve bonds for employees with arrest records.[9]

Many employers and government agencies request the prospective employee to sign a "waiver" permitting authorities in possession of his arrest records to reveal them.[10]

Obviously, it is difficult to prove that the arrest record of an applicant was the reason he was not hired. Nevertheless, this reason is clearly established in a number of cases.

Investigations by a legislative committee in California showed that applicants for post office jobs who answered the question on arrest affirmatively were "automatically disqualified because it is simpler and cheaper to hire an applicant without any record whatever than to investigate the circumstances of an arrest." [11]

A college student was arrested while picketing, but the charge was dismissed. Later, after passing the prescribed examination for a position in the New York State civil service, he answered affirmatively the question on whether he had ever been "arrested for any violation of law" and whether he had "ever been a defendant in a criminal proceeding." Thereupon, the Civil Service Commission investigated the circumstances of his arrest, but, before completing this inquiry, it assigned other applicants who had passed the examination to the vacant positions.[12] (Such practices appear to be quite common: employers sometimes go through the motions of investigating the particulars of an arrest but make their decision without waiting for the results of the investigation, thus disqualifying the person with the arrest record.)

An employee of a Chicago prison suddenly found himself suspended from service because of an arrest that had occurred seventeen years ago as a result of mistaken identity. The FBI record showed merely that he had been arrested on a felony charge. (Eventually, after a new investigation, he was reinstated.[13])

The few cases cited here are merely illustrative; the practices are common all over the United States. "Those of us who deal with the daily practicalities presented by the bread-and-butter portions of court calendars find that, in the main, irreparable injury is done a defendant acquitted after a trial; the fact of his arrest is very often sufficient to rule him out of consideration for employment." [14]

The practical effects of arrest, which has been described as the first of a series of "status degradation ceremonies" in the criminal process,[15] on the accused's job-hunting problem are virtually the same as the consequences of a conviction.[16] Employment agencies tend to make no distinction between persons with arrest records and those with convictions, and most employers equate both categories as "persons in trouble" and, consequently, bad employment risks.

Law-enforcement officials contribute to the confusion between arrest and conviction. Concerning the FBI files of persons with police records (including many persons who have been arrested but not convicted), the director of the Federal Bureau of Investigation said, in 1938: "A police record is a record of a man who has been arrested. It does not mean, though, that he has not later been convicted." [17] The wording strongly suggests a presumption of guilt. In 1946, the FBI referred to all persons in its files as "a *criminal army* of six million individuals who have been arrested and fingerprinted—one out of every twenty-three inhabitants in the United States." [18] Even the separately kept "noncriminal" civil files of the FBI have been labeled by the bureau as part of its "reservoir of criminal records." [19]

Abuse of Knowledge

A few years ago a bill introduced in the New York legislature made it a misdemeanor for an employer to ask a prospective employee about previous arrests. Opposing it, a minister asked: "What kind of an example do we hold out to our youth if we make a public law that hides with legal sanction human wrongdoings?" [20]

The department of water supply of a large eastern city asks fishing license applicants about their previous arrests: "The question," it says, "is a very important one. It is related to national defense." [21]

The rightness of considering a previous arrest that did not lead to a conviction is frequently defended on the grounds of "lack of evidence," deals between offender and prosecutor, and "legal technicalities."

Those opposed to asking a person about arrests cite the principle of presumption of innocence, generally considered a basic criterion of the "state of law" as applied in the United States in particular.

An applicant who lists for an employer or licensing agency his previous arrests that have not led to convictions actually places himself in double jeopardy, facing, without procedural safeguards, a "second trial" in which it is up to him to prove his innocence against a presumption of guilt. Many persons with arrest records do not even qualify for such a second trial since the listing of previous arrests disqualifies them per se. [22]

Frequent abuses in law enforcement make some arrest records an unreliable index of misconduct. Arrests merely "for investigation" or "on suspicion"— that is, without a warrant and without probable cause—are widespread. [23] Mass arrests, used by the police as a technique in riot control, particularly affect persons living in ghetto areas, who are also subject to wholesale arrest as vagrants when the police round up suspects after a crime. [24] Such practices may account for the fact that from 50 to 90 per cent of male slum dwellers have arrest records. [25]

Every year countless numbers are arrested under the catch-all provision of disorderly conduct. In New York City alone, many thousands are arrested annually "who, neither homeless nor drunk, get into arguments with neighbors, talk back to police officers, stand around idly, make speeches on street corners, play music on the sidewalk or in the parks, grow long hair on their chin or head, gather in small or large groups, or look like homosexuals." [26] While this practice has changed somewhat concerning alcoholics, the number of arrests for loosely defined "disorderly conduct" is still enormous.

In the United States, the number of illegal arrests far outstrips the number of legal ones. Police administrators admit that three out of four arrests are probably illegal.[27]

Discrimination based on previous arrests hits hardest at the lowest socio-economic level, where the largest numbers of persons with arrest records are to be found. Since the few existing employment opportunities are still further reduced for persons with arrest records, many who have no chance to break out of the vicious cycle of poverty become criminals.

ARREST-RECORD PRACTICES

Local police forces generally report arrests to the FBI, sometimes also to various state agencies. The reporting range varies greatly. Some police departments report only felonies, others go much further. In New York City, the record, at least theoretically, contains the final court disposition; [28] elsewhere this is not always the case. In providing information about arrests, the FBI warns that the record was furnished by local agencies and, where no final disposition is shown, the recipient should contact the appropriate agency for information about it.

FBI identification records are issued only to duly authorized law-enforcement agencies and federal, state, or local government agencies for official purposes. Private employers are not given such information. Similar principles prevail for the New York City police.[29] In practice, however, private employers manage to gain access to arrest records.

It has been argued that, if undertaken for purposes other than identification within the framework of criminal investigation, not only the taking of measurements, a photograph, and fingerprints but also the maintenance of an arrest record before conviction constitutes an infringement of the individual's right of privacy. Most often, however, courts have ruled that "the good have to suffer for the bad" and have argued that an individual should not mind some infringement on his privacy if it helps to maintain a safe society.[30]

Several states have statutes permitting fingerprints, photos, and arrest records to be destroyed, expunged, or returned if the accused is not convicted. A 1963 Connecticut law provides:

> When any criminal case is nolled or the accused is found not guilty in the superior court or in the circuit court, the clerk of the court shall make the record of such nolle or such not guilty finding and the court having jurisdiction, upon petition of the arrested person or his heirs, may order all police and court records and records of the state's or prosecuting attorney pertaining to such case to be erased, provided at least three years have elapsed from the day of arrest.[31]

Similarly, some laws—for example, New York's Youthful Offender statute— require that certain arrest records be sealed.

A different approach was adopted by a bill introduced in the New York State legislature in 1965. This bill, passed by the Assembly but defeated in the Senate, read, in part:

The penal law is hereby amended by inserting therein a new section, to be Section 510b: *Question of arrest as a condition of employment.* No employer shall inquire of or ask any person whether or not he has ever been arrested, as a condition of employment or continuing employment. Any person violating this section is guilty of a misdemeanor punishable by a fine of not more than five hundred dollars or imprisonment of not more than thirty days, or by both such fine and imprisonment.

The New York Civil Liberties Union introduced, as part of its 1966 legislative program, another draft bill making it unlawful for an employer to require a person to answer the question whether he had ever been arrested, as a condition of employment or continuing employment. This bill also was passed by the Assembly but defeated in the Senate.

ARREST RECORDS ABROAD

A questionnaire sent on November 19, 1966, by NCCD's Information Center to its foreign correspondents draws attention to the distinction between convictions and arrests. The correspondent was asked to describe his country's laws and practices, especially in respect to employment and civil service applications, positions of special trust, expungement, safeguards against abuses, and similar practices.

Ninety questionnaires were sent out; replies were received from thirty-nine countries and one international police organization.

The countries represented thirteen common law, twenty-two civil law, and four socialist jurisdictions and included six nations in Africa, four in the Americas, five in Asia and the Far East, fifteen in West Europe, four in East Europe, three in the Middle East, and two in Oceania.

Not all the answers dealt with all the issues in detail. Canada stated it had not studied the handling of arrest records and therefore could say nothing about it. The thirty-eight other countries do not countenance the general discrimination against persons with arrest records common in the United States. When applied at all, it is only within certain extremely narrow limits. There is also no apparent difference among various political systems in this respect.

A "record" in these thirty-eight countries lists only convictions, for the most part, and then only those convictions for serious crimes that cannot be appealed further. These are listed for a limited number of years. There is a seeming consensus to ignore arrests that have not led to conviction, a consensus best expressed in the reply of Interpol:

Arrest, detention prior to official arrest, and police questioning are only initial phases in criminal proceedings and . . . their justification or expediency can be overruled by the judge's decision in cases where such measures were taken on the sole initiative of the police. Even when official arrest or detention prior to arrest have been ordered by the judicial authorities, the trial and verdict of the court can also declare the innocence of the accused and show that the arrest or detention prior to arrest were not justified.

Thus, in our opinion, arrest, detention, or cross-examination by the police cannot be taken into account to the detriment of an individual without prejudging the outcome of the trial and should be completely disregarded.[32]

Expunging the Arrest Record

Few countries abroad have regulations providing for expunging arrest data. This is not surprising since a so-called criminal record includes only convictions. Where arrest records are generally disregarded, their existence creates no problems and expungement appears unnecessary. Only in a few countries, including Australia, New Zealand, Kenya, and Malaysia, does the law provide for the destruction or return of photographs and fingerprints of a person arrested but later acquitted.

Revelation of Arrest Data

Disclosure of arrests is generally restricted to law-enforcement agencies, chiefly for identification purposes. In some countries (Ethiopia, Lebanon), only police can get the relevant information; in others, prosecutors and judicial authorities have the same privilege. The inclusion of the judiciary occurs mainly in countries where judges conduct preliminary investigations.

Only a few countries release arrest data to government agencies other than law-enforcement and judicial authorities. Even where this is the case, the release of arrest records is on a discriminative basis. In Austria, for example, government agencies can obtain information concerning arrest records for the last two years—not including the current one—of prospective employees from a special office of the police (Korrespondenzbüro). However, so the inquiring agencies can check further arrests not followed by a conviction, the file numbers of the public prosecutor or criminal court must be indicated. None of the countries reports giving information on previous arrests to prospective employers.

Arrest data will generally not be disclosed even on persons applying for positions of trust, though in Ceylon and New Zealand data on previous arrests are required for applicants for police or security service positions. A Swedish law of 1965 permits excerpts from the central police files to be released in connection with applications for positions in the post office department, in the field of crime and delinquency, and in the care of mentally ill or retarded young persons and children, provided that satisfactory information regarding the suitability of the applicant for the position in question cannot be obtained in any other way without considerable inconvenience. However, Swedish police records generally do not list arrests but do note whether a person is suspected of serious or habitual crimes. Nonetheless, when excerpts of the files are issued to other than judicial authorities, such suspicion is mentioned only if the crime was prosecuted. If the person was acquitted, the suspicion is not mentioned.

Switzerland reports that private enterprises sometimes hire a private investigation bureau to check on an applicant for responsible positions. These bureaus occasionally obtain information on arrest data unofficially from the police.

In Belgium, disclosure of information on arrests and pretrial detentions, either to a public or private agency or to an individual, constitutes the criminal offense of breach of professional secret.

In the United States mere arrest constitutes "a record"; in other countries criminal files are limited almost exclusively to convictions of serious offenses.

Outside the United States arrest records are maintained for identification purposes within the framework of crime investigation and, as a rule, only law-enforcement authorities, the prosecutor, and sometimes judicial authorities have access. Previous arrests are hardly ever taken into consideration in connection with employment; even in cases where government positions of trust are at stake, their use is limited.

THE PRESUMPTION OF INNOCENCE

The civilized world generally acknowledges presumption of innocence as a human right. Yet, the United States affords this right less protection than countries abroad; indeed, in the United States, protection of this human right is inferior at times to that in Communist countries. This lack of protection, coupled with widespread abuse in making arrests, suggests the United States needs a thorough revision of its handling of arrest records. Such a reform is especially important because in the United States a significant part of the population has arrest records that did not lead to a conviction and finds it difficult to obtain employment, especially if unskilled and untrained.

While the United States claims it respects the right to presumption of innocence, it has not fully realized that the very essence of the presumption of innocence requires that it be applied in all cases where the person has not been adjudicated guilty. The United States has not adopted the age-old maxim *in dubio pro reo*—if in doubt [decide] in favor of the offender. Since countries abroad do not deem it necessary to release arrest records, it is hard to see why the United States should insist on doing so.

PUBLIC EDUCATION

The American attitude toward arrest records has existed for a long time and it will not be easily changed. The problem must be attacked from many sides. The public in general and decision-makers in particular must learn to differentiate arrest and conviction and acknowledge that mere arrest does not mean the person in question is guilty. A special target for this type of education should be decision-makers who require that applicants answer questions about previous arrests: government agencies giving out licenses, the military, probation officers, union officials, employment agencies, and employers. Public education about arrest records should be part of a broad education program on the prevention, control, and treatment of crime and juvenile delinquency.

Such educational methods may also be advisable for law-enforcement personnel. Policemen, while inclined to respect substantive criminal law, display less respect for the legal constraints imposed by procedural provisions. They often act empirically under the justification of *experito credite*. Convinced of his own expertise in making judgments about apprehension, a policeman may be convinced he knows how to distinguish guilt and innocence, thereby justifying any arrests.

While police department rules of procedure admit a presumption of innocence, policemen favor, "presumption of regularity," which assumes a trained policeman knows when to make proper arrests. This "presumption of regularity," however, constitutes a presumption of guilt.[33]

This attitude leads American law-enforcement personnel to consider arrest records highly significant indications of a person's criminal tendencies. However, this assumption cannot be upheld if three fourths of all arrests are illegal.[34]

Measures for Individual Protection

While there appears to be no objection to the use of arrest data for identification purposes by law-enforcement agencies within the framework of criminal investigation, any further disclosure needs careful controls. Rules and regulations of the record-keeping agency should clearly define the limitations for releasing arrest records. Transmission of incomplete information is often misleading and creates a false impression, not easily corrected, exposing the innocent to serious handicaps. Warnings by the transmitting agency about the incompleteness of the record appear utterly ineffective.

The District of Columbia corporation counsel has questioned the practice of the police in giving arrest records of Washington job-seekers to prospective employers who require police clearance as a condition of employment. He declared the action "operates as an effective bar to employment" for many persons because "many employers do not realize that a record of arrest is not a criminal record and, unless the record shows the charge has been dropped, may assume the arrest resulted in a conviction." [35]

Since grave disadvantages may result from the existing confusion about arrest and conviction, an applicant should have the right to withhold information about previous arrests that have not led to convictions. This right should be provided by law in clear nonambiguous language. Such a provision should also take care of certain situations in which applicants do not know whether they must indicate previous arrests—for example, after a "sealing" of records.[36]

An applicant who wants a job or a license is usually in a weak position compared with the person or agency that has the power to grant or withhold it. Legislation granting him the right to withhold information about previous arrests should be worded broadly to cover questions about similar situations, such as "apprehension," "detention," "custody," "investigation," and even "summons." The provision should also cover cases where the question is circumvented by requesting the candidate to sign a "waiver" of confidentiality granting permission to a public agency to release confidential information about his previous records to the employer, and so on. An applicant is hardly in a position to refuse.

Employers could continue to ask questions about previous convictions; if not worded in terms of "arrest," questions about pending criminal trials would also be permitted.

Countries abroad rarely expunge arrest records, mainly because such records are not revealed and are not considered as indicative of criminal behavior. In the United States, a few statutes do provide for the expungement, annulment, sealing, or return of records, but they appear to have little beneficial effect. Sometimes the law provides for expungement of a conviction but not of mere arrest.[37] Often an applicant does not know whether or not he has to list arrests covered by such provisions.

The law may provide for expungement [38] but not notification to all authorities to which information about the arrests has been disseminated, so expungement has little impact. If, for example, the arrest remains listed in the police or FBI files, the expungement is meaningless. Sometimes, as in Connecticut and Ohio, expungement is granted only on request. If the arrestee is ignorant of this right, his arrest record remains available.

Often, prevailing practices may fall short of legal requirements. John A. Franks, director of the Legal Aid Defender Society of Columbus, Ohio, observed to the California Assembly Interim Committee on Criminal Procedure:

> It has been our observation that fingerprints and photographs are . . . taken by local police departments of any person being arrested or booked for any offense, whether a misdemeanor or a felony. . . . Where the defendant is found not guilty after trial, these fingerprints are not usually returned. In a case where a man has been held for investigation . . . the prints are returned upon request. . . . Our statute does not refer to duplicates, nor does it refer to prints which have been forwarded to other agencies. We suspect that, even though fingerprints are returned to the defendant, there is nevertheless a copy retained in the files of the police department, or some copies may have been forwarded to other agencies, which copies are not returned.[39]

Even if a legal provision attempts to give certain protection, its effect may be limited severely by jurisprudence. In Illinois the courts have held that the only agency required to return arrest records is the State Bureau of Criminal Identification (Department of Public Safety).[40] The requirement does not extend to the city police chief or the sheriff. According to the Illinois courts, the keeping of arrest records does not constitute encroachment on the right of privacy so long as the police do not disclose identification records to the general public.[41]

The opinion was ventured at a recent meeting of an NCCD Professional Council committee that expungement may backfire. If an applicant is placed in the situation where *he* must prove to an employer that an arrest was unjustified, he may have difficulties if the record is inaccessible.

Thus, expungement and similar measures are sometimes mildly helpful, often inefficient, and occasionally even harmful. This, however, should not rule them out. A new version of NCCD's Model Act on the Annulment of a Conviction of Crime might also cover arrests that have not led to conviction.[42]

Until recently the federal Civil Service Commission asked the usual questions about arrests. However, on August 15, 1966. John W. Macy, Jr., chairman of the commission, instructed agencies that "good risk" offenders were acceptable in civil service and that each case should be judged on its individual merits. The commission then modified its application forms by asking about previous convictions instead of previous arrests [43] (a step that has since been followed by a number of state and municipal civil services), but went on to say:

> The deletion of this inquiry does not, however, preclude the Commission and the agency concerned, as part of the full consideration of an individual's case, from developing the circumstances relative to arrests and taking them into consideration in determining suitability for federal employment. This is a reasonable and necessary part of a suitability determination as the circum-

stances surrounding some arrests have a genuine bearing on the individual's fitness regardless of the absence of a criminal conviction. For example, some arrested persons are not brought to trial because of the disappearance of witnesses or an unwillingness on the part of those concerned to prosecute. What has been done by the deletion of the arrest inquiry is to allow the unconvicted individual the very real and worthwhile opportunity to have his application considered on an equal basis with all others, while preserving for the Government the right to reject any truly unsuitable person when an evaluation of the facts surrounding an arrest justify that action.[44]

Thus, despite the shortcomings of arrest-record data, and despite the fact that 75 per cent of the arrests made in the United States are illegal, the commission's position perpetuates the harm done by the arrest record.

New York City not only has set up a municipal corporation to provide bonds for men with criminal records but has also revamped hiring practices in existence fifty years by doing away with the question about previous arrests. According to the statement of the acting chairman of the city's civil service commission, the results were "very good." [45]

A Washington, D.C., demonstration project called "Trustworthy, Inc., United Planning Organization," sponsored by the U.S. Office of Juvenile Delinquency and Youth Development, provides fidelity bonds up to $2,500 for its members who pay $10 in dues.[46] Another interesting suggestion in respect to bonding persons with previous arrest records is to apply "auto-pool bonding principles," which would spread the risk to all bonding companies.[47]

These steps indicate that the United States is slowly changing its long-standing practices in the release of arrest records and evincing more than lip service to the presumption of innocence principle it professes to cherish.

NOTES

[1] The figure excludes arrests for traffic offenses but includes arrests for driving under the influence of alcohol.

The term "arrest records" in this article denotes arrests that have not led to conviction of an adult. The apprehension and disposition of juveniles and the handling of records of conviction of adults are outside the scope of this paper. For proposed standards limiting the use of conviction records, see *Annulment of a Conviction of Crime: A Model Act* (New York: National Council on Crime and Delinquency, 1962); it does not attempt to cover the problem of arrest without conviction.

[2] Federal Bureau of Investigation, *Crime in the United States: Uniform Crime Reports 1965* (Washington, D.C.: Government Printing Office, 1966), Tables 1 (p. 51) and 22 (p. 114).

[3] *Ibid.*, p. 107.

[4] President's Commission on Law Enforcement and Administration of Justice, *The Challenge of Crime in a Free Society* (Washington, D.C.: Government Printing Office, 1967), p. 247.

[5] Sol Rubin *et al., The Law of Criminal Correction* (St. Paul, Minn.: West, 1963), pp. 83–84. Juvenile apprehensions are handled the same way even though, according to many statutes and Sec. 33 of the Standard Juvenile Court Act (6th ed., 1959), they are not part of criminal procedure; in spite of this, they are included in the social investigation report, are read and discussed in the hearing, and conceivably lead to a more severe disposition. See Orman W. Ketcham, "The Unfulfilled Promise of the Juvenile Court," *Crime and Delinquency,* (April 1961), pp. 97–110, esp. pp. 102–03.

[6] The text sometimes expressly includes juvenile apprehensions, mere summonses, and petty offenses. In the Eimicke Application for Employment form, "used by more than 15,000 companies throughout the United States," the question reads: "Were you ever arrested? If yes, describe in full." The applicant is given two and a half lines to "describe in full."

[7] Edward V. Sparer, *Employability and the Juvenile "Arrest" Record* (New York: New York University, Center for the Study of Unemployed Youth, 1966), p. 5.

[8] Richard D. Schwartz and Jerome H. Skolnick, "Two Studies of Legal Stigma," *Social Problems* (Fall 1962), pp. 133–42.

[9] Marcel Frym, "The Treatment of Recidivists," *Journal of Criminal Law, Criminology, and Police Science* (May–June 1956), pp. 1–7; see also, *New York Times,* Nov. 22, 1965, pp. 1 and 27, on a proposal to the City Council by Labor Commissioner James J. McFadden for establishment of a municipal corporation to provide bonds for men who had criminal records and whom private surety companies refuse to bond. "The bonding problem had developed into a major drawback on the [Labor Department's] job-training program. . . ." Difficulties in placing 914 men with a police record (20 per cent of the program's registrants) were attributed mainly to refusal of bonding companies to bond them.

[10] Sparer, *op. cit.,* p. 11.

[11] California Assembly Interim Committee on Criminal Procedure, *1959–61 Report* (Sacramento: California Assembly, 1961), p. 68.

[12] Documentation provided by the American Civil Liberties Union.

[13] *Ibid.*

[14] Judge Irving Ben Cooper, U.S. Court, Southern Dist., N.Y.

[15] Joseph Goldstein, "Police Discretion Not to Invoke the Criminal Process," *Yale Law Journal* (March 1960), p. 590.

[16] Schwartz and Skolnick, *op. cit.,* p. 136.

[17] Quoted in Max Lowenthal, *The Federal Bureau of Investigation* (New York: Sloane, 1950), p. 376.

[18] *Ibid.*

[19] *Ibid.,* p. 377.

[20] Quoted in Aryeh Neier, "The Presumption of Innocence," *Civil Liberties in New York* (March 1965), pp. 1–2.

[21] Cited in Robert R. Hannum, "Employment Impediments for Offenders and Public Safety Regulations," *Federal Probation* (March 1963), pp. 28–33.

[22] Sparer, *op. cit.,* p. 5.

[23] Commissioner's Committee on Police Arrests for Investigation, *Report and Recommendations* (Washington, D.C.: Government Printing Office, 1962).

[24] "The Effect on Employment Opportunity of a Record of an Arrest Not Followed by a Conviction," memorandum prepared for a meeting held by the Advisory Council to the New York State Commission on Human Rights (mimeo), March 19, 1966, p. 1.

[25] President's Commission, *op. cit.,* p. 75.

[26] Alan H. Levine, "Disorderly Conduct: Catch-all Device for New York City's 'Undesirables,' " *Civil Liberties in New York* (June 1966), pp. 2–3.

[27] Marshall Houts, *From Arrest to Release: An Analysis of the Administration of Criminal Justice* (Springfield, Ill.: Charles C. Thomas, 1958), p. 24.

[28] New York City Police Department, "Rules and Procedures," 1956, Ch. 9, Rules 54. O ff.

[29] *Ibid.,* Ch. 2, Rules 6. O ff; Ch. 18, Rules 9. O ff.

[30] McGovern v. Van Riper, 140 N.J. Eq. 341, 54 A. 2d 469 (1947).

[31] Conn., Gen. Stat. Ann. 54–90.

[32] This statement is prefaced as follows: "To give you an accurate and full reply we would have to consult to ninety-two Member Countries of our Organization. . . . We can nevertheless give you the opinion of the General Secretariat, which does not commit our General Assembly—the supreme body of the ICPO-Interpol—in the event of its having to express its attitudes on this subject. It is with this important reservation that we propose to reply to certain points in your questionnaire."

33 Skolnick, *Justice Without Trial: Law Enforcement in Democratic Society* (New York: Wiley, 1966), pp. 196–99.

34 Houts, *op. cit.*

35 *Crime Control Digest* (May 1967), p. 10.

36 United Community Fund of San Francisco, Committee on Youth, *Proceedings: Workshop on Arrest Records and Youth Employment* (mimeo), May 13, 1965, p. 7.

37 Peter D. Pettler and Dale Hilmen, "Criminal Records of Arrest and Conviction Expungement from the General Public Access," *California Western Law Review* (Spring 1967), pp. 121–34.

38 "The Expungement of Adjudication Records of Juvenile and Adult Offenders: A Problem of Status," *Washington University Law Review* (April 1966), pp. 147–90, esp. pp. 162 ff.

39 California Assembly Interim Committee, *op. cit.*, p. 61.

40 People v. Lewerenz, 1963, 42 Ill. App. 2d 410, 192 N.E. 2d 401; Kolb v. O'Connor, 1957, 14 Ill. App. 2d 81, 142 N.E. 2d 818.

41 Kolb v. O'Connor, *op. cit.*

42 NCCD, *op. cit.* (note 1).

43 United States Civil Service Commission, "Policies and Procedures Relating to the Federal Employment of Persons with Criminal Records," FPM Letter No. 731–2 (Washington, D.C., Aug. 15, 1966). pp. 3–4.

44 *Ibid.*

45 *New York Times,* January 7, 1967, p. 1.

46 National Council on Crime and Delinquency, *Selected References in Juvenile Delinquency and Youth Development,* Bulletin #3, December, 1966, p. 15.

47 United Community Fund, *supra* note 36, p. 9.

PART THREE
THE JUVENILE COURT

Introduction

At the turn of the century, reform-minded Americans prided themselves on a new social institution—the juvenile court. In 1967, however, a Presidential Commission and the United States Supreme Court questioned whether these self-congratulations were warranted. The assumptions, operational functioning, and consequences of the court's dispositions are now being scrutinized more carefully than at any time since its creation. The readings in this part examine some of the important issues that have emerged from this scrutiny.

Major critics of the Court assert that the juvenile-court reformers promised a great deal more than they could possibly accomplish. They promised that the court would provide treatment and rehabilitation instead of punishment, but they were never able to offer the variety of services that these intentions required. The court was supposed to deal with children *parens patriae* (in the role of parents), but it offered inferior substitutes: an untrained judiciary, uneven and inadequate probationary supervision, and congregate institutions. The court promised to take children away from the harshness and formality of adult criminal-court procedures, but it supplied arbitrary decision-making unconstrained by the traditional and constitutional guarantees of due process. The court promised expertise in the diagnosis and treatment of problem children, but it was unable to provide the necessary knowledge; in fact, that knowledge does not yet exist. The court promised to do away with the old stigma of youthful criminality, but it could not offset the new stigma of youth delinquency. The court promised to keep pursuing its laudable goals, but critics kept setting them aside and insisted on examining the functioning and outcomes of the court's actual operations.

On May 15, 1967, the Supreme Court delivered the first major decision in its history on the fairness of juvenile-court procedures in determining the facts of a delinquency petition. This historic opinion, written by Justice Fortas for an 8-to-1 majority, offered strong legal support to the critics of the court. The case involved a 15-year-old Arizona boy, Gerald Gault, who had been sentenced to stay at a state training school until he was 21 years of age; the charge was that Gerald and a friend had made a lewd telephone call to a woman—an offense that would have cost an adult a maximum of a $50 fine or a 60-day jail sentence. The Court did not rule on the disparate sentence per se but, rather, confined itself to the formal fact-finding part of the hearing, ruling that young Gault had been unfairly denied protection of the following due-process safeguards: prior notice of charges to prepare a defense; representation by counsel; the constitutional privilege against self-incrimination; sworn testimony of witnesses, and the right to cross-examine their testimony.

The Court's majority opinion (selection 1) provides an analysis of the functioning of the juvenile court that transcends the specifics of the Gault case or of Arizona law, attempting to understand the actual consequences of juvenile-court law and functioning rather than focusing merely on the intent of the framers (and founders) of juvenile legislation. The opinion lends support to virtually every criticism made by the President's Task Force on Juvenile Delinquency. The broadside attack on the unfairness of the juvenile proceedings of Arizona and other states relies essentially on two arguments to bring the Fourteenth Amendment into the courtroom. The major argument is based on the thesis that court decisions involve a loss of liberty and therefore require proceedings that offer youth the minimal rights of American citizenship. A secondary argument reasons that traditional safeguards of due process cannot be suspended when the sentences of the court do not provide the care and treatment intended by the framers of juvenile statutes.

Paulsen, in selection 2, contends that two major consequences are likely to follow the decision: juveniles will be given fairer trials, and there will be a growing tendency to view the court as a "last resort" rather than as a "gateway" for treatment services. The trend of the future, he says, will consist of a search for extracourt approaches to deal with the problems of youth rather than reliance on a court-supported, casework, individualized approach to youthful misconduct. Paulsen's appraisal is of some interest since he has been an outstanding, if moderate, critic of the unfair procedures of the courts; his major articles on the topic are cited positively by the Supreme Court. Paulsen's article is also interesting in that, like many other lawyers, he interprets the court's reasoning as based primarily "on the premise that the juvenile court system has failed to provide the care and treatment that the theory underlying it had posited." We have suggested that another thesis forms the major premise of the *Gault* opinion.

The Paulsen article also implies that the Supreme Court ruling will soon be followed by compliance in all the courts of the land. This position seems premature, given this country's experience with lack of compliance with the school-desegregation decision. Judges who believe in "individualized justice" are just as likely to resist the Supreme Court as are judges who believe in the "separate but equal" doctrine. This shared type of resistance is not due to a common ideological position but to the fact that both groups of judges are in strategic positions of power and may be reluctant to give up their judicial versions of fairness and justice under law. Judicial discretion in both the administration of the law and the interpretation of legal opinions can continue to be a problem. The problem of judicial discretion and selective judicial administration of the law is, in fact, quite comparable to the problem of selective law enforcement by the police.

It is not necessary to rely on theoretical reasons alone for expecting noncompliance; evidence exists that the functioning of the court may *not* be appreciably changed by the *Gault* opinion per se. Selection 4, for example, yields strong evidence that noncompliance was prevalent in the period immediately following the decision. In actual court proceedings and in their modes of dealing with juvenile offenders, many judges appeared either to ignore the decision or selectively to administer *some* fair procedures.

Selection 4 provides other grounds for expecting resistance. The authors note that there is an "Achilles heel" in the *Gault* decision; juveniles and/or their parents may waive (i.e., give up) their constitutional rights. The waiver of rights occurred prior to *Gault* in many jurisdictions; it may continue to occur since the Supreme Court did *not* rule out Mrs. Gault's right to waive her constitutional right to counsel. But she was never given the choice, so her rights were violated. It is possible that in many cases juveniles or their parents could be given this choice in appropriate legal language. If they opted for the waiver, then lack of representation could impair their chances of a constitutionally fair trial.

These problems are less likely to occur in states that have drastically revised their juvenile court statutes, as a few states did just prior to *Gault*, in anticipation of the Court's ruling. California and New York courts, for example, were empowered to appoint and pay for counsel before May, 1967, and were actually doing so in many cases. Legislative changes appear to be a viable approach for ensuring greater compliance with the Constitution in regard to court procedures. Nevertheless, it is important to be aware of the impact of these changes on other aspects of the court's operations, particularly the impact of a legalistic court on judges, lawyers, and social workers.

Lemert (selection 3) studied the California court shortly after it had legally stipulated that counsel was to be offered to indigent juveniles and their families and that fairer procedures were to be employed. He was interested particularly in finding out what happened to the decision-making mechanisms when lawyers became part of the proceedings. Lemert found that judges and probation staff continued to make the critical decisions about youngsters. The presence of lawyers tended to force increased precision in the wording of allegations and greater attention to specific evidence. But the greatest impact appeared to occur in regard to actual dispositional decisions—an area not touched on by the *Gault* decision. Rather than disprove allegations of delinquency, lawyers were successful in reducing the charges and the severity of dispositions. This was accomplished by their adapting to the existing working relationship between judges and probation staff. These traditional relationships, with their sharing of decision-making influences, were not drastically disturbed by either the new laws or the presence of a new occupational role partner.

Lemert's conclusion is not readily accepted by many judges and social workers. Since these two groups actually operate the juvenile courts, their opinions are worth taking into account. In general, those who anticipate negative consequences from introducing lawyers and legalistic procedures are concerned about restrictions of jurisdictional scope. Judges are concerned about placing limits on dispositional discretion and narrowing their areas of administrative responsibilities; probation workers are concerned about placing limits on their presentence reports and delimiting their contacts with clients. The case against a legalistic court is made in selection 5, from *Social Work*. Although the authors' viewpoint is shared by many

social workers, their arguments are also supportive of traditional judicial
discretion regarding juveniles.

The fact that the current post-*Gault* debates tend to center on the relative influence of the judge, the social worker, and the lawyer indicates that
one of the major consequences of promoting a legalistic court is the possible diminution of judicial and social-work influence in response to client
advocacy. It is apparent, however, that this loss of influence has not yet
actually occurred in a systematic fashion. Lemert's study indicates that
the judges and social workers of California have continued traditional
working patterns and that lawyers have tended to adapt to the system. In
other jurisdictions, client advocacy has challenged the existing arrangements. Understanding the kinds of social factor that resulted in these
divergent outcomes is important if we are interested in guiding and controlling the administration of justice. Understanding, however, is not sufficient for choosing which outcome is preferred. The guidance and control
of juvenile court personnel involves clarity of goals and the value assumptions underlying the choices.

The President's Task Force favors a legalistic court. In addition, they
attempted to articulate procedures and programs that would shunt youngsters away from formal adjudication. Instead of being referred to a court,
they said, many youngsters should receive a nonjudicial disposition by
being treated by a new municipal agency, the Youth Services Bureau (see
Part II). The Commission is also in favor of strengthening the intake procedures of the court to ensure that they are legally fair and effective in
maximizing pre-judicial dispositions. If youngsters finally emerge from
these carefully controlled screening procedures as candidates for adjudication, legal counsel should be provided. Youth must have a fair trial and
their rights must be ensured *before* there is consideration of treatment
plans. The promotion of the accused offender's legal rights may restrict
judicial and professional discretion, but the Task Force is quite willing to
accept the value of fair play in preference to therapeutic intent.

Selection 6, by Lerman, questions whether the *Gault* decision goes far
enough in promoting the legal rights of children. It argues that the Supreme
Court did not question whether Gault received justice; instead, the Court
restricted its attention to the fairness of the trial. Using empirical data,
Lerman concludes that juveniles convicted of committing minor offenses
are treated much more harshly than adult misdemeanants. He also cites
data to support the contention that current juvenile court practices do not
distinguish between serious and minor offenders once a youngster reaches
the juvenile court. Since fair procedures cannot ensure just dispositions, it
is important that attention be paid to this problem. The courts should
sponsor justice *before* they sponsor any treatment plans. Acceptance of
this approach would sharply reduce the power of judges and the influence
of presentence investigators.

Selection 7, by a California judge, also focuses on the court's legal
functioning. Gardner feels that many serious offenders are not being
treated severely enough and that the court's operations discourage viewing
the offender as a threat to society. He therefore favors transformation of
the juvenile court into a junior section of the adult criminal system.
Juvenile-status offenses would not be heard since they are not deemed to
be crimes, but all other offenses would be processed like adult cases. He

favors constitutional guarantees and the furnishing of counsel, but prosecutors should also be present to protect society's stake in law and order.
Gardner's proposal may seem like a backward step, but his argument
should be examined dispassionately. He appears to value fair play, justice,
and humanitarianism, but he also values protecting potential victims and
community standards. This competition of values is implicit in all of the
proposals. Gardner's is different because he reconciles the value conflict
with a different ordering of priorities. Choosing a specific orientation
toward the juvenile court involves favoring one hierarchy of values over
another. Frank and fair examination of Gardner's proposal may help
readers to examine their own ordering of preferences.

1. *In re Gault (Case No. 116-October Term, 1966)*

U.S. SUPREME COURT OPINIONS (DELIVERED MAY 15, 1967)

In the Matter of the Application of Paul L. Gault and ⎤ On Appeal From the
Marjorie Gault, Father and Mother of Gerald Francis ⎬ Supreme Court of
Gault, a Minor, Appellants. ⎦ Arizona.

[May 15, 1967.]

MR. JUSTICE FORTAS delivered the opinion of the Court.

This is an appeal under 28 U. S. C. § 1257 (2) from a judgment of the Supreme Court of Arizona affirming the dismissal of a petition for a writ of habeas corpus. 99 Ariz. 181, 407 P. 2d 760 (1965). The petition sought the release of Gerald Francis Gault, petitioners' 15-year-old son, who had been committed as a juvenile delinquent to the State Industrial School by the Juvenile Court of Gila County, Arizona. The Supreme Court of Arizona affirmed dismissal of the writ against various arguments which included an attack upon the constitutionality of the Arizona Juvenile Code because of its alleged denial of procedural due process rights to juveniles charged with being "delinquents." The court agreed that the constitutional guarantee of due process of law is applicable in such proceedings. It held that Arizona's Juvenile Code is to be read as "impliedly" implementing the "due process concept." It then proceeded to identify and describe "the particular elements which constitute due process in a juvenile hearing." It concluded that the proceedings ending in commitment of Gerald Gault did not offend those requirements. We do not agree, and we reverse. We begin with a statement of the facts.

I

On Monday, June 8, 1964, at about 10 A.M., Gerald Francis Gault and a friend, Ronald Lewis, were taken into custody by the Sheriff of Gila County. Gerald was then still subject to a six months' probation order which had been entered on February 25, 1964, as a result of his having been in the company of another boy who had stolen a wallet from a lady's purse. The police action on June 8 was taken as the result of a verbal complaint by a neighbor of the boys, Mrs. Cook, about a telephone call made to her in which the caller or callers made lewd or indecent remarks. It will suffice for purposes of this opinion to say that the remarks or questions put to her were of the irritatingly offensive, adolescent, sex variety.

At the time Gerald was picked up, his mother and father were both at work. No notice that Gerald was being taken into custody was left at the home. No other steps were taken to advise them that their son had, in effect, been arrested. Gerald was taken to the Children's Detention Home. When his mother arrived home at about 6 o'clock, Gerald was not there. Gerald's older brother was sent to look for him at the trailer home of the Lewis family. He apparently learned then that Gerald was in custody. He so informed his mother. The two of them went to the Detention Home. The deputy probation officer, Flagg, who was also superintendent of the Detention Home, told Mrs. Gault "why Jerry was there" and said that a hearing would be held in Juvenile Court at 3 o'clock the following day, June 9.

Officer Flagg filed a petition with the Court on the hearing day, June 9, 1964. It was not served on the Gaults. Indeed, none of them saw this petition until the habeas corpus hearing on August 17, 1964. The petition was entirely formal. It made no reference to any factual basis for the judicial action which it initiated. It recited only that "said minor is under the age of 18 years and in need of the protection of this Honorable Court [and that] said minor is a delinquent minor." It prayed for a hearing and an order regarding "the care and custody of said minor." Officer Flagg executed a formal affidavit in support of the petition.

On June 9, Gerald, his mother, his older brother, and Probation Officers Flagg and Henderson appeared before the Juvenile Judge in chambers. Gerald's father was not there. He was at work out of the city. Mrs. Cook, the complainant, was not there. No one was sworn at this hearing. No transcript or recording was made. No memorandum or record of the substance of the proceedings was prepared. Our information about the proceedings and the subsequent hearing on June 15 derives entirely from the testimony of the Juvenile Court Judge,[1] Mr. and Mrs. Gault and Officer Flagg at the habeas corpus proceeding conducted two months later. From this, it appears that at the July 9 hearing Gerald was questioned by the judge about the telephone call. There was conflict as to what he said. His mother recalled that Gerald said he only dialed Mrs. Cook's number and handed the telephone to his friend, Ronald. Officer Flagg recalled that Gerald had admitted making the lewd remarks. Judge McGhee testified that Gerald "admitted making one of these [lewd] statements." At the conclusion of the hearing, the judge said he would "think about it." Gerald was taken back to the Detention Home. He was not sent to his own home with his parents. On June 11 or 12, after having been detained since June 8, Gerald was released and driven home.[2] There is no explanation in the record as to why he was kept in the Detention Home or why he was released. At 5 P.M. on the day of Gerald's release, Mrs. Gault received a note signed by Officer Flagg. It was on plain paper, not letterhead. Its entire text was as follows:

Mrs. Gault:
Judge McGhee has set Monday, June 15, 1964, at 11:00 A.M. as the date and time for further Hearings on Gerald's delinquency.
/s/Flagg

At the appointed time on Monday, June 15, Gerald, his father and mother, Ronald Lewis and his father, and officers Flagg and Henderson were present before Judge McGhee. Witnesses at the habeas corpus proceedings differed in their recollections of Gerald's testimony at the June 15 hearing. Mr. and Mrs. Gault recalled that Gerald again testified that he had only dialed the number and that the other boy had made the remarks. Officer Flagg agreed that at this hearing Gerald did not admit making the lewd remarks.[3] But Judge

McGhee recalled that "there was some admission again of some of the lewd statements. He—he didn't admit any of the more serious lewd statements." [4] Again, the complainant, Mrs. Cook, was not present. Mrs. Gault asked that Mrs. Cook be present "so she could see which boy had done the talking, the dirty talking over the phone." The Juvenile Judge said "she didn't have to be present at that hearing." The judge did not speak to Mrs. Cook or communicate with her at any time. Probation Officer Flagg had talked to her once—over the telephone on June 9.

At this June 15 hearing a "referral report" made by the probation officers was filed with the court, although not disclosed to Gerald or his parents. This listed the charge as "Lewd Phone Calls." At the conclusion of the hearing, the judge committed Gerald as a juvenile delinquent to the State Industrial School "for the period of his minority [that is, until 21], unless sooner discharged by due process of law." An order to that effect was entered. It recites that "after a full hearing and due deliberation the Court finds that said minor is a delinquent child, and that said minor is of the age of 15 years."

No appeal is permitted by Arizona law in juvenile cases. On August 3, 1964, a petition for a writ of habeas corpus was filed with the Supreme Court of Arizona and referred by it to the Superior Court for hearing.

At the habeas corpus hearing on August 17, Judge McGhee was vigorously cross-examined as to the basis for his actions. He testified that he had taken into account the fact that Gerald was on probation. He was asked "under what section of . . . the code you found the boy delinquent?"

His answer is set forth in the margin.[5] In substance, he concluded that Gerald came within ARS § 8–201–6 (a), which specifies that a "delinquent child" includes one "who has violated a law of the state or an ordinance or regulation of a political subdivision thereof." The law which Gerald was found to have violated is ARS § 13–377. This section of the Arizona Criminal Code provides that a person who "in the presence of or hearing of any woman or child . . . uses vulgar, abusive or obscene language, is guilty of a misdemeanor. . . ." The penalty specified in the Criminal Code, which would apply to an adult, is $5 to $50, or imprisonment for not more than two months. The judge also testified that he acted under ARS § 8–201–6 (d) which includes in the definition of a "delinquent child" one who, as the judge phrased it, is "habitually involved in immoral matters." [6]

Asked about the basis for his conclusion that Gerald was "habitually involved in immoral matters," the judge testified, somewhat vaguely, that two years earlier, on July 2, 1962, a "referral" was made concerning Gerald, "where the boy had stolen a baseball glove from another boy and lied to the Police Department about it." The judge said there was "no hearing" and "no accusation" relating to this incident, "because of lack of material foundation." But it seems to have remained in his mind as a relevant factor. The judge also testified that Gerald had admitted making other nuisance phone calls in the past which, as the judge recalled the boy's testimony, were "silly calls, or funny calls, or something like that."

The Superior Court dismissed the writ, and appellants sought review in the Arizona Supreme Court. That court stated that it considered appellants' assignments of error as urging (1) that the Juvenile Code, ARS § 8–201 to § 8–239, is unconstitutional because it does not require that parents and children be apprised of the specific charges, does not require proper notice of a hearing, and does not provide for an appeal; and (2) that the proceedings and order relating to Gerald constituted a denial of due process of law because of the absence of adequate notice of the charge and the hearing; failure to notify appellants of certain constitutional rights including the rights to counsel and to confrontation, and the privilege against self-incrimination; the use of unsworn hearsay testimony; and the failure to make a record of the proceedings. Appellants further asserted that it was error for the Juvenile Court to remove Gerald from the custody of his parents without a showing and finding of their unsuitability, and alleged a miscellany of other errors under state law.

The Supreme Court handed down an elaborate and wide-ranging opinion affirming dismissal of the writ and stating the court's conclusions as to the issues raised by appellants and other aspects of the juvenile process. In their jurisdictional statement and brief in this Court, appellants do not urge upon us all of the points passed upon by the Supreme Court of Arizona. They urge that we hold the Juvenile Code of Arizona invalid on its face or as applied in this case because, contrary to the Due Process Clause of the Fourteenth Amendment, the juvenile is taken from the custody of his parents and committed to a state institution pursuant to proceedings in which the Juvenile Court has virtually unlimited discretion, and in which the following basic rights are denied:

1. Notice of the charges;
2. Right to counsel;
3. Right to confrontation and cross-examination;
4. Privilege against self-incrimination;
5. Right to a transcript of the proceedings; and
6. Right to appellate review.

We shall not consider other issues which were passed upon by the Supreme Court of Arizona. We emphasize that we indicate no opinion as to whether the decision of that court with respect to such other issues does or does not conflict with requirements of the Federal Constitution.[7]

II

The Supreme Court of Arizona held that due process of law is requisite to the constitutional validity of proceedings in which a court reaches the conclusion that a juvenile has been at fault, has engaged in conduct prohibited by law, or has otherwise misbehaved with the consequence that he is committed to an institution in which his freedom is curtailed. This conclusion is in accord with the decisions of a number of courts under both federal and state constitutions.[8]

This Court has not heretofore decided the precise question. In *Kent v. United States,* 383 U.S. 541 (1966), we considered the requirements for a valid waiver of the "exclusive" jurisdiction of the Juvenile Court of the District of Columbia so that a juvenile could be tried in the adult criminal court of the District. Although our decision turned upon the language of the statute, we emphasized the necessity that "the basic requirements of due process and fairness" be satisfied in such proceedings.[9] *Haley v. Ohio,* 332

U.S. 596 (1948), involved the admissibility, in a state criminal court of general jurisdiction, of a confession by a fifteen-year-old boy. The Court held that the Fourteenth Amendment applied to prohibit the use of the coerced confession. MR. JUSTICE DOUGLAS said, "Neither man nor child can be allowed to stand condemned by methods which flout constitutional requirements of due process of law." [10] To the same effect is *Gallegos* v. *Colorado*, 370 U.S. 49 (1962). Accordingly, while these cases relate only to restricted aspects of the subject, they unmistakably indicate that, whatever may be their precise impact, neither the Fourteenth Amendment nor the Bill of Rights is for adults alone.

We do not in this opinion consider the impact of these constitutional provisions upon the totality of the relationship of the juvenile and the state. We do not even consider the entire process relating to juvenile "delinquents." For example, we are not here concerned with the procedures or constitutional rights applicable to the prejudicial stages of the juvenile process, nor do we direct our attention to the postadjudicative or dispositional process. We consider only the problems presented to us by this case. These relate to the proceedings by which a determination is made as to whether a juvenile is a "delinquent" as a result of alleged misconduct on his part, with the consequence that he may be committed to a state institution. As to these proceedings, there appears to be little current dissent from the proposition that the Due Process Clause has a role to play.[11] The problem is to ascertain the precise impact of the due process requirement upon such proceedings.

From the inception of the juvenile court system, wide differences have been tolerated—indeed insisted upon—between the procedural rights accorded to adults and those of juveniles. In practically all jurisdictions, there are rights granted to adults that are withheld from juveniles. In addition to the specific problems involved in the present case, for example, it has been held that the juvenile is not entitled to bail, to indictment by grand jury, to a public trial or to trial by jury.[12] It is frequent practice that rules governing the arrest and interrogation of adults by the police are not observed in the case of juveniles.[13]

The history and theory underlying this development are well-known, but a recapitulation is necessary for purposes of this opinion. The juvenile court movement began in this country at the end of the last century. From the juvenile court statute adopted in Illinois in 1899, the system has spread to every state in the union, the District of Columbia, and Puerto Rico.[14] The constitutionality of juvenile court laws has been sustained in over forty jurisdictions against a variety of attacks.[15]

The early reformers were appalled by adult procedures and penalties and by the fact that children could be given long prison sentences and mixed in jails with hardened criminals. They were profoundly convinced that society's duty to the child could not be confined by the concept of justice alone. They believed that society's role was not to ascertain whether the child was "guilty" or "innocent," but, "What is he, how has he become what he is, and what had best be done in his interest and in the interest of the state to save him from a downward career." [16] The child—essentially good, as they saw it—was to be made "to feel that he is the object of [the State's] care and solicitude," [17] not that he was under arrest or on trial. The rules of criminal procedure were therefore altogether inapplicable. The apparent rigidities, technicalities, and harshness which they observed in both substantive and procedural criminal law were therefore to be discarded. The idea of crime and punishment was to be abandoned. The child was to be "treated" and "rehabilitated" and the procedures, from apprehension through institutionalization, were to be "clinical" rather than punitive.

These results were to be achieved, without coming to conceptual and constitutional grief, by insisting that the proceedings were not adversary, but that the state was proceeding as *parens patriae*.[18] The Latin phrase proved to be a great help to those who sought to rationalize the exclusion of juveniles from the constitutional scheme; but its meaning is murky and its historic credentials are of dubious relevance. The phrase was taken from chancery practice, where, however, it was used to describe the power of the state to act *in loco parentis* for the purpose of protecting the property interests and the person of the child.[19] But there is no trace of the doctrine in the history of criminal jurisprudence. At common law, children under seven were considered incapable of possessing criminal intent. Beyond that age, they were subjected to arrest, trial, and in theory to punishment like adult offenders.[20] In these old days, the state was not deemed to have authority to accord them fewer procedural rights than adults.

The right of the state, as *parens patriae*, to deny to the child procedural rights available to his elders was elaborated by the assertion that a child, unlike an adult, has a right "not to liberty but to custody." He can be made to attorn to his parents, to go to school, and so on. If his parents default in effectively performing their custodial functions—that is, if the child is "delinquent"—the state may intervene. In doing so, it does not deprive the child of any rights, because he has none. It merely provides the "custody" to which the child is entitled.[21] On this basis, proceedings involving juveniles were described as "civil" not "criminal" and therefore not subject to the requirements that restrict the state when it seeks to deprive a person of his liberty.[22]

Accordingly, the highest motives and most enlightened impulses led to a peculiar system for juveniles, unknown to our law in any comparable context. The constitutional and theoretical basis for this peculiar system is—to say the least—debatable. And in practice, as we remarked in the *Kent* case, *supra*, the results have not been entirely satisfactory.[23] Juvenile court history has again demonstrated that unbridled discretion, however benevolently motivated, is frequently a poor substitute for principle and procedure. In 1937, Dean Pound wrote: "The powers of the Star Chamber were a trifle in comparison with those of our juvenile courts. . . ." [24] The absence of substantive standards has not necessarily meant that children receive careful, compassionate, individualized treatment. The absence of procedural rules based upon constitutional principle has not always produced fair, efficient, and effective procedures. Departures from established principles of due process have frequently resulted not in enlightened procedure but in arbitrariness. The Chairman of the Pennsylvania Council of Juvenile Court Judges has recently observed: "Unfortunately, loose procedures, high-handed methods and crowded court calendars, either singly or in combination, all too often, have resulted in depriving some juveniles of fundamental rights that have resulted in a denial of due process." [25]

Failure to observe the fundamental requirements of due process has resulted in instances, which might have been avoided, of unfairness to individuals and inadequate or inaccurate findings of fact and unfortunate prescriptions of remedy. Due process of law is the primary and indispensable foundation of individual freedom. It is the basic and essential term in the social compact which defines the rights of the individual and delimits the powers that the state may exercise.[26] As Mr. JUSTICE FRANKFURTER has said: "The history of American freedom is, in no small measure, the history of procedure." [27] But, in addition, the procedural rules which have been fashioned from the generality of due process are our best instruments for the distillation and evaluation of essential facts from the conflicting welter of data that life and our adversary methods present. It is these instruments of due process that enhance the possibility that truth will emerge from the confrontation of opposing versions and conflicting data. "Procedure is to law what 'scientific method' is to science." [28]

It is claimed that juveniles obtain benefits from the special procedures applicable to them which more than offset the disadvantages of denial of the substance of normal due process. As we shall discuss, the observance of due process standards, intelligently and not ruthlessly administered, will not compel the states to abandon or displace any of the substantive benefits of the juvenile process.[29] But it is important, we think, that the claimed benefits of the juvenile process should be candidly appraised. Neither sentiment nor folklore should cause us to shut our eyes, for example, to such startling findings as that reported in an exceptionally reliable study of repeaters or recidivism conducted by the Stanford Research Institute for the President's Commission on Crime in the District of Columbia. This Commission's Report states:

> In fiscal 1966 approximately 66 per cent of the 16- and 17-year-old juveniles referred to the court by the Youth Aid Division had been before the court previously. In 1965, 56 per cent of those in the Receiving Home were repeaters. The SRI study revealed that 61 per cent of the sample Juvenile Court referrals in 1965 had been previously referred at least once and that 42 per cent had been referred at least twice before.

Certainly, these figures and the high crime rates among juveniles to which we have referred could not lead us to conclude that the absence of constitutional protections reduces crime, or that the juvenile system, functioning free of constitutional inhibitions as it has largely done, is effective to reduce crime or rehabilitate offenders. We do not mean by this to denigrate the juvenile court process or to suggest that there are not aspects of the juvenile system relating to offenders that are valuable. But the features of the juvenile system which its proponents have asserted are of unique benefit will not be impaired by constitutional domestication. For example, the commendable principles relating to the processing and treatment of juveniles separately from adults are in no way involved or affected by the procedural issues under discussion.[30] Further, we are told that one of the important benefits of the special juvenile court procedures is that they avoid classifying the juvenile as a "criminal." The juvenile offender is now classed as a "delinquent." There is, of course, no reason why this should not continue. It is disconcerting, however, that this term has come to involve only slightly less stigma than the term "criminal" applied to adults.[31] It is also emphasized that in practically all jurisdictions statutes provide that an adjudication of the child as a delinquent shall not operate as a civil disability or disqualify him for civil service appointment.[32] There is no reason why the application of due process requirements should interfere with such provisions.

Beyond this, it is frequently said that juveniles are protected by the process from disclosure of their deviational behavior. As the Supreme Court of Arizona phrased it in the present case, the summary procedures of juvenile courts are sometimes defended by a statement that it is the law's policy "to hide youthful errors from the full gaze of the public and bury them in the graveyard of the forgotten past." This claim of secrecy, however, is more rhetoric than reality. Disclosure of court records is discretionary with the judge in most jurisdictions. Statutory restrictions almost invariably apply only to the court records, and even as to those the evidence is that many courts routinely furnish information to the FBI and the military, and on request to government agencies and even to private employers.[33] Of more importance are police records. In most states the police keep a complete file of juvenile "police contacts" and have complete discretion as to disclosure of juvenile records. Police departments receive requests for information from the FBI and other law-enforcement agencies, the Armed Forces, and social-service agencies, and most of them generally comply.[34] Private employers word their application forms to produce information concerning juvenile arrests and court proceedings, and in some jurisdictions information concerning juvenile-police contacts is furnished private employers as well as government agencies.[35]

In any event, there is no reason why, consistently with due process, a state cannot continue, if it deems it appropriate, to provide and to improve provision for the confidentiality of records of police contacts and court action relating to juveniles. It is interesting to note, however, that the Arizona Supreme Court used the confidentiality argument as a justification for the type of notice that is here attacked as inadequate for due process purposes. The parents were given merely general notice that their child was charged with "delinquency." No facts were specified. The Arizona court held, however, as we shall discuss, that in addition to this general "notice" the child and his parents must be advised "of the facts involved in the case" no later than the initial hearing by the judge. Obviously, this does not "bury" the word about the child's transgressions. It merely defers the time of disclosure to a point when it is of limited use to the child or his parents in preparing his defense or explanation.

Further, it is urged that the juvenile benefits from informal proceedings in the court. The early conception of the juvenile court proceeding was one in which a fatherly judge touched the heart and conscience of the erring youth by talking over his problems, by paternal advice and admonition, and in which, in extreme situations, benevolent and wise institutions of the state provided guidance and help "to save him from a downward career." [36] Then, as now, goodwill and compassion were admirably prevalent. But recent studies have, with surprising unanimity, entered sharp dissent as to the validity of this gentle conception. They suggest that the appearance as well as the actuality of fairness, impartiality, and orderliness—in short, the essentials of due process— may be a more impressive and more therapeutic attitude so far as the juvenile is concerned. For example, in a recent study, the sociologists Wheeler and Cottrell observe that when the procedural laxness of the *parens patriae* attitude is followed by stern disciplining, the contrast may have an adverse effect upon the child, who feels that he has been deceived or enticed. They conclude as follows: "Unless appropriate due process of law is followed, even the juvenile who has violated the law may not feel that he is being fairly treated and may therefore resist the rehabilitative efforts of court personnel." [37] Of course, it is not suggested that juvenile court judges should fail appropriately to take account, in their demeanor and conduct, of the emotional and psychological attitude of the juveniles with whom they are confronted. While due process requirements will, in some instances, introduce a degree of order and regularity to juvenile court proceedings to determine delinquency, and in contested cases will introduce some elements of the adversary system, nothing will require that the conception of the kindly juvenile judge be replaced by its opposite, nor do we here rule upon the question whether ordinary due process requirements must be observed with respect to hearings to determine the disposition of the delinquent child.

Ultimately, however, we confront the reality of that portion of the juvenile court process with which we deal in this case. A boy is charged with misconduct. The boy is committed to an institution where he may be restrained of liberty for years. It is of no constitutional consequence—and of limited practical meaning—that the institution to which he is committed is called an "industrial school." The fact of the matter is that, however euphemistic the title, a "receiving home" or an "industrial school" for juveniles is an institution of confinement in which the child is incarcerated for a greater or lesser time. His world becomes "a building with white-washed walls, regimented routine and institutional laws. . . ." [38] Instead of mother and father and sisters and brothers and friends and classmates, his world is peopled by guards, custodians, state employees, and "delinquents" confined with him for anything from waywardness [39] to rape and homicide.

In view of this, it would be extraordinary if our Constitution did not require the procedural regularity and the exercise of care implied in the phrase "due process." Under our Constitution, the condition of being a boy does not justify a kangaroo court. The traditional ideas of juvenile court procedure, indeed, contemplated that time would be available and care would be used to establish precisely what the juvenile did and why he did it—was it a prank of adolescence or a brutal act threatening serious consequences to himself or society unless corrected? [40] Under traditional notions, one would assume that in a case like that of Gerald Gault, where the juvenile appears to have a home, a working mother and father, and an older brother, the Juvenile Judge would have made a careful inquiry and judgment as to the possibility that the boy could be disciplined and dealt with at home, despite his previous transgressions. [41] Indeed, so far as appears in the record before us, except for some conversation with Gerald about his school work and his "wanting to go to . . . Grand Canyon with his father," the points to which the judge directed his attention were little different from those that would be involved in determining any charge of violation of a penal statute. [42] The essential difference between Gerald's case and a normal criminal case is that safeguards available to adults were discarded in Gerald's case. The summary procedure as well as the long commitment were possible because Gerald was fifteen years of age instead of over eighteen.

If Gerald had been over eighteen, he would not have been subject to juvenile court proceedings. [43] For the particular offense immediately involved, the maximum punishment would have been a fine of $5 to $50, or imprisonment in jail for not more than two months. Instead, he was committed to custody for a maximum of six years. If he had been over eighteen and had committed an offense to which such a sentence might apply, he would have been entitled to substantial rights under the Constitution of the United States as well as under Arizona's laws and constitution. The U.S. Constitution would guarantee him rights and protections with respect to arrest, search and seizure, and pretrial interrogation. It would assure him of specific notice of the charges and adequate time to decide his course and action and to prepare his defense. He would be entitled to clear advice that he could be represented by counsel, and, at least if a felony were involved, the state would be required to provide counsel if his parents were unable to afford it. If the court acted on the basis of his confession, careful procedures would be required to assure its voluntariness. If the case went to trial, confrontation and opportunity for cross-examination would be guaranteed. So wide a gulf between the state's treatment of the adult and of the child requires a bridge sturdier than mere verbiage and reasons more persusasive than cliché can provide. As Wheeler and Cottrell have put it, "The rhetoric of the juvenile court movement has developed without any necessarily close correspondence to the realities of court and institutional routines." [44]

In *Kent v. United States,* we stated that the juvenile court judge's exercise of the power of the state as *parens patriae* was not unlimited. We said that "the admonition to function in a 'parental' relationship is not an invitation to procedural arbitrariness." [45] With respect to the waiver by the juvenile court to the adult of jurisdiction over an offense committed by a youth, we said that "there is no place in our system of law for reaching a result of such tremendous consequences without ceremony—without hearing, without effective assistance of counsel, without a statement of reasons." [46] We announced with respect to such waiver proceedings that while "we do not mean . . . to indicate that the hearing to be held must conform with all of the requirements of a criminal trial or even of the usual administrative hearing; but we do hold that the hearing must measure up to the essentials of due process and fair treatment." [47] We reiterate this view, here in connection with a juvenile court adjudication of "delinquency," as a requirement which is part of the Due Process Clause of the Fourteenth Amendment of our Constitution.[48]

We now turn to the specific issues which are presented to us in the present case.

III

NOTICE OF CHARGES

Appellants allege that the Arizona Juvenile Code is unconstitutional or alternatively that the proceedings before the Juvenile Court were constitutionally defective because of failure to provide adequate notice of the hearings. No notice was given to Gerald's parents when he was taken into custody on Monday, June 8. On that night, when Mrs. Gault went to the Detention Home, she was orally informed that there would be a hearing the next afternoon and was told the reason why Gerald was in custody. The only written notice Gerald's parents received at any time was a note on plain paper from Officer Flagg delivered on Thursday or Friday, June 11 or 12, to the effect that the judge had set Monday, June 15, "for further hearings on Gerald's delinquency."

A "petition" was filed with the court on June 9 by Officer Flagg, reciting only that he was informed and believed that "said minor is a delinquent minor and that it is necessary that some order be made by the Honorable

Court for said minor's welfare." The applicable Arizona statute provides for
a petition to be filed in Juvenile Court, alleging in general terms that the child
is "neglected, dependent, or delinquent." The statute explicitly states that such
a general allegation is sufficient, "without alleging the facts." [49] There is no
requirement that the petition be served and it was not served upon, given, or
shown to Gerald or his parents.[50]

The Supreme Court of Arizona rejected appellants' claim that due process
was denied because of inadequate notice. It stated that "Mrs. Gault knew the
exact nature of the charge against Gerald from the day he was taken to the
detention home." The court also pointed out that the Gaults appeared at the
two hearings "without objection." The court held that because "the policy of
the juvenile law is to hide youthful errors from the full gaze of the public and
bury them in the graveyard of the forgotten past," advance notice of the
specific charges or basis for taking the juvenile into custody and for the hearing is not necessary. It held that the appropriate rule is that

> the infant and his parent or guardian will receive a petition only reciting a
> conclusion of delinquency.[51] But no later than the initial hearing by the
> judge, they must be advised of the facts involved in the case. If the charges
> are denied, they must be given a reasonable period of time to prepare.

We cannot agree with the court's conclusion that adequate notice was given
in this case. Notice, to comply with due process requirements, must be given
sufficiently in advance of scheduled court proceedings so that reasonable
opportunity to prepare will be afforded, and it must "set forth the alleged
misconduct with particularity." [52] It is obvious, as we have discussed above,
that no purpose of shielding the child from the public stigma of knowledge
of his having been taken into custody and scheduled for hearing is served by
the procedure approved by the court below. The "initial hearing" in the
present case was a hearing on the merits. Notice at that time is not timely;
and even if there were a conceivable purpose served by the deferral proposed
by the court below, it would have to yield to the requirements that the child
and his parents or guardian be notified, in writing, of the specific charge or
factual allegations to be considered at the hearing, and that such written
notice be given at the earliest practicable time, and in any event sufficiently
in advance of the hearing to permit preparation. Due process of law requires
notice of the sort we have described—that is, notice that would be deemed
constitutionally adequate in a civil or criminal proceeding.[53] It does not allow
a hearing to be held in which a youth's freedom and his parents' right to his
custody are at stake without giving them timely notice, in advance of the
hearing, of the specific issues that they must meet. Nor, in the circumstances
of this case, can it reasonably be said that the requirement of notice was
waived.[54]

IV

RIGHT TO COUNSEL

Appellants charge that the Juvenile Court proceedings were fatally defective
because the court did not advise Gerald or his parents of their right to counsel,
and proceeded with the hearing, the adjudication of delinquency and the

order of commitment in the absence of counsel for the child and his parents
or an express waiver of the right thereto. The Supreme Court of Arizona
pointed out that "there is disagreement [among the various jurisdictions] as
to whether the court must advise the infant that he has a right to counsel." [55]
It noted its own decision in *State Dept. of Public Welfare* v. *Barlow,* 80 Ariz.
249, 296 P. 2d 298 (1956), to the effect "that *the parents* of an infant in a
juvenile proceeding cannot be denied representation by counsel of their choosing." (Emphasis added.) It referred to a provision of the Juvenile Code that
it characterized as requiring "that the probation officer shall look after the
interests of neglected, delinquent and dependent children," including representing their interests in court.[56] The court argued that "the parent and the
probation officer may be relied upon to protect the infant's interests." Accordingly it rejected the proposition that "due process requires that an infant
have a right to counsel." It said that juvenile courts have the discretion, but
not the duty, to allow such representation; it referred specifically to the situation in which the Juvenile Court discerns conflict between the child and his
parents as an instance in which this discretion might be exercised. We do not
agree. Probation officers, in the Arizona scheme, are also arresting officers.
They initiate proceedings and file petitions which they verify, as here, alleging
the delinquency of the child; and they testify, as here, against the child. And
here the probation officer was also superintendent of the Detention Home. The
probation officer cannot act as counsel for the child. His role in the adjudicatory hearing, by statute and in fact, is as arresting officer and witness against
the child. Nor can the judge represent the child. There is no material difference in this respect between adult and juvenile proceedings of the sort here
involved. In adult proceedings, this contention has been foreclosed by decisions of this Court.[57] A proceeding where the issue is whether the child will
be found to be "delinquent" and subjected to the loss of his liberty for years
is comparable in seriousness to a felony prosecution. The juvenile needs the
assistance of counsel to cope with problems of law,[58] to make skilled inquiry
into the facts, to insist upon regularity of the proceedings, and to ascertain
whether he has a defense and to prepare and submit it. The child "requires
the guiding hand of counsel at every step in the proceedings against him." [59]
Just as in *Kent* v. *United States,* we indicated our agreement with the U.S.
Court of Appeals for the District of Columbia Circuit that the assistance of
counsel is essential for purposes of waiver proceedings, so we hold now that
it is equally essential for the determination of delinquency, carrying with it
the awesome prospect of incarceration in a state institution until the juvenile
reaches the age of twenty-one.[60]

During the last decade, court decisions,[61] experts,[62] and legislatures [63] have
demonstrated increasing recognition of this view. In at least one third of the
states, statutes now provide for the right of representation by retained counsel
in juvenile delinquency proceedings, notice of the right, or assignment of
counsel, or a combination of these. In other states, court rules have similar
provisions.[64]

The President's Crime Commission has recently recommended that in order
to assure "procedural justice for the child," it is necessary that "counsel . . .
be appointed as a matter of course wherever coercive action is a possibility,
without requiring any affirmative choice by child or parent." [65] As stated by
the authoritative *Standards for Juvenile and Family Courts,* published by the
Children's Bureau of the Department of Health, Education, and Welfare:

As a component part of a fair hearing required by due process guaranteed under the 14th Amendment, notice of the right to counsel should be required at all hearings and counsel provided upon request when the family is financially unable to employ counsel. [Standards, p. 57.]

This statement was "reviewed" by the National Council of Juvenile Court Judges at its 1965 convention and they "found no fault" with it.[66] The New York Family Court Act contains the following statement:

This act declares that minors have a right to the assistance of counsel of their own choosing or of law guardians[67] in neglect proceedings under article three and in proceedings to determine juvenile delinquency and whether a person is in need of supervision under article seven. This declaration is based on a finding that counsel is often indispensable to a practical realization of due process of law and may be helpful in making reasoned determinations of fact and proper orders of disposition.[68]

The Act provides that "at the commencement of any hearing" under the delinquency article of the statute, the juvenile and his parent shall be advised of the juvenile's "right to be represented by counsel chosen by him or his parent . . . or by a law guardian assigned by the court. . . ." [69] The California Act (1961) also requires appointment of counsel.[70]

We conclude that the Due Process Clause of the Fourteenth Amendment requires that in respect of proceedings to determine delinquency that may result in commitment to an institution in which the juvenile's freedom is curtailed, the child and his parent must be notified of the child's right to be represented by counsel, that counsel will be appointed to represent the child.

At the habeas corpus proceeding, Mrs. Gault testified that she knew that she could have appeared with counsel at the juvenile hearing. This knowledge is not a waiver of the right to counsel which she and her juvenile son had, as we have defined it. They had a right expressly to be advised that they might retain counsel and to be confronted with the need for specific consideration of whether they did or did not choose to waive the right. If they were unable to afford to employ counsel, they were entitled, in view of the seriousness of the charge and the potential commitment, to appointed counsel, unless they chose waiver. Mrs. Gault's knowledge that she could employ counsel is not an "intentional relinquishment or abandonment" of a fully known right.[71]

V

CONFRONTATION, SELF-INCRIMINATION, CROSS-EXAMINATION

Appellants urge that the writ of habeas corpus should have been granted because of the denial of the rights of confrontation and cross-examination in the Juvenile Court hearings and because the privilege against self-incrimination was not observed. The Juvenile Court Judge testified at the habeas corpus hearing that he had proceeded on the basis of Gerald's admissions at the two hearings. Appellants attack this on the ground that the admissions were obtained in disregard of the privilege against self-incrimination.[72] If the confession is disregarded, appellants argue that the delinquency conclusion, since it was fundamentally based on a finding that Gerald had made lewd remarks during the phone call to Mrs. Cook, is fatally defective for failure to accord the rights of confrontation and cross-examination which the Due Process Clause of the Fourteenth Amendment of the Federal Constitution guarantees in state proceedings generally.[73]

Our first question, then, is whether Gerald's admission was improperly obtained and relied on as the basis of decision, in conflict with the Federal Constitution. For this purpose, it is necessary briefly to recall the relevant facts.

Mrs. Cook, the complainant, and the recipient of the alleged telephone call, was not called as a witness. Gerald's mother asked the Juvenile Court Judge why Mrs. Cook was not present and the judge replied that "she didn't have to be present." So far as appears, Mrs. Cook was spoken to only once, by Officer Flagg, and this was by telephone. The judge did not speak with her on any occasion. Gerald had been questioned by the probation officer after having been taken into custody. The exact circumstances of this questioning do not appear but any admissions Gerald may have made at this time do not appear in the record.[74] Gerald was also questioned by the Juvenile Court Judge at each of the two hearings. The judge testified in the habeas corpus proceeding that Gerald admitted making "some of the lewd statements . . . [but not] any of the more serious lewd statements." There was conflict and uncertainty among the witnesses at the habeas corpus proceeding—the Juvenile Court Judge, Mr. and Mrs. Gault, and the probation officer—as to what Gerald did or did not admit.

We shall assume that Gerald made admissions of the sort described by the Juvenile Court Judge, as quoted above. Neither Gerald nor his parents was advised that he did not have to testify or make a statement, or that an incriminating statement might result in his commitment as a "delinquent."

The Arizona Supreme Court rejected appellant's contention that Gerald had a right to be advised that he need not incriminate himself. It said: "We think the necessary flexibility for individualized treatment will be enhanced by a rule which does not require the judge to advise the infant of a privilege against self-incrimination."

In reviewing this conclusion of Arizona's Supreme Court, we emphasize again that we are here concerned only with proceedings to determine whether a minor is a "delinquent" and which may result in commitment to a state institution. Specifically, the question is whether, in such a proceeding, an admission by the juvenile may be used against him in the absence of clear and unequivocal evidence that the admission was made with knowledge that he was not obliged to speak and would not be penalized for remaining silent. In light of *Miranda* v. *Arizona,* 384 U.S. 436 (1966), we must also consider whether, if the privilege against self-incrimination is available, it can effectively be waived unless counsel is present or the right to counsel has been waived.

It has long been recognized that the eliciting and use of confessions or admissions require careful scrutiny. Dean Wigmore states:

> The ground of distrust of confessions made in certain situations is, in a rough and indefinite way, judicial experience. There has been no careful collection of statistics of untrue confessions, nor has any great number of instances been even loosely reported . . . but enough have been verified to

fortify the conclusion, based on ordinary observation of human conduct, that under certain stresses a person, especially one of defective mentality or peculiar temperament, may falsely acknowledge guilt. This possibility arises wherever the innocent person is placed in such a situation that the untrue acknowledgement of guilt is at the time the more promising of two alternatives between which he is obliged to choose; that is, he chooses any risk that may be in falsely acknowledging guilt, in preference to some worse alternative associated with silence.

*   *   *

The principle, then, upon which a confession may be excluded is that it is, under certain conditions, *testimonially untrustworthy.* . . . [T]he essential feature is that the principle of exclusion is a testimonial one, analogous to the other principles which exclude narrations as untrustworthy. . . .[75]

This Court has emphasized that admissions and confessions of juveniles require special caution. In *Haley* v. *Ohio, supra,* where this Court reversed the conviction of a fifteen-year-old boy for murder, MR. JUSTICE DOUGLAS said:

What transpired would make us pause for careful inquiry if a mature man were involved. And when, as here, a mere child—an easy victim of the law —is before us, special care in scrutinizing the record must be used. Age 15 is a tender and difficult age for a boy of any race. He cannot be judged by the more exacting standards of maturity. That which would leave a man cold and unimpressed can overawe and overwhelm a lad in his early teens. This is the period of great instability which the crisis of adolescence produces. A 15-year-old lad, questioned through the dead of night by relays of police, is a ready victim of the inquisition. Mature men possibly might stand the ordeal from midnight to 5 A.M. But we cannot believe that a lad of tender years is a match for the police in such a contest. He needs counsel and support if he is not to become the victim first of fear, then of panic. He needs someone on whom to lean lest the overpowering presence of the law, as he knows it, crush him. No friend stood at the side of this 15-year-old boy as the police, working in relays, questioned him hour after hour, from midnight until dawn. No lawyer stood guard to make sure that the police went so far and no farther, to see to it that they stopped short of the point where he became the victim of coercion. No counsel or friend was called during the critical hours of questioning.[76]

In *Haley,* as we have discussed, the boy was convicted in adult court, and not a juvenile court. In notable decisions, the New York Court of Appeals and the Supreme Court of New Jersey have recently considered decisions of juvenile courts in which boys have been adjudged "delinquent" on the basis of confessions obtained in circumstances comparable to those in *Haley.* In both instances, the state contended before its highest tribunal that constitutional requirements governing inculpatory statements applicable in adult courts do not apply to juvenile proceedings. In each case, the state's contention was rejected, and the juvenile court's determination of delinquency was set aside on the grounds of inadmissibility of the confession. *In the Matters of Gregory W. and Gerald S.,* 19 N.Y. 2d 55, —— N.E. 2d —— (1966) (opinion by Keating, J.), and *In the Interests of Carlo and Stasilowicz,* 48 N.J. 224, 225 A. 2d 110 (1966) (opinion by Proctor, J.).

The privilege against self-incrimination is, of course, related to the question of the safeguards necessary to assure that admissions or confessions are reasonably trustworthy, that they are not the mere fruits of fear or coercion, but are reliable expressions of the truth. The roots of the privilege are, however, far deeper. They tap the basic stream of religious and political principle because the privilege reflects the limits of the individual's attornment to the state and—in a philosophical sense—insists upon the equality of the individual and the state.[77] In other words, the privilege has a broader and deeper thrust than the rule that prevents the use of confessions that are the product of coercion because coercion is thought to carry with it the danger of unreliability. One of its purposes is to prevent the state, whether by force or by psychological domination, from overcoming the mind and will of the person under investigation and depriving him of the freedom to decide whether to assist the state in securing his conviction.[78]

It would indeed be surprising if the privilege against self-incrimination were available to hardened criminals but not to children. The language of the Fifth Amendment, applicable to the states by operation of the Fourteenth Amendment, is unequivocal and without exception. And the scope of the privilege is comprehensive. As MR. JUSTICE WHITE, concurring, stated in *Murphy* v. *Waterfront Commission*, 378 U.S. 52 (1964), at 94:

> The privilege can be claimed in *any proceeding*, be it criminal or civil, administrative or judicial, investigatory or adjudicatory . . . it protects *any disclosures* which the witness may reasonably apprehend *could be used in a criminal prosecution or which could lead to other evidence that might be so used*. [Emphasis supplied.] [79]

With respect to juveniles, both common observation and expert opinion emphasize that the "distrust of confessions made in certain situations," to which Dean Wigmore referred in the passage quoted above, is imperative in the case of children from an early age through adolescence. In New York, for example, the recently enacted Family Court Act provides that the juvenile and his parents must be advised at the start of the hearing of his right to remain silent.[80] The New York statute also provides that the police must attempt to communicate with the juvenile's parents before questioning him,[81] and that a confession may not be obtained from a child prior to notifying his parents or relatives and releasing the child either to them or to the Family Court.[82] In *In the Matters of Gregory W. and Gerald S.*, referred to above, the New York Court of Appeals held that the privilege against self-incrimination applies in juvenile delinquency cases and requires the exclusion of involuntary confessions, and that *People* v. *Lewis*, 260 N.Y. 171 (1932), holding the contrary, had been specifically overruled by statute.

The authoritative "Standards for Juvenile and Family Courts" concludes that

> Whether or not transfer to the criminal court is a possibility, certain procedures should always be followed. Before being interviewed [by the police] the child and his parents should be informed of his right to have legal counsel present and to refuse to answer questions or be fingerprinted [83] if he should so decide.[84]

Against the application to juveniles of the right to silence, it is argued that juvenile proceedings are "civil" and not "criminal," and therefore the privilege in the Fifth Amendment, which is applicable to the states by reason of the Fourteenth Amendment, is that no person "shall be compelled in any *criminal case* to be a witness against himself." However, it is also clear that the availability of the privilege does not turn upon the type of proceeding in which its protection is invoked, but upon the nature of the statement or admission and the exposure which it invites. The privilege may, for example, be claimed in a civil or administrative proceeding, if the statement is or may be inculpatory.[85]

It would be entirely unrealistic to carve out of the Fifth Amendment all statements by juveniles on the ground that these cannot lead to "criminal" involvement. In the first place, juvenile proceedings to determine "delinquency," which may lead to commitment to a state institution, must be regarded as "criminal" for purposes of the privilege against self-incrimination. To hold otherwise would be to disregard substance because of the feeble enticement of the "civil" label-of-convenience which has been attached to juvenile proceedings. Indeed, in over half of the states, there is not even assurance that the juvenile will be kept in separate institutions, apart from adult "criminals." In those states juveniles may be placed in or transferred to adult penal institutions [86] after having been found "delinquent" by a juvenile court. For this purpose, at least, commitment is a deprivation of liberty. It is incarceration against one's will, whether it is called "criminal" or "civil." And our Constitution guarantees that no person shall be "compelled" to be a witness against himself when he is threatened with deprivation of his liberty—a command which this Court has broadly applied and generously implemented in accordance with the teaching of the history of the privilege and its great office in mankind's battle for freedom.[87]

In addition, apart from the equivalence for this purpose to commitment as a juvenile delinquent and exposure to imprisonment as an adult offender, the fact of the matter is that there is little or no assurance in Arizona, as in most if not all of the states, that a juvenile apprehended and interrogated by the police or even by the juvenile court itself will remain outside of the reach of adult courts as a consequence of the offense for which he has been taken into custody. In Arizona, as in other states, provision is made for juvenile courts to relinquish or waive jurisdiction to the ordinary criminal courts.[88] In the present case, when Gerald Gault was interrogated concerning violation of a section of the Arizona Criminal Code, it could not be certain that the Juvenile Court Judge would decide to "suspend" criminal prosecution in court for adults by proceeding to an adjudication in Juvenile Court.[89]

It is also urged, as the Supreme Court of Arizona here asserted, that the juvenile and presumably his parents should not be advised of the juvenile's right to silence because confession is good for the child as the commencement of the assumed therapy of the juvenile court process, and he should be encouraged to assume an attitude of trust and confidence toward the officials of the juvenile process. This proposition has been subjected to widespread challenge on the basis of current reappraisals of the rhetoric and realities of the handling of juvenile offenders.

In fact, evidence is accumulating that confessions by juveniles do not aid in "individualized treatment," as the court below put it, and that compelling the child to answer questions, without warning or advice as to his right to remain silent, does not serve this or any other good purpose. In light of the observations of Wheeler and Cottrell,[90] and others, it seems probable that where children are induced to confess by "paternal" urgings on the part of officials and the confession is then followed by disciplinary action, the child's reaction is likely to be hostile and adverse—the child may well feel that he has been led or tricked into confession and that despite his confession, he is being punished.[91]

Further, authoritative opinion has cast formidable doubt upon the reliability and trustworthiness of "confessions" by children. This Court's observations in *Haley* v. *United States* are set forth above. The recent decision of the New York Court of Appeals referred to above, *In the Matters of Gregory W. and Gearld S.,* deals with a dramatic and, it is to be hoped, extreme example. Two twelve-year-old Negro boys were taken into custody for the brutal assault and rape of two aged domestics, one of whom died as the result of the attack. One of the boys was schizophrenic and had been locked in the security ward of a mental institution at the time of the attacks. By a process that may be described as bizarre, his confession was obtained by the police. A psychiatrist testified that the boy would admit "whatever he thought was expected so that he could get out of the immediate situation." The other twelve-year-old also "confessed." Both confessions were in specific detail, albeit they contained various inconsistencies. The Court of Appeals, in an opinion by Keating, J., concluded that the confessions were products of the will of the police instead of the boys. The confessions were therefore held involuntary and the order of the Appellate Division affirming the order of the Family Court adjudging the defendants to be juvenile delinquents was reversed.

A similar and equally instructive case has recently been decided by the Supreme Court of New Jersey, *In the Interests of Carlo and Stasilowicz, supra.* The body of a ten-year-old girl was found. She had been strangled. Neighborhood boys who knew the girl were questioned. The two appellants, aged thirteen and fifteen, confessed to the police, with vivid detail and some inconsistencies. At the Juvenile Court hearing, both denied any complicity in the killing. They testified that their confessions were the product of fear and fatigue due to extensive police grilling. The Juvenile Court Judge found that the confessions were voluntary and admissible. On appeal, in an extensive opinion by Proctor, J., the Supreme Court of New Jersey reversed. It rejected the state's argument that the constitutional safeguard of voluntariness governing the use of confessions does not apply in proceedings before the juvenile court. It pointed out that under New Jersey court rules, juveniles under the age of sixteen accused of committing a homicide are tried in a proceeding that "has all of the appurtenances of a criminal trial," including participation by the county prosecutor, and requirements that the juvenile be provided with counsel, that a stenographic record be made, and so on. It also pointed out that under New Jersey law, the confinement of the boys after reaching age twenty-one could be extended until they had served the maximum sentence that could have been imposed on an adult for such a homicide, here found to be second-degree murder carrying up to thirty years' imprisonment.[92] The court concluded that the confessions were involuntary, stressing that the boys, contrary to statute, were placed in the police station and there interrogated; [93] that the parents of both boys were not allowed to see them while they were being interrogated; [94] that inconsistencies appeared among the various statements of the boys and with the objective evidence of the crime; and that there were protracted periods of questioning. The court noted the state's contention that both boys were advised of their constitutional rights before they made their statements, but it held that this should not be given "significant weight in our determination of voluntariness." [95] Accordingly, the judgment of the Juvenile Court was reversed.

In a recent case before the Juvenile Court of the District of Columbia, Judge Ketcham rejected the proffer of evidence as to oral statements made at police headquarters by four juveniles who had been taken into custody for alleged involvement in an assault and attempted robbery. *In the Matter of Four Youths*, Nos. 28–776–J, 28–778–J, 28–783–J, 28–859–J, Juvenile Court of the District of Columbia, April 7, 1961. The court explicitly stated that it did not rest its decision on a showing that the statements were involuntary, but because they were untrustworthy, Judge Ketcham said:

> Simply stated, the Court's decision in this case rests upon the considered opinion—after nearly four busy years on the Juvenile Court bench during which the testimony of thousands of such juveniles has been heard—that the statements of adolescents under 18 years of age who are arrested and charged with violations of law are frequently untrustworthy and often distort the truth.

We conclude that the constitutional privilege against self-incrimination is applicable in the case of juveniles as it is with respect to adults. We appreciate that special problems may arise with respect to waiver of the privilege by or on behalf of children, and that there may well be some differences in technique—but not in principle—depending on the age of the child and the presence and competence of parents. The participation of counsel will, of course, assist the police, juvenile courts and appellate tribunals in administering the privilege. If counsel is not present for some permissible reason when an admission is obtained, the greatest care must be taken to assure that the admission was voluntary, in the sense not only that it has not been coerced or suggested but also that it is not the product of ignorance of rights or of adolescent fantasy, fright or despair.[96]

The "confession" of Gerald Gault was first obtained by Officer Flagg, out of the presence of Gerald's parents, without counsel and without advising him of his right to silence, as far as appears. The judgment of the Juvenile Court was stated by the judge to be based on Gerald's admission in court. Neither "admission" was reduced to writing, and, to say the least, the process by which the "admissions" were obtained and received must be characterized as lacking the certainty and order which are required of proceedings of such formidable consequences.[97] Apart from the "admission," there was nothing upon which a judgment or finding might be based. There was no sworn testimony. Mrs. Cook, the complainant, was not present. The Arizona Supreme Court held that "sworn testimony must be required of all witnesses including police officers, probation officers and others who are part of or officially related to the juvenile court structure." We hold that this is not enough. No reason is suggested or appears for a different rule in respect of sworn testimony in juvenile courts than in adult tribunals. Absent a valid confession adequate to support the determination of the Juvenile Court, confrontation and sworn testimony by witnesses available for cross-examination were essential for a finding of "delinquency" and an order committing Gerald to a state institution for a maximum of six years.

The recommendations in the Children's Bureau's "Standards for Juvenile and Family Courts" are in general accord with our conclusions. They state that testimony should be under oath and that only competent material and relevant evidence under rules applicable to civil cases should be admitted in evidence.[98] The New York Family Court Act contains a similar provision.[99]

As we said in *Kent* v. *United States,* 383 U.S. 541, 554 (1966), with respect to waiver proceedings, "there is no place in our system of law for reaching a result of such tremendous consequences without ceremony. . . ." We now hold that, absent a valid confession, a determination of delinquency and an order of commitment to a state institution cannot be sustained in the absence of sworn testimony subjected to the opportunity for cross-examination in accordance with our law and constitutional requirements.

VI

Appellate Review and Transcript of Proceedings

Appellants urge that the Arizona statute is unconstitutional under the Due Process Clause because, as construed by its Supreme Court, "there is no right of appeal from a juvenile court order. . . ." The court held that there is no right to a transcript because there is no right to appeal and because the proceedings are confidential and any record must be destroyed after a prescribed period of time.[100] Whether a transcript or other recording is made, it held, is a matter for the discretion of the juvenile court.

This Court has not held that a state is required by the Federal Constitution "to provide appellate courts or a right to appellate review at all." [101] In view of the fact that we must reverse the Supreme Court of Arizona's affirmance of the dismissal of the writ of habeas corpus for other reasons, we need not rule on this question in the present case or upon the failure to provide a transcript or recording of the hearings—or, indeed, the failure of the juvenile court judge to state the grounds for his conclusion. Cf. *Kent* v. *United States, supra,* at 561, where we said, in the context of a decision of the juvenile court waiving jurisdiction to the adult court, which by local law, was applicable: ". . . it is incumbent upon the Juvenile Court to accompany its waiver order with a statement of the reasons or considerations therefor." As the present case illustrates, the consequences of failure to provide an appeal, to record the proceedings, or to make findings or state the grounds for the juvenile court's conclusion may be to throw a burden upon the machinery for habeas corpus, to saddle the reviewing process with the burden of attempting to reconstruct a record, and to impose upon the juvenile judge the unseemly duty of testifying under cross-examination as to the events that transpired in the hearings before him.[102]

For the reasons stated, the judgment of the Supreme Court of Arizona is reversed and the cause remanded for further proceedings not inconsistent with this opinion.

It is so ordered.

Notes

[1] Under Arizona law, juvenile hearings are conducted by a judge of the Superior Court, designated by his colleagues on the Superior Court to serve as Juvenile Court Judge. Arizona Const., Art. 6, § 15; Arizona Revised Statutes (hereinafter ARS) §§ 8–201, 8–202.

2 There is a conflict between the recollection of Mrs. Gault and that of Officer Flagg. Mrs. Gault testified that Gerald was released on Friday, June 12; Officer Flagg, that it had been on Thursday, June 11. This was from memory; he had no record, and the note was undated.

3 Officer Flagg also testified that Gerald had not, when questioned at the Detention Home, admitted having made any of the lewd statements, but that each boy had sought to put the blame on the other. There was conflicting testimony as to whether Ronald had accused Gerald of making the lewd statements during the June 15 hearing.

4 Judge McGhee also testified that Gerald had not denied "certain statements" made to him at the hearing by Officer Henderson.

5 Q. All right. Now, Judge, would you tell me under what section of the law or tell me under what section of—of the code you found the boy delinquent?

A. Well, there is a—I think it amounts to disturbing the peace. I can't give you the section, but I can tell you the law, that when one person uses lewd language in the presence of another person, that it can amount to—and I consider that when a person makes it over the phone, that it is considered in the presence, I might be wrong, that is one section. The other section on which I consider the boy delinquent is Section 8–201, Subsection (d), habitually involved in immoral matters.

6 ARS § 8–201–6, the section of the Arizona Juvenile Code that defines a delinquent child, reads:

" 'Delinquent child' includes:

" (a) A child who has violated a law of the state or an ordinance or regulation of a political subdivision thereof.

" (b) A child who, by reason of being incorrigible, wayward, or habitually disobedient, is uncontrolled by his parent, guardian, or custodian.

" (c) A child who is habitually truant from school or home.

" (d) A child who habitually so deports himself as to injure or endanger the morals or health of himself or others."

7 For example, the laws of Arizona allow arrest for a misdemeanor only if a warrant is obtained or if it is committed in the presence of the officer. ARS § 13–1403. The Supreme Court of Arizona held that this is inapplicable in the case of juveniles. See ARS § 8–221 which relates specifically to juveniles. But compare *Two Brothers and a Case of Liquor,* Juv. Ct. D.C., Nos. 66–2652–J, 66–2653–J, Dec. 28, 1966 (opinion of Judge Ketcham); Standards for Juvenile and Family Courts, Children's Bureau Pub. No. 437–1966 (1966), p. 47 (hereinafter cited as Standards); New York Family Court Act § 721 (McKinney's, Vol. 29A, 1963) (hereinafter cited as N.Y. Family Court Act).

The Court also held that the judge may consider hearsay if it is "of a kind on which reasonabe men are accustomed to rely in serious affairs." But compare Note, Juvenile Delinquents: The Police, State Courts, and Individualized Justice, 79 Harv. L. Rev. 775, 795 (1966) (hereinafter cited as Harvard Law Review Note).

"The informality of juvenile court hearings frequently leads to the admission of hearsay and unsworn testimony. It is said that 'close adherence to the strict rules of evidence might prevent the court from obtaining important facts as to the child's character and condition which could only be to the child's detriment.' The assumption is that the judge will give normally inadmissible evidence only its proper weight. It is also declared in support of these evidentiary practices that the juvenile court is not a criminal court, that the importance of the hearsay rule has been overestimated, and that allowing an attorney to make 'technical objections' would disrupt the desired informality of the proceedings. But to the extent that the rules of evidence are not merely technical or historical, but like the hearsay rule have a sound basis in human experience, they should not be rejected in any judicial inquiry. Juvenile court judges in Los Angeles, Tucson, and Wisconsin Rapids, Wisconsin, report that they are satisfied with the operation of their courts despite application of unrelaxed rules of evidence." (Footnotes omitted.)

It rules that the correct burden of proof is that "the juvenile judge must be persuaded by clear and convincing evidence that the infant has committed the alleged delinquent act." Compare the less stringent "preponderance of the evidence" test, N.Y. Family Court Act § 744 (where maximum commitment is three years, §§ 753, 758). Cf. Harvard Law Review Note, p. 795.

[8] See, e.g., *In the Matters of Gregory W. and Gerald S.,* 19 N.Y. 2d 55; —— N.E. 2d —— (1966); *In the Interests of Carlo and Stasilowicz,* 48 N.J. 224, 225 A. 2d 110 (1966); *People* v. *Dotson,* 46 App. D. Cal. 2d 891, 299 P. 2d 875 (1956); *Pee* v. *United States,* —— U.S. App. D.C. ——, 274 F. 2d 556 (1959); *Wissenburg* v. *Bradley,* 209 Iowa 813, 229 N.W. 205 (1930); *Bryant* v. *Brown,* 151 Miss. 298, 118 So. 184 (1928); *Dendy* v. *Wilson,* 142 Tex. 460, 179 S.W. 2d 269 (1944); Application of Johnson, 178 F. Supp. 155 (D.C.D.N.J. 1957).

[9] 383 U.S., at 553.

[10] 332 U.S., at 601 (opinion for four Justices).

[11] See Report of the President's Commission on Law Enforcement and Administration of Justice, "The Challenge of Crime in a Free Society" (1967) (hereinafter cited as Nat'l Crime Comm'n Report), pp. 81, 85–86; Standards, p. 71; Gardner, The Kent Case and the Juvenile Court: A Challenge to Lawyers, 52 A.B.A.J. 923 (1966); Paulsen, Fairness to the Juvenile Offender, 41 Minn. L. Rev. 547 (1957); Ketcham, The Legal Renaissance in the Juvenile Court, 60 Nw. U. L. Rev. 585 (1965); Allen, The Borderland of Criminal Justice (1964), pp. 19–23; Harvard Law Review Note, p. 791; Note, Rights and Rehabilitation in the Juvenile Courts, 67 Col. L. Rev. 281 (1967); Comment, Criminal Offenders in the Juvenile Court: More Brickbats and Another Proposal, 114 U. Pa. L. Rev. 1171 (1966).

[12] See *Kent* v. *United States,* 383 U.S. 541, 555 and note 22 (1966).

[13] See *supra* note 7.

[14] See National Council of Juvenile Court Judges, Directory and Manual (1964), p. 1. The number of juvenile judges as of 1964 is listed as 2,987, of which 213 are full-time juvenile court judges. *Id.,* at 305. The Nat'l Crime Comm'n Report indicates that half of these judges have no undergraduate degree, a fifth have no college education at all, a fifth are not members of the bar, and three quarters devote less than one quarter of their time to juvenile matters. See also McCane, Profile of the Nation's Juvenile Court Judges (monograph, George Washington University, Center for the Behavioral Sciences, 1965), which is a detailed statistical study of juvenile court judges, and indicates additionally that about a quarter of these judges have no law school training at all. About one third of all judges have no probation and social work staff available to them; between 80 and 90 per cent have no available psychologist or psychiatrist. *Ibid.* It has been observed that while "good will, compassion, and similar virtues are . . . admirably prevalent throughout the system . . . expertise, the keystone of the whole venture, is lacking." Harvard Law Review Note, p. 809. In 1965, over 697,000 delinquency cases (excluding traffic) were disposed of in these courts, involving some 601,000 children, or 2 per cent of all children between ten and seventeen. Juvenile Court Statistics—1961, Children's Bureau Statistical Series No. 85 (1966), p. 2.

[15] See Paulsen, Kent v. United States: The Constitutional Context of Juvenile Cases, 1966 Sup. Ct. Review 167, 174.

[16] Julian Mack, The Juvenile Court, 23 Harv. L. Rev. 104, 119–20 (1909).

[17] *Id.,* at 120.

[18] *Id.,* at 109; Paulsen, *op. cit., supra* note 15, at 173–74. There seems to have been little early constitutional objection to the special procedures of juvenile courts. But see Waite, How Far Can Court Procedure Be Socialized Without Impairing Individual Rights, 13 J. Am. Inst. of Crim. L. & Crim. 339, 340 (1922): "The Court which must direct its procedure even apparently to do something *to* a child because of what he *has done,* is parted from the court which is avowedly concerned only with doing something *for* a child because of what he *is* and *needs,* by a gulf too wide to be bridged by any humanity which the judge may

introduce into his hearings, or by the habitual use of corrective rather than punitive methods after conviction."

19 Paulsen, *op. cit., supra* note 15, at 173; Hurley, Origin of the Illinois Juvenile Court Law, in The Child, The Clinic, and the Court (1925), pp. 321, 328.

20 Julian Mack, The Chancery Procedure in the Juvenile Court, in The Child, The Clinic, and the Court (1925), p. 310.

21 See, e.g., Shears, Legal Problems Peculiar to Children's Courts, 48 A.B.A.J. 719, 720 (1962) ("The basic right of a juvenile is not to liberty but to custody. He has the right to have someone take care of him, and if his parents do not afford him this custodial privilege, the law must do so."); *Ex parte Crouse,* 4 Whart. 9, 11 (Sup. Ct. Pa. 1839); *Petition of Ferrier,* 103 Ill. 367, 371–73 (1882).

22 The Appendix to the opinion of Judge Prettyman in *Pee v. United States,* —— U.S. App. D.C. ——, 274 F. 2d 556 (1959) lists authority in fifty-one jurisdictions to this effect. Even rules required by due process in civil proceedings, however, have not generally been deemed compulsory as to proceedings affecting juveniles. For example, constitutional requirements as to notice of issues, which would commonly apply in civil cases, are commonly disregarded in juvenile proceedings, as this case illustrates.

23 "There is evidence . . . that there may be grounds for concern that the child receives the worst of both worlds: that he gets neither the protections accorded to adults nor the solicitous care and regenerative treatment postulated for children." 383 U.S., at 556, citing Handler, The Juvenile Court and the Adversary System: Problems of Function and Form, 1965 Wis. L. Rev. 7; Harvard Law Review Note; and various congressional materials set forth at 383 U.S., at 546, note 5.

On the other hand, while this opinion and much recent writing concentrate on the failures of the juvenile court system to live up to the expectations of its founders, the observation of the Nat'l Crime Comm'n Report should be kept in mind:

"Although its shortcomings are many and its results too often disappointing, the juvenile justice system in many cities is operated by people who are better educated and more highly skilled, can call on more and better facilities and services, and has more ancillary agencies to which to refer its clientele than its adult counterpart." *Id.,* at 78.

24 Foreword to Young, Social Treatment in Probation and Delinquency (1937), p. xxvii. The 1965 Report of the U.S. Commission on Civil Rights, "Law Enforcement—A Report on Equal Protection in the South," pp. 80–83, documents numerous instances in which "local authorities used the broad discretion afforded them by the absence of standards [in the juvenile process]" to punish, intimidate, and obstruct youthful participants in civil rights demonstrations. See also Paulsen, Juvenile Courts, Family Courts, and the Poor Man, 54 Calif. L. Rev. 694, 707–09 (1966).

25 Lehman, A Juvenile's Right to Counsel in a Delinquency Hearing, 17 Juvenile Court Judges Journal 53, 54 (1966).

Compare the observation of the late Arthur T. Vanderbilt, Chief Justice of the Supreme Court of New Jersey, in a foreword to Virtue, Basic Structure for Children's Services in Michigan (1953), p. x:

"In their zeal to care for children neither juvenile judges nor welfare workers can be permitted to violate the Constitution, especially the constitutional provisions as to due process that are involved in moving a child from its home. The indispensable elements of due process are: first, a tribunal with jurisdiction; second, notice of a hearing to the proper parties; and finally, a fair hearing. All three must be present if we are to treat the child as an individual human being and not to revert, in spite of good intentions, to the more primitive days when he was treated as a chattel."

We are warned that the system must not "degenerate into a star chamber proceeding with the judge imposing his own particular brand of culture and morals on indigent people. . . ." Judge Marion G. Woodword, letter reproduced in 18

Social Service Review 365, 368 (1944). Doctor Bovet, the Swiss psychiatrist, in his monograph for the World Health Organization, Psychiatric Aspects of Juvenile Delinquency (1951), p. 79, stated that: "One of the most definite conclusions of this investigation is that few fields exist in which more serious coercive measures are applied, on such flimsy objective evidence, than in that of juvenile delinquency." We are told that "the judge as amateur psychologist, experimenting upon the unfortunate children who must appear before him, is neither an attractive nor convincing figure." Harvard Law Review Note, p. 809.

26 The impact of denying fundamental procedural due process to juveniles involved in "delinquency" charges is dramatized by the following considerations: (1) In 1965, persons under eighteen accounted for about one fifth of all arrests for serious crimes (Nat'l Crime Comm'n Report, p. 55) and over half of all arrests for serious property offenses (*id.,* at 56), and in the same year some 601,000 children under eighteen, or 2 per cent of the total population of that age, came before juvenile courts (Juvenile Court Statistics—1965, Children's Bureau Statistical Series, No. 85, p. 2 [1966]). About one out of nine youths will be referred to juvenile court in connection with a delinquent act (excluding traffic offenses) before he is eighteen (Nat'l Crime Comm'n Report, p. 55). Cf. also Wheeler & Cottrell, Juvenile Delinquency—Its Prevention and Control (Russell Sage Foundation, 1965), p. 2; Report of the President's Commission on Crime in the District of Columbia (1966) (hereinafter cited as D.C. Crime Comm'n Report), p. 773. Furthermore, most juvenile crime apparently goes undetected or not formally punished. Wheeler and Cottrell, *supra,* observe that "Almost all youngsters have committed at least one of the petty forms of theft and vandalism in the course of their adolescence." *Id.,* at 28–29. See also Nat'l Crime Comm'n Report, at p. 55, where it is stated that "self-report studies reveal that perhaps 90 per cent of all young people have committed at least one act for which they could have been brought to juvenile court." It seems that the rate of juvenile delinquency is also steadily rising. See Nat'l Crime Comm'n Report, p. 56; Juvenile Court Statistics, *supra,* pp. 2–3. (2) In New York, where most juveniles are represented by counsel (see note 69, *infra*) and substantial procedural rights are afforded (see, e.g., notes 80, 81, 99, *infra*), out of a fiscal year 1965–1966 total of 10,755 juvenile proceedings involving boys, 2,242 were dismissed for failure of proof at the fact-finding hearing; for girls, the figures were 306 out of total of 1,051. New York Judicial Conference, Twelfth Annual Report, pp. 314, 316 (1967). (3) In about one-half of the states, a juvenile may be transferred to an adult penal institution after a juvenile court has found him "delinquent" (Delinquent Children in Penal Institutions, Children's Bureau Pub. No. 415 [1964], p. 1). (4) In some jurisdictions a juvenile may be subjected to criminal prosecution for the same offense for which he has served under a juvenile court commitment. However, the Texas procedure to this effect has recently been held unconstitutional by a federal district court judge, in a habeas corpus action. *Sawyer* v. *Huack,* 245 F. Supp. 55 (D.C.W.D. Tex. 1965). (5) In most of the states the juvenile may end in criminal court through waiver (Harvard Law Review Note, p. 793).

27 *Malinski* v. *New York,* 324 U.S. 401, 414 (1945) (concurring opinion).

28 Foster, Social Work, the Law, and Social Action, in Social Casework, July 1964, p. 286.

29 See Note, Rights and Rehabilitation in the Juvenile Courts, 67 Col. L. Rev. 281, 321, and *passim* (1967).

30 Here again, however, there is substantial question as to whether fact and pretension, with respect to the separate handling and treatment of children, coincide. See generally, *infra.*

While we are concerned only with procedure before the juvenile court in this case, it should be noted that to the extent that the special procedures for juveniles are thought to be justified by the special consideration and treatment afforded them, there is reason to doubt that juveniles always receive the benefits of such a *quid pro quo.* As to the problem and importance of special care at the adjudicatory stage, cf. *supra* notes 14 and 26. As to treatment, see Nat'l Crime

Comm'n Report, pp. 80, 87; D.C. Crime Comm'n Report, pp. 665–76, 686–87 (at p. 687 the Report refers to the District's "bankruptcy of dispositional resources"), 692–95, 700–18 (at p. 701 the Report observes that "The Department of Public Welfare lacks even the rudiments of essential diagnostic and clinical services"); Wheeler & Cottrell, Juvenile Delinquency—It's Prevention and Control (Russell Sage Foundation, 1965), pp. 32–35; Harvard Law Rev. Note, p. 809; Paulsen, Juvenile Courts, Family Courts, and the Poor Man, 54 Calif. L. Rev. 694, 709–12 (1966); Polier, A View from the Bench (1964). Cf. also, In the Matter of the Youth House, Inc., Report of the July 1966 "A" Term of the Bronx County Grand Jury, Supreme Court of New York, County of Bronx, Trial Term, Part XII, March 21, 1967 (cf. New York Times, March 23, 1967, p. 1, col. 8). The high rate of juvenile recidivism casts some doubt on the adequacy of treatment afforded juveniles. See D.C. Crime Comm'n Report, p. 773; Nat'l Crime Comm'n Report, pp. 55, 78.

In fact, some courts have recently indicated that since treatment is the essential *quid pro quo*, a juvenile may challenge the validity of his custody on the ground that he is not in fact receiving any special treatment. See *Creek* v. *Stone,* —— U.S. App. D.C ——, —— F. 2d —— (1967); *Kautter* v. *Reid*, 183 F. Supp. 352 (D.C.D.C. 1960); *White* v. *Reid*, 125 F. Supp. 647 (D.C.D.C. 1954). See also *Elmore* v. *Stone,* —— U.S. App. D.C. ——, 355 F. 2d 841 (1966) (separate statements of Bazelon, C.J.); *Clayton* v. *Stone,* —— U.S. App. D.C.——, —— F. 2d —— (1966) (separate statement of Bazelon C.J.). Cf. Wheeler & Cottrell, *supra,* at pp. 32, 35; *In re Rich*, 125 Vt. 373, —— A. 2d —— (1966). Cf. also *Rouse* v. *Cameron,* —— U.S. App. D.C. ——, 373 F. 2d 451 (1966).

[31] ". . . the word 'delinquent' has today developed such invidious connotations that the terminology is in the process of being altered; the new descriptive phrase is 'persons in need of supervision,' usually shortened to 'pins.' " Harvard Law Review Note, p. 799, note 140. The N.Y. Family Court Act § 712 distinguishes between "delinquents" and "persons in need of supervision."

[32] See, e.g., the Arizona provision, ARS § 8–228.

[33] Harvard Law Review Note, pp. 784–85, 800. Cf. Nat'l Crime Comm'n Report, pp. 87–88; Ketcham, The Unfulfilled Promise of the Juvenile Court (Nat'l Council on Crime and Delinquency, 1961), pp. 102–3.

[34] *Id.,* at 785–87.

[35] *Id.,* at 785, 800. See also, with respect to the problem of confidentiality of records, Note, Rights and Rehabilitation in the Juvenile Courts, 67 Col. L. Rev. 281, 286–89 (1967). Even the privacy of the juvenile hearing itself is not always adequately protected. *Id.,* at 285–86.

[36] Mack, The Juvenile Court, 23 Harv. L. Rev. 104, 120 (1909).

[37] Juvenile Delinquency—Its Prevention and Control (Russell Sage Foundation, 1966), p. 33. The conclusion of the Nat'l Crime Comm'n Report is similar: "[T]here is increasing evidence that the informal procedures, contrary to the original expectation, may themselves constitute a further obstacle to effective treatment of the delinquent to the extent that they engender in the child a sense of injustice provoked by seemingly all-powerful and challengeless exercise of authority by judges and probation officers." *Id.,* at 85. See also Allen, The Borderland of Criminal Justice (1964), p. 19.

[38] *Holmes' Appeal*, 379 Pa. 599, 616, 109 A. 2d ——, 530 (1954) (Musmanno, J., dissenting). See also *The State (Sheerin)* v. *Governor,* Supreme Court of Ireland, July 28, 1966; *Trimble* v. *Stone*, 187 F. Supp. 483, 485–85 (D.C.D.C. 1960); Allen, The Borderland of Criminal Justice (1964), pp. 18, 52–56.

[39] Cf. the Juvenile Code of Arizona; ARS § 8–201–6.

[40] Cf., however, the conclusions of the D.C. Crime Comm'n Report, pp. 692–93, concerning the inadequacy of the "social study records" on which the juvenile court judge must make this determination and decide on appropriate treatment.

[41] The Juvenile Judge's testimony at the habeas corpus proceeding is devoid of any meaningful discussion of this. He appears to have centered his attention on whether Gerald made the phone call and used lewd words. He was im-

pressed by the fact that Gerald was on six months' probation because he was with another boy who allegedly stole a purse—a different sort of offense, sharing the feature that Gerald was "along." And he even referred to a report that he said was not investigated because "there was no accusation . . . because of lack of material foundation."

With respect to the possible duty of a trial court to explore alternatives to involuntary commitment in a civil proceeding, cf. *Lake* v. *Cameron,* —— U.S. App. D.C. ——, 364 F. 2d 657 (1966), which arose under statutes relating to treatment of the mentally ill.

42 While appellee's brief suggests that the probation officer made some investigation of Gerald's home life, etc., there is not even a claim that the judge went beyond the point stated in the text.

43 ARS §§ 8–201, 8–202.

44 Juvenile Delinquency—Its Prevention and Control (Russell Sage Foundation, 1966), p. 35. The gap between rhetoric and reality is also emphasized in the Nat'l Crime Comm'n Report, pp. 80–81.

45 383 U.S., at 555.

46 383 U.S., at 554. THE CHIEF JUSTICE stated in a recent speech to a conference of the National Council of Juvenile Court Judges, that a juvenile court "must function within the framework of law and . . . in the attainment of its objectives it cannot act with unbridled caprice." Equal Justice for Juveniles, 15 Juvenile Court Judges Journal, No. 3, 14, 15 (1964).

47 383 U.S., at 562.

48 The Nat'l Crime Comm'n Report recommends that "juvenile courts should make fullest feasible use of preliminary conferences to dispose of cases short of adjudication." *Id.,* at 84. See also D.C. Crime Comm'n Report, pp. 662–65. Since this "consent decree" procedure would involve neither adjudication of delinquency nor institutionalization, nothing we say in this opinion should be construed as expressing any views with respect to such procedure. The problems of pre-adjudication treatment of juveniles, and of postadjudication disposition, are unique to the juvenile process; hence what we hold in this opinion with regard to the procedural requirements at the adjudicatory stage has no necessary applicability to other steps of the juvenile process.

49 ARS § 8–222 (B).

50 Arizona's Juvenile Code does not provide for notice of any sort to be given at the commencement of the proceedings to the child or his parents. Its only notice provision is to the effect that if a person other than the parent or guardian is cited to appear, the parent or guardian shall be notified "by personal service" of the time and place of hearing. ARS § 8–224. The procedure for initiating a proceeding, as specified by the statute, seems to require that after a preliminary inquiry by the court, a determination may be made "that formal jurisdiction should be acquired." Thereupon the court may authorize a petition to be filed. ARS § 8–222. It does not appear that this procedure was followed in the present case.

51 No such petition was served or supplied in the present case.

52 Nat'l Crime Comm'n Report, p. 87. The Commission observed that "The unfairness of too much informality is . . . reflected in the inadequacy of notice to parents and juveniles about charges and hearings." *Ibid.*

53 For application of the due process requirement of adequate notice in a criminal context, see, e.g., *Cole* v. *Arkansas,* 333 U.S. 196 (1948); *In re Oliver,* 333 U.S. 257 (1948). For application in a civil context, see, e.g., *Armstrong* v. *Manzo,* 380 U.S. 545 (1965); *Mullane* v. *Central Hanover Tr. Co.,* 339 U.S. 306 (1950). Cf. also *Chaloner* v. *Sherman,* 242 U.S. 455 (1917). The Court's discussion in these cases of the right to timely and adequate notice forecloses any contention that the notice approved by the Arizona Supreme Court, or the notice actually given the Gaults, was constitutionally adequate. See also Antieau, Constitutional Rights in Juvenile Courts, 46 Cornell L. Q. 387, 395 (1961); Paulsen, Fairness to the Juvenile Offender, 41 Minn. L. Rev. 547, 557 (1957). Cf. Standards, pp. 63–

65; Procedures and Evidence in the Juvenile Court, A Guidebook for Judges, prepared by the Advisory Council of Judges of National Council on Crime and Delinquency (1962), pp. 9–23 (and see cases discussed therein).

[54] Mrs. Gault's "knowledge" of the charge against Gerald, and/or the asserted failure to object, does not excuse the lack of adequate notice. Indeed, one of the purposes of notice is to clarify the issue to be considered, and as our discussion of the facts, *supra*, shows, even the Juvenile Court Judge was uncertain as to the precise issues determined at the two "hearings." Since the Gaults had no counsel and were not told of their right to counsel, we cannot consider their failure to object to the lack of constitutionally adequate notice as a waiver of their rights. Because of our conclusion that notice given only at the first hearing is inadequate, we need not reach the question whether the Gaults ever received adequately specific notice even at the June 9 hearing, in light of the fact they were never apprised of the charge of being habitually involved in immoral matters.

[55] For recent cases in the District of Columbia holding that there must be advice of the right to counsel, and to have counsel appointed if necessary see, e.g., *Shioutakin* v. *District of Columbia*, —— U.S. App. D.C. ——, 236 F. 2d 666 (1956); *Black* v. *United States*, —— App. D.C. ——, 355 F. 2d 104 (1965); *In re Poff*, 135 F. Supp. 224 (D.C.D.C. 1955). Cf. also Interest of Long, 1894 So. 2d 861, 862 (Sup. Ct. Miss., 1966); *People* v. *Dotson*, 46 Cal. 2d 891, 299 P. 2d 875 (1956).

[56] The section cited by the court, ARS § 8-204-C, reads as follows:

"The probation officer shall have the authority of a peace officer. He shall:

"1. Look after the interests of neglected, delinquent and dependent children of the county.

"2. Make investigations and file petitions.

"3. Be present in court when cases are heard concerning children and represent their interests.

"4. Furnish the court information and assistance as it may require.

"5. Assist in the collection of sums ordered paid for the support of children.

"6. Perform other acts ordered by the court."

[57] *Powell* v. *Alabama*, 287 U.S. 45, 61 (1932); *Gideon* v. *Wainwright*, 372 U.S. 335 (1963).

[58] In the present proceeding, for example, although the Juvenile Judge believed that Gerald's telephone conversation was within the condemnation of ARS § 13-377, he suggested some uncertainty because the statute prohibits the use of vulgar language "in the presence of or hearing of" a woman or child.

[59] *Powell* v. *Alabama*, 287 U.S. 45, 69 (1932).

[60] This means that the commitment, in virtually all cases, is for a minimum of three years since jurisdiction of juvenile courts is usually limited to age eighteen and under.

[61] See cases cited in *supra* note 55.

[62] See, e.g., Schinitsky, 17 The Record (N.Y. City Bar Assn.) 10 (1962); Paulsen, Fairness to the Juvenile Offender, 41 Minn. L. Rev. 547, 568-73 (1957); Antieau, Constitutional Rights in Juvenile Courts, 46 Cornell L. Q. 387, 404–07 (1961); Paulsen, Kent v. United States: The Constitutional Context of Juvenile Cases, 1966 Sup. Ct. Rev. 167, 187–89; Ketcham, The Legal Renaissance in the Juvenile Court, 60 Nw. U. L. Rev. 585 (1965); Elson, Juvenile Courts and Due Process, in Justice for the Child (Rosenheim. ed.) 95 103–05 (1962); Note, Rights and Rehabilitation in the Juvenile Courts, 67 Col. L. Rev. 281, 321–27 (1967). See also Nat'l Prob. and Parole Assoc., Standard Family Court Act (1959) § 19, and Standard Juvenile Court Act (1959) § 19, in NPPA Journal 99, 323 (1959) (hereinafter cited as Standard Family Court Act and Standard Juvenile Court Act, respectively).

[63] Only a few state statutes require advice of the right to counsel and to have counsel appointed. See N.Y. Family Court Act §§ 241, 249, 728, 741; Calif. Welfare & Inst'ns Code §§ 633, 634, 659, 700 (1966) (appointment is mandatory only if conduct would be a felony in the case of an adult); Minn. Stat. Ann. § 260.155 (2) (1966 Supp.) (see Comment of Legislative Commission accompanying this

section); District of Columbia Legal Aid Act, D.C. Code § 2-2202 (1961) (Legal Aid Agency "shall make attorneys available to represent indigents . . . in proceedings before the juvenile court . . . ." See *Black* v. *United States*, —— U.S. App. D.C. ——, ——, 355 F. 2d 104, 106–07 [1965], construing this Act as providing a right to appointed counsel and to be informed of that right). Other state statutes allow appointment on request, or in some classes of cases, or in the discretion of the court, etc. The state statutes are collected and classified in Riederer, The Role of Counsel in the Juvenile Court, 2 J. Fam. Law 16, 19–20 (1962), which, however, does not treat the statutes cited above. See also Note, Rights and Rehabilitation in the Juvenile Courts, 67 Col. L. Rev. 281, 321–22 (1967).

[64] Skoler and Tenney, Attorney Representation in Juvenile Court, 4 J. Fam. Law 77, 95–96 (1964); Riederer, The Role of Counsel in the Juvenile Court 2 J. Fam. Law 16 (1962).

Recognition of the right to counsel involves no necessary interference with the special purposes of juvenile court procedures; indeed, it seems that counsel can play an important role in the process of rehabilitation. See Note, Rights and Rehabilitation in the Juvenile Courts, 67 Col. L. Rev. 281, 324–27 (1967).

[65] Nat'l Crime Comm'n Report, pp. 86–87. The Commission's statement of its position is very forceful:

"The Commission believes that no single action holds more potential for achieving procedural justice for the child in the juvenile court than provision of counsel. The presence of an independent legal representative of the child, or of his parent, is the keystone of the whole structure of guarantees that a minimum system of procedural justice requires. The rights to confront one's accusers, to cross-examine witnesses, to present evidence and testimony of one's own, to be unaffected by prejudicial and unreliable evidence, to participate meaningfully in the dispositional decision, to take an appeal have substantial meaning for the overwhelming majority of persons brought before the juvenile court only if they are provided with competent lawyers who can invoke those rights effectively. The most informal and well-intentioned of judicial proceedings are technical; few adults without legal training can influence or even understand them; certainly children cannot. Papers are drawn and charges expressed in legal language. Events follow one another in a manner that appears arbitrary and confusing to the uninitiated. Decisions, unexplained, appear too official to challenge. But with lawyers come records of proceedings; records make possible appeals which, even if they do not occur, impart by their possibility a healthy atmosphere of accountability.

"Fears that have been expressed that lawyers would make juvenile court proceedings adversary. No doubt this is partly true, but it is partly desirable. Informality is often abused. The juvenile courts deal with cases in which facts are disputed and in which, therefore, rules of evidence, confrontation of witnesses, and other adversary procedures are called for. They deal with many cases involving conduct that can lead to incarceration or close supervision for long periods, and therefore juveniles often need the same safeguards that are granted to adults. And in all cases children need advocates to speak for them and guard their interests, particularly when disposition decisions are made. It is the disposition stage at which the opportunity arises to offer individualized treatment plans and in which the danger inheres that the court's coercive power will be applied without adequate knowledge of the circumstances.

"Fears also have been expressed that the formality lawyers would bring into juvenile court would defeat the therapeutic aims of the court. But informality has no necessary connection with therapy; it is a device that has been used to approach therapy, and it is not the only possible device. It is quite possible that in many instances lawyers, for all their commitment to formality, could do more to further therapy for their clients than can the small, overworked social staffs of the courts.

*   *   *

"The Commission believes it is essential that counsel be appointed by the juvenile court for those who are unable to provide their own. Experience under the prevailing systems in which children are free to seek counsel of their choice reveals how empty of meaning the right is for those typically the subject of juvenile court proceedings. Moreover, providing counsel only when the child is sophisticated enough to be aware of his need and to ask for one or when he fails to waive his announced right are not enough, as experience in numerous jurisdictions reveals.

"The Commission recommends:
"COUNSEL SHOULD BE APPOINTED AS A MATTER OF COURSE WHEREVER COERCIVE ACTION IS A POSSIBILITY, WITHOUT REQUIRING ANY AFFIRMATIVE CHOICE BY CHILD OR PARENT."

[66] Lehman, A Juvenile's Right to Counsel in a Delinquency Hearing, 17 Juvenile Court Judge's Journal 53 (1966). In an interesting review of the 1966 edition of the Children's Bureau's "Standards," Rosenheim, Standards for Juvenile and Family Courts: Old Wine in a New Bottle, 1 Fam. L. Q. 25, 27 (1967), the author observes that "The 'Standards' of 1966, just like the 'Standards' of 1954, are valuable precisely because they represent a diligent and thoughtful search for an accommodation between the aspirations of the founders of the juvenile court and the grim realities of life against which, in part, the due process of criminal and civil law offers us protection."

[67] These are lawyers designated, as provided by the statute, to represent minors. N.Y. Family Court Act § 242.

[68] N.Y. Family Court Act § 241.

[69] N.Y. Family Court Act § 741. For accounts of New York practice under the new procedures, see Isaacs, The Role of the Lawyer in Representing Minors in the New Family Court, 12 Buffalo L. Rev. 501 (1963); Dembitz, Ferment and Experiment in New York: Juvenile Cases in the New Family Court, 48 Cornell L. Q. 499, 508–12 (1963). Since introduction of the law guardian system in September of 1962, it is stated that attorneys are present in the great majority of cases. Harvard Law Review Note, p. 796. See New York Judicial Conference, Twelfth Annual Report, pp. 288–91 (1967), for detailed statistics on representation of juveniles in New York. For the situation before 1962, see Schinitsky, The Role of the Lawyer in Children's Court, 17 The Record (N.Y. City Bar Assn.) 10 (1962). In the District of Columbia, where statute and court decisions require that a lawyer be appointed if the family is unable to retain counsel, see *supra* note 63, and where the juvenile and his parents are so informed at the initial hearing, about 85 to 90 per cent do not choose to be represented and sign a written waiver form. D.C. Crime Comm'n Report, p. 646. The Commission recommends adoption in the District of Columbia of a "law guardian" system similar to that of New York, with more effective notification of the right to appointed counsel, in order to eliminate the problems of procedural fairness, accuracy of fact-finding, and appropriateness of disposition which the absence of counsel in so many juvenile court proceedings involves. *Id.*, at 681–85.

[70] See *supra* note 63.

[71] *Johnson* v. *Zerbst*, 304 U.S. 458, 464 (1938); *Carnley* v. *Cochran*, 369 U.S. 506 (1962); *United States ex rel. Brown* v. *Fay*, 242 F. Supp. 273 (D.C.S.D. N.Y. 1965).

[72] The privilege is applicable to state proceedings. *Malloy* v. *Hogan*, 378 U.S. 1 (1964).

[73] *Pointer* v. *Texas*, 380 U.S. 400 (1965); *Douglas* v. *Alabama*, 380 U.S. 415 (1965).

[74] For this reason, we cannot consider the status of Gerald's alleged admissions to the probation officers. Cf., however, Comment, Miranda Guarantees in the California Juvenile Court, 7 Santa Clara Lawyer, 114 (1966).

[75] Wigmore on Evidence § 822 (3d ed. 1940).

[76] 332 U.S., at 599–600 (opinion of MR. JUSTICE DOUGLAS, joined by JUSTICES BLACK, Murphy, and Rutledge; Justice Frankfurter concurred in a separate opinion).

[77] See Fortas, The Fifth Amendment, 25 Cleveland Bar Assn. Journal 91 (1954).

[78] See *Rogers* v. *Richmond*, 365 U.S. 534 (1961); *Culombe* v. *Connecticut*, 367 U.S. 568 (1961) (opinion of Frankfurter, J., joined by MR. JUSTICE STEWART): *Miranda* v. *Arizona*, 384 U.S. 436 (1966).

[79] See also *Malloy* v. *Hogan*, 378 U.S.1 (1964); *McCarthy* v. *Arndstein*, 266 U.S. 34, 40 (1924).

[80] N.Y. Family Court Act § 741.

[81] N.Y. Family Court Act § 724. In *In the Matter of Williams*, 49 Misc. 2d 154, 267 N.Y.S. 2d 91 (1966), the New York Family Court held that "the failure of the police to notify this child's parents that he had been taken into custody, if not alone sufficient to render his confession inadmissible, is germane on the issue of its voluntary character. . . ." *Id.*, at ——; 267 N.Y.S. 2d, at 106. The confession was held involuntary and therefore inadmissible.

[82] See *In the Matter of Addison*, 20 A.D. 2d 90, 245 N.Y.S. 2d 243 (1963).

[83] The issues relating to fingerprinting of juveniles are not presented here, and we express no opinion concerning them.

[84] Standards, p. 49.

[85] See *supra* note 79, and accompanying text.

[86] Delinquent Children in Penal Institutions, Children's Bureau Pub. No. 415 (1964), p. 1

[87] See, e.g., *Miranda* v. *Arizona*, 384 U.S 436 (1966); *Garrity* v. *New Jersey*, 385 U.S. 493 (1967); *Spevack* v. *Klein*, 385 U.S. 511 (1967); *Haynes* v. *Washington*, 373 U.S. 503 (1963); *Culombe* v. *Connecticut*, 367 U.S. 568 (1961); *Rogers* v. *Richmond*, 365 U.S. 534 (1961); *Malloy* v. *Hogan* 378 U.S. 1 (1964); *Griffin* v. *California*, 380 U.S. 609 (1965).

[88] Arizona Constitution, Art. 6, § 15 (as amended 1960); ARS §§ 8-223, 8-228 (a); Harvard Law Review Note, p. 793. Because of this possibility that criminal jurisdiction may attach it is urged that ". . . all of the procedural safeguards in the criminal law should be followed." Standards, p. 49. Cf. *Harling* v. *United States*, —— U.S. App. D.C. ——, 295 F. 2d 161 (1961).

[89] ARS § 8-228 (a).

[90] Juvenile Delinquency—Its Prevention and Control (Russell Sage Foundation, 1966).

[91] *Id.*, at 33. See also the other materials cited in *supra* note 37.

[92] N.J. Stats. 2A:4–37 (b) (2) (Supp. 1966); N.J. Stats. 2A:113–4.

[93] N.J. Stats. 2A:4–32, 33. The court emphasized that the "frightening atmosphere" of a police station is likely to have "harmful effects on the mind and will of the boy," citing *In the Matter of Rutane*, 234 N.Y.S. 2d 777 (Fam. Ct. Kings Co., 1962).

[94] The court held that this alone might be enough to show that the confessions were involuntary "even though, as the police testified, the boys did not wish to see their parents" (citing *Gallegos* v. *Colorado*, 370 U.S. 49 [1962]).

[95] The court quoted the following passage from *Haley* v. *Ohio*, *supra*, at 601: "But we are told that this boy was advised of his constitutional rights before he signed the confession and that, knowing them, he nevertheless confessed. That assumes, however, that a boy of fifteen, without aid of counsel, would have a full appreciation of that advice and that on the facts of this record he had a freedom of choice. We cannot indulge those assumptions. Moreover, we cannot give any weight to recitals which merely formalize constitutional requirements. Formulas of respect for constitutional safeguards cannot prevail over the facts of life which contradict them. They may not become a cloak for inquisitorial practices and make an empty form of the due process of law for which free men fought and died to obtain."

[96] The New York Family Court Act, § 744 (b), provides that "an uncorroborated confession made out of court by a respondent is not sufficient" to constitute the required "preponderance of the evidence."

See *United States* v. *Morales*, 233 F. Supp. 160 (D.C. Mont. 1964), holding a confession inadmissible in proceedings under the Federal Juvenile Delinquency Act because, in the circumstances in which it was made, the District Court could not conclude that it "was freely made while Morales was afforded all of the requisites of due process required in the case of a sixteen-year-old boy of his experience." *Id.*, at 170.

[97] Cf. *Jackson* v. *Denno*, 378 U.S. 368 (1964); *Miranda* v. *Arizona*, 384 U.S. 436 (1966).

[98] Standards, pp. 72–73. The Nat'l Crime Comm'n Report concludes that "the evidence admissible at the adjudicatory hearing should be so limited that findings are not dependent upon or influenced by hearsay, gossip, rumor, and other unreliable types of information. To minimize the danger that adjudication will be affected by inappropriate considerations, social investigation reports should not be made known to the judge in advance of adjudication." *Id.*, at 87 (bold face eliminated). See also Note, Rights and Rehabilitation in the Juvenile Courts, 67 Col. L. Rev. 281, 336 (1967): "At the adjudication stage, the use of clearly incompetent evidence in order to prove the youth's involvement in the alleged misconduct . . . is not justifiable. Particularly in delinquency cases, where the issue of fact is the commission of a crime, the introduction of hearsay—such as the report of a policeman who did not witness the events—contravenes the purpose underlying the Sixth Amendment right of confrontation." (Footnote omitted.)

[99] N.Y. Family Court Act § 744 (a). See also Harvard Law Review Note, p. 795. Cf. *Willner* v. *Committee on Character*, 373 U.S. 96 (1963).

[100] ARS § 2-238.

[101] *Griffin* v. *Illinois*, 351 U.S. 12, 18 (1956).

[102] "Standards for Juvenile and Family Courts" recommends "written findings of fact, some form of record of the hearing" "and the right to appeal." Standards, p. 8. It recommends verbatim recording of the hearing by stenotypist or mechanical recording (p. 76) and urges that the judge make clear to the child and family their right to appeal (p. 78). See also Standard Family Court Act §§ 19, 24, 28; Standard Juvenile Court Act §§ 19, 24, 28. The Harvard Law Review Note, at p. 799, states that "the result [of the infrequency of appeals due to absence of record, indigency, etc.] is that juvenile court proceedings are largely unsupervised." The Nat'l Crime Comm'n Report observes, at p. 86, that "records make possible appeals which, even if they do not occur, impart by their possibility a healthy atmosphere of accountability."

2. *Children's Court: Gateway or Last Resort?**

MONRAD G. PAULSEN

IN JUNE 1964, fifteen-year-old Gerald Francis Gault allegedly telephoned Mrs. Cook, a neighbor of the Gault family in Gila County, Arizona, and made remarks to her said to be lewd or indecent. That phone call caused Gerald a great deal of trouble. He was adjudicated a delinquent in juvenile court and ordered committed to the State Industrial School for Boys "for the period of his minority [that is until he was 21] unless sooner discharged by due process of law." An adult guilty of the same offense would, under the Arizona Criminal Code, be subject to a maximum punishment of a $50 fine or imprisonment for not more than two months.

That phone call also made it certain that Gerald will enjoy a kind of im-

* Reprinted by permission of the author from Monrad G. Paulsen, "Children's Court; Gateway or Last Resort?" *Columbia Forum*, Summer, 1967, Vol. 10, No. 2. Copyright 1967 by the Trustees of Columbia University in the City of New York.

mortality. His name is appended to the first juvenile case ever reviewed by the U.S. Supreme Court on constitutional grounds and is thus forever linked to the decision that brought the requirements of the Fourteenth Amendment to juvenile court hearings.

The constitutionality of the procedures employed in juvenile courts had never been tested under the federal Constitution until May 1967, when *In the Matter of Gault* was decided, although some forty state supreme courts had upheld these procedures against the principal challenges. Most of the opinions echoed sentiments similar to those found in a classic Pennsylvania case, *Commonwealth* v. *Fisher:*

> The natural parent needs no process to temporarily deprive his child of his liberty by confining it in his home, to save it and to shield it from the consequences of persistence in a career of waywardness; nor is the state, when compelled, as *parens patriae*, to take the place of the father for the same purpose, required to adopt any process as a means of placing its hands upon the child to lead it into one of its courts . . . the court determines the [child's] salvation, and not its punishment.

The *Gault* decision works a revolutionary change in the law applicable to erring children by establishing that all "fact-finding" hearings in juvenile courts (i.e., hearings in which it is determined what the respondent has done) "must measure up to the essentials of due process and fair treatment." The decision is built upon the premise that the juvenile court system has failed to provide the care and treatment that the theory underlying it had posited. The language of uplift has masked an ugly reality. "Training" schools are often nothing more than prisons for the young, and children may be incarcerated there by proceedings containing few of the safeguards provided for adult offenders. "So wide a gulf between the State's treatment of the adult and of the child," the opinion of Mr. Justice Fortas states, "requires a bridge sturdier than mere verbiage and reasons more persuasive than clichés can provide."

"The essentials of due process and fair treatment" include, in the Court's eyes, the giving of adequate and timely notice of the petition so the youngster and his parents have the opportunity to respond. Further, in fact-finding hearings "which may result in commitment" the child is entitled to be represented by counsel and, if the parents are unable to afford a lawyer, the state must provide one. Due process will require that the "constitutional privilege against self-incrimination is applicable in the case of juveniles as it is with respect to adults." Without a valid confession, a determination of delinquency cannot be sustained "in the absence of sworn testimony subjected to the opportunity for cross-examination."

Mr. Justice Stewart's lone dissenting opinion . . . is based on the view that procedural formalism will "invite a long step backwards into the nineteenth century" by undoing the work of those who established the system of juvenile courts to protect children from nineteenth-century criminal justice.

The reformers of the turn of the century and those who were persuaded by them held the highest hopes. Until a "better and finer agency may be evolved . . . the juvenile court will remain to serve as a fountain of mercy, truth and justice to our handicapped children." This sentiment appears in the final words of the final chapter of Herbert Lou's *Juvenile Courts in the United*

States. Published in 1927, the book was until recently the most widely consulted work in its field. Every page of it reflects the sure conviction that these specialized courts for children are among man's most noble creations.

The juvenile court was created near the turn of the century by men and women possessed of a passion for social justice. The concerned citizens who secured the passage of juvenile court acts in almost every state within a few years after the landmark Illinois Act of 1899 were aroused by women's rights, prison reform, the plight of the immigrant poor, as well as by the need to protect children. The reformers were optimists. They saw the social order as basically good but believed that it ought to be brought up to date and some of the cruelty taken out of it. Women should have the vote, prisoners should be taught a trade, immigrants should be afforded equal opportunity, and wayward youth should be saved.

A child in trouble was not likely to be saved in 1899. If he were over seven, he could be convicted of crime. After conviction he would find himself branded for life with the criminal's stigma; he might be placed in an institution designed for hardened criminals and mixed with the general prison population. In part, the juvenile court movement was a reaction to this harsh and cruel system of cutting off a life's potential before the life had truly begun.

And in part, the reformers were skeptical about the entire process of criminal justice. Obviously, the system of conviction, punishment, and release had not contained crime. If anything, it made men worse. It embraced in its operation nothing designed to lift men up or to help them with their difficulties. Certainly this arrangement, based on uncertain theories of deterrence, in turn founded on a medieval conception of free will, would not in the reformers' eyes be appropriate to the twentieth century.

The new court was to emphasize correctional change in the individual child. The source of each young offender's forbidden deeds was to be discovered and eliminated by treatment. Medical attention was to be given those whose misbehavior resulted from physical ills. Psychological techniques were to be applied to the mentally disturbed. Special teaching would overcome behavior problems rooted in miseducation. A probation officer's guidance and counsel would strengthen the youth's own resources. Indeed, the juvenile court was often compared to a clinic or a school. The reformers had a firm and naive belief that a body of science—medical, social, and psychological—did exist that could work beneficial changes in troubled children if only the law would open the door to its application. "The problem for determination by the judge is not," wrote Judge Julian Mack in 1908, "has this boy or girl committed a specific wrong, but what is he, how has he become what he is, and what had best be done in his interest and in the interest of the state to save him from a downward career." The child should be changed and restored, not branded and lost.

The juvenile court was to be staffed by expert, specialized judges knowledgeable in the behavioral sciences, filled with love for children; by probation officers with extensive training and light caseloads; by medical and psychological personnel who were to provide the needed auxiliary services.

The specialized court was to employ a flexible procedure geared to the individual case. Nothing should remind a respondent youngster of a criminal court—no jury, no robes, no formal courtroom trappings. The rules of evidence which exclude much relevant information only made more difficult the task of getting to the bottom of things. Lawyers were not needed because the court did not employ an adversary procedure. The aim of the process was to help the youngster. Lawyers would only introduce a useless element of conflict. Even the trial hearing itself was perceived as part of the treatment process. "Seated at a desk, with the child at his side, where he can on occasion put his arm around his shoulder and draw the lad to him, the judge, while losing some of his judicial dignity, will gain immensely in the effectiveness of his work." The words are again those of Judge Mack.

How could such a court meet the standards of American constitutions? After all, a youngster could lose his liberty by procedures far too streamlined to pass muster in the criminal courts. The juvenile court, asserted the reformers, was a civil not a criminal court. It employed chancery doctrines, in particular, the concept of *parens patriae*—the idea that the state is the ultimate parent of all. Constitutional guarantees, in short, were traded for rehabilitation, education, and salvation.

These rosy dreams have turned to troubled sleep. A few months ago a fifteen-year-old boy in Wisconsin killed his mother with a rifle shot. A delinquency petition was filed against him and the young man's lawyer moved to dismiss the petition on the ground that the youth was insane at the time of the shooting. The corporation counsel, seeking to sustain the petition, urged that the boy's mental state would provide him with a defense only in a criminal case.

If the question is not "what has a boy done" but "what is he, how has he become what he is, and how can we help him," the corporation counsel should have prevailed. Clearly, the boy performed the act. Now we ought simply ask what are his needs for rehabilitation.

But the Wisconsin Supreme Court saw more to the problem:

Retribution, in practice, plays a role in the function of the juvenile court. The judgment of juvenile courts do serve as deterrents. . . . The adjudication of delinquency carries with it a social stigma. This court can take judicial notice that in common parlance "juvenile delinquent" is a term of opprobrium and it is not society's accolade bestowed on the successfully rehabilitated.

The failure of the juvenile court to achieve its goals and the distressing substitution of cant for correction has moved not only the Supreme Court and the Wisconsin judges, but legislators as well. In recent years three of the country's more populous states, California, New York, and Illinois, have recast their juvenile court laws. In each state more formality has been introduced into the court process and various legislative limitations have been placed on the juvenile court judge's discretionary power.

The 1967 Report of the President's Commission on Law Enforcement and the Administration of Justice also makes a sharp break with the traditional theory regarding the juvenile court. Herbert Lou said that youngsters were brought to court so that "the handicapped children of the community who come before it may be adjusted, protected, corrected, and developed into useful members of society." In contrast, the report of the President's Commission affirms that "delinquency is not so much an act of individual deviancy as a pattern of behavior produced by a multitude of pervasive societal influences well beyond the reach of action by any judge, probation officer, correctional counsellor or psychiatrist." The chief weapons in the fight against delinquency are to be social and economic means rather than attempts to effect change in individual offenders. The report urges improvement in schools, housing, employment opportunities, occupational training programs, and the strengthening of the family.

The formal juvenile court system and its pronouncements of delinquency, the report said, "should be used only as a last resort." The report does not present the juvenile court as an instrument for saving youth; instead it cites numerous studies that indicate that the court is a corrupter of youth. The draftsmen of the report recommend that children be kept away from the juvenile court's formal adjudication in as many cases as possible. They recommend the establishment of youth service bureaus, to be located in neighborhood community centers and required to receive both delinquent and non-delinquent children referred by police, parents, schools, and other agencies. Each bureau would embrace a broad range of services designed to assist young people in their problems. The report further recommends that juvenile courts should make the fullest feasible use of "preliminary conferences" to allow for out-of-court adjustments and settlements at the level of court intake. A further device to avoid adjudication is contained in the suggestion that juvenile courts should employ consent decrees wherever possible in the hope that the agreements to undertake rehabilitative treatment might free the respondent from the stigma of adjudication and at the same time make certain that an erring youth who needs it will undertake a treatment plan. For the cases that must come to court the report urges the introduction of procedures that will guarantee a fair hearing for finding the facts regarding the child's acts as well as a just process for determining questions of disposition. In particular, the Commission urges that lawyers be provided for juveniles. "It is essential," the report states, "that counsel be appointed by the juvenile court for those who are unable to provide their own."

Whatever hope there was (and I think there was little) for the juvenile court to be a gateway to a supermarket of services for regeneration has been drained away by the passing of time and the emergence of a new order of social values.

"Delinquency," invented as a soft substitute for the word "crime," is now a cruel term itself. Why?

The dreams were inflated dreams—cut off from the hard realities of the world. The cities, counties, and states were never willing or able to provide the juvenile court with the resources its theory required. Few judges have reached the level of performance that the reformers expected. Probation staffs have been inadequately trained and given such large numbers to supervise that nothing but the most perfunctory attention can be given most cases. Most courts do not have access either to adequate auxiliary services or to a wide range of institutions for the help of the adjudicated delinquent.

Would the problem of today's juvenile court disappear suddenly if immense new resources would be made available? No, I think not.

The dream believed too much in man's capacity—here and now—to effect correctional change. Within the population of teen-agers there are a number of dangerously antisocial persons who present a great threat to the community and about whose rehabilitation no one has a firm idea. A youth can inflict a grievous injury which cannot go unremarked and yet the tools are not at hand "to save him from a downward career." Thus we have in fact employed juvenile court adjudications to express rather than to re-educate. The desire to save outruns the possibility of doing so.

The aspirations of the reformers have, in fact, been turned upside down. A contact with the juvenile court not only is unlikely to assist a youngster to become a better citizen but, according to respectable theory today, it is likely to lead him into further delinquency. The "saving" institution may be a corrupter of youth. A recent publication of the Russell Sage Foundation puts the matter this way: "If the labeling hypothesis is correct, official intervention may further define the youth as delinquent in the eyes of neighbors, family members, and peers, thus making it more difficult for him to resume conventional activities."

The reformers thought of most criminal procedure as a product of a dark age—technical, impeding the discovery of truth, useful only to pettifogging lawyers. Today, the aspects of the Bill of Rights that set standards in criminal procedure are perceived as milestones marking the progress of man's march to freedom.

Little by little we have learned again that informality can become the curtain behind which error, weariness, indifference, unseemly hate, and prejudice can operate. The misuse of power by juvenile court judges in the South, little inhibited by statutory or constitutional norms, has been documented by the Civil Rights Commission. A trickle of appellate cases further suggests that injustice flowing from an abundance of discretionary power is not regional in this country.

Indeed, the drive of the reformers to make certain that juvenile court procedures be informal, far removed from the practices in criminal cases, is no longer an article of faith. In 1967 a majority of the Supreme Court does not believe that the unique benefits children can receive from specialized courts will be impaired when the courts are subject to "constitutional domestication." "The essentials of due process," the Court said, may be an "impressive and . . . therapeutic attitude so far as the juvenile is concerned." Fairness and simple justice may draw out the best in children as it does in adults.

The stance of the reformers no longer fits the 1960's. Listen to Judge Mack again.

> Most of the children who come before the court are, naturally, the children of the poor. In many cases the parents are foreigners, frequently unable to speak English, and without an understanding of American methods and views. What they need, more than anything else, is kindly assistance. . . .

Is this the way we see delinquency, the delinquent, and the remedy for the problem? The respondent in the juvenile court, especially in the city, is apt to be of the poor; he is often a Negro. His parents are unlikely to be foreigners and may speak English reasonably well. The problem of the slum-bred delinquent will not yield to an offer of "kindly assistance."

The demand for more legal norms has also been fed by an old American practice: the unconscionable manipulation of law and legal process. *Gault* provides a moving example. The juvenile court judge who committed him was unclear about the exact statute under which young Gault was adjudicated. He took into account an unproved prior instance of alleged misconduct. He did not require the complaining witness to testify. Gault's parents were not given notice according to the proper legal form. The events fit the suspicion: The judge believed young Gault should be disciplined. It did not matter much how it was to be accomplished.

The Court, legislatures, and the President's Commission all point to a new juvenile court that will be quite different from the one proposed by the reformers. The new court is to be a court of last resort, not a gateway to rehabilitation and re-education. It will be a court very much like other courts, differing principally in its great emphasis upon (but not exclusive concern with) the rehabilitation of children *before* the formal trial. The new court will be challenged by the old problem: What can the state, in fact, do to help the youthful offender and reduce crime among the young. Orderliness can correct some abuses but surely it cannot create new opportunities.

Like the reformers, the Supreme Court, the legislatures, and the President's Commission are moved by a concern to serve children. They would do it differently, of course: Where the intention was once to get the troubled child into the courts as fast as possible, the aim will now be to keep him out of court altogether, if that is possible. There is a deeper difference, however, than in the method of proceeding. Fundamentally, the conviction is no longer shared that crime can be reduced or children, in large numbers, "saved" by the tactic of treating the individual deviant. Institutional rehabilitation, if not a myth, is at least unreachable in practice. More than law is required. Cure is not the characteristic of "last resort" expedients. Patient attack on basic social evils, together with sorrowful, helpful but firm response to those who cause serious harm, are the actions that commend themselves to the 1960's. Like the recommended programs of 1900, they will take money, determination, and love. Whether the outcome will be happier is in the balance.

3. *Legislating Change in the Juvenile Court* *

EDWIN M. LEMERT

INTRODUCTION

IN THE EARLY HISTORY of American social science and sociology the view that social reforms could be achieved by legislation had sturdy partisans. Among them were Lester F. Ward and Ernst Freund, both of whom believed that "scientific legislation," or a science of legislation, was a distinct possibility.[1] In time, however, the less sanguine views of Sumner, Dicey, Pound, and L. L. Bernard came to prevail in sociology.[2] They emphasized the limited efficacy of law as a means of inducing social change and the dependence of law upon moral growth and public opinion. More recently, particularly since the Supreme Court's 1954 school desegregation decision,[3] some social scientists have returned to the idea that legislation and judicial fiat can produce

* Edwin M. Lemert, "Legislating Change in the Juvenile Court," *Wisconsin Law Review*, No. 2 (1967), pp. 421–49.

significant social changes and that the changes need not be gradual nor supported by public opinion, given the circumstances of clarity of goals, firmness in enforcement policy, and a pluralistic social structure.[4]

Events immediately past have raised doubts about the validity of the predictions of the social scientists who advised the Supreme Court on probable outcomes of a judicial policy of "immediate," as opposed to gradual, school desegregation. Resistance to social change in this area has been as impressive as compliance. More important, it appears that coercive control may generate new forms of behavior equally undesired, or less desired, than those that the agencies of law have sought to change.[5] It is correct to say that the question of the relation of law to social change remains an open one.

The acceleration of change from regional pluralism to functional pluralism in American society probably has prompted social scientists to question the older Sumnerian concepts of cultural continuity and the organic dependence of law on moral consensus. Yet to substitute for one large generalization another that is largely antithetical misses the deeper message of modern pluralism: Complex aggregations of values underlie social action for change and for resistance.[6] Under these conditions, "clarity of goals" and "firmness in enforcement policy" become problematical, to be explained and not assumed.

If pluralism assumes that there is no longer a supervening structure in American society, it does not minimize the importance of *structures,* some tied to locality, but more connected with functional associations. Their entry into social action as limiting factors depends on the nature of the issues raised. For this reason, research on directed social change through law requires designs or models derived from reasonably homogeneous bodies of data. These models must distinguish: (1) the type of human activity subject to control (i.e., economic, sumptuary, health, welfare, public protection, political participation); (2) the number and extent of the changes (ends) sought and their communicability; and (3) the geographic areas affected and the nature of the social structures therein. Observations will be guided less by the captional question "whether morality can be legislated" than by queries whether the changes provoke resistance, what forms resistance takes, what the costs of overcoming resistance are, and what the costs or consequences of new adaptations are in terms of the extinction of existing values and their means of satisfaction.

The changes under consideration here were incorporated in a comprehensive revision of the California Juvenile Court Law in 1961.[7] While the changes cast into law dealt mainly with jurisdiction and procedures, their legislative history reveals the underlying aims to have been the guarantee of greater justice or a fuller measure of civil rights for juveniles and their parents.[8] In essence, the new statutes restricted the power of police and the juvenile court to intervene in parent-child relationships, forbade unnecessary detention and separation of children from their parents (without "reasonable cause"), and specified the form of hearings to detain, declare wardship, and make case dispositions. The changes called for substantial redress in power relations between youths, parents, police, probation officers, judges, and treatment agencies. From a sociological view, they radically altered the basic "rules of the game" for most, if not all, the juvenile courts in California's fifty-eight counties. Among the more crucial changes were those requiring mandatory advice about right to counsel and requiring provision of counsel in certain kinds of cases. The following discussion focuses on the effects of these changes and associated procedural changes.

*   *   *

THE ADVERSARY SYSTEM IN JUVENILE COURT

Role Confusion and Role Conflict

A great deal of underlying confusion and uncertainty arises in California juvenile court hearings due to lack of clarity and to structured conflict in the roles of attorneys, probation officers, and judges. This is most painfully apparent in the actions of private attorneys without previous juvenile court experience. They usually are at a complete loss to know how to proceed; one confided to the writer after a hearing, "What can you do in this kind of a court? Downtown [in adult courts] I know what the rules are and what I can do. Here you come in, hat in hand, and hope for the best." Apart from lacking ideas about how to exploit the court to their clients' advantage, attorneys often confront cases in which there is literally nothing that can be done. Their inactivity may confirm the skepticism of judges who believe they have no place in the court. One such judge sarcastically observed: "They sit there like bumps on logs. They take the client's money and do nothing."

Attorneys undoubtedly feel pressure to do something for their clients, but if they become contentious in true adversary style they slow down the proceedings. Insisting on the right to cross-examine witnesses adds greatly to the work of the probation officer. He, as well as the witnesses and even the judge, may become irritated, particularly if he regards the case as open-and-shut and the intended disposition as lenient. Such problems grew critical in one county shortly after the new law went into effect because the tactics of private attorneys piled up cases and heavily overloaded the calendar. The county bar association was drawn into the discussion of the problem, with the result that one law firm was given a contract to serve as public defender for all assigned cases. Thereafter, the work of the court went forward with less delay.

Although employing public defenders for assigned cases makes for a more "efficient" court, this can cause counsel to be co-opted into the organization of the court, even becoming its superficial appendage. Factors encouraging this are the low priority public defenders give to juvenile work and the growth of interdepartmental or informal reciprocity with probation officers. Public defenders may come to justify their passive roles on the grounds that they do not want to add to the work of already overburdened probation officers, but more important is the arousal of a differential reaction towards juvenile offenders. The following statement is illustrative:

> Ordinarily I stipulate that the probation officer's report is acceptable in the jurisdictional hearings. Otherwise he would have to bring in witnesses. In many such cases, perhaps most, the evidence would not support the judgment, but I hate to see a young kid get the idea that he can get away with something. One fifteen year old boy who broke into a bar and took a case of beer told me in an interview that his problem was that he got caught. I became indignant and asked him if he wasn't too young to drink. The boy said, "No, only too young to buy." I decided he needed to be jolted—maybe with a stay in detention—so I encouraged him to admit his guilt in court. No corpus delecti needed to be established. If it had been an adult

case I would have taken the position that the D.A. could not prove his case because the beer was never found and not even reported until a month after it disappeared.

The Emergent Role of the Attorney

Disregarding the gratuitous aspects of the attorney's role in the juvenile court, exigencies and a growing organizational hiatus (to an extent developed by the law change itself) push the attorney toward the role of negotiator, mediator, or interpreter of court decisions and actions to clients. This view is supported by the author's court observations, by interview findings, and by questionnaire responses of probation officers. The latter are summarized in Table 1.

In nearly half of the responses, counsel was thought to be helpful as an interpreter of the meaning of court decisions to parents and minors and as a source of psychic support. At the same time, in nearly a quarter of the replies the probation workers took a more jaundiced view of the attorney's presence in court—it was of "little real value" or "disruptive." Probation officers' approval of counsel's mediator role and their disapproval of his adversary role reflect both the adaptations and the problems that have evolved with the more formalized structure in the juvenile court.

TABLE 1. EVALUATIONS BY PROBATION OFFICERS OF THE USEFULNESS OF COUNSEL IN JUVENILE COURT HEARINGS IN 56 CALIFORNIA COUNTIES, 1965

Usefulness of Counsel	Number of Responses	Per cent
Helps in clarifying evidence	17	14.0
Helps in suggesting dispositions	17	14.0
Helps in interpreting court decisions to minors and parents	34	28.1
Simply makes parents and minor feel better	24	19.8
Counsel is of little real value	8	6.6
Counsel in some instances is disruptive and time-consuming	21	17.3
	121	99.8

Asymmetry in the Adversary System

One of the major problems accompanying revision of the juvenile court law arises from complications in adversary proceedings where juveniles deny the allegations of the petition. The law made no provision to present the case against minors or parents or to "represent the interests of the state." This has left a kind of asymmetry or imbalance sorely felt by many probation officers and a number of judges. It was much decried by law-enforcement people, who in 1965 made a determined but unsuccessful effort to have the law amended so that the prosecuting attorney could be required to assist probation officers in contested hearings. Meantime, a variety of adaptations to the problem have evolved, the nature and distribution of which are displayed in Table 2. Probation officers generally have had to assume the unpleasant burden of fighting the case; either as case investigators or as court officers, they have been

TABLE 2. Official Who Presents Case Against Juveniles and Parents in Jurisdictional Hearings in 56 California Counties, 1965 California Counties, 1965

	Probation officer who investigates case	Probation officer alternates with prosecutor	Probation officer alternates with court officer	Judge	Combinations of judge, probation officer, court officer, and prosecutor
Per cent	41.0	21.4	14.2	12.5	10.7

responsible for stating and sustaining allegations of the petition in nearly three fourths of the counties in the state.

The role of the investigating officer in presenting the case against parents and juveniles is both anomalous and stressful, for ordinarily he does not have the legal knowledge, training, temperament, or experience to play what in reality is a prosecutor's role. In adversary hearings he may be subjected to rough, embarrassing, even humiliating treatment at the hands of a defense attorney, or he may be called to account sharply by the judge.[9] Moreover, by attacking the integrity of parents and charging crimes by juveniles he frequently loses whatever chance he may have had to establish rapport. While instituting a court officer role obviates some of this difficulty, it does not work too well from an administrative point of view.[10] Furthermore, it increases bureaucratization and impersonality in handling cases and may introduce errors by attenuating the processing of cases. As greater social distance separates the probation officer from persons he theoretically is supposed to help, the need for a mediator's role in the court system intensifies. Attorneys move into the vacuum, but not without conflicts of their own.

The Judge

The American judge, in contrast to the English or continental judge, has traditionally conceived his ideal role as that of an umpire or presiding officer who decides questions of procedure and law rather than adducing facts or evidence. The prosecutor is the chief interrogator in criminal cases. Although the new juvenile court law clearly allows criminal-type adversary hearings, the unwillingness of many prosecutors to try juvenile cases, coupled with the legal ineptitude of probation officers, means that the judge himself frequently not only "presents the case" (see Table 2) but must intervene to take over questioning of the "defendant" or witnesses when the probation officer falters. At the same time, because the court is charged with protecting the interests of the child, the judge may pre-empt or intervene in the role of the defense attorney if one is present.

In contested cases and in those involving serious issues, experienced juvenile court judges are likely to alternate between a managerial role, in which they attempt to insure that all interests will be represented, and a hearing role, in which they seek to actualize the interplay of these interests. However, it is doubtful that many judges are prepared to let hearings become full-dress, protracted, adversary contests. Such considerations shape their decisions to appoint attorneys and their control of court procedures. In unfit home cases and some cases where incorrigibility is charged, the judge may assign counsel because the contest would otherwise become unequal, reduced to the child's words against his parents or a set of relatives solidly aligned. On the other hand, the judge may feel that he and the probation officer can properly defend the interest of the child even though the parents have engaged an attorney.

Observations suggest that in unfit home cases judges tend to structure the situation so that their own roles become much more neutral. That declaring wardship or removing a child from the authority of parents runs contrary to the traditional conservatism of courts in such matters may underlie this. Unfit home cases have a strong potential for conflict, and the hearings may be used for extraneous purposes, such as custody fights. This may explain the reluctance of judges to appoint attorneys for parents as well as children. One judge comments: "I am very reluctant to appoint an attorney for parents because this could very easily turn the hearing into a real adversary fight."

Rules of Evidence

While conflict has always been implicit in the role of the juvenile court judge, it has been made explicit as a consequence of the mandates of the new juvenile code. It results not just from the presence of counsel in court, but also from rules of evidence specified by the new law. In the case of youth alleged to have committed offenses equivalent to felonies, the statute requires that a "preponderance of evidence, legally admissible in the trial of criminal cases, must be adduced to support a finding. . . ." [11] In the first year or two after its passage, this provision led to considerable confusion among judges and attorneys because it seemed to envision standard criminal procedure for such cases.[12]

Conflict arose over the kind of evidence subject to objection and the way objections should be made and ruled on. A conspicuous contradiction emerges if the judge takes over the role of interrogator, for logically he must rule on objections to his own questions, objections that can weaken the case he is making. A judge speaks to the difficulty as follows:

> I start out by telling attorneys: "I don't like this any more than you, but I am sitting up here in the role of interrogator because there's no other provision in the law. You've got to object to the judge's question. And of course I am in a pretty good position to rule here, but I want you to object whenever you think the objection is good and you would have objected if this question had been asked by the District Attorney, and I'll give you a ruling on it." Well, they do some, but it does put counsel obviously at a disadvantage. And it puts the judge in a very awkward and embarrassing position.

If no attorney is present at the contested hearing and the law is followed closely, the judge may find himself in the position of interrogator, yet constrained to think of possible objections to his own questions and to rule on them. The problem is accentuated because much, if not most, evidence in juvenile cases, especially the evidence in the probation report, is legally only hearsay. With passing time most judges have adapted to these difficulties, usually by simply "admitting everything." This is justified by reference to precedents that exist for admitting hearsay evidence in other kinds of cases and by statements that they, as judges, are capable of "sifting," excluding, or otherwise weighing various items in terms of their degree of competence.

Inasmuch as the probation report often is the only evidence presented, many judges seek to validate it by securing admissions from the youth. According to questionnaire information from probation officers, ten courts in the state relied upon admissions of the minor alone to making findings. Twenty-two courts used admissions of minors plus independently established evidence. Five courts relied on evidence other than the minor's admissions. The remaining nineteen courts proceeded "according to the case," with corroborating evidence required in addition to admissions in the more serious cases or in those cases where allegations of the petition were denied.

Although attorneys in juvenile court now have access to probation reports and theoretically can dispute evidence much as in adult criminal hearings, it is doubtful if they are completely free to do so, especially if they must enter a contest with the judge or if they suspect that the judge already concurs with the probation officer's recommended disposition.[13] Furthermore, if an attorney represents or expects to represent more than one case in juvenile court, his actions are likely to be modified by his direct relationship with the probation officer or by what he perceives to be a policy of the probation department. If he pursues an aggressive line of action he may alienate the probation people and do his client more harm than good. An illustrative case is summarized by a probation officer:

> The case was a return from camp for another hearing and new disposition, and the attorney really raised hell with us. He insisted on cross-examining all of the witnesses, which meant that we had to bring about ten people fifty miles in from camp. One woman, a cook, was so upset by the attorney's cross-examination that she said she would bring in her own attorney if she had to come again. Everyone was sore, and now the people out at camp are going to get the boy dead to the right. They'll watch him like a hawk and make it so unpleasant he can't help doing something which will get him out of there.

In understanding the probation officer's often ill-concealed rancor towards the attorney's single-minded pursuit of evidence according to the rules, due heed must be given to his nonlegalistic orientation. Moreover, the police sometimes send him "bad cases" or pass onto him the job of investigation, and the production of witnesses is often an almost hopeless task. Frequently, perhaps typically, the case rests upon the testimony of teen-age witnesses who, as a probation officer observed, "blow hot and cold." It is not unusual for a probation officer to go into court in contested matters not knowing whether he has a case or not. The probation officer's sense of frustration with disputatious attorneys typically is expressed by the plaint that "they do not understand the philosophy of the juvenile court."

Jurisdictional and Dispositional Hearings

Presumably, the separation of jurisdictional and dispositional hearings was designed to make juvenile procedure more nearly like adult criminal procedure. In particular, it would exclude the possible prejudicial effects of the so-called social report of the probation officer on findings of fact. The judge theoretically must first consider only jurisdictional facts contained in a separate report; he then proceeds to facts relevant to disposition submitted in a second report, known variously as the social report or the dispositional re-

port. The "facts" in the second report may include impressionistic and typological judgments by teachers, psychologists, psychiatrists, and camp and
juvenile hall counselors, as well as by probation officers themselves. It is
doubtful that this part of the law has even approximated in actual practice the
results intended. In their first experience with the new law, some judges tried
to hear cases without first reading the social report. But they gave it up as a
bad practice, joining the majority of judges who currently read both reports
prior to hearings. A minority of judges comply with the criminal procedure
prototype to the extent of setting aside the social report in contested cases for
later reading; however, this device breaks down where the contest does not
become apparent until the time of the hearing. One conscientious judge under
these circumstances offers the youth or parents the option of a hearing by the
second judge in his court, but this alternative is absent in one-judge counties
or where otherwise available judges have full and pressing calendars. A
smaller minority of judges do not receive social reports on any cases before
adjudication.[14]

One reason why most judges do not postpone study of the social report has
to do with time and convenience. In most counties the jurisdictional hearing
ordinarily phases right into the dispositional. If the judge has not read the report on the latter, he must take a recess while he reads it, awkwardly try to
digest it while the hearing proceeds, or order a continuance. None of these
techniques is a satisfactory use of the time, energies, and personnel of the
court. Furthermore, since the great majority of youth admit the allegations of
the petition, the focal problem most commonly presented to the court is not
whether an offense has been committed but what should be done with the
youth in question.

Despite the change in the law, formal adjudication at hearings remains a
marginal function of the California juvenile court. Since the judge reads the
entire probation report, it must be concluded that he responds to the configuration of perspectives, facts, and circumstances upon which the probation
officer makes his recommendation. In most cases the judge decides before the
hearing what action he plans and simply reserves a right for others to try to
change his mind. Although judges are unlikely to say so flatly, they make their
conviction clear that the work of the juvenile court could not be done without reading the complete social report before hearings. This was illustrated in
extensive discussions of intercounty transfer cases in the 1962 and 1964 Institutes for Juvenile Court Judges and Referees. It was discovered that many
judges believed that declaring wardship by the transferring county tied the
hands of the receiving county and could lead to imposing a stigma that might
be avoided in the light of additional evidence available in the home county.

Interaction of Judge and Probation Officer

One byproduct of separating the dispositional and jurisdictional hearings
in juvenile court has been to make the probation officer's recommendations
more definitive and less flexible because now disposition has to rest upon
findings. A chief probation officer of long experience in a large county in-
sightfully raised the point at a juvenile court judge's conference:

A bifurcated report . . . prevents the probation officer from commingling
fact and fiction. You [the judge] don't have to eliminate all the things that

aren't fact. It has one other advantage to the judge—it avoids the oldtime distinction we used to have—that if the court finds, then so-and-so, and if the court doesn't find, do such-and-such. The court already has to find, so the probation officer has to stick his neck out and make a definite recommendation. He can't hide behind that "If the court finds. . . ." [15]

Another result of the changed form of the probation report has been to promote a closer coordination between the views of judges and probation officers. Speaking of agreement between judicial dispositions and recommendations by his department, a probation officer summarized his sensitivity to the issues:

> Right now we are running somewhere between 90 and 95 per cent [agreement]. I have always felt that if we drop below 85 per cent it is time to talk with judges to see whether or not we're interpreting their philosophies and approaches the right way. One time we went down with one judge to 64 per cent and that was a rather unfortunate situation.

Probation officers must try to accomplish their goals yet satisfy the values to which judges give their allegiance. The new law requires that more factual evidence be presented if they are to do so; yet the changed law does not and cannot specify what substantive evidence demonstrates such things as "dependency," "unfit home," or "delinquent tendencies." The philosophy of the judge and the values he brings to bear in court continue to have a selective effect upon the kinds of information included in the probation officer's report. Nowhere does this become more apparent than where a probation officer has to bring cases before more than one judge or when judges are changed. To quote a probation officer in a central valley county: "Getting a different judge calls for a lot of readaptation by the probation officer. Judges differ greatly in the kinds of facts and information they ask for. This means that both the investigation and the manner of writing up the case are affected."

Probation officers make judgments that the community must be protected, that a boy needs some detention time to "cool off," that a youth needs protection from the community, that parents should be punished, that county welfare costs must be kept down, or that illegitimacy should not be encouraged. Normally, they do not separate value judgments from judgments of fact. One officer thus stated, "I can tell in twenty minutes what type of case it is," meaning whether the youth was destined for simple probation, foster home placement, boys camp, or the California Youth Authority. Unlike judges, probation officers are not constrained by their training to discover an explicit rationale for the decisions and actions; hence they are freer to tailor their investigation, allegations, and procedures to the ends sought. Procedures required by a judge or by the presence of an attorney in contested cases may simply become obstacles to overcome or circumvent. In legally weak cases probation officers are not above "finagling," as one harassed worker serving as court officer put it, or, as another explained, a "little star chambering."

A more crucial question is the extent to which juvenile judges are willing and able under the new law to accommodate the ends of probation officers or to fulfill through extralegal means the various purposes of the juvenile court as they see them or as they sometimes unavoidably emerge. While some judges, even before the law was changed, carefully observed "due process" in the juvenile courts, the new law undeniably has made all judges more conscious of requirements of procedure and proof.[16] This tendency was strengthened by the retirement of a number of older judges at about the time the law was changed and the appointment as their successors of younger judges, many of whom were favorable to the new law.

Constraint on the juvenile court judge now is operationally or situationally induced or reinforced by the required presence of a clerk and reporter.[17] It is far more greatly induced or reinforced by the presence of counsel and the possibility that he will object and argue or bargain on evidence or procedural points. This was illustrated by the comments of a judge, reputed for his careful attention to procedure and proof, about a case in which he found parents to have neglected their children as alleged:

> If this case had been strongly defended or if an attorney had been present, I might not have been able to sustain a finding. However, the charge downtown [under the penal code] will probably be dismissed and then I would have no hold over these parents. As it is, the children will be dependent for one year only, and there will be some visits by the probation officer. I don't really think that being dependent children for a year will harm them.

CONCLUSIONS

. . . The author's observations of about 120 hearings in this one court and of several dozen scattered in other courts underscore the idea that opportunities for use of adversary skills by attorneys in juvenile court are limited. Occasionally attorneys can get dismissals, but more often they succeed in getting allegations reduced in number or modified, which allows them then to argue for a more favorable disposition They also have some negative power to alter dispositions by an implied threat to contest evidence and slow down the work of the court. Occasionally this takes the form of barefaced bargaining at the hearing.

Attorneys in juvenile court appear at their best when they make positive contributions by bringing new evidence into the dispositional hearing and by proposing alternatives to the probation officer's recommendations. These may include finding relatives to take a child in preference to foster home placement or proposing that psychiatric counseling paid for by the parents be substituted for commitment to Boys Ranch. Attorneys also help their clients by convincing them to accept a recommended disposition where refusal would lead to a more draconic order by the court. These things may be done before, during, or after hearings.

Sometimes attorneys get overinvolved in juvenile court cases, either as civil rights crusaders or as attorney-turned-social worker. In one small county, an attorney became a kind of local *bête noire*, haunting the probation office and striking fear into the heart of the probation officer, who happened to be a woman. Attorneys elsewhere have requested that youths be paroled to them, but an unfortunate experience in one county, having sexual overtones, suggests that this is a spurious development of their role.

The Idealization of Legislative Intent

Whether the role of counsel in juvenile court has emerged along lines intended by those who revised the law poses a question whose answer is obscured by the American tendency to idealize due process of law. The role of counsel as primarily a mediator and negotiator in disposing of cases was not publicly represented nor anywhere clearly stated as the intended result of the law change. Proposals of the Juvenile Justice Commission to introduce counsel into the court were, on their face, part of a concerted effort of legally minded persons in the state to engineer changes to prevent the court from assuming jurisdiction over juveniles unless legally competent evidence was at hand to justify the action and unless the court had adequate facilities to accomplish its purposes.[18] In the same vein, legislators were persuaded to accept the recommendations of the law change largely on the grounds that legal rights of juveniles were being jeopardized and needed more protection.

In the controversies preceding passage of the new law, the role of counsel as envisioned in the juvenile court became polarized, mainly due to anxieties many people held over the possible unwanted effects of instituting adversary proceedings. Discussion in legislative hearings and elsewhere conjured up the image of counsel either as a dauntless courtroom protagonist, disputing evidence and invoking traditional advocacy techniques, or a reverse, darker picture—the scheming manipulator of procedure, helping guileless youth "beat the rap" and making them crimewise. Yet these ideas were derived from popular stereotypes rather than from the reality of due process of law as it operates in adult criminal courts, where the overwhelming majority of convictions (usually over 90 per cent) are not products of adversary proceedings but follow from negotiated, bargained pleas of guilty. A realistic view might have predicted some comparable development in juvenile courts, where questions of fact are not likely to be disputed with any greater frequency than in criminal courts. . . .

NOTES

[1] L. WARD, APPLIED SOCIOLOGY 337–39 (1896); E. FREUND, LEGISLATIVE REGULATION (1932); Freund, *Prolegomena to a Science of Legislation,* 13 ILL. L. REV. 264 (1918).

[2] W. G. SUMNER, FOLKWAYS 55–56 (1906); A. DICEY, LAW AND PUBLIC OPINION IN ENGLAND 17–47 (Macmillan and Company, Ltd., ed. 1952; R. Pound, *The Limits of Effective Legal Action,* in 22ND ANNUAL REPORT OF THE PENNSYLVANIA BAR ASSOCIATION 221 (1916); L. L. BERNARD, SOCIAL CONTROL 580–81 (1939). See also F. PARSONS, LEGAL DOCTRINE AND SOCIAL PROGRESS 17–25 (1911). These references are only representative of the large number of writers who have taken a conservative view of legislation as a means of social control.

[3] Brown v. Board of Educ., 347 U.S. 483 (1954).

[4] Appendix to Appellants' Brief at 13–24, Brown v. Board of Educ., 347 U.S. 483 (1954) ("The Effects of Segregation and the Consequences of Desegregation: A Social Science Statement"). For those who have explicitly discussed pluralism in relation to legally directed social change, see Rose, *The Use of Law to Induce Social Change,* in 6 TRANSACTIONS OF THE THIRD WORLD CONGRESS OF SOCIOLOGY 52 (1956); Breed, *Group Structure and Resistance to Desegregation in the Deep South,* 10 SOC. PROBLEMS 84 (1962); Honigmann, *Value Conflict and Legislation,* 7 SOC. PROBLEMS 34 (1959).

[5] *See* Goldblatt and Cromien, *The Effective Social Reach of the Fair Housing Practices Law of the City of New York,* 9 SOC. PROBLEMS 365 (1961); Hager, *Housing Discrimination, Social Conflict, and the Law,* 8 SOC. PROBLEMS 80 (1960). For a discussion of studies showing tangential or undesired consequences of

changes in court procedures introduced by legislatures or by the courts themselves, see Rosenburg, *Court Congestion: Status, Causes, and Proposed Remedies, in* THE COURTS, THE PUBLIC AND THE LAW EXPLOSION 29, 46–59 (H. Jones ed. 1965).

6 F. COTTRELL, MEN CRY PEACE 112–24 (1954).

7 CAL. WELFARE & INST'NS CODE §§ 500–914 (West 1966). For an outline of the law's provisions, see Comment, *1961 California Juvenile Court Law: Effective Uniform Standards for Juvenile Court Procedure?*, 51 CALIF. L. REV. 421 (1963). Recommendations upon which the changes were based are found in GOVERNOR'S SPECIAL STUDY COMM'N ON JUVENILE JUSTICE, REPORT, pt. I (Cal. 1960). [hereinafter cited as REPORT].

8 *See* e.g., REPORT 9–11.

9 One female probation officer spoke of being reduced to tears in court by her judge's rough manner and of going sleepless for a month after she began to present cases. A male probation officer described his feelings during a fast interchange between judge and defense attorney in a murder hearing: "Suddenly I thought, 'What am I doing here?'"

10 The court officer has other duties and cannot become fully informed on all aspects of the cases investigated by others. As one said, "There isn't time to do the homework." Public defenders may have the same problem, but they are not regarded by the court as the chief source of information about the case.

11 CAL. WELFARE & INST'NS CODE § 701 (West 1966).

12 The recommendations of the Juvenile Justice Commission were much stronger than the change made by the legislature. Originally the statute was proposed to read: "A preponderance of evidence not subject to timely objection by competent counsel under rules of evidence observed in the trial of criminal cases . . . ." Proposed but later omitted was a statement that no findings were to be made upon uncorroborated extrajudicial admissions or confessions of minors unless they were represented by counsel. REPORT 73.

13 The juvenile court might be likened to a mediation system of justice in which the judge acts as interrogator, counsel, and jury. According to Schwartz and Miller, to serve as counsel in this setting is "painful as well as superfluous," and "even where specialized counsel emerge, their role tends to be ambiguous." Schwartz and Miller, *Legal Evolution and Societal Complexity*, 70 AM. J. SOCIOLOGY 167 (1964).

14 The questionnaire replies from fifty-four counties showed that thirty-three judges read the dispositional report in all or most cases before jurisdictional hearings; thirteen judges did not read the dispositional report before jurisdiction was determined in contested cases; and nine judges did not see the dispositional report prior to the jurisdictional hearing in all cases. In a few counties the dispositional report was not even brought to the court until after jurisdiction had been established.

These figures may be compared with a study of New York judges in 1957, in which 67 per cent of those surveyed at a judges' conference stated they saw the "background report" before juvenile court hearings; 8 per cent read the report during the hearings; and 25 per cent made use of the report only after adjudication. Yehle, *Some Practices and Procedures in Children's Court*, 9 SYRACUSE L. REV. 1 (1957).

15 CALIFORNIA JUDICIAL COUNCIL, PROCEEDINGS OF THE SECOND ANNUAL INSTITUTE FOR JUVENILE COURT JUDGES AND REFEREES 134 (1963) (statement by Lorenzo Buckley).

16 The law change, passed after considerable professional controversy, was popularly conceived as "Civil Rights for Juveniles," or a "Little Bill of Rights for Juveniles."

17 One judge averred that he no longer could "put on his act" because he had to watch his language with a reporter present. Occasional older practices in which judge and probation officer played "good guy and bad guy" in hearings are unlikely to occur now.

¹⁸ In fairness to the commission, it generally recommended strengthening services of
the juvenile court. However, its main contribution along this line was recommendations to strengthen the position of the probation officer, e.g., giving him exclusive right to initiate petitions.

4. *In Search of Juvenile Justice*—Gault *and Its*
Implementation *

NORMAN LEFSTEIN, VAUGHAN STAPLETON,
AND LEE TEITELBAUM

INTRODUCTION

ON MAY 15, 1967, THE U.S. Supreme Court rendered, in *In re Gault,* its first
decision in the area of juvenile delinquency procedure. Commentators have
repeatedly construed the rulings in *Gault* as requiring juvenile courts to adopt
new and more liberal practices. The privilege against self-incrimination, and
the rights to notice of charges, counsel, confrontation, and cross-examination
were heretofore primarily regarded as the cornerstones of an adversary system
of justice. The extension of these rights to juvenile courts would have seemed
to require an overnight transformation of the court procedures.

This article examines the response of three urban juvenile courts—referred
to as Metro, Gotham and Zenith—to the *Gault* decision. The data presented
here—drawn from numerous observations of court hearings—provide some
indication of the extent of the changes in juvenile proceedings. Particular attention is paid to what the Supreme Court seems to have required in *Gault,*
to what juvenile courts should now be expected to do under that decision,
and to what was actually done in the observed courts. This study also provides insight into the problems encountered in the implementation of *Gault,*
as well as a commentary on the structure of the juvenile hearing process. . . .

In Zenith, the dearth of cases falling within our sample (youths without

* From Norman Lefstein, Vaughan Stapleton, and Lee Teitelbaum, "In Search of
Juvenile Justice—*Gault* and Its Implications," *Law and Social Review,* Vol. 3, No.
4 (May, 1969), pp. 491–537. Reprinted by permission of the authors.

AUTHORS' NOTE: The material for this article was gathered during a research and
demonstration project made possible by a Ford Foundation grant to the National
Council of Juvenile Court Judges. The opportunity to complete this article was
made possible through the Russell Sage Program in Law and Social Science at the
Yale Law School. Until the project's termination in the summer of 1968, Norman
Lefstein and Vaughan Stapleton shared responsibility for administration. Lee Teitelbaum served as a staff attorney in one of the project cities.

We are indebted to Jack Hill, Karen L. Frederick and Helene Stoffey for their
assistance in the collection and analysis of field materials, and to the project's attorneys: Stephen Bing, Mark Gasarch, Marsha and William Meckler, Robert Shuker,
Alan Silverman, and Clarence Rogers.

lawyers) testifies to that city's unique position vis-à-vis traditional juvenile court practices, while in Gotham the changes in court rules created a non-comparable sample after their implementation. Ultimately, however, in order to determine the long-term impact of *Gault*, this study will have to be validated through replication over time.

Observer Interference

. . . It may be argued that an observer's presence causes judges to alter their behavior and interferes with the normal court procedure so that the report does not accurately reflect court proceedings that are unobserved. We concede that there may be some truth to this, and there is at last one instance where interference was documented.[1] In general, however, all three courts by the time of the *Gault* decision were reasonably accustomed to the presence of note-taking observers because, as mentioned earlier, field workers had been assigned to the courts since early 1966. But more importantly, to the extent that our observers did interfere, we claim the error is irrelevant for purposes of this study, in light of the fact that our data reveal widespread violations of *Gault*'s requirements. We submit that if judges know their words and actions are being recorded, they will attempt to speak and act in the manner most favorable to a positive image, and therefore the data contained in this study reflect juvenile courts at their best. There is no reason to suppose that judges consciously go out of their way to violate *Gault*'s requirements in the presence of note-taking observers.

RIGHT TO COUNSEL

In discussing the right to counsel, the Supreme Court in *Gault* commented:

A proceeding where the issue is whether the child will be found to be "delinquent" and subjected to the loss of his liberty for years is comparable in seriousness to a felony prosecution. The juvenile needs the assistance of counsel to cope with problems of law, to make skilled inquiry into the facts, to insist upon regularity of the proceedings, and to ascertain whether he has a defense and to prepare and submit it. *The child "requires the guiding hand of counsel at every step in the proceedings against him."* [2]

The court then directed its attention toward ensuring that this right, established in principle, would be meaningful in operation. Rejecting the view of some courts that even if a youth does have the right to counsel there is no requirement that he be so informed,[3] the majority opinion expressly required that the juvenile and his parent be told of the child's right, and further that they be instructed that if they could not afford an attorney, one would be appointed for them.[4] The opinion also imported to the juvenile courts the concept of waiver; henceforth, counsel could be withheld from the parties only if they validly waived their rights to a lawyer.

In the delinquency cases reported in this study, compliance with the right to counsel was determined from the initial court hearings where juveniles and their parents appeared without counsel. However, two of the courts sent to the accused's parents, in advance of the first hearing, a notice which included reference to the right of counsel. In Metro, a form entitled *Notice:*

Legal Rights and Privileges was delivered by a probation officer to the minor's parents, and the parents were asked to sign a return indicating their receipt of the notice. The part of the form relevant to the right to counsel reads as follows:

> You and/or your child have the right to be represented by a lawyer who will advise you as to the law and present your case in Court. If you wish to have a lawyer but are financially unable to employ one, we suggest that you contact the Legal Aid Defender's Office [giving address and phone number] or consult the yellow pages of the telephone book under "attorneys" for a listing of the Legal Aid Society Office nearest your home.

The Gotham juvenile court at the time of this study sent a summons by regular mail to the respondent and his parents containing the following information: "PARENTS, GUARDIAN or CUSTODIAN, of the juvenile and the juvenile _____, have the right to retain and be represented by counsel at every stage of the proceedings."

Neither notice complies satisfactorily with the right-to-counsel requirement imposed by *Gault*.[5] The first carefully avoids mentioning the court's duty to appoint a lawyer for the minor, if for financial reasons one cannot be retained; the latter simply makes no mention at all of that duty. But even if the notices were complete, it is doubtful that the court's responsibility to inform the parents and juvenile of the right to counsel would be reduced. In federal criminal cases, the judge bears the responsibility of ascertaining that the defendant in fact knows of, and adequately understands, this right.

> When a defendant appears before the court without counsel, we think, as a minimum, the court, in order to discharge its duty, must advise the defendant of the seriousness of the charge, that the Constitution of the United States guarantees him the right to have the assistance of counsel for his defense, and that if he is unable to employ counsel, it is the duty of the court to appoint, and the court will appoint, counsel for him. Ordinarily, only by such an inquiry can the court be sure that the defendant understands his constitutional right. . . .[6]

While it may be argued that the states are not bound to exercise all the precautions of federal criminal practice,[7] it would seem clear that the accused juvenile must be offered the right to counsel before it can be said that he has knowingly and intelligently waived it,[8] and that every presumption against such waiver must be indulged.[9] Similarly, it would seem that juvenile courts must insure that the minor and parents knew of their right to counsel, and that they understood its significance.[10] Indeed, particular care is necessary in cases involving minors in order to be assured that the youth knows he is entitled to a lawyer; in criminal prosecutions involving juveniles, it has frequently been held that the trial judge must so inform the defendant, or a subsequent waiver is invalid.[11] Since minors in delinquency proceedings are almost always younger than those prosecuted criminally, the need for a careful appraisal of rights is, if anything, more pronounced. Further support for this proposition may be found where, as in most delinquency cases, the respondent and his parents are indigent. Reliance upon written notification presupposes that the recipient can read and understand the notice, that he does so if he can, and that, if it is the parent who is given notice, the parent conveys the information in an intelligible manner to the child. These assumptions, when applied to the population typically appearing before juvenile courts, are most dubious.

Degree of Compliance

"Full advice" has been used to describe those cases where the respondent and his parents were fully informed of the child's right to retained or appointed counsel. The following colloquy from a case in Zenith illustrates full advice:

> The judge, "You understand this is a serious charge, don't you?" "Yes." [This is response by father.] Now speaking to both the father and the boy, he continued, "I want you to know that you have the right to a private attorney, I'll appoint a public defender for you."

This case may be taken as an exemplar: the advice of rights is directed to both the parent and the youth, and it is made clear that the judge will appoint an attorney if the respondent is indigent. Although every warning should be as straightforward and complete as this one, instances where compliance was not so satisfactory have been treated as "full" for the purposes of this article. For example, it is certainly not sufficient to tell only the parent that he has a right to counsel; the right to be informed runs equally to the child. Thus, if the judge specifically addresses only the parent in rendering advice of counsel, the requirements of *Gault* have not fully been met. On the other hand, if full advice was given and no person singled out, full compliance was assumed, even though only the parent responded and even though it was unclear that the child comprehended in any real sense that the right was *his*.

The judge also must clearly state that the respondent and his parent not only have the right to retained counsel, but that if they cannot afford an attorney, one will be appointed for them. If the court does not state that counsel will be appointed but merely says that a legal aid lawyer is available, the effect may not be the same. If appointment is made, the attorney is generally under an obligation to appear and either provide representation or satisfy the court that he cannot.[12] If the latter occurs, the court will be bound to appoint a substitute for him, and the defendant is assured of representation. Further, some legal aid offices require a registration fee, and in the absence of outright appointment the respondent or his parents may be required to absorb that expense or forego the legal services. Nevertheless, consistent with our practice of analyzing the data conservatively, a statement by the judge that a legal aid attorney was available has been treated as satisfying *Gault*'s requirements.

On the basis of the above categorization, Zenith was found to have the highest degree of compliance with *Gault*'s mandate. Of the eighteen youths in the sample of cases analyzed, 10 (or 56 per cent) were fully advised of the right to counsel. In Metro, the extent of compliance was substantially less. Only two youths of a sample of seventy-one (3 per cent) were fully advised of the right to representation. Gotham was the least diligent in complying with *Gault*'s requirements. In not one case among fifty-nine were the parents and minor adequately advised of their right to counsel. One of two things happened: Either no mention at all was made of the right to counsel or there was "partial advice" of the right, meaning that necessary elements of the warning were omitted. A case from Metro in which the judge asked: "Mrs. C——, did you know that you have a right to have a lawyer?" illustrates what we have termed "partial advice." The warning, phrased in the form of a question, was directed solely and explicitly to the parent, and the judge failed to state that the boy and his parent were entitled to appointed counsel if they were indigent.[13] A breakdown of the degree of compliance with the right to counsel for all three cities is shown in Table 1.

TABLE 1. COMPLIANCE WITH THE RIGHT-TO-COUNSEL REQUIREMENT

Type of Compliance	Gotham		Metro		Zenith	
	N*	%	N	%	N	%
Full advice	(0)	0	(2)	3	(10)	56
Partial advice	(9)	15	(46)	65	(7)	38
No advice	(50)	85	(23)	32	(1)	6
Total Number of Youths	(59)		(71)		(18)	

* N = number of youths.

Thus, a greater attempt at compliance was made in Zenith and Metro than in Gotham. Only one case was found in Zenith where a hearing was held without any mention of the right to counsel, and in Metro, at least some form of advice was given, albeit incompletely, in more than two thirds of the cases. Gotham, in contrast, emerged as the most resistant to the newly imposed constitutional requirements.

The failure of the courts in Metro and Gotham to comply with the right to counsel requirements cannot be dismissed as a technical matter. In one third of the sample cases in Metro, and in 85 per cent of the Gotham cases, the error cannot be ascribed to faulty terminology nor even to imperfect comprehension of the rules set out in *Gault;* neither the parent nor the child was informed in any fashion by the courts of the right to retained or appointed counsel. Even in those instances where partial but inadequate advice was rendered, the omission cannot be considered insignificant. Failure to inform the child of the right, or to state that a "free lawyer" is available as a matter of right, is a most critical omission.[14]

Prejudicial Advice

Heretofore, we have been concerned with the relevant legal content of the communication regarding the right to counsel. Successful communication of a message from one person to another depends on many factors other than content of the message itself. Verbal and nonverbal cues may transform a statement's meaning into something altogether different from the actual words used. In considering the extent of meaningful as well as literal compliance with *Gault,* the manner of communication is highly relevant.

Advice of the right to counsel may be rendered in such a way as to encourage the exercise of that right. When the judge says (as he did in a Zenith case), "Larry, I'd like to advise you that you are entitled to a lawyer and I'll be happy to appoint a free lawyer for you if you have no money," it may be supposed that any trepidation on the part of the youth or his parent concerning exercise of the right does not derive from the court.

The advice may be essentially neutral in quality. Consider this Zenith case:

The judge continued that the law obliges him to tell them that they have a

privilege of engaging an attorney. If they wish to get an attorney, the proceedings would be continued for them to do so. If they didn't have sufficient
funds, he would appoint one.

Conversely, the advice may be given in such a manner as to discourage
exercise of the right to counsel. Perhaps the most common is "a question so
framed, or uttered with such emphasis, or accompanied by such non-verbal
conduct of the questioner as to suggest the desired answer." [15] The following
excerpt from a Zenith case is illustrative:

> After the judge informed the boys and their mothers of the charges against
> them, he continued very rapidly, "At this time, I'd like to inform you that
> you have a right to have an attorney. If you cannot afford an attorney, I'll
> appoint an attorney for you. Or, on the other hand, if you'd like, we can
> have the case heard today."
> The woman said something and the judge said, "I can't hear you."
> Then the woman said that she would like to have it heard today.
> The judge said, "Let the record show that Mrs. G_____, the mother
> of A_____, waives the right to an attorney."

It is arguable here that the judge is merely performing his duty to inform
the respondent of all possible courses of action open to her. Nevertheless,
the effect of a rapid delivery plus the judge's invitation that "we can have
the case heard today," suggesting that proceeding without a lawyer will
expedite matters and that the case can competently be placed in his hands,
tend to preclude a positive consideration of the right to counsel.

By failing to respond to the misapprehensions and questions of parties,
judges may effectively discourage the use of counsel. Consider the following
case from Metro:

> The judge begins by saying, "Mrs. C_____, did you know that you have
> a right to have a lawyer?"
> She replied that she "didn't know." She paused, then she said, "Well,
> Mr. _____ [the probation officer] said that it was up to me, and I said
> that I didn't have any money."
> The judge said, "Well, one thing you have here is all kinds of lawyers."
> He said that they could get some at the Legal Aid Society.
> The mother replied, "Well, I have one, but he's so expensive."
> And the judge left it at this, and they went ahead and heard the case.

In this case the judge's failure to inform the respondent that the court
would appoint an attorney if she could not afford one, taken with his
failure to respond to her oblique reference of an inability to pay, militated
against exercise of that right.

In Metro the judges consistently assumed that the written notice of right to
counsel delivered before the hearing fully satisfied *Gault*. Communication between judge and respondent during the court hearing reflected an assumption
by the judge that the parents and child had read the notice, understood their
rights, and were waiving these rights by appearing at the hearing without
an attorney. The following is a simple illustration of this:

> Addressing himself to the mother the judge states, "I take it that you came
> without a lawyer because you think you didn't need it."
> Mrs. H_____ replies, "Right."

The effect of this formulation is to discourage further and positive consideration of the right to an attorney, and the statement's directive quality is strengthened by the judge's status vis-à-vis those appearing before him.[16]

Still another case from Metro embodies a different type of prejudice. The judge not only failed to inform the respondents that a free attorney could be appointed but was obviously unwilling to continue the case for such an appointment.

> The judge begins by saying, "We sent a notice out to you which stated that you can get a lawyer, and furthermore that if you can't afford one that we would get you one."
> The father stands up and says in broken phrases, "Well we—I can't afford . . ."
> The judge breaks him off and says, "That's no objection, we're able to get you one, but you've decided not to have one. Right?"
> The father replies, "Yes."

A case from Gotham presents a classic example of a judge leading the respondent to the position desired by the court. Before the case began, a bailiff entered the court and told the judge that Mr. *X*, a legal aid attorney, had been assigned to the case, but no one from the legal aid office had appeared. A private attorney, Mr. G————, learned that the court might hear the case without counsel, and asked the bailiff to request an adjournment until such time as the legal aid attorney could be present. The following material is from our field notes:

> The judge, "I will not adjourn it."
> The bailiff, "Your honor, G———— is not the attorney."
> The judge, "He needn't come in. We have proof of the matter?"
> The police officer, "Yes."
> The father and the boy entered the courtroom. The bailiff told them to be seated.
> The judge said, "Tell me about this charge."
> The police officer said that the youth before him was ————.
> He was 17 years of age. There were two complaints against the boy, one was illegal possession of marijuana, the other was illegal use of marijuana.
> The judge said, "What are the two charges?"
> The police officer answered, "Possession and unlawful use."
> The judge turned to the boy and his father, "Are you the boy's father?"
> The father said, "Yes. Can I say something? We were supposed to have an attorney here, but he's not here."
> The judge said, "Did you get notice of the hearing today?"
> The father said he didn't, but I don't think he understood the word notice, and so the boy explained it to him. And then he said he did.
> The judge, "When did you get notice?"
> The father said, "Some time ago. Our attorney was supposed to be here, but he didn't show up."
> The judge then read off the new notice which says that they're entitled to have an attorney, Mr. *X*, etc.
> The man said yes he knew about that, and he said, "I talked with Mr. *X* Monday, but there's been a mix-up." He went on to explain that there was supposed to have been someone here today. It sounded as if he had not discussed in detail the content of the case, but he had actually contacted him on Monday.
> The judge said, "The important thing is whether the boy had possession of narcotics or not."

The father said that the boy stated that he did not have it, and he got scared when he was brought into the police station and then said it.

The judge said, "I'm going to hear testimony. If Mr. X's office wants to take the blame, O.K. Swear them in. . . ." [Testimony concerning the charges was then heard by the judge.] After hearing some of the evidence during which time the boy denied that he had smoked marijuana, the judge turned to the father and said, "Now sir, I'm prepared today to place this boy on probation and let him go home. If you want to come back here next week and have this detective. . . ." He continued on to say that if he wanted to come back here and say the same thing over while the father had an attorney he may do so. The judge then said that he didn't know what he would do next week, however. [After some more conversation, the judge said], "We can go through the mechanics of the court and have cross-examination and all the rest, but this court's interest is what is best for the boy. . . . I think what I'm trying to do is save everybody's time."

The father then said that probation would be all right. The judge stated that he could sign the waiver. The father said that he wondered if the boy went on probation could he leave town. He said he had been planning on going to see his grandfather.

The probation officer present spoke up and said that this would present no problems. The judge agreed, and he stated that otherwise, we'll make a federal case out of this. And if we bring the boy back with an attorney, well, after an hour, I'll still have to make a decision and it's probably not going to be so different from what I make here. Then he went on to explain that he wanted the father to understand that the boy should sign a waiver which would save him from a criminal record and from going into an adult court since this was a criminal offense. The boy went over to the table and signed it, apparently without question, and then the father was asked to come over to the table.

The foregoing case illustrates fully the coercive power of suggestion. Obviously the judge thought the case sustainable on the evidence presented by the detective and did not wish to be bothered by an attorney. The field notes also indicate that the judge had knowledge of a social record on the juvenile, which revealed that the youth had previously been before the court on a narcotics charge, but had not been adjudicated delinquent.[17]

Bureaucratic pressures may sometimes provide the impetus for biased communication. To avoid delay, a judge may fail to fully advise the child and his parents of their right to an attorney:

The probation officer stated, "Mrs. G——— mentioned the fact that she might want to have a lawyer."

The judge, "Well, we can't have them coming down here at the last minute." The judge then commented about how hard it is to get them down here.

The mother said something. The judge said, "Have you changed your mind?" The mother replied, "Yes."

Finally, the content of a message may be compromised by the manner in which it is delivered. When rights are communicated to respondents in a rapid fashion, allowing no time for an answer, the communication must be deemed prejudicial. In the following example (a case in Metro), the rapidity with which the information was given plus the obvious desire to hear the case without delay undoubtedly discouraged exercise of the rights mentioned:

Referee, "You have the right to be represented by an attorney and the right to cross-examine witnesses, and you do not have to say anything, either an admission or denial, if you don't want to. All right, officer, what is the situation?"

"Prejudicial advice" of the right to counsel was found almost uniformly where less than "full advice" of the right was rendered. Only three cases were observed where full advice was given in a manner deemed to be prejudicial, two in Zenith and one in Metro. A complete breakdown reflecting "prejudicial advice" together with "full," "partial," and "no advice," reveals the patterns in Table 2.

TABLE 2. COMPLIANCE WITH THE RIGHT-TO-COUNSEL REQUIREMENT *

Type of Compliance	Gotham		Metro		Zenith	
	N	%	N	%	N	%
Full advice	(0)	0	(1)	1	(8)	44
Full advice—also prejudicial	(0)	0	(1)	1	(2)	11
Partial advice	(7)	12	(15)	21	(6)	33
Partial advice—also prejudicial	(2)	3	(31)	44	(1)	6
No advice	(50)	85	(23)	32	(1)	6
Total Number of Youths	(59)	—	(71)	—	(18)	—

* Percents may not add to 100 due to rounding.

PRIVILEGE AGAINST SELF-INCRIMINATION

The privilege against self-incrimination was largely unrecognized in delinquency proceedings before the Supreme Court's decision in *Gault*.[18] Even those courts and authorities that held that the privilege was in some way appropiate in juvenile court hearings felt it unnecessary or even inadvisable to inform the minor of this right.[19] In *Gault*, the Supreme Court rejected the argument that the youth and his parent should not be advised of the right to silence,[20] and held that: "The constitutional privilege against self-incrimination is applicable in the case of juveniles as it is with respect to adults." [21]

In criminal prosecutions, the defendant is exempt from answering all questions, since each may be incriminating.[22] While in principle the prosecution could call the defendant to the stand to determine whether he chose to exercise his right of refusing to answer any questions, no court has approved this practice.[23] Even the calling of a codefendant in a criminal case, without his having made a valid waiver, is a violation of the defendant's privilege.[24] Furthermore, the prosecutor is barred from commenting upon the accused's failure to testify, and no inference may properly be drawn from such failure.[25]

Now that *Gault* has extended the privilege against self-incrimination to delinquency proceedings, it seems clear that an uncounseled juvenile must be informed that he need not say anything before a single question is asked and, if he does testify, a valid waiver of the privilege must have been made. In *Johnson v. Zerbst*,[26] the Supreme Court established that every reasonable presumption against waiver of basic constitutional rights must be indulged.

Relying upon the *Johnson* case, a federal court of appeals has held that: "Waiver of the privilege [against self-incrimination] must be informed and intelligent. There can be no waiver if the defendants do not know their rights. The rule must be the same, we think, when the record is silent or inconclusive concerning knowledge." [27] In *Miranda* v. *Arizona*,[28] invoking the *Johnson* decision and *Carnley* v. *Cochran*,[29] the Supreme Court held that waiver of the privilege against self-incrimination during in-custody interrogation, in the absence of an attorney, cannot be presumed from a silent record.

State courts have come to much the same conclusion. In *People* v. *Chlebowy*,[30] an unrepresented defendant was asked by the court if he wished to take the stand at the conclusion of the prosecution's case. He said that he did, and was thereupon sworn and examined by the judge. The reviewing court reversed, holding that the trial judge was required to inform the accused that he did not have to testify, that no inference could be drawn from his failure to testify, and that what he said could be used against him:

> When a defendant goes to trial upon a charge of a criminal nature without the benefit of counsel, it is the duty of the court to be alert to protect the defendant's rights. Good practice requires that any suggestion by the court that the defendant take the stand be coupled with advice as to his privilege against self-incrimination. The defendant may not be called to the stand in a criminal case unless he waives his privilege. He cannot be charged with a waiver of the privilege unless it appears that he was aware of its existence and its surrounding safeguards and voluntarily and intelligently elected to refrain from asserting it.[31]

Surely these rules applied to protect adults are even more appropriate when a juvenile is involved.

In this study, advice of the privilege against self-incrimination was considered relevant in all cases in our final sample, except those continued for a lawyer or witness, or dismissed without a hearing. It may appear that this approach fails to take into account the effect of a respondent's guilty plea which, in criminal prosecutions, is usually said to waive the privilege against self-incrimination. When an uncounseled defendant in a criminal case enters a guilty plea, attack on an ensuing conviction normally is directed to the validity of the plea itself, or to the competency of the waiver of counsel pursuant to which the plea was accepted. The issue of self-incrimination does not arise, since the guilty plea is not considered testimonial in nature and, once entered, it is deemed to waive the privilege. However, in many juvenile courts, certainly in Gotham and Metro, we are persuaded that the relevancy of the privilege against self-incrimination should not be related to whether the respondent admits the offense. The informality in these courts all too often leads to a blurring of procedural lines. It is often unclear whether the juvenile admits or denies the offense, and occasionally he is never even asked. Sometimes when a youth is asked to state his position, the judge has already heard the evidence against him. In criminal cases, by contrast, the plea-taking process occurs at a separate arraignment hearing; if a defendant subsequently wishes to plead guilty and withdraw a not-guilty plea entered at arraignment, the record provides a clear statement of what has happened.

Although the procedure in Zenith provided that a definite plea be taken before the adjudication hearing, no such hearing existed in either Metro or Gotham. Thus no plea was taken in the usual sense in these two cities, but during the proceedings the youth usually was asked whether he committed the alleged act, or if he had anything to say. While sometimes there was an "admission" by the respondent, it was not a guilty plea, but a self-incriminatory statement in the testimonial sense. Therefore these admissions have been seen to pose self-incrimination issues. Similarly, in *Gault,* the alleged admissions by the respondent to the juvenile court judge were viewed as self-incriminatory statements.[32] *In re Butterfield,*[33] a recent decision of a California appellate court, provides a further illustration. After the respondent and her mother were advised of and purportedly waived the right to counsel, the charges were read. At this point, there was the following dialogue:

> MR. PALMA [Deputy Probation Officer]: Now, Rachelle, did you understand the petition that was read?
> THE MINOR: Yes.
> MR. PALMA: Are these allegations true?
> THE MINOR: Yes.
> MR. PALMA: Will you explain to the Court what happened at the time?
> THE MINOR: I just got suspended from school, and my aunt came and picked me up and she said that she thought she was going to put me back in Juvenile Hall and I just—she left the house and I got in the cabinet and took some medication.
> MR. PALMA: What was your reason for taking the medication, Rachelle?
> THE MINOR: I didn't want to go back to Juvenile Hall.
> MR. PALMA: All right. . . .[34]

The reviewing court, in reversing the adjudication, analyzed the case as follows:

> No evidence other than the minor's admission was received. The adjudication was one of "delinquency" because it found her guilty of disobedience to a court order and committed her to confinement in a correctional institution. It was used "against" her in the sense that it formed the entire evidentiary basis for the judgment. *The statement was self-incriminating. She had no prior warning and there is no evidence that she had any awareness of her right to refrain from self-incrimination. Evidentiary use of her self-incriminating statement without that awareness infected the hearing with a violation of due process.*[35]

Degree of Compliance

Full advice of the privilege against self-incrimination requires that the minor be informed that he need not answer any questions before any questions are in fact put to him. We did not assume in our analysis that the judge was bound to advise the respondent that no inference would be drawn from his failure to speak, although this is arguably required by *Gault.* The Supreme Court stated the issue as: "whether . . . an admission by the juvenile may be used against him in the absence of clear and unequivocal evidence that the admission was *made with knowledge that he* was not obliged to speak and *would not be penalized for remaining silent.*"[36] The import of the Court's language seems to be that unless a youth has been so informed, any statement he may make is improperly obtained.[37] Had this criterion been used there would not have been any case in the three cities where the privilege was fully implemented.

In Zenith, the relevant sample for purposes of the privilege against self-incrimination contained only six cases, due to the large number continued for an attorney. In two of these the youths were fully advised of the privilege. The remaining four juveniles were not advised at all, and all entered admissions. Since Zenith employs a formal plea-taking procedure, it can forcefully be argued that the requirements of the privilege did not apply in these cases.

TABLE 3. COMPLIANCE WITH THE PRIVILEGE-AGAINST-SELF-INCRIMINATION REQUIREMENT

Type of Compliance	Gotham		Metro		Zenith	
	N	%	N	%	N	%
Full advice	(0)	0	(18)	29	(2)	33
No advice	(53)	100	(44)	71	(4)	67
Total Number of Youths	(53)		(62)		(6)	

In Metro, of a relevant sample of sixty-two cases, eighteen respondents (29 per cent) were advised of the right to remain silent. In forty-four cases (71 per cent), the privilege was never mentioned. In Gotham, the sample contained fifty-three relevant cases, and in not one of these was mention made of the privilege against self-incrimination. As explained previously, in neither Metro nor Gotham was an admission by the juvenile considered a waiver of the privilege.

Prejudicial Advice

We found that advice of the privilege invariably was communicated in a prejudicial manner in Metro. Frequently the warning was transmitted very quickly, and the proceeding continued without further reference to the privilege. Both the speed with which the information was communicated and the abrupt change of subject, without waiting for an answer, clearly tended to discourage exercise of the privilege. In one hearing a judge informed eight boys involved in a single offense of their privilege not to testify in the following way:

> Initially, the judge made comments to the effect that all boys were involved in the arson, although some may have taken part in different ways. After these statements, the judge stated, "Now, none of you have to answer anything. You don't have to say anything. I'll start with A_____." The judge asks A_____ if he was involved saying, "A_____?" And A_____ says, "Yes."

The judge then received admissions or denials from all eight boys without first ascertaining whether any of the youths actually wanted to invoke the privilege. Subsequently all of the boys testified. The privilege against self-incrimination was particularly relevant in this case because there was no presentation of evidence, with the exception of extrajudicial confessions made to police officers by five of the boys. Three of the boys during the hearing repudiated their confessions and denied involvement, but all were adjudicated delinquent.

Advice of the privilege also was classified as prejudicial when the judge, after giving the warning, immediately invited the respondent to forego his right of silence. Consider these examples from Metro:

> The judge first asked the boy if it was true that he stole the merchandise in question from the company. After receiving a response from the boy which is unclear [although the statement of the child was unclear, the judge treated the case as a denial], the judge stated, after a detective from the department store was sworn in, "B———, you don't have to tell us anything unless you want to, but you can tell us if you want to."

*   *   *

> The judge says, "All right, B———, you don't have to say a word here, but you may do so if you wish. Swear them in. You can talk or be quiet."

The court's conduct here cannot be considered neutral. By swearing the respondent, the uniform rule in criminal cases that a defendant has a right not to be called or sworn as part of his privilege is breached.[38] In addition, an explicit invitation to testify may make it difficult for some juveniles to decline. During a coroner's inquest in a South Dakota case,[39] the state's attorney observed that the eighteen-year-old defendant was present, but stated that he would not call him to testify. The coroner then said: "Did you hear what the state's attorney said, Mr. Halvorsen? He's not going to call on you to testify. You have the right if you so wish on your own behalf to come up and be sworn and testify." [40] The Supreme Court of South Dakota held that the information given was insufficient, and further that: "After . . . it was announced that he would not be called, but had a right to come forward and testify in his own behalf, he was not free to exercise an uncoerced volition." [41] The status of the juvenile court judge, as perceived by those appearing before him, may be expected to strengthen the impact of the invitation to testify, thereby weakening or entirely negating any previous statement of the right.

While there were no youths in Gotham who were fully or even prejudicially advised of their right to remain silent, there was one case that demonstrated a unique and imaginative response to the privilege against self-incrimination requirement:

> The judge began, "Are you the boy's mother?"
> "Yes."
> "Have you talked with the boy about this?"
> "Yes."
> "Does he admit it?"
> "Yes."

By asking the boy's mother if the child had admitted his involvement, the judge circumvented the self-incrimination issue. Subsequently, the youth testified, denied his guilt, but was adjudicated delinquent.

Table 4 reveals patterns of compliance for the following three categories: full advice of the privilege, full advice—also prejudicial, and no advice.

In Metro, consideration of literal compliance with the requirement, (i.e, whether the privilege was mentioned to the respondent) revealed that in seventeen cases (27 per cent) the privilege was accorded.[42] However, when an analysis is made of the manner and meaningfulness of the communication,

TABLE 4. COMPLIANCE WITH THE PRIVILEGE-AGAINST-SELF-INCRIMINATION REQUIREMENT

Type of Compliance	Gotham		Metro		Zenith
	N	%	N	%	N
Full advice	(0)	0	(1)	2	(2)
Full advice—also prejudicial	(0)	0	(17)	27	(0)
No advice	(53)	100	(44)	71	(4)
Total Number of Youths	(53)		(62)		(6)

the instances of full nonprejudicial compliance with the privilege are reduced to one case (2 per cent).

RIGHT OF CONFRONTATION

In *Gault*, the only evidence against the respondent, except for an invalid admission, was a probation officer's second-hand account of the respondent's conversation with the complaining witness. The complainant, a woman, allegedly told the probation officer that Gerald Gault had spoken obscene words to her over the telephone, but she failed to testify in court, and the trial judge explicitly stated that her presence was unnecessary.[43] Noting its recent extension of the Sixth Amendment Confrontation Clause to state criminal prosecutions,[44] the Supreme Court held: "Absent a valid confession adequate to support the determination of the Juvenile Court, confrontation and sworn testimony by witnesses available for cross examination were essential for a finding of 'delinquency.' . . ."[45]

The Court's holding may be interpreted as differentiating between evidence that the juvenile court may receive and evidence upon which a constitutionally sufficient delinquency adjudication must be founded.[46] In any event, it is clear that a delinquency finding must, in light of *Gault*, satisfy normal standards of confrontation.

The principal objective of the right to confrontation is to secure an opportunity for the accused to cross-examine the witnesses against him.[47] To that extent, constitutional significance is accorded to the evidentiary rule against hearsay.[48] In criminal cases, failure of confrontation typically occurs where statements of a third party are related by a witness. The impropriety lies in receiving evidence not subject to cross-examination.

The informality of juvenile courts presents a situation rarely found in criminal prosecutions. In delinquency cases a necessary witness frequently does not appear, and no evidence is introduced in lieu of the anticipated testimony. In an auto theft case, for instance, the owner of the stolen car may not be present to testify that the vehicle is his and that it was taken without his authority. Instead, a police liaison officer or some other court official will read the charge at the beginning of the hearing, and the charge will include allegations of ownership and theft. While no testimony has been given, these allegations are nevertheless before the court, and their truth is frequently accepted. In criminal cases, the failure to produce a key witness would be treated as a failure to prove essential elements of the crime and result in dismissal. During this analysis, when we encountered similar failures in proof that were ignored by the juvenile courts, the confrontation was classified as inadequate.

The same standards of relevancy used to identify the privilege against self-incrimination cases were applied to determine cases in the right to confrontation category. Although a guilty plea excuses confrontation in criminal cases by making it unnecessary for the state to prove its case, for reasons noted in the discussion of the privilege against self-incrimination in Gotham and Metro, a juvenile's admission or denial was not considered decisive.

Degree of Compliance

Satisfactory implementation of the right to confrontation normally requires that every essential witness testify whenever there is not a guilty plea. Because formal pleas were never rendered in Metro and Gotham, it could be argued that all necessary witnesses should have testified in every hearing. However, we rejected this argument, principally because we wanted to know whether all necessary witnesses were *present*, not whether in fact they *testified*. The objective was to determine to what degree the action of juvenile court judge in *Gault*, when he stated that the complainant did not have to be present, was unusual, or whether it would occur even after the Supreme Court's decision. Moreover, it was not difficult to report accurately who was present during a hearing, but our observers sometimes did experience difficulty in reporting everyone who spoke and the complete substance of what they said. If, during an informal hearing with multiple parties, suddenly everyone spoke at once, the observer might have missed one or more "witness's testimony." With these concerns in mind, the following categories were formulated: "full confrontation"—all essential witnesses present in the courtroom regardless of whether they testified; "partial confrontation"—one or more of several essential witnesses present regardless of whether any testified; and "no confrontation"—no essential witnesses present. Table 5 shows the data analyzed according to these categories.

TABLE 5. COMPLIANCE WITH THE RIGHT-TO-CONFRONTATION REQUIREMENTS

Type of Compliance	Gotham		Metro		Zenith	
	N	%	N	%	N	%
Full confrontation	(20)	38	(14)	22	(3)	70
Partial confrontation	(16)	30	(42)	68	(0)	43
No confrontation	(17)	32	(6)	10	(4)	0
Total Number of Youths	(53)		(62)		(7)	57

In Zenith, of the seven cases deemed relevant for purposes of the right to confrontation, full opportunity for cross-examination of witnesses was found in three cases, and no confrontation in four. But in the four cases lacking confrontation, admissions to the offense were entered by the respondent, and, as noted previously, the plea-taking procedure is sufficiently formalized in Zenith to make it comparable with criminal cases. Indeed, the pattern in Zenith is normally what one expects in a formal prosecutorial system—full confrontation afforded when there is a denial and no confrontation if an admission is entered.

In Gotham, the right to confrontation was more frequently afforded the respondent than were the other requirements of *Gault*. In twenty of fifty-three cases (38 per cent), there was full confrontation; but in sixteen cases (30 per cent), only some of the necessary witnesses were present and available for cross-examination, and none were present in seventeen cases (32 per cent). In Metro, by contrast, the majority of cases, forty-two (68 per cent), fell into the "partial confrontation" category. Complete failure of confrontation was relatively rare, occurring in only six cases (10 per cent), and full confrontation was found in fourteen cases (22 per cent).

* * *

THE WAIVER CONCEPT

We have thus far ignored what is perhaps the most troublesome issue in implementing *Gault's* rulings—the proposition that minors and their parents can waive their newly guaranteed constitutional rights. Our study of *Gault's* implementation, however, has strengthened the credibility of the alternative proposition—that the concept of waiver of rights in juvenile delinquency proceedings is unrealistic. The Supreme Court in *Gault* assumed without discussion that the waiver doctrine could be imported to juvenile court hearings. Only with respect to the privilege against self-incrimination did the Court concede that "special problems" might be encountered because minors were involved.[49] We submit that these special problems are extremely serious, and that a review of the appropriateness of this doctrine for juvenile courts is necessary.

If, as the Court assumed, minors can relinquish the rights guaranteed by *Gault*, their action must be "knowing and intelligent,"[50] a standard implying a sophistication and capacity not usually associated with children. Following a waiver, the Court necessarily assumed that the rights relinquished would still be meaningful in operation. To the extent *Gault* sanctioned parental participation in the decisional process, the Court assumed a unity of interest between parent and child that is not only frequently absent, but the presence of which may be impossible to determine with any real confidence. The Court implicitly assumed that minors and their parents are capable of intelligent and objective waivers of their rights, despite the social factors present in juvenile court proceedings that militate against such results. Nor did the Court consider the minor's capacity in the light of established legal principles deemed applicable to minors. . . .

Parent-Child Relations and the Waiver Doctrine

In suggesting that the rights guaranteed by *Gault* were subject to waiver, at least in some circumstances, the Court appeared to place substantial reliance on the participation of the parents in the decision process. In holding that Mrs. Gault's knowledge that she could have appeared with counsel did not constitute a waiver of the right "which she and her juvenile son had," the majority seemed to indicate that had the Gaults been properly informed of the

right to retained or appointed counsel, Mrs. Gault could have effectively relinquished "their right." [51] With regard to the privilege against self-incrimination, the Court stated: "We appreciate that special problems may arise with
respect to waiver of the privilege *by or on behalf of* children, and that there
may well be some differences in technique—but not in principle—depending
upon the age of the child and the presence and competence of parents." [52]
The thrust of this statement appears to be that, where the respondent is ex-
tremly young, and it is evident that he cannot be found to make an "intelligent
and competent" waiver of the privilege, a parent may do so on his behalf, assuming the latter's relinquishment is "intelligent" under ordinary standards.
But such a rule cannot easily be dismissed as a matter of "technique" if, as the
Court maintains, the privilege applies to juveniles as it does to adults. The
privilege against self-incrimination, as all other privileges, is personal to the
claimant,[53] and ordinarily no person can claim the privilege for, or on behalf
of, another.[54] It may be argued, however, that the adult in this situation can be
thought to act, in a sense, as the youth's attorney, since the parent would not
be exercising the child's privilege for the benefit of another person.[55]

Placing reliance on parental participation in the exercise of these rights is
not only unusual (the very existence of this practice indicates, in a sense, the
difficulties in applying waiver in the juvenile court context) but fraught with
danger. In a substantial number of cases, the parent is himself the complaining witness, and probably hostile to the respondent's position. A case from
Zenith illustrates this problem. The minor was charged with the theft of $80
from his mother, who brought the charges. The mother stated that she did not
want the child at home. It further appeared that the mother was responsible
for keeping the child in detention pending adjudication and that she had refused the services of a lawyer for her son. The same situation arises in almost
all cases where the delinquency petition alleges "incorrigibility" or "runaway,"
since the parent is necessarily the complainant. It is obviously no guarantee
of the right to counsel, or of the other rights, to allow the parent to waive
these rights where his position is obviously antagonistic to the child's.[56]

It may be suggested that where there is what we have termed an "explicit
conflict" (i.e., the parent is the complaining witness), the court can adequately respond by appointing a guardian ad litem or counsel. Regardless
of whether this suggestion provides a desirable basis for deciding whether a
minor will enjoy the benefit of legal assistance, it does not satisfactorily
dispose of those cases where conflict is present, but the parent does not
happen to be the complaining witness. It frequently occurs that parents manifest hostility toward the child, and disapprobation of his conduct, generally
or particularly. This "implicit conflict" may take many forms. In a glue-
sniffing prosecution in Metro, the father volunteered that "the boy would
not tell him anything" and further stated that his wife had found "a bag in
the basement," thereby implying the use of glue in the home. In another
Metro case, the police officers present stated that they had enjoyed the cooperation of both parents, and further recalled that the father had previously
brought his son to the police "for discipline." Again, another mother complained to the probation officer (and repeated to the court) that the boy
continued to roam the street at night, and "was definitely out of her control."
All this is not to say that the parents somehow acted wrongly; but rather
that we cannot with great confidence entrust the child's legal rights to their

custody, since their expressed feelings are to some extent inimical to what may be the child's legal interest.

Table 6 indicates the extent of explicit and implicit conflict in the cases observed.

TABLE 6. INCIDENCE OF CONFLICT BETWEEN PARENTS AND CHILD

Type of Conflict	Gotham		Metro		Zenith	
	N	%	N	%	N	%
No apparent conflict	(40)	68	(54)	76	(16)	89
Implicit conflict	(9)	15	(9)	13	(0)	0
Explicit conflict	(10)	17	(8)	11	(2)	11
Total Number of Youths	59		71		18	

It appears that in approximately 10 per cent of the cases in Zenith, one fourth of those in Metro, and one third of those in Gotham, significant hostility was expressed by the parent concerning the minor respondent. In 17 per cent of those in Gotham and in 11 per cent in Metro and Zenith, the parent was at the same time the complaining witness. It will be appreciated that these are rough measures indicating only evident conflict; that is, conflict manifested during the proceeding itself. As such, they may be taken as understating, if anything, the extent of such conflict. In addition, there are many instances in which the parent may be largely disinterested or apathetic toward the proceedings, or where he feels embarrassed or inconvenienced by the necessity of appearing at court. If the parent is so affected, he may wish to get the ordeal over with as quickly as possible in order to get home to other children, or back to work, or to avoid further expenses which he can ill afford, or to avoid further embarrassment. He may find further justification for his actions in the belief that his child would not be before the court if he had not done *something* wrong, and in a concomitant disinclination to "uphold" the child's wrongdoing, whatever it may be. In these situations, the parent's concern, while understandable and indeed not blameworthy from his point of view, obviously does nothing to ensure that the respondent makes an intelligent and informed decision as to either his plea or his conduct of the case generally.

This conflict, even where manifest, typically does not become evident until the adjudication has progressed to some extent. Witnesses may have been heard, and the opportunity for cross-examination lost. If the problem is to be cured by appointment of counsel when conflict becomes evident, a new trial will be required in almost all cases, greatly increasing the expenditure of time and resources. Moreover, it should be recognized that this solution is available only where the conflict becomes apparent to the court; otherwise, the court simply must assume that the parent is devoted to the protection of his child's rights and interests—a position that cannot be taken with great confidence.

Even where the parent is inclined to support the child, the "competence" required on the part of adult to waive his right is very different from the "competence" of an attorney. It is not assumed that the average, or even the educated, intelligent layman can effectively plead and try his own cause; indeed, the contrary has expressly been stated in Supreme Court decisions.[57] Competence in the former sense generally means only that the adult is of adequate or normal intelligence and apparently suffers from no gross mental disorder. The latter, of course, implies far more knowledge and experience of the specialized sort involved in legal proceedings. While it may be acceptable to say that the first will suffice as a basis for allowing the adult to accept the risk of conducting his defense, it by no means necessarily follows that this standard can meaningfully be transferred to his waiver of the rights of others. . . .

CONCLUSION

The present movement toward procedural due process in juvenile court hearings did not begin with the *Gault* decision. Prior to May 15, 1967, several populous states revamped their juvenile codes and included greater legal protections for children.[58] During the past decade representation of the poor by legal aid and legal service program members has been increasingly extended to juvenile delinquency cases. Even before the *Gault* decision there was a marked increase in the number of state court appellate decisions dealing with delinquency procedures.

These observations, however, should not overshadow the revolutionary dimensions of the *Gault* decision. The privilege against self-incrimination (the lever by which the adversary-minded lawyer can silence his young client and put the state to its proof) was almost totally unrecognized. While a few courts frequently appointed lawyers as a matter of practice, and several states had statutes that required the appointment of counsel upon request, the requirement that counsel be appointed in the absence of a legally valid waiver was virtually unknown. While rights to cross-examination, confrontation, and sworn testimony were generally acknowledged before *Gault*, their faithful implementation, as the data in this study suggest, very likely depended upon the presence of an attorney.

If there is one central conclusion which emerges from our study, it is that total compliance with the word and spirit of the pronouncements in *Gault* will come gradually. Our data, of course, are taken from juvenile courts in only three cities, and in these courts, as well as in juvenile courts throughout the country, the process of change, begun before the *Gault* decision, is continuing. Indeed, *Gault* appears to have greatly accelerated the trends towards legislative reform and increased legal representation.[59] In the three courts discussed in this study, for example, we excluded observation of numerous cases involving attorneys. While there are no statistics available, we doubt that before *Gault* we would have seen as many cases with counsel present. But having acknowledge all of this, the fact remains that in the Metro and Gotham juvenile courts—and in courts like Metro and Gotham—children are frequently and sometimes flagrantly denied their constitutional rights.[60] Moreover, if we are correct in the belief that resistance to change is related to deep-seated adherence to *parens patriae* concepts, nurtured over long years of service on the juvenile bench,[61] then the changing of judges from their present ways may be painfully slow. In many courts the need undoubtedly is for new juvenile court judges, less oriented to a traditional juvenile court philosophy and more disposed to a "legalistic" approach in their courtroom procedure.

The problem of achieving compliance with changes in the law is not peculiar to the implementation of *Gault*. Recent studies concerned with the impact of *Miranda* v. *Arizona* [62] have demonstrated that overnight compliance with Supreme Court decisions is not always the rule.[63] A study of the impact of legislative changes on California juvenile courts concluded that "compliance has been partial and inconsistent." [64] In short, depending upon the content of the new rule and the degree of commitment to the old, we have come to expect a lack of conformity between institutional practices and new legal norms.

It is in this context that we speculate on what would have happened had the Supreme Court in *Gault*, recognizing that a child cannot intelligently waive his rights, made the requirement of counsel in delinquency cases non-waivable. As the Supreme Court surely realized, this would have precipitated a crisis of grave proportions. In most jurisdictions there simply would not have been sufficient lawyers available for appointment. Ironically, the situation probably would have been badly exacerbated because the judges would have found it virtually impossible to circumvent the counsel requirement.

But what was true in 1967 need not necessarily be true in the future. The time may soon come when the recommendation of the President's Crime Commission, that "counsel should be appointed as a matter of course whenever coercive action is a possibility, without requiring any affirmative choice by child or parent," [65] may be capable of implementation. As legal representation in juvenile courts increases, and as judges, lawyers, and probation officers become more familiar with each other's roles, the way will be smoothed for altering the concept that a child can validly relinquish all of his rights, including the right to legal representation. While it may only be premature speculation, we predict that in the not too distant future, either as a result of legislative changes or court decisions, juveniles will not be permitted to waive their right to an attorney. Other constitutional rights, such as the privilege against self-incrimination, confrontation, and cross-examination, will be validly relinquished only upon legal advice. Through these—perhaps only through these rules—will the objectives of *In re Gault* be realized.

NOTES

[1] In Metro, following a case that had been continued for the appointment of an attorney, the probation officer assigned to the case approached the observer and stated: "You're a real doll. You just messed up my case." He said that because I [the observer] was in there, "he [the judge] really bawled me out." I [observer] said, "You think so?" and he [probation officer] said, "Yea. He would have heard it." And I said, "Well, why didn't he have them waive it then?" And he said, "Well, he could have done that. . . . but he gave me a hard time and it's all because of you. Thanks a lot, doll." [Observer speaking:] This probation officer carries on that way. It's obvious that my presence is an interference with the on-going way of handling things.

[2] 387 U.S. 1, 36 (emphasis added).

[3] See Note, *Juvenile Delinquents: The Police, State Courts, and Individualized Justice*, 79 HARV. L. REV. 775, 797 (1966).

[4] 387 U.S. 1, 41.

[5] Nor did the notices in these two cities or in Zenith satisfy *Gault's* requirement that the parent and the child be served written, timely, and specific notice of the charges. 387 U.S., at 32–33. In Metro, a written notice was served with a

copy of the petition attached, but it was not directed to the child as the Supreme Court in *Gault* required. Although in Gotham both parent and child were afforded written and timely notice, the charge frequently was indicated only by the initials of the offense. For example, the offense of "deportment endangering health and general welfare" appeared in notices as "Juvenile Delinquency: DEHGW." Moreover, even when the offense could be deciphered, a specific factual description of the conduct was still missing. See *In re Wylie*, 231 A. 2d 81 (D.C. Ct. App. 1967); N. Dorsen and D. Rezneck, *In re Gault and the Future of Juvenile Law*, 1 FAM. L. Q. 1, 14 (Dec. 1967). In Zenith, written notice of the charge was not sent to the youth or his parents. Instead, the parties were informed verbally of the date and time of their first scheduled court hearing, and when a parent appeared a bailiff thrust into his hand a printed form to sign, which purposed to waive service of process. The substance of the form was rarely—if ever—explained, and the consequences of waiver never discussed. The child typically was not asked to sign the waiver form. Only after the parent had signed was a copy of the petition containing the charge given to the parent or child. Clearly this procedure did not constitute timely fulfillment of *Gault's* notice of charges requirement. Nor did the purported waiver of service by the parent appear to have been "knowing and intelligent." See Carnly v. Cochran, 369 U.S. 506 (1962); Johnson v. Zerbst, 304 U.S. 458 (1938). The procedure also failed to circumvent a statutory requirement that summons and a copy of the petition be served on the parties at least three days before the first court hearing.

[6] Cherrie v. United States, 179 F. 2d 94, 96 (10th Cir. 1949). See W. Thompson, *The Judge's Responsibility on a Plea of Guilty*, 62 W. VA. L. REV. 213, 216 (1960).

[7] See Comment, *Waiver of the Right to Counsel in State Court Cases: The Effect of* Gideon v. Wainwright, 31 U. CHI. L. REV. 591, 594–95 (1964).

[8] See Carnley v. Cochran, 369 U.S. 506 (1962).

[9] *Id.,* Johnson v. Zerbst, 304 U.S. 458 (1938).

[10] See Von Moltke v. Gillies, 332 U.S. 708, 723–24 (1948) (plurality opinion by Black, J.); Cherrie v. United States, *supra* note 6; Snell v. United States, 174 F. 2d 580 (10th Cir. 1949); People v. Hardin, 207 Cal. App. 2d 336, 24 Cal. Rptr. 563 (Dist. Ct. App. 1962).

[11] See Uverges v. Pennsylvania, 335 U.S. 437 (1948) (17 years old); People v. Devanish, 285 App. Div. 826, 136 N.Y.S. 2d 759 (1955) (16 years old); *In re Gooding*, 338 P. 2d 114 (Okla. Crim. 1959) (18 years old). *Accord* United States *ex rel.* Brown v. Fay, 242 F. Supp. 273 (S.D.N.Y. 1965) (16 years old); People v. Byroads, 24 App. Div. 2d 732, 263 N.Y.S. 2d 401 (1965) (17 years old) (mem.); United States *ex rel.* Slebodnik v. Pennsylvania, 343 F. 2d 605 (3rd Cir. 1965) (applying Pennsylvania law to a 17-year-old).

[12] See Powell v. Alabama, 287 U.S. 45, 73 (1932): "Attorneys are officers of the court, and are bound to render services when required by such appointment."

[13] See United States *ex rel.* Brown v. Fay, 242 F. Supp. 243 (D.C.N.Y. 1965); People v. Byroads, 24 App. Div. 2d 732, 263 N.Y.S. 2d 401 (1965).

[14] See Cherrie v. United States, 179 F. 2d 94 (10th Cir. 1949); Thompson, *supra* note 6.

[15] E. D. MORGAN, BASIC PROBLEMS OF EVIDENCE (Joint Committee on Continuing Legal Education of the American Law Institute and the American Bar Association 1963), quoted in E. Webb, The Interview, or The Only Wheel in Town, 23 (unpublished ms. Northwestern University, undated).

[16] The significance of the judge's status vis-à-vis those appearing before him is discussed later in this article, in a section not reprinted here.

[17] Although foreknowledge of a juvenile's prior history may well constitute prejudicial error, traditional juvenile court philosophy and practice has tended to support procedures whereby the judge becomes familiar with the youth's background before an adjudication hearing. See generally, E. Krasnow, *Social Investigation Reports in the Juvenile Courts: Their Uses and Abuses*, 12 CRIME &

DELIN. 151 (1966); Teitelbaum, *The Use of Social Reports in Juvenile Court Adjudications,* 7 J. FAM. L. 425 (1967).

[18] See *In re Santillanes,* 47 N.M. 140, 138 P. 2d 503 (1943).

[19] See Application of *Gault,* 99 Ariz. 181, 407 P. 2d 760 (1965); U.S. CHILDREN'S BUREAU, STANDARDS FOR JUVENILE AND FAMILY COURTS 72 (1966).

[20] 387 U.S. 1, 51–52.

[21] *Id.,* at 55.

[22] 8 J. WIGMORE, EVIDENCE § 2260, at 369 (McNaughten Rev. 1961).

[23] *Id.,* at § 2268, p. 406, and cases cited at note 6. THE UNIFORM RULES OF EVIDENCE, rule 23 (I), provides a typical statement of the principle: "Every person has in a criminal action in which he is an accused a privilege not to be called as a witness and not to testify."

[24] See United States v. Housing Foundation of America, 176 F. 2d 665 (3d Cir. 1959).

[25] Griffin v. California, 380 U.S. 609 (1965).

[26] 304 U.S. 458 (1938).

[27] Wood v. United States, 128 F. 2d 265, 277 (D.C. Cir. 1942).

[28] 384 U.S. 436, 475 (1966).

[29] 369 U.S. 506 (1962).

[30] 78 N.Y.S. 2d 596 (Sup. Ct. 1948).

[31] *Id.,* at 600. See People v. Glaser, 238 Cal. App. 2d 819, 48 Cal. Rptr. 427 (1965), *cert. denied,* 385 U.S. 880, *reh. denied,* 385 U.S. 965; State v. De Cola, 33 N.J. 335, 164 A. 2d 729 (1960) (grand jury investigation); People v. Morett, 69 N.Y.S. 2d 540 (App. Div. 1947); State v. Halvorsen, 110 N.W. 2d 132 (S.D. 1961) (coroner's inquest).

[32] 387 U.S., at 42–57, *passim.*

[33] 61 Cal. Rptr. 874 (1967).

[34] *Id.,* at 877, note 5.

[35] *Id.,* at 877 (emphasis added).

[36] 387 U.S. 1, 44 (emphasis added).

[37] Cf. People v. Chlebowy, *supra* note 27.

[38] 8 WIGMORE, EVIDENCE § 2268, at 406.

[39] State v. Halvorsen, 110 N.W. 2d 132 (S.D. 1961).

[40] *Id.,* at 134.

[41] *Id.,* at 136–37.

[42] See Table 3 *supra.*

[43] 387 U.S., at 43.

[44] Pointer v. Texas, 380 U.S. 400 (1965); Douglas v. Alabama, 380 U.S. 415 (1965).

[45] 387 U.S., at 56.

[46] See Dorsen and Rezneck, *supra* note 5, at 20; Teitelbaum, *supra* note 18, at 431. Cf. CAL. WELF. & INST'NS. CODE § 701 (1966), which permits the juvenile court to admit any evidence that is relevant and material, but requires that a finding of delinquency be supported by a preponderance of the evidence admissible in criminal cases.

[47] 5 WIGMORE, EVIDENCE § 1395 (3d ed. 1940).

[48] See Pointer v. Texas, 380 U.S. 400 (1965); Dorsen and Rezneck, *supra* note 5, at 20; Note, *Confrontation and the Hearsay Rule,* 75 YALE L. J. 1434 (1966); Comment, *Federal Confrontation: A Not Very Clear Say on Hearsay,* 13 U.C.L.A. L. REV. 366, 372 (1966).

[49] *In re Gault,* 387 U.S. 1, 55 (1967). The failure to consider the waiver issue with care is especially surprising because several of the justices displayed great interest in the question during oral argument.

[50] *Id.,* at 42.

[51] 387 U.S., at 41–42.

[52] *Id.,* at 55.

[53] "The privilege is that of the person under examination as witness . . . is intended for his protection alone." 8 WIGMORE, EVIDENCE § 2270, at 414–15.

[54] *Id.,* note 1.

[55] If the child is of very tender years, and as a practical matter could not be found to make a valid waiver, and appeared through counsel, the attorney, should he decide to have the youth testify, would in effect waive the minor's privilege on his behalf. The child himself, by hypothesis, is not capable of making an effective waiver, and if he is incompetent for that purpose, it is clear that the decision to take the stand is for all intents and purposes made by the lawyer, though for the child's benefit. The Supreme Court apparently suggests that this decision can be made by a parent as well as by counsel, assuming he is present and competent.

[56] See *In re* Sippy, 97 A. 2d 455 (D.C. Mun. Ct. App. 1953).

[57] See, e.g., Powell v. Alabama, 287 U.S. 45, 69 (1932); Johnson v. Zerbst, 304 U.S. 458 (1938); Gideon v. Wainwright, 372 U.S. 355, 344 (1963).

[58] E.g., CAL. WELFARE & INSTITUTIONS CODE § 500 *et seq.* (1961); ILL. REV. STAT. ch. 37 § 701 *et seq.* (1966); N.Y. Family Court Act (1962).

[59] At least three states undertook substantial revision of their juvenile court laws during 1967, apparently in response to the Gault decision. Colorado enacted a new Children's Code, COLO. REV. STAT. ch. 22, § 22–1–1 *et seq.* (Supp. 1967), explicitly guaranteeing the right to retained or appointed counsel (§ 22–1–6), and providing generally that the rules of evidence applicable to civil proceedings shall apply to delinquency hearings (§ 22–1–7). Vermont added a new chapter to its Code, specifically devoted to juvenile court procedures. VT. STAT. ANN. tit. 33, ch. 12 (Supp. 1968). This chapter contains provisions relating to notice of charges (§§ 645–48), the privilege against self-incrimination (§ 652), and the right to counsel (§ 653). California's Welfare and Institutions Code was amended to further guarantee the rights to notice of charges (CAL. WELF. & INST. CODE §§ 630, 630.1, 658 [Supp. 1967]), counsel (§§634, 679, 700), confrontation and cross-examination (§ 702.5) and the privilege against self-incrimination (§702.5). It is also noteworthy that other amendments were directed to assuring that a juvenile to be charged with delinquency would be afforded Miranda-type rights. (CAL. WELF. & INST. CODE §§ 625, 627.5 [Supp. 1967]). The practical effect of Gault's requirements, particularly the right to counsel, have not gone unnoticed. One observer states that "Already the trend is clear. In Philadelphia, only about 5 per cent of the children appearing in juvenile court had been represented by counsel in the period'immediately preceding 1967. At present, close to 40 per cent of the children are represented." S. Coxe, *Lawyers in Juvenile Court,* 13 CRIME & DELIN. 488 (1967). Presumably statutory modifications of the sort mentioned above will further reinforce this trend.

[60] Is it conceivable that what we have reported observing in Metro and Gotham is terribly unusual, so much so that one would have great difficulty finding other courts that indulged in the same practices? The answer is yes—it is conceivable —but we strongly doubt it. First, we know of nothing extraordinary about these courts, save perhaps that they frequently functioned under the gaze of our observers. In addition, frequent conversations during the past several years with juvenile court judges and occasional observations of delinquency hearings in various parts of the country have substantiated our belief that the courts in Metro and Gotham are quite typical. Significantly, in the only study we have seen of actual court hearings made subsequent to Gault, substantially the same findings as our own are reported. During October and November 1968, the *Washington Post* published a series of articles based on a five-month survey of the six suburban juvenile courts in the metropolitan area surrounding Washington, D.C. (Incidentally, none of the courts studied was in Metro, Gotham, or Zenith.) . . .

[61] See generally, Sect. 1, *supra.*

[62] 384 U. S. 436 (1966).

[63] R. Medalie, L. Zeitz, and P. Alexander, *Implementation of Miranda in D.C.,* 66 MICH. L. REV. 1347 (1968); A. Reiss and D. Black, *Interrogation and the Criminal*

Process, 374 ANNALS 47 (1967); and *Interrogation in New England: The Impact of Miranda,* 76 YALE L. J. 1519 (1967).
[64] E. Lemert, *Legislating Change in the Juvenile Court,* 1967 WIS. L. REV. 421, 431.
[65] PRESIDENT'S COMMISSION ON LAW ENFORCEMENT AND ADMINISTRATION OF JUSTICE, THE CHALLENGE OF CRIME IN A FREE SOCIETY 87 (1967).

5. Law-Guardian Representation and the Treatment of Delinquent Children *

PHYLLIS R. SNYDER AND ANTONIA F. MANGANO

EVEN BEFORE THE May 1967 decision rendered by the United States Supreme Court *In re* Gault, it was becoming clear that procedural rights guaranteed to adults were about to be granted to delinquent children. The rights to be implemented for these children were the rights to (1) be informed of charges against them, (2) confront their accusers and for these accusers to be cross-examined, (3) have legal representation, (4) avoid self-incrimination, and (5) be protected against involuntary confession, unnecessary detention, and the like.

Although for the greater number of this country's three thousand juvenile courts this was a landmark decision that would require radical changes to be made immediately, this was not the case in New York State. In New York, the Family Court Act of 1962 provided for legal representation for the child in the juvenile term of family court. This lawyer was designated a "lawyer guardian," a term that has led to misconceptions about his traditional role as a lawyer, as will be shown later in this paper.

At the outset, praise for the idea of legal representation came from judges, probation officers, and lawyers. Judge Justine Wise Polier described the law guardian's role as being "of great value in assuring full presentation of the evidence, interpreting the court's role to the child and his family, and securing a fair hearing at the initial stage of the proceedings."[1]

Social workers were active in encouraging the requirement of legal representation for children. Bernard Fisher of Community Service Society, New York, says in stressing the need for defense counsel: "So preoccupied have some of our juvenile court jurists become with personality assessment and formulation of treatment plans that serious departures from rules of evidence may occur and the facts of the case may not be properly established."[2]

Renée Berg examines the way changes leading toward the formulation of the juvenile court would affect social work practice in the court. She not only concedes this will occur but cites advantages that are expected to accrue from it.[3]

* From "Effect of Law Guardian Representation on the Treatment of Delinquent Children" by Phyllis R. Snyder and Antonia F. Mangano. Reprinted with permission of the authors and the National Association of Social Workers from *Social Work,* Vol. 13, No. 3 (July, 1968), pp. 102–8.

Yet it would appear that these advantages and rights are obtained at a high cost. In the operation of the juvenile term of family court in New York City, the "law guardian" protects the rights of the delinquent child, but the price may be no service at all. At the fact-finding hearing, a petition may be found inadmissible because it is incorrectly drawn. If the case is dismissed, what happens to the boy whose acting out signals a need for help? What happens to his need for help?

THE LAW GUARDIAN–CHILD RELATIONSHIP

Protecting a delinquent child's right not to incriminate himself casts question on the entire conception of the juvenile court, as contrasted with a criminal court. It casts question on the role of the judge as "wise parent" and on the role of the probation officer as the court's social worker. The law guardian is presented as the delinquent child's friend—his *only* friend—the one who protects his rights (against whom?), who defends him against the charges alleged in the petition (are allegations an attack?). What relation has this stance to a delinquent child's view of the world?

This view of the law guardian and his "adversaries" suggests that the other persons in the legal proceedings are not his friends and are not interested in his welfare: They are out to "get" him, to establish his guilt and punish his wrongdoing. Surely this view of a hostile world and punitive adults is abetted by insisting on his right to remain silent; surely this is treating a delinquent child like a junior ciminal and encourages the taunt of "Let them prove it!" The price of this child–law guardian versus judge-probation officer dichotomy is paid at the dispositional hearing, when the child is led to regard disposition as punishment, whatever the judge's intent may be.

The relationship between the delinquent child and his law guardian is, unfortunately, all too similar to that of the adult criminal and the attorney who defends him. It tends to confirm a child's delinquent values by stressing the acceptability of denying wrongdoing (placing the burden of proof on the petitioner) and seeking to avoid the consequences of his delinquent behavior, rather than teaching him to eschew the behavior itself.

Moreover, it is confusing to the child that the legal process sometimes prevents expected consequences from following specific acts. It may disrupt his understanding of the simple cause-and-effect relationship that underlies many therapeutic ideas. A delinquent child is helped by the awareness that a given act brings expectable consequences and that he, therefore, has some choice as to whether he will experience these consequences or not. It is a simple device to underscore a young person's feelings about himself and his power to influence what happens to him. All too often, these children come to court feeling they are powerless victims of circumstance. Change cannot take place until it is demonstrated to them that they can control their behavior and that their behavior in turn affects what happens to them.

Recently a "petition for transfer" to a closed institution was instituted by an open institution for delinquent boys. Robert had been in the program for fourteen months, and his aggressive behavior had become more pronounced as the anticipated date of his return home approached. When this date was finally set, Bob attacked two teachers. The staff considered the possible meaning of this behavior, and also determined that the boy should not go home then.

The discussion with Bob centered on his dread of returning to public school. Institution staff told him that another institutional placement would be recommended in court, and it was likely that he would remain in such an institution until he was 16 and was no longer legally required to attend school. Bob thought that a court hearing would result in this outcome and accepted it as a reasonable expectation. (It may even have been the result his behavior was unconsciously meant to accomplish.)

Bob was advised by the law guardian of his right to remain silent. He looked bewildered, but said nothing about the allegations that had brought him back to court. When the petitioning institution was asked to produce witnesses, Bob admitted hitting both teachers.

A finding was made. Bob had expected to be remanded to the detention facility to await the dispositional hearing. Instead, he was paroled to his parents who were as bewildered as their son. They were worried about their ability to handle him and even more concerned about the court's order to place him in public school. Bob's return home was therefore clouded by his bewilderment at unexpectedly finding himself there and his fear of facing the difficulties of returning to public school.

It is not legal representation that is the issue, but rather the form it has taken and the risks that accompany this form.

THE LAW GUARDIAN'S ROLE

The role of the law guardian and the performance of a private attorney retained by the family differ in significant ways. It is important to recognize that the private lawyer would not expect to employ his own investigator and social worker in order to legally represent a delinquent child; he would utilize the knowledge and expertise of those who were part of the court service and indeed were charged with these functions.

The law guardian, on the other hand, does not seek to fill gaps in his knowledge by using those who are part of the court services, but rather *duplicates* the investigatory services, questions the psychiatrist's examination and recommendations, and, indeed, has his own manual of institutions for referring delinquent children. Seeing this as his professional responsibility as a lawyer representing a juvenile before the court, the law guardian must consider the probation officer as an adversary when their findings, evaluation, or recommendations differ.

The probation officer, neither equipped nor trained to be a legal adversary, is undercut and undermined in his role. The effect of this contest with the law guardian is damaging indeed; if the child perceives him as a prosecutor, how will the child relate to him if he is placed on probation? Can he be a helping person if he has been made to look like a prosecutor?

Similarly, the law guardian, neither trained nor equipped to offer treat-ment, evaluates the expertise of those who are. When his efforts to clear his client result in the child and family perceiving him as the only helpful per-son, he cannot make therapeutic use of this beginning relationship, which terminates as soon as he leaves the courtroom. Beyond the role of legal representation at the initial hearing emerges the law guardian's attempt to keep his client in the community when disposition is at issue.

DISPOSITION

At the disposition hearing, the law guardian's activity contradicts the notion that disposition of juvenile cases is meant to be therapeutic, not punitive. Such activity suggests that the judge, equipped with the social study prepared by the probation officer, is not able to evaluate the alternatives available to him and choose the most helpful course. The law guardian's intervention implies that he has some means of evaluating the probation officer's recommendations and derogates the expertise of the probation officer—the social service arm of the court.

What special knowledge can the law guardian draw on to question the probation officer's recommendations? Legal interference with recommended disposition is based on the assumption that the lawyer's role is to keep his client free, to "get him off." While compounding the notion that the delinquent child is a junior criminal, this approach denies that probation supervision, referral to a social agency as a condition of probation, and, especially, placement outside his home are resources that can be helpful to the delinquent child; they are viewed as punitive actions or confinement to penal institutions.

The law guardian's actions at the disposition hearing appear to be aimed at *preventing* disposition—and disposition within the jurisdiction of the court —as is shown in the following example:

Byron, a 13½-year-old boy, had been known to the juvenile term of family court since he was 10. Two incidents in which he was involved were adjusted without court action at intake by the probation department. The third, an assault that resulted in court action, was still pending when a fourth offense occurred, another assault. A finding was made after a hearing at which Byron was represented by a law guardian. On recommendation of the court clinic psychiatrist, Byron was observed at a city psychiatric hospital.

His parents then had him admitted voluntarily to a nearby state mental institution in which he remained about two months. When he returned home on convalescent status, he had no contact with aftercare and attended school only about half of the time. Probation was ordered. Byron reported to his probation officer infrequently, and the seriousness of his situation was discussed with him. Byron told his probation officer that, were he a judge, he would "send up" a boy who behaved as he did. Before their next interview he was arrested for a new offense.

Byron denied the allegations in the new petition, although the police apprehended him in the place into which he was accused of breaking and entering. While awaiting the hearing, he ran away from the court waiting room. Two days later he was returned to court on a warrant; a finding was made on admission.

State training school placement was recommended. The law guardian objected, and the judge ordered an inpatient psychiatric observation. On recall, the law guardian proposed a psychiatric examination by his own psychiatrist. The boy was held in detention until the law guardian arranged an interview with a psychologist who had no connection with the court.

The psychologist's report described Byron as a boy with dull-normal intelligence, who was not psychotic. The recommendation was made that he be placed in a "milder institution," but no specific institution was named. The law guardian planned for the mother to take the boy to a state mental hospital, to which the psychologist was to arrange admission.

Since Byron was not psychotic, the state hospital refused to accept him. State training school placement was successfully avoided, but so was help for Byron, whose aggression could again be expected to lead to assaultive behavior.

Institutional placement is regarded as punishment. It appears to be the law guardian's aim to avoid placement of the delinquent child, despite the failure of therapeutic measures tried within the community.

When attempts to foil placement are successful, a delinquent youth will often be retained on probation and there is little possibility that he will attain good adjustment to the community. When such a child commits another delinquent act—as predicted by the probation officer who had recommended placement—a new petition is drawn or a violation of probation is heard at a new hearing. What has happened to the child by this time? It can be assumed that his image of himself as a troublemaker—one who is always getting into conflict with established authority—has been reinforced. Furthermore, it would seem that the possibilities of his being accepted by a "therapeutically oriented residential facility," which is less likely to view a boy with a history of repeated delinquences as being able to respond to its program, would be slim. Whether this is a valid judgment or not, private institutions that accept delinquent youngsters are indeed less likely to regard a child who has committed many reported delinquent acts as helpable and, therefore, as an admissible candidate. A child who has been held in the community beyond the time recommended by a knowledgeable probation officer may be rejected by those institutions that have the power to reject him. If such a child is then placed in a public training school, how much chance is there for him to use its rehabilitation program?

When Placement Is Inevitable

When placement appears inevitable even to the law guardian, this effort to achieve acceptance by a private institution can have damaging results. Experienced probation officers can individualize the treatment programs of the private residential facilities serving delinquent youngsters and can try to match the child with the program. It is their job to know the admissions criteria of these facilities as well as the strengths and limitations of their programs.

When a probation officer recommends a state training school as the placement of choice, he is more likely to be realistic about the child's needs and how they will be perceived by other trained personnel. He is also giving the school's program its fullest opportunity to be effective. The child who knows that every private institution has rejected him is entitled to feel "dumped" at the state training school and is unlikely to feel that it has anything helpful to offer him, since every possible effort was expended by the law guardian to prevent this placement. What can be the effect of this "last-resort" placement on a youngster's image of himself, his expectations of the training school, and his feelings about his future chances?

The law guardian's role in creating this situation cannot be evaded, as can be seen in the following case:

> Against the recommendation of the probation officer, 14-year-old Don had been referred to all private·institutions that accept delinquent boys, although his IQ of 77 and his second-grade reading level made him unable to benefit from the programs of these facilities. In addition, Don had a history of running away from home whenever his parents confronted him with school reports—he could not face the consequences of what he had done. While placement resources were being explored. Don continued to be truant from school and to disrupt classes when he did attend. He ran away when his parents attempted to discuss this behavior with him and to explain how this was affecting the plans for his placement. When the last private institution turned him down, the judge placed Don at the state training school. The law guardian turned to Don and his parents, shook her head, murmured gratuitously, "I did the best I could for you," and walked away.

Both the actions and parting words of the law guardian compounded the difficulties the state training school had in reaching the boy and its community worker had in reaching his parents.

Restraint of the law guardian's prejudices against the public facilities can be expected to reduce to some extent the feeling of a child's being dumped into such an institution and to enhance the helpfulness of the structured program. If it were not viewed as punishment, the improved image of the rehabilitative and preventive possibilities of training school placement would lead to further improvements in program, for much of the initial energy of the professional staff must be used to handle resentment at the placement.

Consider the effect of the law guardian's role and his view that placement is punishment on Carmella and her parents:

> Carmella, age 12, was brought to family court because she was having sexual relations with her 16-year-old school dropout boyfriend. Her parents, born in Puerto Rico, were unsuccessful in preventing her from seeing this boy, were worried that she would meet him on the days she was truant from school, and were frightened that she would become pregnant. Psychological testing done at the court clinic revealed that Carmella had an IQ of 70; her borderline intelligence interfered with her ability to do classwork in the slowest sixth-grade class and made it hard for her to understand the risks to which she was exposing herself. She had great difficulty in giving up the affection of her boyfriend, especially when there were so few comparable satisfactions for her.
>
> When her parents filed a "violation of probation" petition because Carmella's truancy and sexual involvement persisted, the probation officer recommended that she be removed from the community and placed in the state training school. The law guardian remonstrated, protesting that the girl was "only truanting" and "did not deserve to go to the training school."

What can be expected of Carmella if she remains with her frustrated, angry parents? At what price would she remain home? If she became pregnant, who would care for her baby and what kind of life would she have? What other means exist to prevent Carmella from becoming a thirteen-year-old mother? What does the judge decide in the absence of a less-stigmatized resource for a girl too dull and unmotivated for private programs? What does the law guardian reveal about his lack of understanding of the girl, the meaning of her behavior, and the difficulties of rehabilitation?

PROFESSIONAL ETHICS

When the law guardian upholds such principles as protection of constitutional rights, he must as equally maintain his obligations to his professional ethics. He cannot maneuver to get his client freed at all costs, although this has been known to happen. In a manner reminiscent of criminal cases, a law guardian recently represented a fifteen-year-old boy accused of raping an eighteen-year-old girl. Three years prior to this event, the girl had been adjudicated as a "person in need of supervision," and had been represented by a law guardian. Disposition in the girl's case had been placement at the state training school. The law guardian's knowledge of these circumstances was used to attack her credibility in the boy's case in which she was the complaining witness—a flagrant violation of professional ethics, the confidentiality of the material known to the lawyer, and the privileged lawyer-client relationship. Was this the price paid to obtain "liberty" for the boy? What about the girl's view of the lawyer who had previously protected her rights? Are rights to be protected only if they are deemed expedient by the law guardian? How much clearer can the danger signals be that personal liberty is being held more sacred than professional conscience, the rights of children not to be treated as criminals, or the welfare of the community?

CONCLUSION AND QUESTIONS

The need for legal representation of the delinquent child is "documented" by descriptions of the worst conditions, practices, and resources from studies that illustrate conditions in the most backward or overburdened courts. But it is poor statesmanship to look to courts that are run by the least qualified judges, served by the least adequate probation departments, and have no intake services and propose legal safeguards as a remedy. The remedy for these problems continues to be better qualified judges, trained probation officers with manageable case loads, intake services that can be used without adjudication, and innovative treatment programs.

It is illogical to leap to the conclusion that the need for improved services within the court will be met by preventing an adjudicated child from receiving services recommended by the probation department. Legal interference with the process of helping a delinquent child within the structure of the court will not encourage improved services, additional treatment facilities in the community, or a wider range of institutional resources because it denigrates the value of these services and is hardly likely to encourage recruitment of trained personnel or the development of innovative programs.

Should the legal profession assume some responsibility for defining the lawyer's role in representing a juvenile in a delinquency proceeding? Is it the judgment of the legal profession that the traditional role of the lawyer will not work in this setting and requires a new design, title, and function to safeguard due process of law for the delinquent child?

In what sense are social workers failing to recognize the plight of their colleagues in juvenile probation and corrections? Is there not a dilemma? The social workers' concern for the legal rights of the child combined with their lack of knowledge of the lawyer's function blinds them to the real issue: the law guardian-court social worker role conflict. If each profession recognizes the contribution it can make in the context of its own discipline, perhaps both will be able to achieve a truer measure of justice for children.

NOTES

[1] *A View from the Bench: The Juvenile Court* (New York: National Council on Crime and Delinquency, 1964), p. 67.
[2] Bernard C. Fisher, "Juvenile Court: Purpose, Promise, and Problems," *Social Service Review*, 34 (March 1958), 78–79.
[3] "Social Work Practice and the Trend Toward a Legalistic Juvenile Court," *Social Casework*, 47 (Feb. 1966), 93–97.

6. *Beyond* Gault: *Injustice and the Child* *

PAUL LERMAN

ON MAY 15, 1967, the U.S. Supreme Court rendered a decision that highlighted the procedural defects characteristic of many juvenile courts.[1] A majority of the court ruled that fifteen-year-old Gerald Gault—accused of having placed, with a friend, an anonymous phone call to a woman and making lewd remarks to her—had been denied the following "basic rights" by the state of Arizona: (1) notice of charges; (2) right to counsel; (3) right to confront and cross-examine the complainant; and (4) protection against self-incrimination. This far-reaching decision will probably have important effects on the procedural justice accorded to juveniles throughout the United States. However, it will not restrain the fifty states from exercising enormous discretion in the detention and institutionalization of youth. Although the issues of procedural justice for juveniles have been faced, the problems of substantive justice have scarcely been addressed, legally or empirically. This paper will not analyze problems of juvenile justice from a legal perspective; rather, we shall approach three problems empirically by using available data. The problems and the data, however, become meaningful only by utilizing traditional standards of justice as a frame of reference. Therefore, the problems and standards will be briefly discussed before presenting evidence concerning the court's actual decisions concerning detention and institutionalization.

* This work was assisted by a special grant from the Center for Demonstration and Research of the Columbia University School of Social Work and the Metropolitan Applied Research Center.

The First Problem: Equal Treatment for Comparable Offenses

In the Gault case, the Supreme Court deliberately avoided dealing with the substantive issues arising from the detention and lengthy incarceration of a fifteen-year-old boy. As Justice Fortas, writing for the majority, states:

> We do not in this opinion consider the impact of these constitutional provisions upon the totality of the relationship of the juvenile and the state. We do not even consider the entire process relating to juvenile "delinquents." For example, we are not here concerned with the procedures or constitutional rights applicable to the pre-judicial stages of the juvenile process, nor do we direct our attention to the post-adjudicative or dispositional process.[2]

Specifically, this restriction of the issues to procedural rights governing court hearings means that the court refrained from deciding whether young Gault had been unreasonably detained for four or five days prior to his trial; they also refrained from deciding whether the dispositional sentence of six years in a state institution was unreasonable as compared to the penalty for a similar offense by an adult: a fine of $5 to $50 or a jail sentence of not more than sixty days. Because of the Supreme Court decision, Gerald Gault was released from Arizona's State Industrial School for Delinquents before he had reached adulthood. But he was released because his trial was adjudged "unfair"—not because the disposition was deemed unreasonable.

Had fifteen-year-old Gault been accorded a "fair" trial, he might still have been sentenced to a six-year term for a sixty-day misdemeanor. Although procedural justice can have a great impact on the substantive justice rendered to suspected offenders, it is important not to confuse "fairness" and "justice."[3] The Supreme Court has not yet ruled on how much deprivation of liberty (before and after a "fair trial") can be imposed on the juveniles of America.[4] How soon it will rule on the "pre-judicial stages" and on the "post-adjudicative or dispositional process" *may* depend on how sensitive the friends of the court are to the issues of arbitrary detention and lengthy incarceration of juveniles.

Justice is not an easy concept to define, much less measure, but two central aspects of its meaning in relation to criminal adjudication can be identified as providing standards: (1) equal punishment should be accorded to all those who commit comparable offenses; and (2) the penalties imposed should be graded according to the degree of social harm the defendant has actually done or clearly threatens to do to the community.[5] To the extent that actual cases depart from these two tenets, our own sense of justice is affronted. Regarding the first standard, the Gault case affects our sense of justice because Gault did not receive treatment equal to what would have been given to an *adult* committing the same act. On the basis of an adult standard of punishment, Gault should have received a maximum sentence of sixty days—not six years. Empirical research can supply the facts for ascertaining whether this type of unreasonable disposition is prevalent.

THE SECOND PROBLEM: MATCHING EXTENT OF PUNISHMENT WITH DEGREE OF SOCIAL HARM

Adherence to traditional standards implies that a day's "imprisonment" in a county jail or state prison is equal to a day's "placement" in a county detention home, state training school, or residential treatment facility. Semantic differences, as well as actual differences in personnel, food, housing, programs, and general amenities, should not obscure the central fact that deprivation of liberty—even for twenty-four hours—is an extreme form of punishment. Both adult and juvenile facilities involve custodial management, as well as loss of liberty, as part of the judicial intervention authorized by the court. There is no logical reason to regard a stay at a "residential treatment center" as any less depriving of liberty than a stay of the same duration at a state training school. In brief, a court-imposed "treatment plan" is actually a *type of punishment*.

For those who question this equation, we point out that the first question that "placed" youngsters in "treatment" institutions invariably ask their social workers is: "When am I going home?" We also recommend that they accept the many runaways occurring at these institutions at face value —as attempts to be free of a "home" they never freely chose. These verbal and nonverbal actions are strong reminders—if any are required—that children, as well as adults, are capable of feeling deprived of their liberty. A legal scholar has summarized this point of view quite ably:

> . . . When, in an authorative setting, we attempt to do something *for* a child "because of what he is and needs" we are also doing something *to* him. The semantics of socialized justice are a trap for the unwary. Whatever one's motivation, however elevated one's objectives, if the measures taken result in the compulsory loss of the child's liberty, the involuntary separation of a child from his family, or even the supervision of a child's activities by a probation worker the impact on the affected individual is essentially a punitive one. Good intentions and a flexible vocabulary do not alter this reality. . . . We shall escape much confusion here if we are willing to give candid recognition to the fact that the business of the juvenile court inevitably consists, to a considerable degee, in dispensing punishment. If this is true, we can no more avoid the problem of unjust punishment in the juvenile court than in the criminal court.[6]

If we accept the fact that any deprivation of liberty is actually a punishment, then a sense of justice also requires a proportionate relationship between the seriousness of the actual or clearly potential "social harm" and the penal sanction. If traditional beliefs about justice prevailed in the juvenile system, as they do in the regular criminal court system, convicted misdemeanants like Gerald Gault would spend less time in detention and "training" than a juvenile burglar would. We are here concerned, not with a comparison of the judicial outcomes of juveniles and adults, but with the relative severity of judicial intervention within a juvenile offender population. Empirical data can also be employed to assess the prevalence of this type of unreasonable outcome.

THE THIRD PROBLEM: DETENTION AND SEVERITY OF FINAL DISPOSITION

Juveniles can be legally detained (i.e., deprived of liberty) at three stages of the adjudication process, even in a "fair" jurisdiction: (1) prior to a hearing to determine whether the offender is guilty of delinquency; (2) after conviction but prior to dispositional hearing, while the court assembles information that will guide it in handing down sentence; and (3) after sentencing but prior to institutionalization, while court personnel attempt to "place" the offender in a state or private facility. Whether youngsters should be detained to the degree that they are has been widely discussed in the literature.[7] The possibility that many juveniles may be detained at a greater rate and for longer periods of time at all stages of the adjudication process has been implicitly covered under the discussion of the disparity in the punishment of juveniles and adults. The problem with which we are here concerned focuses on the influence of detention per se on the likelihood that the offender will be found guilty and sentenced to an institution. This problem also refers to the standard of equal punishment for comparable offenses. But the problem is sufficiently important to warrant separate treatment.

Adults have access to bail, as well as the possibility of release on their own recognizance, to lend support to the assumptions that a person is "innocent until proven guilty" and that imprisonment should be avoided whenever possible. Recently the adult bail system has become the focus of practice reforms and study. Studies of the denial of bail have offered convincing evidence that when offense and previous record are controlled, adults who post bail are much more likely to escape conviction and a prison sentence than are suspects who are detained and unable to post bail.[8] From the viewpoint of traditional standards, whether a juvenile has been detained or released to his parents should not influence the findings of guilt or the dispositional decision.

AVAILABLE EVIDENCE

These three types of problems have never been studied directly.[9] However, available evidence indicates that the juvenile court system is probably characterized by these types of unreasonable outcomes in many cases.

Unequal Punishment of Juveniles and Adults

The President's Commission on Law Enforcement and Administration of Justice had the Gault case and others in mind when it argued that the juvenile courts should institute fairer proceedings to avoid overly severe dispositions:

> . . . The essentials of fair procedures are most imperative in light of the fact that the juvenile court's broad jurisdiction and indefinite commitment power lead not infrequently to sanctions more severe than those an adult could receive for like behavior . . .[10]

Monrad G. Paulsen, a prominent legal authority on the juvenile court system, highlighted the problem of unequal treatment in a West Virginia case:

> The juvenile court judge has great discretion in respect to disposition of delinquents, and sometimes a relatively minor offense forms the basis for excessive and arbitrary treatment.
>
> A case from West Virginia provides an unhappy example. A 14-year-old youngster was found "guilty" on the charge of "delinquency" and sent to the Industrial School for Boys until age 21, unless discharged sooner. Responding to a dare, the boy had telephoned police and told them that a bomb was planted in each of two local schools. Police, school officials and townspeople were put to much inconvenience. A section of the West Virginia Code provides that anyone who "molests or disturbs" a school is guilty of misdemeanor and upon conviction shall be fined between $10 and $50 and may, in the judge's discretion, be confined in jail for not more than 30 days. The boy violated the state law; hence he was a juvenile delinquent, but with a consequence more severe to him than to an offending adult.[11]

Paulsen also notes that some states have "reacted against harsh dispositions for minor infractions of law" by rewriting their statutes to refer to a "habitual" course of antisocial conduct as a basis for the conviction and sentencing of youngsters who have not violated criminal statutes.[12]

The problem of disparate punishment has also been noted by sociologists and social workers. Bloch and Flynn, in 1956, stated the issue in the following manner:

> . . . Large numbers of children are sent to training schools for long periods of time for treatment that they do not receive in fact, while if adults were involved in the same offense, the "punishment" meted out by a court might well be 10 days or 30 days in jail. Without doubt, many criminal careers begin as a result of a rankling sense of injustice that comes to a child when he realizes that he is being "imprisoned" for many years for relatively trivial offenses.[13]

Evidently, youth are aware of the disparity in treatment, as the following excerpt from an interview with two youth officers indicates:

> . . . A youth's motives for lying about his age are generally practical in nature; for example, Chicago youth officers indicated that juveniles taken into custody for minor offenses such as disorderly conduct often claim to be over the age limit, reasoning that if they are treated as adults they will simply be forced to spend a night in jail and to hear a lecture by the judge in the morning, but that if they are identified as juveniles the interference with their liberty may well be more substantial.[14]

These reports and case studies gain further credence from the data released after a national survey conducted for the President's Commission on Law Enforcement:

> The average institutional stay before first release among the (adult) misdemeanant institutions covered by the National Survey (which excluded those handling persons sentenced for less than 30 days) was slightly less than 8 weeks, as compared to 20.9 months for adult felons and 9.3 months for juveniles.[15]

Since it is a well-known fact that the bulk of offenses handled by the juvenile court are of a minor nature, it is difficult not to infer that many juveniles are being punished about four times as severely as adult misdemeanants. This, of course, is a gross estimate of the disparity. In cases of youngsters "placed" at private residential treatment centers (at public expense), the disparity may even be greater. One private facility studied by the author kept youngsters who completed "treatment" for an average of two and a half years, whereas those who did not complete treatment were released after sixteen months.[16] Such lengthy stays rival the average national figure for the incarceration of convicted *felons* (as revealed by the national survey). If special programs of this kind yielded higher rates of successful rehabilitation, we might be confronted by an ethical dilemma; however, there is *no* convincing evidence that greater success actually occurs.[17] It appears, then, that juveniles may be institutionalized for minor offenses four to sixteen times as long as adult misdemeanants.

These estimates of disparities in punishment, it should be noted, are based on actual sentences served—not on sentences imposed at the time of dispositional adjudication. The distinction is important, for both juveniles and adults. In New York State, for example, juveniles can be held for a maximum of three years under the usual sentence imposed; however, the actual length of stay at *public* institutions averages about nine months. But the difference between sentences imposed and sentences served holds for adults, too—even for convicted felons, according to the President's Commission on Law Enforcement:

. . . More than one-half of the adult felony offenders sentenced to state prisons in 1960 were committed for maximum terms of 5 years or more; almost one third were sentenced to terms of at least 10 years. And more than one-half of the prisoners confined in state institutions in 1960 had been sentenced maximum terms of at least 10 years . . . [However] there are indications that despite the long sentences initially imposed, the administrators of penal systems in this country in practice have relied on shorter periods of confinement. Of the approximately 80,000 felony prisoners released in 1960 from state institutions, the median time actually served before first release was about 21 months; only 8.7 per cent of the prisoners actually served five years or more.[18]

It is important to recognize that on a relative basis the "nontreated" felon is punished much less severely than the law allows, in comparison to the "treated" juvenile offenders "placed" for two and a half years of a maximum three-year term. Whether we apply an absolute or a relative standard, the youngsters who probably experience the greatest disparity are those minor offenders who purportedly receive the *best* treatment. As Allen has noted, "One with reason may inquire as to the value of therapy purchased at the expense of justice." [19]

Failure to Match Punishment and Degree of Social Harm

The criminal statutes that exist or are proposed as models attempt to establish a range of penalties based on the relative harmfulness of the criminal conduct or the probable degree of danger represented by repeated offenders. Although the range and inconsistency of sentencing distinctions are often deplored, there is little doubt that in dealing with adult offenders all fifty states make some attempt to fit the penalty to the degree of social harm inflicted by the crime.[20] However, juvenile delinquency statutes are not drawn up in this manner. Paulsen suggests that the principle is worth introducing into the framework of juvenile court law:

> In the writer's opinion, harsh disposition ought not to depend solely on guesses as to "need." Rather, some relationship between conduct and disposition ought to be established. Is it not possible to classify certain kinds of cases involving breaches of the criminal law that do not support training school disposition without further allegations and findings of facts, although an adjudication of delinquency accompanied by less severe disposition would be permitted? Violations of municipal ordinances might be one example of this "second-degree delinquency." [21]

It is possible, of course, that in actual practice juvenile court personnel attempt to assess degree of social harm and to pass sentence accordingly. Available national data suggest that differences in degree of punishment probably occur at the *initial* stages of processing—where the decision to "adjust" the cases unofficially or to bring the offender before the court is made. Once the juveniles are placed on petition before the court, there do *not* appear to be any differences in the dispositional outcomes.[22] Table 1 provides the data for these inferences. Based on a secondary analysis of information published by the Children's Bureau for nineteen of the thirty largest cities reporting in detail, offenders are classified as follows: (1) *Part I type* refers to the offenses considered most serious by the FBI (homicide, rape, armed robbery, burglary, aggravated assault, and theft of more than $50); (2) *All other adult types* refers to offenses that would be crimes if committed by an adult, but not serious crimes; (3) *Juvenile-status offenses* refers to acts deemed harmful but not criminal if committed by an adult (e.g., running away, truancy, incorrigibility, disobedience). Three stages in the processing of juveniles are depicted in Table 1: (1) whether an official petition is drawn; (2) whether the juvenile is found guilty, if brought before the court; and (3) whether he is placed or committed to an institution, if convicted. The rates are computed for each offense type at each of the stages.

TABLE 1. DISPOSITION OF JUVENILE CASES AT THREE STAGES OF ADJUDICATION IN 19 OF 30 LARGEST CITIES, 1965

| | Offense Categories * | | |
Stage of Adjudication	Part 1 Type	All Other Adult Types	Juvenile-Status Offenses
Per cent court petition	57 N = (37,420)	33 (52,862)	42 (33,046)
Per cent convicted—if petition	92 N = (21,386)	90 (17,319)	94 (13,857)
Per cent placed or committed—if convicted †	23 N = (19,667)	18 (15,524)	26 (12,989)

* See text for definition of each category.
† All suspended sentences are considered as noncommitments.
SOURCE: Juvenile Court Statistics, 1965.

As Table 1 makes clear, the only major difference between offense categories exists at the stage of unofficial adjustment or petition (57 per cent versus 33 per cent and 42 per cent). Convictions and commitment rates do not vary greatly. These data suggest that once an offender reaches the judge's bench, the relative seriousness of his offense does *not* influence the likelihood of his becoming an official delinquent or receiving the maximum penalty—deprivation of liberty. The results depicted in Table 1 are not peculiar to 1965; similar results are obtained if 1964 data are used.[23]

The national data summarized in Table 1 do not refer to cities like New York where some differentiation of offenders has begun. Beginning in September 1962, New York's Family Court has been labeling juvenile-status offenders as "persons in need of supervision" (PINS) rather than as delinquents.[24] But has this change in labels led to less severe punishment of youth? Official data of the Family Court for New York City indicate that the *reverse* appears to be occurring.[25] Since this court has implemented "fair hearings" to the extent of providing legal counsel for virtually all court cases, the available comparisons are of some interest.

TABLE 2. DISPOSITION OF JUVENILE CASES AT TWO STAGES OF ADJUDICATION, NEW YORK CITY FAMILY COURT CASES, JULY 1, 1965–JUNE 30, 1966 (BOYS AND GIRLS COMBINED)

	Type of Court Petition	
Stage of Adjudication *	Delinquency	PINS
Per cent convicted	58 — N= (6,604)	81 — (3,545)
Per cent placed or committed— if convicted	21 — N= (3,832)	26 — (2,859)

* The following cases of both types are excluded: discharged to another petition, discharged to mental institution, and transfers.

SOURCE: State of New York, "Report of the Family Court" (Report of the Administrative Board of the Judicial Conference for the Judicial Year July 1, 1965–June 30, 1966), reprint from 12th Annual Report, pp. 52–59.

In Table 2, New York City youth are classified according to their petition labels, whether "delinquency" or "PINS." As with the national data reported in Table 1, stages of the adjudication process are considered. Unfortunately, the "petition" stage has had to be omitted because this information is not available by offense category.

The conviction rate for "delinquents" shown in Table 2 is much lower than the national rate reported in Table 1, but this may occur because New York City adjusts fewer cases unofficially. However, "PINS" youth do not fare as well as the "delinquents"; 81 per cent are convicted as compared to only 58 per cent of the youth who commit offenses that are regarded as crimes if committed by an adult. The actual rates of commitment disclose a 5 per cent difference to the disadvantage of PINS youth.

If actual length of stay in the institution is considered, the comparisons again reveal that the PINS label is not a benign one. In a pilot study that focused on a 1963 random sample of officially adjudicated PINS and delinquent boys appearing in Manhattan Court, the author gathered data on the range, median, and average length of stay for institutionalized boys. The *range* of institutional stay was 2 to 28 months for delinquents and 4 to 48 months for PINS; the *median* was 9 months for delinquents and 13 months for PINS; and the *average* length of stay was 10.7 months for delinquents and 16.3 months for PINS. Regardless of the mode of measurement, it is apparent that more boys convicted and sentenced for juvenile offenses are actually punished for longer periods of time than juveniles convicted for criminal-type offenses.

The President's Commission on Law Enforcement, agreeing that any formal court conviction is stigmatizing (with perhaps lifelong effects on employment and military service), has suggested that "serious consideration should be given to complete elimination from the court's jurisdiction of conduct illegal only for a child."[26] Until this occurs, the invention of the "PINS" label may only be increasing the disparity between conduct and disposition inherent in present juvenile court legislation and administration. (In the next section, this inference is supported by further evidence.)

Detention and Severity of Final Disposition

There have been many studies of juvenile detention practices in the United States. The general conclusions emanating from these studies are stated in the survey conducted recently by the National Council on Crime and Delinquency for the President's Commission on Law Enforcement:

> At one time, detaining an accused person was based on the fear that, if left at liberty, he would fail to appear for trial or might commit other violations. Times have changed. Pre-trial release on bond or recognizance is now commonplace for adults, especially those with money or influence. Not so for children, who may be detained—no matter how inadequate the place of detention or the type of care given—by exercise of the *parens patriae* doctrine upon which the juvenile courts were established.
>   . . . Confusion and misuse pervade detention. It has come to be used by police and probation officers as a disposition; judges use it for punishment, protection, storage, and lack of other facilities. More than in any other phase of the correctional process, the use of detention is colored by rationalization, duplicity, and double talk, generally unchallenged because the law is either defective or not enforced, and because it is always easy to make a case for detaining on the grounds of the child's offenses or the demands of the public as interpreted by the police or the press.[27]

Given this strong tendency to use juvenile detention for a variety of reasons that have nothing to do with whether the accused (presumed to be innocent until proved guilty) will appear at his trial or dispositional hearing, it would not be surprising to find that unequal treatment exists in comparison to adult detention practices. But comparisons of this type cannot be made with available data.

More reliable inferences can be drawn about detention and the second type of problem (i.e., failure to match punishment and degree of social harm). Table 3 indicates the proportion of New York City youth detained for any length of time, comparing those who appear in court on "delinquency" and "PINS" petitions; in addition, these two offender categories are compared according to the per cent detained for more than thirty days, if they are detained. It is quite evident that substantial differences exist in

TABLE 3. COMPARISON OF DETENTION DATA FOR DELINQUENT AND PINS YOUTH APPEARING IN COURT, NEW YORK CITY, JULY 1, 1965–JUNE 30, 1966 (BOYS AND GIRLS COMBINED)

Detention Data	Type of Court Petition	
	Juvenile Delinquents	Juvenile PINS
Per cent detained—if petition	$\dfrac{31}{N=(6,497)}$	$\dfrac{54}{(3,849)}$
Per cent detained more than thirty days—if detained	$\dfrac{25}{N=(2,024)}$	$\dfrac{50}{(2,067)}$

SOURCE: State of New York, "Report on the Family Court" (Report of the Administrative Board of the Judicial Conference for the Judicial Year, July 1, 1965–June 30, 1966), reprint from 12th Annual Report, pp. 44–51.

the detention rates of the two offender groups. Those charged with the least socially harmful offenses (i.e., noncriminal) are, in fact, detained much more often—and for longer periods of time.

Whether detention per se also makes it more likely that a youngster will be found guilty and sentenced to an institution has not been studied, except for the author's pilot study. Using the same type of sample as reported in the discussion of length of stay, data were also gathered concerning previous court appearance and detention prior to final disposition. Boys that have never appeared, or appeared once, are much more likely to be institutionalized if they have also been detained prior to their dispositional hearing. Apparently, if boys have appeared two or more times then detention is not related to institutionalization. Detention per se can have an impact, but not as consistently strong as was found in the bail studies.

TRADITIONAL STANDARDS OF JUSTICE AND JUVENILE COURT PHILOSOPHY

If the conventional standards of justice are used as a norm, there exists sufficient evidence for indicating that the current system of juvenile adjudication probably operates unreasonably in many cases. However, it is important to recognize that the type of evidence presented refers to problems of juvenile justice *only* if we utilize the standards of conventional criminal justice.

Proponents of the traditional juvenile court philosophy might suggest that these traditional standards of justice should not be employed. The juvenile court, they might argue, does not punish the offender but, rather, hands down treatment-oriented decisions according to individual need. The court's philosophy of "justice" is to treat the offender's underlying needs, irrespective of the legal distinctions among offenses. Some proponents of this philosophy might even argue that a boy who has committed a fairly trivial offense might, nevertheless, need a correctional or treatment regime of long duration, whereas another boy who has engaged in an act of serious wrongdoing might not need institutional treatment at all.

By utilizing the conventional standards of justice we have implicitly rejected this traditional juvenile court philosophy. On what grounds do we challenge this philosophy and adopt instead the standards of the adult system of justice?

1. It can hardly be disputed that court-imposed treatment plans are not freely chosen by juvenile offenders and their families but are based on a coercive deprivation of liberty. Therefore, court-imposed "treatment" is actually a type of punishment—however benign the intentions or rhetoric of the court personnel.

2. If probation and institutionalization—the two basic "modalities of treatment"—involve restrictions on the liberty of parents and children, then care must be taken that punishment not be meted out unfairly and unreasonably. Adherence to the standards of fairness and justice can provide important safeguards ensuring that the deprivation of liberty will not be arbitrary and unreasonable. The treatment ethos does not contain safeguards that can be consistently applied to prevent arbitrary and unreasonable "treatment" of offenders. Therefore, even benign treatment of offenders will be less arbitrary and unreasonable if rehabilitation plans are introduced *after* a fair and just adjudication limits their imposition and duration.

3. To oppose unregulated punishment implies that one adheres to a moral position in favor of reasonable standards. But morality aside, it is critically important for the juvenile court philosophy that the treatment personnel be capable of accurately diagnosing the presumed treatment needs of offenders. If their diagnoses are not reliable and valid, then the rationale for utilizing criteria that do not contain safeguards against unregulated punishment is weakened even further. Empirical studies that test this assumption of expertise are notably absent in the delinquency literature. However, in the general field of mental health there is sufficient empirical evidence that diagnoses can be, and often are, quite unreliable and invalid. Why should the juvenile court system with its well-known personnel problems be expected to perform any better than trained psychiatrists in providing diagnoses that are reliable and valid? [28]

4. Practically, there appears to be substantial doubt that the juvenile court system has been able to inaugurate and sustain treatment programs that are sufficiently individualized to meet "needs" as idealized by professional treatment personnel. Since institutional programs are operated on a congregate basis, it is doubtful that on a practical level *individualization* of every offender can even occur.

5. When empirical studies attempt to evaluate the effectiveness of the actual treatment regimes provided to juveniles, the following conclusion tends to emerge: The treatment programs geared to juvenile offenders do not appear to be successful in curbing renewed delinquency. [29]

The foregoing assessment indicates that the modern juvenile court philosophy is based on assumptions that are unreasonable and an operational system that is questionable on moral, empirical, and practical grounds. We contend, therefore, that the current system should be assessed by the traditional norms of criminal justice in regard to judicial outcomes, as well as procedures.

IMPLICATIONS FOR RESEARCH

Although the evidence we have cited strongly suggests that problems are prevalent, there remains a need to control for prior court appearances, to categorize offenses more precisely, and to conduct comparisons by specific locales of court jurisdiction. With these controls, the direct study of the three types of problems could be geared to testing explicit hypotheses. The hypotheses might state that even when juvenile offenders are provided with a defense counsel and due process is observed, the following types of outcomes will be found in jurisdictions that attempt to implement the juvenile court philosophy of treatment:

1. *Unequal punishment of juveniles as compared to adults.* Juveniles who are found guilty of a minor (i.e., nonfelonious) offense and are institutionalized are likely to spend a longer period of time in the institution than adults in the same position.

2. *Failure to match punishment and degree of social harm.* In the juvenile court system, once cases reach the adjudication stage, there is virtually no difference in severity and duration between the punishments meted out for minor and serious offenses.

3. *Detention and severity of final disposition.* Detained juveniles are much more likely to be found guilty and institutionalized than are accused persons who are permitted to remain free prior to adjudication.

These hypotheses could be tested easily in any juvenile court jurisdiction that meets minimum procedural standards of justice as defined by the Gault case.

Besides these descriptive studies, a good case could also be made for conducting explanatory research with an historical focus. We do not know whether the problems of today are peculiar to the modern era, with its "rehabilitation" and "treatment" ethos. There is a strong likelihood that many juveniles have been unintentionally dealt with more severely by well-meaning reformers for a long time.

Special facilities for the "reformation" and "saving" of juveniles preceded the first juvenile court law by many years. New York City set up a house of refuge in 1825; the Lyman School for Boys, in Massachusetts, opened in 1847; the first juvenile court came into being more than fifty years later.[30] If investigation of available historical records revealed unequal treatment of juvenile offenders vis-à-vis adults for a century or more, then an explanation of the problem would have to take this into account. Crucial to an understanding of the continuity between "child-saving" justice and "rehabilitative" justice would be the status of juveniles and their parents in America. Juveniles have always held an inferior status, particularly if they come from poor or migrant households. How the resulting powerlessness is linked, historically, with the judicial handling of juveniles would probably be a rewarding subject for study.[31]

SOCIAL POLICY IMPLICATIONS

If the hypotheses regarding problems are upheld, there are a number of policy issues that will probably confront those interested in changing the status quo. Some of them are as follows.

1. *The values of traditional justice* versus *the values of rehabilitation.* Every policy choice is based on value preferences. In many instances the values implicit in a given policy conflict with other cherished values. Many years ago, the system of juvenile justice began to be shaped by values associated with "child-saving" and "rehabilitation." It was argued that traditional conceptions

of criminal justice were secondary to these rehabilitative values. However, the Supreme Court opinion in the Gault case emphasized values associated with justice and argued that rehabilitative values were secondary. Any re-shaping of the societal response to juvenile misbehavior will have to come to grips with this basic conflict of values. Proponents of the values of traditional justice will have to focus on substantive outcomes, as well as on procedural aspects of adjudication.

2. *New laws* versus *new interpretations*. The juvenile court law in New York State, as in other states, permits a great deal of discretion regarding detention and institutionalization. If there were a concerted effort to realize the ideals of justice in the daily functioning of the system, it could be directed at obtaining new laws or new interpretations of existing laws. It is conceivable that judges could agree on administrative rules that sharply limit the extent and length of detention, as well as the duration of institutional commitments for minor offenses. On the other hand, a case could also be made for legislating these limits.

3. *Fixed penalties* versus *indeterminate punishment*. The current scale of penalties for juvenile misbehaviors or PINS offenses can be questioned. The juvenile court systems do not tend to sentence youth for short, fixed terms, as is done in adult misdemeanor proceedings. An indeterminate approach to punishment that yields many unreasonable outcomes is certainly open to question. Pragmatically, it is unclear how the interests of justice are served by imposing unclear penalties for clearly defined offenses. Perhaps they would be much better served by evolving a broader range of fixed penalties that would include one-day to two-day, weekend, and one-week sentences, as well as longer sentences with a fixed maximum. Short, fixed penalties could also be included in a determinate probation disposition; a special treatment ex-periment in California has unwittingly begun to demonstrate the feasibility of such an approach.

4. *Rehabilitative philosophy* versus *social accountability*. If the major ra-tionale for the current treatment accorded to children rests on the assumption of rehabilitation, then there ought to be empirical evidence to support the treatment-oriented decisions. However, empirical evidence is lacking that long-term treatment is more successful than short-term treatment; that private residential treatment centers yield better results than the average state institu-tion; or that any court-sanctioned intervention is superior to no intervention. At a minimum, there should be social accountability for *all* the youth proc-essed through the court system to determine empirically whether justice is actually operative and intervention schemes are worthwhile. The public cur-rently pays for a system of rehabilitative operations of unproved value; is it willing to pay for research to make certain that the juvenile court system is socially accountable?

SUMMARY AND CONCLUSIONS

The Supreme Court has highlighted the procedural injustice associated with the juvenile court tradition; this article has attempted to provide evidence that substantive injustice is also associated with the juvenile court. It appears quite likely that even in fair jurisdictions—like New York City—minor juvenile offenders are deprived of their liberty for much longer periods of time than adult misdemeanants. If one is concerned about traditional standards of justice it appears that our current juvenile court system is an unjust one; the Gerald Gaults of America have yet to be counted in their entirety.

From a theoretical perspective, the juvenile court tradition affords another example of how unintended consequences can flow from benign intentions. The juvenile court reformers were successful in taking children out of the traditional criminal court jurisdictions; however, on behalf of humanitarian motives they engaged in unregulated "treatment." In the process they have probably caused juveniles to be detained more frequently and institutionalized for longer periods of time than adults. By paying little heed to the seriousness of the youngster's offenses they have unwittingly been "easy" on the felonious delinquent and "hard" on the misdemeaning youngster.

Our societal response to youthful deviations has always been subject to the influence of competing interest groups. It is time to reshape that response so that professional language does not obscure punishment as a palpable fact, and benign intentions do not disguise the operation of an unjust system.

NOTES

1 "In re Gault (Supreme Court of the United States, May 15, 1967)," in *Task Force Report: Juvenile Delinquency and Youth Care,* President's Committee on Law Enforcement and Administration of Justice (Washington, D.C.: Government Printing Office, 1967), Appendix A, pp. 57–76.

2 *Ibid.,* p. 59.

3 See John W. Chapman, "Justice and Fairness," in Carl J. Friedrich and John W. Chapman (eds.), *Justice* (New York: Atherton, 1963), pp. 147–69.

4 The problem is an acute one for the traditional criminal system as well, since discretion is quite prevalent at the precharging and postconviction stages of both the criminal and the juvenile court processes. See Sanford Kadish, "Legal Norm and Discretion in the Police and Sentencing Processes," *Harvard Law Review,* 75 (March 1962), 904–31.

5 For example, see the following: Monrad G. Paulsen, "The Delinquency, Neglect, and Dependency Jurisdiction of the Juvenile Court," in Margaret K. Rosenheim, *Justice for the Child* (New York: The Free Press, 1962), pp. 44–81; Chapman, *op. cit.; Task Force Report, op. cit.,* p. 23; Jerome Hall, *General Principles of Criminology,* 2d ed. (Indianapolis: Bobbs-Merrill, 1960), p. 310; *Task Force Report: The Courts,* President's Committee on Law Enforcement and Administration of Justice (Washington, D.C.: Government Printing Office, 1967), pp. 23–24; and Paul W. Tappan, *Crime, Justice and Correction* (New York: McGraw-Hill, 1960), pp. 392–93.

6 Francis A. Allen, "The Borderland of the Criminal Law: Problems of 'Socializing' Criminal Justice," *Social Service Review,* 32 (June 1958), 110. Author's emphasis.

7 For a convenient summary of the general problems of detention, see *Task Force Report: Corrections,* President's Committee on Law Enforcement and Administration of Justice (Washington, D.C.: Government Printing Office, 1967), pp. 119–29.

8 See Anne Rankin, "The Effect of Pretrial Detention," *New York University Law Review,* 39 (June 1964), pp. 641–56; Daniel J. Freed and Patricia M. Wald, *Bail in the United States: 1964* (New York: The Vera Foundation, 1964), pp. 45–48.

9 We are *not* claiming that others have been unaware of juvenile court problems related to justice. However, a fair reading of the literature indicates that the issues of substantive justice had not been operationally defined so that empirical data could provide assessments of the court's operation.

10 *Task Force Report: Juvenile Delinquency, op. cit.,* p. 23.

11 Paulsen, *op. cit.,* p. 52.

12 *Ibid.,* p. 55.

13 Herbert A. Bloch and Frank T. Flynn, *Delinquency: The Juvenile Offender in America Today* (New York: Random House, 1956), p. 357.

14 David R. Barrett, William J. T. Brown, and John M. Cramer, "Notes. Juvenile Delinquents: The Police, State Courts, and Individualized Justice," *Harvard Law Review*, 79 (Feb. 1966), 778, n. 13.

15 *Task Force Report: Corrections, op. cit.,* p. 76.

16 Paul Lerman, "Evaluating Institutions for Delinquents: Implications for Research and Social Policy," *Social Work*, 13, (July 1968), 55–64. The irony that degree of professionalization is strongly related to severity of "treatment" is not restricted to the institutional sphere. Similar relationships have been found for police and judges; the more their outlook is similar to a treatment orientation, the greater the likelihood that police will file arrests and judges will institutionalize. See two studies reported in Stanton Wheeler (ed), *Controlling Delinquents* (New York: Wiley, 1968), pp. 9–30 and 31–60.

17 Lerman, *op. cit.*

18 *Task Force Report: The Courts, op. cit.,* p. 17.

19 Allen, *op. cit.,* p. 117.

20 See *Task Force Report: The Courts, op. cit.,* pp. 14–28.

21 Paulsen, *op. cit.,* p. 56.

22 *Juvenile Court Statistics, 1965,* Children's Bureau Statistical Series 83, Department of Health, Education and Welfare (Washington, D.C.: Government Printing Office, 1966), Table B.

23 *Juvenile Court Statistics, 1964.*

24 See *Task Force Report: Juvenile Delinquency, op. cit.,* pp. 25–27.

25 State of New York, "Report of the Family Court" (Report of the Administrative Board of the Judicial Conference for the Judicial Year July 1, 1965–June 30, 1966), reprint from 12th Annual Report.

26 *Task Force Report: Juvenile Delinquency, op. cit.,* p. 27.

27 *Task Force Report: Corrections, op. cit.,* pp. 119 and 129.

28 For example, see Leo Srole, Thomas S. Langner, Stanley T. Michael, Marvin K. Opler, and Thomas A. C. Rennie, *Mental Health in the Metropolis* (New York: McGraw-Hill, 1962), esp. pp. 127–51 and pp. 395–407.

29 Lerman, *op. cit.*

30 *Task Force Report: Juvenile Delinquency, op. cit.,* pp. 2–4.

31 The juvenile courts of today are still mainly the courts of the poor—even if the accused are provided with a new name, fair laws and procedures, and defense counsel. See Monrad G. Paulsen, "Juvenile Courts, Family Courts, and the Poor Man," *California Law Review*, 54 (May 1966), 649–716.

7. Let's Take Another Look at the Juvenile Court *

ROBERT GARDNER

IN JULY OF THIS YEAR [1964], the first session of the National College of State Trial Judges was held on the campus of the University of Colorado. I was a member of the staff of that college. For one week during that month,

* Hon. Robert Gardner, "Let's Take Another Look at the Juvenile Court," *Juvenile Court Judges Journal*, Vol. 15, No. 4 (Winter, 1964), pp. 13–18. Reprinted by permission of the author.

an institute for juvenile court judges took place on the same campus. As a trial judge with a juvenile court background, I was constantly shocked when the judges from the college referred to the juvenile court judges as "those juvenile *people*." Finally, this attitude became crystallized in a conversation I had with a Texas judge at lunch one day. I was defining the juvenile court when the Texan terminated the conversation with this statement: "Gardner, the trouble with the juvenile court is that it isn't a *court*."

I am afraid that this attitude . . . reflects a rather widespread attitude on the part of the bench, the bar, and the public, that the juvenile court is not a court in the traditional sense, but is some kind of a social-worker adjunct to a sociological concept in the handling of young people—an arm of the probation department, as it were.

I deny the truth of these charges. I think, however, it would be unrealistic to deny the existence of these charges or to deny that their very existence harms the entire juvenile court movement. The questions to be asked are: Do juvenile court judges wish to admit the existence of these charges; do they consider them of sufficient gravity to attempt to do something about them; and what, if anything, can be done to answer them without destroying the effectiveness of the juvenile court process? With full knowledge of the sensitivity to criticism and suggestion of some juvenile court judges, I do feel that the charges should be recognized, examined, and if there are any steps that may be taken which will effectively answer them without damaging the juvenile court, that these steps should at least receive serious consideration. With this thought in mind and with full recognition of the fact that some of my suggestions may not only be unpopular but may be without merit, I submit herewith with a series of proposals for consideration.

As a background for a proper frame of reference for the author, I should say that my own experience in the juvenile court covers a span of seventeen years, from a time when our juvenile court hearings consumed only part of one day per week (with a half dozen probation officers and no specialized services) to a highly specialized full-time court serving over a million people (with a large probation staff and a vast complex of services).

ELEVATE JUVENILE COURTS

First, in an effort to upgrade the juvenile court, to enhance its status, and to improve its image . . . I would suggest that wherever possible the juvenile court be a part of the highest trial court in the state. The juvenile court should *never* be an "inferior" court. It is my firm belief that the responsibilities of the judge of the juvenile court are the most important of any in our judicial system. Each decision of a judge of this court is of vital and lasting importance to a child, to a family, and to society. Because of this importance, it is little enough to expect that in each state these responsibilities be placed in the hands of the court of the highest trial jurisdiction.

ROTATE THE JUDGES

My second suggestion is that in those states in which the juvenile court is a part of the general trial court the practices of assigning judges to full-time careers in the juvenile court be discontinued. I am aware that in 1963 the

National Council of Juvenile Court Judges adopted a resolution supporting
the nonrotation of juvenile court judges into other assignments. This policy
does offer the advantage of permitting the judge to develop some expertise in
his role and of establishing some continuity to his program. On the other
hand, it fosters alienation and loss of communication with the balance of the
bench and lends itself to the attitude expressed in the first paragraph of this
article. When one judge is removed physically (and usually geographically)
from the rest of the bench, an invisible wall grows up between him and the
other members of the bench. This situation lends itself to the statement made
recently by Dean Joseph Lohman of the School of Criminology of the University of California: "Ordinarily, the people who occupy the juvenile court are
persons who have found their way there because for some reason or other
they have been shunted aside."

RESTORE COURTROOM FORMALITY

My third suggestion is that traditional court formality be restored to the
juvenile court. There is a dignity, a solemnity, and a symbolism in formal
judicial proceedings which are now being lost in the informality of the
juvenile court. The judge should remove himself from his "informal" status
and should resume his traditional position on the bench—not as a protector,
advisor, guardian, or friend but as a fair, impartial, detached, objective, and,
if necessary, stern conscience of society. There should never be any question
in the mind of anyone in the courtroom but that the man in the black robe is
a judge in the truest sense of the word. Incidentally, if there is any court in
which the wearing of the robe is essential, it is in the juvenile court.

As part of this formality, at least during the jurisdictional phase of the case,
there should not only be the symbolism mentioned, but there should be formal
attention paid to all traditional judicial processes and procedures. At this
stage of the proceeding, only legal evidence should be received, and this
should be received under time-tested and constitutionally approved safeguards.
Hearings should be prompt, fair, and in accordance with due process.

ESTABLISH SEPARATE COURTS

My next suggestion is that the present juvenile court which handles abandoned, neglected, dependent, and delinquent children in the same court should
be divided . . . into two separate legal entities with two separate names and
two separate legal philosophies—one court for dependent children and another for delinquents.

With headlines screaming of mounting juvenile crime, the public understandably takes a dim view of anyone who has been in juvenile court. There
is a stigma to juvenile court proceedings, a stigma that may well be carried
through life in spite of well-intentioned efforts to keep these proceedings
confidential. To the average citizen, a young person who has been in juvenile
court is a "juvie" with all that word connotes—the switchblade knife, the
gang rumble, senseless violence and total disregard for authority and the
rights of others. While in some jurisdictions, such as California, the juvenile
court law distinguishes between dependents and delinquents and rigorously

keeps the two categories physically separated, it is submitted that this fine distinction in the law is not clear to the public. I have answered enough employment and military questionnaires plus private inquiries to realize that society does not make the legal distinction between dependents and delinquents. The unfortunate dependent child who is handled at the present time in a court with the same name as the delinquent bears, insofar as the uninformed public is concerned, the brand of "juvie" even though this child has committed no offense and has broken no law. It is a very real injustice that these children must go through life with the stigma of having been in juvenile court.

I suggest that it take something far more obvious and far more dramatic than a fine legal distinction between a dependent and a delinquent to make the necessary distinction between the offender and the nonoffender. It is submitted that another name could and would make this distinction. The present juvenile court with its guardianship philosophy (assuming at all times that judicial procedures are followed) is admirably suited to handle the neglected child. This court, however, should be given a new name so that the whole world will know that the youngster brought into it is not an under-age criminal but is simply the tragic result of environmental factors over which he has no control. Recognizing that juvenile courts go by various names in various jurisdictions, I would suggest as a generality that the court handling the dependent child be called the children's court and the one handling the delinquent child be called juvenile court. Into children's court let us bring the unfortunate, the neglected, abused, abandoned, the victims of cruelty, neglect, and depravity—but let us exclude from this court the delinquents.

Admittedly, many of the roots of dependency and delinquency reach into the same unhealthy social background. This reason, it is assumed, was the basis of comingling these categories in the first juvenile court in Chicago in 1899—and slavishly followed since. However, it is submitted that, sociological philosophy to the contrary notwithstanding, the coincidence of an unhealthy background is not sufficient cause to handle these two categories of young people in the same court. It is simply not fair to the dependent, neglected, or abandoned child.

Legalize the "Juvenile" Court

My next suggestion is that, having removed the dependent, neglected, or abandoned child into another court, the juvenile court which would then handle only delinquents conduct itself, insofar as its procedures are concerned, by the same standards as the criminal court (still remaining separate, of course, from the adult criminal court.) This new juvenile court, however, should be divorced from the guardianship and protective philosophy of the present court, while at the same time keeping its rehabilitative functions.

A very necessary part of the procedures of this new juvenile court would be to afford the young people charged with crime the same constitutional rights afforded adults charged with crime.

While the law provides that an adjudication in juvenile court is not to be termed conviction of a crime, nevertheless, for all practical purposes, this is a legal fiction presenting, as Justice Thomas White of the Supreme Court of California once said, "a challenge to credibility and doing violence to reason."

One of the most persistent charges made against the juvenile court is that in this court young people are being treated as second-class citizens. I find it difficult in all honesty to deny this charge. *Time* magazine in a recent article on the juvenile courts said, "All too often protectiveness has made them so unjudicial that they are accused of dispensing injustice." Certainly it is a fact that in the present juvenile court the young person charged with a public offense is denied the right afforded to an adult charged with the same offense.

For example, since the child is not charged with a crime, he is not entitled to bail, pending the determination of his guilt or innocence, but is often "detained" pending this determination. Also, since he is not charged with a crime, he is not entitled to the presumption of innocence or to demand that the proof of the crime charged be beyond a reasonable doubt and to a moral certainty. And, again, since he is not charged with a crime, he is not entitled to a trial by jury. In many jurisdictions he is not entitled to be confronted by the witnesses against him and the question of the truth or falsity of the charges contained in the petition are often tried on the basis of a probation officer's report. To me as a judge, a lawyer, and a citizen, this is patently unfair. In spite of a mountain of appellate decisions approving present practices under the *parens patriae* philosophy, it would appear basic that whether an individual is seventeen or seventy he should be entitled to exactly the same rights when his name, his reputation, and his liberty are at stake as a result of the charge of a criminal offense. A denial of these rights under the guise of "protecting" the minor is no answer. Any person, young or old, charged with a criminal offense should have a right to a determination of this charge by time-tested and constitutional methods. This can be done only by taking the delinquent category from the present philosophy of the juvenile court and putting this category into another court operated on the same procedural basis as the adult criminal court.

To the cry that this will result in a young person suffering a conviction of a crime, I can only say that the distinction between crime and delinquency has long since evaporated. As a matter of fact, in the current connotation of the two words, I would rather have my child stand convicted of a crime than be branded as a juvenile delinquent.

In this regard, when the jurisdiction of the juvenile court depends on an allegation of commission of a crime, I can see no possible legal, philosophical, or moral ground for any judge considering a social history until after the fact-finding hearing. This, to me, smacks of reading a probation officer's report in adult court before the accused has either pleaded guilty or been convicted. This practice, which we must admit does exist, certainly lends itself to the charge that the juvenile court is not a court.

I am aware that some juvenile courts fear the presence of counsel not so much from the standpoint of desiring to deny the young person his rights, as [from] the fear that counsel will make the matters unduly time-consuming. In this regard our experience in California may be relevant. In 1961 our juvenile court law was amended to provide that the juvenile and his parents be advised at each and every stage of the proceeding as to their right to counsel and their right to the appointment of counsel in cases of indigency. Experience has shown that in spite of these constant admonitions few attorneys appear in juvenile court. In the first two years after the new law went into effect, I handled several thousand juvenile court cases; weeks went by without the appearance of counsel. Nevertheless, the knowledge that juveniles were entitled to counsel was a big step forward in curtailing criticism.

It is submitted that/ the same result would ensue were bail permitted. At one time, when bail was a matter of discretion in the juvenile courts of this state, I established a bail schedule in Juvenile Hall. During the course of the year that this program was in existence, bail was used only three times. Nevertheless, the existence of a right to bail removed that criticism from my court.

So, also, would be the result of the right to a jury trial. It is submitted that the number of times parents and child would wish to have their case presented to a jury would be extremely limited. Nevertheless, the fact that one could say of the juvenile court that the young person who comes before that court charged with a crime has all of the constitutional rights of an adult charged with the same crime would very effectively put an end to all criticism from bench, bar, and public in this regard and, it is submitted, would not in the least hamper the efficiency of the juvenile court.

Focus on Individual Responsibility

My next suggestion is that, having established the juvenile court for the handling of delinquents as a court with full constitutional rights, the focus of this court should change from the present guardianship philosophy to one of self-responsibility of the individual.

The philosophy of the present juvenile court is one of protection for the minor—protection from outside influences as well as protection from himself and, it is submitted, inevitably protection from self-responsibility. While the emphasis should, of course, remain on rehabilitation (rather than retribution), the focus should be on the responsibility of the individual. Eventually, the child grows into a man. Someday he is going to have to face responsibility. Why should this not start while he is still a child?

In both courts, juvenile and criminal, the judge now attempts to use all of the modern tools aimed at reformation and rehabilitation, not necessarily for any humanitarian purpose but simply because a successful program of rehabilitation is obviously the most effective way to protect society in the long run. Blind, unthinking retribution or punishment for the sake of vengeance has no part in the thinking of a judge of any court.

There should, however, be restored to the juvenile court the power to punish when the judge feels that reasonable punitive measures are called for as a part of a program of therapy. Strangely enough, even though the juvenile court philosophy has completely abandoned the punitive approach, most authorities agree that reasonable punishment does have value in the treatment and control of delinquency, be it adult or juvenile. Of course, for an intelligent and effective use of punishment, it must be used only as an integral part of a program of therapy and should never be harsh or degrading.

The concept of punishment has a place in our culture and to ignore it is unrealistic. The behaviorial sciences come to the same result, but with the use of another word—sanctions. In either case, be it punishment or sanction, the result is often the same—loss of liberty. To the individual who has lost his liberty, the distinction becomes fine indeed. In a good many years of handling several thousand cases in the juvenile court, I have experienced great difficulty in persuading the young person whose liberty is being taken from him (for his own protection) that he is not being punished. It is submitted that approaching the situation from a standpoint of punishment would mean a more honest, understandable approach to the juvenile than an esoteric philosophical concept completely beyond his comprehension. While we talk about treatment in a nonpunitive environment, the juvenile sent to a training school sees himself as confined and punished for something he did wrong. Of course, the judge sitting in this juvenile court must have the right to transfer cases from this court to the children's court when the facts indicate that the child, even though he has committed an offense, is basically in need of the protection of the other court. However, this must be a one-way street. Juvenile court to children's court—yes. Children's court to juvenile court—no.

ALTER POLICE AND PROBATION PRACTICES

Once the procedures outlined above are established, then my next suggestion is that certain changes be made in present practices existing in the handling of young people by police and probation agencies. This suggestion is that "informal" handling of young persons charged with crime by police officers and probation officers be terminated, and in its place there be substituted a simple arraignment procedure in the court wherein the offender, either by arrest or by citation, appears in court in *all* cases where he is advised of his rights, these rights are recognized and protected, and a determination made as to his guilt or innocence of the crime charged. To the objection that this would necessitate the hiring of a large number of juvenile court judges, attention is merely invited to the new juvenile traffic courts of this state and the present adult municipal courts wherein vast numbers of people are handled expeditiously by a small number of judges with a meticulous recognition at all times of their constitutional rights, yet with prompt determination of the merits of the cases. Obviously, most of the cases not now being referred to court are of a minor nature and a court appearance would not involve any prolonged hearing or any intensive, costly, or extensive probation investigation. The suggested procedure is one that affords the juvenile full protection of his rights in court proceedings with a judicial determination of the truth or falsity of the charge and at the same time establishes an orderly court disposition of his case. The "informal" handling of juveniles in this jurisdiction has grown to the extent that 50 per cent of all young people who come to the attention of the law-enforcement authorities are handled informally by the police agency. In those cases in which a referral is made to the probation department, here again roughly 50 per cent are handled informally by the probation officer.

This informal handling of juveniles by police agencies and probation officers is objectionable in three respects:

1. There is never a judicial adjudication as to the truth or falsity of the charge. Thus, the juvenile is left with the stigma of a criminal record in a police agency or a probation department for an offense of which he may or may not be guilty. If the juvenile is cited directly into court, a proper judicial adjudication can be made in each case. To the horrified cry that this will result in too many young people getting juvenile court records, I can only say that I would prefer that my child have a juvenile court record after proper adjudication than a police department or probation department record with no adjudication.

2. Having brought the juvenile into court, the court record and all police records are thereafter subject to expungement. The power and right to expunge the casual offense of the average irresponsible young person is extremely important. There exists in this state a law by which the person who has appeared in juvenile court may petition the court for an order sealing all records relating to such person's case including not only the court and probation records but all law-enforcement agency records as well. Each of the agencies must report back to the court that the record has been expunged. The law further provides that "thereafter the proceedings in such case shall be deemed never to have occurred and the juvenile may thereafter so reply according to any inquiry about the event, the records of which have been ordered sealed." In view of the fact that the court now receives a small percentage of all juveniles handled, this means that the majority of young people being handled informally by police and probation agencies carry a record that is *not* subject to expungement.

3. The present policy of police and probation officers handling juveniles informally results in an attitude on the part of the juvenile by the time he finally reaches the juvenile court by which he is completely indifferent to authority. Having been warned and counseled a half-dozen times by police and probation agencies, his respect for authority is completely gone by the time he finally arrives in court. Were he to be cited directly into court with its austere symbolism on his first contact with the law, it is submitted that some of the disrespect for authority might well be changed.

It is submitted that the above procedure by which each arrest of a juvenile by a police agency is made subject to judicial scrutiny might well cut down on the volume of under-age arrests, many of which are unnecessary and unjust. It is common knowledge that some police agencies engage in rather widespread practices in which juveniles are arrested ("picked up," "handled," "detained"—the result is the same) for situations in which no adult would be touched.

REDEFINE DELINQUENCY

My last suggestion is that each state and each judge might well review the types of cases which are being brought into juvenile court. Someone once referred to a great deal of the juvenile court caseload as a "lot of garbage." I have had the distinct impression from time to time that as a juvenile court judge I found myself acting as a glorified babysitter, a woefully inadequate substitute parent, an agency for advice to the lovelorn, a judicial truant officer, and a general catch-all for many problems which should be handled and would be handled by the average family were they not able to turn their responsibilities over to the juvenile court. And I think each of us has suffered the frustrating experience of trying to oversee the sexual activities of a large group of uncooperative young ladies who were "in danger of leading idle, lewd, dissolute or immoral lives" when they came before us and who were not much better when they left. Since each of the fifty states has a different definition of that which is dependency (that state at one time had fourteen different categories) and each judge is entitled to exercise his own discretion as to the type of case he is going to handle in his court, I am unable to comment further on this general subject. I think, however, that many juvenile court judges would agree that throughout the years our jurisdiction has become much too broad. We have attempted to become all things to all men, and in so doing we have diluted our efficiency in doing the basic job for which we were created.

The above suggestions are not an attack on the juvenile court. Rather, they are submitted with the thought that they may be of service to the whole juvenile court movement by challenging some of the ideas which have been accepted without question for the last sixty-five years. The patina of age does not necessarily prove the value of a philosophical or a legal concept, and intelligent questioning is still considered the best vehicle our society has developed to ascertain truth. Unhappily, there is an attitude on the part of a very considerable number of persons in the juvenile field that any questioning of the status quo is heresy. However, it is only through informed, intelligent controversy that a fair determination can be made.

PART FOUR

CORRECTIONS

Introduction

It is customary to think of corrections as taking place primarily in residential institutions, after a juvenile court has weighed the charges and the evidence, formally made a finding of delinquency, and rendered a decision concerning disposition. However, earlier Parts have indicated that the social workers and cottage parents in institutions are not the sole agents of official attempts to influence youth. A variety of persons engage in correctional decisions at earlier stages of processing. Many youth, in fact, are even institutionalized in a detention facility prior to an adjudication of fact and during the period of presentence investigation. Although these presentence dispositions are legitimated as judicial decision, it is evident that holding youth in custody for 24 hours or more is also the result of a correctional decision. It is possible analytically to separate the judicial and correctional aspects of youth handling; in practice, however, it may be more difficult when courts administer correctional facilities as well as juvenile justice, as is the case currently in 32 states.

Detention and probation are the two largest correctional programs in use today. Perhaps because of the close association of detention and probation with the courts, corrections has often been identified solely with post-sentence institutional programs. However, for the purposes of this reader, corrections begins with decisions concerning detention and ends with decisions terminating parole (*i.e.,* aftercare).

Historically, the operation of a separate juvenile correctional system is much older than autonomous juvenile adjudications. The document supporting the creation of the New York City House of Refuge is dated 1824; the first juvenile court began operating in Illinois almost 75 years later. The philosophy of the juvenile court borrowed heavily from existing correctional views. As the court developed, it began to exercise an influence on correctional philosophy and practice.

Selection 1, by Empey, provides a brief review of important trends in American corrections. Until recently, the dominant ideological approach to offenders can be summarized as a program of three R's: Revenge, Restraint, and Rehabilitation. A fourth R is being increasingly emphasized— Reintegration of the offender into the community after a period of incarceration. As Empey points out, this progression has occurred mainly on the level of intention. On a practical level, there has also been a trend toward

261

more humane handling of offenders, but unfortunately, this has been mitigated by the tendency to confuse humanitarianism with specific programs of rehabilitation. It is possible to be humane to offenders without offering counseling, guided group interaction, or residential treatment.

Despite the growth of more humane practices and attempts at rehabilitation, coercion and sanctions remain a part of correctional programs. The sanctions used today appear to be more humane than the practices of a hundred years ago; but it is important to recognize that detention stays, institutionalization in therapeutic programs, and even probation all involve restrictions on personal liberty. The restrictions, of course, can vary from being in custody twenty-four hours a day to being forced to obey the rules for living accompanying a legal probation order. Whatever their nature, restrictions on liberty, as Lerman notes in Part III, involves the coercion of individuals by the state and in effect comprise types of punishment. If it is true that punishment occurs in all correctional programs sanctioned by the courts, it is useful to consider why this is so. Is it just for revenge or to be punitive—as some argue—or are there other reasons? Toby deals with this issue in selection 2 by asking, "Is punishment necessary?"

In general, it is apparent that correctional programs are not only rehabilitative in intent or practice. Three orientations tend to govern current efforts: control, reformation, and humane treatment of offenders. If each goal could be pursued separately, the correctional task would be greatly simplified. But this is not the case; all three are expected simultaneously of any effective program. Since these goals may often be in conflict, it is not surprising that correctional programs can vary enormously in their attempts to accommodate this complex assignment. These basic dilemmas are often beclouded by the conventional rhetoric, which emphasizes rehabilitation as the sole goal of corrections. The result is often great disparity between rhetorical intention and actual practices. In this respect, corrections is quite similar to the juvenile courts.

The complexity and dilemmas confronting corrections are acute in regard to detention decisions and practices. The National Council on Crime and Delinquency, as part of a nationwide survey of corrections for the President's Commission, documented the enormous diversity in the use of detention. According to this authoritative survey excerpted in selection 3, some communities detain only a small fraction of accused offenders prior to adjudication while others detain almost all of the juveniles scheduled to appear in court. The rationales offered by the high-detention communities range from "just teaching them a lesson" to holding youth as a matter of convenience while working up diagnostic and presentence reports. The legal impropriety of detaining youngsters on such grounds is worth noting, since decisions to deprive youngsters of liberty should presumably address the issue of whether accused youth will appear for a trial (where they are presumed to be innocent until legally found guilty). The irony evident in these rationales should also be highlighted. The punitive argument ("teaching them a lesson") is usually associated with a *control* orientation to corrections. The diagnostic argument is, of course, associated with a *rehabilitative* orientation. However, these apparently divergent ideologies can lead to the same consequence—a decision to detain prior to adjudication. Just as rehabilitation should not be confused with humaneness, neither should it be confused with fairness or justice. (See, in this connection, the Lerman article in Part III).

Selection 3 also offers another example of how the response to a social problem becomes an intrinsic part of the problem. If jurisdictions refrained —or were restrained—from detaining so many youngsters, there would be fewer overcrowded facilities. Communities that do not critically examine their criteria for detaining may decide to build new facilities. But communities that permit an enormous array of nonlegal reasons to legitimate the detention of youngsters are likely to find that the new facilities can also become overcrowded. Many communities could solve their "detention problem" by redefining detention criteria.

The survey on probation also reveals some dilemmas of correctional practice. It points out that probation departments, whether or not they are administered directly by juvenile courts, are generally charged with three important functions: (1) intake and screening youngsters out of the judicial system; (2) social study, diagnosis, and presentencing reports; and (3) supervision and treatment of adjudicated offenders. Many large departments are specialized, so that the intake and screening function is carried out relatively independently of the other functions. (Problems in screening are described in the readings in Part III, on the court.) The other functions are usually carried out as part of a probation officer's caseload. The possibility that zeal in carrying out the diagnostic function can lead to the probation officer's recommending control measures (*i.e.,* detention) has already been discussed. The major probation task of "supervision and treatment" also involves difficulties.

The survey suggests that supervision involves "surveillance, service, and counseling." Service and counseling imply a goal of rehabilitation; surveillance implies social control as a goal. The survey asserts that these two goals are interrelated; it does not clearly point out that they are often in conflict. The probation officer is often forced to choose between acting as an enforcement officer and as a service-counseling officer. It is clearly difficult to develop and maintain a confidential relationship for the purpose of helping youngsters while at the same time using privileged information as an officer of the court. The dilemma is clearly revealed when probation officers petition the court to revoke a delinquent's probationary status on the ground that the youngster has failed to obey the rules set down by the court. Often, the conditions for remaining on probation are more stringent than those implied in the original law defining delinquency; in effect, the probation officer is expected to enforce a special administrative definition of delinquency over and above the sociolegal definition that prevails in the community.

Without reasonable guidelines, probation officers probably utilize their discretion to selectively play enforcement or service roles and to decide which rules will be ignored or noticed. It may be that reasonable guidelines cannot be set down, and that the enforcement function and the service function should be split apart into two distinct jobs. It is evident that these problems are important, since they involve the basic tasks of probation agencies.

The survey of state juvenile institutions indicates that many states have yet to evolve a "working philosophy" that emphasizes humane treatment and rehabilitative programs, rather than just custodial control. In practice,

the ratio of custodial personnel to youngsters is far higher than the combined ratio of teachers and clinical personnel. Ten states still authorize
the use of corporal punishment, one indication of inhumane treatment. The
survey also reveals that external interest groups and problems have a
strong influence on correctional programs. Many public institutions are
used as a dumping ground by communities (and the state) to take care of
child-welfare, mental-health, and even medical problems; they do not have
the power to control their population at intake. Custodial-control procedures are often stricter than correctional administrators desire because they
fear that runaways will damage the institution's image and perhaps its
chances of obtaining financial resources. Even the location of facilities may
not be in their control. In general, the survey provides evidence that, besides the internal difficulties of reconciling conflicting values, the institutions must also accommodate to more powerful external forces. Many of
the important policy decisions that affect institutions are, therefore, made
in a political rather than a correctional context.

The Task Force surveys also deal with a number of other issues—
recruiting qualified manpower, organizing services, and the relative distribution of costs among programs—all of sufficient importance to warrant
the inclusion of readings devoted only to them. There is one issue, however, that the surveys do not regard as problematic that warrants special
attention—the National Council's use of standards. At numerous points in
the survey, references are made to national standards; these standards, in
turn, are used to evaluate existing practices or to propose changes. It is
useful to be aware of these standards and how they are used in policy
analysis and recommendations. Standards should not be accepted at face
value; they require as much scrutiny as any other set of policy recommendations. There are at least three useful questions that can be posed
regarding standards:

1. What groups are proposing and sponsoring them?
2. What evidence, if any, exists on behalf of the proposed standards?
3. What value preferences are implicit—or explicit—in the standards?

The standards offered in these surveys are generally proposed by experts
called together by the NCCD; experts assembled by the President's Commission or the Department of Health, Education, and Welfare; and individuals attempting to summarize the best thinking in the field. Usually the
credentials of these groups are impeccable; that is why there is a tendency
to accept their proposals so readily.

Answers to the second question, however, should persuade readers to
assume a critical stance toward the standards. It is difficult to think of any
standards that are supported by acceptable empirical evidence. Size of
institution, caseloads for probation and aftercare workers, ratio of professional personnel to children, organization of services, and length of stay at
institutions—none of these recommendations is based on empirical evidence. Instead they are all based on "practice wisdom." But practice wisdom is grounded not in facts but in shared beliefs, norms, and values; the
standards may therefore represent a preferred way of practicing corrections
based on a priority of values. If this is so, then the ordering of values
should be examined by potential users of the standards. It is possible that
some standards would lead to an undesirable value conflict or even undermine cherished values.

For example, in the discussion of aftercare, the survey cites the standard that youngsters should be held for no more than three years but that there should be no minimum. Aftercare or post-institutional parole should be linked to such a policy, according to the NCCD. This standard, however, is based on the preference of occupational groups, particularly social work and psychiatry, that deem such a stay useful for the practice of their techniques of rehabilitation. There are sound reasons for sharply questioning an indeterminate sentencing standard. First, there is no empirical support for the underlying premise that youngsters are more likely to be rehabilitated if they are unsure about their length of incarceration than if they are faced with a determinate period of custody; even if normlessness could be defended psychologically, there remains the moral issue of whether it is humane to inculcate this kind of anxiety. Second, there is no evidence that lengthy institutional stays, whether determinate or indeterminate, are any more effective than shorter stays; even if we are not persuaded by the efficient use of resources, it is apparent that paying extra costs for no apparent benefits is not a very attractive standard. Third, this kind of standard disregards the elementary considerations of justice, since no distinctions are offered between minor and serious offenders; it appears unreasonable to trade off the traditional values of justice in favor of an unproved benefit. In summary, this NCCD standard is questionable—probably harmful—because it probably induces unnecessary anxiety, incurs extra costs without any increase in benefit, and promotes the practice of treating many juveniles unjustly.

It is quite unlikely that the experts who participated in the writing and dissemination of these standards intended these consequences. Unfortunately, unintended consequences are as real as any intended outcomes. Not all of the standards, of course, have unintended negative outcomes; some standards can result in unforseen benefits. The standards relating to detention could, for example, not only reduce overcrowding; they might also lead to the introduction of fairer legal procedures to circumscribe excessive judicial discretion.

Through attention to the results of correctional practices and programs —not just the stated intention—fresh ideas and approaches are gaining in acceptability as alternatives to incarceration. In selection 4, Empey discusses these approaches, which attempt to keep youngsters in the community by providing a variety of services more flexible and intensively. A close reading of this selection reveals that the programs are experimenting with new forms of social control as well as new modes of delivering rehabilitative services.

The new approach also emphasizes the offender's successful integration in the community where he must eventually live. Empey emphasizes the general problems of re-entry of institutionalized offenders. One implication of his analysis is that institutions and social groups external to corrections and the offender must assist in the reintegration process. Parole officers and aftercare workers, regardless of their professional knowledge and expertise, cannot magically reintegrate offenders by interpersonal influence techniques alone. Community change—not just offender and correctional change—may become necessary.

The relative effectiveness of old and new approaches to corrections is discussed in selection 5. Lerman's analysis of the problem of assessing effectiveness reveals that residential treatment centers are no more effective than state training schools; that short-term residential programs are no less effective than long-term institutional stays; and that intensive community treatment programs (i.e., intensive probation) do not pose greater social-control risks than traditional institutional programs. His analysis also reveals how not paying attention to the problem of discretion can cause problems for evaluative research as well as for social policy and correctional practice.

The next group of articles focuses on the issue of changing corrections to accord with the newer approaches. The NCCD's analysis of the distribution of costs in corrections (selection 6) indicates that there is an extreme imbalance between expenditures for institutional and for community-based programs. If the costs were apportioned according to need, virtually all states would have to engage in a drastic redistribution of funds. The likelihood that this will occur is lessened by the dispersed centers of authority and responsibility for corrections in each state. The general problem of state responsibility for correctional planning change is discussed by the NCCD in selection 7.

The shift to the newer approaches also requires increased manpower. A traditional manpower policy assumes that college-trained persons constitute the desirable manpower pool to recruit and train. This conventional view is challenged by critics of the old corrections. In selection 8, Sigurdson argues in behalf of devising new careers for offenders and utilizing untrained manpower for correctional tasks. He claims that in many cases the use of nonprofessionals is preferable, not just expedient.

1. Correctional History *

LA MAR T. EMPEY

CURRENT TRENDS in reactions to crime are best understood in terms of an historical perspective. Correctional practices have been revolutionized twice in the past two centuries and these revolutions have important implications for contemporary development.[1]

The first revolution occurred in the late eighteenth and early nineteenth centuries and was generated, in part, by the growth of Western democracy and, in part, by the rational philosophers and legalists of that period. The latter had two objectives in mind. First, they wished to establish a more rational and equitable legal system. They reacted against the practice of basing penalties for crime on whether the offender and his victim were noblemen or commoners. All men, they believed, should be treated equally, not according to their stations in life but according to the crimes they had committed.

Second, they wished to make punishment more humanitarian. They believed that imprisonment should be substituted for the earlier forms of exile, execution, and corporal punishment. Imprisonment would serve as the means of eliminating the cruelties and excesses of that time. Accordingly, imprisonment became the predominant penalty for felonies in most of the Western world during the nineteenth century.[2]

The causation assumptions on which these philosophers based their corrective policies were that men are rational beings who operate on a pleasure-pain principle, doing that which gives them pleasure and avoiding that which gives them pain. They believed, therefore, that reactions to crime should be rationally based on the same principle: light punishment for light crimes, heavy punishment for serious crimes, making sure in each case that the pain of punishment slightly exceeds the pleasure of the crime. By utilizing imprisonment and establishing, by statute, a prescribed punishment for each kind of offense, they believed that they could control crime effectively.

Given this conceptual framework, the objectives which were imposed on correctional facilities were relatively clear and straightforward: The offender was to be punished and society was to be protected. Imprisonment would not

* LaMar T. Empey, *Studies in Delinquency: Alternatives to Incarceration*, U.S. Department of Health, Education and Welfare, Office of Juvenile Delinquency and Youth Development, Publication No. 9001, 1967, pp. 1–11.

only be more humane but would also help to deter other rational men from crime. It would be a lesson, teaching that crime does not pay.

This approach pervaded the legal practices of Western civilization and it has by no means been totally abandoned. It is still very much a part of our normative and legal structure today. Nevertheless, it has been shown to have several deficiencies.

Imprisonment has not worked out as an impartial and uniform reaction to crime. All criminals are not caught and legislatures cannot prescribe, like a pill, the way courts and correctional organizations should react to each offender depending not on situational or personal characteristics but on the crime he committed. It is simply too mechanistic a procedure to deal with the complex problems that characterize crime and criminals.

Second, the desired deterrent and rehabilitative effect of imprisonment was not borne out by accumulated evidence. Crime did not decrease, especially where long and repeated imprisonment was involved. It seemed to increase rather than decrease the likelihood of further violations. Furthermore, punishment through imprisonment was not universally applicable or adequate for such offenders as drug addicts, sexual psychopaths, the mentally deficient, or the mentally ill.

Finally, the number of prisoners confined continued to increase, resulting in constantly overcrowded prisons. The result not only questioned whether imprisonment was a more humanitarian response to crime but made it clear that the cost of imprisonment would eventually be prohibitive. The cost of housing, guarding, and meeting all the needs of prisoners would eventually become too great for society to bear.

The late nineteenth and early twentieth centuries, therefore, were marked by a decline in this classical approach to corrections and a second revolution was introduced. In addition to the problems generated by the first revolution, the second revolution gained impetus through the growth of Freudian psychology and the social sciences. Freudian psychology, for example, suggested that crime is not always a deliberate defiance of social norms but may be an unconscious response to personal problems. The offender may be *sick* rather than *wicked*. His violation of rules is more an illness than a conscious choice to do wrong.[3]

The social sciences, meanwhile, pointed to the influence of complex learning processes, to conflicting subcultural influences, and to conditions of class and ethnicity as sources of nonconformity, rather than a deliberate misuse of free will. The result was a tendency to view the offender as a deprived or handicapped person whose major deficiencies were to be found in his mental or emotional make-up. Treatment rather than punishment was called for, professionalism and specialization rather than a generalized response.

The treatment orientation that was introduced resulted in two striking changes in legal and correctional decision-making: (1) a *deferral* of correctional decisions from the time of sentencing, and (2) a *division* of responsibilities among more persons for making those decisions about the offender.[4] Prior to the second revolution, a criminal's fate was almost always decided once his guilt was established. The court was expected to impose sentence as defined by statute. If imprisonment was used, the legal system not only specified an exact duration for the penalty but even designated the institution to be used and the program to be followed, such as solitary confinement or hard labor.

With the introduction of the second revolution, however, all of this began to change. Statutes were introduced that permitted the court to defer sentencing decisions until the offender could be studied and recommendations made to the judge. Probation officers, psychiatric consultants, and others became advisors to the court. Decision responsibility was divided. Furthermore, it was divided not only among people close to the court but throughout the whole correctional process. The indeterminate sentence was also introduced so that classification processes and decision-making within correctional systems were the means by which an offender's fate was decided.

In many systems, specialized treatment programs were added and housed in diversified correctional institutions. Maximum, medium, and minimum-security prisons were established; forestry camps, farms, or small-cottage programs were designed. Hypothetically, these were expected to respond to classes of offenders, rather than to classes of crimes: juveniles, addicts, sex offenders, habitual criminals. Specialized treatment also made use of professional counseling, psychotherapy, and medical care, as well as the more conventional academic and vocational training.

The result was such specialized roles for correctional people as administration, care and feeding, control, casework, education, therapy, vocational training. Planning was separated from operations, and treatment separated from custody. Even after incarceration, the use of parole further deferred the sentencing decision formerly exercised by the court and lodged it, instead, in parole boards and parole officers. Thus, at least in theory, the response of corrections during the second revolution concentrated much more on the individual than on his crime, more on divided and deferred decision-making than on legal prescription and court action.

The shift of large masses of people from rural to urban environments contributed also to the increases in professionalization and specialization. As the informal controls and functions of the rural family and neighborhood diminished, such complex formal systems as police, court, welfare, juvenile court, probation, and parole were given the responsibility of responding formally to the commission of crime. In the larger cities these formal systems became complex bureaucracies and the people who manned them became the formal agents of social control.

Yet, despite these developments, there has been a disturbing accumulation of negative evidence relative to the efficacy of the second revolution. Current practices are undoubtedly more humane than earlier forms of punishment, but delinquency and recidivism seem to have continued at a high rate, and the few studies of individualized treatment that are available present discouraging results.

On one hand, there is some indication that, through specialization, the occupational and educational skills of offenders are being increased and that, within correctional programs, attitudes are being changed. But somehow, these changes are not translated to the community where the offender's adjustment is submitted to the ultimate test. Programs do not seem to address adequately what seem to be some of his most important problems, those having to do with his interaction with, and reintegration into, the law-abiding community.

There is a long list of difficult, unanswered questions: Is individualized and specialized treatment the answer? Do our efforts result in a correctional approach which constitutes a coherent system throughout? Are specialized functions related logically to each other and to the factors that lead to crime? Are the criminals with whom we deal a representative population or only the tip of a criminal iceberg which remains largely unstudied and untouched? In our concern with individual offenders, are we not missing other variables which may be crucial in determining the success or failure of correctional programs?

Current trends seem, even if indirectly, to be in response to such questions. It is Schrag's opinion, therefore, that we are in the early stages of a third major correctional revolution,[5] one whose philosophy is characterized by two main features. The first suggests that society, itself, is badly in need of change. As Schrag puts it:

> It is generally recognized that various kinds of unconventional behavior are sometimes richly rewarded. Wealth, power and prestige are frequently highly regarded irrespective of the means by which they are achieved. Political corruption and white collar crime are often viewed as unavoidable nuisances. But there is also increasing evidence of public demand for control in these areas. New attention is being devoted to the tendency for some respected and influential persons to be favorably disposed toward illegitimate activities if they provide sufficient material benefits and good prospects for escaping detection or censure. These are some of the previously neglected aspects of crime and correction that are attracting the systematic attention of correctional experts.

The second feature of the rising philosophy places more emphasis on the compelling pressures that are exerted on the offender by persons living in his community, by the social groups to which he belongs, by our overall culture and, within it, a host of dissonant subcultures. It is the cultural and subcultural matrix from which the offender comes that prescribes his goals and his standards of conduct. And it is this matrix which will heavily influence whether he will become a success or a failure, a criminal or a law-abiding citizen.

Delinquency and crime and reactions to them are social products and are socially defined. Society, not individuals, defines rules, labels those who break rules, and prescribes ways for reacting to the labeled person. There are times when the societal process of defining, labeling, and reacting is problematic, times when it is far more influential in determining who shall enter the correctional process and what its outcome will be than techniques designed solely to change offenders.[6]

The labeling process is often a means of isolating offenders from, rather than integrating them in, effective participation in such major societal institutions as schools, businesses, unions, churches, and political organizations. These institutions are the major access to a successful, nondelinquent career. Those who are in power in them are the gatekeepers of society and, if offenders and correctional programs are isolated from them, then the personal wishes and characteristics of offenders will have only marginal bearing on whether correctional programs succeed or fail.

This is not to deny individual differences, nor the importance of inculcating individual responsibility, but it does make clear that correctional techniques are terribly nearsighted which fail to take into account the offender's social and cultural milieu. Successful adjustment on his part will require some kind of personal reformation but it will also require conditions within the community that will encourage his reintegration into nondelinquent activities and institutions. Fundamentally, this is a community function. Reintegration may succeed or fail depending on the community's labeling and reacting processes. If they are such as to permit the offender to discard the label of criminal and to adopt another label, the integration process will be aided. But, if they insist on holding the former offender at arm's length, then any desire on his part for reintegration may be of little consequence. Until the labeling and reacting processes are changed he will remain, by definition, an offender, an outsider. . . .

IMPLICATIONS OF CORRECTIONAL HISTORY

Our historical review has indicated, as Glaser suggests, that man's historical approach to criminals can be conveniently summarized as a succession of three R's: Revenge, Restraint, and Reformation. Revenge was the primary response prior to the first revolution in the eighteenth and nineteenth centuries. It was replaced during that revolution by an emphasis on restraint.

When the second revolution occurred in the late nineteenth and early twentieth centuries, reformation became an important objective. Attention was focused upon the mental and emotional make-up of the offender and efforts were made to alter these as the primary sources of difficulty.

Finally, we may be on the verge of yet another revolution in which a fourth concept will be added to Glaser's list of R's: Reintegration.[7]

Students of corrections, like those of mental health, feel that a singular focus on reforming the offender is inadequate. Successful rehabilitation is a two-sided coin, including reformation on one side and reintegration on the other. Unless both are used, correctional programs will fail.

There are some who will argue that movement into a third revolution at this time is premature. For example, society itself is still very ambivalent about the offender. It has never really replaced all vestiges of revenge or restraint, simply supplemented them. Thus, while it is unwilling to kill or lock up all offenders permanently, it is also unwilling to give full support to the search for alternatives.

On the other hand, there are those who argue that the treatment philosophy of the second revolution has never really been implemented, that true diagnosis followed by individualized treatment has never been possible in correctional settings. If it were, better results would ensue.

But this argument overlooks one very important problem which, if uncorrected, will undoubtedly thwart efforts to make the treatment model work. The problem is the lack of knowledge and comprehensive correctional theory on which to base clinical treatment models. They are in a primitive state. Consequently, as Gibbons has pointed out, more personnel, smaller caseloads, higher salaries, and better training can never solve the correctional problem until the conceptual deficiency is worked out. Until improvements are made in the theories that underlie treatment, changes in correctional structures, by themselves, will be unlikely to produce dramatic reductions in delinquency and criminality.[8] Instead, we will have more refined failure.

In a similar vein, Korn and McKorkle agree that our thinking is very muddy. The bleak facts are, they say, that just as the monstrous punishments of the eighteenth century failed to curtail crime, so, during the twentieth century, we have failed likewise to do so.[9] The reason, they say, is that we have equated humanitarianism with treatment and failed to recognize that the humane care of offenders is not necessarily the same thing as reducing crime, that our practices relative to reducing the problems are sadly lacking.

Perhaps it would be important, therefore, to try to focus more pointedly on just what our difficulties have been. The ones that stand out most clearly are our lack of knowledge and the unsystematic approaches we have taken to corrections. We have been guided, primarily, by what John C. Wright calls "intuitive opportunism," a kind of goal-oriented guessing, a strategy of activity.[10]

Instead of proceeding systematically, to define and then to solve our correctional problems, we have made sweeping changes in correctional programs without adequate theoretical definitions of the causes of crime or the development of logical strategies to deal with them.

The problem, however, is not inherent in some kind of human perversity. Society is far less sophisticated in the development of scientific procedures by which to deal with such human problems as crime than it is in the development of scientific methods to alter the technological elements of culture. The social sciences are just coming into their own. There is not only a profound lack of scientific knowledge about ways to develop better correctional methods, but a general disinclination to approach the search for that knowledge in a disciplined way. That is why a strategy of activity has prevailed.

Correctional units—police, courts, rehabilitative programs—have seldom been considered on any total or comprehensive basis as constituting a single system. Theory has rarely been used. New practices such as casework, psychotherapy, remedial education, group counseling, have all been added piecemeal to existing systems and, instead of replacing older philosophies, have simply supplemented them. As a result, it is difficult to tell whether new practices contribute to, or only confuse, older objectives and practices.

The possibility has not been adequately considered that the impact of new techniques may be overwhelmed by negative influence already existing in correctional system, or the possibility that their introduction may produce negative effects on procedures already present. Individual practices, which by themselves might have been helpful, often seem to generate conflict when joined irrationally with other practices. For example, the tendency for custody and treatment people to conflict with each other in correctional institutions often contributes to the cynicism, rather than the reformation, of inmates. Inmates are encouraged to concentrate on means for exploiting the rift among staff members, rather than working with staff people to resolve common problems. What has been lacking in the past, therefore, is some consideration of correctional problems in organizational teams and the lack of adequate knowledge and theory-building by which to approach solutions in a more systematic way. . . .

NOTES

[1] For a broader development of issues, see Clarence Schrag, "Contemporary Correction: An Analytical Model," preliminary draft of paper prepared for the President's Commission on Law Enforcement and the Administration of Justice, Feb. 1966 (mimeo).

[2] Daniel Glaser, "The Prospect for Corrections," paper prepared for the Arden House Conference on Manpower Needs in Corrections, 1964 (mimeo).

[3] Jackson Toby, "Is Punishment Necessary?" *The Journal of Criminal Law, Criminology, and Police Science,* 55 (Sept. 1964), 332–37.

[4] Glaser, *op. cit.,* pp. 2–3.

[5] Schrag, *op. cit.,* p. 12.

[6] For a summary of the subject, see Howard S. Becker, *Outsiders* (New York: The Free Press, 1963), Chap. 1.

[7] Glaser, *op. cit.*

[8] Don C. Gibbons, *Changing the Lawbreaker* (Englewood Cliffs, N.J.: Prentice-Hall, 1965), pp. 14–16.

[9] Lloyd W. McCorkle and Richard Korn, "Resocialization Within Walls," *Annals of the American Academy of Political Science,* 293 (May 1954), 94–95.

[10] John C. Wright, "Curiosity and Opportunism," *Trans-Action,* 2 (Jan–Feb. 1965), 38–40.

2. *Is Punishment Necessary?* *

JACKSON TOBY

OF ELEVEN CONTEMPORARY TEXTBOOKS in criminology written by sociologists, ten have one or more chapters devoted to the punishment of offenders.[1] All ten include a history of methods of punishment in Western society and, more specifically, a discussion of capital punishment. Seven discuss punishment in preliterate societies. Seven include theoretical or philosophical discussions of the "justification" of punishment—usually in terms of "retribution," "deterrence," and "reformation." These theoretical analyses are at least as much indebted to law and philosophy as to sociology. Thus, in considering the basis for punishment, three textbooks refer both to Jeremy Bentham and to Emile Durkheim; three textbooks refer to Bentham but not to Durkheim; and one textbook refers to Durkheim but not to Bentham. Several textbook writers express their opposition to punishment, especially to cruel punishment. This opposition is alleged to be based on an incompatibility of punishment with scientific considerations. The following quotation is a case in point:

> We still punish primarily for vengeance, or to deter, or in the interest of a "just" balance of accounts between "deliberate" evildoers on the one hand and an injured and enraged society on the other. We do not yet generally punish or treat as scientific criminology would imply, namely, in order to change antisocial attitudes into social attitudes.[2]

Most of the textbook writers note with satisfaction that "the trend in modern countries has been toward humanizing punishment and toward the reduction of brutalities."[3] They point to the decreased use of capital punishment, the

* Reprinted by special permission of the author and the *Journal of Criminal Law, Criminology and Police Science* (Northwestern University School of Law). Copyright © 1964, Vol. 55, No. 3.

introduction of amenities into the modern prison by enlightened penology, and the increasing emphasis on nonpunitive and individualized methods of dealing with offenders, for example, probation, parole, psychotherapy. In short, students reading these textbooks might infer that punishment is a vestigial carryover of a barbaric past and will disappear as humanitarianism and rationality spread. Let us examine this inference in terms of the motives underlying punishment and the necessities of social control.

The Urge to Punish

Many crimes have identifiable victims. In the case of crimes against the person, physical or psychic injuries have been visited on the victim. In the case of crimes against property, someone's property has been stolen or destroyed. In pressing charges against the offender, the victim may express hostility against the person who injured him in a socially acceptable way. Those who identify with the victim—not only his friends and family but those who can imagine the same injury being done to them—may join with him in clamoring for the punishment of the offender. If, as has been argued, the norm of reciprocity is fundamental to human interaction, this hostility of the victim constituency toward offenders is an obstacle to the elimination of punishment from social life.[4] Of course, the size of the group constituted by victims and those who identify with victims may be small. Empirical study would probably show that it varies by offense. Thus, it is possible that nearly everyone identifies with the victim of a murderer but relatively few people with the victim of a blackmailer. The greater the size of the victim constituency, the greater the opposition to a nonpunitive reaction to the offender.

It would be interesting indeed to measure the size and the composition of the victim constituencies for various crimes. Take rape as an illustration. Since the victims of rape are females, we might hypothesize that *women* would express greater punitiveness toward rapists than *men* and that degrees of hostility would correspond to real or imaginary exposure to rape. Thus, pretty young girls might express more punitiveness toward rapists than homely women. Among males, we might predict that greater punitiveness would be expressed by those with more reason to identify with the victims. Thus, males having sisters or daughters in the late teens or early twenties might express more punitiveness toward rapists than males lacking vulnerable "hostages to fortune."

Such a study might throw considerable light on the wellsprings of punitive motivation, particularly if victimization reactions were distinguished from other reasons for punitiveness. One way to explore such motivation would be to ask the same respondents to express their punitive predispositions toward offenses that do not involve victims at all, that is, gambling, or which involve victims of a quite different kind. Thus, rape might be balanced by an offense the victims of which are largely male. Survey research of this type is capable of ascertaining the opposition to milder penalties for various offenses. It would incidentally throw light on the comparatively gentle social reaction to white-collar crime. Perhaps the explanation lies in the difficulty of identifying with the victims of patent infringement or watered hams.[5]

THE SOCIAL-CONTROL FUNCTIONS OF PUNISHMENT

Conformists who identify with the *victim* are motivated to punish the offender out of some combination of rage and fear. Conformists who identify with the *offender*, albeit unconsciously, may wish to punish him for quite different reasons. Whatever the basis for the motivation to punish, the existence of punitive reactions to deviance is an obstacle to the abolition of punishment. However, it is by no means the sole obstacle. Even though a negligible segment of society felt punitive toward offenders, it might still not be feasible to eliminate punishment if the social control of deviance depended on it. Let us consider, therefore, the consequences of punishing offenders for (1) preventing crime, (2) sustaining the morale of conformists, and (3) rehabilitating offenders.

Punishment as a Means of Crime Prevention

Durkheim defined punishment as an act of vengeance. "What we avenge, what the criminal expiates, is the outrage to morality." [6] But why is vengeance necessary? Not because of the need to deter the bulk of the population from doing likewise. The socialization process prevents most deviant behavior. Those who have introjected the moral norms of their society cannot commit crimes because their self-concepts will not permit them to do so. Only the unsocialized (and therefore amoral) individual fits the model of classical criminology and is deterred from expressing deviant impulses by a nice calculation of pleasures and punishments.[7] Other things being equal, the anticipation of punishment would seem to have more deterrent value for inadequately socialized members of the group. It is difficult to investigate this proposition empirically because other motivationally relevant factors are usually varying simultaneously, for example, the situational temptations confronting various individuals, their optimism about the chances of escaping detection, and the differential impact of the same punishment on individuals of different status.[8] Clearly, though, the deterrent effect of anticipated punishments is a complex empirical problem, and Durkheim was not interested in it. Feeling as he did that *some* crime is normal in every society, he apparently decided that the crime-prevention function of punishment is not crucial. He pointed out that minute gradation in punishment would not be necessary if punishment were simply a means of deterring the potential offender (crime prevention). "Robbers are as strongly inclined to rob as murderers are to murder; the resistance offered by the former is not less than that of the latter, and consequently, to control it, we would have recourse to the same means." [9] Durkheim was factually correct; the offenses punished most severely are not necessarily the ones that present the greatest problem of social defense. Thus, quantitatively speaking, murder is an unimportant cause of death; in the United States it claims only half as many lives annually as does suicide and only one-fifth the toll of automobile accidents. Furthermore, criminologists have been unable to demonstrate a relationship between the murder rate of a community and its use or lack of use of capital punishment.

Most contemporary sociologists would agree with Durkheim that the anticipation of punishment is not the first line of defense against crime. The socialization process keeps most people law-abiding, not the police—if for no other reason than the police are not able to catch every offender. This does not mean, however, that the police could be disbanded. During World War II, the Nazis deported all of Denmark's police force, thus providing a natural experiment testing the deterrent efficacy of formal sanctions.[10] Crime increased greatly. Even though punishment is uncertain, especially under contemporary urban conditions, the possibility of punishment keeps some conformists law-abiding. The empirical question is: *How many* conformists would become deviants if they did not fear punishment?

Sustaining the Morale of Conformists

Durkheim considered punishment indispensable as a means of containing the demoralizing consequences of the crimes that could not be prevented. Punishment was not for Durkheim mere vindictiveness. Without punishment Durkheim anticipated the demoralization of "upright people" in the face of defiance of the collective conscience. He believed that unpunished deviance tends to demoralize the conformist and therefore he talked about punishment as a means of repairing "the wounds made upon collective sentiments." [11] Durkheim was not entirely clear; he expressed his ideas in metaphorical language. Nonetheless, we can identify the hypothesis that the punishment of offenders promotes the solidarity of conformists.

Durkheim anticipated psychoanalytic thinking as the following reformulation of his argument shows: One who resists the temptation to do what the group prohibits, to drive his car at 80 miles per hour, to beat up an enemy, to take what he wants without paying for it, would like to feel that these self-imposed abnegations have some meaning. When he sees others defy rules without untoward consequences, he needs some reassurance that his sacrifices were made in a good cause. If "the good die young and the wicked flourish as the green bay tree," the moral scruples which enable conformists to restrain their own deviant inclinations lack social validation. The social significance of punishing offenders is that deviance is thereby defined as unsuccessful in the eyes of conformists, thus making the inhibition or repression of their own deviant impulses seem worthwhile. Righteous indignation is collectively sanctioned reaction formation. The law-abiding person who unconsciously resents restraining his desire to steal and murder has an opportunity, by identifying with the police and the courts, to affect the precarious balance within his own personality between internal controls and the temptation to deviate. A bizarre example of this psychological mechanism is the man who seeks out homosexuals and beats them up mercilessly. Such pathological hostility toward homosexuals is due to the sadist's anxiety over his own sex-role identification. By "punishing" the homosexual, he denies the latent homosexuality in his own psyche. No doubt, some of the persons involved in the administration of punishment are sadistically motivated. But Durkheim hypothesized that the psychic equilibrium of the *ordinary* member of the group may be threatened by violation of norms; Durkheim was not concerned about psychopathological punitiveness.

Whatever the practical difficulties, Durkheim's hypothesis is, in principle, testable. It should be possible to estimate the demoralizing impact of nonconformity on conformists. Clearly, though, this is no simple matter. The extent of demoralization resulting from the failure to punish may vary with type of crime. The unpunished traffic violator may cause more demoralization than the unpunished exhibitionist—depending on whether or not outwardly conforming members of society are more tempted to exceed the speed limit than to expose themselves. The extent of demoralization may also vary with position in the social structure occupied by the conformist. Thus, Ranulf suggested that the middle class was especially vulnerable:

> [T]he disinterested tendency to inflict punishment is a distinctive characteristic of the lower middle class, that is, of a social class living under conditions which force its members to an extraordinarily high degree of self-restraint and subject them to much frustration of natural desires. If a psychological interpretation is to be put on this correlation of facts, it can hardly be to any other effect than that moral indignation is a kind of resentment caused by the repression of instincts.[12]

Once the facts on the rate and the incidence of moral indignation are known, it will become possible to determine whether something must be done to the offender in order to prevent the demoralization of conformists. Suppose that research revealed that a very large proportion of conformists react with moral indignation to *most* violations of the criminal laws. Does this imply that punishment is a functional necessity? Durkheim apparently thought so, but he might have been less dogmatic in his approach to punishment had he specified the functional problem more clearly: making the nonconformist unattractive as a role model. If the norm violation can be defined as unenviable through some other process than by inflicting suffering upon him, punishment is not required by the exigencies of social control.

Punishment can be discussed on three distinct levels: (1) in terms of the motivations of the societal agents administering it, (2) in terms of the definition of the situation on the part of the person being punished, and (3) in terms of its impact on conformists. At this point I am chiefly concerned with the third level, the impact on conformists. Note that punishment of offenders sustains the morale of conformists only under certain conditions. The first has already been discussed, namely, that conformists unconsciously wish to violate the rules themselves. The second is that conformists implicitly assume that the nonconformity is a result of *deliberate defiance* of society's norms. For some conformists, this second condition is not met. Under the guidance of psychiatric thinking, some conformists assume that norm violation is the result of illness rather than wickedness.[13] For such conformists, punishment of the offender does not contribute to their morale. Since they assume that the nonconformity is an involuntary symptom of a disordered personality, the offender is automatically unenviable because illness is (by definition) undesirable. Of course, it is an empirical question as to the relative proportions of the conforming members of society who make the "wicked" or the "sick" assumption about the motivation of the offender, but this can be discovered by investigation.

In Western industrial societies, there is increasing tendency to call contemporary methods of dealing with offenders "treatment" rather than "punishment." Perhaps this means that increasing proportions of the population are willing to accept the "sick" theory of nonconformity. Note, however, that the emphasis on "treatment" may be more a matter of symbolism than of substance. Although the definition of the situation as treatment rather than punishment tends to be humanizing—both to the offender and to the persons who must deal with him—there are still kind guards and cruel nurses. Furthermore, it would be an error to suppose that punishment is invariably experienced as painful by the criminal whereas treatment is always experienced as pleasant by the psychopathological offender. Some gang delinquents consider a reformatory sentence an opportunity to renew old acquaintances and to learn new delinquent skills; they resist fiercely the degrading suggestion that they need the services of the "nut doctor." Some mental patients are terrified by shock treatment and embarrassed by group therapy.

What then is the significance of the increasing emphasis on "treatment"? Why call an institution for the criminally insane a "hospital" although it bears a closer resemblance to a prison than to a hospital for the physically ill? In my opinion, the increased emphasis on treatment in penological thinking and practice reflects the existence of a large group of conformists who are undecided as between the "wicked" and the "sick" theories of nonconformity. When they observe that the offender is placed in "treatment," their provisional diagnosis of illness is confirmed, and therefore they do not feel that he has "gotten away with it." Note that "treatment" has the capacity to make the offender unenviable to conformists whether or not it is effective in rehabilitating him and whether or not he experiences it as pleasant. Those old-fashioned conformists who are not persuaded by official diagnoses of illness will not be satisfied by "treatment"; they will prefer to see an attempt made to visit physical suffering or mental anguish on the offender. For them, punishment is necessary to prevent demoralization.

Reforming the Offender

Rehabilitation of offenders swells the number of conformists and therefore is regarded both by humanitarians and by scientifically minded penologists as more constructive than punishment. Most of the arguments against imprisonment and other forms of punishment in the correctional literature boil down to the assertion that punishment is incompatible with rehabilitation. The high rate of recidivism for prisons and reformatories is cited as evidence of the irrationality of punishment.[14] What sense is there in subjecting offenders to the frustrations of incarceration? If rehabilitative programs are designed to help the offender cope with frustrations in his life situation, which presumably were responsible for his nonconformity, imprisoning him hardly seems a good way to begin. To generalize the argument, the status degradation inherent in punishment makes it more difficult to induce the offender to play a legitimate role instead of a nonconforming one. Whatever the offender's original motivations for nonconformity, punishment adds to them by neutralizing his fear of losing the respect of the community; he has already lost it.

Plausible though this argument is, empirical research has not yet verified it. The superior rehabilitative efficacy of "enlightened" prisons is a humanitarian assumption, but brutal correctional systems have, so far as is known, comparable recidivism rates to "enlightened" systems. True, the recidivism rate of offenders who are fined or placed on probation is less than the recidivism rate of offenders who are incarcerated, but this comparison is not merely one of varying degrees of punishment. Presumably, more severe punishment is meted out to criminals who are more deeply committed to a deviant way of life. Until it is demonstrated that the recidivism rates of strictly comparable populations of deviants differ depending on the degree of punitiveness with which they are treated, the empirical incompatibility of punishment and rehabilitation will remain an open question.

Even on theoretical grounds, however, the incompatibility of punishment and rehabilitation can be questioned once it is recognized that one may precede the other. Perhaps, as Lloyd McCorkle and Richard Korn think, some types of deviants become willing to change only if the bankruptcy of their way of life is conclusively demonstrated to them.[15] On this assumption, punishment may be a necessary preliminary to a rehabilitative program in much the same way that shock treatment makes certain types of psychotics accessible to psychotherapy.

It seems to me that the compatibility of punishment and rehabilitation could be clarified (although not settled) if it were considered from the point of view of the *meaning* of punishment to the offender. Those offenders who regard punishment as a deserved deprivation resulting from their own misbehavior are qualitatively different from offenders who regard punishment as a misfortune bearing no relationship to morality. Thus, a child who is spanked by his father and the member of a bopping gang who is jailed for carrying concealed weapons are both "punished." But one accepts the deprivation as legitimate, and the other other bows before superior force. I would hypothesize that punishment has rehabilitative significance only for the former. If this is so, correctional officials must convince the prisoner that his punishment is just before they can motivate him to change. This is no simple task. It is difficult for several reasons:

1. It is obvious to convicted offenders, if not to correctional officials, that *some* so-called criminals are being punished disproportionately for trifling offenses whereas *some* predatory businessmen and politicians enjoy prosperity and freedom. To deny that injustices occur confirms the cynical in their belief that "legitimate" people are not only as predatory as criminals but hypocritical to boot. When correctional officials act as though there were no intermediate position between asserting that perfect justice characterizes our society and that it is a jungle, they make it more difficult to persuade persons undergoing punishment that the best approximation of justice is available that imperfect human beings can manage.[16]

2. Of course, the more cases of injustice known to offenders, the harder it is to argue that the contemporary approximation of justice is the best that can be managed. It is difficult to persuade Negro inmates that their incarceration has moral significance if their life experience has demonstrated to them that the police and the courts are less scrupulous of *their* rights than of the rights of white persons. It is difficult to persuade an indigent inmate that his incarceration has moral significance if his poverty resulted in inadequate legal representation.[17]

3. Finally, the major form of punishment for serious offenders (imprisonment) tends to generate a contraculture that denies that justice has anything to do with legal penalties.[18] That is to say, it is too costly to confine large numbers of people in isolation from one another, yet congregate confinement results in the mutual reinforcements of self-justifications. Even those who enter prison feeling contrite are influenced by the self-righteous inmate climate; this may be part of the reason recidivism rates rise with each successive commitment.[19]

In view of the foregoing considerations, I hypothesize that punishment—as it is now practiced in Western societies—is usually an obstacle to rehabilitation. Some exceptions to this generalization should be noted. A few small treatment institutions have not only prevented the development of a self-righteous contraculture but have managed to establish an inmate climate supportive of changed values.[20] In such institutions punishment has rehabilitative significance for the same reason it has educational significance in the normal family: it is legitimate.

To sum up: The social control functions of punishment include crime prevention, sustaining the morale of conformists, and the rehabilitation of offenders. All of the empirical evidence is not in, but it is quite possible that punishment contributes to some of these and interferes with others. Suppose, for example, that punishment is necessary for crime prevention and to maintain the morale of conformists but is generally an obstacle to the rehabilitation of offenders. Since the proportion of deviants is small in any viable system as compared with the proportion of conformists, the failure to rehabilitate them will not jeopardize the social order. Therefore, under these assumptions, sociological counsel would favor the continued employment of punishment.

Conclusion

A member of a social system who violates its cherished rules threatens the stability of that system. Conformists who identify with the victim are motivated to punish the criminal in order to feel safe. Conformists who unconsciously identify with the criminal fear their own ambivalence. If norm violation is defined by conformists as willful, visiting upon the offender some injury or degradation will make him unenviable. If his behavior is defined by conformists as a symptom of pathology they are delighted not to share, putting him into treatment validates their diagnosis of undesirable illness. Whether he is "punished" or "treated," however, the disruptive consequence of his deviance is contained. Thus, from the viewpoint of social control, the alternative outcomes of the punishment or treatment processes, rehabilitation or recidivism, are less important than the deviant's neutralization as a possible role model. Whether punishment is or is not necessary rests ultimately on empirical questions: (1) the extent to which identification with the victim occurs, (2) the extent to which nonconformity is prevented by the anticipation of punishment, (3) what the consequences are for the morale of conformists of punishing the deviant or of treating his imputed pathology, and (4) the compatibility between punishment and rehabilitation.

Notes

[1] Barnes and Teeters, New Horizons in Criminology (3d ed. 1959); Caldwell, Criminology (1956); Cavan, Criminology (1955); Elliot, Crime in Modern Society (1952); Korn and McCorkle, Criminology and Penology (1959); Reckless, The Crime Problem (2d ed. 1955); Sutherland and Cressey, Principles of Criminology (5th ed. 1955); Taft, Criminology (3d ed. 1956); Tappan, Crime, Justice, and Correction (1960); von Hentig, Crime: Causes

and Conditions (1947); Wood and Waite, Crime and Its Treatment (1941).

[2] Taft, *op. cit., supra* note 1, at 359.

[3] Reckless, *op. cit., supra* note 1, at 450.

[4] Gouldner, *The Norm of Reciprocity: A Preliminary Statement,* 25 Am. Soc. Rev. 161 (1960).

[5] In this connection, it is well to recall that there is less reluctance to steal from corporations than from humans. See A. W. Jones, Life, Liberty, and Property (1941).

[6] Durkheim, The Division of Labor in Society 89 (1947).

[7] Parsons, The Structure of Social Action 402–03 (1949).

[8] Toby, *Social Disorganization and Stake in Conformity: Complementary Factors in the Predatory Behavior of Young Hoodlums,* 48 J. Crim. L., C. & P.S. 12 (1957).

[9] Durkheim, *op. cit., supra* note 6, at 88.

[10] Trolle, Syv Maneder Uten Politi (Seven Months Without Police) (Copenhagen, 1945), quoted in Christie, *Scandinavian Criminology,* 31 Sociological Inquiry 101 (1961).

[11] Durkheim, *op. cit., supra* note 6, at 108.

[12] Ranulf, Moral Indignation and Middle-Class Psychology 198 (Copenhagen, 1938).

[13] Talcott Parsons has repeatedly suggested the analogy between illness and criminality. See also Aubert and Messinger, *The Criminal and the Sick,* 1 Inquiry 137 (1958), and Wootton, Social Science and Social Pathology 203–67 (1959).

[14] Vold, *Does the Prison Reform?* 293 Annals 42 (1954).

[15] McCorkle and Korn, *Resocialization Within Walls,* 293 Annals 88 (1954).

[16] See the interesting discussions of human fallibility in the works of Reinhold Neibuhr—e.g., The Children of Light and the Children of Darkness (1950).

[17] Trebach, *The Indigent Defendant,* 11 Rutgers L. Rev. 625 (1957).

[18] For a discussion of the concept of contraculture, see Yinger, *Contraculture and Subculture,* 25 Am. Soc. Rev. 625 (1960).

[19] Sellin, *Recidivism and Maturation,* 4 Nat'l Probation and Parole A. J. 241 (1958).

[20] McCorkle, Elias, and Bixby, The Highfields Story (1958), and Empey and Rabow, *Experiment in Delinquency Rehabilitation,* 26 Am. Soc. Rev. 679 (1961).

3. *Juvenile Corrections Today: A National Survey* *

NATIONAL COUNCIL ON CRIME AND DELINQUENCY

Juvenile Detention

Juvenile detention is the practice of holding children of juvenile court age in secure custody for court disposition. The most common reason for its misuse and overuse is that it is allowed to function as a substitute for probation and other community services and facilities.

* Appendix A, "Correction in the United States: Data Summary," *Task Force Report: Corrections,* prepared by the National Council on Crime and Delinquency for the Task Force on Corrections of the President's Committee on Law Enforcement and Administration of Justice, Washington, D.C.: Government Printing Office, 1967, pp. 115–54.

Unlike statutes pertaining to adults, juvenile court law permits a child to be taken into custody for his protection from situations that endanger his health and welfare. This purpose can be served by two distinctly different types of temporary care:

1. *Detention.* Temporary care, of a child who has committed a delinquent act and requires secure custody, in a physically restricting facility pending court disposition or the child's return to another jurisdiction or agency. Any place for temporary care with locked outer doors, a high fence or wall, and screens, bars, detention sash, or other window obstruction designed to deter escape is a detention facility. If a substantial part of a building is used for detention as defined above, it is a detention facility no matter how flimsy the restricting features may be.

2. *Shelter.* Temporary care in a physically unrestricting facility pending the child's return to his own home or placement for longer term care. Shelter care is generally used for dependent and neglected children in boarding homes, group homes, and, in the larger cities, temporary care institutions; it is also used for children apprehended for delinquency whose homes are not fit for their return but who, with proper handling, are not likely to run away and therefore do not need secure custody.

Juvenile detention, properly used, serves the juvenile court exclusively; shelter care is a broader child welfare service not only for the court but also for child and family agencies, both public and private.

*   *   *

Divided Authority

Ultimate responsibility for detention rests with the judge but, in practice, probation and police officers often make decisions to detain for which the court takes no responsibility.

The first decision to detain or release is usually made by the police. Unlike probation services, which are technically subject to court control, police services are administered by a separate agency. Therefore, unless an authorized person is available to make a decision for the court shortly after apprehension, a child may be detained as a result of a police officer's judgment or a police agency's practice. When the source of referrals to a single juvenile court is more than a hundred police agencies, the use of detention as an initial step in the court process is far from uniform. The exception occurs where court control over detention has been achieved through cooperation with the law-enforcement agencies so that common practice prevails and authorization for detention. during or after court hours, rests with a court intake service. Without such court intervention at the point of intake, some children are detained overnight only to be released the following morning by a probation officer after an interview with the child and the parent which could have taken place the day before had probation staff been available. In some jurisdictions children, once placed in detention by the police, remain there until released by the court at a hearing, which may not take place for a week or more.

The second point of decision is reached when a probation officer releases a child or continues the detention initiated by the police. Only in a few states does legislation require the judge to review this decision.

According to the standards, a petition should be filed for every child detained.

In twenty-one states, children may be detained without the filing of a petition. Police and probation officers in these jurisdictions are free to exercise what should be exclusively a court prerogative.

The third point of decision, after a petition is filed, rests with the court itself. According to the committee standard, the juvenile court is responsible for detention admissions and releases and for establishing written policies and procedures for detention. The Standard Juvenile Court Act requires that, when a child is taken into custody, both the parents and the court are to be notified immediately, and, should the child be detained, the parents must be notified in writing that they are entitled to a prompt hearing regarding release or continued detention. The act provides, furthermore, that no child shall be held in detention longer than twenty-four hours unless a petition has been filed, or twenty-four hours beyond that (excluding nonjudicial days) unless the judge signs a detaining order.

Data are not available to show the proportion of jurisdictions in which children and parents are, in fact, assured or denied these legal protections. Professional observers note that once police or probation officers detain a child, the court seldom challenges the wisdom of their decision even though it may release the youngster pending disposition of the case. Furthermore, when a child is detained and social information justifying his release is not available to the judge, chance revelation in the brief fact-finding or detention hearing will usually determine his continued detention or release. Court rules make the acquisition of preliminary social data by the probation officer a mandatory requirement for the initial hearing.

Inconsistency in Rate of Detaining

The rate of detaining is the total number of children detained for delinquency divided by the total number apprehended and booked for delinquent acts. (Both figures exclude dependent children, traffic cases, and material witnesses.) Much as police statistics vary, the arrest base is generally more satisfactory for establishing a rate of detaining than is county population or court referrals for delinquency. Where arrest figures are not available, court referrals can be used, modified by estimates of the police-to-court referral rate.

NCCD's recommended rate of detaining—10 per cent of juvenile arrests—is merely an indicator of the need to examine intake practices when the detaining rate rises significantly above it.

Inconsistency in the use of detention from one jurisdiction to another raises serious question about the validity of detaining in many cases. Judges and court personnel in counties with low detaining rates were questioned to find out whether released children fail to appear in court or commit other offenses while awaiting hearings. Replies consistently said "rarely," "less than with adults released on bond," and so on.

In some jurisdictions all arrested children are detained routinely; in others, less than 5 per cent are detained. A 30 per cent rate is not uncommon. Whatever rate of detaining is customary in one jurisdiction is usually defended to the death, by the judge and the probation or law-enforcement officers, against another wholly different concept defended with equal fervor in another state or in another county in the same state. No research has been designed to prove the efficacy of either practice. Since removal of a child from his home before all the facts are available is drastic action, the burden of proof rests on judges whose courts have high detaining rates, not on judges who detain sparingly.

An increasing rate of detaining often creeps up on a court after the construction of a new building without anyone aware of the change. The courts usually explain the increase by a rise in population or an increase in delinquency. They rarely compute the rate of detaining and compare it with the alleged increase in the alleged causes.

Even the recommended 10 per cent rate referred to above may some day be regarded as too high. Where intake is held down, by design or by custom, the rate can drop below this figure.

A Midwestern county judge, who believed in making children responsible for their own behavior and parents responsible for their children pending court disposition, reduced the overcrowded population of the detention home from a previous average of fifty-three to an average of thirty-six delinquent children within two weeks and suffered no repercussions about lack of community protection.

Of all the children detained in a Western county, approximately two-thirds were referred to the probation department after adjudication; of these, less than half were placed under official supervision. A governor's commission suggested that most of the two-thirds originally detained could have been left at liberty to await court hearings without endangering the community. Following a juvenile court law revision that eliminated the free use of detention by the police, the statewide rate of detaining dropped from an average of 41 per cent to 29 per cent; in some counties there, the rate is considerably lower and is still going down.

A 1965 study of detention in New York City showed a detaining rate of less than 13 per cent (computed on the total number of juvenile arrests). The intake service established by the New York City Office of Probation under the New York Family Court Act reduced the volume of delinquency referrals to the court by 37 per cent in one year and reduced the daily detention population of boys from 554 to 316.

A recently conducted intensive study of all types of detention, including detention of juveniles, made the following observation:

> Out of all children detained overnight or longer, 43 per cent are eventually released without ever being brought before a juvenile court judge, and half of all cases referred to juvenile courts are closed out at the intake stage before any judicial hearing.

It is evident from the above, as well as from a case-by-case examination of detained children in almost any court, that the minor or first offender constitutes the largest group unwisely detained. Many youngsters who have committed more serious offenses are detained when they could have been released under the close supervision of a probation officer, without danger to the community.

Where backed up by proper probation services, such release helps parents to assume greater responsibility for the supervision of their child during a crucial period, and helps the child to assume responsibility for his own behavior pending the court hearing. Examples of effective intake procedures have been developed at the Lane County Juvenile Court in Eugene, Oregon; the Summit County Juvenile Court in Akron, Ohio; the Kent County Juvenile Court in Grand Rapids, Michigan; and the Harris County Juvenile Court in Houston, Texas. Other and somewhat different but comparatively effective intake practices adapted to the special conditions in each jurisdiction can be seen in the New York City Family Court, the juvenile court for the State of Connecticut, and a number of juvenile courts in Massachusetts recently studied by the Special Delinquency Branch of the U.S. Children's Bureau. . . .

Length of Stay

Theoretically, the detention stay is the length of the predisposition period, usually ten days to two weeks in a court with good probation and clinical services—and in a court where juvenile sessions are held only twice a month. In some courts without adequate probation services, the average length of stay may be only two or three days at most.

The average length of detention stay may be lowered by a number of overnight to three-day police detentions, or it may be raised by a number of cases waiting for psychological or psychiatric interviews. More frequently, the reason for long average stays is the large number of children who have been committed by the court to a state institution but cannot be sent there because of lack of room. For this situation the counties that have high commitment rates are usually as responsible as the state through its failure to provide correctional treatment resources. Detention, inappropriately, is left holding the bag.

Another reason for long detention stay is the time spent on looking for an appropriate foster home or private institution placement for a child. Frequently, after considerable time the child either is returned to his home on probation or is committed to a state institution for delinquents. A partial solution to this problem is a thirty-day statutory length of stay. A better solution is for the courts to demand, more clearly and forcefully than they have in the past, the kind of probation and placement resources they need and to encourage citizen action for appropriation of funds to obtain them.

The range of stay in the detention places in counties studied in the survey, which included jails as well as detention homes, was from one day to sixty-eight days; the average was eighteen days. Nearly all the smaller county jails reported stays of usually one to three days. Longer average stays were consistently found in the detention homes and other facilities. These survey data raise questions about the purposes for which detention homes are used.

High ratios of admission to detention homes and long stays there usually stem from the mistaken notion, held by many judges, that these facilities are all-purpose institutions for (1) meeting health or mental health needs, (2) punishment or treatment in lieu of a training-school commitment, (3) retarded children until a state institution can receive them, (4) pregnant girls until they can be placed prior to delivery, (5) brain-injured children involved in delinquency, (6) protection from irate parents who might harm the child, (7) a material witness in an adult case, (8) giving the delinquent "short sharp shock" treatment, (9) educational purposes ("He'll have to go to school in detention"), (10) therapy, (11) "ethical and moral" training, and (12) lodging until an appropriate foster home or institution turns up.

The problems of proper care for these children can hardly be imagined. The comings and goings of detained children fresh from encounters with the police make a place of detention inappropriate for rehabilitation. Program geared to short stays does not lend itself to long-term treatment, particularly when the treatment called for is so varied. No research has yet proved the validity of extensive or long-term detention. Hence, standards do not endorse the construction or use of detention homes for dependent and neglected children or for a variety of other purposes. . . .

JUVENILE PROBATION

Juvenile probation, which permits a child to remain in the community under the supervision and guidance of a probation officer, is a legal status created by a court of juvenile jurisdiction. It usually involves (1) a judicial finding that the behavior of the child has been such as to bring him within the purview of the court, (2) the imposition of conditions upon his continued freedom, and (3) the provision of means for helping him to meet these conditions and for determining the degree to which he meets them. Probation thus implies much more than indiscriminately giving the child "another chance." Its central thrust is to give him positive assistance in adjusting in the free community. . . .

Goals and Functions

The dominant purpose of the total correctional process is promotion of the welfare and security of the community. Within this overall goal, juvenile probation's specific assignment includes (1) preventing a repetition of the child's delinquent behavior, (2) preventing long-time deviate or criminal careers, and (3) assisting the child, through measures feasible to the probation service, to achieve his potential as a productive citizen.

Thus, the central services of probation are directed to the child found delinquent by the court and, often, to his family. However, in some jurisdictions probation departments are also assigned responsibilities in broader, delinquency-prevention programs. Though the proper boundaries of probation's services in this role are not clear and may vary from one jurisdiction to another, it seems clear that a probation department should at least assume the responsibility for assembling and reporting its special knowledge about delinquent children, their needs, and the community conditions that produce delinquency. It is also vitally necessary for the department to be an active partner in the process of community planning for meeting the needs of young people.

The modern probation department performs three central—and, sometimes, several auxiliary—functions. Its central services are (1) juvenile court, probation department, and detention intake and screening, (2) social study and diagnosis, and (3) supervision and treatment. . . .

Standards for Evaluating Practice

Universally accepted standards proven by research methods to correlate with movement toward specified goals have not been developed for the field of juvenile probation. The same statement can be made of all other aspects of correction, as well as of education, public administration, political science, and most other fields concerned with human behavior. This does not mean that the quality of a probation system cannot be assessed. However, the criteria by which such assessment is made must be recognized as a sort of distillate of current "practice wisdom" rather than the product of definitive inquiry. This process has resulted in standards generally accepted among experienced practitioners and eminently applicable to today's practice. Among the most useful compilations of such standards are (1) the one prepared by the Special Committee on Standards (President's Commission on Law Enforcement and Administration of Justice), (2) NCCD's "Standards and Guides for Juvenile Probation," and (3) the Children's Bureau's "Standards for Juvenile and Family Courts." . . .

SURVEY FINDINGS

Probation Coverage

Juvenile probation service is authorized by statute in each of the fifty states and the Commonwealth of Puerto Rico. The study conducted in conjunction with the preparation of this report shows that in one recent year some 192,000 written social studies were made on behalf of children referred to our courts and that some 189,000 children were placed under probation supervision. At the time of the survey, approximately 223,800 children were under such supervision. Supervision usually extends over significant periods of the child's life. Among the agencies included in the sample, the average period of supervision ranged from three months to three years, with a median of thirteen months. In the sample of 250 counties, 233 had probation services.

Fundamental to any definition of desirable probation practice is the availability of paid, full-time probation service to all courts and all children needing such service.

The survey reveals that, though every state makes statutory provision for juvenile probation, in many states probation service is not uniformly available in all counties and localities. The data on this point may be summarized as follows:

1. In thirty-one states all counties have probation staff service.
2. A total of 2,306 counties (74 per cent of all counties in the United States) theoretically have such service. In some of these the service may be only a token.
3. In sixteen states that do not have probation staff coverage in every county, at least some services are available to courts in some counties from persons other than paid, full-time probation officers. The sources of such services include volunteers (in six states), child welfare departments (in five states), and a combination of child welfare, sheriff, and other departments (in five states).

4. In 165 counties in four states, no juvenile probation services at all are available.

Generally, the country's more populous jurisdictions are included among the counties served by probation staff. However, in the smaller counties service may be expected to be spotty. Comments such as the following occur in the observations of the experienced practitioners gathering the survey data:

> The . . . State Department of Public Welfare does provide, upon request, probation and aftercare services to the courts and to institutions. These services are part of the child welfare program, and no differentiation is made as to specific caseloads. A general impression is that . . . there is not an acceptance of this service, and it is not used in many counties.

Many of the state agencies that are theoretically responsible for providing services are not prepared to do so. Yet some child welfare departments acknowledge the provision of probation services as a major responsibility, assign capable staff to the function, and provide services of good caliber. Yet the development of practitioners in the court setting who have specialized knowledge of the diagnosis and treatment of acting-out, behavior-problem children remains a challenge to probation practice. This task is doubly difficult when the staff is not oriented specifically to these problems. It is particularly inappropriate to expect specialists in law enforcement (sheriffs, police, and so on) to become skilled in probation diagnosis and treatment as well as in their own specialized functions. And rare is the volunteer who has the time, energy, and resources to so equip himself (though the volunteer often plays a valuable role when working on carefully defined problems in cooperation with a trained and experienced member of the probation staff).

Whether a child subjected to the truly awesome powers of the juvenile court will be dealt with on the basis of knowledge and understanding, usually the product of a good probation social study, is determined by chance—the accident of his place of residence. The same accident determines whether the community treatment resource of probation as an alternative to incarceration will be available to him. The following observation about one state was made by a member of the survey team:

> In the entire State, only two counties have probation services. The other counties have no service. A child placed on probation in these counties is presumed to be adjusting satisfactorily until he is brought back to the court with a new charge. . . . The Department of Welfare will not accept referrals of delinquent children from the courts.

Organization of Services

Juvenile probation services are organized in a state in one of the following ways:

1. A centralized, statewide system.
2. A centralized county or city system, the services of which are strengthened and supported by state supervision, consultation, standard-setting, re-

cruitment, assistance with in-service training and staff development, and partial state subsidy of the local department.

3. A combination of the above systems, with the more populous and prosperous jurisdictions operating their own departments and with service being provided by the state in the other areas.

Which of the three organizational plans is to be preferred is a question that has to be resolved by such factors as prevalent state administrative structures, political patterns and traditions, and population distribution. However, for many states, a well-coordinated state plan appears preferable. Such a pattern (a) has greater potential for assuring uniformity of standards and practice, including provision of service to rural areas; (b) makes certain research, statistical and fiscal control, and similar operations more feasible; (c) best enables recruitment of qualified staff and provision of centralized or regional in-service training and staff development programs; (d) permits staff assignment to regional areas in response to changing conditions; and (e) facilitates relationships to other aspects of the state correctional program.

In some states, it may be that local agencies are in a better position to respond to changing local conditions and to assure investment of local resources in the solution of essentially local problems. These benefits usually occur in a city or county relatively high in tax potential and progressive leadership; corresponding progress does not take place in adjoining jurisdictions. To assure at least acceptable performance throughout a state where probation is a local responsibility, state supervision, standard-setting, consultation, assistance in staff recruitment and in-service training, and similar services are required. The problems all too often resulting from the absence of either a centralized state probation service or adequate standard-setting for local services are illustrated by another comment emerging from one of the state studies:

> In [the small State of . . .] juvenile probation . . . offers 11 different programs, with widely differing philosophies of institutional use, much variation in procedures, and no possibility of influencing the quality of probation work through any centralized training effort. Political appointment of officers is standard practice and there is no merit system offering the possibility of a career in probation.

Intrastate uniformity in achieving acceptable standards often requires that local probation be subsidized by the state. State expenditure for this purpose is an excellent investment, for it militates against the ever-present danger of indiscriminate commitment to the state correctional program. This and similar benefits seem to have been obtained by such a program recently introduced in one state, where the conference with correction officials held in connection with the survey produced the following observation:

> Juvenile probation has . . . seen substantial improvement in the past few years with the help of a State subsidy that provides that in order to participate the local county must add to its existing staff. A number of small counties which had never had probation services prior to this study have now created departments. Larger counties have been able to expand their services. . . . The general effect of the subsidy has been to generate consider-

able interest on the part of some judges where little or no interest previously existed.

1. *Court Administration Versus Administrative Agency.* County and city systems are organized mainly acccording to two patterns. In the prevalent one, probation services are administered by the court itself or by a combination of courts; in the other, the services are provided to the court by an administrative agency, such as a probation department established as a separate arm of local government.

The survey reveals that juvenile probation is administered as follows:

	In States
By courts	32
By state correctional agencies	5
By state departments of public welfare	7
By other state agencies	4
By other agencies or combination of agencies	3

Some authorities arguing in behalf of the first pattern, in use in most jurisdictions, hold that administration by the court is necessary and desirable since it is the court that is responsible for determining which delinquents are to remain in the community and under what circumstances they are to be permitted to do so. Proper discharge of this responsibility, they say, means that the judge must have the authority to select and control the probation officer, who functions as an extension of the court.

Other authorities argue that the more widespread use of the first pattern may well be the result of historical accident rather than careful analysis of the advantages and disadvantages of the two plans. They point out that conditions have changed since the administration-by-the-court pattern was first established and that now many probation departments are large, complex organizations. Their administration requires a background of training and experience in, as well as an inclination toward, administration—qualifications that do not necessarily accompany judicial function. The judge should be an impartial arbiter between contending forces. His administration of an agency often party to the issues brought before him in the courtroom may thus impair —or may seem to one or the other of the parties to impair—performance of his judicial function. Further, if the court is composed of many judges, it is likely that the juvenile court judgeship assignment will rotate frequently, so that true assumption of administrative leadership may never take place.

In any event, the major, administrative, leadership role in the operation of probation services must be clearly recognized. The total juvenile court function is rendered almost impossible without good probation service, which cannot develop without good administration. It may be that some judges can perform both the judicial and the administrative function effectively. But, as Keve points out:

It seems that at this point in its history, the juvenile court must face its growing administrative task and decide whether it is to relinquish its administrative duties to a separate administrative body, or accept the administrative character of the juvenile court and deliberately develop the structure and capacities of the court to a greater extent than is usually true now.

2. *State Standard-Setting.* In thirteen of the forty-five states in which some or all of the courts are served by local departments, an agency of the state government sets at least some standards governing probation performance. The aspects of the local departments' functions so governed are as follows:

	States
Staff qualifications only	6
Standards of practice only	2
Combination of staff qualifications, salary, and so on	5

Efforts were made during the course of the survey to discover whether, in the professional opinion of the experienced practitioners gathering survey data, the introduction of state standard-setting had resulted in the improvement of local probation service. In nine of the thirteen states, such improvement was considered to have taken place; in two, no change could be observed; and in two, evaluation could not be secured.

3. *State Subsidy of Local Probation.* In nineteen of the forty-five states offering probation on a local basis, some subsidization of the service is available from state funds. The items covered by such subsidies are as follows:

	States
Personnel	7
Personnel and other items	5
New personnel only	1
Operational costs	2
Other items	4

Complete data on the proportion of the local department's budget coming from state subsidy are not available. In six states this proportion is 50 per cent or less; in one, it is more than 50 per cent; and in three, the total costs of local probation services are subsidized by state funds.

In nine states professional judgments were generally to the effect that subsidy programs had resulted in the improvement of probation service. In two states no change was considered to have resulted.

* * *

JUVENILE INSTITUTIONS

A juvenile-training facility is normally part of a system separate from other state and local juvenile correctional services, which usually include, at a minimum, the courts, juvenile probation, and supervision (aftercare) of those released from the training facility. Together these services provide resources for the differential treatment required for juvenile offenders committing offenses from various levels of motivation.

The role of the training school is to provide a specialized program for children who must be held to be treated. Accordingly, such facilities should normally house more hardened or unstable youngsters than should be placed, for example, under probation supervision.

The juvenile institutional program is basically a preparation and trial period for the ultimate test of returning to community life. Once return has been effected, the ultimate success of the facility's efforts is highly dependent on good aftercare services. These are needed to strengthen changes started in the institution; their value can be proved only in the normal conditions of community life. . . .

SURVEY FINDINGS

The survey findings are organized around three factors that significantly affect the operation of juvenile-training facilities: (1) the presence of working philosophies that are consistent with what makes change possible; (2) a use of juvenile institutions by the courts and related groups that allows a program focused on change to operate; and (3) the presence of personnel, physical facilities, administrative controls, and other resources tailored to the job of producing change.

Working Philosophy

A good working philosophy clearly relates the institution's activities to its purpose and to the problems it must meet in serving this purpose.

Such a relationship between purpose and program is clearly outlined in the operations of some facilities. As a general matter, however, the absence of a clear working philosophy that ties programs to the achievement of more responsible attitudes is a significant weakness crucial to the problem of improving services.

Lack of understanding concerning the practicality of newer philosophies is a major problem. The difficulty of securing their acceptance is clearly illustrated by developments in the issue of discipline. For some years standards have declared that "corporal punishment should not be tolerated in any form in a training school program." The misbehaving youngster should see, to the greatest degree possible, the reason for a rule and its meaning for the particular brand of difficulty he encounters on the "outs." In this way discipline can become an avenue to new behavior having the force of personal meaning. The use of force shifts the emphasis away from the youngster and onto the smooth running of the institution. For someone with antagonistic attitudes, hitching behavior to the good of something he dislikes can be expected to have little lasting effect.

Thus, apart from the issue of whether physical abuse results, use of corporal punishment can reasonably be taken as a rough statistical indicator of the degree to which treatment viewpoints are actually operating. The survey found that corporal punishment is authorized in juvenile institutions in ten states.

Another indicator of working philosophy is found in an institution's answer to the question, "How much security?" The institution's need to develop the youngsters' self-control often collides with the public's concern over escapes. Caught between the two, the administrator may set up a system of tight management which, he rationalizes, is for the youngsters' "own good." Thus the juvenile is used to serve the institution instead of the other way around.

A solution can be achieved by public and professional education. Though public expectations toward training facilities are often unrealistic, they must be met by the administrator if he wants to hold his job. Therefore, maximum efficiency—doing the best that current knowledge will allow—cannot be reached until this blurring effect is looked at honestly. If training facilities are to change youngsters, they must be allowed to operate out of philosophies consistent with this purpose. The public needs to learn that treatment approaches that allow "breathing room" are not naive but are, on the contrary, extremely practical. Properly conceived, they are directed at getting the trainee to assume more responsibility for his life rather than assigning it later to the police.

Uses Being Made of Training Schools

In theory, training schools are specialized facilities for changing children relatively hardened in delinquency. In practice, as the survey shows, they house a nonselective population and are primarily used in ways that make the serving of their theoretical best purpose, that of "change," beside the point.

This is not to say that other purposes being served by the typical training facility are not important in themselves. Rather, the point is whether they can best be served by a training facility, and, if they cannot, the effect of this extraneousness on the facility's prime reason for existence, the basic job for which it is intended. The extent to which its ability to do this job is diminished becomes clear from the following list of its "other" expedient purposes:

Use as a detention or holding facility for youngsters awaiting completion of other plans for placement.

Providing basic housing for youngsters whose primary need is a foster home or residential housing.

Housing large numbers of youngsters whose involvement in trouble is primarily situational rather than deep-seated and who could be handled more effectively under community supervision.

Caring for mentally retarded youngsters committed to training school because there is no room in a mental retardation facility or because no such institution exists.

Providing care for youngsters with severe psychiatric problems who are committed to the training school because of no juvenile residential treatment program.

Use of girls' facilities to provide maternity services.

The problem of varied intake is further complicated by differences in court commitment philosophies, each of which is a working view of "the best purpose a training facility should ideally serve." In summary, the effects of the diverse elements cited contribute to training facilities wherein no one is best served and most are served in default.

Variations in use of training schools are found among the states as a whole, as well as among the counties of a single state, and further show that many reference points other than "change" are the determiners of practice. If juvenile institutions were actually working in allegiance to a common "best use," statistics that reflect practice would have some uniformity of meaning. That this is not true is revealed by some of the statistical sketches below. For example, length-of-stay statistics do not now reflect differences in time needed to effect "change." If they did, one system's length of stay could be compared with another's, as a guideline for the efficacy of a given program. Rather, the data show that length of stay reflects some extraneous factor such as "overcrowding," or a population whose primary need is "housing," or children awaiting unavailable placements, or children who, though better suited to a probation program, must be held "long enough" to avoid court or community problems.

Resources to Produce Change

1. *Capacity*. The survey covers 220 state-operated juvenile institutional facilities in all states, Puerto Rico, and the District of Columbia. These facilities, constituting 86 per cent of the juvenile training capacity in the United States, had a total capacity of 42,423 in 1965 and a total average daily population of 42,389, which was 10.7 per cent more than the population reported to the Children's Bureau in 1964 by 245 state and local facilities.

The overcrowding suggested by daily population figures is not uniform. In seventeen jurisdictions, in programs housing total average daily populations of 7,199 children (17 per cent of the total), the average daily population is more than 10 per cent below each system's capacity. Conversely, in eleven states, in programs housing 9,165 children (22 per cent of the total reported by all fifty-two jurisdictions), the average daily population is 10 per cent or more above their respective systems' capacities.

In many states, the capacity of state and locally run training facilities is extended through use of private facilities. In some instances these are publicly subsidized, but control of the program remains in private hands. During the survey, thirty-one states reported using private facilities for the placement of delinquents. An estimate of the use of private facilities was not possible in eight of these states. The twenty-three states submitting estimates reported they had placed 6,307 youngsters in private facilities in 1965.

Concern about the increasing numbers of delinquents being housed in training facilities is growing. Only eight states at present have no plans for new construction which would increase the capacity of their institutional programs. Construction under way in seventeen states will add space for 4,164 youngsters at a cost of $41,164,000. Thirty-one states report that they have $70,090,000 of construction authorized for an additional capacity of 7,090. Projecting still further ahead, 21 states report plans for additional capacity of 6,606 by 1975 at an anticipated cost of $66,060,000.

Thus, new construction, under way or authorized, will increase the present capacity (42,423 in state-run facilities) by 27 per cent. By 1975, planned new construction will have increased present capacity by slightly over 42 per cent.

2. *Program*. a) Diversification. In contrast to the diversified program "balance" recommended by the standard, juvenile-training facilities in most states present limited diversity of programs. Six of the larger jurisdictions now have nine or more facilities, but eight states have only one facility serving juveniles and fourteen states have only two facilities—a boys' school and a girls' school, a pattern that characterized state juvenile institutional systems for many years.

In states that have expanded their facilities further, the most numerous separate new programs are small camps for boys and reception centers. The camp is one of the fastest growing developments in the institutional field; forty-nine camps have been established in twenty states, with Illinois alone operating ten of then. Ten states now have a total of fourteen separate reception programs.

The rapid growth of camp programs has been attributed to low cost of operation, often half that of a training school in the same state, and to a good success rate, which in turn has been attributed to size and selection of population. Many of the camps have a capacity of fifty or less; standards call for capacities of forty to fifty.

b) Average stay. The length of stay for children committed to state training facilities ranges from four to twenty-four months; the median length of stay is nine months. The number of children at the extremes of the range is relatively small. Five state systems, housing 3 per cent of the total, report an average length of stay of six months or less; eight state systems, housing 8 per cent of the total, report average lengths of stay of more than twelve months. The remainder of the state systems—three-fourths of the total, housing nine-tenths of the institutional population—have an average length of stay of six months to a year.

Reception centers which serve primarily placement diagnostic purposes and do not include a treatment program for segments of their population report a surprisingly uniform average length of stay, ranging from twenty-eight to forty-five days.

c) Actual availability of service. Services that look the same "on paper" are revealed by the survey to differ widely in quality. For example, 96 per cent of the facilities contacted report the provision of medical services, and 94 per cent report that dental services are provided. In fact, however, examination of operating practice in each jurisdiction shows major differences in the quality of these services. Where medical and dental services represent an especially expensive drain on hard-pressed budgets, as is true in many programs, the decision that treatment is "needed' may be reached less quickly than where services are routinely available and "paid for." Thus quality differences are born.

Similar differences between what is available "on paper" and what is available "in fact" are to be found among other services offered by training facilities. The survey data indicate that nearly all programs (95 per cent) provide recreational services; 88 per cent, educational programs; 86 per cent, casework, and 79 per cent, counseling services; and 75 per cent, psychological, and 71 per cent, psychiatric services. The question of concern, however, is not their provision "on paper" but their adequacy for the problems being faced. From this viewpoint, with the possible exception of education, improvement of all types of services seems badly needed. Support for this view is based on the existing ratios of treatment personnel to training-school population.

d) Costs. Regardless of the adequacy of services, the cost of care in a training facility is high. The fifty-two jurisdictions report a total operating cost of $144,596,618 to care for an average daily population of 42,389 youngsters. This means an average per capita operating expenditure of $3,411. The national average, however, conceals considerable variation in costs among the states. Forty-two jurisdictions operate training facility systems without a separate reception and diagnostic center, at an average per capita cost ranging from $871 to $7,890. Within this group, six states operate juvenile institutional systems for average per capita costs falling below $1,600 per year; eight report average costs between $1,600 and $3,000; thirteen report costs between $3,000 and $4,500; and thirteen report average annual per capita costs above $4,500.

The inclusion of a reception and diagnostic center as part of a diversified juvenile institutional system helps to individualize institutional placements. Ten jurisdictions have set up programs consistent with the idea of specialized facilities, and another ten are on the verge of doing so. This trend makes especially significant the costs experienced in states with separate reception programs. Among the ten that operate such systems, per capita costs range from $1,757 to $5,723. Average per capita cost is less than $2,000 in three of these states; from $2,000 to $2,500 in two states; from $3,900 to $4,500 in three states; and $4,877 and $5,723 in the two remaining states.

*   *   *

JUVENILE AFTERCARE

Juvenile aftercare is defined as the release of a child from an institution at the time when he can best benefit from release and from life in the community under the supervision of a counselor. Use of the term "aftercare" rather than "parole," though not yet fully accepted even within the field of juvenile correction, has been encouraged by persons interested in social service in order to separate juvenile programs from the legalistic language and concepts of adult parole. The concept of aftercare has wider acceptance than the term, but the survey of aftercare programs in the United States today reveals wide variations in structure and program content.

Aftercare service for juveniles first appeared in the United States in the early nineteenth century, but it has become an integral part of correctional rehabilitation for the young offender only in the past decade. In most states, aftercare is the least developed aspect of correction; in the opinion of many observers, it is less adequate than its counterpart, adult parole.

Aftercare originated in New York and Pennsylvania, where houses of refuge indentured child inmates to work in private homes for several years. The child's daily regimen rarely included anything but work. Total responsibility for the child was vested in the family that undertook to feed and clothe him, and it was the family that determined when he had earned his freedom. This form of postinstitutional treatment persisted for over half a century.

An Overview of Aftercare Today

. . . Any study of aftercare today at the national level is plagued by inadequate statistics coming from the fifty states and Puerto Rico. As long as this situation persists, attempting a thorough study of juvenile aftercare can be described only as an exercise in futility. The gaps in vital information are so great that the reliability and validity of the few national statistics that can be gathered must be viewed with extreme caution. Efforts are being made to change this condition, but extensive organizational programing for statewide data collection is needed.

State operating costs range from $7,000 to over $4 million a year. Together the states are spending about $18 million a year. Average per capita cost is $320 a year.

This expenditure is small in comparison with the cost of state-operated juvenile institutions, which spend over $144 million a year to care for an average daily population of slightly over 42,000 at an average per capita cost of about $3,400 a year.

The fact that aftercare costs less than one-tenth as much as institutional care is nothing to be proud of. As reported by the forty states, its relative cheapness reflects the inadequacy of the programs at least as much as it demonstrates inherent economy. It is not uncommon for 250 adolescents to be assigned to a program staffed by only two or three aftercare counselors located at the state capital or training school, which may be hundreds of miles from the communities where the juveniles are supposedly under supervision. Aside from the excessiveness of the supervisors' caseloads, sheer distance reduces the effectiveness of the program. . . .

Organizational Arrangements

According to the standard, responsibility for aftercare should be vested in a state agency that is administratively responsible for institutional and related services for delinquent children.

As shown in Table 1, the organizational arrangements through which juvenile aftercare services are administered vary widely among the states. In contrast to other programs for juveniles, such as public education, which is always administered by the state educational agency, juvenile aftercare has no clear organizational pattern. Administration may be the responsibility of, for example, a lay board, an adult correction program, a public welfare agency, a youth authority, or the training school itself.

TABLE 1. Organizational Arrangement for Administration of Aftercare

Type of structure	No. of States
State department of public welfare	13
State youth correction agency	12
State department of correction	10
Institution board	6
State training-school board	4
State department of health	1
Other	5
Total	51

The issue of administration is further complicated by the survey finding that in only thirty-four states does the state department that administers the state juvenile institutions also provide aftercare services for juveniles released from these institutions. For example, in five states local probation departments are given responsibility for aftercare even though they have no official relationship to the agency administering the training schools. Patterns of local jurisdiction have developed for various reasons. In some states, there was no state agency that could provide supervision at the local level, and therefore a local social service agency was asked to perform this function. In other states, state officials preferred to give jurisdiction to local agencies because they believed the youth would receive better care from local agencies than from centralized, state-operated programs. In their opinion, local programs helped avoid duplication of services at the state level.

According to the standard, the law under which a juvenile enters a state training school should provide that the agency granted legal custody should have the right to determine when he shall leave the institution.

The opportunity for legal and jurisdictional disputes is always present. In nine states, the problem is complicated by the fact that the committing judge becomes involved in the decision to release a juvenile for aftercare services. If he is thus involved in the release decision, he must be thoroughly aware of the child's behavior and growth at the training school as well as of the factors in his home community; actually, in the nine states where this procedure is followed, he rarely has this information. In five of the nine states, the committing judge must approve all releases; in the others, he must approve only certain ones. A training-school staff which has worked daily with a ward may find its aftercare plan disapproved by a judge unfamiliar with all the circumstances of his case. Where the state provides aftercare services, it should be unnecessary for the committing judge to approve aftercare plans for children released from state institutions.

Length of Commitment

According to the standard, the law under which a juvenile enters a state training school should provide that the child remain there for an indefinite period of not more than three years and of no specified minimum before being released on aftercare.

The survey found that specific minimums are authorized by law in three states: In one, the specified minimum is twelve months; in another, it is eighteen months; in the third, it varies. And in many other states, the survey found, specific minimum length of stay in the training school has been established informally—without legal authorization of any kind but firmly established nonetheless—by superintendents, classification committees, and other groups or individuals. . . .

4. *Alternatives to Incarceration* *

LA MAR T. EMPEY

. . . In choosing among the sentencing alternatives which are open to it, the court is influenced by three kinds of forces. The first is the penal law. The law distinguishes, for example, between crimes according to their seriousness, classifying them into felonies and misdemeanors. It also distinguishes among offenders, the most notable distinction being between juvenile and adult. As one alternative, the law provides that imprisonment for a misdemeanor may be set in a local jail or a workhouse for any period up to a year. Ordinarily, sentences are of a fixed duration—thirty, sixty, or ninety days, six months, or a year. In some cases, habitual misdemeanants may receive indefinite sentences for periods longer than a year.[1] If the crime is a felony, the law provides for imprisonment in a state prison or reformatory for a period longer than one year. For the most serious felonies, especially crimes punishable by death or life imprisonment, the court must sentence to prison rather than consider any other alternative.

* LaMar T. Empey, *Studies in Delinquency: Alternatives to Incarceration,* U.S. Department of Health, Education and Welfare, Office of Juvenile Delinquency and Youth Development, Publication No. 9001, 1967, pp. 12–77.

Second, the decision making of the court is influenced by the conflicting pressures which play on it: the police, the probation department and its supporting services, the prosecutor's office, public opinion, and the defendant's counsel and his family. These groups feel differently about the offender. They lack consensus as to what should be done with him and make recommendations to the court which range from those that are extremely lenient to those that are extremely punitive.

Finally, court decision-making is limited by the variety of resources to which the court has access. If community alternatives to incarceration are nonexistent, then imprisonment may be the only course. If resources are great, the range of choices may be greatly extended.

SENTENCING ALTERNATIVES

The historical trend has been away from imprisonment and toward other alternatives. The three most common, traditional ones have been the suspended sentence, fines, and the use of probation.

Suspended sentence. The power to suspend sentence preceded the development of probation, but today it is most frequently coupled with probation. Tappan reports that there are statutory provisions for the suspended sentence in at least eighteen states but that, in addition, other states employ such a sentence under their common-law powers.[2] This type of sentence occurs in two different forms: the suspension of the imposition of sentence and the suspension of the execution of sentence.

Suspension of the imposition of sentence means that the court withholds decisions on the length of the prison term at the time of conviction so that if it is necessary to revoke the suspended sentence, the period of imprisonment will be fixed at that time. By taking this step, the court is able to consider the subsequent misconduct of the offender if it finds it necessary to revoke the suspended sentence. If, after having been given a second chance, the offender gets into further trouble, it is likely he will receive a more severe penalty upon revocation than he would have received under a commitment in the first place.

In suspending the execution of a sentence, the court fixes a sentence of imprisonment and then suspends execution during the good behavior of the offender. If the court subsequently finds it necessary to revoke the suspension, it must ordinarily impose the term originally fixed.

Fines. Fines constitute a second distinct form of sanctions. The offender may be fined either on the theory that he does not require imprisonment or that he will be deterred through the imposition of a monetary sanction. The alternative to the fine is imprisonment. If the offender cannot or will not pay, he is imprisoned. Fines are also used frequently in association with probation sentences, the payment of the fine constituting one of the conditions of probation.

Restitution. The money received from fines generally goes to the state. However, the court sometimes makes provision for the offender to pay restitution to the victim of his crime. Restitution is not ordinarily provided as a sentence-alternative in penal codes, but not uncommonly it is set as one of the conditions of probation. This is often a sensible course since it confronts the offender with consequences of his act and requires that he make good the loss he has caused. Surprisingly, however, little use has been made of restitution, either as a possible correctional device for the offender or as a means of compensating the victim. Under some circumstances it may be a preferable alternative to incarceration since incarceration removes any chance for reparation by the offender. In the event he fails to comply with the restitution order, his failure ordinarily represents a breach of probation and may become the basis for imprisonment. The use of restitution, in conjunction with probation, would be cheaper to the state, more satisfactory to the victim, and probably more preferable to the offender than incarceration. Certainly, for those who can afford to pay, restitution among other restrictions may be a sensible alternative.

Probation. Probation is the most common alternative to incarceration. It is the disposition available to the courts in virtually every jurisdiction. For juveniles, probation terms tend to be indeterminate, depending on the decision of the probation officer. For adult misdemeanants, terms are usually from one to three years. For adult felons, the ordinary term is for a period of five years or less. Probation resembles the suspended sentence in the sense that an offender may serve one or more years and then, because of a breach of the conditions of probation, may be imprisoned.

Current probation techniques had their origin in the quasi-probationary measures of an earlier day. The Prisoners' Aid Association of Maryland was established in 1869 and assisted offenders in the Baltimore courts. In 1894, a statute was passed that permitted any court to release first offenders "on probation of good conduct." This law was very similar to one passed in Great Britain for first offenders in 1887. In 1897, Missouri passed legislation that made it possible to suspend the execution of sentence for young and for minor offenders. But all of these statutes were only quasi-probationary in the sense that they made no provision for the supervision of probationers. However, Vermont established such a plan on a county basis in 1898, and Rhode Island established a state-administered system in 1899.[3]

After the turn of the century the spread of probation was accelerated by the juvenile court movement. Thirty-seven states and the District of Columbia had enacted children's court acts by 1910. Forty of them had also introduced probation for juveniles, reflecting the greater concern for the rehabilitative needs of the young. By 1925, probation for juveniles had become universal although it was delayed for adults until 1956. Nevertheless, there is extremely wide variation in the laws and in the ways probation is practiced.

This variation introduces many perplexing and contradictory problems. Probation was introduced initially as a humanitarian measure, not as a scientific endeavor to discover more effective rehabilitative techniques. Early proponents wished simply to keep first offenders and minor recidivists from undergoing the corrupting effects of jail.[4] They were volunteers—ministers and others—whose untrained efforts to help guide and moralize with their probationers were considered adequate. Their philosophy was that the offender was a deprived, perhaps uneducated person, who needed help in adjusting to his environment. Their orientation was social in nature.

During and after World War I, however, a marked change occurred in this orientation. As probation work continued to expand there was an ever increasing demand for professionally educated people, especially trained social workers, to serve as probation officers. And the training of social workers, in turn, was profoundly influenced by the introduction of psychiatric and especially psychoanalytic theory. Freud and his associates were preoccupied with the individual and his emotional makeup, and the training of the professional caseworker reflected this concern.

The offender was seen as a disturbed person in whom emotional healing was necessary, and the professional probation caseworker, therefore, became associated with his capacity to offer psychiatrically oriented therapy. Thus, the philosophy and administration of probation became a highly complex admixture of psychotherapeutic theory and an older concern with helping the offender to adjust economically and socially to his environment. They remain that way today. The ideology of probation is broad and amorphous, one of generalized beneficence. Ideally, it is supposed to help the offender with all phases of his life, as well as monitoring his capacity for discipline and self-control. Yet in practice the individual officer may be expected to maintain a caseload of from 75 to 200 probationers, to conduct presentence investigations, to maintain extensive paperwork, and perhaps to carry out other functions as well. It is obvious that the ideology of beneficence has not been reconciled with probation in practice. A logical deduction would be, therefore, that probation is destined to fail. But the available evidence does not support the deduction.

First of all, probation is widely used. It is used for the preponderant majority of all juveniles and not insignificantly for adult first-time felons. Between one third and two thirds of the latter receive probation. But despite its wide use there are surprisingly few studies of probation effectiveness and surprisingly few record systems by which such studies could be made. In many jurisdictions probation is a county function, in others a city or court function, and in others a state function. Thus, there are few central record repositories by which to follow up court dispositions for purposes of evaluating probation effectiveness.

In a summary analysis of fifteen probation studies conducted in a variety of jurisdictions, Ralph England found reported success rates to vary between 60 and 90 per cent.[5] A survey of probation effectiveness in such states as Massachusetts, California, and New York, or in a variety of foreign countries provides similar reported results with the modal success rate at about 75 per cent.[6]

These findings are not totally valid because they were not obtained under controlled conditions, nor were they supported by data that distinguished among the types of offenders who succeeded or the types of services that were rendered. Nevertheless, the success rates were rather uniform and relatively high and cannot, therefore, be discounted totally. They are the product of a variety of kinds of probation administered in different times and places. Even when interpreted skeptically, therefore, they raise some real issues relative to current policy and practice which can be answered only through further use of the technique accompanied by research and experimentation. The issues are these:

1. What proportion of those now being placed on probation could do just as well on a suspended sentence without any supervision? England suggests that many offenders are probably "self-correcting" individuals who, having once committed a crime, would not be likely to do so again. Still others would be dissuaded from further criminality merely through exposure to the limited surveillance of the suspended sentence.[7]

2. How can one identify those who do not require intensive supervision in order to prevent their future violation of the law, and, more important, how can one identify those who do require intensive supervision? Obviously, current correctional systems cannot provide the answer. Knowledge-building resources are lacking. Yet, if these systems are to be improved, some kind of quality control is needed. Hopefully, the day will come when it will be possible to identify those who are most likely to fail, and, conversely, those who do not require extended surveillance. Probation departments could then concentrate upon that segment of the population for whom probation is most appropriate.

3. Is it not possible that many offenders who are now commonly committed to institutions rather than receiving probation might be dealt with safely and effectively in the community? If the majority of probationers can succeed without much intensive supervision, then perhaps many of those who were incarcerated could do likewise if supervision in the community were intensified. What, therefore, is the picture for incarcerated offenders? How might it be related to the foregoing information on probation and reflect on correctional procedures as a total system?

INCARCERATION AND ITS IMPACT

It has been assumed almost universally that two-thirds of those who are incarcerated eventually commit new crimes and are returned to prison. Yet Glaser says that this assumption is myth. Evidence does not support it. The information heretofore has been inadequate and incorrectly reported.[8]

First of all, he points out that the only conclusive way to find out how many offenders eventually return to prison is to follow, for a number of years, all those released in a given period. If this is not done, we make the mistake of basing our statistics upon the percentage of men in prison at any given time rather than studying the percentage of men received by the prison in a given period. The two are much different. What happens is that two- and three-time losers tend to accumulate in prison because they get longer sentences and are much less readily paroled than first-timers. Consequently, when the focus is only upon those who are in prison, we get a biased sample, one which overestimates failures and underestimates successes. Thus, when Glaser looked at the number of men being received, he discovered that only about a third had previously been imprisoned, a figure which is only about half as large as has been assumed traditionally.

Glaser reviewed a number of different studies in making his analysis. He found that adults and juveniles being released from diverse institutions in Massachusetts, Minnesota, Wisconsin, California, New York, Washington, and the federal system had reimprisonment rates varying between 15 and 45 per cent, with the modal category being about 35 per cent. However, it is his position that we could become even more certain about the issue by constructing a national information system to which corrections research people could have access so as to be able to follow more carefully what happens to parolees.

But even without total confirmation, the evidence, when coupled with that presented on probation, confirms the need to think more realistically about corrections as a total system. Again it raises a number of policy issues, suggesting that we could make a much better utilization of our resources.

It has been estimated, for example, that the cost of maintaining an offender in an institution is anywhere from three to ten times as great as that of supervising him in the community. Therefore, if a more efficient job could be done of separating hard-core from less dangerous offenders, a more effective allocation of resources might be devised. A heavier concentration of community alternatives might be set up at no extra cost simply by reducing the number of people who must be incarcerated.

In setting up such alternatives, there is no doubt that the hard-core group of offenders against whom society must be protected cannot be ignored. But the need to guard against such people works two ways; that is, they must be identified and kept out of community programs as well as in prison. The only answer, therefore, is research that will provide more discriminating criteria for the classification of offenders into the categories of those who do not require supervision, those who require differing degrees of supervision, and those who require highly concentrated controls. Similarly, research is needed about the programmatic counterparts for types of offenders. Obviously, generic casework as it is practiced in probation is not the total answer. Other programmatic designs are needed of which casework is only one. A coherent system of alternatives should be sought, ranging from nonsupervisory measures such as fines and the suspended sentence, through increasingly structured community programs, to total incarceration.

Fortunately, we are not without some experience in setting up such a system of alternatives. A rather wide variety of programs has been tried and the following section is devoted to their brief categorization and description.

OTHER ALTERNATIVES

It is difficult to categorize, along one dimension, all of the various programs that have been tried. They have involved both juveniles and adults, misdemeanants and felons, one-time and persistent offenders. Therefore, the list which follows is not meant to be exhaustive nor completely descriptive of all programs, but simply to illustrate the kinds of programs that might be implemented. Wherever possible, evidence as to the efficacy of the various programs will be presented. The major objective of the analysis is to distill basic issues—obstacles to innovation, strengths and weaknesses, research issues—as a means of establishing a baseline for future developments.

Fines and Restitution by Installment

One very elemental device for avoiding imprisonment for the misdemeanant offender, or complex probationary procedures for the juvenile, is to provide for the payment of fines or restitution by installment. In the case of the adult, there is some evidence that over two-thirds of all offenders committed to jail for short terms were incarcerated as a result of their inability to pay fines. The use of jails for such commitment, especially for brief periods of time, could be greatly reduced through the use of this alternative.

There is nothing new about the approach. Tappan cites a study in which imprisonment in England for default of payments of fines dropped from 79,583 cases in 1913 to 15,261 in 1923 as the result of legislation providing for time payment. He notes also that additional legislation in 1935, requiring the courts to inquire into the offender's ability to pay, reduced such commitments still further to 2,646 in 1946.[9] He also cites an American study that showed that in those states where fines are based on the ability to pay and where installment paying is allowed, fewer than 5 per cent of those who would otherwise have been incarcerated actually had to be committed.[10]

Juvenile judges have probably been more concerned with using fines and restitution as a teaching device than adult judges. They have felt that having a youthful offender compensate the victim or the state would be rehabilitative. If he has committed an act of vandalism, the judge may assign him to repair the damage. If he has committed a traffic violation for which fine is levied he may be assigned to work for a governmental jurisdiction. Judges feel these activities have served successfully as a deterrent to the juveniles in question.

The important consideration in setting up such alternatives concerns the necessity to write statutes or find administrative mechanisms by which to carry them out. The problems in setting up such mechanisms should not be minimized. Despite the relative simplicity of this alternative, the potential savings, both to the offender and to the state, are not inconsequential. For example, the tremendous number of offenders in England who were not required to serve sentences in jail undoubtedly represented a tremendous saving to the state. The cost of housing, feeding, and clothing prisoners was eliminated, to say nothing of the probable social and economic savings to the offenders themselves and their families.

Work Furlough

The work furlough is more complex than fines by installment in the sense that the offender does lose some liberty. However, the concept of maintaining his integration in the community remains prominent. Under this alternative, the offender is confined in jail only at night or on weekends, but is permitted to pursue his normal life in the remainder of the time. In this way, while some punishment is being levied, the punishment does not totally disrupt his domestic and economic relationships.

The concept of the work furloughs, like fines by installment, is not new. It dates back first to the Huber Law which was enacted in Wisconsin in 1913. This law sought to accomplish two objectives: (1) to provide for reformation and rehabilitation of the prisoner, and (2) to provide means of financial support, other than public relief, for the prisoner's dependents.[11] However, the work furlough was not used extensively until World War II when workers were sorely needed. Today at least twenty-four states formally provide for some form of work release, and in addition to this judges and sheriffs informally make use of it in handling various cases. Work-release laws ordinarily apply only to misdemeanants, but some states have extended their laws to include felons.[12]

In Wisconsin, the earnings of the employed prisoner are kept in a trust fund and dispersed in accordance with the statutes of the Huber Law. They provide for the board of the prisoner in the jail; necessary travel expenses; support of the prisoner's dependents, if any; payments of the prisoner's obligations acknowledged by him in writing or which have been reduced to judgment; and the balance of payment due the prisoner upon his discharge.[13]

Again the effects of the work furlough have not been assessed under strict experimental conditions. However, in Wisconsin where it has been most widely practiced, there seems to be considerable satisfaction with it. In 1960, for example, about one third of almost 10,000 persons who were sentenced to county jails were sentenced under the Huber Law. Of the 3,215 prisoners involved, 2,281 were actually employed. The remainder remained unemployed primarily because jobs were unavailable. Over $600,000 was earned that year by Huber-Law prisoners. Over a third of that amount went to support the dependents of prisoners, one-quarter to pay for his board and room, one-fifth to the prisoner upon release, and the rest to pay for debts and personal expenses.[14]

One important point to be remembered about both the use of fines by installments and work-furlough programs is that they are relatively simple, mechanistic approaches of dealing with offenders. Those who write about these approaches often speak of their rehabilitative impact, but one can scarcely expect significant personal change to be the most important consequence of them.

This is not to depreciate these programs, but to note simply that they are not designed as complex change strategies such as those that will be discussed below. Instead, the most significant thing about them is their alteration of correctional organizations and policies. When some offenders are provided with a mechanism by which to exercise decision-making and responsibility, the consequences are not always bad. Many offenders are capable of utilizing an installment plan or work furlough without complex personal change. They can already meet, at least on a minimal level, their conventional responsibilities. They do not need more complex devices. The available evidence, therefore, by no means suggests that simple changes such as these are inferior to more complex strategies. They are only inferior for certain types of offenders. Everything possible should be done, therefore, to identify these types and their numbers so as to maximize the attention that must be paid to them and to minimize the attention devoted to offenders who can benefit from simple strategies. Only when that is done will society be better protected and justice more effectively rendered.

Nonresidential Community Programs

A relatively recent development has been the creation of intensive, nonresidential community programs. They have been used primarily for juvenile offenders who have not succeeded on regular probation and are candidates for incarceration. These programs, in the main, are considerably more concentrated in design than regular probation or work-furlough programs. They involve definite strategies that are designed to change the offender and facilitate his reintegration into the community.

Provo Experiment and Essexfields. The most pronounced innovations have divided themselves into two general types. The first type is built more or less around sociological tradition and is illustrated by such programs as the Provo Experiment [15] or Essexfields.[16] These two programs are designed for older adolescents, ages fifteen to eighteen. They are by no means exact duplicates but, in the main, they are based on two sets of postulates, one having to do with causation, the other having to do with strategies for intervention. These postulates would not necessarily be applicable to very young children or older adults.

The Provo Experiment, for example, postulated: (1) that most older delinquents who are eventually processed through the courts are from low-income homes; (2) that the lives of these offenders have been characterized by failure in such conventional institutions as the school or world of work; and (3) that membership in a delinquent group develops as an alternative means for acquiring many of the social, emotional, and economic goals which are acquired by other young people through conventional means. The prevailing theme is that the greater part of delinquent behavior consists of patterns that are socially proscribed and that have evolved out of experiences in a working environment, in peer groups, and in the community.

The home may have had an early negative influence, but rather than attempt to reconstruct that relationship, the implication is that steps must be taken to alter the identification of the offender with the antisocial group and behavior through which he has found compensating satisfactions. The focus is upon the here-and-now. Postulates for intervention, therefore, suggested that a program should try: (1) to make the delinquent group the target of change—that is, attempt to change shared standards, points of view, rewards and punishments; (2) to give the delinquent group a stake in what happens to its members by permitting participation with staff in solving problems, exerting controls, and making basic decisions; and (3) to open up conventional opportunities for delinquents in the school, the world of work, and other conventional institutions. Reformation on the part of offenders is only one side of the coin. Certain aspects of the community will have to be changed if the offenders are to be successfully reintegrated.

In implementing these assumptions, the Provo and Essexfields programs were generally the same. Program activities included gainful employment in the community, school, and daily group meetings built around the technique of Guided Group Interaction.[17] This technique differs considerably from traditional group psychotherapy in the sense that all group members, not just staff, are responsible for defining problems, dealing with difficult questions, and finding solutions. An effort is made to provide means by which offenders can assume more responsibility for their lives and to reward them for help that they are able to give others. The offender is sponsored in an active, reformative role rather than in a passive one in which he is acted upon by others.

The fact that these two programs were located in the community meant that problems with which the groups were struggling were those that confront them in their daily lives: families, friends, school, work, leisure time. That is one very important strength of a community over an institutional program. The artificiality of institutional life is avoided and concentration can be placed upon the problems of successful community reintegration rather than upon adjustment to institutional norms.

The available evidence is that the two programs had a generally positive effect. The Provo Experiment was one of the first to set up an experimental design by which to examine outcome. Offenders who were assigned to the experimental program were compared with two control groups, one of which was left in the community on probation and a second that was incarcerated in a training school. The initial design was such that all three groups could be drawn randomly from a common population of persistent offenders residing in the same county.

As a background for comparing the three groups, a study of court records was made prior to the introduction of the experiment. It revealed that only about 50 to 55 per cent of the persistent offenders who were assigned to the program were succeeding on probation. It will be recalled from the success and failure rates presented earlier that this was a lower success rate than the case for probation in general. It explains why the more intensive experiment was started.

The experiment improved the success rate. Six months after release, 72 per cent of those who were initially assigned and 84 per cent of those who eventually completed the program had no record of arrest. None of the remainder had been arrested more than once and none had been incarcerated. But these were probably not the most interesting findings.

During the same period the success rate for the control group under regular probation had gone up almost as precipitously. From its original success rate of 55 per cent, the probation department developed a success rate of 73 per cent for all those who were initially assigned to probation and 77 per cent for those who completed it.

Apparently the introduction of the experiment, and the research which accompanied it, had some influence on the operation of court and probation personnel. Their work, perhaps as a result of a sense of competition with the experiment, resulted in a higher success rate. At any rate, there was a halo effect, not uncommon in social experiments, which affected everyone concerned and not just the offenders who were subjected to the experimental stimulus. Such findings, of course, indicate the importance of replicating the experiment elsewhere.

On the other hand, the second control group, made up of incarcerated offenders, was not nearly so successful as the experimental and control groups that were left in the community. Six months after release, only 42 per cent of the incarcerated group had not been arrested, and half of the 58 per cent who had been arrested had been arrested two or more times. This finding, however, must be tempered by the fact that the original experimental design had to be altered during the experiment because the court was not assigning enough boys to the institutional control group. Consequently, it became necessary to complete this control group with boys randomly selected from other jurisdictions. This change may have biased results considerably.

Nevertheless, the findings are strong enough to raise important issues. Both community programs not only resulted in significantly less recidivism but cost only a fraction of the money. The experimental program was anywhere from two to four times cheaper than institutions in California, Utah, Colorado, and elsewhere. Probation, of course, was much cheaper still.[18]

Essexfields has not made a detailed presentation of its success and failure rates. However, it has consistently graduated approximately 75 per cent of all of the offenders assigned to it. This is very similar to the Provo study, which graduated 73 per cent. It may be, therefore, that the two kinds of programs are operating at approximately the same level.[19] Their presence in the community makes a graduated range of correctional controls available so that courts do not have to make an either/or choice between the limited controls of probation versus the total controls of a training school, but can individualize sentencing procedures more successfully.

Community Treatment Project. Another type of community project which has probably drawn more attention in recent years than any other is the Community Treatment Program sponsored by the California Youth Authority. This project is exciting, not only because it represents an alternative to incarceration for Youth Authority wards but because it is founded on a classic, clinical design prescribing specific types of treatment for specific types of offenders. While its orientation is generally psychological in nature, it departs from traditional personality classifications and defines offenders according to personal maturity levels.[20]

The maturity typology includes nine subtypes of delinquents classified according to their interpersonal maturity level and the mode of behavior that typifies their interaction with the world.[21] The nine delinquent subtypes fall into three larger groupings, including Low, Middle, and High Maturity delinquents. Each of the larger groupings, and to some extent the subtypes within it, calls for distinctly different approaches to treatment and control. Treatment methods that are regarded as appropriate for an individual in any one of the subtypes would be considered highly inappropriate for an individual in another subtype.

Each experimental delinquent is diagnosed prior to admission to the project and, on the basis of the diagnosis, is assigned to a parole agent who is thought to be skilled in working with that type of delinquent. Thus, types of delinquents are matched with types of agents. Each agent carries an average caseload of eight to ten wards. Contacts may vary from two to five weekly and may involve full-day as well as part-time programing for youth. A given case, for example, may require—singly or in combination—surveillance and firm discipline, individual counseling, psychotherapy, family group therapy, guided group interaction, occasional confinement, or foster home placement.

The effort to make treatment consistent with design has extended to the development of specially designed group homes for those who need them. For the type of client who makes his way by manipulating others, a specific home will be set up with parents who are trained to frustrate such behavior by exerting firm controls. For the child who needs a considerable amount of assurance and freedom, placement would be in another home designed to operate warmly and permissively. Such homes will operate only for special cases since most wards will probably continue to live at home.

In summary, then, the design of this program is extremely complex. It calls for the differential diagnosis of offenders into subtypes, the selection and training of agents to work with these subtypes, the definition of a treatment plan for each of the subtypes, the development of a host of program resources to be used singly or in combination for the different subtypes, and perhaps even the development of specialized homes in which certain wards would be housed.

This project is utilizing experimental controls. All subjects come from a common pool of eligibles who have been assigned by the courts to the Youth Authority for what traditionally has been an institutional program. However, the design now permits random assignment of experimental subjects to the Community Treatment Project and control subjects to a traditional institutional program. Comparative effectiveness of the two programs is being assessed is a variety of ways, by parole performance and by attitudinal and behavioral changes.

The latest reported figures show that 29 per cent of the experimentals, as contrasted to 48 per cent of the controls, have been parole failures within fifteen months on parole. Failure means that their paroles have been revoked and they have been recommitted. This difference in favor of the community program is an important one and, in statistical terms, is highly significant.

Experimental subjects also showed a significantly higher level of social and personal adjustment in terms of psychological test scores than did the control subjects. For example, the experimental group was significantly ahead of controls on ten of eighteen individual scales of the California Psychological Inventory, while control subjects were ahead on two of the eighteen.

One debatable difference between experimentals and controls was observed with respect to parole suspensions. Suspensions refer to temporary, rather than permanent, revocations of parole and usually result in a short period of detention. The experimental group had an average of 2.6 suspensions per ward, while the control group had an average of only 1.4 suspensions. Furthermore, 61 per cent of all experimental group suspensions were the direct result of arrest action taken by experimental staff, as contrasted to only 25 per cent of the suspensions for the control group.

These differing rates of suspension are thought to be due to differences in the philosophy and procedures of experimental and control staffs. Experimental agents may be more inclined than control agents to use temporary detention as a part of their treatment and control strategies.

However, there are pro and con arguments relative to the use of suspension in this way. If temporary suspensions result in fewer long-term revocations, as is hoped in this case, and are a part of a long-term treatment scheme, they would seem to be justifiable on therapeutic grounds. But the question is whether such suspensions violate constitutional rights, and should be permitted only after proof of new violations, not on the basis of clinical judgment.

The problem is complex. Suspensions have their paradoxical qualities. For example, one that becomes clear in intensive programs, such as the Community Treatment Program, Provo, and Essexfields, is that staff members are a party to much greater information about their wards than they would be if they operated with traditional, large caseloads. Therefore, in the event they find that wards are doing things that will lead eventually to official detection, staff must decide whether to suspend the ward or to let him continue without control. The problem is that judgment must be based on information or behavioral characteristics which ordinarily do not come to the attention of the regular agent or the police. The real problem hinges on whether the ward or community is in danger. If either is, then failure to control him through brief periods of detention may mean that, eventually, he will be incarcerated permanently. If he is not in danger or his behavior is not supportable in court as illegal, then perhaps he should not be submitted to temporary losses of freedom. But since the decision to suspend or revoke parole obviously involves some subjectivity on someone's part, and since it seems almost certain that intensive community programs will be used increasingly in the future, more attention will have to be paid to both the clinical and legal issues that are involved.

In summary, the Community Treatment Project provides an interesting and valuable contrast to such programs as those at Provo and Essexfields in terms of both theory and design. Yet all three seem to indicate two very important things: (1) that serious delinquents can be treated in the community without undue danger to the community; and (2) that apparently the majority of them can successfully be changed without having to subject either them or the state to the costly and negative consequences of incarceration.

On the other hand, many questions remain unanswered, one of which has to do with the complexity of community programs. Are the relatively similar success rates of these two vastly different types of programs due to the programs themselves or to the fact that juveniles in both simply escape the negative influences of incarceration? Some of both is probably involved. But if programs per se are to be made more efficient, answers must be sought. One very encouraging development is the fact that the California Youth Authority, in an effort to assess the relative merits of these two approaches, has recently set up a study in which Provo-type and Community Treatment-type programs will be implemented and results compared. The problem, of course, is in achieving accurate replication. Both programs require a trained staff whose philosophy and interest will permit them to operate according to theoretical design. The mere statement on paper does not guarantee that the programs can be implemented.

Another important question is whether programs such as these must be restricted to juveniles. Is it not possible that some modification of them could be used with adults? Must the alternatives for adults always be extreme, either the almost total freedom of probation or the total loss of freedom through incarceration? Except for an isolated residential program here and there, intensive community programs for adults, as will be seen below, have not been tried. The above evidence seems to imply that they should be tried.

Residential Group Centers

The final type of alternative that is used in place of total incarceration is the residential group center. Such centers are now restricted mostly to juveniles and range from boarding-type homes in the community to the more treatment-oriented centers such as Highfields or the Kentucky Camp Programs. The latter are unlike training schools, in that they are small and in open settings and are removed from the community.

Such states as Washington and Michigan operate group centers that serve as a home base for delinquents. These homes are probably the most familylike of any residential centers. They do not operate elaborate programs but draw upon the community for education, training, jobs, or recreation. Some are staffed by employees of the state correctional agency and serve in place of training-school commitments for some delinquents or as a halfway parole facility for delinquents who are leaving an institution. Such homes, on occasion, are also operated by private agencies and are especially useful as places to which juveniles, whose problems may be as much dependency and neglect as law violation, can be assigned.

Highfields-Type Centers. The prototype for more treatment-oriented but small residential group centers is the Highfields program which was begun in 1950. Highfields limits its population to twenty boys, age sixteen and seventeen, who are assigned directly from the juvenile court. Boys with former commitments to correctional schools are not accepted. The program is not designed for deeply disturbed nor mentally deficient youths.[22]

Highfields was established on the premise that, with intensive methods, rehabilitation could be accomplished in three or four months. The daily routine is like that described earlier for the Provo and Essexfields programs. The major difference, of course, is that the boys live in residence rather than in their own homes.

During the day, the boys work at the New Jersey Neuro-Psychiatric Institute. In the evening, the population is broken into two groups of ten boys, each of which then meets for its daily group meeting. On Saturday, the boys clean up the residence. Saturday afternoon is free. Sunday they may attend church at nearby Hopewell and receive visitors. Formal rules are few. Control instead is exercised informally through the development of a culture that is presumably peer-centered, therapeutic, and antidelinquent.

Not all boys are able to adjust to the Center. Some run away, others do not fit into the program. A few commit delinquencies of a serious nature. The Highfields response, therefore, is that staff members and other boys should be free to reject certain of these people (because such rejection is necessary as a means of reinforcing an antidelinquent culture) and working with those who are willing to change. Consequently, boys who cannot adjust are returned to court for some other disposition.

In order to test the effectiveness of the program, Highfields graduates were compared to a group of boys who had been committed to the New Jersey State Reformatory for Males at Annandale. A lower percentage of Highfields than of Annandale boys recidivated. However, the results of the comparison have been debated because both groups were not selected under experimental conditions such as they were in the Community Treatment Program in California. Without such selection, there is some doubt as to whether the groups are comparable. For example, the Annandale boys tended to be a little older, perhaps more experienced in delinquency, and from poorer social backgrounds than the Highfields boys. It is difficult to say, therefore, whether success and failure differences were due to the treatment approaches or the differences in the youth populations.

It should not be forgotten, however, that the Highfields method was at least as successful as the Reformatory and that it accomplished its results in a much shorter period of time and at much less expense. These factors alone, quite apart from more subtle personal changes which might have occurred, seem justification enough for further work with such methods.

The Highfields model has been widely adopted in other places in New Jersey, New York, and Kentucky.[23] One of the most significant adoptions has been the creation of the Turrell Residential Group Center for Girls at Allaire, New Jersey.[24] This Center utilizes the same general approach as Highfields and apparently has been reasonably satisfactory. It has not been studied, however, under experimental conditions. Therefore, empirical results cannot be presented either regarding recidivism or alterations that may have to be made in the use of Highfields techniques with girls.

The Silverlake Experiment. Another small residential group center called the Silverlake Experiment is being tried in Los Angeles. This experiment was begun in 1964 and is an alternative to institutionalization for those who attend.[25]

The experiment attempts to combine the contributions of theory, action, and research. As a result, it is built upon four main building blocks: (1) a series of theoretical assumptions about persistent offenders; (2) a series of assumptions as to what should be done to change them; (3) the development of a basic strategy for producing that change; (4) a systematic plan for testing this approach.

In one way, the program is very much like the Provo, Highfields, and Essexfields programs. It attempts to involve delinquents actively in looking at problems, exerting controls, and making decisions. It attempts to create an antidelinquent culture in which offenders, as well as staff, play important roles. For that reason the staff is small, including only two professionals, a part-time cook, and a part-time work supervisor.

One marked difference between this and the foregoing programs is its concentration upon school rather than work. Attendance at school is mandatory for boys, with volunteer tutors assisting in the evening. As might have been anticipated, many problems have been encountered and it remains to be seen whether this facet of the experiment can succeed. Virtually every boy was in serious difficulty with school when he came and it remains a formidable task to reintegrate him in the school.

In addition to action, considerable attention has been paid in the experiment to the problems of research. An attempt has been made to establish a more functional relation between the two. Both are joined by a common administrative and theoretical structure and offenders assigned to the program are a party to the joint operation. The role of research in understanding and improving correctional programs is explained to them and they realize that research information is privileged.

The research endeavor is concentrating on four areas. The first might be called input research and is concerned with the characteristics of offenders and whether the assumptions made about them are confirmed by empirical findings. If basic assumptions made about offenders have no basis in fact, then theoretically at least the treatment program might be relatively ineffective. Revisions would have to be made.

The second might be called process research that is concerned with program operation itself and is a form of quality control. It determines whether actual operation conforms to program design and what the consequences for staff and offenders are.

The third is outcome research concerned, in this case, with determining the relative effectiveness of the experimental program as contrasted to that of an institutional program with which it is being compared. Experimental and control groups have been randomly chosen from a common pool of eligibles as a means of making the comparison.

At this writing, results are inconclusive because the experiment is only about half completed. However, some items of interest have emerged. First, in terms of process research, an analysis of "critical incidents" reveals that the majority of delinquent and other problem-acts at the experiment are committed by a minority of offenders. This small correctional residence is apparently like society in microcosm. Most of those who are present are generally conformist with only a small proportion continuing to be persistently deviant.

Second, unauthorized absences from the residence and the school have been a problem but preliminary input and process research suggest that it may eventually be possible to do a more effective job of identifying the offenders and situations in advance that are most likely to contribute to absences. At present, for example, selection criteria are broad, excluding only addicts, sex, and violent offenders. It may be that certain kinds of offenders are less likely to benefit from a program of this type, and it would be important to be able to identify them.

Finally, in terms of success and failure rates, the experimental and control groups are doing about the same. Approximately three-quarters of both groups are succeeding after completion of their programs. But while boys in the experimental residence are remaining only about six and one-half months, those in the control group are staying in an institution about fifteen and one-half months, a period over twice as long and much more costly.

These findings are highly tentative, however, because numbers remain small. Furthermore, the success rates of both groups are sullied by the fact that both programs, being open and without guards, are struggling with a runaway problem. If runaways are taken into account, some of whom leave on the first or second day, then overall success rates drop sharply. Such findings highlight the importance of intensive research because until offender and organizational problems can be straightened out, until types of offenders can be related to types of programs, problems of this kind will persist. It is one thing to retain tight and effective control in a closed setting but quite another to hold on to offenders because they see some benefit in staying. . . .

Miscellaneous Alternatives

Other miscellaneous alternatives to incarceration are emerging very rapidly; it is almost impossible to keep abreast of them. Most, however, are not far from total incarceration and represent only a small step from complete loss of freedom.

The California Youth Authority launched an experiment some years ago at its Southern Reception Center in which it randomly selected an experimental group and kept it separate from other institution-bound juveniles. It then established a program that gave principal emphasis to a combination of group and individual counseling and to limited work activities. Instead of staying six to nine months, the average stay for Youth Authority wards, those assigned to this program were held for five months. Upon release, and fifteen months of elapsed time, the recidivism rate for the experimental group was less than that of the control group, with only about one fifth of the experimental cases requiring recommitment, as contrasted to approximately one third of the control cases.

This encouraging development led to an expanded and modified effort known as the Marshall Program which is now in progress. This program minimizes formal academic and trade training and concentrates, instead, on personal changes induced through a therapeutic community model. The program is housed in a fifty-bed cottage and those assigned to it are expected to stay only a few months. Thus, the program will process 180 to 200 wards per year, as contrasted to traditional programs that process only 75 to 80 boys through facilities of the same size.

Los Angeles County is experimenting with similar short-term programs for serious delinquents. One such program for disturbed delinquent girls at Lathrop Hall involves only a short stay of two and one-half to three months, yet produces results that seem to be notably superior to traditional placement for such girls.[26]

Los Angeles County is now beginning a short-term program for boys at Juvenile Hall. It is also experimenting with a program in which it buses apparent probation failures from their homes each day to one of its probation camps. Rather than having to house, feed, guard, and care for these wards, this approach permits them to live at home, thus concentrating solely on a school and counseling program.

Other correctional day-care programs are in operation in San Mateo and Contra Costa counties in California and in the Parkland Project in Louisville, Kentucky. These programs can be used for probation failures in place of commitment or they can be adapted to parole programs. They can be administered locally with state subsidy or by the state itself.

Summary

It seems clear that the numbers of alternatives and the amount of experimentation in the post-trial phase of the correctional process are greater than in any other phase. Nevertheless, more questions remained unanswered than answered.

1. *What kinds of programs are needed for what kinds of offenders?* The findings cited above were generally encouraging in the sense that they implied that, with careful programing, the number of offenders who might safely be kept in the community could be enlarged. Yet, at the same time, they shed little light on the problems of relating types of offenders to types of programs. Errors are probably occurring in two directions; first in seeking complex programing for offenders who, because they are not basically criminal, could be corrected with only minimal controls; and, second, in failing to provide enough controls and direction for potentially dangerous offenders who must be carefully supervised.

The search for solutions is not a simple one. We tend to operate in extremes. If the minimal controls of the suspended sentence or probation do not work, we tend either to incarcerate or to plan elaborate therapeutic treatment. Neither extreme may be warranted for the majority of cases. The need, then, is for careful research that concentrates not only on offenders but on the nature of programs as well.

In considering types of offenders, the focus should not be narrow but concerned with the offender in a broad social context involving familial, educational, economical, and peer as well as personality variables. Similarly, with respect to programs, we need to know what their goals, methods, and outcomes are, what the evidence is to indicate that they are addressing fundamental problems, and whether it can be demonstrated that they are more effective than resources already available in the community.

2. *What can be done to create programmatic controls in the community that will adequately replace those now provided by prisons and training schools?*

Some offenders are predatory and must be controlled, but it does not necessarily follow that permanent and extended incarceration is the best answer. It may be a relatively poor choice. By contrast the few experiments mentioned above for serious offenders attempted to make the control function a part of the change strategy. Instead of incarceration, they used peer group and staff rewards and punishments, work details, temporary detention, and other measures of social control. Their idea was that control is successfully achieved only when it is made a part of a total program. It cannot be a separate function, as is a jail sentence, from the activities of daily living. Furthermore, the offender must have the chance to recognize and accept it as a legitimate part of living.

There are many problems, practical, legal, and ethical, in establishing community controls. For example, while it is customary for the court to incarcerate an offender indefinitely, and to permit prison and parole officials wide latitude in determining when he shall be released, it is much less customary to permit occasional incarceration of short duration in community programs. Paradoxically, constitutional and bureaucratic questions are likely to be raised. Conversely, it is extremely difficult within existing constraints to reward acceptable behavior by offenders in some special way. This, also, is paradoxical. In light of learning theory, the problem of extinguishing old patterns of behavior is difficult if nothing can be done to reward new patterns.

Finding ways to effectuate community controls are fundamental issues that confront those who work with offenders in any stage of the correctional process. If community programs are to succeed, then policies and statutes as well as research efforts must be directed to their discovery and implementation. Effective methods are not now available.

3. *To what extent will successful programs and reintegration for the offender require some form of social reconstruction?*

The fundamental logic of the third revolution in corrections is that reintegration for the alienated offender is a necessity. Reintegration, in turn, implies some form of social reconstruction, some change in community institutions other than those that are strictly legal-correctional in nature.

Community acceptance of the offender, changes in educational programs, or genuine career opportunities may be a necessary counterpart to personal reformation.

The kinds of changes that are needed and how they can be induced are not known. They are a part of a number of broader societal problems relative to education, poverty, and employment. Not only does each of them require attention in its own right but also changes in the traditional policies and practices which make it difficult for the offender to benefit from advances that are made. . . .

CONCLUSION

Given all of the innovations that are now being developed, the ingredients are probably available for a more efficient development of alternatives to incarceration. But taken singly, these innovations would not constitute a solution to the correctional problem. Ways must be sought by which to relate them together in some systematic way. Thus, what is needed is a long-range perspective and the commitment of resources that would result in a better understanding of the whole correctional process, a better conception of the key decision points in that process, the development of more specific kinds of programs for specific kinds of offenders, and a careful study of whatever steps are taken to improve the system. The changes that are needed, therefore, are philosophical as well as practical. Political, economic, and humanitarian pressures which impel society to "do something" must be accompanied by a more disciplined recognition of the complexities involved and the need for careful study of whatever steps are taken.

NOTES

[1] Paul W. Tappan, *Crime, Justice and Correction* (New York: McGraw-Hill, 1960), p. 422.

[2] *Ibid.*

[3] For a more detailed summary and a list of bibliographical sources, see *ibid.,* pp. 546–49.

[4] See Sheldon Glueck (ed.), *Probation and Criminal Justice* (1933), p. 228; and Ralph W. England, "What Is Responsible for Satisfactory Probation and Post-Probation Outcome?" *Journal of Criminal Law, Criminology, and Police Science,* 47 (March–April 1957), 675.

[5] England, *ibid.,* pp. 667–77.

[6] Max Grunhut, *Penal Reform* (New York: The Clarendon Press, 1948), pp. 60–82. For an additional summary, see Tappan, *op. cit.,* pp. 576–84.

[7] "What Is Responsible for Satisfactory Probation and Post-Probation Outcome," *op. cit.,* pp. 667–77.

[8] Daniel Glaser, *The Effectiveness of a Prison and Parole System* (Indianapolis: Bobbs-Merrill, 1964), Chap. II.

[9] Tappan, *Crime, Justice and Correction, op. cit.,* p. 661.

[10] Charles H. Miller, "The Fine—Price Tag or Rehabilitative Force," *NPPA Journal,* 2 (Oct. 1956), 377–85.

[11] *Wisconsin's Huber Law in Action* (Milwaukee: Wisconsin Service Association, 1958); and V. A. Verhulst, "Report on Progress and Promotion of a Country Work Release Program (Wisconsin's Huber Law)," (Madison: State Department of Public Welfare, 1963) (mimeo).

[12] Stanley E. Grupp, "Work Release—Statutory Patterns, Implementation, and Problems," *The Prison Journal,* 44 (Spring 1964), 4–25; and Grupp, "Work Release in the United States," *The Journal of Criminal Law, Criminology, and Police Science,* 54 (Sept. 1963), 267–72.

[13] Verhulst, *op. cit.,* p. 4.

[14] *Ibid.*

[15] LaMar T. Empey and Jerome Rabow, "The Provo Experiment in Delinquency Rehabilitation," *American Sociological Review,* 26 (Oct. 1961), 679–96; "Ethics and the Provo Experiment," an exchange of letters, *American Sociological Review,* 27 (April 1962), 256–58; Empey, Maynard L. Erickson, and Max Scott, "The Provo Experiment: Evolution of a Community Program" in *Correction in the Community,* Monograph No. 4 (Sacramento: California State Board of Corrections, 1964), pp. 29–38.

[16] Albert Elias and Saul Pilnick, "The Essexfields Group Rehabilitation Project for Youthful Offenders," in *Correction in the Community, op. cit.,* pp. 51–57, "Essexfields Group Rehabilitation Center," New Jersey Department of Institutions and Agencies, Division of Correction and Parole, Annual Report, 1963; and Saul Pilnick, "The Essexfields Concept: A New Approach to the Social Treatment of Juvenile Delinquents," (Newark: Essexfields Group Rehabilitation Center, 1964) (mimeo). The latter are available in the Information Library of NCCD.

[17] F. Lovell Bixby and Lloyd W. McCorkle, "Guided Group Interaction and Correctional Work," *American Sociological Review,* Vol. 16 (August, 1951), pp. 455–59; Lloyd W. McCorkle, Albert Elias, and F. Lovell Bixby, *The Highfields Story* (New York: Henry Holt, 1958).

[18] All of the above findings are summarized in LaMar T. Empey, "The Provo Experiment: A Book Review" (Los Angeles: Youth Studies Center, University of Southern California, mimeo., 1965).

[19] "Essexfields Group Rehabilitation Center," *op. cit.*

[20] See Clyde Sullivan, Marguerite O. Grant, and J. Douglas Grant, "The Development of Interpersonal Maturity: Applications to Delinquency," *Psychiatry,* 20 (Nov. 1957), 1–15.

[21] Several publications have been made on the Community Treatment Project. For a

general description, see Marguerite C. Warren, "An Experiment in Alternatives to Incarceration for Delinquent Youth: Recent Findings in the Community Treatment Project," in *Correction in the Community, op. cit.,* pp. 39–50. For greater detail and current progress reports, see Community Treatment Project Reports Nos. 1–6 (Sacramento: California Youth Authority).

22 For a more complete description of Highfields, see Lloyd W. McCorkle, Albert Elias, and F. Lovell Bixby, *The Highfields Story: A Unique Experiment in the Treatment of Juvenile Delinquency* (New York: Holt, Rinehart & Winston, 1957).

23 For some description of New York's programs, see Alexander Aldrich, "The Opportunity and Rehabilitation Center Program," New York State Division for Youth, 1960; and Milton Luger, "Launching a New Program: Problems and Progress," *Syracuse Law Review*. Both publications on file in the Library of the National Council on Crime and Delinquency.

24 Rosemary McGrath, "Residential Group Center for Delinquent Girls," *The Welfare Reporter,* 84 (July 1963), New Jersey Institutions and Agencies, 66–73.

25 This experiment was begun in 1964 and joins in a common enterprise the Boys Republic, a private institution for delinquents, and the Youth Studies Center of the University of Southern California. Research funds are provided by the Rosenberg and Ford Foundations. See LaMar T. Empey, George E. Newland, and Steven G. Lubeck, *The Silverlake Experiment,* Youth Studies Center, University of Southern California, Progress Report No. 2, 1965.

26 *Development of a Program Research Service in Probation,* Los Angeles County Probation Department, Research Report No. 27, Jan. 1966, pp. 18–22.

5. *Evaluative Studies of Institutions for Delinquents* *

PAUL LERMAN

EVALUATIVE RESEARCH IS USUALLY undertaken for the purpose of gathering evidence of a program's success in achieving its avowed goals.[1] This approach can be questioned, however, unless a more basic question has first been answered in the affirmative: Is there any empirical evidence that the program under consideration is more likely to be associated with success than with failure? It is not sufficient merely to assume that assessing success is the relevant evaluative problem. One must be willing to face the possibility that the program is associated with high rates of failure. Instead of the success of a program, it might be more relevant to evaluate its failure.

This point of view can be applied to any program of interest to social workers. It is especially appropriate in studying institutions that seek to transform delinquents into law-abiding youths. This paper will provide evidence that supports the following conclusions: Regardless of the type of program investigated, residential institutions for delinquents (under eighteen years of age) are characterized by high rates of potential failure. On the basis of this evidence, it will be argued that researchers interested in evaluating new programs should focus on the problem of whether (and how)

* Reprinted from *Social Work,* Vol. 13, No. 3 (July, 1968).

failure rates have been reduced—not whether an institution can claim success. In addition, this paper will propose that the issue of humanitarianism be considered apart from the ideologies of treatment and success.

What Is Organizational Failure?

It has become virtually a custom in the delinquency field to measure the success of correctional organizations by determining whether boys released from custody have refrained from known law violations.[2] From an evaluative perspective this approach is quite misleading. Boys released from a residential institution who are not "renoticed" by the legal system *might* be regarded as successes, but it still must be demonstrated that their success is attributable to the organization. Boys can be successful in this respect for many reasons that have little to do with their residential experiences. It is the task of evaluative research to demonstrate that the organization was actually responsible for the boys' achievements.[3]

The crucial difference between potential and actual organizational success becomes even clearer when the boys who *are* renoticed are examined. Residential organizations will not readily agree that renoticed boys constitute evidence of the organizations' *actual* failure to rehabilitate. Rather, they argue (and correctly so) that the failure may be due to many factors—some of which may be beyond the power of the institution to control. Without further evidence, it is no less unfair to attribute the failures to the organization than to credit it with the successes. But organizations cannot claim unnoticed boys as their successes without also claiming renoticed boys as their failures. Again, it is the task of evaluative research to demonstrate that the organization was responsible for the boys' failure or success.

At the stage of formulating the evaluative problem to be investigated, interest is in estimating *potential* organizational failures. To carry out this purpose, *all the boys whom the organization cannot reasonably claim as evidence of success must be identified.*

Recontact with the criminal-justice system constitutes one measure of potential failure. Although this is a crude measure, it is difficult to deny its social utility. If it is granted that there is social utility in assessing failure by indications of renewed delinquent activity, it is still appropriate to question the usual measure utilized in evaluation studies. Most delinquency studies rely on recidivist data—the reinstitutionalization of released boys. This type of measure implies that boys who are known to the police and/or courts but who were not reinstitutionalized should be counted as successes, which is a dubious practice. Sophisticated criminologists are well aware that indications of delinquency or criminality decrease in reliability as the level of enforcement takes one further away from the offense itself. Sellin, the dean of American criminology, states this position as follows:

> The difficulty with statistics drawn from later stages in the administrative process is that they may show changes or fluctuations which are not due to changes in criminality but to variations in the policies or the efficiencies of administrative agencies.[4]

In classifying boys as potential successes or failures, it is important that one avoid confounding the issue of renewed delinquent behavior with discretionary reactions to that behavior by court personnel. Whenever possible, studies must be analyzed to obtain indications of failure regardless of whether boys were reinstitutionalized. In brief, the notion of counting as successes boys whose behavior indicates that the institution has probably failed is rejected.

The importance of making these distinctions explicit can be highlighted by reviewing the results of a major current study.[5] For the past six and one-half years the California Youth Authority's research department has been continually engaged in evaluating the Community Treatment Project, in which, since September, 1961, first-commitment youths have been randomly assigned to experimental services in their own communities or to a control situation that involves residence in an institution away from home. As of March 31, 1966, 241 in the experimental group and 220 in the control group had been paroled to Sacramento and Stockton, the two major sources of the sample; the former had been on parole for an average of 16.4 months and the latter for an average of 17.9 months. As of May, 1967, 33 per cent of the experimentals and 55 per cent of the controls had violated parole (that is, the boys' parole was officially revoked, they were recommitted, or they had received an unfavorable discharge from the youth authority). A more detailed analysis sustains this difference, but regardless of the refinement the findings are quite misleading about the behavior of the two groups.

The difference in parole violation figures suggests that the experimentals as a group were less delinquent in their behavior than the controls, but this is not the case. As a matter of fact, the experimentals had more known delinquent offenses per boy than the controls (2.81 to 1.61).[6] When the seriousness of the offenses is considered, then the rates for "low-serious" offenses are 1.56 per boy for the experimentals and .52 for the controls; for "medium-serious" offenses, .61 per boy for the experimentals and .45 for the controls; and for "high-serious" offenses, .64 per boy for both groups.[7] The authors present convincing evidence that the parole officers of the experimentals were much more likely to know about their boys' offenses than the parole officers of the controls.[8] In effect, they argue that the delinquent *behavioral output* was probably the same, but that the *rate of being noticed* was different.

The report could go a step further: It could demonstrate that the noticed offenses were reacted to differently by the experimental and control organizations. The parole violation rates differ because the modes of reacting to and handling the offenses are different. Table 1 compares the experimental and control groups by the seriousness of the offenses officially known; using known offenses as the base, the table then indicates the proportion of parole violations for each offense category for experimentals and controls. The table attempts to answer the following questions: Are noticed offenses of varying degrees of severity more or less likely to be judged parole violations when committed by the experimental group?

As the table clearly shows, the chance that an experimental boy's offense will be handled by revocation of parole is lower than for a control boy if the offense is low or moderate in seriousness; experimentals are judged similarly to the controls *only* when the offenses are of high seriousness. It is difficult not to conclude that the experimental boys have a lower parole-violation rate because offenses of low and medium seriousness are evaluated differently by adults according to organizational context.

TABLE 1. RATES OF PAROLE VIOLATION PER OFFENSE CATEGORY FOR EXPERIMENTALS
AND CONTROLS, CALIFORNIA COMMUNITY TREATMENT PROJECT

Seriousness of Offense *	Experimentals		Controls	
	Number	Rate	Number	Rate
Low	376	.02	114	.17
Medium	146	.10	100	.40
High	156	.37	140	.44

* Seriousness-of-offense ratings are those used in the CTP study, but they have been trichotomized to highlight the trends. The low category includes California Youth Authority ratings 1–2, medium includes ratings 3–4, and high includes ratings 5–10.

SOURCE: Marguerite Q. Warren, Virginia V. Neto, Theodore B. Palmer, and James K. Turner, "Community Treatment Project: An Evaluation of Community Treatment for Delinquents," CTP Research Report No. 7 (Sacramento: California Youth Authority, Division of Research, Aug. 1966) (Mimeo).

Instead of the misleading conclusion derived from using only parole-violation differences, it appears that the potential rates of failure of the two programs are similar (at this point in time). The behavioral outputs of the experimentals and controls are probably the same; however, the experimentals' parole agents notice more of this behavior and therefore give the impression that the experimentals are more delinquent. But even though the behavior of experimentals attracts more notice, it is not evaluated in the same way as the behavior of the controls. This important study may have exercised excellent control over the random selection of boys; unfortunately, the ideology of treating boys in the community spilled over into the postexperimental phase. The experimental and control groups appear to differ in the behavior of the parole agents with respect to revocation of parole—not in the delinquent behavior of the boys.

In addition to officially noticed delinquent actions that are not regarded as parole violations, there is another measure of potential failure that has been disregarded: boys who do not "complete treatment." The following section will describe this additional source of measurement; a subsequent section will then provide data from published and unpublished studies that highlight the importance of measuring *all* the potential failures.

COUNTING ALL OUTCOMES

Before measurement of this other type of failure is discussed, the social bookkeeping of institutions must be understood. The literature on delinquency reveals a curious bookkeeping habit: Boys who do not complete treatment are usually *not counted* in evaluations of organizational effectiveness. These boys are treated statistically as if they never existed; in a sense they are dealt with as Orwellian "no-persons." It is difficult to think of such outcomes as successes, but organizations do not like to count them as failures. Therefore, these boys are set aside and ignored. If this group were small, this accounting fiction might be accepted; unfortunately, it is not. The rate of no-persons in an institutional population can exceed 30 per cent. Discarding a third of an agency's budget as nonaccountable would never be tolerated; should one tolerate discarding a third of its clients?

The problem of how to count boys who are labeled as not completing treatment is especially acute in the private sector. Although private institutions for delinquents are heavily subsidized by public funds, they have been permitted an enormous amount of discretion in controlling the population they treat, especially with regard to intake and maintenance. These agencies choose the boys who will enter into residence and those who will remain in residence and complete treatment (and, of course, those who will not do so). By contrast, most public institutions, unless they are special experimental programs, are forced to accept into residence all boys the private institutions reject at intake; even if the boys do not "work out," they are usually maintained in the institution, since there are few if any other places that will take them. State training schools rarely have reason to use the classification "not completing treatment."

One private residential center in New York State studied by the author controls its population to the extent of rejecting seventeen boys for every one accepted for residential treatment. This institution (hereafter referred to as "Boysville") considers many nonpsychological factors in exercising discretion at intake; that is, age, previous record, ethnicity, space in the cottages. Having exercised this population control at intake, Boysville then proceeds to use its freedom to reject boys who "resist treatment." An unpublished study by the author of Boysville found that 31 per cent (51 out of 164) of the boys in the study sample released from the institution were classified as not completing treatment. Most of these boys (40) were sent to state training schools. The average length of their stay at the private institution was sixteen months, far exceeding the customary remand period of ninety days. Had these boys been sent to nearby "Statesville" at intake, their average stay would have been only nine months.

This outcome was not unique to the specific time chosen for the Boysville study. The administrative staff was so surprised by the findings that they examined their records for a different time period. This unusual replication— conducted surreptitiously—revealed an almost identical rate of boys classified as not completing treatment released from the institution (33 per cent).

Nor is this problem unique to private nonsectarian organizations in New York State; it is just more acute at Boysville. A study of Highfields, a special public organization located in New Jersey, reveals that 18 per cent of the population released did not complete treatment.[9] A study of another special public program located in Michigan reveals a rate of 18 per cent.[10] An unpublished study of a sectarian residential treatment center in New York State disclosed a rate of 25 per cent.[11] Street, Vinter, and Perrow comment that in one treatment institution "many boys were screened out in the first three months."[12] These organizations share one characteristic: Each exercised control at intake and was also able to "get rid of" boys who were "untreatable." In a less sophisticated period these boys might have been called "incorrigible."

This shift in semantic labels should suggest to the researcher the need to seek his own definition of this outcome. It is suggested that boys classified as not completing treatment have been granted "dishonorable discharges" from the institution, whereas those who have completed treatment are released as "honorably discharged." Only the latter boys can reasonably be conceived of as contributing to an organization's potential success. Redefining boys not completing treatment as dishonorably discharged permits counting

TABLE 2. Potential Failures of Boysville Residential Treatment Center by Two Counting Methods (Percentage)

Type of Failure	All Boys Released (N=164)	Honorable Discharges Only (N=113)
Internal	31	0
External *	23	34
Total	54	34

* Refers to boys officially rated as having violated the law between six and twenty-four months after their release to one of the five boroughs of New York City. Institutional records and the state files at Albany furnished the data.

TABLE 3. Comparison of Potential Failures of Two New Jersey Public Institutions (Percentage)

Type of Failure	Highfields (N=229)	Annandale (N=116)
Internal	18	3
External *	34	59
Total	52	62

* The external failures include all law violators, both institutionalized and non-institutionalized, who had been released for at least eight months.
Source: H. Ashley Weeks, *Youthful Offenders at Highfields* (Ann Arbor: University of Michigan Press, 1958), pp. 46–50, 52, and 60. This table does not appear in Weeks but is derived from data appearing in the cited pages.

of *all* the boys admitted to an institution in evaluating its success. Once this is done, it is clear that institutions yield two types of potential failures:

1. *Internal potential failures*—boys released from residential institutions via the route of a dishonorable discharge.
2. *External potential failures*—boys released with an honorable discharge who later engage in criminal or delinquent violations.

Internal failures can easily be identified in the everyday records of residential institutions. However, the type of discharge will not be stamped on the folders. Of the fifty-one boys in the Boysville sample who did not receive the usual honorable discharge—release to aftercare—forty were reinstitutionalized in state training schools, five were sent to mental hospitals, and six were purportedly "released to the community," but were actually runaways who could not be found. All these boys are classified as dishonorably discharged; they should be counted as the institution's potential internal failures. Certainly it is unreasonable to view them as potential successes.

Adding Up Failures

The profound differences that can ensue when *all* boys regardless of discharge status are counted are clearly shown in Table 2. When internal failures are taken into account, the minimum estimate of the total potential failures of Boysville is 54 per cent. (If this group of boys had been followed for a longer period of time, there is little doubt that the total failure rate would have been higher.) If the usual custom of "not counting" internal failures in either the numerator or the denominator had been followed, the estimate would have been 34 per cent. Which social bookkeeping method is used obviously matters; the distinction is not just academic.

Although Boysville differs in many ways from its public neighbor, Statesville, the total potential failure rates for the two institutions are quite comparable for similar postrelease periods. The major difference between them is that Boysville's potential failure rate is derived from both internal and external sources; Statesville has an internal failure rate of only 3 per cent. The total rates are similar even though Boysville and Statesville differ in their relative power to control intake and maintenance of population in addition to treatment modalities.

Is this estimate of comparable failure rates a unique finding? Reanalysis of the best evaluation study available in the literature indicates that it is not.[13] In Table 3 data obtained from Weeks's comparison of Highfields, a special public program, and Annandale, a typical state training school—both of which are located in New Jersey—are presented.

The rates of total potential failures differ by only 10 per cent. However, the two institutions differed in their treatment services; Highfields boys worked away from their residence, received "guided group interaction," and stayed only four months; Annandale boys were incarcerated on a routine twenty-four-hour basis and stayed twelve months. The similarity of the failure rates is even more striking when the initial differences between the populations are taken into account: Annandale boys were more likely to have come from urban centers rather than suburban towns, were more likely to be Negro, and had longer and more intense careers as delinquents; Highfields boys tended to be younger and to have completed more years of schooling. In addition to these initial population differences, Highfields was composed of first offenders only; although the Annandale sample was also composed of first offenders, the institution itself contained knowledgeable multiple offenders. Annandale had little control over the maintenance of membership and initial recruitment, while Highfields had a great deal.

Furthermore, the two populations were exposed to different types of parole (or aftercare) services. Highfields parole officers encouraged boys to enlist in the armed services; twenty-seven Highfields boys and only seven Annandale boys entered the armed forces and thus were removed from the risk of failure. Also, Highfields boys, unlike their peers from Annandale, were discharged from postprogram supervision "within only a few months after their release."[14] More Annandale than Highfields boys were actually reinstitutionalized because of parole violations; had these boys not been under longer supervision they might not have been so easily renoticed. In general, Weeks presents an image of the Highfields population as more advantaged before, during, and after treatment. Despite these differences, the total potential failure rates are not too dissimilar and in both cases involve a majority of the boys.

COMPARABILITY OF CONTROL GROUPS

In investigating potential failure, it is not necessary to measure boys "before" and "after." Attempting to assess attitudinal change that can be attributed to an organizational experience is a complex affair; if the potential rates of failure are high, there is scant justification for expending money, personnel, and creative energy in this direction. However, there is one feature of the usual approach to evaluation that cannot be set aside so easily in assessing potential failure: If two organizations are being compared, then it is crucial that the population of boys be quite similar. The Highfields study by Weeks exhibits sensitivity to this requirement; unfortunately, a more recent study indicates that this sensitivity has not yet been translated into a norm of evaluative research.

In 1965, Jesness released a study, sponsored by the California Youth Authority, that attempted to compare "outcomes with small versus large living groups in the rehabilitation of delinquents." [15] The design of the study called for random assignment of ten-to-eleven-year-old boys at Fricot Ranch to either the experimental twenty-boy lodge or the control fifty-boy lodge. For unknown reasons, random processes did not appear to be operating in the actual assignments. Instead of being comparable, the two populations were discovered to have significant background differences: The experimentals were 73 per cent white and the controls only 55 per cent; 35 per cent of the experimentals and 50 per cent of the controls came from the poorest

TABLE 4. Successes and Failures as Reported by William McCord and Joan McCord (Percentage)

Type of Outcome *	Wiltwyck (N=65)	"New England State" (N=228)
Complete success	43	48
Partial success	28	5
Complete failure	29	33
Don't know	0	13

* For definitions of categories, see text.
Source: William McCord and Joan McCord, "Two Approaches to the Cure of Delinquents," in Sheldon Glueck (ed.), *The Problem of Delinquency* (Boston: Houghton Mifflin, 1959), pp. 735–36.

homes; and 67 per cent of the experimentals were from households in which the father was the main provider as compared with only 52 per cent of the controls.[16]

Using revocation of parole as a measure of failure, Jesness found that the experimentals were less likely to fail than the controls up until after thirty-six months of exposure to parole. The rates are as follows: 32–48 per cent after twelve months, 42–58 per cent after fifteen months, and 61–70 per cent after twenty-four months. After thirty-six months the rates were virtually the same—76 and 78 per cent, respectively.[17] Jesness concludes that the "effects of the experimental program tend to fade as the exposure period increases." [18] This may be so, but it seems even more likely that the higher failure rates of the controls reflect the fact that they were actually a higher risk group at the outset of parole, since the group was comprised of more Negroes and Mexican-Americans and came from poorer homes than the experimentals (and probably poorer neighborhoods, too). Unless Jesness presents evidence that these critical background variables, when used as analytical controls, do not change the differential outcomes after twelve or fifteen months of parole exposure, his inference cannot be accepted. These background variables, for which Jesness does not control, have usually been strongly associated with delinquency and recidivism, and these, not the institutional experiences, probably account for the differences in failure. In the language of multivariate analysis, Jesness' findings on early failure are probably spurious (that is, the result of a third, uncontrolled variable).

INSTITUTIONAL INTERESTS

Organizational personnel have a major stake in any evaluative outcome. They want to be associated with potential success, not failure. Researchers are not likely to have a similar stake in the outcome. Although researchers do not purposefully seek to devalue people or organizations, their motto is much more likely to be: "Let's find out the truth and let the chips fall where they may." Their reference group is the scientific community and their ethics are ideally guided accordingly. Administrators, on the other hand— the persons who hire researchers—usually want the evaluators to demonstrate that their operations are successful and worthy of the external community's moral and financial support. Rather than deny this conflict of interest, one ought to be aware of its existence and make sure that biases do not influence empirical studies and written reports.

Biases influenced by organizational interests are especially likely to develop when researchers give up their independence and seek ways to demonstrate program success. Consider the evaluative study of Wiltwyck reported by William and Joan McCord.[19] Employed as the institution's resident psychologists, the McCords seemed so eager to prove its success that they defined one type of *failure* as "partial success." Table 4 presents the data as reported by the McCords for Wiltwyck and "New England State School."

From the McCord text it is learned that "partial success" refers to boys who actually appeared in court for law violations but were not reinstitutionalized; "complete failures" were both noticed and reinstitutionalized. The McCords do not seem to be bothered by this odd use of labels, for they claim that Wiltwyck had a *combined* success rate of 71 per cent whereas New England, a state institution, had a rate of only 53 per cent. A fair appraisal of the data would suggest that there is no appreciable difference between these institutions in potential success, using this writer's definition; the 5 per cent difference—in favor of New England—is small. If all law violations are counted as potential failure, regardless of court disposition, it appears that *both* institutions are characterized by high external failure.

A subtle form of bias can be found in a study reported by Black and Glick.[20] The population of primary interest was composed mainly of Jewish boys sentenced to Hawthorne Cedar Knolls School, a sectarian-sponsored residential treatment institution. Both researchers were regular employees of the Jewish Board of Guardians, the sponsoring agency. In a monograph reporting their results, the investigators describe the selection of their sample as follows: "For purposes of this study the followup period was computed from the date of discharge from after-care." [21] Not surprisingly, Black and Glick report that Hawthorne Cedar Knolls had a higher success rate than a neighboring state school. They excluded from their sample not only all of the internal failures, but also all of the external failures occurring during the period of aftercare. Since the bulk of postrelease failures take place within the first two years, the researchers thus eliminated the chance of finding many failures. In effect, all this study can hope to describe is the potential success rate of an unknown population that has been selectively screened for boys who might be failures. Since the researchers have gone to such lengths to minimize their potential failures, it is reasonable to conclude that they were unwilling to face up to the possibility that their organization, like the state school, is characterized by a high rate of internal and/or external failure.

IMPLICATIONS FOR A HUMANITARIAN POLICY

The consistent finding that treatment programs have not yet been proved to have an appreciable impact on failure rates should not be misinterpreted. For even though institutions for delinquents are probably not highly successful—regardless of treatment type—there is no reason to go back to harsher methods of child handling. It can be argued, rather, that even when boys are kept for only four months and treated with trust (as at Highfields), there is no evidence that this "coddling" will yield greater failure rates.

The case for a humanitarian approach needs to be divorced from any specific mode of treatment. People can be nice to boys with and without engaging in psychotherapy. This point is implicit in the recent work by Street, Vinter, and Perrow.[22] But we should not delude ourselves into adopting the unsubstantiated position that a humanitarian organization for delinquent boys yields lower rates of potential failures. With our present state of knowledge, it makes more sense to advocate a more humanitarian approach on the ground that it does not increase the *risk* of potential failure.

If it is decided to advocate humanitarianism in its own right, the social policy issue becomes much clearer. Given the fact that social work is still unable to influence appreciably the rates of failure of institutions for court-sentenced delinquents, should not ways be sought to make the total criminal-delinquent system more humane? In the name of treatment, boys have actually been sentenced for two and a half years (as at Boysville) for offenses that might bring an adult a sentence of only thirty, sixty, or ninety days. Surely it is time that youths were dealt with as humanely, and with similar regard for equity and due process of law, as adults.[23]

If lighter sentences do not increase the risk of failure, then why not be more humane and equitable? Keeping boys in the community is undoubtedly a lighter sentence than sending them away. But California has found that this probably does not increase the risk of failure. Actually, the California Community Treatment Program has evolved a series of graded punishments. If youngsters in this program misbehave or do not obey the youth officer, they are *temporarily* confined. During the first nineteen months of the program, 57 of 72 experimental cases were placed in temporary confinement a total of 183 times; this was an average of three times each, with an average length of stay of twelve days per confinement.[24] As earlier analysis disclosed, the risk of postprogram failure is not increased by using this kind of approach. It is even conceivable—although this has not been demonstrated—that keeping these boys out of all long-term institutions in itself constitutes treatment and that this treatment may have a payoff much later, when the boys become adults. Spending less time in an all-delinquent community might yield more conforming adults.

Even if communities are not willing to follow the California community approach, one can still argue for shorter "lock-ups." Highfields kept first offenders for only four months, yet the risk of failure was not increased. As long as society is still determined to "teach boys a lesson" by locking them up (or sending them away), why not extend the idea of shorter confinements to a series of graded punishments for offenses? Adults are sentenced for thirty, sixty, or ninety days—why not children? Perhaps we might even come to advocate taking the institutional budgets allocated for food, beds, and clothing (based on lengthy stays) and spending them on boys and their families in their own homes. It is doubtful whether this would add to the risks, but the program would be a great deal more fun to study and run than the old failures.

Whether one embraces the perspective offered here, it is certainly time to address the problem of social accountability, regardless of the type of program. Social welfare institutions are too heavily subsidized, indirectly and directly, for social workers not to take the responsibility for knowing what has happened to the people served. A good start can be made by keeping track of all the people not completing treatment, discontinuing service, dropping out of programs, and running away. Rigorous and nondeceptive social bookkeeping may yield discomforting facts about agency success and reputation. It is hoped that we will be aware of defensive reactions and remind ourselves that we entered social work to serve *people* in trouble—not established agencies, ideologies, and methods.

NOTES

1 Herbert H. Hyman, Charles R. Wright, and Terrence K. Hopkins, *Application of Methods of Evaluation: Four Studies of the Encampment for Citizenship* (Berkeley and Los Angeles: University of California Press, 1962), pp. 3–88.
2 For example, see Bernard C. Kirby, "Measuring Effects of Treatment of Criminals and Delinquents," *Sociology and Social Research*, 38, No. 6 (July–Aug. 1954), 368–75; Vernon Fox, "Michigan Experiment in Minimum Security Penology," *Journal of Criminal Law and Criminology*, 41, No. 2 (July–Aug. 1950), 150–66; William McCord and Joan McCord, "Two Approaches to the Cure of Delinquents," in Sheldon Glueck (ed.), *The Problem of Delinquency* (Boston: Houghton Mifflin, 1959); Bertram J. Black and Selma J. Glick, *Recidivism at the Hawthorne Cedar Knolls School*, Research Monograph No. 2 (New York: Jewish Board of Guardians, 1952); H. Ashley Weeks, *Youthful Offenders at Highfields: An Evaluation of the Effects of the Short-Term Treatment of Delinquent Boys* (Ann Arbor: University of Michigan Press, 1958).
3 This type of research demands careful attention to design to provide evidence that the experimental program had a greater impact on attitudes and values that, in turn, influenced postrelease behavior. This requires control groups and "before-after" measures. At the level of evaluative research herein referred to, in which *potential* outcomes are being assessed, attitudinal measures before and after are *not* necessary. As noted later on, comparability of groups continues to be important at *all* levels of evaluative research. See Hyman, Wright, and Hopkins, *op. cit.*, for a general statement of the problems. See Weeks, *op. cit.*, for the best-detailed example of evaluative research regarding institutions for delinquents.
4 Thorsten Sellin, "The Significance of Records of Crime," in Marvin E. Wolfgang,

Leonard Savitz, and Norman Johnson (eds.), *The Sociology of Crime and Delinquency* (New York: Wiley, 1962), p. 64.

[5] Marguerite Q. Warren, Virginia V. Neto, Theodore B. Palmer, and James K. Turner, "Community Treatment Project: An Evaluation of Community Treatment for Delinquents," CTP Research Report No. 7 (Sacramento: California Youth Authority, Division of Research, Aug. 1966) (mimeo).

[6] *Ibid.*, p. 64.

[7] See *ibid.*, Table 15, p. 68. For an explanation of the ranking of offenses by seriousness on which these figures are based, see Table 1 of this article.

[8] *Ibid.*, p. 65.

[9] Weeks, *op. cit.*

[10] Fox, *op. cit.*

[11] Personal communication from Robert Ontell, former study director of Mobilization for Youth's Reintegration of Juvenile Offenders Project, 1962.

[12] David Street, Robert D. Vinter, and Charles Perrow, *Organization for Treatment: A Comparative Study of Institutions for Delinquents* (New York: The Free Press, 1966), p. 196. This information is presented in a parenthetical comment about "Inland," a private institution. How many of the boys released as not completing treatment are actually excluded or included in this study is difficult to estimate. This study focuses on the attitudes of institutionalized boys about their experiences in residence. It would have been extremely valuable to know whether the screened-out boys differed in their responses to the attitudinal questions. It would also have been valuable to know whether the runaways also differed. Such information might have provided evidence that the attitudinal measures had validity. Presumably boys "resisting treatment" (i.e., those who were screened out or ran away) should have responded differently to questions about themselves and the institutional staff. These kinds of missing data are quite central to the argument concerning the institutional "effectiveness" of Inland.

[13] Weeks, *op. cit.*, pp. 41–62.

[14] *Ibid.*, p. 61.

[15] Carl F. Jesness, "The Fricot Ranch Study: Outcomes with Small Versus Large Living Groups in the Rehabilitation of Delinquents," Research Report No. 47 (Sacramento: California Youth Authority, Division of Research, Oct. 1, 1965) (mimeo).

[16] *Ibid.*, p. 52.

[17] *Ibid.*, pp. 85–90.

[18] *Ibid.*, p. 89.

[19] McCord and McCord, *op. cit.* The Wiltwyck sample is composed only of Negro boys between the ages of eight and twelve (at intake) who presented no "deep-seated psychiatric problems." "New England," on the other hand, is much more heterogeneous and has older boys. The data regarding the Wiltwyck sample can be found in Lois Wiley, "An Early Follow-up Study for Wiltwyck School" (unpublished master's thesis, New York School of Social Work, 1941).

[20] Black and Glick, *op. cit.*

[21] *Ibid.*, p. 4.

[22] *Op. cit.*

[23] See David Matza's insightful description of youthful appraisals of the juvenile court system in the discussion of the "Sense of Injustice," in Matza, *Delinquency and Drift* (New York: Wiley, 1964).

[24] Marguerite Q. Grant, Martin Warren, and James K. Turner, "Community Treatment Project: An Evaluation of Community Treatment of Delinquents," CTP Research Report No. 3 (Sacramento: California Youth Authority, Division of Research, Aug. 1, 1963), p. 38 (mimeo).

6. *The Distribution of Costs in Corrections* *

NATIONAL COUNCIL ON CRIME AND DELINQUENCY

ON ANY ONE DAY in the United States, about one and a quarter million persons—more than the population reported for sixteen states—are under the jurisdiction of state and local correctional agencies and institutions. In addition, many thousands more are serving from a few days to a few weeks in a variety of local lock-ups and jails not included in this survey.

Of the total volume reported, 28 per cent are juveniles and 72 per cent are adults (according to the definitions of each category, which vary from state to state). The number of adults under probation and parole supervision and in correctional institutions (876,412) is more than the number of enlisted personnel (846,684) reported in the U.S. Army for 1965.

DOES IT MAKE A DIFFERENCE WHERE THE OFFENDER IS?

One-third (more than 400,000) of all offenders reported, juvenile and adult, were found in institutions; two-thirds (over 800,000) were in communities under probation or parole supervision (see Table 1). However, about 20 per cent of the latter are on either parole or aftercare status, having first served time in an institution. Judges and juries evidently place a high degree of reliance on institutional commitment.

TABLE 1. AVERAGE DAILY POPULATION OF OFFENDERS IN CORRECTIONAL SYSTEMS

	Juvenile		Adult		Total	
	Number	Per Cent	Number	Per Cent	Number	Per Cent
In the community	283,491	82.16	533,889	60.92	817,380	66.92
In institutions	61,526	17.84	342,523	39.08	404,049	33.08
Total	345,017	100.00	876,412	100.00	1,221,429	100.00

Agencies and institutions receive, during the course of a year, more than 2.5 million persons, whose status as inmate, probationer, or parolee directly affects, in addition, 5,825,000 members of their families.[1] One may well speculate on the number affected over a ten- or twenty-year period and the percentage of the entire population this would represent.

The question of where an offender is—in the community (on probation

* Appendix A, "Correction in the United States: Data Summary," *Task Force Report: Corrections*, prepared by the National Council on Crime and Delinquency for the Task Force on Corrections of the President's Committee on Law Enforcement and Administration of Justice, Washington, D.C.: Government Printing Office, 1967, pp. 192–95.

or parole) or in an institution—makes a profound difference to his family's economic condition and the welfare resources of his community. Although the total commitment rate for the nation cannot be estimated accurately, it would appear that (excluding those sentenced to fines) about two-thirds of all offenders are committed to institutions. That the commitment rate can be lowered has been demonstrated by the Saginaw project,[2] which in addition, offered evidence of the comparatively greater success achieved with offenders through increased use of effective probation. A lower commitment rate produces enormous savings not only in manpower but also in taxes.

How Much Does Correction Cost?

The estimated cost of operating state and local correctional services in 1965 (see Table 2) was almost $1 billion ($940,467,494).

About 80 per cent of the total operating cost is allocated for institutions.

TABLE 2. Annual Expenditures for Correctional Systems

	Juvenile		Adult		Total	
	Number	Per Cent	Number	Per Cent	Number	Per Cent
In the community	$ 93,159,382	29.9	$693,122,837	14.9	$186,282,219	19.9
In institutions	221,410,413	70.1	532,774,862	85.1	754,185,275	80.1
Total	314,569,705	100.00	625,897,699	100.0	940,467,494	100.0

Of that allocation, more than half goes to support state adult correctional institutions. Local institutions and jails account for about 16 per cent of all expenditures; juvenile detention accounts for about 6 per cent of the total. Only 14.4 per cent of correctional costs are allocated for probation services, including supervision of offenders and preparation of social studies to aid courts in making dispositions.

Of the total cost, one-third ($314,569,795) is for juvenile detention, institutions, and aftercare.

Costs for local services for misdemeanant offenders account for 18.7 per cent of the total, with only 3 per cent going for probation services and 15.7 per cent on confinement of misdemeanants.

Per Capita Cost

The figures for per capita cost of all correctional expenditures according to per capita income are not available for all states, but they undoubtedly would show wide variations, with some of the poorer States paying proportionately more than some of the wealthier states. Table 3 compares, regionally, per capita expenditures for state-operated adult and juvenile institutions and parole.

Table 4 illustrates the wide variations in per capita expenditure for these services in the ten largest states, where the average is $2.95 but the range is from $1.75 to $5.31. The average total expenditure is 0.10 per cent of per capita income, but the range extends from 0.06 per cent to 0.17 per cent.

Variations in expenditures for some of the services within each state are shown in Table 5.

TABLE 3. PER CAPITA EXPENDITURES FOR STATE-OPERATED INSTITUTIONS, AFTERCARE, AND PAROLE, BY REGIONS

	Expenditures			Percent of Per Capita Income
	Total	Per Capita	Average Income	
East *	$176,412,231	$3.46	$2,836	0.12
Midwest †	140,770,260	2.40	2,381	.10
South ‡	106,961,398	2.16	1,904	.12
West §	146,950,278	4.81	2,482	.19
Insular ¶	9,824,473	2.65	2,189	.12
Total	580,918,640	3.00	2,386	.13

* Connecticut, Delaware, Washington, D.C., Maine, Maryland, Massachusetts, New Hampshire, New Jersey, New York, Pennsylvania, Rhode Island, Vermont.

† Illinois, Indiana, Iowa, Kansas, Kentucky, Michigan, Minnesota, Missouri, Nebraska, North Dakota, Ohio, South Dakota, West Virginia, Wisconsin.

‡ Alabama, Arkansas, Florida, Georgia, Louisiana, Mississippi, North Carolina, Oklahoma, Tennessee, Texas, South Carolina, Virginia.

§ Arizona, California, Colorado, Idaho, Montana, Nevada, New Mexico, Oregon, Utah, Washington, Wyoming.

¶ Alaska, Hawaii, Puerto Rico.

TABLE 4. PER CAPITA EXPENDITURES FOR STATE-OPERATED INSTITUTIONS, AFTERCARE, AND PAROLE, IN THE TEN LARGEST STATES

State	Per Capita Expenditure	Per Cent of Per Capita Income
A	$1.75	0.08
B	1.89	.06
C	2.37	.09
D	2.46	.09
E	2.56	.08
F	2.69	.10
G	3.03	.13
H	3.16	.11
I	4.29	.14
J	5.31	.17

Greater expenditures in use of probation services could account in some states—not all—for smaller expenditures for institutions and parole. Probation is known to be undeveloped in many states that appropriate either much less or much more than the average percentage of per capita income.

In some states that now expend a disproportionate share of income for correctional services, improvement of services may require even further disparity unless subsidy is obtained from some outside source.

Daily Cost Per Case

The overall daily cost for a juvenile in an institution is ten times more than the cost of juvenile probation or aftercare. For adults, state institutional cost is about six times that of parole and about fourteen times that of probation (see Table 6).

The low cost of probation can be attributed in part to excessively heavy caseloads and low salaries. The average cost per case should be more than doubled to enable probation nationally to become more effective.

The "half-starved" condition of probation services may be one reason why commitment rates are so high. Many judges interviewed during the course of NCCD's state and community surveys report their reluctance to add more offenders to the burdens of an already overburdened probation service. On the other hand, where probation services have been improved, judges have made greater use of them.

If one-third of the prisoners were transferred to probation along with their share of the expenditures, they could be placed in caseloads of ten or less. As has been demonstrated by the California Community Treatment Project, this move would be a more effective disposition and use of public funds.[3]

Are Expenditures for More Institutions Really Needed?

Previous parts of this report have noted the extent of construction underway or planned for local and state institution systems. The total bed capacity

TABLE 5. Per Capita Expenditures for Selected Correctional Services, by State Populations *

States †	Adult Institutions	Parole	Juvenile Institutions	Aftercare ‡
Group I: §				
A	$1.10	$0.15	$0.26	—
B	1.14	.07	.90	—
C	1.16	.06	.48	$0.05
D	1.24	.17	.34	.93
E	1.24	.13	.49	.03
F	1.38	.07	.97	.14
G	1.40	.11	.84	.11
H	1.56	.07	.79	.06
I	1.58	.11	.32	.06
J	1.69	.14	.44	—
K	1.72	.13	.91	.12
L	1.91	.13	.63	.02
M	2.04	.20	.61	—
N	2.30	.21	.49	—
O	2.36	.12	.61	.07
P	2.96	.14	.72	—
Q	3.24	.34	.66	.05
R	3.46	.44	1.14	.27
Group II: ¶				
AA	.26	.25	.22	—
BB	.62	.01	.23	—
CC	.63	.02	.35	.03
DD	1.07	.07	.19	—
EE	1.13	.12	.77	.07
FF	1.14	.12	.49	.07
GG	1.14	.20	.44	—
HH	1.25	.05	.81	.10
II	1.48	.07	.45	.04
JJ	1.52	.15	.72	—

TABLE 5. Per Capita Expenditures *(Continued)*

States †	Adult Institutions	Parole	Juvenile Institutions	Aftercare ‡
KK	1.58	.06	.54	—
LL	1.83	.07	.68	.07
MM	2.04	.09	1.71	—
NN	2.09	.09	.52	.09
OO	2.18	.07	.58	—
PP	2.36	.11	2.02	.17
QQ	2.56	.08	1.85	.36
RR	2.98	.29	1.33	.13
SS	3.11	.30	1.41	—
Group III: #				
AAA	.71	.05	.95	.02
BBB	1.07	.07	.19	.03
CCC	1.19	.14	.90	—
DDD	1.38	.02	1.52	.25
EEE	1.45	.07	1.05	.03
FFF	1.61	.13	1.13	.02
GGG	1.64	.24	.68	.19
HHH	1.68	.93	.74	.07
III	2.00	.09	1.32	.04
JJJ	2.13	.06	1.11	—
KKK	2.28	.17	.87	.10
LLL	2.61	.08	1.54	.11
MMM	2.82	.04	.90	.03
NNN	2.98	.08	3.05	—

* Population figures based on July 1, 1964, estimate.
† Includes Puerto Rico.
‡ Includes only states operating special statewide programs.
§ States having populations over 3,500,000.
¶ States having populations between 1,000,000 and 3,500,000.
# States having populations under 1,000,000.

TABLE 6. Average Daily Costs Per Case

	Juvenile	Adult
Detention	$11.15	—
State institutions	9.35	$5.24
Local institutions (including jails)	10.66	2.86
Probation	.92	.38
Parole or aftercare	.84	.88

of new construction in process or authorized is about 60,000 (see Table 7).

Construction currently being planned for completion by 1975 would add over 50,000 more beds, for a total of almost 114,000 new beds by that date. Some of the new construction will replace obsolete facilities, but probably most of it will add to the present capacity. If all of the units being planned are added, the present capacity of correctional institutions will be increased by 24 per cent. If the cost of correctional institution construction is estimated conservatively at an average of $10,000 a bed, the cost of these added

TABLE 7. CURRENT AND PLANNED CONSTRUCTION OF CORRECTIONAL INSTITUTIONS IN THE UNITED STATES
Construction (Number of Beds)

Type of Facility	Current Estimated Capacity	In Process	Authorized	Total in Process and Authorized	Planned by End of 1975	Total	Estimated Cost *
Local adult institutions	† 192,197	3,196	2,683	5,879	9,982	15,861	$ 158,610,000
Jails ‡	(see above)	4,240	9,824	14,064	17,247	31,311	313,110,000
Adult correctional institutions	213,558	6,360	18,107	24,467	16,909	41,376	413,760,000
Juvenile institutions	43,027	4,164	7,090	11,254	6,606	17,860	178,600,000
Juvenile detention (including jails)	25,932	1,711	2,247	3,958	3,136	7,094	70,940,000
Total	474,714	19,671	39,951	59,622	53,880	113,502	1,135,020,000

* Cost estimated at $10,000 a bed.
† Includes prorated capacity for jails that receive inmates for thirty days or longer.
‡ Jail construction is for persons awaiting trial or serving time.

facilities will be over $1 billion ($1,135,020,000). The added capacity will, of course, increase the operating expense. When fully occupied, the new space will add, on the basis of current per capita costs, over $200 million annually to the operating cost of the institutions. That amount alone is about equal to the total amount now being spent on all probation and parole services, both juvenile and adult.

This trend can be reversed by more adequate staffing of conventional field services and by the development of new and more effective approaches within existing programs. . . .

7. The Degree of State Responsibility *

TASK FORCE ON CORRECTIONS

WHAT IS THE STATE RESPONSIBLE FOR?

BECAUSE OF THE INTERDEPENDENCE of correctional services and the need for statewide coverage, standards call for state governments to have responsibility for the quality of all correctional systems, including those operated by local city and county jurisdictions.

Types of Assistance

The state's responsibility for local service is understood to include consultation, standard-setting, recruitment, and subsidy. In practice, however, the state government's role seems to vary with each type of correctional service. For example, few states set standards for local adult institutions and juvenile detention, but most states (88.2 per cent) either provide all direct services or set standards for adult probation. More than one third of the juvenile probation agencies have no state services (see Table 1).

Where states do provide standards and subsidy, there are marked differences according to the correctional service (see Table 2). For example, 40 per cent of the states inspect jails, but only 25 per cent inspect local correctional institutions. About half of the states (45.5 per cent) subsidize local probation services, yet only 14 per cent subsidize juvenile detention, only 4.5 per cent subsidize local misdemeanant probation services, and only 4 per cent subsidize local correctional institutions. Consultation is given in 61 per cent of the states to juvenile probation and in 57 per cent to adult probation, but in only 32 per cent to misdemeanant probation. State correctional agencies have not been sufficiently concerned with giving direction and leadership necessary to help local communities develop effective short-term institutions or improve adult detention services. While juvenile detention has long been considered a specialized service outside of law enforcement, adult de-

* Appendix A, "Correction in the United States: Data Summary," *Task Force Report:Corrections,* prepared by the National Council on Crime and Delinquency for the Task Force on Corrections of the President's Committee on Law Enforcement and Administration of Justice, Washington, D.C.: Government Printing Office, 1967, pp. 198–202.

TABLE 1. ROLE OF STATE IN PROVIDING DIRECT SERVICES OR SETTING STANDARDS FOR COMMUNITY-BASED PROGRAMS

System	States Providing Direct Service		States Setting Standards for Local Service		Total		States Providing Neither	
	No.	%	No.	%	No.	%	No.	%
Juvenile detention	8	15.7	10	19.6	18	35.3	33	64.7
Juvenile probation	19	37.3	13	25.4	32	62.7	19	37.3
Aftercare	40	78.4	—	—	40	78.4	11	21.6
Misdemeanant probation	22	43.1	9	17.7	31	60.8	20	39.2
Adult probation	37	72.5	8	15.7	45	88.2	6	11.8
Jails *	4	7.8	19	37.2	23	45.0	28	55.0
Local adult institutions	—	—	12	23.6	12	23.6	39	76.4

* For purposes of this table, jails were separated from other local institutions.

TABLE 2. PERCENTAGE OF STATES OFFERING ASSISTANCE OTHER THAN DIRECT SERVICE *

Agencies Providing Direct Service	Services Rendered by States to Improve Local Services				
	Standards	Inspection	License	Subsidies	Consultation
Juvenile detention	23.8	33.3	9.5	14.3	47.6
Jails	40.4	40.4	—	12.8	34.0
Local institutions	27.3	25.0	—	4.3	27.7
Juvenile probation	40.6	—	—	45.5	60.6
Misdemeanant probation	40.9	—	—	4.5	31.8
Adult probation	57.1	—	—	21.4	57.1

* Excludes states providing the given service at the state level.

tention remains primarily a law-enforcement rather than a correctional function. Most of the state standards set for local institutions and jails are for health and construction. It is rare for a state correctional agency to set standards for the operation, programs, or staffing of these institutions. In some states, juvenile probation consultation service is provided by a state welfare department that has no other responsibility—an arrangement that practically guarantees that the consultant will not be in the mainstream of correction.

The leadership role is almost totally absent in some states; in others, it is weakened by the diffusion of consultation and subsidy services among several different state agencies. Thus, in most states, there is no mechanism for providing a better balanced system of correction.

Research and Statistics

The standards call for a central state agency to collect statistical data and to provide for research on the planning and evaluation of correctional programs.

Had the standard been in effect in all states, this survey would have been vastly simplified and the desired information could have been obtained easily from all states. The survey found, instead, that few states have a central source of correctional information and that no state has a central information agency for all its correctional systems (see Table 3).

TABLE 3. STATE'S ROLE IN COLLECTION OF STATISTICS

System	Percentage of States Routinely Collecting Statistics	Agencies Responsible for Collecting Statistics (Per Cent)			
		Department of Public Welfare	Correction Agency	Bureau of Research	Others
Juvenile detention	56.0	46.4	28.6	—	25.0
Juvenile probation	74.5	31.1	44.8	—	24.1
Juvenile institution	73.5	31.1	46.9	6.3	15.7
Aftercare	56.9	23.2	66.4	—	11.4
Misdemeanant probation	35.9	14.3	78.6	—	7.1
Local institutions and jails	25.5	42.9	57.1	—	—
Adult probation	74.5	12.0	80.0	—	8.0
Adult institutions	70.6	7.7	77.0	3.8	11.5

Without going into the quality of the statistical information collected by the states, the survey found that only 25 per cent of the states collect statistics on jails and local institutions, only 36 per cent do so on misdemeanant probation, 57 per cent on aftercare programs, and 75 per cent on probation services. In over one fourth of the states, information on juvenile and adult institutions is available only from each institution.

The agencies responsible for collecting some information and statistics include public welfare departments, correctional agencies, health departments, administrative offices of courts, bureaus of research, boards of control, departments of public safety, and "others." In not a single state is there any one agency responsible for collecting information from all the correctional services or capable of presenting a statistical profile of correction for the state as a whole.

Sensible Administration

In only one state (Alaska) are all nine correctional services organized in a single correctional department; in two states, seven functions are administered by a single correctional agency. At the other extreme, each juvenile institution in five states and each adult institution in three states has a separate board. Between these extremes, we find only six states in which more than three functions are administered by a single state correctional agency (see Table 4).

In a number of states, correctional services are administered by departments that also have other responsibilities, such as welfare, mental health, hospitals, and public safety. In all, there are forty-one state departments whose primary function is not correction but that administer several correctional services.

TABLE 4. PARENT AGENCY RESPONSIBLE

States	Juvenile Detention	Juvenile Probation	Juvenile Institutions	Juvenile Aftercare
Alabama	Local	Department of pensions and security and local	3 separate and independent boards	Department of pensions and security and local
Alaska	Division of youth and adult authority	Division of youth and adult authority	Division of youth and adult authority	Division of youth and adult authority
Arizona	Local	Local	Board of Directors of State Institutions for juveniles	Board of Directors of State Institutions for juveniles
Arkansas	do	State DPW and local	4 independent boards	State DPW and local
California	do	Local	Youth and adult correction agency	Youth and adult correction agency
Colorado	do	do	Department of institutions	Department of institutions
Connecticut	State juvenile court	State juvenile court	2 independent boards of trustees	2 independent boards of trustees
Delaware	Youth service commission	Local	Youth service commission	Youth service commission
Florida	Local	do	Division of child training schools	Division of child training schools
Georgia	Department of family and child service and local	Department of family and child service and local	Department of family and child service	Department of family and child service
Hawaii	Local	Local	Department of social service	Department of social service
Idaho	do	Department of health and local	Department of education	Department of education
Illinois	do	Local	Youth commission	Youth commission
Indiana	do	do	Board of corrections	Board of corrections
Iowa	do	do	Board of control	Board of control
Kansas	do	do	Department of social welfare	Department of social welfare
Kentucky	do	Department of child welfare and local	Department of child welfare	Department of child welfare

TABLE 4. Parent Agency Responsible (*Continued*)

States	Juvenile Detention	Juvenile Probation	Juvenile Institutions	Juvenile Aftercare
Louisiana	do	State DPW and local	Department of institutions	State DPW
Maine	do	Department of mental health and correction and local	Department of mental health and correction	Department of mental health and correction
Maryland	State DPW and local	Department of parole and probation and local	DPW	Department of parole and probation and DPW and local
Massachusetts	Youth service board	Probation commission and local	Youth service board	Youth service board
Michigan	Local	Local	Department of social service	Department of social service
Minnesota	do	Department of correction and local	Department of correction	Department of correction
Mississippi	do	Local	Board of trustees	State DPW and local
Missouri	do	do	Board of training schools	Board of training schools
Montana	do	do	Department of institutions	Department of institutions
Nebraska	do	do	Department of public institutions	Department of public institutions
Nevada	do	do	Department of health and welfare	Department of health and welfare
New Hampshire	Board of trustees	Department of probation and local	Board of trustees	Board of trustees
New Jersey	Local	Local	Department of institutions and agencies	Department of institutions and agencies
New Mexico	do	do	4 separate boards	Local
New York	do	do	Department of social welfare	Department of social welfare
North Carolina	do	do	Board of juvenile correction	Local
North Dakota	do	DPW and local	Board of administration	do
Ohio	do	Local	Youth commission	Youth commission
Oklahoma	do	do	DPW	DPW
Oregon	do	do	Board of control	Board of control

TABLE 4. Parent Agency Responsible (*Continued*)

States	Juvenile Detention	Juvenile Probation	Juvenile Institutions	Juvenile Aftercare
Pennsylvania	do	do	DPW	Local
Rhode Island	Department of social welfare	Department of social welfare	Department of social welfare	Department of social welfare
South Carolina	Local	Local	Board of State industrial schools	Board of State industrial schools
South Dakota	do	do	Board of charities and corrections	Board of pardons and paroles
Tennessee	Local	Department of corrections and local	Department of corrections	Department of corrections
Texas	do	Local	Youth council	Youth council
Utah	do	State juvenile court	DPW	DPW
Vermont	Department of social welfare	Department of social welfare	Department of institutions	Department of institutions
Virginia	Local	Local	Department of welfare and institutions	Local
Washington	do	do	Department of institutions	Department of institutions
West Virginia	do	Department of public assistance and local	Commissioner of public institutions	Commissioner of public institutions
Wisconsin	do	DPW	DPW	DPW
Wyoming	do	Local	Board of charities and reform	Department of probation and parole
Puerto Rico	Department of health	Administration office of courts	Department of health	Department of health

This does not mean that the services are consolidated since seldom is more than one correctional service placed under one correctional administrator. The total number of state departments having correctional functions is 131.

The results of this crazy-quilt administration of correctional services is the absence of any mechanism for planning the development of a well-balanced correctional program.

8. Expanding the Role of the Nonprofessional *

HERBERT R. SIGURDSON

THE WHOLE CONCEPT of professionalism in correction is nebulous. Generally, it is limited to the level of formal education achieved. Persons having a bachelor's degree in any discipline are usually granted professional status and tend to be assigned the higher status roles in the correctional system by virtue of their college degree. They can usually be distinguished from the nonprofessionals by their status and their behavior: They are the ones in the system who talk to the offender in formal situations, whereas the nonprofessionals tend to engage in activities with the offender in informal situations, including the business of escorting the offender to the professional's office. This observation is not meant to imply that nonprofessionals have not made significant contributions to correctional theory and practice. After all, the record informs us that it was a cobbler who first introduced the concept of probation into American correctional practice.[1] Correction has experienced many fads and fancies since 1841, when that profound innovation was presented as an alternative to incarceration, and nonprofessionals have continued to play a significant role in the development of correctional theory and practice.

THERE ARE ALMOST NO PROFESSIONALS

A recent study of correction in the United States, conducted by the National Council on Crime and Delinquency, reports that (1) institutional personnel make up 87 per cent of the entire correctional force, (2) 63 per cent of institutional employees are custodial staff, and (3) virtually no correctional institutions require professional qualifications of their custodial staff. The same study reports that no educational qualifications whatever are required of officers in 8 per cent of juvenile probation agencies and not more than a high school diploma is required in 14 per cent of the agencies. The comparable figures for officers in aftercare are 5 per cent and 10 per cent; in misdemeanant probation, 11 per cent and 13 per cent; in adult probation, 15 per cent and 21 per cent; and in adult parole, 22 per cent and 20 per cent. Finally, a degree beyond the baccalaureate is required of officers by only 4 per cent of the agencies in juvenile probation, 3 per cent in aftercare, 2 per cent in misdemeanant probation, and 0.9 per cent in adult probation; and evidently not a single one of the fifty-one agencies administering adult parole requires parole officers to have a graduate degree.[2]

It is apparent from these findings that the overwhelming majority of correctional personnel do not have a professional degree and that most of those who do are at the baccalaureate level. Further, in jurisdictions where person-

* Herbert R. Sigurdson, "Expanding the Role of the Non-Professional," *Crime and Delinquency*, Vol. 15, No. 3 (July, 1969), pp. 420–29. Reprinted by permission of the author.

nel are required to have a graduate degree, the officers are inundated with heavy caseloads, paper work, and "bureaucratic administrivia." [3]

In some jurisdictions, nonprofessionals are required to perform many professional roles; in others, professionals are required to perform many nonprofessional roles. In the face of this dilemma the NCCD study cited above calls for an additional 16,583 field and institutional personnel to bring ratios of professional, social, and psychological treatment service up to recommended standards.[4] In the light of recruitment problems resulting from low salaries, long working hours, lack of effective contact with colleges and universities, and other special handicaps, the chances of meeting the projected professional manpower need are dim.

THE OFFENDER LOOKS LIKE ME

But if we evaluate correctional practice from another point of view, it may be possible to turn this apparent adversity to advantage. What is required is a major shift in emphasis from a dedication to serving the needs of our various correctional agencies and professional institutions to serving the needs of the people who enter the system. Grant has described traditional correctional practice as a mechanism for "screening out" members of society who get caught in the criminal web—"a servomechanism to keep the main system from having to change." [5] What we have failed to grasp is that, except for having been caught, most of the offender population are not significantly different from the population at large.

Wallerstein and Wyle interviewed 1,700 middle-class adults and discovered that 99 per cent admitted to having committed offenses punishable by one year's imprisonment. About two-thirds of the men and one-third of the women admitted to having committed felonies.[6] Kenneth Polk found no correlation between economic status and delinquency.[7] Nye found some difference in type of offense but no overall class differences in delinquency (more sex delinquency in the lower class, more vandalism in the middle class).[8] Nye's findings were confirmed by the research of Short, in Chicago, and by the New York City Youth Board.[9] Cohen and Porterfield found that 100 per cent of the college students they studied had been involved in offenses serious enough to justify court action.[10] Finally, the President's Crime Commission report reveals that six out of ten children in our population will be officially arrested before their eighteenth birthday, and nine out of ten have committed an offense for which they could have been arrested.[11] It is true that many offenders end up in the system because they *persistently* violate the law; nevertheless, the findings from these studies suggest that, in American society, criminality is normal and noncriminality is deviant.

THE ILLNESS INTERVENTION STRATEGY

Since many who enter the criminal justice system are no "sicker" than the society from which they come, it seems unreasonable for correction to pursue an illness approach to intervention as its major strategy for rehabilitating offenders (for example, suggesting treatment in the form of social worker-patient relationships). We have a rich literature describing the "cold war" between the "inmate culture" and the "staff culture" of correctional institutions, most of whose programs have been unsuccessful in preparing inmates for return to the community.[12] Studies of probation and parole effectiveness have led to a general conclusion that there is little demonstrable relationship between the officer's work and the offender's subsequent criminal behavior.[13] In a national survey of alternatives to incarceration, Empey concludes that "current practices are undoubtedly more humane than earlier forms of punishment, but delinquency and recidivism seem to have continued at a high rate, and the few studies of individualized treatment that are available present discouraging results." [14]

The reasons for successful completion of supervision are explored in a recent study conducted by the University of California's School of Criminology.[15] Seventy-five federally supervised probationers and parolees were asked, "How do you account for your success on supervision?" Similarly, the officers and a friend or relative of each offender were asked, "How do you account for the offender's success on supervision?" The responses were coded and organized into the following categories:

1. Noncriminal Orientation—this is the belief that the offender, even though sustaining a felony conviction, does not characteristically employ illegal methods of handling his affairs.

2. Assistance from Family and Friends—this is the help which accrued to the offender by virtue of his ties to others. This help may come in any form, i.e., emotional acceptance, financial assistance, advice or information.

3. Employment or Training—this means a reasonably satisfying job or an appropriate vocational or educational program which will ostensibly lead to a satisfying occupation.

4. Personal Strengths or Emotional Growth—this includes the emotional stability which the offender has characteristically demonstrated or the greater emotional maturity demonstrated during the supervision.

5. Probation Officer—this category was listed in those instances in which any of the respondents were convinced that the probation officer was significantly beneficial to the offender.

6. Religious or Ethical Principles—this includes those who felt that adherence to religious beliefs or an ethical system reinforced a noncriminal way of life.

7. Social Responsibility—this category contains those responses which indicated that the offender's sense of responsibility to family, friends, or society acted as a deterrent to further criminal activity.

8. Fear of Further Legal Action—this was listed in those instances in which the respondent saw the shame, guilt, or fear engendered by the correctional process as a strong positive influence on the offender's behavior.

9. Other—this category includes an assortment of fortuitous circumstances occurring in the life of the offender which supported legal behavior or limited the opportunity for illegal behavior. Responses ran the gamut from "pure luck" to physical disability.[16]

Table 1 is a summary of the distribution of responses by origin and category of response. One is immediately struck with the high level of agreement in the response pattern of officers, offenders, and the third parties interviewed. What is more significant is that only 20 per cent of the officers themselves and even smaller percentages of offenders and third party respondents—12 per cent and 15 per cent, respectively—associated the efforts of the supervising officer with successful completion of supervision.

TABLE 1. FREQUENCY OF RESPONSE BY ORIGIN AND CATEGORY

Origin of Response	Category of Response								
	Non-criminal Orientation	Assistance from Family and Friends	Employment or Training	Personal Strengths or Emotional Growth	Probation Officer	Religious or Ethical Principles	Social Respon-sibility	Fear of Further Legal Action	Other
75 Officers	41	43	34	34	15	6	9	14	4
75 Offenders	43	40	40	39	9	13	11	21	8
Family or friends *	38	57	53	39	11	11	17	16	9

* For a variety of reasons it was possible to interview only 49 families or friends of the 75 offenders; for purposes of comparison, their responses were projected to a total of 75.

SOURCE: *San Francisco Project, A Study of Federal Probation and Parole,* Research Report No. 13, National Institute of Mental Health, 1967, Tables 13, 14, 15.

It is apparent from these findings that the officer plays a rather insignificant role in the rehabilitation of most of his charges. One would suppose that the type of supervision offered should influence the response pattern, but analysis of offender responses shows that this is not so. Of fourteen offenders assigned to Intensive Supervision (caseload ratio, 25 to 1), none mentioned the probation officer as contributing to the successful completion of supervision; of twenty-five assigned to Ideal Supervision (caseload ratio, 50 to 1), seven mentioned the probation officer as contributing to the successful completion of supervision; of thirty-six assigned to Regular Supervision (caseload ratio, 100 to 1), three mentioned the probation officer as contributing to the successful completion of supervision.

On the other hand, it is instructive to note the high level of agreement among offenders, officers, and third party respondents regarding the significance of elements in the community setting that facilitate the successful completion of supervision. Assistance from family or friends was mentioned 43, 40, and 57 times by officers, offenders, and third-party respondents, respectively; employment or training was mentioned 34, 40, and 53 times, respectively. These response patterns not only emphasize the importance of community resources in the rehabilitation process, but also raise questions about the training qualifications required of correctional workers.

That large numbers of additional personnel are needed for correction to do a more effective job is certain; where they will come from and what the training requirements should be remain uncertain. But one can reasonably conclude from the above study that graduate training is not an essential prerequisite for helping to rehabilitate offenders.

In social work, "manipulating the environment" is generally viewed as the nonprofessional part of the practice. Accordingly, it would be quite feasible to train nonprofessionals to facilitate the integration or reintegration of offenders into society. The range of opportunities for negotiating conditions in the environment is extensive. Among the specific functions are vocational counseling, job training and placement, interviewing to keep a youngster in school, arranging needed transportation, and so on. The nonprofessional would need to become aware of the various community resources and be trained in strategies for dealing with community agencies and institutions, labor, industry, and other parts of the private sector.

The nonprofessional occupying linking roles with resources in the community has an opportunity to meet some of the basic survival needs of the offender. His participation in the rehabilitation process becomes significant because a tangible benefit accrues to the offender. On the other hand, the professional is handicapped by the burden of his desk work and other middle-class trappings that place social distance between him and his clients. Yet the correctional system has depended upon the professional to deliver service simply because he has acquired four, six, eight, or more years of university education. It may be that the shortcomings of the past are attributable to a dearth of *relevant* services and the failure to involve the offender in the change effort. For the offender, the correctional process has been largely a spectator sport. In summary:

1. Relatively few persons working in correction have academic training beyond the bachelor's degree.

2. Many of those who do have graduate training are burdened with bureaucratic trivia.

3. The offender population does not differ significantly from the community at large.

4. The illness model of intervention has not demonstrated itself to be a promising rehabilitation strategy.

5. The offender population has not been involved in the rehabilitation process.

6. Efforts to integrate the offenders through job training, employment, and other community-based strategies are associated with successful completion of supervision.

EXPANDING THE ROLE OF NONPROFESSIONALS

New approaches to correctional reform are being tested in agencies and institutions across the nation and a new body of knowledge is being written. This paper is principally concerned with program strategies that expand the potential for using nonprofessionals in significant reform roles, an important approach because the preponderance of correctional employees today perform nonprofessional tasks.

A promising model for correction to consider is found in programs where the target of change is also the medium and agent of change. Application of the principle of self-help has had remarkable success in problem areas that traditional agencies have been unable to touch, the most notable examples being Alcoholics Anonymous and Synanon. Synanon's success and failure rates are not known, "so one has no way of comparing its effectiveness with the notably poor results achieved in governmentally sponsored institutions," but. to members of the Synanon system, "such matters may be inconsequential since the living presence of former addicts, free from dope, in Synanon programs in Santa Monica, San Francisco, San Diego, Westport, and Reno is evidence enough of Synanon's success." [17] In light of the failure of traditional programs to reform offenders, a long hard look at self-help programs is called for.

The theory on which these self-help programs are based was first and perhaps best described by Donald Cressey in 1955. The essence of the theory follows:

1. If criminals are to be changed, they must be assimilated into groups which emphasize values conducive to law-abiding behavior and, concurrently, alienated from groups emphasizing values conducive to criminality. Since our experience has been that the majority of criminals experience great difficulty in securing intimate contacts in ordinary groups, special groups whose major common goal is the reformation of criminals must be created.

2. The more relevant the common purpose of the group to the reformation of criminals, the greater will be its influence on the criminal members' attitudes.

3. The more cohesive the group, the greater the members' readiness to influence others and the more relevant the problem of conformity to group norms. The criminals who are to be reformed and the persons expected to effect the change must, then, have a strong sense of belonging to one group; between them there must be a genuine "we" feeling. The reformers, conse-

quently, should not be identifiable as correctional officers or social workers.

4. Both reformers and those to be reformed must achieve status within the group by exhibition of "pro-reform" or anti-criminal values and behavior patterns. As a novitate . . . he is a therapeutic parasite and not actually a member until he accepts the group's own system for assigning status.

5. The most effective mechanism for exerting group pressure on members will be found in groups so organized that criminals are induced to join with non-criminals for the purpose of changing other criminals. A group in which criminal A joins with some non-criminals to change criminal B is probably most effective in changing criminal A, not B. In order to change criminal B, criminal A must necessary share the value of the anti-criminal members.[18]

These are some of the basic principles that undergird the work of self-help programs like Alcoholics Anonymous and Synanon except that the latter does not use professionals. The same principles apply to a number of experimental programs in correction in which the approach is variously referred to as the therapeutic community, sensitivity training, or guided group interaction. The research that has been done in this area of correctional experimentation suggests that typically the control group does about as well as the experimental group, but uniformly the experimental programs accomplish results much more quickly and much less expensively. "These factors alone, quite apart from more subtle personal changes which might have occurred, seem justification for further work with such methods."[19]

THE NEW CAREERS MOVEMENT

In the "new careers" program developed by J. Douglas Grant and his associates, the offender is employed in the correctional process.[20] His training covers a period of eight months—four while he is still confined and four while on parole.

The trainees, as teams, learn through projects and study groups where they work together and teach each other. The teams take turns preparing group studies on organization change, interviewing, group dynamics, research and social trends . . . [and] the entire training group discusses the problems they have had working with each other.[21]

The skills developed during the training are used to solve a variety of problems in the community. Illustrative of new careers community programs are (1) studies in the genesis of violence, (2) job and career development for the poor in state service, (3) developing nonprofessionals for work in California State Vocational Rehabilitation, and (4) the use of the poor as elementary school teaching assistants.

For the offender, says Empey, the new careers movement would:

1. Seek to use his knowledge as a resources rather than a liability;
2. Involve him actively as a reformer rather than as a perpetual enemy or a persistent dependent;
3. Constitute a rite of passage back from a criminal to a noncriminal status; and
4. Provide him with a career which could be a source of personal and social esteem rather than a source of stigma and degradation.[22]

Many offenders, of course, are neither suited for nor interested in the new careers movement. The new careers approach, therefore, is only a partial answer to the problem. Other sources of recruiting correctional manpower must be developed.

RECRUITING NONPROFESSIONALS

"Goodness" and "badness" are to be found in situations, not just in people. Grant suggests that the new model of correction will be designed to "screen in" the "bad" persons of society and assume greater responsibility for influencing and controlling the "bad situations" in the community where the offender is so often found. Perhaps what is needed is a strategy that simultaneously addresses the "bad situation" found in the community and in the correctional process.[23]

It is more than a coincidence that large numbers of hard-core unemployed persons live in the poverty ghettos of our urban centers and that these ghettos are the "bad situations" from which society has traditionally "screened out" the offender population. Many of these same people lack the education and training required of jobs in industry. But because they too have lived in the "bad situation," they understand the personal and social problems of the offender population. Thus they would appear to have excellent credentials for occupying leadership roles in reform groups. Correction could recruit and train at least 25,000 persons to perform self-help reform roles for the same amount of money that it would take to hire the 16,583 professionals recommended by the NCCD study. Thus it not only would deal with its own problem but also would attack the problem of ghetto poverty and unemployment. A further benefit is that both offenders and nonoffenders from the ghetto community would be adopting prosocial values. Their new status would have a positive impact on friends, neighbors, and associates, thus benefiting the community at large.

A STRATEGY FOR IMPLEMENTATION

Expanding the role of nonprofessionals in correction may constitute a threat to the system's professionals—who, as we can see by glancing at the record, have every reason to feel threatened. However, if the manpower needs of correction are to be met, expanding the role of the nonprofessional is the most realistic alternative available. The reasons are that (1) there is a large pool of untrained, unemployed nonprofessionals from which to recruit, (2) it is possible to train nonprofessionals to perform significant reform roles, and (3) it would be economically efficient to use nonprofessionals in the reformation process. Therefore, a strategy must be developed for reducing the threat to professionals and legitimating a career in correction for nonprofessionals.

Terwilliger has, at least in part, defined what the professional role could be in this new alliance. "The role of the professional," he says, "becomes one of coordinating and directing subprofessional activities, providing specialized training for nonprofessional team members, and rendering those services and judgments which are exclusively professional." [24] Unfortunately he fails to specify the conditions that would demand the exclusive judgment of a professional. It is reasonable to conclude that no judgments in correction are exclu-sively professional; rather, decisions are to be made in the administration of correctional programs.

Pathologically disturbed individuals who enter the criminal-justice system require special treatment and attention and might appropriately be assigned to the professionals. The presence of nonprofessionals in the system to work with the great bulk of offenders should free the professionals to engage in a variety of innovative programs. Carefully conceptualized experimental pro-grams are needed as a basis for developing knowledge about these particular offenders and how they can be helped.

Career professionals in correction have opportunities for both lateral and upward mobility. Similiar opportunities must be made available for nonpro-fessionals who choose to make a career out of correctional work. The Na-tional Committee on Employment of Youth has developed a three-step career ladder for nonprofessionals that may serve as a useful model for adoption or modification by personnel departments and civil service commissions. In this model the entry level serves primarily as a screening device to test the appli-cant's interest in and suitability for correctional work, and the steps relate to higher levels of proficiency and responsibility. Upon entering the third level, the worker is viewed as a semiprofessional. Those having unusual talent should be offered opportunities for additional training and advancement into pro-fessional status.

There is no longer any question that nonprofessionals can be trained to occupy significant roles in correction as links to community resources, as leaders of reform groups, and in other capacities. The pilot testing has already been done, but in most jurisdictions these new roles have not been officially legitimated. However, there are new forces in our society that will increasingly demand changes in the correctional system to make it more relevant and responsive to the needs of the offender. With increased research, society will eventually discover the madness of spending millions of dollars each year on programs that literally make no constructive difference in the lives of the offender population. The Joint Commission on Correctional Manpower and Training reports that while the public is generally uninformed about correc-tional agencies and services, it nevertheless favors an emphasis on rehabilita-tion over punishment.[25] Further, many people, particularly the youth of our society, have adopted a value system in which *people* are more important than *institutions* or *possessions*. Correctional practice will eventually be influenced by these values.

NOTES

[1] National Council on Crime and Delinquency, *John Augustus: First Probation Officer* (New York: NCCD, 1939).

[2] National Council on Crime and Delinquency, *Correction in the United States,* in *Crime and Delinquency,* Jan. 1967, pp. 237, 242.

[3] J. D. Lohman, A. Wahl, R. M. Carter, and A. E. Elliott, "An Afterview of Super-vision," Research Report No. 10, *The San Francisco Project: A Study of Federal Probation and Parole* (Berkeley: University of California, School of Criminology, 1966), p. 10.

[4] *Op. cit., supra* note 2, p. 240.

[5] J. Douglas Grant, "Changing Times and Our Institutions: Participants, Not

Recipients," presented at the 12th National Institute on Crime and Delinquency, June 14, 1965, p. 3 (mimeo).

[6] J. S. Wallerstein and C. J. Wyle, "Our Law-Abiding Law-Breakers," *Probation* (April 1947), pp. 107–12.

[7] Cited in H. E. Salisbury, *The Shookup Generation* (New York: Harper, 1958).

[8] F. Ivan Nye, *Family Relationships and Delinquent Behavior* (New York: Wiley, 1958).

[9] James F. Short, Jr., "Street Corner Gangs and Patterns of Delinquency," Progress Report, NIMH Grant M-3301, University of Chicago Department of Sociology, 1961 (mimeo); New York City Youth Board, *Reaching the Fighting Gang* (New York, 1960).

[10] A. K. Cohen, *Delinquent Boys* (New York: The Free Press, 1955); A. L. Porterfield, "Delinquency and Its Outcome in Court and College," *American Journal of Sociology* (Nov. 1943), pp. 199–208.

[11] President's Commission on Law Enforcement and Administration of Justice, *The Challenge of Crime in a Free Society* (Washington, D.C.: Government Printing Office, 1967), p. 55.

[12] G. Sykes, *Society of Captives, A Study of a Maximum Security Prison* (Princeton, N.J.: Princeton University Press, 1958); R. Giollombardo, *Society of Women —A Study of a Women's Prison* (New York: Wiley, 1966); D. Cressey, *The Prison* (New York: Holt, Rinehart & Winston, 1961).

[13] D. Street, R. D. Vinter, and C. Perrow, *Organization for Treatment* (New York: The Free Press, 1966); D. Glaser, *The Effectiveness of a Prison and Parole System* (Indianapolis: Bobbs-Merrill, 1964); A. W. McEachern, "The Juvenile Probation System, Simulation for Research and Decision Making," *American Behavioral Scientist* (Jan.–Feb. 1968).

[14] LaMar T. Empey, *Alternatives to Incarceration* (Washington, D.C.: Government Printing Office, 1967).

[15] *Op. cit., supra* note 3, Research Report No. 13 (1966).

[16] *Id.*, pp. 37–38.

[17] Empey, *op. cit., supra* note 14, p. 45.

[18] Donald R. Cressey, "Changing Criminals: The Application of the Theory of Differential Association," *American Journal of Sociology* (Sept. 1955), pp. 116–20.

[19] Empey, *op. cit., supra* note 14, p. 45.

[20] J. D. Grant, "New Careers Development in the Change Agent Field," presented at the 42nd Annual Meeting of the American Orthopsychiatric Association, New York, March 1965 (mimeo).

[21] J. D. Grant, "The Offender as Participant, Not Recipient, in the Correctional Process," presented at *Recent Developments in Criminology and Corrections*, lectures sponsored by the Center of Criminology, University of Toronto, Feb. 7, 1966, pp. 7–8.

[22] LaMar T. Empey, "Offender Participation in the Correctional Process: General Theoretical Issues," in *Offenders As a Correctional Manpower Resource* (report of a seminar convened by the Joint Commission on Correctional Manpower and Training, Washington, D.C., March 7–8, 1968), pp. 11–12.

[23] Grant, *op. cit., supra* note 21.

[24] Carl Terwilliger, "The Nonprofessional in Correction," *Crime and Delinquency* (July 1966), p. 285.

[25] Joint Commission on Correctional Manpower and Training, *The Public Looks at Crime and Corrections*, Washington, D.C., 1968.

PART FIVE

COMMUNITY RESPONSES
TO YOUTHFUL MISBEHAVIOR

Introduction

Previous readings have pertained to subsystems of the official response to youthful misbehavior. In this part attention is directed to community responses to the problem. By community responses we mean primarily public attitudes and voluntary organizational efforts. Readings organized around these two perspectives can be useful in assessing public support for control, correctional, and preventive programs; in addition, they can help us to understand some of the problems of citizen participation and interagency cooperation that emerge in a community working on youth problems. These insights are especially important because of the current emphases on treating youngsters in the community and improving the relationships between the community and official agencies.

Selection 1, by the President's Task Force on the Assessment of Crime, summarizes a number of studies of public attitudes toward the problem of crime and delinquency and the official responses. The report provides strong empirical support for the commonsense belief that there is national and local concern about crime and delinquency as major problems. At a local level, in fact, the public's concern about delinquency exceeds its concern about adult crime. This concern about delinquency, as well as crime in general, is not necessarily based on personal experience as a victim. Rather, it appears to emanate from vicarious sources that provide subjective and evaluative images of community events. One of the images of crime involves a fear of violence from a stranger. In fact, there is greater statistical probability that people will kill themselves than that they will be homicide victims. They are also much more likely to be physically harmed by acquaintances, friends, and relatives than by strangers. Statistically, they have a much better chance of being killed in an accident, either directly or as a result of inadequate emergency care. It is clear that subjective images are primary elements in ranking social problems.

Evaluations of group interest can also play a part. Negroes and whites may rank social problems quite differently, and these rankings need not accord with objective reality. For example, poorer Negroes rank crime as a less important national problem than either race relations or education; poorer whites, however, rank crime as far more important than education. These disparities occur despite the fact that Negroes express more fear of leaving their homes at night because of crime and the further fact that official rates of crimes against the person are highest in ghetto communities. In policy terms, the finding implies that low-income whites and blacks might support different modes of allocating resources; blacks might advocate spending more for the education of youth, while whites might support increased expenditures for reducing youth crime.

The intrusion of race relations and group interest into the public response to crime and delinquency should not be surprising. As earlier readings indicate, the police and the courts may also use delinquency as a means of obtaining nonlegal goals. Since public officials and citizens are subject to similar cultural influences, it is certainly understandable that attitudes toward the problem can be affected by orientations regarding race and ethnocentric interests. These are not the only influences on public attitudes, but they are perhaps more significant than the Task Force report suggests.

The discrepancy between objective reality and the public definition of the crime and delinquency problem has an additional implication for social policy. If the public is more concerned about the problem than facts warrant, how can this misperception be corrected? The Task Force suggests that careful attention to the public presentation of facts might be useful. This proposal assumes that there is clarity and agreement about the facts concerning the problem. However, the readings on the statistical meaning of delinquency in Part I provide evidence that measurement of official rates is problematic. It may therefore be prudent to obtain agreement among the experts on the technical aspects of problem assessment before attempting to correct inaccurate public definitions of delinquency. Support of basic research might yield greater benefits than an educational approach that utilizes unclear concepts and measurements.

Besides assessing public concern about crime and delinquency, the Task Force summary analyzes public attitudes toward attempts to deal with the problems. The public apparently supports control, rehabilitation, and humaneness, but responses vary according to the types of question posed. There is a tendency to treat youthful first offenders with greater leniency and attention to rehabilitation than adult criminals; however, the surveys did not determine whether this humane and rehabilitative orientation extended to youthful repeaters and recidivists, the group to which the newer correctional approaches stressing alternatives to incarceration are primarily geared.

Of all the agencies that are trying to deal with the crime problem, the public generally regards the police as the most important. There is a pronounced tendency to view crime as primarily a police problem and to believe that there is little that citizens can do about it; there is even a reluctance to report many criminal acts to the police. Summarizing the first nationwide study of the nonreporting of crime, the Task Force report concludes that Americans frequently fail to take the one essential action that they can take as citizens to help the police. Victims cited the following reasons for not reporting crimes: reluctance to get involved or to take the time; unwillingness to cause trouble for the offender, particularly for family and sex offenses and when the offenders were personally known; fear of reprisal; and a general belief in police ineffectiveness. Even businessmen are reluctant to call the police when they are the victims of thefts by employees, bad checks, or shoplifting.

In general, there is less reluctance to report serious crimes against the person than crimes against property. But if the public responded to a campaign to report more of the known crimes, not only would there be a dramatic increase in the workload of the police, the rise in the crime statistics could be precipitous. Whether the public would feel that their persons and property were indeed safer if they acted more "responsibly" is unknown. It is evident, however, that the public is willing to tolerate a great deal of illegal activity. When this tolerance decreases, there is an enormous potential for increased law enforcement. An increase in public concern about crime and delinquency as a problem may, therefore, be strongly influenced by shifts in community tolerance regarding types of offense or offender rather than reflect a real increase in illegal activities. In this sense, community tolerance of delinquent activities is part of the delinquency problem.

Theoretically, it is conceivable that community tolerance is analogous to police discretion. The police are more likely to arrest serious offenders; the public is more likely to report them. The police tend to be lenient toward first offenders; the public responds in similar fashion. The police in many cities treat minority-group youth more harshly for less serious offenses; perhaps the public's behavior is similar. If so, then shifts in the absolute and relative numbers of minority youth residing in a community could affect public tolerance for illegal activity by such youth. It is possible, too, that community tolerance is affected by shifts in police tolerance, as implied in the Wilson readings in Parts I and II. If social policy should address the guidance and control of police discretion (or tolerance), then perhaps community tolerance is also a likely target for change. Do we want the public to be legalistic, watchman, or service in their attitudes regarding delinquent youth? The question is worth posing, even though the answer would be based on fragmentary information and hypothetical consequences. And if we were clear about the type of public tolerance to be sought, how would the goal be implemented? The Task Force report does not deal with these questions directly, but they emerge quite naturally from reading the survey of public attitudes in the context of earlier readings and discussions.

Selection 2, by Campbell and Schuman, attempts to differentiate public attitudes toward law enforcement by race. This information is important because, as selection 1 indicates, law enforcement is perceived as the dominant method for dealing with illegal activities; in addition, heterogeneous communities are not necessarily unified in their attitudes toward the primary law enforcers, the police. The reading yields potent evidence that there is much more negativism toward the police in ghetto communities than in white areas, as was publicly demonstrated in the urban riots of the 1960's. However, in both black and white communities, the young express the greatest distrust of police behavior. To overcome this distrust, many police departments have begun to involve ghetto adults in community-relations meetings. These efforts may be useful beginning steps, but unless there is meaningful involvement of minority youth the salient target groups will be missing. Apparently, there is also a broader need for involving all types of youth, white and black, in police-community discussions to overcome distrust. Again, the dialogues may not be very fruitful unless police administrators take steps to ensure that police discretion is exercised with fairness and justice. It is possible that police attitudes and behavior toward minority groups and youth may have to change before there can be a diminution of distrust among these disaffected groups. The police—not minority and white youth—may have to take the first steps to demonstrate that a change in police-community relations is desirable.

The next group of readings consider some of the problems involved in voluntary community efforts to deal with youthful misbehavior. Selection 3, by Gans, provides insight into the workings of a suburban middle-class community. Selections 4 and 5, by Spergel and Miller, focus on low-income areas. All three readings reveal that cooperative efforts among groups are difficult to obtain because of a lack of ideological unity, competing interests, and intergroup distrust. In the absence of a common definition of the problem and meaningful goals, adherence to a minimal set of common interests, and a sense of trust, it is difficult to envisage a coalition of effort. Involving citizens and groups cooperatively, however, depends on building successful coalitions; if they cannot be built, the call for community cooperation may become merely an exercise of rhetoric and good intentions. The problem of building and maintaining coalitions occurs among professional as well as nonprofessional groups; middle-income as well as low-income communities; and at a citywide level as well as local level.

The Gans selection is taken from a larger study of how people live and politick in a new suburban community, Levittown, New Jersey. The community was built by a single developer in an open area of an existing township. Gans moved into the new community with the express purpose of studying its social, cultural, and political development, so as to be able to comment on suburban communities in general. His description of Levittown's youth problem, as the children of the newcomers entered adolescence, appears to be relevant for an array of such communities; many older suburbs have also proved incapable of forging a community coalition to deal with adolescent interests and waywardness.

According to Gans, adult groups are divided on whether the problem occurs in the recreational sector or is part of family discipline, a merchant problem, or just a police responsibility. They are also divided on how much autonomy they are willing to grant adolescents in operating dances and recreational facilities, and whether public facilities and dollars should be set aside for youth. The police would like to enforce a curfew but are fearful of increasing distrust among youth by "bugging" them on street corners. Unable to act in unison, the community has apparently settled for a policy of tolerating an array of rowdy and vandalous acts, using police authority to keep youth in their place, relying on the attractiveness of other areas to lure youth out of the community, and providing special-interest activities by competing church groups. Gans is pessimistic about the likelihood that suburban communities will behave any differently until their juvenile problems mount and federal money becomes available. He might have added that it is unlikely that youth will be dealt with as a special-interest group until they are granted the right to participate and influence community decision-making.

Spergel's statement (selection 4) is based on an assessment of the use of the delinquency problem for political purposes. He argues that individuals and groups that obtain influence in the field of delinquency control, prevention, and treatment may use this power in other areas of decision-making. Awareness of this possibility can influence, in turn, the way in which they approach joint efforts to deal with aspects of the delinquency problem that affect their interests. It may also mean that individuals and groups will seek to make a "rep" in dealing with the problem in order to reap other rewards. Because of the political potential of delinquency, Spergel discerns the development of new political roles in low-income, high-rate areas of the city. Civil-rights, black-nationalist, and radical political groups have attempted to use delinquent-gang members to support and even to staff their organizations and movements. Members of these groups, as well as executives of gang-control agencies, have attempted also to use their connections with the delinquency problem for their own political advancement. Ex-gang leaders have also tried to benefit from their position. With the addition of massive federal funds, many agency executives attempted either to corner the delinquency market in their areas or to gain a good "cut" of the funds; by building their reputations— with or without merit—they attempt to expand their general influence and that of their agencies in the field of welfare organization. Spergel argues that further politicalization of the delinquency problem may attract attention away from community failures at the local and national levels. For example, he argues that we have failed to focus on the important target populations; insufficient resources have been provided; delinquents have not been sufficiently involved in solving their own problems; planned and coordinated approaches have not developed; evaluational efforts and experimentation have been minimal; and education of public and professional groups has not occurred. Spergel also indicates that politicalization of the delinquency problem has contributed to these community failures.

Selection 5, by Miller, specifically deals with a program of delinquency prevention in Roxbury, Massachusetts, in the 1950's, but his inferences about interorganizational conflict are germane to virtually every large urban area. According to Miller, not only does conflict occur among youth-welfare agencies, but the competition is a major impediment to community programs for prevention. His penetrating study highlights how ideological disagreement, competing interests, and organizational distrust prevent cooperation at the local level. In a sense, Miller points out, agencies have a great deal to lose by cooperating. Until we can devise effective rewards to offset these threatened losses, interorganizational conflict will continue to impede delinquency prevention, control, and treatment.

1. *Public Attitudes Toward Crime and Law Enforcement* *

TASK FORCE ON ASSESSMENT

AT VARIOUS PERIODS in history, there are surges of public alarm about crime, such as the national concern about gangland crime in the 1920's. More frequently, however, alarm about "crime waves" has been localized. A few cases of terrible offenses can terrorize an entire metropolis, and rising crime rates in once safe areas can arouse new fears and anxieties. At other times in the past, however, some of these crises have been synthetic ones, manufactured as circulation-building devices by the "yellow press." Lincoln Steffens, for example, recounts how he created crime waves by giving dramatic banner-headline play to crimes that were actually ordinary occurrences in the metropolis.[1]

Although it is not possible to identify all the factors that affect the rise and fall in public alarm about crime, it is a constantly recurring public theme.[2] A legal scholar recently took a look over the literature of the past fifty years and noted that each and every decade produced prominent articles about the need for strong measures to meet the then current crisis in crime.[3] Periodically throughout the century, there have been investigating committees of the Congress, of the state legislatures, and special commissions of cities to deal with the particular crime problem of the time. It may be that there has always been a crime crisis, insofar as public perception is concerned.

CRIME AS A NATIONAL ISSUE

Many circumstances now conspire to call greater attention to crime as a national, rather than a purely local, problem. Concern with crime is more typically an urban than a rural phenomenon, and the rural population of the

* Task Force on Assessment of the President's Committee on Law Enforcement and Administration of Justice, *Crime and Its Impact—An Assessment*, Washington, D.C.: Government Printing Office, 1967, pp. 85–95.

358

country is declining. At one time, for a majority of the population, reports of crime waves related only to those remote and not quite moral people who inhabited cities.

Now, also, more people are informed by nationally oriented communications media and receive crime reports from a much wider territorial base. In recent years news of the violent and fearful mass killing of eight nurses in a Chicago apartment, five patrons of a beauty shop in Mesa, Arizona, and thirteen passersby on the University of Texas campus in Austin received detailed coverage throughout the country. The fear of the people of Boston in 1966 of the brutal attacks of the "Boston Strangler" must have been sympathetically shared and understood in many homes across the land. Some part of the public fear of crime today is undoubtedly due to the fact that the reports of violent crime we receive daily are drawn from a larger pool of crime-incident reports than ever before. But perhaps most important has been the steady stream of reports of rising crime rates in both large and small communities across the nation. From all this has emerged a sense of crisis in regard to the safety of both person and property.

Heightened Concern About Crime

The national public opinion polls provide evidence of the heightened concern today about the crime problem. International problems have invariably been at the top whenever open-ended questions were asked by the Gallup poll about the problems facing the nation. Crime problems were not mentioned as an important problem by enough people to appear among the list. When the National Opinion Research Center conducted a national survey for the Commission during the summer of 1966, interviewers asked citizens to pick from a list of six major domestic problems facing the country the one to which they had been paying most attention recently.[4] [See Table 1.] Crime was second most frequently picked from among the list of domestic problems; only race relations was selected by more people. (Lower income nonwhites placed more emphasis on education than crime.)

TABLE 1. MOST IMPORTANT DOMESTIC PROBLEM BY RACE AND INCOME

Domestic Problem	White		Nonwhite	
	Under $6,000	Over $6,000	Under $6,000	Over $6,000
Poverty	9%	5%	7%	8%
Inflation	15	17	4	4
Education	12	19	23	21
Crime	27	22	19	22
Race relations	29	34	32	38
Unemployment	8	3	15	7
Total	100%	100%	100%	100%
Number	(3,925)	(6,461)	(1,033)	(462)

SOURCE: Philip H. Ennis, "Attitudes Toward Crime," Interim Report to the President's Commission on Law Enforcement and Administration of Justice, 1966 (mimeo).

In a consideration of local rather than national problems, people rank juvenile delinquency higher on the scale than almost any other issue, including adult crime. Gallup polls reported in 1963 that when persons were asked to name the top problems in their community from a list of thirty-nine, juvenile delinquency was second in frequency of selection—exceeded only by complaints about local real estate taxes. The third most frequently mentioned problem was a not completely unrelated matter in the public's perception—the need for more recreation areas.

Whether more concerned about adult or juvenile crime, most people think the crime situation in their own community is getting worse, and, while substantial numbers think the situation is staying about the same, hardly anyone sees improvement. A Gallup survey in April 1965, showed this pessimistic perception of the problem prevailed among men and women, well educated and less well educated, and among all age, regional, income, and city-size groupings.

Sources of Public Attitudes About Crime

From analysis of the results of its surveys of the public, the Commission tried to determine to what extent this increased public concern about crime was a reflection of personal experience as a victim or of vicarious impressions received from acquaintances, the mass media, or other sources. . . . The available data indicate that for most people attitudes about serious crimes and crime trends come largely from vicarious sources. This is especially the case with the crimes of violence which, although the focus of the public's concern, are relatively rare.

Very few incidents in which citizens have been victimized by crime were of such great significance in their lives as to be readily remembered for any length of time. This conclusion is one of the findings from the intensive methodological work undertaken for the Commission by the Bureau of Social Science Research in Washington, D.C., in preparation for surveys of the public regarding victimization.[5] This was first observed in pretest interviewing that showed extremely pronounced "recency effects"; that is, the bulk of such incidents as respondents did report . . . had occurred within the very recent past —in the space of just the last few months. A very steep decline occurred when the number of cases of victimization were plotted by month of occurrence from the present into the past—even for as short a period as one year. While the investigators were ultimately able to achieve far greater exhaustiveness of reporting through methods that facilitated recall and led their respondents to give more time and effort to the task of remembering, even these revised methods showed pronounced effects of forgetting.

This effect is even very evident in the dates victimized citizens gave for crimes mentioned in response to questions about the worst crime that had ever happened to them or to any member of their household. . . . Over half had occurred during the previous eighteen-month period and 60 per cent in the past two years. Only 21 per cent of all incidents described as "the worst ever" were said to have happened more than five years ago.[6]

The seriousness of most crimes reported by the citizens interviewed by BSSR also led to the inference that people generally do not readily remember minor incidents of victimization, though relatively trivial criminal acts, such as vandalism and petty larcenies from automobiles and of bicycles, are undoubtedly much more prevalent than are more serious offenses.[7]

These observations may help to explain why the surveys of citizens conducted for the Commission found little statistical relationship between having been directly victimized by crime and attitudes toward most aspects of the crime problem. Undoubtedly, if there had been sufficient cases to relate reliably the personal experiences and attitudes of persons suffering victimization from the most serious crimes of rape, aggravated assault, robbery, and so on, a direct relationship would have been found in such cases. However, for all victims as a group in contrast to nonvictims, having been personally victimized did not influence perceptions of whether crime was increasing or not, or the degree of a person's concern with the crime problem in most instances. The NORC national survey did show that victims tended to have somewhat more worry about burglary or robbery. This was true for both males and females, as can be seen in Table 2, though females, whether they had been victimized or not, were more concerned about their safety than males. However, other data from the NORC survey show that recent experience of being a victim of crime did not seem to increase behavior designed to protect the home. Almost identical proportions, 57 per cent of victims and 58 per cent of nonvictims, took strong household security measures.[8]

TABLE 2. CONCERN OF VICTIMS AND NONVICTIMS ABOUT BURGLARY OR ROBBERY

	Victim	Nonvictim
Males		
Worried	69%	59%
Not worried	31	41
	100%	100%
Number	(1,456)	(3,930)
Females		
Worried	84	77
Not worried	16	23
	100%	100%
Number	(2,399)	(6,189)

In its Washington study BSSR found similar results. An index of exposure to crime was developed based on having personally witnessed offenses or on whether oneself or one's friends had been victimized. Scores on this index, in general, were not associated with responses to a variety of questions on attitudes toward crime and toward law enforcement that respondents were asked. Nor did exposure to crime appear to determine the anxiety about crime manifested in the interviews. The one exception appeared in the case of the Negro male. Negro men showed a tendency to be influenced in their attitudes and behavior according to whether they had been victims of some type of crime or not.[9]

In addition, the BSSR study found that the average level of concern with crime in a predominantly Negro police precinct that had one of the highest rates of crime in the city, according to police data, was lower than it was in another Negro precinct that had a low rate relative to the first.[10]

All of these observations suggest that people's perception of the incidence and nature of crime and even to some extent their concern about it may be formed in large part by what they read or hear about from others. This does not mean, of course, that what people learn to think and feel about the crime problem in this way is any less valid or important as grounds for launching renewed efforts at crime control and prevention, or that either the extent of the crime problem or people's fears about it should be minimized. It does indicate the need for a greater public responsibility to insure that people have a chance to learn facts about crime that are not only accurate and trustworthy but also most relevant to the situations in which they live and work. It also means, because of the apparent importance of vicarious impressions in forming public attitudes about crime, that we need many more intensive studies to determine what it is that most influences people's views and feelings about crime.

A further indication of the importance of vicarious impressions in forming the public's perceptions of crime is that a majority of citizens almost everywhere think that the situation right where they live is not so bad. While the predominant opinion is that the crime situation is terrible and getting worse, most people tend to think of the situation as one that characterizes places other than their own immediate neighborhood. In the nationwide NORC study for the Commission, 60 per cent of those questioned compared their own neighborhood favorably to other parts of the community in which they lived with regard to the likelihood that their home would be broken into, while only 14 per cent thought their area presented a greater hazard.[11] This is the case even in areas that are regarded as very crime-ridden by the police. In the BSSR survey of residents of areas in Washington, D.C., that have average to high crime rates, only one out of five of those interviewed thought his neighborhood was less safe than most in the city.[12] Surveys conducted for the Commission by the Survey Research Center of the University of Michigan concerning public attitudes about crime in four medium to high crime-rate police precincts in Boston and Chicago found that 73 per cent of the respondents thought their own neighborhoods were very safe or average compared to other neighborhoods in relation to the chances of getting robbed, threatened, beaten up, or anything of that sort.[13]

Almost half of the nationwide sample contacted by the NORC survey said there was no place in the city in which they lived (or suburb or county for those not living in cities) where they would feel unsafe. Two thirds of the respondents say they feel safe walking alone when it is dark if they are in their own neighborhood. Responses to the question: "How likely is it that a person walking around here at night might be held up or attacked—very likely, somewhat likely, somewhat unlikely or very unlikely?" were very heavily weighted toward the "unlikely" direction.

Personal Fear of Crime

The core of public anxiety about the crime problem involves a concern for personal safety and to a somewhat lesser extent the fear that personal property will be taken. Perhaps the most intense concern about crime is the fear of being attacked by a stranger when out alone. According to the NORC survey, while two-thirds of the American public feel safe about walking alone at night in their own neighborhoods, the remaining third does not. . . . As noted above, women worry more than men about the risk of burglary or rob- bery. According to an April 1965 Gallup survey, the percentage of people feeling unsafe at night on the street is higher in large cities than in smaller ones and higher in cities than in rural areas.

Recently studies have been undertaken to develop an index of delinquency based on the seriousness of different offenses.[14] They have shown that there is widespread public consensus on the relative seriousness of different types of crimes, and these rankings furnish useful indicators of the types of crime that the public is most concerned about. Offenses involving physical assaults against the person are the most feared crimes and the greatest concern is ex- pressed about those in which a weapon is used.

Fear of crime makes many people want to move their homes. In the four police precincts surveyed for the Commission in Boston and Chicago, 20 per cent of the citizens wanted to move because of the crime in their neighbor- hoods, and as many as 30 per cent wanted to move out of the highest crime- rate district in Boston.[15]

Fear of crime shows variations by race and income. In the survey in Wash- ington, the Bureau of Social Science Research put together an index of anx- iety about crime. It found that Negro women had the highest average score, followed by Negro men, white women, and white men. Anxiety scores were lower at the higher income levels for both Negroes and whites.[16]

The NORC survey asked people whether there have been times recently when they wanted to go somewhere in town but stayed at home instead be- cause they thought it would be unsafe to go there. Sixteen per cent of the re- spondents said that they had stayed home under these conditions. This type of reaction showed marked variation with race; one out of every three Negro respondents had stayed home as contrasted with one in eight whites.[17]

People also take special measures at home because of the fear of unwanted intruders. The national survey showed that 82 per cent of the respondents al- ways kept their doors locked at night and 25 per cent always kept their doors locked even in the daytime when the family members were at home. Twenty- eight per cent kept watch-dogs and 37 per cent said they kept firearms in the house for protection, among other reasons.[18]

The special city surveys disclosed that a substantial number of people take other measures to protect themselves from crime. In Boston and Chicago 28 per cent had put new locks on their doors primarily, as one might expect, be- cause they had been victimized or were worried about the high crime rate in the area. Another 10 per cent had put locks or bars on their windows; this occurred primarily in the highest crime-rate areas. Nine per cent said they car- ried weapons, usually knives, when they went out, and this figure rose to 19 per cent in the highest crime-rate district in Boston.[19]

The close relationship between worry about crime and the taking of strong precautionary measures is further demonstrated by the results from the na- tional survey. Respondents were asked how much they worried about being victimized by robbery or burglary and their responses were related to their tendency to take strong household security measures. Persons worried about both burglary and robbery are most likely to take such precaution, about 50 per cent more likely than those who are worried about neither.[20]

Perhaps the most revealing findings on the impact of fear of crime on peo- ple's lives were the changes people reported in their regular habits. In the high-crime districts surveyed in Boston and Chicago, for example, five out of every eight respondents reported changes in their habits because of fear of crime, some as many as four or five major changes. Forty-three per cent reported they stayed off the streets at night altogether. Another 21 per cent said they always used cars or taxis at night. Thirty-five per cent said they would not talk to strangers any more.[21]

Conclusions

The Task Force cannot say that the public's fear of crime is exaggerated. It is not prepared to tell the people how fearful they should be; that is something each person must decide for himself. People's fears must be respected; certainly they cannot be legislated. Some people are willing to run risks that terrify others. However, it is possible to draw some general conclusions from the findings of the surveys.

The first is that the public fears the most the crimes that occur the least—crimes of violence. People are much more tolerant of crimes against property, which constitute most of the crimes that are committed against persons or households or businesses. Actually, the average citizen probably suffers the greatest economic loss from crimes against business establishments and public institutions, which pass their losses on to him in the form of increased prices and taxes. Nevertheless, most shoplifters never get to court; they are released by the store managers with warnings. Most employees caught stealing are either warned or discharged, according to the reports of business and organizations in the Task Force's survey in three cites.[22]

Second, the fear of crimes of violence is not a simple fear of injury or death or even of all crimes of violence, but, at bottom, a fear of strangers. The personal injury that Americans risk daily from sources other than crime are enormously greater. The annual rate of all Index offenses involving either violence or the threat of violence is 1.8 per 1,000 Americans.[23] This is minute relative to the total accidental injuries calling for medical attention or restricted activity of one day or more, as reported by the Public Health Service.[24] A recent study of emergency medical care found the quality, numbers, and distribution of ambulances and other emergency services severely deficient, and estimated that as many as 20,000 Americans die unnecessarily each year as a result of improper emergency care.[25] The means necessary for correcting this situation are very clear and would probably yield greater immediate return in reducing death than would expenditures for reducing the incidence of crimes of violence. But a different personal significance is attached to deaths due to willful acts of felons as compared to the incompetence or poor equipment of emergency medical personnel.

Furthermore, . . . most murders and assaults are committed by persons known to the victims, by relatives, friends, or acquaintances. Indeed, on a straight statistical basis, the closer the relationship, the greater the hazard. In one sense the greatest threat to anyone is himself, since suicides are more than twice as common as homicides.

Third, this fear of strangers has greatly impoverished the lives of many Americans, especially those who live in high-crime neighborhoods in large cities. People stay behind the locked doors of their homes rather than risk walking in the streets at night. Poor people spend money on taxis because they are afraid to walk or use public transportation. Sociable people are afraid to talk to those they do not know. In short, society is to an increasing extent suffering from what economists call "opportunity costs" as the result of fear of crime. For example, administrators and officials interviewed for the Commission by the University of Michigan survey team report that library use is decreasing because borrowers are afraid to come out at night. School officials told of parents not daring to attend PTA meetings in the evening, and park administrators pointed to unused recreation facilities.[26] When many persons stay home, they are not availing themselves of the opportunities for pleasure and cultural enrichment offered in their communities, and they are not visiting their friends as frequently as they might. The general level of social interaction in the society is reduced.

When fear of crime becomes fear of the stranger, the social order is further damaged. As the level of sociability and mutual trust is reduced, streets and public places can indeed become more dangerous. Not only will there be fewer people abroad but those who are abroad will manifest a fear of and a lack of concern for each other. The reported incidents of bystanders indifferent to cries for help are the logical consequence of a reduced sociability, mutual distrust, and withdrawal.

However, the most dangerous aspect of a fear of strangers is its implication that the moral and social order of society are of doubtful trustworthiness and stability. Everyone is dependent on this order to instill in all members of society a respect for the persons and possessions of others. When it appears that there are more and more people who do not have this respect, the security that comes from living in an orderly and trustworthy society is undermined. The tendency of many people to think of crime in terms of increasing moral deterioration is an indication that they are losing their faith in their society. And so the costs of the fear of crime to the social order may ultimately be even greater than its psychological or economic costs to individuals.

Fourth, the fear of crime may not be as strongly influenced by the actual incidence of crime as it is by other experiences with the crime problem generally. For example, the mass media and overly zealous or opportunistic crime fighters may play a role in raising fears of crime by associating the idea of "crime" with a few sensational and terrifying criminal acts.[27] Past research on the mass media's connection with crime has concentrated primarily on depictions and accounts of violence as possible causes of delinquency and crime. Little attention has thus far been given to what may be a far more direct and costly effect—the creation of distorted perceptions of the risk of crime and exaggerated fears of victimization.

The greatest danger of an exaggerated fear of crime may well reside in the tendency to use the violent crime as a steretotype for crimes in general. For example, there may be a significant interplay between violence, the mass media, and the reporting of general crime figures. Publicity about total crime figures without distinguishing between the trends for property crime and those for crimes against persons may create mistaken ideas about what is actually happening. If burglaries and larcenies increase sharply while violent crimes decrease or remain stable, the total figures will follow the property crime figures, since crimes against property are more than four fifths of the total. Yet under these conditions people may interpret the increases in terms of the dominant stereotype of crimes of violence, thus needlessly increasing their fears. They may not only restrict their activities out of an exaggerated fear of violence but may fail to protect themselves against the more probable crimes. The fact is that most people experience crime vicariously through the daily press, periodicals, novels, radio, and television, and often the reported experiences of other persons. Their fear of crime may be more directly related to the quality and the amount of this vicarious experience than it is to the actual risks of victimization.

The Task Force believes that there is a clear public responsibility to keep citizens fully informed about crime so that they will have facts to go on when they decide what the risks are and what precautionary measures they should take. Furthermore, without an accurate understanding of the facts, they cannot judge whether the interference with individual liberties which strong crime-control measures may involve is a price worth paying. The public obligation to citizens is to provide this information regularly and accurately. And if practices for disseminating information give wrong impressions, resources should be committed to developing more accurate methods.

ATTITUDES TOWARD CAUSES AND CURES

Attitude surveys involving questions on the causes of crime and measures for remedying the situation yield results reflecting differences in fundamental beliefs regarding man and society. Some regard punitive and repressive measures as the best means for coping with the problem while others prefer measures of social uplift. Some see inherent and immutable differences between the character of those who commit crimes, on the one hand, and the ordinary citizen on the other. Others see criminal tendencies as modifiable by instruction or changes in environment circumstances. Some view many current social changes as leading toward a progressively more law-abiding citizenry; others see in them the undermining of moral beliefs and constraints which keep men law-abiding.

While there undoubtedly are some persons whose views fit neatly into this liberal versus conservative polarity, this is by no means universally so. The lack of a rigid polarity is evidenced by conflicting poll and survey results, especially between notions of causes and cures, and between ideas of appropriate actions in general or in concrete cases.

A Gallup poll in August 1965 asked people what they thought was responsible for the increase in crime in this country. The major reasons people mentioned were things having directly to do with the social or moral character of the population rather than changes in objective circumstances or in law enforcement. Gallup classified more than half of all the answers given under the category "Family, poor parental guidance." About 6 per cent of the answers gave breakdown in moral standards as the reason for increased crime. A variety of other directly moral causes were given in addition, such as people expect too much, people want something for nothing, and Communism. Relatively few (12 per cent) of the responses were in terms of objective conditions such as unemployment, poverty, the automobile, or the population explosion. Inadequate laws and the leniency of the courts were mentioned by 7 per cent and not enough police protection by only 3 per cent.

The responses to a query by Harris the same year were classified differently, but a similar pattern emerges. Disturbed and restless teen-agers was mentioned by more persons than any other cause and poor police departments by very few.

Harris later asked specifically why people become criminal rather than the reasons for an increase in crime. Most respondents attributed criminality to environmental and developmental factors rather than inborn characteristics, emphasizing such factors as poor training and companions, sometimes simply bad environments. [See Table 3.]

TABLE 3. WHY PEOPLE BECOME CRIMINALS

	Total public
Upbringing	38
Bad environment	30
Mentally ill	16
Wrong companions	14
No education	14
Broken homes	13
Greed, easy money	13
Too much money around	11
Not enough money in home	10
Liquor, dope	10
Laziness	9
For kicks	8
No religion	8
No job	8
No chance by society	7
Born bad	5
Feeling of hopelessness	4
Moral breakdown of society	3
Degeneracy, sex	2
Failure of police	2

NOTE: Percentages add to more than 100 because people volunteered more than one cause.
SOURCE: Harris poll, conduced in 1965 and reported in 1966.

Although a majority of persons queried tended to think of inadequate moral training rather than inherent weaknesses when asked about the cause of crime, their response concerning the best way to cope with the problem tended to depend on how the issue was phrased. For example, the BSSR survey in Washington asked citizens what they thought was the most important thing that could be done to cut down crime in the city.[28] Their responses were classified as to whether a repressive measure, a measure of social amelioration, or one of moral inculcation was being advocated. (Repressive measures included such things as more police, police dogs, stiffer sentences, cracking down on teen-agers. Social amelioration included advocacy of such things as more jobs, recreation and youth programs, better housing, and improved police-community relations. Moral measures were better child training, religious training and revival, community leadership, and, most simply, teach discipline.) Sixty per cent of the respondents recommended repressive measures as compared with 40 per cent who suggested social and amelioration or moral inculcation.

Further, evidence of this tendency to think of repressive measures as the way to deal with some aspects of the crime problem is contained in the answers to the question. "In general, do you think the courts in this area deal too harshly or not harshly enough with criminals?" asked in a 1965 Gallup survey. The majority of responses was not harshly enough; only 2 per cent said too harshly. The BBSR study in Washington avoided the use of the word criminal by asking whether the sentences given by courts in Washington were generally too lenient or too harsh. Again, most respondents, including Negroes, thought the courts too lenient.[29]

However, when survey items pose alternative rather than general open-ended questions, they have yielded somewhat different results. The NORC national study asked people whether the main concern of the police should be with preventing crimes from happening or with catching criminals. All but 6 per cent of those asked felt they could make a choice between these two emphases—61 per cent chose preventing crimes and 31 per cent catching criminals.[30]

Another question by the Harris poll in 1966 posed these alternatives:

Leading authorities on crime feel there are two ways to reduce crime. One way is to head off crime by working with young people to show them that nothing can be gained through a life of crime. Another way is to strengthen our law enforcement agencies to make it hard for criminals to get away with crime. While both ways might be desirable, if you had to choose, which one would you favor: trying to stop criminals before they begin or strengthening the police force to crack down on crime?

More than three-fourths of respondents chose "work with young people," and only 16 per cent "strengthen police." Eight per cent were not sure which was preferable.

A nonpunitive approach was also evident in a third question in the same survey that asked people to choose between corrective and punitive goals for prisons. Again, over three-fourths of the respondents chose correction as the alternative, only 11 per cent punishment. Apparently, when the alternatives are put sharply enough, especially in dealing with the misbehavior of young people, the general preference of the public for preventive or rehabilitative rather than repressive measures emerges.

The tendency to be nonpunitive and repressive when considering the handling of youthful offenders is strikingly illustrated by the results of a 1963 Gallup survey. A sample was drawn from 171 communities across the nation to sit in judgment on a hypothetical case. The respondents were asked how they would deal with a seventeen-year-old high school student from their own community who was caught stealing an automobile. They were told he had no previous record. Fewer than 10 per cent recommended confinement of any sort: the largest number said they would give him another chance (Table 4).

These survey results indicate the existence of public attitudes endorsing current trends in the criminal-justice field that would increase the effectiveness of law enforcement and at the same time greatly expand preventive and rehabilitative efforts, particularly with young people. Though at first glance public attitudes toward the causes and cures for crime might appear contradictory, a more careful analysis suggests that the public assumes different attitudes toward different aspects of the crime problem. This provides po-

TABLE 4. How Public Would Deal with Youth Caught Stealing a Car
(Rank Order of Answers)

1. Give him another chance, be lenient.
2. Put him on probation; give him a suspended sentence.
3. Put him under care of psychiatrist or social worker.
4. Put him in an institution: jail, reformatory, etc.
5. Release him in the custody of his parents.
6. Punish his parents; fine them.

tential support for many different types of action programs ranging all the way from increased police powers and more severe penalties for crime to the benign types of treatment and preventive programs.

Citizen Involvement in Crime Prevention

Public concern about crime can be a powerful force for action. However, making it one will not be easy. The Washington survey asked people whether they had ever "gotten together with other people around here or has any group or organization you belong to met and discussed the problem of crime or taken some sort of action to combat crime?" [31] Only 12 per cent answered affirmatively, although the question was quite broad and included any kind of group meeting or discussion. Neither did most persons believe that they as individuals could do anything about the crime in their own neighborhoods. Just over 17 per cent thought that they could do something about the situation.

The question of what could be done to reduce crime was put to administrators and officials of public and quasi-public organizations in three cities.[32] These officials suggested ameliorative measures, such as greater equality of opportunity, rehabilitative, recreational and youth programs more frequently than did the sample of the general population. These citizens in positions of responsibility also relied to a great extent on the police; almost as many suggested improved and augmented police forces as suggested the social measures. There was, however, much greater emphasis on improvement in the moral fiber and discipline of the population than was true of the sample of the general population. Administrators of parks, libraries, utility companies, and housing projects frequently stressed greater respect for property, for persons, or for the police; they believed that education could inculcate these values in the population. As these officials were responsible for organizations that suffered considerable loss through vandalism, it seemed reasonable to them that greater respect for property would solve much of the crime problem. School officials proposed more alternative activities for youth while park and traffic officials emphasized more police activity and better police-community relations, reflecting their own perceived need for their province.

These administrators and officials who were interviewed also acknowledged a number of ways in which they might help to reduce crime. Some suggested that they might cooperate with the police in ways calculated to make law enforcement easier. Others thought that they might cooperate in neighborhood and community programs, particularly by donating money for youth activities. The largest number of suggestions, however, involved what might be termed extension of the organizations' services. Electric companies considered more and brighter street lights, park officials more parks and recreational programs, and school principals more youth programs and adult education. Another category of responses by officials concerned participation in activities directed toward community goals. They thought that integration of work crews and the support of community relations programs might be helpful. Interestingly, some of these suggestions were not offered until the officials were specifically asked what their organizations might do. Park officials, for example, did not suggest recreational and other alternative activities as a means of reducing crime until asked what park departments might do. Nonetheless, these administrators and officials did see the potential of their own organizations as useful in reducing crime, creating the possibility that they might do something other than rely on the police. They also take a broader view of crime prevention than does the general public. Understandably, they might as citizens and organizations feel more competent to participate effectively in these broader programs while other segments of the public are more likely to believe that control and prevention is not within their province.

Ambivalence Regarding Police Practices

The public surveys show that there is a considerable willingness to permit practices the police and law-enforcement agencies consider important—but not an unqualified willingness. The complexity of the feelings about the relative rights of the police and the accused person is apparent in the responses of persons questioned by the BSSR in Washington and also in the results of the national study.

As one might expect, a substantial majority of the respondents in Washington, 73 per cent, agreed that the police ought to have leeway to act tough when they have to.[33] In addition, more than half—56 per cent—agreed that there should be more use of police dogs, while less than one-third (31 per cent) disagreed. However, the person who takes a strong position on one question may refuse to do so on another. Further, there is little consistency between a general respect and sympathy for police and willingness to enlarge police powers. Table 5 shows that there is some tendency for those with high police support scores to be willing to give the police greater power, but that there are also many who regard the police favorably who would restrict their power. The public's attitudes seem to be more responsive to particular issues than to anything which might be called a generalized high or low attitude toward supporting the police.

A similar ambivalence was observed in the results of the national survey conducted for the Commission.[34] There were four questions concerned with the power of the police. Forty-five per cent favored civilian review boards (35 per cent opposed them, 30 per cent had no opinion or were indifferent); 52 per cent believed that the police should have more power; 42 per cent that police should risk arresting an innocent person rather than risk missing a criminal; and 65 per cent favored the ruling that police may not question a suspect without his lawyer being present or the suspect's consent to be questioned without counsel. These percentages indicate that individuals vary considerably from one issue to the next as to the desirability of enlarging or restricting police powers.

TABLE 5. ATTITUDES TOWARD SUPPORTING POLICE AND APPROVAL OF
CERTAIN POLICE PRACTICES

"The police should have leeway to act tough when they have to."

	Agree		Disagree	
Low police support score *	136	(36.5%)	59	(53.6%)
High police support score	237	(63.5)	51	(46.4)
Total	373	(100.0)	110	(100.0)

"There should be more use of police dogs."

	Agree		Disagree	
Low police support score	100	(35.1%)	86	(53.4%)
High police support score	185	(64.9)	75	(46.6)
Total	285	(100.0)	161	(100.0)

* A police support score was assigned each respondent depending on whether he gave a positive or negative response to six statements about the police.

SOURCE: BSSR study, *supra* note 5, p. 148.

To test this notion, the answers of each respondent were combined to form a scale of restrictiveness or permissiveness regarding law-enforcement policy. Those consistently in favor of expanding police powers would score 0 and those most restrictive of police power would score 8. The distribution of scores in Table 6 illustrates the variations in attitudes about different law-enforcement policies or issues. Only 11 per cent of the respondents show extreme scores advocating expansion of police power and 15 per cent show extreme restrictive scores. Many give restrictive answers to some questions and permissive answers to others.

TABLE 6. PER CENT DISTRIBUTION, POLICE POLICY INDEX

Most in favor of increasing police powers (index value):	
0	7.5
1	3.6
2	16.4
3	10.7
4	16.9
5	17.1
6	12.5
7	13.1
8	2.2
Most in favor of restricting police power:	
Total	100.0
N	(11,742)

The public surveys also show that most people believe that the police do not discriminate in the way they treat members of different groups. About half of the Negro and 20 per cent of the white citizens interviewed in Washington thought that Negroes get no worse treatment than other people. Among the comments of those respondents who do believe the police discriminate were that the police pick on Negroes more, they are rude to Negroes, use brutality and physical force, or else ignore Negroes more than other people. Half of the Washington respondents believed that people who have money for lawyers don't have to worry about police. Somewhat fewer but nonetheless almost half of the respondents in Boston and Chicago said that the way police treat you depends on who you are.[36] In these cities, 35 per cent saw rich and respectable persons as being favored by the police while 38 per cent said that being a Negro makes a difference.[37] In the predominantly Negro districts in each of these cities, more persons thought that Negroes receive less than equitable treatment while in the predominantly white areas more persons spoke of favorable treatment of rich persons.[38]

The single most outstanding finding of the survey in Washington, however, was not the differenecs between groups but rather the generally high regard for the police among all groups, including Negro men. Although the BSSR survey found that more than half of the Negro men believed that many policemen enjoy giving people a hard time, 79 per cent said that the police deserve more thanks than they get. And 74 per cent thought that there are just a few policemen who are responsible for the bad publicity that the police force sometimes gets.[39] It is not so surprising to find this potential for good will toward the police when it is remembered that Negroes expressed the most worry about being the victims of crime and a general reliance on the police to prevent and control crime. This was the case even among Negro men who are not well educated and who live in the poorer areas of the city with relatively high rates of crime.

In general, the surveys found public concern for safeguarding individual rights. Only 38 per cent of the respondents agreed that too much attention is paid to the rights of persons who get in trouble with the police, when that question was asked in Washington, Boston, and Chicago.[40] The questions that comprised the law-enforcement policy scale in the national survey also were concerned with various aspects of the relative rights of the accused and the police.[41] When asked several questions in which various extensions of police powers were posited against protections of individual rights, in only one case did a majority favor the enlargement of police power.[42] Barely more than half, 52 per cent, thought that police should have more power to question people. A pronounced concern with the rights of citizens is particularly apparent when the rights issue is very explicit. It also is apparent that most persons do not perceive this concern with rights of citizens as being derogatory toward the police. Of those persons questioned in Washington who took a prorights position, more than half indicated strong respect and sympathy for the police.[43]

Negroes were somewhat more likely to take the rights position than white respondents but the differences were not great. The survey in Washington found that 49 per cent of the Negroes and 46 per cent of the white respondents did not think that too much attention was being paid to the rights of people who get into trouble with the police.[44] The same question was asked in Boston and Chicago; in both cities there were more prorights replies in the districts that were predominantly Negro than in those that were predominantly white. In Boston the proportions of prorights replies were 46 per cent in the predominantly Negro district and 20 per cent in the predominantly white area.[45] In Chicago it was 40 and 33 per cent in predominantly Negro and white areas, respectively.[46] The differences between the mean scores on the police policy index also reflected more concern with the rights of citizens on the part of nonwhite than white persons in the national sample.[47]

Another form of concern with the rights of citizens in recent years has been the question of allowing political and civil rights demonstrations. People who were questioned in the national study were asked whether such demonstrations should be allowed no matter what, should be allowed only if the demonstrators remain peaceful, or should not be allowed at all.[48] A majority of both whites and nonwhites would allow the demonstrations, most with the proviso that they remain peaceful. Among white persons there was a relationship between income and tolerance toward demonstrations. Those persons with higher incomes would more frequently allow demonstrations if they were peaceful and less frequently prohibit all demonstrations. Nonwhites tended to be more permissive regarding demonstrations regardless of income level. The upper income nonwhites, however, more often qualified their tolerance by requiring that demonstrations be peaceful. The tolerance of demonstrations as an indication of concern for rights was far from synonymous with a desire to restrict police powers as they related to the rights of citizens, however. More than 50 per cent of the white respondents who would allow demonstrations would also enlarge police powers. (More of the nonwhites would restrict police powers.)

The national survey also found a strong preponderance of favorable opinion toward the Supreme Court's decision regarding right of counsel.[49] Almost three-quarters of the persons questioned approved the decision that the state must provide a lawyer to suspects who want one but cannot afford to pay the lawyer's fee. Not only does a strong majority approve the decision but no income, sex, or racial group opposes it.

NONREPORTING OF CRIMES TO THE POLICE

Americans believe that the crime problem is a matter for police rather than citizen action. They nevertheless frequently fail to take the one essential action that they as citizens must take if the police are to intervene in any particular criminal instance. Fewer than half of the incidents of victimization uncovered by NORC in the national survey conducted for the Commission had been reported while the residents of Washington had notified the police of only 65 per cent of the incidents they disclosed to BSSR interviewers.[50] NORC found considerable variation by type of crime.[51] Generally the more serious the crime the more likely the police were called. A higher percentage of grand than petty larcenies and of aggravated than simple assaults were reported, for example. Except for the more serious crimes against the person, however, crimes that were completed were reported no more frequently than the attempted crimes. It is apparent that the simple desire to recover losses or damages is not the only factor in a victim's decision for or against police notification. This study did not find that any racial or income group was any more likely than another to report or decline to report crimes.[52]

The victim's or witness' reluctance to get involved was one of the most frequently cited reasons for nonreporting.[53] Sometimes he did not want to take the time to call the police and present evidence, perhaps spending time in court and away from his work. Some persons who said they had witnessed incidents that might have been crimes did not feel it was their responsibility to intervene, that it was not their business to call the police or take any other action. A few persons expressed this sentiment by stating to the interviewers, "I am not my brother's keeper."

Others said they did not think the victim would want the police to be notified or they indicated a concern for the offender. Victims, too, were sometimes reluctant to cause trouble for the offender. In half the cases of family crimes or sex offenses (other than forcible rape) reported to NORC interviewers the police were not notified, and the reason most frequently given was that it was a private rather than a police matter.[54] Similarly for all classes of offenses except serious crimes against the person, the police were less likely to be called if the offender were personally known to the victim than if he were a stranger.

The fear of reprisal or other unfortunate consequences sometimes deterred victims or witnesses from notifying the police of an incident. Some feared personal harm might come from the offender or his friends. Some feared that they themselves would become the subject of police inquiry or action. In the case of property offenses the fear of increased insurance rates or even of cancellation of insurance was more likely to be the reason. Businessmen often refrained from reporting burglaries, believing that it was less expensive to absorb some of these losses than to pay more for their insurance.[55]

The most frequently cited reason for not reporting an incident to the police is the belief in police ineffectiveness; 55 per cent of the reasons given for nonreporting by respondent in the national study fell in this category. This does not necessarily constitute evidence of a pervasive cynicism regarding police. The victim may instead have simply accepted that the damage had been done, there were no clues and the police could not be expected to apprehend the offender or undo the damage. For example, in malicious mischief where it is unlikely the offender will be caught, police ineffectiveness is the preponderant reason for nonreporting.

For similar reasons, businessmen interviewed by the University of Michigan survey team said that they rarely called the police to handle cases of employee dishonesty.[56] In 46 per cent of the cases where the police were not called, the reason given questions the capability of the police to do anything in the situation.[57] They do not queston that the police will respond to their call but doubt whether the police would or could accept the kind of evidence they have, or they do not feel that the courts would accept the evidence even if the police formally made an arrest. These businessmen also frequently responded in terms of not wanting to get involved and preferring to handle the matter themselves. Dismissal of the employee apparently requires less time and effort than referral of the matter to the police. Their feeling that it was not worthwhile to call the police, then, did not always indicate a negative evaluation of the police. Ironically, many of these same businessmen who do not report instances of employee dishonesty use police records as a screening device for selecting potential employees.[58]

Another factor which may be operating here is the relationship between the employer and employee. The employer has in a sense taken some responsibility for the relationship by engaging the employee; what happens then is seen as a matter between himself and the person he has hired. Similarly, when a businessman agrees to cash a customer's check he infrequently calls the police when the check is returned for insufficient funds or other reasons. Only 19 per cent of the owners and managers said they called the police when they are given a bad check and another 8 per cent said they would do so if they could not collect.[59] By far the most frequent response is to request that the offender make good. This is also the most frequent response in the case of shoplifting, but here there is a greater willingness to call the police. Nonetheless, only 37 per cent say they call the police and another 5 per cent will call them if they cannot make the offender pay for the goods. Half of them try to make the offender pay for the goods.[60] There is, of course, greater reliance on law-enforcement agencies than is apparent in these figures on nonreporting. Some businessmen suggested that they could threaten to call the police if the offender did not make restitution; in other instances the threat would be implicit.

CONCLUSION

Analysis of the findings of public opinion polls and surveys of the measures citizens take to cope with the threat of crime shows an increased concern about the crime problem and greatly aroused fears of being victimized, especially from the violent acts of strangers. This fear leads many people to give up activities they would normally undertake particularly when it may involve going out on the streets or into parks and other public places at night. The costs of this fear are not only economic, though a burdensome price may be paid by many poor people in high crime-rate areas who feel compelled to purchase protective locks, bars, and alarms, who reject an attractive night job because of fear of traversing the streets or who pay the expense of taxi transportation under the same circumstances. In the long run more damaging than costs are the loss of opportunities for pleasure and cultural enrichment, the reduction of the level of sociability and mutual trust, and perhaps even more important, the possibility that people will come to lose faith in the trustworthiness and stability of the social and moral order of the society.

At the same time most people seem to feel that the effort to reduce crime is a responsibility of the police, the courts, and other public or private agencies engaged in the tasks of crime prevention and control. Though the people generally see little they can do as individuals, they are prepared to endorse a variety of programs to remedy the situation. These range all the way from stricter policies of law enforcement to expensive crime prevention and treatment programs for offenders. Public attitudes about various programs or policies reflect both a desire for a better system of protection against crime and an interest in protecting individual rights and freedom. For this reason the pattern of public attitudes is complex and varies considerably from one issue to another. Thus, a majority of citizens believe the police should have more power to question people; but a somewhat greater majority favor the Supreme Court ruling regarding access to legal counsel as a pre-condition to police questioning following arrest. A majority feel that courts are too lenient in sentencing criminals, and yet they overwhelmingly prefer rehabilitative rather than punitive goals in corrections, and in the case of a young first offender the largest number would give him another chance.

Much more should be known about these public attitudes, how they vary from issue to issue, and how they differ for various social, economic, ethnic, and other groupings of the population. Nevertheless, it seems reasonable to conclude that there is substantial public support for a vigorous program of law enforcement, for more intensive use of rehabilitative treatment methods, and for broad programs of social, educational, and economic reforms that will help prevent youth from becoming enmeshed in delinquent and criminal careers.

NOTES

1 Lincoln Steffens, *The Autobiography of Lincoln Steffens* (New York: Harcourt, Brace, & World, 1931), pp. 285–91.

2 E.g., Daniel Bell, "The Myth of Crime Waves," in *The End of Ideology* (2d rev. ed.; New York: Collier, 1962), pp. 151–74.

3 Yale Kamisar, "When the Cops Were Not 'Handcuffed,'" *New York Times Magazine*, No. 7, 1965.

4 Philip H. Ennis, "Criminal Victimization in the United States: A Report of a National Survey," President's Commission on Law Enforcement and Administration of Justice, Field Survey 2 (Washington, D.C.: Government Printing Office, 1967), hereinafter referred to as the NORC study.

5 Albert D. Biderman, Louise A. Johnson, Jeanie McIntyre, and Adrianne W. Weir, "Report on a Pilot Study in the District of Columbia on Victimization and Attitudes Toward Law Enforcement," President's Commission on Law Enforcement and Administration of Justice, Field Survey 1 (Washington, D.C.: Government Printing Office, 1967), hereinafter referred to as the BSSR study.

6 *Ibid.*, p. 40.

7 *Ibid.*, p. 33.

8 Ennis, *op. cit.*, source note Table 1.

9 BSSR study, *op. cit.*, p. 127.

10 *Ibid.*, p. 125.

11 NORC study, *op. cit.*, Table 47, p. 76.

12 BSSR study, *op. cit.*, p. 121.

13 Albert J. Reiss, Jr., "Studies in Crime and Law Enforcement in Major Metropolitan Areas," President's Commission on Law Enforcement and Administration of Justice, Field Survey 3 (Washington, D. C.: Government Printing Office, 1967), vol. 1, sec. 2, p. 30. Hereinafter referred to as the Reiss studies.

14 Thorsten Sellin and Marvin E. Wolfgang, *The Measurement of Delinquency* (New York: Wiley, 1964), Table 69, p. 289.

15 Reiss studies, *op. cit.*, p. 31.

16 BSSR study, *op. cit.*, p. 124.

17 NORC study, *op. cit.*, Table 44, p. 74.

18 Ennis, *op. cit.*, source note to Table 1.

19 Reiss studies, *op. cit.*, pp. 103–06.

20 NORC study, *op. cit.*, Table 48, p. 77.

21 Reiss studies, *op. cit.*, p. 103.

22 Donald J. Black and Albert J. Reiss, Jr., "Problems and Practices for Protection Against Crime Among Business and Organizations" (Ann Arbor: University of Michigan, 1966). A report to the President's Commission on Law Enforcement and Administration of Justice (mimeo).

23 "UCR, 1965," p. 3.

24 National Safety Council, *Accident Facts* (Chicago: National Safety Council, 1966), p. 2.

25 Data obtained by interview from American College of Surgeons, Washington, D.C., 1966.

26 Stephen Cutler and Albert J. Reiss, Jr., "Crimes Against Public and Quasi-Public

Organizations in Boston, Chicago, and Washington, D.C." (Ann Arbor: University of Michigan, 1966). A report to the President's Commission on Law Enforcement and Administration of Justice (mimeo).

[27] It is also possible at the same time that overexposure of the public to accounts of violent crime creates a dullness and indifference to the crime problem that only news of the most violent crimes can penetrate. For a discussion of this possible effect and a review of studies of crime and the mass media, see Edwin H. Sutherland and Donald R. Cressey, *Principles of Criminology* (7th ed.; New York: Lippincott, 1966), pp. 257–65.

[28] BSSR study, *op. cit.,* p. 134.

[29] *Ibid.,* p. 135.

[30] NORC study, *op. cit.,* p. 59.

[31] BSSR study, *op. cit.,* unpublished supplement.

[32] Cutler and Reiss, *op. cit.*

[33] BSSR, *op. cit.,* p. 146.

[34] NORC study, *op. cit.,* pp. 64–72.

[35] BSSR study, *op. cit.,* p. 144.

[36] Reiss studies, *op. cit.,* p. 42.

[37] *Ibid.,* pp. 43–47.

[38] *Ibid.,* pp. 42–47.

[39] BSSR study, *op. cit.,* p. 137.

[40] *Ibid.,* p. 149; and Reiss studies, *op. cit.,* p. 82.

[41] For a description of the police policy index, see NORC study, *op. cit.,* pp. 64–65.

[42] *Ibid.,* p. 64.

[43] BSSR study, *op. cit.,* p. 150.

[44] *Ibid.,* p. 149.

[45] Reiss studies, *op. cit.,* p. 82.

[46] *Ibid.*

[47] NORC study, *op. cit.,* p. 68.

[48] *Ibid.,* Table 36, p. 63.

[49] *Ibid.,* Table 40, p. 70.

[50] *Ibid.,* p. 42; and BSSR study, *op. cit.,* p. 40.

[51] See Table 5 in Chap. 2.

[52] NORC study, *op. cit.,* Table 27, p. 46.

[53] *Ibid.,* Table 24, p. 44.

[54] *Ibid.,* Table 26, p. 46.

[55] Black and Reiss, *op. cit.*

[56] *Ibid.*

[57] *Ibid.*

[58] *Ibid.*

[59] *Ibid.*

[60] *Ibid.*

2. *Attitudes of Negroes Toward the Police**

ANGUS CAMPBELL AND HOWARD SCHUMAN

THIS IS A PRELIMINARY REPORT of a survey of the perceptions and attitudes of more than 5,000 Negroes and whites in fifteen major American cities. In each city a cross-section of the population of each race, aged sixteen to sixty-nine, was interviewed in early 1968. For the present report the results for all fifteen cities have been combined. Suburban white samples were also drawn around two of the cities in order to study city and suburban differences in attitude. . . .

THE POLICE

In view of the importance of the police in the complicated social problems of the cities, our survey invested a considerable segment of the questionnaire in exploring the experiences of our Negro and white respondents with the police of their community. Our data make it clear that this is an area of urban life that looks quite different to white and Negro citizens.

We began this series with a question dealing with what we thought would be the most common complaint that might be offered concerning the police: They do not come quickly when they are called. We asked our respondents first whether they thought this happened to people in their neighborhood, then whether it had ever happened to them personally, and finally whether it had happened to anyone they knew. As Table 1 demonstrates, Negroes are far more likely than whites to feel that people in their neighborhood do not receive prompt police service, one in four of them report they have experienced poor service themselves (compared to about three-fifths as many whites), and they are twice as likely as whites to say they know people to whom this has happened.

The second question dealt with the incidence of the show of disrespect or use of insulting language by the police. The racial differences in response to this inquiry are even more pronounced (see Table 2). While relatively few white people felt this sort of thing happened in their neighborhood and even fewer reported it had happened to them or to people they know, substantial numbers of Negroes, especially men, thought it happened in their neighborhoods and many of these reported that they had experienced such treatment themselves.

The third question asked if the police "frisk or search people without a good reason" and the same pattern of racial differences emerges (see

* Angus Campbell and Howard Schuman, "A Comparison of Black and White Attitudes and Experiences in the City," Chapter 4 in The National Advisory Commission on Civil Disorders, *Supplemental Studies for the National Advisory Commission on Civil Disorders*, New York: Praeger, 1968.

Table 3). This is not an experience that occurs to many white people and they do not think it happens in their neighborhoods. Three times as many Negroes do believe it happens in their neighborhoods and report that it has happened to them personally.

TABLE 1. "Now I want to talk about some complaints people have made about the (Central City) police. First, some people say the police don't come quickly when you call them for help. Do you think this happens to people in this neighborhood?" (In Per Cent)

	Negro			White		
	Men	Women	Total	Men	Women	Total
Yes	51	52	51	29	24	27
No	36	31	34	58	62	60
Don't know	13	17	15	13	14	13
"Has it ever happened to you?"						
Yes	24	27	25	16	13	15
No	39	42	40	25	24	24
Don't know	1	0	1	1	1	1
Don't think it happens in their neighborhood	36	31	34	58	62	60
"Has it happened to anyone you know?"						
Yes	31	35	33	18	15	17
No	27	30	28	20	20	20
Don't know	6	4	5	4	3	3
Don't think it happens in their neighborhood	36	31	34	58	62	60

TABLE 2. "Some people say the police don't show respect for people and use insulting language. Do you think this happens to people in this neighborhood?" (In Per Cent)

	Negro			White		
	Men	Women	Total	Men	Women	Total
Yes	43	33	38	17	14	16
No	38	41	39	75	75	75
Don't know	19	26	23	8	11	9
"Has it ever happened to you?"						
Yes	20	10	15	9	5	7
No	40	49	45	15	19	17
Don't know	2	0	1	1	1	1
Don't think it happens in their neighborhood	38	41	39	75	75	75
"Has it happened to anyone you know?"						
Yes	28	23	26	12	9	11
No	29	34	32	11	13	12
Don't know	5	2	3	2	3	2
Don't think it happens in their neighborhood	38	41	39	75	75	75

TABLE 3. "Some people say the police frisk or search people without good reason. Do you think this happens to people in this neighborhood?" (In Per Cent)

	Negro			White		
	Men	Women	Total	Men	Women	Total
Yes	42	30	36	12	9	11
No	41	40	41	78	75	76
Don't know	17	30	23	10	16	13
"Has it ever happened to you?"						
Yes	22	3	13	6	1	4
No	36	55	45	16	24	20
Don't know	1	2	1	0	0	0
Don't think it happens in their neighborhood	41	40	41	78	75	76
"Has it happened to anyone you know?"						
Yes	28	20	24	8	6	7
No	28	36	32	12	17	14
Don't know	3	4	3	2	2	2
Don't think it happens in their neighborhood	41	40	41	78	75	75

Finally, we asked a direct question about "police brutality"—do the police rough up people unnecessarily when they are arresting them or afterwards? Over a third of the Negro respondents reported this happened in their neighborhoods, while 10 per cent of whites so reported (see Table 4).

TABLE 4. "Some people say the police rough up people unnecessarily when they are arresting them or afterwards. Do you think this happens to people in this neighborhood?" (In Per Cent)

	Negro			White		
	Men	Women	Total	Men	Women	Total
Yes	37	32	35	10	9	10
No	42	41	41	80	76	78
Don't know	21	27	24	10	15	12
"Has it ever happened to you?"						
Yes	7	1	4	2	0	1
No	50	56	53	18	23	20
Don't know	1	2	2	0	1	1
Don't think it happens in their neighborhood	42	41	41	80	76	78
"Has it happened to anyone you know?"						
Yes	27	20	24	7	6	7
No	28	35	32	11	15	13
Don't know	3	4	3	2	3	2
Don't think it happens in their neighborhood	42	41	41	80	76	78

Much smaller numbers of both races reported that they had experienced unnecessary roughness themselves, but Negroes were four times more likely to report such treatment. Far more Negroes than whites report knowing someone who had been roughed up by police. The great discrepancy which we find between the number of Negroes who say they were themselves unnecessarily frisked or roughed up and the numbers who testify that they know someone to whom this has happened reflects the manner in which reports of such incidents travel through the Negro community.

Reports of unfavorable experiences with the police are clearly more numerous among the younger members of both racial groups than among their elders (see Table 5). Younger people are more likely to think police offenses occur in their neighborhoods, to report that offenses have been committed against them personally, and to know other people against whom they have been committed. As we see in Table 5, abrasive relations with the police are not only a racial problem in these northern cities, they are also a problem of youth. Negro young people are much more likely to complain of police offenses than the older generations of their race, especially of those police actions that involve bodily contact. However, the same age trend, about equally pronounced, is found in the white population. These findings are consistent, of course, with police records of the age characteristics of arrestees of both races. . . .

TABLE 5. COMPLAINTS ABOUT POLICE BEHAVIOR AMONG AGE CATEGORIES
(Results for Men and Women Combined, in Per Cent)

	White					
	16–19	20–29	30–39	40–49	50–59	60–69
Police don't come quickly						
Believe this happens in their neighborhood	35	32	29	24	24	16
Say it has happened to them	20	16	16	16	11	10
Say it has happened to people they know	27	19	17	15	12	9
Police use insulting language						
Believe this happens in their neighborhood	24	24	14	13	9	8
Say it has happened to them	14	11	7	3	6	3
Say it has happened to people they know	22	19	11	7	4	3
Police frisk and search without good reason						
Believe this happens in their neighborhood	25	15	7	9	7	4
Say it has happened to them	12	5	2	2	1	1
Say it has happened to people they know	21	10	3	5	3	2
Police rough up people unnecessarily						
Believe this happens in their neighborhood	25	13	7	5	6	3
Say it has happened to them	3	1	3	0	1	0
Say it has happened to people they know	18	12	6	4	3	1

TABLE 5. COMPLAINTS ABOUT POLICE BEHAVIOR (*Continued*)

| | Negro | | | | | |
	16–19	20–29	30–39	40–49	50–59	60–69
Police don't come quickly						
Believe this happens in their neighborhood	64	51	50	52	43	48
Say it has happened to them	27	22	24	28	20	21
Say it has happened to people they know	44	33	32	32	27	28
Police use insulting language						
Believe this happens in their neighborhood	55	45	37	36	26	24
Say it has happened to them	24	19	14	15	7	5
Say it has happened to people they know	43	32	24	21	15	10
Police frisk and search without good reason						
Believe this happens to their neighborhood	51	43	33	32	28	24
Say it has happened to them	22	18	11	9	4	8
Say it has happened to people they know	42	30	23	18	17	9
Police rough up people unnecessarily						
Believe this happens in their neighborhood	49	43	33	30	26	20
Say it has happened to them	8	7	3	2	4	1
Say it has happened to people they know	38	32	23	17	15	9

3. *The Juvenile Problem in Levittown* *

HERBERT J. GANS

LEVITTOWN IS "ENDSVILLE": THE ADOLESCENT VIEW

THE ADULT CONCEPTION OF Levittown's vitality is not shared by its adolescents. Many consider it a dull place to which they have been brought involuntarily by their parents. Often there is no place to go and nothing to do after school. Although most adolescents have no trouble in their student role, many are bored after school and some are angry, expressing that anger through thinly veiled hostility to adults and vandalism against adult property. Their relationship to the adults is fraught with tension, which discourages community attempts to solve what is defined as their recreational problem.

Essays which students in grades 6–12 wrote for me early in 1961 suggest that most children are satisfied with Levittown until adolescence.[1] Sixty-eight per cent of the sixth-graders liked Levittown, but only 45 per cent of

* Herbert J. Gans, *The Levittowners,* New York: Random House, 1967, pp. 206–16.

the eighth-graders, 37 per cent of the tenth-graders, and 39 per cent of the twelfth-graders did. In comparison, 85 per cent of the adults responded positively to a similar question.[2] Likes and dislikes reflect the state of recreational and social opportunities. Girls make little use of recreational facilities until they become adolescents, and before the tenth grade, they like Levittown better than the boys. Dislikes revolve around "nothing to do." The sixth- and eighth-grade boys say there are not enough gyms, playing fields, or hills, and no transportation for getting to existing facilities. Both sexes complain about the lack of neighborhood stores and that the houses are too small, lack privacy, and are poorly built. By the twelfth grade, disenchantment with the existing facilities has set in; those who like Levittown stress the newness and friendliness of the community, but references to the pool, the shopping center, and the bowling alley are negative.[3] As one twelfth-grader pointed out, "Either you have to pay a lot of money to go to the movies or the bowling alley, or you go to too many parties and that gets boring." Lack of facilities is reported most often by the older girls, for the boys at least have athletic programs put on by civic groups.[4]

But the commonest gripe is the shortage of ready transportation, which makes not only facilities but, more important, other teen-agers inaccessible. One girl complained, "After school hours, you walk into an entirely different world. Everyone goes his own separate way, to start his homework, take a nap, or watch TV. That is the life of a vegetable, not a human being." A car, then, becomes in a way as essential to teen-agers as to adults. Moreover, many small-town teenagers like to meet outside the community, for it is easier to "have fun" where one's parents and other known adults cannot disapprove. A high school senior who took a job to buy a car put it dramatically:

> I had no choice, it was either going to work or cracking up. I have another week of boring habits, then [when I get the car] I'll start living. I can get out of Levittown and go to other towns where I have many friends. . . . In plain words, a boy shouldn't live here if he is between the ages of 14 and 17. At this age he is using his adult mind, and that doesn't mean riding a bike or smoking his first cigarette. He wants to be big and popular and go out and live it up. I am just starting the life I want. I couldn't ask for more than being a senior in a brand new high school, with the best of students and teachers, and my car on its way. . . .

The adults have provided some facilities for teen-age activities, but not always successfully. One problem is that "teen-age" is an adult tag; adolescents grade themselves by age. Older ones refused to attend dances with the younger set, considering forced association with their juniors insulting.[5] Some adolescents also found the adult chaperones oppressive. At first, the chaperones interfered openly by urging strangers to dance with each other in order to get everyone on the floor and to discourage intimate dancing among couples. When the teen-agers protested, they stopped, but hovered uneasily in the background.[6]

Specifically, adolescent malcontent stems from two sources: Levittown was not designed for them, and adults are reluctant to provide the recreational facilities and gathering places they want. Like most suburban communities, Levittown was planned for families with young children. The bedrooms are too small to permit an adolescent to do anything but study or sleep; they lack the privacy and soundproofing to allow him to invite his friends over. Unfortunately, the community is equally inhospitable. Shopping centers are intended for car-owning adults, and in accord with the desire of property owners, are kept away from residential areas. Being new, Levittown lacks low-rent shopping areas which can afford to subsist on the marginal purchases made by adolescents. In 1961, a few luncheonettes in neighborhood shopping centers and a candy store and a bowling alley in the big center were the only places for adolescents to congregate.[7] Coming in droves, they overwhelmed those places and upset the merchants. Not only do teen-agers occupy space without making significant purchases, but they also discourage adult customers. Merchants faced with high rent cannot subsist on teen-age spending and complain to the police if teen-agers "hang out" at their places. Street corners are off limits, too, for a clump of adolescents soon becomes noisy enough to provoke a call to the police. Eventually they feel hounded and even defined as juvenile delinquents. Said one twelfth-grade girl, "I feel like a hood to be getting chased by the police for absolutely nothing."

The schools were not designed for after-hours use, except for adults and for student activities that entertain adults, such as varsity athletics. The auditoriums were made available for dances, although when these began, the school administration promptly complained about scuffed floors and damaged fixtures. Only at the swimming pool are teen-agers not in the way of adult priorities, and during the day, when adults are not using it, it is their major gathering place. But even here, smoking and noisy activities are prohibited.

The design deficiencies cannot be altered, and should not be if they are a problem only for teen-agers, but there is no inherent reason why teen-age facilities cannot be provided. However, adults disagree on what is needed and, indeed, on the desirability of facilities, for reasons partly political but fundamentally social and psychological. For one thing, adults are uncertain about how to treat teen-agers; for another, they harbor a deep hostility toward them which is cultural and, at bottom, sexual in nature.

There are two adult views of the teen-ager, one permissive, the other restrictive. The former argues that a teen-ager is a responsible individual who should be allowed to run his own affairs with some adult help. The latter, subscribed to by the majority, considers him still a child who needs adult supervision and whose activities ought to be conducted by adult rules to integrate him into adult society. For example, when one of the community organizations set up teen-age dances, there was some discussion about whether teen-agers should run them. Not only was this idea rejected, but the adults then ran the dances on the basis of the "highest" standards.[8] Boys were required to wear ties and jackets, girls, dresses, on the assumption that this would encourage good behavior, whereas blue jeans, tee shirts, and sweaters somehow would not. The adults could not resist imposing their own norms of dress in exchange for providing dances.

The advocates of restriction also rejected the permissive point of view because they felt it wrong to give teen-agers what they wanted. Believing that teen-agers had it "too easy," they argued that "if you make them work for programs, they appreciate them more." Logically, they should, therefore, have let the teen-agers set up their own activities, but their arguments were not guided by logic; they were, rather, rationalizations for their fear of teen-agers. Although the "permissives" pointed out that teen-agers might well set up stricter rules than adults, the "restrictives" feared catastrophes: fights, the "wrong crowd" taking over, pregnancies, and contraceptives found in or near the teen-age facility. These fears accounted for the rules governing dances and inhibited the establishment of an adult-run teen-age center, for the voluntary associations and the politicians were afraid that if violence or sexual activity occurred, they would be blamed for it.

The problem is twofold: Restrictive adults want adolescents to be children preparing for adulthood, and are threatened by the teen-age or youth culture they see around them. By now, adolescents are a cultural minority like any other, but whereas no Levittowners expect Italians to behave like Jews, most still expect teen-agers to behave like children. They are supposed to participate in the family more than they do and, legally still under age, to subsume their own wishes to the adults'. The failure of teen-agers to go along is blamed on the parents as well. If parents would only take more interest in their adolescent children, spend more time with them, be "pals" with them, and so on, then misbehavior—and even youth culture—would not develop. This argument is supported by the claim that delinquency is caused by broken homes or by both parents' holding full-time jobs.

Such views are espoused particularly by Catholics, who share traditional working-class attitudes; the parochial school, with its emphasis on discipline to keep children out of trouble, is their embodiment. Even adult-devised programs are considered undesirable, for, as one Catholic working-class father put it, "In summer, children should either work or be at home. Summer arts and crafts programs are a waste of time. My kid brother brought home dozens of pictures. What's he going to do with so many pictures?" The adolescents' social choices are also restricted. Adults active in youth programs frequently try to break up their groups, damning them as cliques or gangs, and even separating friends when athletic teams are chosen. Some teen-agers react by minimizing contact with adults, pursuing their activities privately and becoming remarkably uncommunicative. In essence, they lead a separate life which frees them from undue parental control and gives an air of mystery to the teen-ager and his culture.

Among restrictive adults, the image of the teen-ager is of an irresponsible, parasitic individual, who attends school without studying, hangs out with his peers looking for fun and adventure, and gets into trouble—above all, over sex. There were rumors of teen-age orgies in Levittown's school playgrounds, in shopping-center parking lots, and on the remaining rural roads of the township. The most fantastic rumor had forty-four girls in the senior class pregnant, with one boy singlehandedly responsible for six of them. Some inquiry on my part turned up the facts: Two senior girls were pregnant and one of them was about to be married.

If the essays the students wrote for me have any validity, the gap between adult fantasy and adolescent reality is astonishing. Most teen-agers do not even date; their social life takes place in groups. Judging by their comments about the friendliness of adult neighbors, they are quiet youngsters who get along well with adults and spend most of their time preparing themselves for adulthood. Needless to say, these essays would not have revealed delinquent activities or sex play. However, I doubt that more than 5 per cent of the older teen-agers live up to anything like the adult image of them.

What, then, accounts for the discrepancy? For one thing, adults take little interest in their children's education; they want to be assured that their children are getting along in school, but not much more. The bond that might exist here is thus absent. Changes in education during the last two decades have been so great that even interested parents can do little to help their children with their schoolwork. Consequently, adults focus on teen-agers in their nonstudent roles, noting their absence from home, the intensity of their tie to friends and cliques, and their rebelliousness.

Second, there is the normal gap between the generations, enlarged by the recent flowering of youth culture, much of which is incomprehensible or unaesthetic to adults. Despite the parents' belief that they should be responsible for their adolescents' behavior, they cannot participate in many joint activities or talk meaningfully with them about the experiences and problems of teen-age life. This gap is exacerbated by a strange parental amnesia about their own—not so distant—adolescence. I recall a letter written by a twenty-one-year-old mother who wanted to help the Township Committee set up a delinquency-prevention council because she was concerned about teen-age misbehavior.

Third, there is enough teen-age vandalism and delinquency to provide raw material for the adult image, although not enough to justify it. According to the police and the school superintendent, serious delinquency in Levittown was minimal; in 1961, about fifty adolescents accounted for most of it. Many were children from working-class backgrounds who did poorly in school or from disturbed middle-class families. From 1959 to 1961, only twelve cases were serious enough to go to the county juvenile court, and some were repeaters. Vandalism is more prevalent. The first victim was the old Willingboro YMCA, which was wrecked twice before it was torn down. Schools have been defaced, windows broken, garbage thrown into the pools, flowerbeds destroyed, and bicycles "borrowed." The perpetrators are rarely caught, but those who are caught are teen-agers, thus making it possible for adults to suspect all adolescents and maintain their image.

Finally, some adults seem to project their own desires for excitement and adventures onto the youngsters. For them, teen-agers function locally as movie stars and beatniks do on the national scene—as exotic creatures reputed to live for sex and adventure. Manifestly, teen-agers act as more prosaic entertainers: in varsity athletics, high school dramatic societies, and bands, but the girls are also expected to provide glamour. One of the first activities of the Junior Chamber of Commerce was a Miss Levittown contest, in which teen-age girls competed for honors in evening gown, bathing suit, and talent contests—the "talent" usually involving love songs or covertly erotic dances. At such contests unattainable maidens show off their sexuality—often unconsciously—in order to win the nomination. Men in the audience comment *sotto voce* about the girls' attractiveness, wishing to sleep with them, and speculating whether that privilege is available to the contest judges and boyfriends. From here, it is only a short step to the conviction that girls are promiscuous with their teen-age friends, which heightens adult envy, fear, and the justification for restrictive measures. The sexual function of the teen-ager became apparent when the popularity of the Miss Levittown contest led to plans for a Mrs. Levittown contest. This plan was quickly dropped, however, for the idea of married women parading in bathing suits was thought to be in bad taste, especially by the women. Presumably, young mothers are potential sexual objects, whereas the teen-agers are, like movie stars, unattainable, and can therefore serve as voyeuristic objects.

Although suburbia is often described as a hotbed of adultery in popular fiction, this is an urban fantasy. Levittown is quite monogamous, and I am convinced that most suburbs are more so than most cities.[9] The desire for sexual relations with attractive neighbors may be ever-present, but when life is lived in a goldfish bowl, adultery is impossible to hide from the neighbors— even if there were motels in Levittown and babysitters could be found for both parties. Occasionally such episodes do take place, after which the people involved often run off together or leave the community. There are also periodic stories of more bizarre sexual escapades, usually about community leaders. . . . However, . . . no cases ever appeared on the police blotters during the two years I saw them.[10]

"The Juvenile Problem" and Its Solution

The cultural differences between adults and adolescents have precipitated an undeclared and subconscious war between them, as pervasive as the class struggle, which prevents the adults from solving what they call "the juvenile problem." Indeed, putting it that way is part of the trouble, for much of the adult effort has been aimed at discouraging delinquency, providing recreational activities in the irrational belief that these could prevent it. Sports programs were supposed to exhaust the teen-agers so that they would be too tired to get into trouble (harking back to the Victorian myth that a regimen of cold showers and sports would dampen sexual urges, although, ironically, varsity athletes were also suspected of being stellar sexual performers); dances were to keep them off the street. When delinquency did not abate, a Youth Guidance Commission to deal with "the problem" and a Teen-Age Panel to punish delinquencies too minor for court actions were set up. The police chief asked for a curfew to keep youngsters off the street at night, hoping to put pressure on parents to act as enforcing agents and to get his department out of the crossfire between teen-agers, merchants, and home owners. Chasing the teen-agers from shopping centers and street corners was useless, for having no other place to go they always returned the next night, particularly since they knew people would not swear out complaints against their neighbors' (or customers') children. The police chief also did not want·"the kids to feel they are being bugged," for they would come to hate his men and create more trouble for them.[11] If he cracked down on them, they would retaliate; if he did not, the adults would accuse him of laxity. Although the curfew was strongly supported by parents who could not control their children, it was rejected as unenforceable.

Adult solutions to the juvenile problem were generally shaped by other institutional goals which took priority over adolescent needs. The organizations that scheduled dances wanted to advertise themselves and their community-service inclinations, even competing for the right to hold them, and the churches set up youth groups to bring the teen-agers into the church. Indeed, those who decide on adolescent programs either have vested interests in keeping teen-agers in a childlike status (parents and educators, for example) or are charged with the protection of adult interests (police and politicians). The primacy of adult priorities was brought out by a 1961 PTA panel on "How Is Our Community Meeting the Needs of the Adolescents?" With one exception, the panelists (chosen to represent the various adults responsible for teen-agers) ignored these needs, talking only about what teen-agers should do for *them*. For example, the parent on the panel said, "The needs of adolescents should first be met in the home and young energies should be guided into the proper normal channels." The teacher suggested that "parents should never undermine the authority of the teacher. Parents should help maintain the authority of the school over the child, and the school will in turn help maintain the authority of the parent over the child." The minister urged parents to "encourage youth leadership responsibilities within the church," and the police chief explained "the importance of teaching adolescents their proper relationship to the law and officers of the law." [12]

Political incentives for a municipal or even a semipublic recreation program were also absent. Not only were prospective sponsors afraid they would be held responsible for teen-age misbehavior occurring under their auspices, but in 1961 not many Levittowners had adolescent children, and not all of them favored a public program. Middle-class parents either had no problems with their youngsters or objected to the working-class advocacy of municipal recreation, and some working-class parents felt that once children had reached adolescence they were on their own. The eventual clients of the program, the adolescents, had no political influence whatsoever. They were too young to vote, and although they might have persuaded their parents to demand facilities for them, they probably suspected that what their parents wanted for them was more of what had already been provided.

In the end, then, the adults got used to the little delinquency and vandalism that took place, and the teen-agers became sullen and unhappy, complaining "This place is Endsville," and wishing their parents would move back to communities that had facilities for them or pressuring them for cars to go to neighboring towns.

The best summary of what is wrong—and what should be done—was stated concisely by a twelfth-grade essayist: "I think the adults should spend less time watching for us to do something wrong and help us raise money for a community center. We're not asking for it, we only want their help." If one begins with the assumption that adolescents are rational and responsible human beings whose major "problem" is that they have become a distinctive minority subculture, it is not too difficult to suggest programs. What else the teen-agers want in the way of recreation can be readily inferred from their essays: besides the center, a range of inexpensive coffeehouses and soda shops and other meeting places, bowling alleys, amusement arcades, places for dancing, ice- and roller-skating rinks, garages for mechanically inclined car owners (all within walking or bicycling distance or accessible by public transportation), and enough of each so that the various age groups and separate cliques have facilities they can call their own. Since adolescents are well supplied with spending money, many of these facilities can be set up commercially. Others may need public support. It would, for example, be possible to provide some municipal subsidies to luncheonette operators who are willing to make their businesses into teen-age social centers.

Recreational and social facilities are not enough, however. Part of the adolescents' dissatisfaction with the community—as with adult society in general—is their functionlessness outside of school. American society really has no use for them other than as students and condemns them to spend most of their spare time in recreational pursuits. They are trying to learn to be adults, but since the community and the larger society want them to be children, they learn adulthood only at school—and there imperfectly. Yet many tasks in the community now go unfilled because of lack of public funds—for example, clerical, data-gathering, and other functions at city hall; and tutoring children, coaching their sports, and leading their recreational programs. These are meaningful duties, and I suspect many adolescents could fill them, either on a voluntary or a nominal wage basis. Finally, teen-agers want to learn to be themselves and do for themselves. It should be possible to give them facilities of their own—or even land on which they could build—and let them organize, construct, and run their own centers and work places.

Needless to say, such autonomy would come up against the very real political difficulties that faced the more modest programs suggested in Levittown, and would surely be rejected by the community.[13] The ideal solution, therefore, is to plan for teen-age needs outside the local adult decision-making structure, and perhaps even outside the community. It might be possible to establish Teen-age Authorities that would play the same interstitial role in the governmental structure as other authorities set up in connection with intercommunity and regional planning functions. Perhaps the most feasible approach is to develop commercially profitable facilities, to be set up either by teen-agers or by a private entrepreneur who would need to be less sensitive to political considerations than a public agency. If and when the "juvenile problem" becomes more serious in the suburbs, federal funds may become available for facilities and for programs to create jobs, like those now being developed for urban teen-agers. Most likely, this will only happen when "trouble" begins to mount.

NOTES

[1] The students were asked what they liked and disliked about living in Levittown, and what they missed from their former residence. Since they were not asked to sign their names, and the questions were general, I believe the essays were honest responses. I purposely included no questions about the schools, and teachers were instructed not to give any guidance about how the questions should be answered. (One teacher did tell the children what to write, and these essays were not analyzed.) The data presented here are based on a sample of one sixth and one eighth-grade class from each of the three elementary schools, and of all tenth- and twelfth-grade classes.

[2] The data are not strictly comparable, for the adults were asked outright whether they liked or disliked living in Levittown, whereas the teen-agers' attitudes were inferred from the tone of the essays.

[3] Twenty-eight per cent of the boys liked the community's newness; 18 per cent, the friendly people. Among the girls, 34 per cent liked the people; 20 per cent, Levittown's newness.

[4] Twenty-five per cent of the tenth-graders and 50 per cent of the twelfth-graders say there is nothing to do, and 25 per cent and 46 per cent, respectively, mention the lack of recreational facilities. Among the twelfth-grade girls, 56 per cent mention it.

[5] Similarly in the elementary schools, seventh- and eighth-graders complained about having to go to school with "immature" and "childish" students; when they were moved to the high school, the older students objected to their presence in the same terms.

[6] There was also a dispute over programing: The adults wanted slow music and the traditional dances they knew best; the teen-agers wanted the latest best-selling records and the newest dances. They signed petitions for the ouster of the man who chose the records, but the adults refused to accept the petitions, arguing that they would be followed by petitions to oust the school superintendent.

[7] Indeed, the existing teen-age hangouts in little luncheonettes resulted from the lucky accident that the builder and the township planner were unable to regulate

and limit the number of small shopping centers which sprang up on the edge of the community.

[8] At one point adult-run dances failed to attract teen-agers, and a group of teen-age leaders was delegated to run the dances themselves. This foundered because other teen-agers disagreed with the rules and program set up by these leaders, and since only one opportunity for dancing was provided, they could express their disagreement only by nonattendance.

[9] A comparison of urban and suburban marriages indicated that extramarital affairs occur principally in older and well-educated populations, and that place of residence is irrelevant. (Earl Ubell, "Marriage in the Suburbs," *New York Herald Tribune,* January 4–8, 1959). For another observer's skepticism about suburban adultery, see W. H. Whyte, Jr., *The Organization Man* (New York: Simon & Schuster, 1956), pp. 355–57.

[10] Since the blotter listed adolescent promiscuity, adult suicide attempts, and even drunkenness and family quarrels among community leaders, I assume it was not censored to exclude adultery.

[11] Actually, since the police usually sided with the merchants against the teen-agers, the latter did feel "bugged."

[12] "Panel Features Junior High P.T.A. Meeting," *Levittown Herald,* Jan. 26, 1961.

[13] In 1966, no teen-age centers had yet been established in Levittown, and campaigning politicians were still arguing about the wisdom of doing so.

4. *Politics, Policies, and the Gang Problem* *

IRVING A. SPERGEL

THE PERSISTENCE OF juvenile delinquency in our society may be due, in large measure, to its importance for certain political purposes. The delinquency problem is more than the rate of antisocial acts or the aggregate of delinquents at a given time. It is more than the variety of psychological, social, cultural, educational, and legal causes of and effects on the delinquent. It is also the value of these factors for certain political purposes. Unless we understand clearly the uses of delinquency, particularly the gang problem, for certain organizational and political ends, we shall not grasp an essential element of the problem. This paper examines some of these political uses, the bases for their development, and the policies that are appropriate to significant change in the conditions that cause or contribute to the delinquency problem.

Some youth gangs today have become—or are becoming again—a political force in the urban ghetto. This is so because of their potential for violence, their new interest in community affairs, and the political interests of other community groups. A number of gangs, sensitized to the power they possess

* This is a revised version of Irving A. Spergel, *Politics, Policies and the Delinquency Problem,* Washington, D.C.: Office of Juvenile Delinquency and Youth Development, Welfare Administration, Department of Health, Education and Welfare, Sept., 1966, mimeographed. Used by permission of the author.

as a threat to the community, are learning to extract benefits from established and official groups. Gangs are becoming, in some cases, a corporate entity concerned with the economic, political, ideological, and social development of its membership and slum residents generally. New opportunities, roles, and access to success status are being provided, at least to gang leaders. It is possible that the gang structure is coming to be a kind of transitional institution permitting the delinquent adolescent to move more directly into—or at least to make an impact on—adult society.

The term politics, in this paper, is meant to suggest that he who wages battle against delinquency in the open community may accrue power or influence in decision-making related not only to delinquency-control, prevention, or treatment programs but to other community issues and problems. Power derives from the fact that whoever successfully engages in reducing delinquency, or creates the "myth" that his program is curtailing delinquent activity, gains the respect, prestige, and gratitude of the community at large. The community, and especially the establishment that speaks and acts for it, is beholden to and rewards the leaders of these efforts at delinquency control.

There is a reservoir of deep psychological and moral concern in urban communities over the problem of delinquency. Delinquents, especially aggressive gang youths, are regarded with fear, if not terror. They are conceived as evil incarnate. They focus and symbolize fundamental human conflicts over good and evil. The hard-core gang youth or the notorious delinquent serves as the projected image of the community's concern with its own impulses to commit murder, mayhem, and violence. These impulses are more readily stimulated in a period of rapid societal change, when deep frustration and aggravated failure result from inability to understand or to cope adequately with the myriad of new and complex problems of daily living.

In other words, the program that is "successful" in engaging and controlling delinquents represents, in moral and psychological terms, a reordering or restabilizing of the human condition. Everyone shares in the surcease of anxiety and dread when a delinquency crisis has been resolved and the world seems "right" and under control again. The chief architects, warriors, or missionaries of these battles, when they are "successful," and, in general, they almost always claim to be "successful," are accorded a special lien on the community's good will. The reward for these community heroes is public prestige, new jobs, salary increases, opportunity to expand a program, public acceptance of a point of view, or even commitment to a social cause.

On the other hand, on certain infrequent occasions, when the community or its representatives view a given program as no longer "successful," extreme hostility, denigration, and even destruction of a staff person's position or the specific agency itself, although not the general type of program, may ensue.

Thus, delinquency and gang conflict come to represent the irrational in our everyday living, the immoral equivalent of war on the local scene. It is a phenomenon we think, feel, and speak much about but seem unable to comprehend or adequately control. Despite varied researches, descriptive and analytic efforts, the nature and basis of the problem have been only partially delineated. We still depend on myths to generate, sustain, and justify many of our community programs that "combat" delinquency. With partial knowledge, great consternation, and little will, apparently, for genuine solutions, we resort to politics for management or pseudo-solution of the problem.

Historical Perspectives

Man creates his own social environment and thereby the form and intensity of the problems of deviancy he must confront. In each generation, however, the community appears to produce or highlight different patterns of deviant behavior. The youth gang, for example, appears to retain certain characteristics over time, yet modifies its purpose and form in response to shifting social, economic, cultural, and political conditions. The delinquent gang is basically a friendship and status-seeking group. It provides excitement, fun, adventure, recognition, and meaningful social roles for its members. It serves as a release from the frustrations and failures induced by defective family backgrounds, inadequate schools, lack of job opportunities, and unresponsive community agencies. It has functioned poorly in recent decades to prepare adolescents for legitimate adult roles and hardly better in their preparation for successful criminal adult roles. The gang as a socializing institution loses much of its force unless it is intimately connected to a power base and commands resources for its members.

Youth gang members subscribe ordinarily to a delinquent subculture which determines the nature of the social satisfactions to be sought and the activities to be carried out. Gang members interact with other members, girls, family members, neighborhood adults, and representatives of official agencies according to prescribed norms of the delinquent subculture. The specific character of the gang, however, seems to vary not only according to the particular constellation of youths, group norms, values and opportunities available to it at a given time and place, but also according to certain organizational and political interests.

The political nature of the gang in the United States has been noted by various observers. When the consensus over fundamental values and norms begins to break down and the basic structure of social and economic opportunities and civil liberties is seriously questioned, elements of the population, for example, gang members, may no longer define themselves or come to be defined by others as deviants. The problem of illegitimacy, including youth gang activity, tends to become part of and also resolved through the political process. Herbert Asbury claimed that many of the election disorders in New York City in the nineteenth century were stimulated by politicians in alliance with large gangs. Age-grade distinctions were not reported for the earlier gangs. Undoubtedly, adolescents as well as adults were members of these street groups.

> By 1855 it was estimated that the metropolis contained at least thirty thousand men who owed allegiance to the gang leaders and through them to the political leaders of Tammany Hall and the Know-Nothing or Native American Party who kept the political pot boiling furiously by their frantic and constant struggles for the privilege of plundering the public funds.
>
> At every election gangs employed by the rival factions rioted at the polling places, smashing ballot boxes, slugging honest citizens who attempted to exercise the right of franchise themselves. . . .[1]

The draft riots of July 1863 in New York City involved predominantly young men from the streets under twenty years of age. Asbury speaks of the "controlling inspiration of the mob" which was *not* directly related to the

Military Conscription Law.[2] The vast majority of the youthful street groups were Irish. The sense of frustration against middle- and upper-class groups was joined with a political desire to support the South's cause.

It came from sources quite independent of that law (Conscription) or any other law—from malignant hate toward those in better circumstances, from craving for plunder, from a barbarous spite against a different race, from a disposition to bolster up the failing fortunes of the Southern rebels. . . .[3]

A relatively stable system of working relationships was established between politicians and the youth gangs by the turn of the century. Local politicians provided ready and relatively safe access to opportunities. Gang leaders established relations with politicians with "the prospect of obtaining a 'soft job' or a lucrative job." Frederic Thrasher writes of conditions in Chicago:

The influence of the boy or adult gang in city politics has arisen largely through its ability to trade some advantage in the way of votes, influence, money, or what not, with the politicians in return for subsidies, immunities and so on. In this way gang influence has been enlisted in the support of the political machine, whose potential development is one of the weaknesses of democracy in cities. . . .[4]

According to Thrasher, politicians encouraged and controlled the development of youth gangs.

. . . There can be little doubt that most of the 302 so-called athletic clubs listed in this study have first developed as gangs, many of them still retaining their gang characteristics. The ward "heeler" often corrals a gang like a beeman does his swarm in the hive he has prepared for it. The boss pays the rent and is generous in his donations for all gang enterprises. He is the "patron Saint" of the gang and often leads the grand march or makes a speech at gang dances and picnics. In return his protegés work for him in innumerable ways and every gang boy in the hive is expected to gather honey on election day. It is doubtful if this sort of athletic club could long survive if it had to depend solely upon the financial backing of its own members.[5]

With election reform, the more complex organization of urban communities, the growing governmental investment in social welfare programs, and the rise of neighborhood and social agencies, the direct connection between politics and youth gangs was weakened. The neighborhood organization in the 1930's and the social agencies in the 1940's and 1950's assumed increasing responsibility for socialization of delinquents and control of youth gang behavior. Clifford Shaw's area projects in Chicago used indigenous adult leadership and developed welfare programs to rehabilitate gang youths. Social agencies, adapting certain of the techniques of the area project's, began to experiment with a professional street gang-worker approach.[6]

Prior to World War II, according to Frederic Thrasher,[7] Clifford Shaw,[8] Solomon Kobrin,[9] and others, it was possible for delinquent adolescents, especially those in youth gangs, to follow careers of crime into adulthood. There seemed to be greater integration of adolescent and adult norms and roles. It was possible for slum youths who could not "make it" through legitimate channels to find adequate access to success status through meaningful criminal roles. Delinquency took varied forms but seemed to possess a strong economic character. Youth gang violence and extremely disruptive activity appeared to be relatively contained.

During World War II and especially later, with the influx of the new minority groups to the large northern slum areas, established systems of legitimate opportunity seemed to break down. Subcultures of violence or gang fighting arose. Youth gangs were concerned with the creation and maintenance of new routes to reputation and status. Status depended on success in gang fighting rather than through traditional criminal means. Gang conflict, which had never been absent in the slum, now became more lethal, systematic, and particularly distressing to middle-class groups and official agencies, as well as to residents generally in such areas.

Community agencies with gang work programs in the 1940's and 1950's based their approaches on psychoanalytic and small-group theories of behavior. Notions of the delinquent's defective personality, lack of adequate individual socialization, absence of positive role models, and lack of opportunities for positive group development were at the heart of agency strategies of intervention. A variety of devices—counseling, recreation, job referral, work projects—were employed by workers to establish relationship with gangs, prevent and control warfare, and redirect the energies of youths. This period saw the flowering of gang control projects under some type of public or voluntary social agency auspices in almost every major urban area in the country.[10]

In the mid–1950's and early 1960's, sociological theories of status frustration, lack of social and economic opportunities, and lower-class culture began to replace older theories. But it was not always clear that writers as Albert Cohen,[11] Richard Cloward and Lloyd Ohlin,[12] and Walter Miller [13] were talking about the same types of lower-class delinquent groups. The forms of delinquent gang behavior—malicious mischief, vandalism, adolescent rebellion, as well as gang conflict—were not carefully distinguished. It is also possible that youth gangs began to change. They were breaking up in some cities. They were less oriented to gang fighting, some were more "cool" and committed to drug use, and others became increasingly integrated into the social change efforts of various community groups in the ghettoes.

The interventions of the social agency workers and police may have contributed to the "break-up" of the gangs in some of the cities, although not apparently in Chicago [14] and Philadelphia [15] where strong political machines may have made it extremely difficult for dissident neighborhood groups, including gangs, to coalesce, or at least for gangs to be absorbed. The increased use of drugs, particularly in some of the coastal cities, also made less imperative the need to externalize aggression. The drug user or addict could no longer maintain his commitment as a gang fighter, since he had to devote great energy to "hustling" or stealing in order to support his habit.

In the 1960's many gang youths were caught up in the mainstream of national concern about civil rights and poverty. They became significantly involved in a variety of local community activities, where this was permitted by the formal political structure. They no longer perceived themselves or were perceived as so different from other ghetto residents. These youths were viewed as among the indigenous elements which could contribute to community self-determination and development. Undoubtedly delinquent youths were involved in the ghetto riots and insurrections, but they also aided in the prevention and control of other riots and disorders, for example, through community youth patrols.[16] There was some evidence that the better organized the youth gang, the more its members could be mobilized for riot prevention —protecting neighborhood "turf" and thereby existing community arrangements.

In short, gangs were politicized. They became important sources for the disruption and change or the control and stability of communities. Efforts by the local agencies and neighborhood groups, the Office of Economic Opportunity, Departments of Labor and Health, Education, and Welfare, Southern Christian Leadership Conference, Student Nonviolent Coordinating Committee, and the Black Panthers to involve gangs served to sensitize them not only to the affronts, indignities, and discrimination against black and Spanish-speaking members of the ghettoes, but to their own rights and privileges both in their local community and in the city at large. The youth gangs suddenly became participants in the significant efforts to solve manpower, recreation, health, housing, education, and race problems. In the turmoil of rapidly evolving, changing, and shifting organizations, in the competitions for federal funds and the conflicts over local control, the youth gangs came to recognize themselves as a new and important urban interest group.

POLITICAL ROLES

At least five major types of political roles have recently arisen or been redeveloped in response to the problems of lower-class delinquency, particularly gang violence. Whether and how the youth gang and its violence are defined as social problems depend on the utility of gang phenomena for the political purposes of a variety of organizations, particularly for their leaders. Each political role is becoming socially structured and provides at least some opportunities for the achievement of political ends for its occupants. These roles are the civil rights or extremist leader, the new liberal politician, the gang or exgang leader, the agency executive, and the professional reformer.

Civil Rights or Extremist Leader

Civil rights, black power, and current revolutionary leaders have attempted to use delinquent gang members to support and sometimes to staff their various organizations or movements. The evidence is clear, for example, that the Southern Christian Leadership Conference (SCLC), the Student Nonviolent Coordinating Committee (SNCC), black power, Maoist or Castro Communist, and most recently SDS groups on university campuses have sought to capture or co-opt gang members. Gang youths, delinquents, and other lower-class members historically have constituted significant elements of revolutionary efforts. They have been useful as the shock troops, the *putschist* element, the essence of the rabble or the mob that serves to topple the existing regime or that at least seriously threatens the existing political structure. Certain civil rights leaders, for example, have sought to capture these youths probably because of their availability, their vigor, and especially for their willingness to participate in direct action. Some black power groups see gangs with their violence potential as a useful means for influencing and controlling low-income populations in an urban area.

Delinquent gangs, however, have not yet been systematically captured or used by civil rights or militant groups. In other words, gangs or delinquent street groups, as such, have not been fully converted or subverted to support these various organizational programs or causes. During the early and mid–1960's, the conversion of established groups of street-corner delinquents had occurred spasmodically in areas such as Central Harlem and Watts, where former gang members were reported members of small Malcolm X or ultra-militant black power young adult groupings that were, however, poorly organized, elusive, transitory groups, more like "near groups" than solidary entities. Often these militant organizations were able to draw off only a few of the older youth gang leaders.

The most significant influence on gang members had been through co-optation of certain gang leaders. These individuals in many cases were separating themselves from gang life patterns and were available for new young adult roles. Staff position or status that provided some subsistence or prestige was offered by the civil rights or militant organizations. Subsequently, many of these former gang leaders were employed, though not specifically, to convert other gang members or leaders. They were to help in the general community organizing and staffing activities of these organizations.

The early efforts to capture and retain gang youths as organizers for militant organizations seem not to have been particularly successful. A former SNCC official (an exnational chairman) and another SNCC worker who had considerable experience in the South reported that efforts were made to recruit selected gang members from northern and southern communities to work in the South. After relatively short periods of organizing experience, they gravitated to northern urban centers and found employment in conventional pursuits. In other words, these youths were apparently not deeply committed to the cause. They saw their employment as routes to other, more conventional and lucrative careers. They were looking for ways out of poverty and the ghetto.

Further evidence for the early lack of success of these organizations to capture or convert existing gangs to civil rights and black power causes derives from reports of gang workers and antipoverty officials in Chicago and Washington, D.C. One SNCC worker in Washington was unsuccessful in penetrating a former gang that developed a strong community action orientation. The group preferred to develop programs in association with a social agency. Apparently, there were difficulties in establishing positive working relationships with the group, and the SNCC worker was "driven out."

Sustained and controversial efforts at co-optation—controversial in the sense that they were opposed by most law-enforcement and social agencies in the city—occurred in Chicago. The Revolutionary Action Movement (RAM) attempted with little or no success to interest gang youths in its highly militant, possibly revolutionary program. Also, well-publicized attempts by staff of the SCLC several years ago were largely unsuccessful. A variety of workers from the civil rights movement sought to establish relationships with leaders of warring gangs. The effort was to redirect intergang hostility into controlled hostility against the system. At an early stage, staff strategy was to stimulate participation in protests, sit-ins, tent-ins, vigils, and so on, in relation to school housing, welfare, and other problems afflicting intercity ghettoes. But significant involvement by gang youths in these activities did not materialize, although on several occasions individual gang youths participated as guardians or "disciplined" protectors of the marchers against hostility and attack from white "onlookers." One of the dangers of gang participation in these demonstrations, apparent to some of the civil rights leaders, was that these youths might invite or precipitate countergang formation and hostility from gangs of white youths. The purpose and meaning of nonviolent civil rights demonstrations might be open to question, should these youth gang marchers lose their "cool" and resort to strongly defensive or even counteraggressive activity. Furthermore, gang members, particularly leaders, tended to be unreliable in their commitment to civil rights objectives. They sought to serve their own interests, for example, in the course of a boycott or demonstration against a grocery chain discriminating against blacks. They could "sell out," and have been known to support the interests of the establishment against protesters.

Early attempts by SCLC workers to bring ghetto gang leaders together to settle their disputes, establish treaties of peace, and orient them to the principles of the nonviolent movement met with failure in Chicago. Indeed, several of the meetings arranged with the gang leaders—unfortunately ill-prepared and uncontrolled—resulted in knifings, shootings, injuries, arrests, and consequent heightening of gang friction. Parenthetically, in 1967, the attempts of the Chicago Police Commissioner to negotiate with gang leaders were unsuccessful. Tragically, a series of shootings and injuries ensued.

Negotiations with gangs by militant organizations primarily served the interests of gang leaders to obtain additional status, prestige, and advantages on their own terms. Gang leaders were generally unable or unwilling to influence the membership of their own groups and were at first little identified, nor did they cause others to be identified with the ideas and principles of civil rights or militant organizations.

The most successful early efforts to co-opt delinquent youths probably occurred in Watts by militant groups, such as those included in an umbrella organization called the Temporary Alliance of Local Organizations (TALO), that were strongly neighborhood-based, where leadership of organizations was in close communication and understood the need and strivings of such youths. The elements of protest and personal "race" expression, however, appeared insufficient over time to sustain the allegiance of gang youths, without program success and especially without financial return or jobs.

The least successful efforts thus far have probably been sponsored by groups such as the Progressive Labor Movement, pro-Mao or Castro Communist, and SDS groups. These efforts have been launched, for example, through a recreational program or a bookstore located in a slum area, or more recently through requests for participation in university sit-ins or protest actions. The doctrines of radical dissent and the intellectualism of revolution, however, are ordinarily foreign and incomprehensible to delinquent youths, who generally seek not to overthrow but to gain more adequate—often quick and exploitive—entry into the existing economic, social, and political system. These organizations have succeeded primarily in being exploited themselves by delinquents, for example, through use of facilities for "blowing pot" or getting drunk or as a target for aggression and property destruction. Gangs have used situations of confrontation to express their presence and to demonstrate that outside neighborhood or community interference would not be tolerated. They have at times served, therefore, the interests of the establishment by preventing wider organizational coalitions of interest.

The reasons for the limited success, until recently, of civil rights, black power, and revolutionary groups in obtaining the support of delinquent gangs may be summarized as follows:

1. The causes of these organizations were not sufficiently understood nor attractive to rank-and-file gang members. Scratch a gang youth and you find a conservative, not a radical. He wants basically to get into, use, and especially to manipulate the system, not to change it.

2. Civil rights leaders were not sufficiently sensitive to the psychological problems of lower-class delinquents. They did not at first understand the complexity and intransigence of delinquent-conflict subcultures. Nor did they adequately understand the dimensions of personal and social deprivation of these youths. Civil rights workers were primarily concerned with dialogue and militancy. They tended to be articulate, intellectual, idealistic, and middle-class in their habits and orientations. Gang youths tend to be nonverbal, pragmatic, materialistic, and interested in immediate gratification, and strangely enough in the integrity of day-to-day human relationships rather than causes. They were more interested in certain qualities of relationship than in ideals and organizational interests.

3. Jobs, income, and other tangible rewards or evidences of status were not forthcoming to gang youths by the civil rights or extremist organizations. Gang youths required immediate gratifications or concrete rewards as well as altruistic motivations to obtain their services.

4. Management or utilization of hard-core delinquents requires intensive, skilled, and multidimensional involvement in various social aspects of their life experience. A great many problems must be attended to in dealing with delinquents, including change of group norms, literacy training, job or career development, as well as personal self-fulfillment. Civil rights groups were not at first sufficiently prepared, knowledgeable, or skilled in their work with delinquents.

Nevertheless, the problems of successful use of youth gangs by civil rights and militant community groups may not be insolvable. There is evidence in the past year of more effective communication and working relationships between the gangs and these organizations. Civil rights leaders, for example, the Reverend Jesse Jackson of Operation Breadbasket, are learning to speak the language of gang youths. Issues of poverty, job discrimination, and urban renewal can be communicated to and made meaningful for delinquent youths. Rewards of status, income, and notoriety can be forthcoming for participants. The complexities of dealing with volatile gang youths can be learned by militant organizers. Delinquents are susceptible to radical ideology when it is supported by a rhetoric of militancy and social justice which directly affects them and their families.

The participation of leaders of the Young Lords, a Spanish-speaking gang in Chicago, in a community sit-in at the McCormick Theological Seminary for day care and 500 members of the Black P. Stone Nation (Blackstone Rangers) in a Poor People's March on the Illinois Legislature in Springfield, organized by Operation Breadbasket, both during May of 1969, are cases in point. Also, hundreds of members of the Black P. Stone Nation, Disciples, and Conservative Vicelords participated in demonstrations against the construction industry and unions during the summer and fall of 1969. They were a well-disciplined group organized by the Black Coalition (The Coalition for United

Community Action) for purposes of bringing pressure to bear for more black persons in construction jobs.

New Liberal Politician

These are executives of gang control and law-enforcement agencies, community action groups, and civil rights organizations, committed to liberal causes and social change, but who have also attempted to use their connections with the delinquency problem for their personal political advancement. These leaders tend to view themselves as directly or indirectly heading a youth movement against entrenched establishment leadership. The object of such a movement is to legally force a change in the political structure, in particular to drive out incumbent city councilmen, state assemblymen or congressmen who are opposed to civil rights and progressive legislation. These aspiring politicians usually view elected officials as corrupt, inefficient, or irrelevant and as a major contributory cause of the social problems that afflict low-income ghetto communities, including delinquency. The capture and assumption of political power is viewed as the *sine qua non* of curing the social ills of the community.

The new politician has certain distinguishing characteristics. He is very sensitive to and directly familiar with the problem of hard-core delinquency in the slum. He is articulate, intelligent, ambitious, and highly committed to a progressive social point of view. He regards his own direct experience with people in the ghetto, including delinquents, as his best qualification for efforts to change the system.

That this type of politician is rising in slum communities is evidenced by the following:

An ex-gang worker supervisor in Chicago attempted unsuccessfully to gain the democratic nomination for Congress. He sought major support from gang youths, their parents, friends, as well as nongang youths. Gang youths directly participated in distribution of literature and in other activities related to his campaign, such as a protest march, when he was shot by an unknown assailant. Recently he was elected as an independent alderman to the City Council.

The executive director of a city youth commission—one of the country's largest public delinquency-control and prevention agencies—personally directed a program to organize youths throughout the city, comprising many delinquent youths and gang representatives. His staff members were convinced that its purpose was to build political support for the mayor or even to develop a cadre of young men and women who would support his own bid for public office in the not-too-distant future.

The executive of an antipoverty program in a small eastern city, formerly a gang worker, was building a youth movement, comprising mainly delinquent youths from the ghetto. He planned to encourage the young people to bring pressure on the political system for the ouster of local aldermen who represented white, corrupt power interests. He saw his major mission as bringing increased social and economic opportunities to young people in the ghetto. He viewed himself as available for political office or at least instrumental in directing efforts to unseat elected officials presently in office.

A former action program director encouraged and sponsored the organization of a youth movement, composed mainly of gang members and delinquents. The youth groups engaged in protest marches and demonstrations for improved recreation facilities and additional job opportunities. He indicated these were only the first efforts in a campaign to develop political power by himself and these youths.

Some of these aspiring politicians have already been successful in election campaigns; however, it is too soon to determine whether commitments to the interests of youth gangs in the ghettoes will be fulfilled. Very early indications suggest that the youth problem was primarily a device for personal political advancement. Youth gangs generally comprise too elusive and transient a constituency to constrain the newly elected liberal politicians, some of whom have already joined forces with established political interests.

The strength of these new politicians, further, is open to question. They tend to underestimate the power of the existing political structure and governmental bureaucracy. They have not developed viable organizational machinery. There is some tendency to self-deception about available resources, staff, organizing ability, indigenous neighborhood support, and the strength of the opposition. These leaders have not yet acquired sufficient support from dissident or new elements within the established political or governmental structure. But the potential for political success based on support of gang youth interest and manpower clearly exists. For example, elected liberal politicians representing the ghetto community, when under extreme attack from other elements in the city, may call on, or find themselves receiving, the support of youth gangs. The *Chicago Sun-Times* reported:

> Gary Mayor Richard G. Hatcher declared Wednesday he saw no threat of any kind in the appearance before the city council Tuesday night [of] about 60 tough-looking motorcycle gang members.
>   The council had been meeting to decide on a bill to strip Hatcher of nine of his fifteen appointments to the Gary Human Relations Commission.
>   . . . Included in the speeches made by the gang spokesman were statements that all Hatcher had to do was "Pull our chain and we'll bark, and we bark hard." [17]

Gang and Ex-Gang Leaders

Usually leaders of youth gangs, especially fighting gangs, have sought and claimed influence over delinquent youths and groups in the neighborhood or immediate community. The president of a gang, who is talented and ambitious, may also attempt to extend his hegemony to other gangs in areas throughout the city. Gang affiliates, divisions, or subgroups are recruited or incorporated as a function of intergang hostilities. Also, the power of the gang for community relations and political purposes may depend on its size and fighting reputation.

In the last several years, many of these gang leaders have obtained positions as program aides or community workers performing a variety of recreational, social welfare, and organizational tasks, mainly in relation to other youths. Social agencies, churches, and community action agencies have attempted to capitalize on the influence of the gang leaders to expand their own organizational programs. On the other hand, the gang leaders, highly sensitive to opportunities that enhance gang interests, are quick to learn political techniques which build their own organizations. They play a complex game of serving the agency, building their own following, and augmenting personal political interests. The youth decides he can develop his own youth or young adult movement. He makes connections with politicians and executives of various public bureaucracies. A Republican nominee for Congress in 1966 solicited the leaders of a major gang in Chicago for help in his fall election campaign. A picture of the Congressional nominee, surrounded by the gang leaders, appeared in a citywide newspaper. The gang leader is called upon as an advisor, consultant, or molder of youth opinion. He is asked for ideas and participation in solving recreational, sanitation, and other local problems. He may even be elected honorary youth-alderman or mayor of his neighborhood, or even to the local or citywide antipoverty action council.

The leaders of the Blackstone Rangers (now the Black P. Stone Nation), one of the most politically sensitive gangs in Chicago, if not the country, have engaged in a variety of important and controversial community affairs. They have supported candidates for City Council, Congress, Mayor. Leaders have participated in Model Cities planning discussions. They have negotiated with a ward committeeman and a state assemblyman for legal assistance and public support of gang activities. Leaders have engaged in a running public battle with the Chicago Police Department, especially its Gang Intelligence Unit, over the issue of police brutality and harassment. A legal suit was recently filed by the president of the gang against the mayor and the police department.

The leaders of the Black P. Stone Nation have also claimed that their gang is a community organization—indeed, that it is the most representative organization in their community. Its leaders have elicited the support of churches, university professors, social agencies, and federal bureaucrats in their efforts to develop organizational potential. It also aroused the curiosity and ire of Senator McClellan's Permanent Subcommittee on Investigations of the Committee on Government Operations during the summer of 1968.[18] The leader of the Blackstone Rangers, Jeff Fort, was cited by the committee and the Senate for contempt in refusing to answer the committee's questions. What greater evidence for the role of the gang leader as political actor!

The following problems arise, however, in the development of the role of political or community leader by the gang chieftain:

1. At the point where the gang leader firmly identifies with the role of community organizer, political leader, or business entrepreneur and seeks to solve a variety of community problems, he initiates a process of alienation from his delinquent group and the delinquent subculture. The base of his power with other gang delinquents rapidly evaporates, unless many of the other members of his gang are also provided with alternate roles and access to opportunities. In this case, the base is no longer the delinquent group but usually a young adult neighborhood interest group. Also, the political power of the gang may depend in large measure on its continuing threat as a force for violence.

2. It is important to understand, furthermore, that the gang leader, despite his and the claims of others to the contrary, is not really head of an efficient or well-disciplined organization. Almost all gangs are diffuse, transitory, organizationally weak entities except during times of gang warfare or when receiving support from external organizational sources. The power of the youth gang in the community or political arena is ordinarily quite fragile.

3. The gang leader, or, more accurately, the ex-gang leader, is not ordinarily prepared by his own limited background of education, experience, or tem-

perament for the complex maneuvering, negotiating, pressuring, cajoling, bargaining, and administering required of the political leader. It is the rare gang leader who has sufficient ability, community support, and good fortune to overcome the limitations of his social environment and gang training.

4. Also, the gang leader is usually not firmly committed to a cause, an ideology, a social or even a business program. He is easily co-opted by a fairly well-paying job, which may provide him immediately with better clothes, his own apartment, and a down payment on a car. He is loath to devote long hours to planning and preparation, to politicking, especially for community betterment. He is usually interested in his own immediate personal advantage, the easiest way he knows how.

However, participation by gang leaders or ex-gang leaders in a new type of politicoeconomic process is growing. In the past two years, gangs have graduated to economic development organizations and nonprofit corporations; their leaders have learned how to negotiate with federal and local agencies, businesses, chambers of commerce, politicians, private foundations, police commanders, and others to obtain sanction and support for various enterprises, for example, small businesses, job-training programs, community planning, housing, and recreation services, theater and art groups, youth patrol operations. The budgets of the more successful ex-gang or quasi-gang corporations may be a hundred thousand dollars or more a year. Professional and technical expertise may be hired by these corporations. Political problems are minimized if the gang does not challenge the existing political structure.

Communication and bonds of solidarity are growing between certain youth organization leaders and radical groups. Leaders of the Young Lords, for example, are identified with the ideology of the Black Panther Party and revolutionary groups of the Third World. Organization of other youth groups for political and ideological purposes rather than to enhance gang fighting reputation is developing.

Agency Executive

Most gang control or service programs in the major cities have arisen in response to community concern and alarm over serious gang conflicts and depredations. These programs, initiated in the 1940's and 1950's as pilot projects, were rapidly expanded to become major, if not massive, components of citywide youth welfare and control systems. In the process, administrators of these expanding youth-serving agencies have sought and achieved a large measure of influence in the definition of the community delinquency problem and in decisions about resources to cope with it.

The development of the political role of these agency executives, moreover, has often been a result of the ignorance of the community about the complex causes of delinquency and of the ineffectiveness of various remedies. The agency administrator has successfully perpetuated this condition by systematic avoidance of evaluation of his program or of the implications of program failure and by conscious exploitation of the community's dread of youth gangs. Extensive public relations campaigns demonstrating the value of gang control activities, frequent fund-raising drives to sustain the program, and ingenious stimulation of crises and playing on community fears about delinquency constitute the stock-in-trade of the successful executive. The mayor's office, board of directors of his agency, the newspapers, and citizen groups all play a collusive role in the drama of purgation of the community's fears and anxieties about delinquent gangs. The gang fight crises, the newspaper pronouncements, the high-level community meetings, and the crash programs which result serve to maintain collective inattention to the forces that make for and sustain delinquency.

More public attention has probably been centered on gang control efforts in the past twenty years than on any other welfare program, with the possible recent exception of public assistance. Most gang work programs, and their expansion, have been devices by executives to acquire funds for other agency programs—community organization, recreation, casework, day care—less likely to be adequately funded. Settlements, Boys Clubs, YMCA's, traditionally not engaged in outreach service to gangs, have enlarged the scope of their activities to capitalize on the community's interest and concern with gangs. At the same time, there is some evidence, dating from the Cambridge-Somerville study [19] before World War II, to indicate that the bulk of existing community-based delinquency control, treatment, and prevention programs, particularly those concentrating on recreation, intra- or interpersonal approaches, may be of marginal or even negative value.

A strange process of accountability occurs in which extravagant claims are made by the executive for the value of the program. He is concerned with every gang fracas that takes place in his jurisdiction, but at the same time it is extraordinarily difficult to assign specific responsibility to him or his agency. Each gang outbreak or program failure becomes an opportunity for the executive to exploit community anger and anxiety to obtain more funds for program expansion. Problems do arise, however, in the competitive arena of human welfare and gang control services. Other agency directors are threatened by the expansiveness of a particular administrator. Each agency seeks to maintain or enlarge its cut of the pie of voluntary or public funds. Competition, hostility, and open "warfare" among agencies may result. More than one police chief has accused and attacked a street gang work agency or a church program for increasing the incidence of delinquency and gang warfare. The police department itself may be internally divided on the best approach for dealing with gangs. The push, the thrust, and the politicking for survival may diminish only when the aggressive or ambitious executive has been removed from power, when a particular agency or a particular department has been stripped of its sanction to deal with gangs, or when a carefully worked out division of resources and responsibilities has been temporarily developed among the agencies.

Without clear criteria of effective service, without community knowledge of what constitutes appropriate means or appropriate goals of service, the director is left to operate on the basis of what captures the interest, serves the whims, or mollifies the fears of fund-controlling or fund-giving groups or individuals. The role of the executive is primarily that of a bargaining and political agent who sees that his program survives and obtains the largest share of public or private resources available.

Also, it may be argued that some control-oriented social agency programs have increased rather than diminished delinquency in a given area. For example, on the rare occasions when an evaluation is conducted, research evidence indicates that the sudden termination of gang worker service, for example, by the Los Angeles Probation Department resulted in lowering of delinquent activity by a virulent, cohesive gang.[20] The very presence of the street worker apparently served to cohere the group and consequently increase its commitment to delinquent norms. Also, there is some evidence from another city that an agency director's efforts to expand programs stimulated a process of labeling young people as delinquents not previously so defined. The director, to justify program expansion, found even more delinquents in the community. Youngsters suddenly received attention and status for reputed antisocial activities or tendencies which previously would have gone unnoticed. A self-fulfilling prophecy resulted. The paradox is that delinquency may be encouraged by the very agency and system established to reduce it.

Professional Reformer

Finally, a new breed of professional reformer has arisen, concerned with innovative and basic solutions or changes in institutional systems. Various priests, ministers, university professors, bureaucrats, and social agency and business personnel, dissatisfied with past attempts, including their own, to cope with problems of the ghetto and focusing on gang delinquency, support the notion of maximum feasible participation of the most alienated members of the ghetto in community decision-making. The problems of gang delinquency, race, housing, and others are to be resolved by the gangs themselves, often on their own terms. The professional reformer assumes the weakness of other local neighborhood organizations and sees the gang as the most powerful group in the ghetto with positive potential for changing slum conditions.

These reformers carry out organizational and political activities in support of the corporate development of the gang. Proposals for gang projects are written and funds negotiated with private foundations and governmental agencies; support for these projects is obtained through a variety of devices, including not only persuasion but political manipulation and threat of violent consequences. For example, the Youth Manpower proposal on behalf of the Blackstone Rangers and East Side Disciples, sponsored by the Woodlawn Organization in Chicago, was written by a staff member of the Office of Economic Opportunity. Furthermore, he "rammed through" the proposal on the threat that prevention of a riot in Woodlawn could not be guaranteed unless the mayor's office permitted funding and implementation of the project. The mayor acceded to pressure from this federal bureaucrat, although he was "equivocably unopposed" to the project. The federal official was less successful in obtaining support for the project from other community and national groups. While the ostensible purpose of the project was youth manpower training, its underlying intent apparently was to provide gangs with resources to develop their capacities on their own terms. The assumption possibly was that such development would serve to rearrange youth-serving agencies' patterns, even political patterns in the city, as well as lead to some new, undefined but positive, type of transitional teen-age and young adult institution.

The professional reformer regards existing social agencies and political groups as ineffective. He tends to view himself as a knight in shining armor doing battle with a host of reactionary or do-nothing forces both within and outside his own organization. He tends to operate alone or with limited institutional or community support as yet. He makes a cardinal virtue of supporting the underdog and weak groups. As a rule, his influence tends to be situational, depending on the availability of resources, lack of significant opposition from his own organization, and strength of the gangs. The gangs, playing their own political game of expanding group interests, may "cut loose" from the professional reformer when opposition pressures are too great or when resources are available from other sources.

It may be argued that this kind of professional reformer is a social rebel without a strong power base. He is also using the gang as an instrument of social change, but the gang is not always clearly committed to social change. The professional reformer tends to be a loser in this kind of enterprise, unless he can mobilize a considerable amount of community or federal support. In a period of political conservatism, fiscal control, and fear of radical subversion, widespread political and organizational support is not likely to be forthcoming. . . .

CONCLUSION

. . . In large measure, the problem of the politicization of the gang is ultimately the problem of lack of resources for a deprived population. The gang is the volatile and combustible edge of the larger problem of poverty and racism, which can be solved only by the input of additional or the redistribution of existing societal resources.

The consequences of the great social and technological changes for our time are not yet fully apparent. What is evident, however, is that youth gang members in our slums are somehow part of the problem and are at the same time being asked and want to participate in coping with the effects of these changes. To what extent they will heed the call, how positive their involvement in new structures and strategies, and how positive official and establishment responses will be are still to be determined. Ghetto youths seem no longer content to sit on the political sidelines and engage only in delimited and periodic gang fighting, assaults, robberies, and burglaries. The civil rights movement, black power and black nationalist efforts, and antipoverty programs have raised the aspirations of these youths and stimulated them to seek a larger share in their affluent society. For example, a national coalition of street youth groups, Youth Organizations United (YOU), has been created recently with over 200 member groups to facilitate this process. Delinquents have been urged to awaken to the potentials of their mass power. A force for good in the further enhancement of our political democracy or a force for evil in its destruction may have been let loose. Either communities will better aid in fulfilling the social potentials of these ghetto youths or communities ridden with riot, revolt, and vast human waste will result. Only enlightened and progressive-minded citizens, politicians, professionals, and bureaucrats can possibly make the right decisions. The decisions must be guided, furthermore, by a set of public policies obviously different from those that presently prevail at the federal level. The specific program devices may well be incidental to the general social purpose and magnitude of the efforts that need to be undertaken.

NOTES

[1] Herbert Asbury, *The Gangs of New York: An Informal History of the Underworld* (New York: Alfred A. Knopf, 1927), p. 105.

[2] *Ibid.*, p. 118.

[3] *Ibid.*

[4] Frederic M. Thrasher, *The Gang* (Chicago: University of Chicago Press, 1927), pp. 462–63.

[5] *Ibid.*, p. 456.

[6] For a description of the role of the worker and his practice, see Irving A. Spergel, *Street Gang Work: Theory and Practice* (Reading, Mass.: Addison-Wesley, 1966).

[7] Thrasher, *op. cit.*

[8] Clifford R. Shaw, *The Jack-Roller* (Chicago: University of Chicago Press, 1930); Shaw and Henry D. McKay, *Juvenile Delinquency and Urban Areas* (Chicago: University of Chicago Press, 1969).

[9] Solomon Kobrin, "The Conflict of Values in Delinquency Areas," *American Sociological Review*, 16 (1961), 653–61.

[10] See Irving A. Spergel, "Street Gang Work," *Encyclopedia of Social Work* (forthcoming 1971).

[11] Albert K. Cohen, *Delinquent Boys: The Culture of the Gang* (New York: The Free Press, 1955).

[12] Richard A. Cloward and Lloyd E. Ohlin, *Delinquency and Opportunity*, (New York: The Free Press, 1960).

[13] Walter B. Miller, "Lower Class Culture as a Generating Milieu of Gang Delinquency," *Journal of Social Issues*, 14, No. 3 (1958), 5–19.

[14] *Chicago Journalism Review*, 2, No. 6 (June 1969), 7–12.

[15] Dennis Neil, "Gang Control: Out of Control," *Philadelphia Magazine* (Oct. 1969), pp. 1–3.

[16] Terry Ann Knopf, *Youth Patrols: An Experiment in Community Participation*, (Waltham, Mass.: Brandeis University, The Lemberg Center for the Study of Violence, 1969).

[17] *Chicago Sun-Times*, May 8, 1969.

[18] Permanent Subcommittee on Investigations of the Committee on Government Operations, U.S. Senate, Twentieth Congress, Second Session, *Riots, Civil and Criminal Disorders*, Pts. 9–13 (June, July, Sept., and Oct., 1968).

[19] Edwin Powers and Helen Witmer, *An Experiment in the Prevention of Delinquency: The Cambridge-Somerville Youth Study* (New York: Columbia University Press, 1951).

[20] Malcolm W. Klein, *From Association to Guilt: The Group Guidance Project in Juvenile Gang Intervention* (Los Angeles: Youth Studies Center, University of Southern California, 1968).

5. Inter-institutional Conflict and Delinquency Prevention *

WALTER B. MILLER

JUVENILE DELINQUENCY is a major area of concern in the United States today. Although there is evidence of some increase in the actual incidence of juvenile crime, it is equally evident that the intensity of public concern over this issue has increased far more rapidly than the demonstrated statistical increase. This paper will focus, not on juvenile crime as such, but on the larger adult community that maintains explicit responsibility in this area.

It is the thesis of this paper that the nature of current concern over juvenile delinquency serves important latent functions for substantial segments of the adult community. If this thesis is true, we would expect to find, as in all areas where a significant discrepancy exists between the overt or recognized aspects of a phenomenon and its covert aspects or latent functions: (1) discrepancies and contradictions between officially stated policy and actual operating procedure; (2) recurrent failure to follow through on plans whose objectives conform to officially stated positions but whose execution would in fact run counter to the latent function; and (3) much conflict over goals and methods both between concerned institutional systems and between subunits within these systems. The net result of these forces would be to produce action stalemates both through failure to take action and through mutual blocking of efforts to the end that the latently functional status quo is preserved.

That public concern over juvenile delinquency serves *psychological* functions for adults as individuals has been maintained by several investigators. This paper will attempt to show that the nature of current institutional practice regarding delinquency serves important *structural* functions as well; that is, for the great majority of organized institutions that maintain programs directed at juvenile delinquency, the adoption of operating procedures and philosophies that would be effective in reducing juvenile crime would, in fact, pose severe threats to the viability of the institution. The focus here will be on the area of delinquency *prevention* rather than on methods of dealing with the adjudicated delinquent. Since the area of prevention is far less structured and has developed fewer established operating procedures than the area of treatment or disposition, the dynamics of institutional functioning in this area are revealed in much sharper relief.

It has been established that there is far more law-violating behavior by adolescents than is officially acted on; according to one study, the actual number of potentially arrestable delinquents is three times that of those actually arrested. Once an individual is officially apprehended for the commission of a delinquent act or acts, a whole series of established procedures are set into motion; the individual may be released with a warning, put on probation, or sentenced to undergo a variety of corrective measures ranging

* Reprinted from *Human Organization*, Vol. 17, No. 3 (Fall, 1958), pp. 20–23, by permission of the author.

from a citizenship course through psychiatric treatment to straight confinement. But in the area of "prevention" things are much less well established. There is growing sentiment to the effect that "prevention" of juvenile crime would be a much sounder procedure than attempting to deal with the individual once he has already committed a crime, and would be much more economical in the long run. But then the question becomes—how does one "prevent"? Once something has happened you can take steps as a consequence of that occurrence, but what steps should you take for something that has not happened yet, but that might? Thus, while there are many well-established institutions—courts, police, correctional institutions, psychiatric agencies—whose operating procedures and philosophies are geared to handling individuals who have committed delinquent acts and been apprehended, there are, with a few exceptions, *no* established institutional structures whose major responsibility is delinquency prevention, and whose institutional values and operating philosophies are geared to that objective. Existing organizations undertake prevention, if at all, as a relatively minor adjunct to major institutional responsibilities which lie elsewhere—a fact that has important bearing on the potential effectiveness of prevention programs.

Following sections will describe very briefly the experience of one large eastern city in attempting to institute and maintain a "preventive" program on the community level. In 1950, rising public apprehension over juvenile delinquency in general, and gang violence in particular, produced demands for action from many quarters. Since gang activity was a focus of concern, and much gang delinquency is undetectable or undetected, traditional approaches based on restriction or treatment were seen as unfeasible, and pressures to institute some sort of community-based preventive program were exerted on the major institutional structures with assumed or assigned responsibility in the area of juvenile crime.

I

The city contained scores of intricately interrelated organizations, both public and private, varying widely in size, scope, and method of operations, and in assigned or claimed area of jurisdiction or concern with juvenile crime. Of these, about a dozen public and private organizational groupings maintained major responsibility in the area of juvenile crime. The principal public agencies were the municipal government, the recreation department, the police department, the courts, the public schools, and the state youth corrections division. Major private groupings were medical and psychiatric clinics, social work agencies, churches, universities, and various special cause groups, such as ethnic associations and crime-prevention societies.

Initial pressures produced a variety of statements as to the desirability of a preventive program, but no action. A complex set of maneuvers was carried on for about three years, usually involving the appointment of special committees which then appointed a study group which turned in a set of recommendations strongly affirming the desirability of a preventive program, and at the same time explaining why such a program was not the responsibility of that particular organization. This continuing stalemate was finally broken early in 1953, primarily through combined pressures from two ethnic groups, the Jews and the Negroes, after a prominent Jewish clergyman had been murdered, allegedly by a Negro teen-age gang. The Jews, acting through their organized representative groupings, inferentially charged the Negroes with anti-Semitism; the Negroes, through their organized group- ings, intimated that this charge indicated anti-Negro sentiment on the part of the Jews. Two other groups whose interests were being threatened by gang activity—the public schools and the settlement houses—added their pressures to those of the Jews and Negroes, and, in the spring of 1953, a central de- linquency committee was created, comprising representatives of over one hundred youth-concerned groupings in the metropolitan area, including the major groups cited above. At the time this committee was formed, many statements were made by all groupings—police, courts, the municipal admin- istration, churches, private agencies—pledging their fullest mutual cooperation in this enterprise aimed at coping with the city gang problem.

Despite the sense of urgency and crisis which attended the organization of the central committee, no concrete action was taken for more than a year. This year was filled with indecision, groping for direction, and constant mutual blocking and conflict, sometimes veiled, sometimes overt, among the agencies represented on the central committee. A great variety of proposals was forwarded and debated, reflecting many divergent conceptions of the causes and proper treatment of juvenile crime, and the group seemed unable to reach any agreement on a positive course of action. After six months, a sociology professor at a local university was persuaded to accept responsibil- ity for formulating a plan of action, and in June of 1954—four and a half years after the initial moves, and a year and a half after the murder which had broken the stalemate—a special demonstration project in delinquency prevention was set up in one district of the city. By this time, several of the major organizations originally represented on the central committee had terminated active affiliation principally, the police and the Jewish clergy. The Jews lost interest rapidly when it developed that anti-Semitism had played a relatively small role in gang attacks on Jews.

The prevention project, which was to operate for three years, was staffed primarily by social workers, and included three service programs—a program of direct service to selected "delinquogenic" families, a community organiza- tion program, and, as a major effort, a program of direct work with delin- quent corner gangs. Although it was the creation of the central committee, once project operations actually started, the committee became progressively disenchanted with its offspring. As the project took action in more definite and visible ways, it became clear that many of its methods and the operating philosophies behind them were in radical conflict with the institutional ideals of the various groups represented on the central committee. This was evi- denced in responses ranging from passive nonparticipation, through with- drawal, to active opposition.

During the three years of the project's existence, the executive board of the central committee became a battleground for its component organizations, with the project and its methods serving as a pawn in these conflicts. After the first meeting, at which a project worker presented a report on his ac- tivities, the representative of the Catholic Archdiocese resigned in indignation from the executive board. Following this incident, a watchdog committee was set up to oversee the project; the chairman of this committee was a Protestant clergyman who was strongly opposed to major methods of the project. About a year later the project became involved in direct conflict with the state division of corrections, with enmity reaching sufficient intensity that the corrections division issued an order forbidding its parolees to participate in project activities, and, in fact, jailed one parolee who defied this order. The social agencies initially regarded the program with great suspicion, as did the schools. During the latter part of the program the city recreation department representative on the central committee, incensed by a report issued by the project, demanded that no further reports be issued unless approved by the central committee. During the second year, funds to support the project, which were raised by the central committee, became increasingly difficult to obtain, and about this time the committee's original chairman, who had been active in initiating and supporting the project, was replaced, without his prior knowledge, by another man who was far less assertive.

Shortly after the start of the project's third year, its director resigned, partly because of increasing difficulties in obtaining financing, and no attempt was made to replace him with a person of equivalent status. Before the director left, he formulated a detailed proposal for the establishment of a permanent delinquency-prevention agency under state and municipal auspices, using the project's experience as the basis of recommendations. The three-man committee chosen to present this program to the mayor and governor consisted of an amiable but aged chairman and the two most outspoken opponents of the project on the central committee. The recommendations for a state-municipal program presented under these auspices were rejected both by the mayor and governor. Once the program was officially terminated, the central committee appeared eager to forget that it had ever existed. Although federal support for postproject research had been obtained, members of the central committee were most reluctant to permit such continuation and questioned the right of the project to have sought these funds, despite the fact that authorization had been officially voted.

During the period when the project was subject to increasing opposition by its parent organizations on the central committee, these agencies were also engaged in attacking one another both in the arena of central committee meetings and through other media. A judge accused the police of inefficiency in dealing with delinquents and in keeping adequate crime statistics; a police chief accused the social welfare agencies of coddling delinquents; the director of a medical group accused the corrections division of increasing the delinquency of those in their care; a Catholic prelate accused the social work agencies of neglecting religion in their dealings with delinquents; a psychiatric agency head accused the police of harmful advocacy of punitive measures; the Archbishop accused enforcement agencies of politically motivated laxness in prosecuting delinquents; a group of legislators attempted to oust major officials of the youth corrections department over the issue of personnel qualifications. In addition, subunits within these larger organizations feuded with one another; a judge accused other judges of excessive leniency in dealing with juvenile offenders; a committee of the school department claimed that some teachers were fostering delinquency by being unable or unwilling to cope with school behavior problems; the Police Commissioner castigated and demoted a sizable group of patrolmen, charging them with inefficiency in dealing with juveniles in their area of jurisdiction; a Protestant clergyman claimed that some Protestant sects were failing in the fight against delinquency by remaining too aloof from community involvement.

II

We have, then, a situation that involves these elements: first, a social phenomenon—gang violence—that is universally condemned; a crisis incident that arouses deep feelings and provides a spur to direct action; the mobilization and pledged cooperation of all the major concerned institutional groupings of a major American city; and then—much delay and misdirected energy by these institutions in setting up a project to which they become progressively more hostile; constant interinstitutional conflict over a variety of issues; and finally a virtual stalemate in launching any sort of effective action to cope with the problem. This situation is by no means unique; it is found in many cities faced with similar problems—in particular, conflicts between the police, churches, courts, social agencies, and schools in the New York City gang situation have been widely publicized. This prevalent phenomenon—apparently universal agreement on a basic objective, gang control, coupled with mutual conflict leading to almost complete blocking of action—may be explained by focusing on the *means* proposed to secure the end, means that derive from the operating philosophies of the various concerned organizations. This paper suggests that operating philosophies may be *non*functional for the purpose of reducing juvenile crime, and that a consequence of differences in institutional philosophies is that a significant proportion of energy potentially directable to delinquency reduction is instead expended in conflict between institutions.

The nature of these differences may be illuminated by specifying six dimensions along which conflict takes place: these relate to differences in conceptions of the *etiology* of delinquency; of the *disposition* of the delinquent; of the *approach priority;* of the appropriate *organizational method;* and of the proper *status of personnel.*

Morality-Pathology. A major difference in assumptions as to the etiology of juvenile crime, as well as other forms of behavior, involves fundamental concepts of human nature. According to one school of thought, deviant or criminal behavior must be viewed in terms of morality and immorality; an individual is morally responsible for his own behavior, and failure to conform to norms and standards represents a triumph of evil forces over good in an inner struggle for which the individual is held personally responsible. The opposing school maintains that deviant or criminal behavior should be viewed in terms of sickness and health; that an individual who violates social and legal norms is, in fact, driven by inner forces over which he has relatively little control and which have their origins in pathological conditions of the organism.

Individual Locus-Social Locus. A second important difference involving etiological concepts relates to the locus of deviant behavior. One school attributes criminal behavior to forces within the *individual*—moral or physical-psychological—which may be dealt with by corrective measures directed at the individual; the other school finds the significant factors in the nature of the *social milieu* and sees basic alterations in social conditions as the necessary course of action.

Restriction-Rehabilitation. This dimension relates to the proper method of dealing with offenders. The restrictive school of thought advocates the separation or isolation of the individual from normal social intercourse on the assumption, first, that the *protection of society* is the paramount necessity and second, that punishment both serves as a deterrent to future violation and is merited in consequence of transgression. This dispositional prescription is generally forwarded by those espousing the morality concept of etiology. The treatment or rehabilitative school, basing procedure on the "pathology" conception of etiology, postulates "cure" or directed efforts to modify behavior patterns of the offending individual as of prime importance, with his restoration to normal social interaction a desired objective.

Action-Research. This dimension relates to consideration of priority in approaching the problem. One school maintains that the urgency of the situation, or the intensity of need, demands immediate action, based on the best knowledge currently available; the other maintains that far too little reliable information exists as the nature of the involved phenomena and methods of treatment, and that the most productive expenditure of energy can be made by undertaking systematic research to gain essential knowledge.

Localization-Centralization. This dimension concerns the issue of the most desirable method for organizing preventive programs. One school believes that programs should be undertaken within and by the local community, on the grounds that only local people are sufficiently familiar with the special conditions of the local situation for adequate understanding, and that local autonomy must be maintained. The centralization school maintains that the nature and magnitude of the problem demand mobilization of resources which local groups, operating independently, could not afford, and that, to be effective, resources must be pooled and efforts coordinated to avoid duplication and overlap.

Lay-Professional. This dimension relates to the qualifications and status of personnel who are to implement preventive programs. One school holds that only those who manifest characteristics similar to those of the subject population—either through similarities in class or locality status—can be effective, and that attributes essential to effectiveness, such as warmth and sympathy are independent of training. The other school maintains that work in so difficult an area demands that practitioners be exposed to a course of professional training that both imparts knowledge as to specialized procedures and eliminates those whose personality characteristics would be detrimental to this kind of work.

The various institutional structures related to delinquency tend to maintain characteristic syndromes of these etiological and procedural positions. The described positions are seldom maintained in the "pure" form, since they are presented here as polar extremes that define variable dimensions—and "middle positions," such as equal stress on action and research, may be taken, but most institutions involved do maintain definitely identifiable positions of varying intensity along these dimensions. Conflicts along the varying dimensions take place both *between* and within concerned institutions, but intrainstitutional differences are generally concealed from public notice. The most severe conflict occurs between institutions that take extreme opposing positions on all or most of these dimensions; conflict is less severe when there is disagreement on only one or two. For example, the major juvenile court of the city described above strongly supported the "morality" and "individual locus" concepts of etiology: the restrictive dispositional method, action priority, and localized organization. The major child psychiatry clinic supported the "pathology" etiological concept: rehabilitative treatment method, centralized organization, and use of professional implementary personnel. These positions put the two organizations in direct conflict in four of the six dimensions; in agreement over one—individual etiological locus—and in minor opposition over the action-research issue. Similar comparisons could be made between each set of involved institutions.

SUMMARY

The argument of this paper may be summarized as follows: There is much conflict over the issue of proper procedure among the different groups that maintain varying orders of responsibility for delinquency prevention. This conflict results in a lack of coordination and mutual blocking of efforts leading to a stalemate in reference to a community-supported objective. But these conflicts over method derive from the basic institutional philosophies of the several institutions; although these philosophies may be effective in facilitating achievement of the stated objectives of the institution, their maintenance is vital to the institution's continued existence and this latent objective has greater priority than the achievement of the institution's explicit objectives, and much greater priority than achieving objectives only peripherally related to the institution's primary explicit aims.

This situation would appear to have important implications for delinquency prevention. It would imply that the major impediment to effectiveness in this field relates more to the nature of relations among the various concerned institutions than to a lack of knowledge as to effective procedure. Much is now known about the causes of delinquency and promising ameliorative techniques have been developed. The principal difficulty lies in the *application* of these techniques, and any realistic possibility of such application depends almost entirely on existing institutional structures. This would suggest a shift in emphasis in current research and action efforts from a primary focus on the relations between implementing institutions and the subject population to the relationships among the institutions themselves. Both research and action efforts involve severe difficulties since they will touch on areas intimately related to the viability of the institution—areas all the more charged and sensitive, since they are frequently unconscious or implicit.

PART SIX

SOCIAL PLANNING AND THE PREVENTION AND CONTROL OF DELINQUENCY

Introduction

In a society that places great value on science and technology, it is not surprising that there is increasing support for developing a rational approach to many of the nation's social problems. In the field of delinquency prevention, control, and treatment, a rational approach stresses coordination and integration of efforts as well as problem-focused planning. Besides prizing rationality, however, Americans also favor dispersal of centers of authority, participation by citizens in community affairs, and the right to compete for social attention and economic resources—values associated with democracy and pluralism. The coexistence of these competing value orientations is a basic fact of life in America. Advocates of a planning perspective who do not recognize it may be acting as irrationally as those who oppose any attempts at centrally planned change. Given the fact that the value conflict is a real one, the newly emerging profession of social planning will have to live with value accommodations and trade-offs in the same fashion as do policemen, judges, correctional workers, and legislators.

Actually, the advocates of social planning at present comprise a rather weak interest group. Very few schools in the country are currently training students to fill the jobs that are becoming available on the city, state, and federal level. Although the supply may soon catch up with the demand, as departments of city planning, social work, and public administration adapt their programs, one difficulty exists that is not so easy to overcome—the low level of current planning technology in dealing with social problems such as delinquency. Instead of possessing a proved social-planning technology for the field of delinquency prevention, control, and treatment, we only have suggested approaches. Therefore, this section includes readings on suggested strategies that *could* set the goals for planning, readings about the ideal model for planning that *could* serve as a technical planning guide, and readings that highlight the problems in implementing planning approaches that *could* add to planning expertise.

The first two selections outline suggested strategies for dealing with delinquency. In an article addressed primarily to social workers, Kahn stresses four policy proposals: (1) expanding opportunities for disadvantaged youth, (2) exercising social control through individualization and treatment, (3) protecting individual legal rights, and (4) developing a system of case-finding, evaluation, and treatment through coordinated and integrated programs and services. Although Kahn provides ample evidence that he is aware of the inconsistencies in defining and labeling youth as delinquent, he appears to be reluctant to follow out the implications of his analysis by reducing the jurisdictional scope of the court, the law, or any of the other control agencies. In general, he places major reliance on expanding, improving, and coordinating existing services within the current system of handling delinquents. Kahn wants to save children, as did the founders of the system, but he is willing to add legal safeguards. If society provided more jobs, better education, and other opportunities for all youth, then Kahn would favor resources for case-by-case planning as an "untried weapon against delinquency."

The case-planning approach of Kahn is quite different from the strategy suggested by Wheeler, Cottrell, and Romasco in selection 2. Instead of focusing on individual motivation and treatment, they favor spending resources on altering the physical and social environment surrounding youth, including efforts to reduce delinquent opportunities. They cite evidence that youth often misbehave according to the attractiveness or temptation inherent in a situation; if street lights were more abundant at night or cars were built with tamper-proof locks, then fewer youngsters might get into trouble. Reducing the number of risk situations might also reduce the risk groups.

The evidence on behalf of expanding youth opportunities is not yet available, but it is clear that the programs involved are to be made available to *all* disadvantaged youth, not just the high-risk groups. While Kahn (selection 1) argues that this is morally right, Wheeler, Cottrell, and Romasco question whether this shotgun approach can yield many hits if the target is delinquency (selection 2). As a strategy to reduce delinquency, the youth-opportunities approach may not be efficient, even if it is eventually evaluated as effective. If the evidence for this conclusion were forthcoming, then the strategy for expanding youth opportunities might have to involve a choice between the values of efficiency and of equality of opportunity. On the other hand, if it is not effective, then planners would be faced with a quite different choice. They might be able to opt for the expansion of youth opportunity if it were effective although inefficient, but they would have difficulty advocating the spending of antidelinquency funds for an ineffective and inefficient program. If the latter were true, other grounds for expanding opportunities might have to be found—for example, the ground that it promotes education, citizenship, resource development, or individual growth.

Three readings provide approaches to the rational ideal of social planning. In selection 3, Robert MacIver, an elder statesman of American sociology, emphasizes the importance of coordinative planning. His emphasis is strongly influenced by the findings that emerged from an evaluation of the functioning of agencies charged with controlling and treating New York City delinquents. The study found lack of communication, coordination, and integrated effort. MacIver's approach to planning is therefore geared to ensuring that the city will create a responsible center of authority that will bring order and rationality to the current system.

Zweig and Morris, in selection 4, attempt to deal with more technical problems. However, their model of a planning guide assumes that the planner is separate from the ongoing agencies and possesses a mandate from an "innovating organization." The ideal guide assumes that the planner can define problems at any level, but the example offered is at a neighborhood level. The advantage of this problem-focused approach is that the planner is not theoretically bound to accept the existing arrangement of services. A disadvantage of this model is that it does not strive to be comprehensive; problems are attacked in piecemeal fashion, perhaps even on an opportunistic basis.

In selection 5, Skoler attempts to state the case for a more comprehensive model. His views are of some importance, since at the time the article appeared, in July, 1968, Skoler was deputy director of the Law Enforcement Assistance Administration of the U.S. Department of Justice; this is the federal agency that is legally responsible for approving and funding state planning and program grants to combat crime and delinquency. Skoler argues that the police, courts, and correction agencies should be treated as a criminal-justice system with interdependent linkages and consequences. While subsystem planning is necessary, the major goal is to provide a master plan of criminal justice. This guide for super-rationality is quite similar to the city planner's ideal that urban-renewal programs be fitted into a master plan. The goals are laudable; however, it appears doubtful whether legislators and program administrators will wait patiently for the completion of comprehensive plans before urging program expenditures. Furthermore, it is unclear which groups would benefit from a comprehensive program and which would lose influence as a result.

The differences between planning methods could, of course, influence the kind of social planning that would actually occur at the local, city, state, or federal level. The competition may appear irrational and wasteful; however, in the absence of much experience with any of the suggested planning guides, it might be useful to experiment. At this point, we lack evidence that any one approach will yield especially effective results in the treatment, control, or prevention of delinquency. It is even conceivable that one or more planning methods might prove effective in controlling delinquency but not in treating or preventing it. Other combinations of goal achievement are also possible.

From a broad perspective, social planning is another programmatic approach to the delinquency problem. Why shouldn't planning methods be evaluated scientifically with as much dispassion as community treatment programs, police-community advisory boards, nonjudicial dispositions, and other program proposals? A premature decision on planning method may prove as retrogressive as maintaining that the residential treatment center is the ideal program for rehabilitating delinquents. In the absence of certain knowledge, encouraging a competitive search for effective solutions is a sound social policy. As we gain knowledge about planning methods, we can attempt to implement a policy of rational restriction on the competition between technologies.

In evaluating the effectiveness of planning method (and competence), it is important to distinguish between the plan as a recommendation for action and the actual implementation of the guide for action. A variety of nontechnical influences can shape the recommendations and implementation. Many of these influences can be perceived as representing competing interest groups or individuals. In effect, the purity of the plan's recommendations and implementation may depend on the outcome of the value conflict between democratic pluralism and centrally planned change. These realities of social planning are vividly described in selection 6 as the "dilemmas of social reform."

Marris and Rein describe the complexities of social planning in major cities in the early 1960's, when the Public Affairs Department of the Ford Foundation and the President's Committee on Juvenile Delinquency jointly and separately funded community-planning and action programs in a number of cities. The "gray areas" programs of the Foundation and the "opportunity" programs of the President's Committee proved to be the forerunners of the War on Poverty.

Both programs were broadly conceived to deal with urban problems affecting inner-city youth. The President's Committee operated from the assumption that inner-city delinquency stemmed primarily from frustration experienced in striving to overcome barriers to opportunity; the social environment, rather than individual personality, required change. The Ford Foundation was willing to rely mostly on its promise of funds to negotiate a workable program that its staff approved. But the President's Committee attempted to reform the social environment of youth by engaging in a formal planning process that analyzed problems and evaluated solutions. As Marris and Rein note, although they differed in their emphasis on planning, both funding agencies were forced to recognize that reform of social institutions required (1) recruitment of a coalition of power strong enough to obtain the goals; (2) respect for the democratic tradition that expects citizens to play a part in the determination of policies; and (3) presenting the policies as based on rationality and scientific analysis.

The programs experienced conflict in starting the planning process, developing plans, and realizing the plans. In Philadelphia, for example, there was a year-long fight over the choice of director of the agency that would set up a comprehensive program. In Los Angeles, in order to avoid conflicts between existing agencies, programs were included in the plan that were not demonstrably innovative or even appropriate. In other cities, where there was agreement over the proposed reforms, conflict arose over control of the program's operation and funds.

Marris and Rein, after discussing political intrusions on rational planning, conclude that planning cannot insist on formal coordination of conflicting groups as a prerequisite for their working together. Which groups dominate in the coordination is an outcome of shifts in the balance of political power in a community. Coordination, integration of effort, and rational planning are most likely to occur when a stable coalition of power is in favor of this approach. Social planning cannot achieve a new coalition of power merely by appealing to a commitment to intellectual rationality. Marris and Rein contend that realizing new plans may have to depend on placing new men in positions of power, not just proposing new ideas. They argue for a planning process that is pragmatic, sensitive to political opportunities, and selective in choosing targets.

Supporters of comprehensive criminal-justice planning will find little intellectual comfort in the Marris and Rein analysis. And those who sponsor the ideal of coordinating and integrating services may also be disappointed by their findings. These sorrowful conclusions, however, need not lead to outright pessimism and intellectual inertia. Rather, what is required is search and experimentation to evolve a variety of social-planning models that can be used adaptively to deal with the existing realities of interest groups, power conflicts, and scarce resources. In pursuit of this strategy, planners may have to trade off a value they cherish—rationality—in order to realize other values they prize—humanitarianism, fairness, and effective treatment. As we noted earlier in this book, other participants in the criminal-justice system have been engaged in trade-offs for a long time. If planners want to have a voice in guiding the system, they may have to become participants and act like an interest group, too. This might compromise their adherence to rationality—but they may have no other choice if they are to exercise influence.

1. *Social Work and the Control*
of Delinquency *

ALFRED J. KAHN

STRATEGY FOR THE control of a social problem or for its prevention assumes some clarity as to the nature of the problem. In the instance of delinquency conceptual ambiguities and confusion dominate the field.

The "facts" of delinquency appear simple at first: 1.5 to 2 million children reported to the police each year, about 600,000 juvenile court cases annually (traffic matters excluded) involving about 518,000 children, a nationwide court-referral rate of over 2 per 100 children. Nor are explanations for its existence difficult to come by. While there are styles and fads in theory for this, as in all other human arenas, a reasonable sampling of sermons, lectures, magazine articles, and television panel shows yields many of the following "causes," often as part of one presentation and not in any sense ranked or interrelated: the home, a general decline in moral and spiritual values, excessive free time and lack of responsibility of youth, poorly guided leisure time, violence and sadism on television, failure of the schools to teach citizenship, compulsory education laws which keep poorly motivated youth in school too long, racial and ethnic tensions, delinquency and crime as a "normal" way of life for those living in the "lower-class culture," and basic personality disturbances of an identifiable type.

And so it goes. One is tempted to phrase a new "law of delinquency interpretations" to the effect that the simplicity and degree of confidence in a theory advanced on the public platform is proportionate to the square of the distance from the phenomenon being described! . . .

SOCIAL CONTROL AS THE UNIFYING FACTOR

While no one theoretical perspective on delinquent behavior is useful for all purposes, a social perspective on this very phenomenon has value: How can

* Alfred J. Kahn, "Social Work and the Control of Delinquency: Theory and Strategy," *Social Work*, Vol. 10 (April, 1965), pp. 3–13. Reprinted by permission of the author.

one account for the tendency to group so many things together, to act as though they are one thing, to create competing theories and methods of intervention, to allow and to accept so many different and apparently discriminatory modes of definition, discovery and action? The hypothesis may be suggested that the unity is of only one kind: *society's social control objectives at a given time.* The various phenomena recognized, reported, and subsumed under delinquency constitute that deviance in children toward which society wants to apply relatively potent sanctions. This is the unifying social control motive that brings into police complaint listings, juvenile courts, or clinics that admixture of acts of omission and commission, as well as situational problems, that constitutes delinquency.

Why does society provide an authoritative mode of intervention that unifies this admixture? Ultimately one would have to answer in terms of the social changes that came about with industrialism and the decrease of primary-group controls. More immediately, society has defined certain circumstances or acts as endangering itself or its members and is willing to apply potent sanctions if necessary. The cut-off point on definitions of delinquency may be determined to be that point at which actions are perceived as undermining social control at what are sensitive spots. This may account for some of the regional, social class, and ethnic differences: society's control mechanisms take a different view of the significance and hazard in deviant behavior depending on where it is socially located. And behavior "normal" for a social subgroup may be seen as delinquent if it threatens the mores that prevail in the community power structure.

The analysis of delinquency is complicated by the inclusion of acts and phenomena that on the surface seem to endanger nobody and are not necessarily thought to be predictive of future hazard. Courts are used as leverage for social intervention in connection with such problems important to social control, broadly conceived—even though there is no physical danger, property danger, or property relationship change implied—as learning difficulty, psychosis, illegitimacy, and parent-child problems. Only analysis of the challenge to mores implied in these patterns clarifies why they, too, are grouped with more aggressive attacks on society or its members and demand court intervention. In effect, changes in socialization processes and in the competences of the primary group have been followed by public assumption of certain social responsibilities; the courts are the assigned instrument. It may be expected that a similar process will be seen increasingly in the adult field. (Whether delinquency jurisdiction is necessarily the best rationale for action will be discussed later.)

What is especially interesting about delinquency as a unifying concept is that twentieth-century society has been willing to develop a treatment rationale for its broad control measures. It is thus the readiness to impose relatively potent sanctions that characterizes the delinquency network—but also the search for rehabilitative and curative results in so doing. Only this can justify inclusion of the other forms of deviance mentioned.

It is a documented fact that positive action following case-finding in instances of alleged or emerging delinquency is a complex process involving the careful integration and coordination of schools, police, courts, social and medical agencies, clinics, institutions, child-care facilities, and so on. Many observers are agreed that in this sense a scientific, rehabilitative approach as a way to deal with this problem is as yet an "untried weapon." [1] There is a gap between humanitarian rationale and actual practice. Facilities are in short supply, are poorly staffed, and have partially developed programs. All the components of a necessary intervention network are seldom present in one place at one time, or are not adequately coordinated. Whatever the philosophy and objectives of the juvenile court movement or of individual agencies and treatment facilities, for the parent and child brought into the network of delinquency services the impact is largely one of punishment, deprivation, and control. What is defined as social control through individualization, help, and therapy emerges as control through threat, separation, and surveillance.

Incomplete implementation of announced intent and the simultaneous following of mutually contradictory courses reflect the fact that actually many publics are involved and that they do not have the same objectives. The premises of delinquency statutes are not always accepted. Moreover, values and goals are in transition, so that one overall policy is not dominant nationally. Some elements in society stress punitive approaches. Others affirm deterrence, moral reform, and treatment simultaneously. Still others are openly discriminatory in their enforcement of social and legal codes between groups.

OBJECTIVES AND PRACTICE

How does the social work profession view all this? A reasonable sampling of yearbooks, journals, texts, and policy statements discloses that the profession is almost unanimous in its commitment to a humanitarian, individualizing, nonpunitive treatment approach to delinquency. In short, it takes literally the rationale that supports the delinquency umbrella as a broadly conceived device for social control through protection and helping. Social workers were among the founders of the juvenile court movement and have sought to assure that the philosophy of the juvenile court dominates and unifies the work of police, detention, probation, institutions, and the like. The policy statement of the National Association of Social Workers is quite clear: Delinquency programs are seen in fact as part of public welfare provision. When prevention is not successful, programs are to emphasize the goal of rehabilitation.[2]

On one level, the profession has continued conscientiously and systematically in the endeavor to implement these objectives. Because of the implied premise that anything that promotes the "good life" decreases antisocial behavior, social workers have always related their efforts for housing, public welfare, recreation, and the like to positive prevention. And, as already described, case treatment strategies consistent with development of knowledge and the promise of effectiveness have been chosen. Movement has been from an emphasis on character-building services to clinical treatment to the current eclecticism in which community organizers, group workers, caseworkers, and policy-planning personnel all make their contributions. The profession is involved in intensive clinical efforts, institutional milieu experimentation, "reaching out" in casework and group work, "higher horizon" programs, vocational guidance, and new "opportunity" services.

There has been a tendency, also, toward a different approach to delinquency. Concern has been with some of the aimlessness and undirected conduct of middle-class youth when their parents were not concerned. Withdrawal behavior in the classroom is considered as noteworthy as acting-out behavior in its long-term meaning. In short, self-realization and mental health are valued objectives even if not quite as important in the value hierarchy as social control.

To summarize all this does not, however, tell the whole story. Programs of the kind listed are carried out with energy, imagination, and good faith. Social workers would expand them, given resources and personnel. At the same time, nonetheless, other relevant phenomena may be noted: the relatively small commitment of professionally trained social workers to work with delinquents; the fact that the bulk of institutions and detention facilities are large, custodial, and delegate most responsibility for service and treatment to subprofessionals who are poorly prepared; the extent to which social workers in their capacities as agency directors, institution superintendents, and state administrative officers cooperate with and actually serve as "fronts" for essentially punitive, segregated, and deterrent-oriented programs.

Social workers are thus only members of the larger society, in some ways different but also in a sense an instrument of society's ambivalence. Ideologically, they express the individualized treatment objectives and the best programs embody these. Organizationally, the profession also reflects the push toward use of courts, police, and the like for differential social control through custody, deterrence, and punishment, not through help. It is not the controlling profession in many of the services under discussion. Within these parameters slow progress is made from the socially imposed realities toward professionally defined objectives and implied promises. Where does the profession go next? What social policy does the analysis suggest?

POLICY PROPOSALS

Expanding Opportunities

It is obviously inadequate to talk only of services and agencies, since also involved is administrative social control applied differentially. In one sense, delinquency statistics—when analyzed geographically, racially, ethnically, or in stratification terms—are an index of social inequities. Considerable energies must be devoted to dealing with the ramifications of such inequities. Institutional-change strategies become an alternative to use of control as a way of coping with social developments.

Fortunately, this point has been understood in the past several years as community mobilizations have moved from control and treatment alone to a concern with expanding opportunities. Especially helpful is the present interest in improved job opportunities and job counseling, "higher horizons" in education, and expanded cultural opportunities. Social workers, among others, should continue to promote these developments on their own merit.

To put the point somewhat differently, delinquency reflects social-structural factors that need to be dealt with at the level of social policy and social provision. To respond only on the level of individual treatment is unsound.

Need we add that efforts along these lines are self-defeating if organized under the banner of preventing or treating delinquency? Such labeling affects both self-definition and social definition and tends to block upward mobility. It also leads to only partial commitment on the part of those to whom potential delinquents and "competent citizens" are categories in an incompatible dichotomy.

Social Control Through Individualization and Treatment

Turning to policy *within* the correctional field, it may also be useful to reconsider the legal bases of the interventions defined as necessary, as these affect what next occurs. If detection and reporting are followed by stigma, custodial care, or punishment and not by helpful measures, the wisdom of use of the delinquency status as opposed to that of an adult criminal comes into question. Experts such as Tappan would therefore remove from juvenile courts (and thus also presumably from the entire network of related police-detention agencies) all conduct that is not the equivalent of a crime or an offense in adults.[3]

Such proposals tend, however, to ignore the need for potent sanctions and the potential for protective intervention in a relatively wide range of circumstances. Society's social control requirements in relation to youth are not met by such delimitation because society has had to assume certain socialization and protective responsibilities that some or all families are no longer able to carry. The problem is to do this without discrimination and to assure that the intervention occurs in helpful fashion. Thus, rather than follow Tappan's solution, it would seem desirable to assure that court jurisdiction and intervention by any of the other agencies in the network mean social control through individualization and treatment, not stigma or custody. Several paths might be followed to achieve this, although some may eventually prove more effective than others:

1. Removal of all conduct that is not the equivalent of crime or offense in an adult (such as truancy, waywardness, and incorrigibility) from the "delinquency" to the neglect jurisdiction of juvenile courts. The strategy here is to delimit "delinquency" but not the courts.[4]

2. Assuring that "delinquency" adjudication is followed by treatment and rehabilitative measures.

3. Eliminating all juvenile court adjudication labels, so that the allegations become not the definers of possible "remedies" but merely the bases for the "care and protection" of the state. Specific treatment would be determined diagnostically. In short, the court's protective role would be seen as necessary but would not be hampered by excessive parallelism with criminal procedures.

Protection of Individual Legal Rights

Social work objectives suggest the need to strengthen throughout the process protections for individual legal rights. Juvenile courts are not criminal courts in this country. Detention need not be defined as arrest. However, to be served, treated, or "handled" by the police-detention-court network does involve deprivation of freedom and exposure to strong sanctions. It is important that allegations about behavior or home conditions be sustained reasonably and fairly in accord with the standards of a civil court, that there be no dispositions or compulsory treatment until jurisdiction is formally assumed, that appeal be available, and that possible court action be defined and delimited.

Social workers have traditionally been concerned more with diagnosis than with legalities, yet the misuse of the authority system when there is no basis for so doing is as much a diagnostic error as an infringement on rights. Furthermore, it is in this realm that discrimination (and, therefore, differential impact) is most blatant. Social workers would do well to help develop legal aid and public defender systems and to help define how they may work in family and children's courts.

Evaluation and Treatment

The policy to be adopted should also give high priority to the development of an effective system of case-finding, evaluation, and treatment through coordinated and well-integrated programs and services.[5] The theoretical basis for the evaluations and treatment prescriptions should be eclectic, derived from the understanding that to be dealt with are *delinquencies,* not one homogeneous psychiatric or social entity.

To limit oneself to these case measures is to ignore the degree to which delinquency is more than an individual, family, or peer group problem. However, once action along the lines of the above discussion is initiated, that is, once we move truly to convert delinquency from a differential instrument of social control to a social category for special service or help, then it is also possible to conceive, organize, and implement that community provision for intervention that comes into play when potent sanctions are needed. Definitions may change with time, but provision will persist and can become a useful aspect of social organization. Social work experiences and values would seem to support this.

Both Policy and Case Approach

The analysis suggests, in short, that the delinquency phenomenon requires both a policy and a case approach. Basic attention to social institutions and definitions and the development of alternative responses to our social patterns will affect the uses of this type of categorization of people and the numbers and types who fall into the group considered to require handling as delinquents via potent sanctions. Thus, given clearer recognition of how the delinquency label is used, social workers will be in a position to develop differentiated case measures suitable to the variety of types of individuals thus labeled. To move in this direction is to decrease the gap between ideologies and what social workers now help society to do far too often—to announce the need for but not to implement rehabilitative measures.

NOTES

[1] See Alfred J. Kahn, "The Untried Weapon Against Delinquency," *Federal Probation,* 22, No. 3 (Sept. 1958), 11–14; Kahn, *When Children Must Be Committed* (New York: Citizens Committee for Children of New York, 1960); Oram W. Ketcham, "The Unfilled Promise of the American Juvenile Court," in Margaret Rosenheim (ed.), *Justice for the Child* (New York: The Free Press, 1962).

[2] *Goals of Public Social Policy* (New York: National Association of Social Workers, 1963), pp. 20–21.

[3] Paul W. Tappan, *Juvenile Delinquency* (New York: McGraw Hill, 1949), Chap. 9. See also Sol Rubin, "Legal Definition of Offenses by Children and Youth," *Indiana Law Forum,* Pt. 1 (Winter 1960), pp. 512–23; and Rubin, *Crime and Juvenile Delinquency* (Dobb's Ferry, N.Y.: Oceana, 1958), Pts. 1 and 2.

[4] The British Inglesby Commission suggests that the label "delinquent" not be applied to a child under the age of twelve. See *Report of the Committee on Children*

and Young Persons (London: Her Majesty's Stationary Office, 1960), pp. 30–33. See also *Recommendations for Change in California's Juvenile Court Law,* Report of the Governor's Special Study Commission on Juvenile Justice (Sacramento: California State Printing Office, 1960); and *Standard Juvenile Court Act* (New York: National Council on Crime and Delinquency, 1959), Sects. 8 and 24.1.

[5] Alfred J. Kahn, *Planning Community Services for Children in Trouble* (New York: Columbia University Press, 1963).

2. *Juvenile Deliquency—*
Its Prevention and Control *

STANTON WHEELER, LEONARD S. COTTRELL, JR., AND ANNE ROMASCO

CURRENT DELINQUENCY-PREVENTION PROGRAMS

. . . THERE WAS NO major federal effort directed toward the prevention of juvenile delinquency until passage of the Juvenile Delinquency and Youth Offenses Control Act of 1961. Many action programs have been supported in local communities, and occasionally there has been sustained support by private philanthropy, but the efforts have been spasmodic. An occasional program has been sustained for some period of time, and a few of these have been evaluated, at least in part. But there have been very few preventive efforts that were based on any systematic theory of delinquency, and very little evaluation of their success or failure.

Most of the programs could be classified very simply into one of two broad categories. On the one hand, there were programs directed toward changing the feelings, attitudes, and eventually the reactions of individual delinquents or predelinquents. These programs were based on a theory that emphasized the emotional problems of individual children, allegedly resulting primarily from pathological elements in family relationships. The earliest clinics that directed attention to delinquents derived their theoretical support from individual psychology, and later from psychoanalytic or other psychiatric views. They worked primarily on the pathology of the individual in treating delinquency. The other major category of programs emphasized sociogenic theories of delinquency causation. These theories stress the broader social environment as a source of delinquent behavior and concentrate on the need for changing the nature of that environment in order to control delinquency. The setting for these programs is the streets and neighborhoods of slum communities rather than the confines of medical and psychological clinics. Many of these programs were first developed in Chicago, where they received theo-

* Excerpted from *Juvenile Delinquency: Its Prevention and Control* by Stanton Wheeler and Leonard S. Cottrell, Jr., with the assistance of Anne Romasco, Russell Sage Foundation, Publishers, New York, 1966.

retical support and backing from the social sciences at the University of Chicago.[1]

Although much more could be said about earlier work on theories of delinquency causation and programs of prevention, it seems appropriate to begin our discussion of delinquency prevention by analyzing the programs supported under the Juvenile Delinquency and Youth Offenses Control Act and the conceptions on which they were based. That act established funds for support of planning and demonstration projects in delinquency prevention in a number of our largest urban centers. It also provided funds for training in the skills relevant for preventive and correctional activities.

The basic position taken by the President's Committee on Juvenile Delinquency and Youth Crime was that juvenile delinquency and youth crime are two of many symptoms that emerge from the community's failure to provide the conditions, services, and experiences that enable a person to participate competently in American life. The weight of the findings of systematic research as well as the operating experience of the educational, welfare, political, and economic institutions clearly pointed to the inner areas of the great cities as the settings in which the burden of failure fell most heavily. The impact of this failure was most acutely felt by the young people in these areas.

With this general orientation, it is not surprising that the Committee directed its efforts, on the one hand, toward demonstration programs aimed at increasing the capability of the community and its component institutions to provide the services and conditions needed by its youth if they were to gain the required competence; and, on the other, to aid the people of the demonstration areas in making effective use of the programs undertaken. A significant element in these comprehensive programs was the attempt to involve the people themselves in the process of increasing and improving the capabilities of the community.

Specific programs directed toward delinquents were included in the comprehensive programs but were not a central focus. As a community became more competent to function as such, it was assumed it would cope more effectively with all its problems—including the problem of delinquency.

The situations clearly seemed to require a coordinated, concentrated, and comprehensive approach. Since delinquency was so closely tied to the other social problems that beset the residents of these areas, it could not be conquered without attempts at solving these other problems as well. Any possible solution would require a coordination of social agencies and programs. In many communities, therefore, new agencies were set up to administer funds. Private and public agencies that had competed with one another in the project areas were drawn together.

The specific focus of the programs supported by the President's Committee fell into three chief areas: employment opportunities, educational services, and community organization. . . . A key concept relevant to all three of these programs is the provision of opportunity—opportunity to develop the necessary abilities and skills to participate meaningfully in the society, and thereby to gain a sense of personal dignity and competence.[2]

The Committee made significant efforts to apply a broad theoretical orientation to the problem of delinquency. The programs were comprehensive in scope and bold in their vision, but the success of the venture remains unknown, in part because many of the plans were too broad to be easily evaluated. Further, the demonstrations had barely got under way before they were virtually inundated by the massive federal poverty program, which so changed the available services and the pressures on the agencies that evaluation programs could not be carried out. Thus, although the Committee developed highly significant ideas for a basic approach to the problem of delinquency, it was largely unable to carry through any tested demonstrations of its conceptions.

Among those who were either directly responsible for these comprehensive programs, or who were close enough to them to be able to provide an informed opinion regarding their adequacy as delinquency preventives, two different views have been expressed. One view is that the idea underlying the themes of opportunity and community competence are still the most useful and promising orientation toward work on delinquency. Those holding this view feel that delinquency is indeed bound up with a host of related problems, that only a comprehensive and coordinated set of programs can make any real impact, and that unless some other program is shown to be effective as a preventive, we should continue our attempt to test this set of ideas.

This group agrees that there are severe problems in the implementation of programs, largely because this approach requires a whole series of changed attitudes on the part of established agencies. It is argued that many of those who are in powerful positions within the established organizations do not have the knowledge and manipulative skills to work at the level of community organization necessary to achieve the desired results. The demonstration programs were thrust into competition with entrenched traditional bureaucracies, found in many schools and welfare systems, and the leaders did not command the power and political skills required for the successful launching of these new programs. But those who support these programs feel that the problems they present are only temporary. Once those skills are developed, or new ways are found to make established agencies responsive to the comprehensive programs, the efforts will be successful as delinquency preventatives.

Those holding the other view of the Committee's work feel that the specific target for the program was lost from sight in the diffuse activities addressed to the general community of underprivileged youths. These persons point out that only some of those reared in even the worst conditions of discrimination and slum life became delinquents. By addressing the total population of youths in such areas, the programs lose focus and increase their costs. Administrators will desire to avoid the delinquency-prone juveniles for fear they will be disruptive elements.

Critics of the comprehensive efforts also feel that the relation between broader community programs and specific acts of auto theft, burglary, and assault is at best indirect and often extremely remote. Problems of successfully implementing long-term programs in the face of high mobility and social change in the inner-city area are very difficult, and the chances great that they will miss the main target population, or if they reach it, that other events will intercede in the lives of those involved to preclude their being greatly affected by the programs. For the small portion that actually complete their experience in a long-term prevention effort, some would succeed without it and others will fail in spite of it, so the long-term payoffs may not be great.

From this point of view, the effort to solve the very broad and basic problems of disadvantaged social status, discrimination, poor housing, and inadequate socialization tends to distract attention from the more immediate and specific conditions relating to the commission of particular types of delinquent acts, and from the most obvious target group—those who are already delinquent, but might be prevented from repeating their delinquency.

Both views are relevant to the formulation of new policies concerned with delinquency prevention. A large part of the delinquency problem does indeed appear to lie in the structure of the community itself, in the frustrations imposed by the lack of development of appropriate skills in a society that increasingly demands high performance from its members, and in the general problems rooted in discrimination against minority groups. But delinquency is not the only response to these conditions. They appear to play an important part in the genesis of mental illness, of adult crime, of family disintegration, of apathy and alienation, and of other social problems. This is one reason why the broad and general programs developed initially by the President's Committee are now also being supported in part by the Office of Economic Opportunity and other federal agencies. The rationale and justification for those programs does not depend on their specific value as delinquency-prevention measures; the provision of minimum health and welfare standards and of equal opportunity for advancement are valuable goals in their own right.

In view of the difficulties of implementing large-scale comprehensive programs, and the relatively long causal chain connecting them with delinquency, quick and sizable reductions in delinquency cannot be expected. It is quite possible that whatever impact they have will not be apparent for several years. In any case it will be necessary to engage in a continued evaluation so that whatever effects they have can become known.

Granted that long-range programs should be continued, there is still the question of whether or not there should be other more direct and specific efforts focused on the prevention and control of delinquent behavior. It appears that there should be. The comprehensive efforts by no means exhaust the range of imaginative ideas, and there still appear to be important avenues open for exploration, implementation, and evaluation.

These avenues relate more closely to the delinquent act itself, to its relatively immediate antecedents and surrounding events, and to more effective programs that operate on those who are already defined as delinquent. They emphasize the relation of the potential or actual delinquent to his immediate environment, rather than the relation of deprived youth to long-range opportunities. But these differences are matters of emphasis, and while some of the suggested new programs move in directions left largely unexplored by the President's Committee, others—the connection of delinquency to schools and to employment—derive quite directly from the concerns reflected in the comprehensive efforts.

AREAS FOR FURTHER DEVELOPMENT

We suggest four areas of concentrated effort toward developing adequate delinquency-prevention programs. These are clarification of the different types of delinquency and the most appropriate prevention techniques for each, use of modern technology to change the immediate environment, improving the school's ability to work with troublesome youths, and further experimentation with youth employment programs. None of these four problem areas is new. Some specialists in delinquency have been concerned with each, and segments of all the problems have received attention from many. Each of the areas offers good theoretical reasons why work on it might be rewarding, but none has received the systematic and sustained effort required to develop and thoroughly test its implications. In some instances the direction of further program efforts is clear, while in others it is only possible to carve out a general problem that appears highly significant, and to suggest that more imagination and constructive effort may yield valuable programs. Finally, some of the areas call primarily for new knowledge, while others more readily suggest immediate action programs. Common to all, however, is the feeling among a significant portion of those familiar with delinquency problems that important progress may be made by their further exploration.

Varieties and Types of Delinquents

The interest in delinquency as a problem of inner-city areas focused attention on the common problems found in delinquent subcultures and away from the variety of forms and types of delinquency, each of which may call for different prevention or correction strategies. Especially because delinquency is a concept that includes a great variety of behavioral forms, it is important to devote attention to the different patterns of delinquent conduct, to the different conditions that may generate the patterns, and to programs of prevention aimed at the particular problems faced by the delinquent in question. Somewhere between the assumption that each juvenile is vastly different from others and the contrary assumption that all juveniles fit a certain pattern lies an important focus on specific types of delinquent careers.

Almost all who have worked closely with delinquents have recognized a distinct group of "aggressive" offenders. They are called "Unsocialized Aggressive Delinquents" by Lester Hewitt and Richard Jenkins, "Children Who Hate" by Fritz Redl and David Wineman, and in a study by Albert Bandura and David Walters they are described as cases of "Adolescent Aggression." [3] Unlike most participants in delinquent subcultures, these children tend to display characteristics associated with psychopathy. They engage in bullying and assaultive conduct, showing little concern for others. They are more egocentric and less peer-oriented than the delinquents dealt with in most studies of delinquency. Although such offenders are less frequent, they are important because they are believed to be unresponsive to usual forms of treatment and they are more likely to continue their patterns of aggression into adulthood. Special rehabilitative efforts are therefore suggested.

Patterns of delinquency in the middle-class areas provide another example of the need to focus on specific types of delinquents.[4] Although delinquency among suburban and middle-class populations is exploited by the mass media, basic facts regarding its frequency are still lacking. It is clear from a variety of sources that official rates of delinquency in such areas are much lower than they are for the inner-city areas. Although studies of unofficial and unrecorded delinquency do indicate that "hidden delinquency" is a typical middle-class phenomenon, other authorities point out that police and youth workers in middle-class areas are more sensitive to indicators of delinquency and therefore intervene and warn potential delinquents about activities which would not be cause for intervention in the urban slums. A balanced judgment would seem to be that, while there is indeed unreported delinquency and slower resort to official police and court sanctions in middle-class areas than in the central sectors of our cities, there is also an absolute difference in the amount and types of crimes committed in each area. In short, the vast differences represented in official statistics cannot be explained by differential police or court actions toward children of varying backgrounds. There are, in fact, real differences leading to more frequent assaults, thefts, and breaking and entering offenses in lower socio-economic areas of our urban centers.

But middle-class delinquency and the delinquency in middle-class communities are not the same thing. Much of the reported increase in suburban delinquency may be due to the movement of lower-class families out of the urban centers into low-status positions in communities dominated by middle-class membership. Thus the family membership context may be lower class, while the community context is middle class.

Dr. Betty Makkay reports from her experimental delinquency treatment program, operating in an education-conscious and middle-class suburb, that two-thirds of the delinquents in the study are from poor families. Special problems arise for delinquents in such communities. Failure in education, in a community where it is prized, puts special pressure on both parents and children. Furthermore, communities with a heavy emphasis on education for the college-bound population may be lacking in services for poor families despite the high average socio-economic level. Since current trends are toward the movement out from the inner city, the pattern of lower-class delinquency in middle-class suburbs may be increasingly important. Efforts to distinguish these problems from those associated with the large inner-city areas and to provide the special services they require would seem to be indicated.

When delinquency is committed by middle-class boys, it may well follow a distinctive form involving the automobile, sexual experimentation, and, perhaps, the use of alcohol and barbiturates. But the mass media reporting of such activities is often based on sporadic episodes. These reports may well be unrepresentative of middle-class adolescent life. Indeed, it is interesting that while the press plays on this theme, there is, of course, a counter theme stressing the extent to which our young people are conforming, serious, and overanxious about college entrance. It seems clear that whatever patterns are represented among middle-class adolescents, they are not primarily the traditional ones associated with delinquency and crime among juveniles. Some of the variation may be due less to social class than to size of community. But, since so little is known about patterns of delinquency in different types and sizes of cities, it is impossible to draw any firm conclusions. There is grave need for more detailed empirical studies designed to provide specific data on the quantity and quality of delinquency in varying types of communities.

The suburban and middle-class delinquent and the aggressive delinquent are familiar common-sense categories which are simply illustrations of the sorts of problems that require further investigation. In these and other cases we lack knowledge of the extent to which homogeneous patterns exist. For example, is there one dominant pattern that characterizes the female delinquent or is there a variety of different types of delinquent girls? Are there identifiable types of delinquent girls? Are there identifiable types of youths with homicidal tendencies? Here we have only the most meager knowledge.

A real advance in our knowledge of patterns of delinquency may be expected only when we become more sophisticated in our efforts to develop classifications and typologies based on personal and social background characteristics, or on modes of personality functioning. Perhaps the most advanced typology in actual use at this time is that developed by Marguerite Warren and others, based on an assessment of maturity levels in interpersonal relations.[5]

One consequence of the recent emphasis on the gang and interaction patterns on the street corner has been the withdrawal of attention from family relations and delinquency. Yet most serious students of delinquency recognize the crucial role played by socialization patterns within the family. Since many of the types may yield distinctive patterns in the relationship of the juveniles to parental authority, patterns of parent-youth interaction and programs of family therapy may emerge as relevant. Preventive or rehabilitative services requiring intensive interaction with family members, either individually or in family units, is likely to be prohibitively expensive as a general rehabilitation device, but it may be essential for certain special subtypes of problem youth. A typological approach focuses attention on such issues.

Delinquency and the Immediate Environment

Most delinquency-prevention programs are based on the assumption that the cause of the misconduct has deep roots, either in the individual or in the structure of the society. Treatment is thought to involve fundamental reorganization of the psyche, the social structure, or the culture.

But if one can commit delinquent acts without having a deep commitment to delinquency and if one can engage in them periodically without making any emotional investment in their expression, perhaps deep underlying forces need not be present for delinquency to occur. One of the major reasons for believing that these forces are not always present is the precipitous decline in delinquency and crime rates as adolescents move into adulthood. Deeply rooted patterns should not be so easily erased.

The concept of the situational delinquent has arisen on the assumption that, for at least a portion of the delinquent population, delinquency is not so deeply rooted as is generally assumed. Rather, delinquency may be, at least in part, an immediate response to an immediate situation. This does not mean that deeper forces are not also at work, but it does suggest that some programs of prevention may be successfully based on concern for the more immediate opportunities for misconduct. To the extent that this reasoning is correct, we may be able to prevent some delinquency, not by acting directly on the delinquent with casework or other services, but by acting on his social and physical environment. And here it should be possible to make good use of modern technology.

Auto theft would seem to provide a good example, since it is predominantly a teen-age crime. It has been suggested that it would not be too difficult to develop an automobile that is reasonably theft-proof—one in which, say, any effort to put a key in the ignition or to "hot wire" it would set off an alarm. If most cars were equipped with such devices, the auto theft rate might decline. Another example is revealed in current efforts to make the setting of false fire alarms less attractive.[6] Other straightforward attempts to limit the opportunities for delinquency could, no doubt, be found.

The employment of modern technology in crime-prevention programs has a common-sense ring. It is likely to be opposed on grounds that the techniques do not really get at the heart of the problem, which is presumed to be the initiation of delinquent attitudes. The budding delinquent, it is feared, will turn to other forms of delinquency if stifled in the chosen one. These are empirical questions in any case, but the possibility of measurable reductions in certain forms of delinquency seems great enough to warrant an expanded effort in this direction. Much of the rest of our lives is governed by a kind of economy of effort, whereby desired activities can become so difficult to complete that the effort is no longer made, and there seems no clear reason that criminal activities should not be governed by analogous principles.

Such measures might be particularly effective if coupled with efforts to make it easier to achieve legitimate access to the desired object. Again the automobile provides a good example. As automobiles are made more difficult to steal, would it not also be possible to make them more readily available in legitimate settings? Training in auto mechanics and driving might be supplemented by designating special settings where used automobiles would be made available for driving.

Programs might also be based on closer examination of the social environment in which delinquency takes place. The apparent effectiveness of detached street workers in reducing the incidence of gang warfare resulted in part from their active efforts in working on the scene with gang leaders when group hostility was at a peak. In a similar fashion, police assignments might be systematically based on delinquency rates and other ecological aspects of juvenile crime.

The common element in all these programs is the concern for short-run opportunities and limits, designed to make it easier for adolescents to gain access to valued experiences or objects by legitimate means, while making it harder for them to do so illegally. To the extent that motivations for the activities are relatively superficial and youths are responsive to the situational elements of their environment, such efforts should succeed. Broader aspects of such programs lead into the theory of deterrence—to legislation prohibiting the sale of weapons save under greatly restricted conditions, or the occasional "stop and identify" programs used by the police to check for stolen autos and to deter auto theft. These latter programs open up obvious constitutional issues, and point to the limits of such measures without basic changes in our evaluation of the importance of preventing crime relative to other desired goals.

The intent of this discussion is simply to open up for review the potential value of technological innovation and programs aimed at the immediate environment of delinquency. Such efforts will not begin to resolve the underlying structural supports for delinquent behavior patterns, but they may prevent a certain portion of delinquent acts, thereby saving both the potential victims and the potential wrongdoers. Furthermore, despite relatively high initial investments in technology, such programs might be much less expensive than those directed toward altering the attitudes and values of potential delinquents. Finally, it should be possible to test the effectiveness of such a program fairly easily.

Delinquency and the Schools

School problems, failure in schoolwork, and misbehavior in school are often judged to be a common source of the frustration and alienation that motivate delinquent conduct. The school is frequently the setting within which children and youth first come to think of themselves as consistently inadequate or dumb, and especially as bad or troublesome. It is also in school that questions arise about the relation between the person's present status and his future career. It is, finally, a sorting station, where some become defined as college material, some as poor but normal students, and others as disturbed ones or troublemakers.[7]

Even though the behavior problems that appear in school usually reflect inadequacies in family and community background, and therefore may not be in a clear sense created by the school itself, the school may still be the most efficient organization through which to work. Through the school system, it may be possible to bring about changes in the life conditions and opportunities of large numbers of youths more effectively than through the individual families.

There are, of course, dangers attendant on any expansion of school functions. Efforts to use the schools to help prevent or control delinquency must be balanced against the other goals that clearly must guide educational policies. But, since we require school attendance of almost all children until they reach the age of sixteen, it seems important that the school accept responsibility for those students for whom it is least rewarding, just as it does for those who are most adapted to its disciplines. Furthermore, the school must find some way of dealing with these problems, and much of what is suggested here is a search for more creative ways. Many with whom we talked view the school as an absolutely critical institution in the development and control of delinquent attitudes and actions. General improvements in teaching, curricula, and special services will naturally benefit those showing learning difficulties, but many of our consultants think there is a need for particular concern about those most likely to be defined as behavior problems.

Some of our consultants feel an urgent need for further development of programs aimed at providing autonomy and responsibility, and thereby a sense of competence in ability to handle life circumstances. Both the home and the school are seen by many near-delinquents as prisons, where dependency rather than opportunity for meaningful experiences is nurtured. Especially for those who are in more vocationally oriented classes, is it possible to find modes of participation that will increase a sense of self-confidence and capacity to control one's own fate?

There is a specific interest in how the school responds to misconduct. How do teachers and guidance counselors put some children into the "problem" category? Is it possible systematically to increase teachers' capacities to deal with these problems? Some authorities report that certain teachers seem to "have a way" with these children, and that for almost all youths who become defined by the system as bad and troublesome, there is at least one teacher who does not hold that definition of the youth in question.

Examination of the process by which suspension and expulsion occurs is particularly important. These decisions are fateful ones, and are usually not lightly made. But some authorities report that delinquent adolescents' sense of injustice and unfairness center much more on how they were handled by the school system than by police or court authorities.

Finally, the whole set of relations that occur between the school, community, police, probation officers and the delinquent and his family needs further examination. Is it possible to study more closely how these groups combine in their impact on children in trouble, and whether new modes of relations between them might not yield improvements? Of particular concern is the provision of modes of exit from the school system that do not necessarily connote failure, and modes of re-entry that might aid the delinquent in his efforts to become reintegrated into the school system.

Solutions to most of these problems will require more than a simple extension and elaboration of current services, for these questions relate to the organization of the school as a system and not simply to the problems of its individual members. Solutions may require, for example, quite new ways of thinking about the division between college preparatory programs and vocational programs, new mechanisms within the school structure for dealing with behavior problems, and the creation of new kinds of relations with family and community agencies. Attention must be focused, therefore, on the social organization of the school, and not on a mere increase in services for troublesome pupils.

It is natural that administrators responsible for any given school, or perhaps school system, feel they cannot give these problems prime attention, for in most school systems misconduct and delinquency are problems of only a minority, and primary attention must lie elsewhere. Viewed from the perspective of those responsible for delinquency-prevention and control efforts, however, a new significance attaches to these issues, for the vast majority of delinquents have experienced earlier problems in school. This is why it is so important that we find new modes of organization within the school system, designed to make the experience more rewarding for more students.

Employment and Delinquency

Income and employment are so basic to society that one naturally supposes they have strong effects on delinquency. It is, however, not easy to specify the connections in detail, for the relationships may operate through a complicated set of intervening processes.[8]

Belton Fleisher has recently found evidence that both high income and employment are correlated with low delinquency rates, and that changes in either may change delinquency rates.[9] In his view the effects are direct, and also operate through other variables, principally family structure. A rise in income is related to lower divorce rates, which, in turn, are related to lower rates of delinquency. Although he concludes that the effect on delinquency of income is greater than that of unemployment, he suggests that unemployment may be the better target for manipulation. The effects are by no means trivial. He estimates that in areas with high tendencies toward crime, a 10 per cent rise in income might produce a 20 per cent drop in delinquency.

In another recent study, Singell found that, among the noncollege group of high school graduates in the Detroit area, ability to get a job, the length of time it takes to find it, and the pay are all related to socio-economic background.[10]

The results of both of these studies indicate the need for continued efforts to develop programs of employment for youth. It appears, however, easier to single out employment as a critical target than to work out feasible and successful programs, for it remains unclear what part of the problem lies with the employability of the youths themselves, and what part lies with general economic conditions which affect availability of jobs.

A detailed analysis of youth work programs suggests some of the major obstacles that have been encountered.[11] It is clear that delinquents or near-delinquents often represent a most difficult group to work with. It was the sixteen- and seventeen-year-olds—often immature, antagonistic, apathetic, and beset by family and other problems—who were most often judged unemployable. The dropout rate during training, often substantial in any event, is even higher for this group. They, more often than other candidates for training, seem to need special attention if they are to accept training and work conditions. New ways must be found to bridge the gap between the relatively middle-class background of many trainers and counselors and the deprived background of the recruits. A special project in learning how to work with such youth may be essential before training them for employment can begin to be successful. It may be necessary, for example, to develop programs which would emphasize teaching the skills necessary for functioning in and mastering an urban environment as a preliminary phase to actual job training.

Employment programs in particular run the risk of raising expectations of the youths who are enrolled to a level that may be difficult to fulfill. The importance of building into the job-training programs the mechanisms that will allow for the fulfillment of the objectives of employment subsequent to training cannot be overemphasized. It is significant that the programs have encountered great difficulties in this respect. Employers, skeptical of those with deprived backgrounds in general, may be even more skeptical of those close to delinquency. Just as the potential employees must learn something about the requirements of stable employment, so must the employer be prepared to handle new problems in working with this 'segment of the population. Bridging the cultural gap between the two requires effort, and perhaps special effort in orienting the employers, for stable employment to result. Certainly a meshing of general employment needs in the local area with the specific training programs is one of the surest ways to increase success. . . .

Education and employment are essential for the assumption of stable adult roles. But the employer, like the educator, may be resistant to participation in programs oriented more toward the solution of a social problem than toward his primary concern. Some of the most important developments in the field of delinquency prevention may involve changing the educator and the employer before they can be successful with delinquents. It may also be necessary to provide employers with incentives in the form of public recognition or economic benefits to encourage them to employ these youths. The potentially close relation between school training and employability suggests, furthermore, that any effort to solve one of these problems must be related to the other. . . .

RESEARCH

It is common to hear from social scientists that more research is needed and it is probably not much less common to hear from practitioners that research is usually inconclusive, and that it is more important to get under way with action programs. But whatever its limitations, the long-term development of the field of delinquency control requires the kind of knowledge that can come only from systematic research efforts. Three particular types of research now seem required. National statistical data are necessary for long-term planning and for keeping the public informed. There is a desperate need for a description and evaluation of alternative programs of prevention and control and for techniques that will aid in the development of such programs. Finally, theoretical research is needed to provide a base for the creation of more meaningful and theoretically sound action programs.

The development of sound public policy regarding all aspects of delinquency prevention and control requires adequate information on which to base decisions. National planning will have to depend on statistical studies of trends in the amount and types of delinquency. There is a need for detailed information on the reasons for referral to juvenile courts, on the length of time spent in detention facilities, on the reasons for the dispositions made by the court, on the personnel who work with juvenile delinquents, and on the character of the training schools and other facilities. All these things call for a collection of local, state, and regional data in a national center which can provide statistical analysis and report the results.

Since 1926 the Children's Bureau has collected a minimal amount of information of this sort, and is, in fact, our principal source of national information on youth crime. Experts in the field agree, however, that while the information produced may be the best possible given the limited resources made available for that purpose, the data are inadequate for the formulation of sound social policy. There are weaknesses in both basic data and statistical treatment.

The information comes on a voluntary basis from juvenile courts throughout the country. The percentage of the child population covered by the reporting courts has risen from approximately 29 per cent in 1952 to roughly 75 per cent in 1964. This increase in reporting agencies was apparently made possible by a reduction in the amount of information the agencies making the voluntary reports were asked to give, so a minimum of information is now collected. Information is not routinely collected, for example, on the reasons for referral to the courts, on the ages and social backgrounds of the children involved, or on many other highly relevant subjects. This information is critically important, especially for juvenile court decisions which are presumably based on such considerations.

An example of the problems in statistical treatment concerns the baseline for computing the delinquency rate. That baseline is the population of ten- to seventeen-year-olds in the country. But since the major delinquency age is approximately fifteen to seventeen, anything that swells that particular age group will give the appearance of a higher rate. What are needed are age-specific rates: the number of fifteen-year-old delinquents in relation to the fifteen-year-old population, and so on.

These are merely examples of areas where vast improvement in the reporting of juvenile delinquency and juvenile court data are needed. Numerous other examples could be enumerated. The essential requirement is for improved quantity and quality of information, improved techniques of analysis, and improved means for dissemination of the resulting information. The technical skills are at hand, but funds are necessary if local jurisdictions are to improve their statistical reporting systems. It would be necessary to provide training and perhaps some personnel to local jurisdictions in order to accomplish this task, but the gain in the quality and utility of the knowledge made available thereby would certainly seem to warrant it.[12]

No responsible business concern would operate with as little information regarding its success or failure as do nearly all of our delinquency-prevention and control programs. It is almost possible to count on one hand the number of true experiments in which alternative techniques are compared; the number of systematic, though nonexperimental, evaluations is not a great deal larger. We spend millions of dollars a year in preventive and corrective efforts, with little other than guesswork to tell us whether we are getting the desired effects.

Two types of program and evaluation research are needed. One is the standard evaluation of impact directed at assessing the effect of the program on delinquency rates, on cost per inmate, on recidivism, or some other relevant criterion. The second kind of research calls for examination of the process whereby the effects are achieved, for it is seldom enough to know what the end results were. Many programs must shift their course in response to changing circumstances, and it is essential to build information that feeds directly into the programs, as well as information pertaining only to the long-term evaluation.

The chief example of a research system designed to produce these research objectives is the Research Division of the California Youth Authority.[13] The Youth Authority has managed to develop a research orientation, a flow of information required for the evaluation of various program efforts, and apparently a commitment on the part of the State of California to research as an important part of its program. Although less than 1 per cent of the Youth Authority budget goes for research, the system has produced a series of experiments in the field of youth correction which exceed those produced anywhere else in the country. The actual program results are still modest at best, but California is at least learning whether it is getting results and where it is getting them.

A very important feature of the California research program is the long-term commitment to such an enterprise. It is very difficult to build effective research teams without such a commitment. Especially at the prevention stage, where programs operate in the community and often on budgets that may not allow much forward planning, it may be necessary to find new institutional forms such as university-based research institutes that are related directly to service agencies. Experimentation with a variety of plans seems called for. Another problem for evaluation research concerns replication, which is essential to any long-term program development. Here it may be necessary to develop cooperative relations among states, so that programs developed and tested in one locale can be replicated elsewhere.

Research on the process and product of actual delinquency-prevention and control programs is essential, but it is not enough. Such programs themselves when rationally designed are based on theories of delinquency causation and control which have their roots in other studies of behavior. Indeed, many of the most important ideas in the field of delinquency causation and control have come from more theoretical works in social science.

It may take special efforts to make sure the necessary theoretical work is stimulated, and to find promising projects and ideas that deserve further development. Leadership in such efforts must really come at the federal level, perhaps in special grant programs operating through the National Institute of Mental Health, which already has a coordinating mechanism and a review committee for delinquency projects. In any such effort it will be essential to build strong ties to scholars and researchers who may not think of themselves as specialists in delinquency, but whose work when appropriately interpreted has valuable implications for delinquency-control programs.

The importance of research designed to fulfill the various purposes described above cannot be overemphasized. When the President's Committee on Juvenile Delinquency and Youth Crime established its grants, there was insistence on adequate research design as a condition for receiving federal funds. But pressure on the agencies to expand before they were prepared for expansion, and to shift directions and goals during the course of the projects, led to the sacrifice of research objectives. The result is that we are still nearly as deep in ignorance regarding the effects of programs and the conditions producing the effects as we were before the programs were launched. It can only be hoped that a high priority is given to research in future projects. so that we can begin to develop the knowledge base that is essential for the creation of successful programs. . . .

The Organization of Delinquency Prevention and Control

The field of delinquency lies at the intersection of a broad variety of disciplines and organizations. It touches problems of youth, urban life, justice, health, education, employment, and welfare. Persons who consider themselves heavily involved in delinquency work may be policemen, psychiatrists, clergymen, or probation officers, to name but a few.

It is therefore natural that work on problems of delinquency knows no unique home or institutional locus. In some states, the more important delinquency services are lodged in a welfare department; in others, they are found in a department of institutions. In some states, there are special children and youth divisions, while in others the alignment is closer to adult crime and corrections.

This state of affairs also exists in federal programs in delinquency. Work touching on delinquency may be found in any number of governmental agencies, though most of them are to be found within the Department of Health, Education, and Welfare. Many of the persons with whom we consulted were worried about the problems of coordination and balance in federal programs for delinquency. Some were fearful lest more bureaucratic struggles be created by new plans, others that the balance between work on prevention and correction would be determined haphazardly. Some wanted a larger role for consideration of justice for juveniles, others a larger role for child welfare.

It seems clear that special efforts must be made to provide coordination of services between all the possible agencies and especially that there be some unit where firm direction and leadership can be lodged. This is necessary if we are to arrive at rational program priorities. Delinquency is too serious a problem to be lodged in a labyrinth of separate bureaucratic settings with little in the name of logic, program, or coordinating mechanism to tie them all together. This does not mean that a new division or department is necessarily essential. It does mean that a mechanism must be found for guiding the development of the field in a responsible and orderly way. Only then can we anticipate that the federal leadership needed in so many areas of concern for delinquency can really emerge. . . .

NOTES

[1] Detailed treatment of the theories of delinquency causation can be found in many standard texts. A good review is found in John Martin and Joseph P. Fitzpatrick, *Delinquent Behavior* (New York: Random House, 1965). A classic psychogenic treatment is William Healy and Augusta F. Bronner, *New Light on Delinquency and Its Treatment* (New Haven: Yale University Press, 1936). Sociogenic views are reviewed in James F. Short, Jr., "Juvenile Delinquency: The Sociocultural Context," in Lois W. Hoffman and Martin L. Hoffman (ed.), *Review of Child Development Research* (Vol. 2; New York: Russell Sage Foundation, 1966).

[2] The theoretical base for much of the opportunity theory came from Richard A. Cloward and Lloyd E. Ohlin, *Delinquency and Opportunity: A Theory of Delinquent Gangs* (New York: The Free Press, 1960). The stress on community organization was a long-standing feature of early efforts in Chicago. See Solomon Kobrin, "The Chicago Area Project—A 25-Year Assessment," *The Annals of the American Academy of Political and Social Science*, 322 (March 1959), 19–29.

[3] Lester Hewitt and Richard Jenkins, *Fundamental Patterns of Maladjustment: The Dynamics of Their Origin* (Springfield: Illinois State Printer, 1947); Fritz Redl and David Wineman, *Children Who Hate* (New York: The Free Press, 1951); and Albert Bandura and David Walters *Adolescent Aggression* (New York: Ronald Press, 1959).

[4] Throughout our discussion on variation in delinquency by social class, we have been aided by discussions with Walter Miller, who provided access to data from his current investigation of delinquency in different types of communities. See also his paper, "Lower Class Culture as a Generating Milieu of Gang Delinquency," *The Journal of Social Issues*, 14, No. 3 (1958), 5–19

[5] Works that are relevant here include Don C. Gibbons, *Changing the Lawbreaker* (Englewood Cliffs, N.J.: Prentice-Hall, 1965); the review in Martin and Fitzpatrick, *op. cit.*; and the work of Marguerite Warren in this area, reviewed in the "6th Annual Report of the Status of Current Research in the California Youth Authority," Department of Youth Authority, April 1966 (mimeo).

[6] These and other ideas for the use of modern technology are contained in a mimeographed report by Albert V. Crewe of Argonne National Laboratory, "Crime as a Scientific Problem" (mimeo). Other works that contain materials relevant for situationally oriented statements include Scott Briar and Irving Piliavin, "Delinquency, Situational Inducements, and Commitment to Conformity," *Social Problems*, 13, No. 1 (1965), 35–45; and James F. Short, Jr., and Fred L. Strodtbeck, *Group Process and Delinquency* (Chicago: University of Chicago Press, 1965).

[7] Albert J. Reiss, Jr., *Schools in a Changing Society* (New York: The Free Press, 1965); Donald G. Woodworth, "The Effects of Laws Governing Youth and Employment and School Attendance on Youth Offenses and Delinquency," Standard Research Institute, Project 1–5332, Menlo Park, Calif., 1965; Aaron Cicourel and John I. Kitsuse, *Educational Decision-Makers* (Indianapolis: Bobbs-Merrill, 1963); and Arthur L. Stinchcombe, *Rebellion in a High School* (Chicago: Quadrangle Books, 1964); and Kenneth Polk, who has been working with Walter E. Schafer on

school and delinquency problems for the National Crime Commission, provided useful comments for the section.

8 Ivar Berg, Columbia University, "Some Reflections on Juvenile Delinquency and Economic Policy" (undated and unpublished paper).

9 Belton Fleisher, *The Economics of Delinquency* (Chicago: Quadrangle Books, 1966).

10 Larry D. Singell, "Some Private and Social Aspects of the Labor Mobility of Young Workers," Quarterly Review of Economics and Business, vol. 6, Spring 1966, p. 26.

11 Melvin Herman and Stanley Sadofsky, *Youth-Work Programs: Problems of Planning and Operation* (New York: Center for the Study of Unemployed Youth, New York University, 1966).

12 We are indebted to Bernard Cohen of the University of Pennsylvania for a detailed review and critique of delinquency statistics, and we have drawn from it at various points throughout the report. We are also indebted to the Children's Bureau and to Richard Perlman for an analysis of the trends and problems in juvenile-delinquency statistics at the national level. Also relevant are Thorsten Sellin and Marvin E. Wolfgang, *The Measurement of Delinquency* (New York: Wiley, 1964).

13 See "6th Annual Report of the Status of Current Research in the California Youth Authority," Department of Youth Authority, April 1966, and Keith Griffiths, "The Role of Research in Corrections," a paper prepared for the President's Commission on Law Enforcement and Administration of Justice.

3. *Planning for the Prevention and Control of Delinquency* *

ROBERT M. MAC IVER

AS THE VOLUME of delinquency has increased, more services have been and are being provided for its control and prevention. These services have grown up sporadically and more or less independently. They are spread out over numerous agencies, public and private, and the public ones are distributed over several main city departments, while the states and the federal government are also actively concerned. On every level of service the question of integrated planning arises. The problem is complex and the need for some kind of coordination is imperative. Any given service is more effective when it is linked up with other services and may be wholly negated unless it is supported by these other services. The lack of integrated planning means discontinuity and the dissipation of energies and funds.

Let us look more specifically at the need and the problem. A disturbed youth may be put under good guidance, but unless something is done at the same time to change his relationship with his family and his family's relationship with him, the value of the guidance may be lost altogether. A youth may learn to form good habits in a custodial school for delinquents, but if he is not

* Robert MacIver, *The Prevention and Control of Delinquency*, New York: Atherton Press, 1967, pp. 191–196. Reprinted by permission of Atherton Press, Inc. Copyright © 1967 Atherton Press, Inc., New York. All Rights Reserved.

provided with aftercare in the form of protection, temporary assistance, and help in finding a job, the benefit may be purely transitory. Delinquency is the result of the accumulation of unfavorable conditions, and if treatment is limited to one or more of these conditions, the others may balk its efficacy.

Similar conditions apply to the series of stages through which a youth proceeds when a charge of delinquency is brought against him. The case may go first to the police, to be followed by detention, and then, after the adjudication of the court, he may be put on probation. At every stage, some screening and diagnosis are necessary but there may be no consistency in the process. The police screening decides whether the youngster is warned, referred to some welfare agency, or arrested. The court screening decides whether he is dismissed, discharged, put on probation, or sent to an institution. Are the police sufficiently trained, sufficiently in touch with the procedures of the court, to decide whether a case should be brought before the court? Does the judge know enough about the case to make the best decision for the welfare of the youth and is he sufficiently in touch with the nature of the institution to which he may commit the youth? Obviously, a close relationship between these stages of service is eminently desirable.

If this statement holds for the treatment process, it is certainly no less valid for the prevention of delinquency. Delinquency cannot be effectively prevented if attention is centered solely on children who already show delinquent tendencies, important as it is to deal with these. An effective system for the prevention of delinquency should be available to all children and will be no less valuable for those who have no delinquency taint than for those who have. In its functioning the school has a large part to play, but so has the family, the church, and all the other agencies attempting to provide opportunities for youth. Again, children who are particularly vulnerable or who are already showing signs of delinquent tendencies should be a concern of the neighborhood as a whole, and the neighborhood should be organized under professional leadership to discover such children, with the aid of the schools and welfare associations; otherwise they are likely to be neglected and uncared for until it is too late to arrest the formation of delinquent habits.

In light of these considerations, let us look at the problem of coordination at it affects the great city. We shall take New York City as our main illustration, since we have had occasion to give it special study. Like all great cities, it has a number of departments offering particular services for the young—the departments that deal with health, mental health, welfare, recreation, and correction. It has various agencies concerned with housing, urban renewal, foster care, day centers; its Board of Education has provided and developed a multitude of services for guidance—social, educational, and vocational.

The Youth Board is the city's major agency for antidelinquency planning and the coordination of services, but for various reasons it has usually understood the function of coordination in an extremely limited sense. This board also has two other functions: contracting special services to private agencies concerned with the welfare of children in trouble, and an operating service concerned with street clubs for work with gangs, multiproblem families, and other activities.

While the Youth Board has contributed some important advances in particular areas and has itself filled some gaps in the city's operative services, it has never undertaken the major task of supervision and presumably was not expected to do so. Instead, it has established a rather loose liaison with various departments of the city and on the whole has been more concerned with the fulfillment of its other functions. It did not possess the status required to undertake full-scale coordination. In any event, whether the broad planning and integrating of closely related services should be conjoined with other functions is questionable.

A further problem has been that other bodies are also engaged in planning operations. The City Administrator's Office has had the special function of surveying and making reports on the efficacy and the interrelation of particular services. The Department of Welfare, in its turn, has been active in the expansion of a variety of services for health and social betterment. Again, the Community Council of Greater New York has been active in the consideration of a wide variety of city services, and its Regional and Neighborhood Planning Board has been concerned with the promotion of coherent local and regional associations. The council, which has an elaborate structure, represents the major voluntary agencies of the city, with members of some city departments on it. Typically, in modern cities, a plethora of agencies arise to meet growing demands but little consideration is given to assuring that they will work together effectively.

The need for some kind of overall supervision is further indicated by what has been happening to the two major enterprises recently set up within the city to provide all-around opportunities and services for the greatly disadvantaged youth of the city regions in which the projects are located. We refer to Haryou Act and Mobilization for Youth. Such organizations should have ample freedom to devise their own plans for the exploration of the needs of the people they serve, to encourage these people to express in their own way their grievances and complaints, and to stimulate them to develop self-help while they are being ministered to by the workers for the projects. But such projects are liable to rouse objections from particular interest groups, political or economic. Moreover, they receive considerable financial contributions from both public and private sources and may be challenged to justify the way these funds are used. If they were under the aegis of a broad-based supervisory authority, they would possess a degree of security they otherwise lack. It is not unreasonable to suppose that if the two programs in question had been under the guardianship of a fully competent top-level unit responsible for the supervision and coordination of youth services, they would have been protected against unfair attacks and at the same time would be in less danger of giving grounds for such attacks. The kind of supervisory unit we have in mind would not interfere with the programs and policies of any responsible enterprise, but would make sure that it worked in proper relationship with sponsors, supporters, and city authorities.

The type of planning unit would vary with conditions but certain considerations are essential. The unit should be composed of persons of recognized standing and wide experience in an endeavor to see that they are given full opportunity to establish the area of youth welfare, including persons who have shown high capacity in administration, citizens recognized for their broad and generous outlook, and one or two leading scholars. It would not carry on any direct operations of its own in the delinquency field, but would be full time devoted solely to overall planning and supervision. It would enter into negotiations with the city's various agencies to develop policies to bridge the gap that so often exists between more or less autonomous city agencies. It would promote standards of service and would see that the conditions of service are such as to attract properly qualified personnel.

The planning unit, if it is to be effective, must be placed at a high level of government, say, within the mayor's executive office. It would not undertake to control individual agencies but would use its influential position to assure their cooperation.

Such a planning unit should have attached to it a research group which would be in direct touch with the programs and operations of the various agencies in order to make recommendations for any necessary improvements, and also keep abreast of the studies being made in the field and bring to the attention of the planning unit any findings that might have a bearing on programs.

In the light of experience and research, the planning unit would seek to establish priorities and to promote policies that would bring them into effect. To give an illustration, a much neglected aspect of our present services is the failure to concentrate on *directed* prevention. By that, we mean those services that discover and give timely guidance and aid to those young persons who are beginning to fall into delinquent ways and who are particularly vulnerable because of their family situation or the tendency to truancy. At this early stage, the chances of rescuing such children are much greater than they are when habits of delinquency have been formed and confirmed.

Finally, the planning unit would take cognizance of the manifold services being rendered by voluntary agencies and would effect cooperation with official agencies.

While the need for the integration of programs may be greatest in the big city, with its multitude of agencies, public and private, it is also important in the state. On the state level, there is often a commission on crime and delinquency, or a council of community services, which has some general supervisory responsibilities. Some states—California and Minnesota, for example—have adopted the youth authority approach as a means of centralizing certain functions of delinquency control and treatment. The mechanisms for coordinating delinquency services vary greatly from state to state. In most states, however, there remains a considerable need for the more effective integration of state, regional, and municipal service.

Finally, on all levels of government, from federal to local, resources and programs are being provided to cope with the problems of youthful delinquency. The federal government has been greatly expanding its services to this end, especially since the establishment in 1961 of the President's Committee on Juvenile Delinquency and Youth Crime. In the same year, Congress passed its Juvenile Delinquency and Youth Offenses Control Act. Following up these initiatives, there are now important federal groups for training programs, special educational programs, many-sided programs for youth employment, and the recently established broad-based antipoverty campaign. The Department of Health, Education, and Welfare, along with its Health Institutes, has been active in furthering these developments.

These programs give new resources for states and localities, and this means an expansion of youth services all down the line. They call also for a redesigning of earlier services and for new liaisons between federal and state and between state and local activities in the field. To give fuller effectiveness to these new resources and opportunities, to avoid waste and overlapping and inefficiency, overall planning is more imperative than ever before, both to assure the linkage between the different levels of public authority and to establish coherence and unity of effort within the operative programs of city and state alike.

4. *The Social-Planning Design Guide* *

FRANKLIN M. ZWEIG AND ROBERT MORRIS

ONE OF THE MOST SALIENT features of social work practice at the community level is the virtual absence of capacity to formulate comprehensive social plans. The literature of community organization, even as it has been modified in recent years, reflects a singular preoccupation with social process and a nearly complete neglect of the technological aspects of social planning.[1] Whatever factors may be cited as playing a part in this situation, it is apparent that the avoidance of plan-making in the curricula of professional schools and in the practice of professional social workers places them in a weak position with respect to formulating designs for social problem solution and prevention.

Unfortunately, this shortcoming exists at a time when innovation aimed at solving massive social problems at the local, metropolitan, and national levels is going full steam ahead. The organizations responsible for the management of innovation—such as those operating antipoverty and community mental health efforts—have created many new roles that place a premium on planning technology. These innovating roles cry out for broad scope and effective imagination. In short, they require practitioners to adopt a planning stance and technological skills beyond those they generally now possess.

AN APPROACH TO PLAN-MAKING

Noting that the frame of reference for the ensuing discussion is the individual social work practitioner performing an innovating role in an innovating organization, it is possible to cite three canons that constitute a planning stance.

The primary canon of the stance is that the social worker must adopt a problem-focused approach to plan-making. This means that he initially explores the nature of the problem at issue,[2] that he does not permit consideration of what to do about the problem to interfere with his full assessment of it, and that he frees his observational capacities to the greatest possible exent.

A second, derived, canon is that the social worker will take nothing for granted about the target social problem. By not allowing his perceptions to be limited by his current knowledge, by the mythology surrounding a given problem, or by the perceptual biases of his close associates, the practitioner opens up an expanded arena for objective analysis.

A final canon relates to the planner's view of the plan. He must be able to view a plan as a rational, deliberate scheme for solving a social problem—an expert's design for intervention and solution. The plan, therefore, must possess the necessary components to describe the target problem, to assess it, to set

* Reprinted, with permission of the authors and the National Association of Social Workers, from *Social Work*, Vol. 11, No. 2 (April, 1966), pp. 13–21.

objectives for its solution, and to set forth the means by which such objectives may be accomplished. Since the nature of the problems with which the social planner deals is never unitary or amenable to simple cause-effect analysis, the plan must set forth the entire range of available alternatives for problem solving, and the planner must be prepared to select among the alternatives according to his best judgment, or according to a standardized decision-making scheme.

A particular set of biases, or stance, is to be attributed to the plan itself. The plan created by the expert cannot be merely a statement of Utopia, although it must be at least that. While it must reflect the utopian objectives of the planning effort, the plan must be geared to offer realistic courses of action. It must hone its ideal types as closely as possible to the margins of reality. The design cannot be perceived as a theory in itself. It must be a design for solution that specifies the theoretical framework upon which it is based. It must constantly guide action, but such guidance must be based on the reality of the target problem rather than on its mythology. The plan must specify in a clear fashion its inputs and outputs and it must structure the expectation of the planner for feedback. Finally, the plan must be specialized according to the problem addressed, but must also be developed within a mosaic of broad economic, social, and political forces.

SOCIAL-PLANNING DESIGN GUIDE

The social-planning design guide is a concept that can be expressed as a plan-making process. It is a means for providing boundaries for professional judgment for social welfare planners who perform innovating roles at the community level.

As a plan-making process, the design guide is a systematic means of citing the relevant tools that can be used in plan-making and for ordering the sequence in which these tools are used. The guide is viewed as a process for integrating different classes of design tools. It is viewed as a means by which the cognitive processes of the planner are mobilized so as to produce problem-specific plans that meet the innovative role expectations for both specialism and holism.

Five classes of design tools appear to exist. They are, in sequential order of input: (1) the statement of the problem, (2) the theories of causation relevant to the problem, (3) intervention alternatives and their possible consequences, (4) information about target population, (5) value considerations. . . .

Statement of the Problem

The statement of the problem sets the conditions for all the additional classes and categories of design tools subsequently to be selected. The statement should explicate the problem, providing answers to the questions "who? what? where? how? and under what conditions?" as these pertain to the problem. The statement should be brief enough to provide a succinct, descriptive overview, yet elaborate enough to describe the problem fully as it is manifested in a particular time and place.[3]

Using the definition of social problem cited earlier, the statement should begin with declarative statements in answer to the following questions: (1) What is the nature of the situation brought to the planner's attention? (2) Which social values are being threatened by the situation? (3) What kind of group recognition and action regarding the problem is extant? Moreover, the statement should include three descriptive elements that can constitute a synopsis of the situation: time scale, geographic scale and locus, and extent of the problem.

Time scale refers to the duration of the problem. Geographic scale refers to its spatial location, specifying both horizontal boundaries and vertical scale.[4] Extent refers to the number of people affected by the problem, including those directly and peripherally affected.

An example is in order. Let us suppose that a planner in an innovative planning role has been told that a horrible situation at the community level exists in *x* neighborhood: Mothers are working full time and young children are left unattended, often from early morning to late evening, to roam the streets and create confusion and mischief. Having engaged in preliminary exploration, the planner sets up the following statement:

Situation. Interviews with fifteen residents of *x* neighborhood, with the precinct police chief, with social agency leaders, and with city and state political representatives from the neighborhood disclose that there is widespread concern about lack of care for children of a large number of working mothers. These children are sometimes expected to be on their own, sometimes are left with neglecting friends or relatives. Concern is evidenced on the part of several mothers interviewed; they claim there is no way to provide adequate care, yet they feel they must work.

Further work using an exploratory, purposive-sample survey indicates that this situation has existed for about six years and has accompanied the high inmobility of one-parent families replacing many two-parent families who moved to the suburbs.

In *x* neighborhood, composed of some 11,500 persons and some 4,200 households, 1,300 one-parent families are resident, and of these, 726 female heads of households are employed full-time. These families average about 2.6 children per family. It is estimated that only about half of these families have permanent care arrangements for their school-aged and preschool children.

Moreover, this situation has been found to exist in two other areas of the community, in *y* neighborhood, and in the semi-industrial area bridging the melting points of census tracts 21, 23, 25.

In all three areas the police have taken thirty-two different preschool children and forty-seven school-aged children into protective custody in the last three months.

Values threatened. (1) Local merchants complain about increased petty thievery on the part of unsupervised children. (2) Many working mothers express guilt about inadequate arrangements for these children; some are fearful they may have to quit work and rely on public welfare; some feel that the care arrangements are adequate. (3) Police are annoyed with after-school vandalism and attribute this to unsupervised children. (4) Several social agencies are concerned that these unsupervised children, especially preschoolers, are deprived of important family relationships. (5) Local school officials feel that widespread neglect curtails preschool children's later ability to use elementary education. (6) Local political leaders feel the "good name" of the neighborhood is being seriously undermined by "these kind of people."

Recognition of need for collective action. All of the above groups expressed the necessity of "doing something about the situation" although none could map a particular course of action which he could call effective.

Summary. Neglect of children of working mothers is a problem in three areas of the central city. There seems to be widespread recognition of the problem and the situation threatens the interests of some institutional units by reflecting poorly on their ability to keep the situation under control.

It is clear that the statement of the problem can be tailored to fit several levels, for example, family, neighborhood, organization, city, state, region, and nation. It would seem to be good practice to attempt to generalize to the level at which the planner's position is located in order to establish horizontal relevance of the problem in terms of intervention resources which the planner may wish to enlist in his plan-making process.

A statement of goals—objectives to be reached by the plan—should accompany the statement of the problem. The goals statement serves by sheer contrast to the problem to highlight the state of affairs desired after the plan has been implemented. Objectives would, of course, be general at first formulation and would be refined increasingly as the plan-making process continues. Initially the statement of objectives serves to explicate terminal goals —ideal end situations. As plan development proceeds, objectives will be increasingly specified and differentiated into terminal and instrumental goals.

Recognition that a given social problem has vertical impacts is an important component in the planner's thinking.[5] A problem located at a neighborhood level, in the example used, will certainly have connections with the larger community and external jurisdictions of government and voluntary associations at state, regional, and federal levels. Conversely, a general problem in the national scale will have its impact for communities and neighborhoods. As a rule of thumb, then, the planner might do best to formulate goals for every level with relevance for the problem at hand, ordering them in terms of their relevance to the locus of his innovating organization. With respect to the problem "neglect of children of working mothers," the planner would order goals (1) at the community level, (2) at the neighborhood level, (3) at the next most relevant upward vertical levels.

Theories of Causation

The second class of design tools is the causal explanation of the problem. The entire *perspective* of the plan is oriented around how the planner explains the etiology and dynamics of the problem. The causal explanation lends meaning to the statement of the problem by providing an analytical vehicle, a cause-effect interpretation.

Theories of causation available to social work are the products of various branches of social science. The term "theory" may be overstating the case a bit, however. *Completed* conceptual schemes are a rarity in social science, and an accepted theory of causation pertaining to a given social problem would obviate the need for a social-planning design guide by providing an explanation so complete that the subsequent classes of design tools—modes of intervention and the like—would automatically be prescribed by the very nature of the theory itself.

As the situation now exists, there are a variety of conceptual tracks that aim at explaining a part of the problem. Every planner, then, has his choice of conceptual stances and each stance dictates a slightly different direction for the making of his plan.

What explanation, for example, can be given for the working mother phenomenon? One conceptual track will hold that mothers work in response to a cultural readjustment of the role of women in Western society; another track will hold that women work in order to meet personal-financial and societal-economic exigencies; still another track will hold that women work because they have not resolved their own feelings about their sexual identity. Which one is right? Perhaps all are to some degree, but the choice of any one predisposes the planner to a particular stance with reference to modes of intervention and the other classes of design tools to be utilized according to the sequence outlined above.

The major point is that in a planning process the causal explanation of the problem implicitly shapes the plan. Tracing out the available explanations utilizing the best available social science orientations provides motive force for different directions for action. Scarcity of resources often makes mandatory a selection of a few solutions from a large range of solutions. When the social-planning practitioner makes such a choice, it is his professional responsibility to select alternatives that can be based on the most clearly stated conceptual formulations of problem causation.

Modes of Intervention

Once the statement of the problem and a given range of causal explanations have been formulated, the planner faces the task of choosing an appropriate mode (or modes) of intervention. For example, if neglect of children of working women is the problem and if the causal explanation of the working-women phenomenon holds that women work in order to overcome financial deficits in family income, a whole series of possible interventions is opened up. At one end of the series, an intervention might be applied by subsidizing the wages of low-income breadwinners, thus "freeing" women to stay at home. At the other end of the series, intervention might be achieved by paying women to stay at home and care for their children. A midseries intervention might be retraining of women to qualify them for better paying jobs so that they in turn can afford to buy child care services for their children.

Analysis of modes of intervention should do more than indicate to the planner a possible course of action. This design tool should indicate "that, given a course of action, the consequences are likely to be these." Elaboration of modes of intervention, then, gives the planner some basis for expecting results and consequences from a given course of action.

The statement was made above, as an example, that one of the possible courses of action that is feasible as an intervention mode is the subsidizing of families with preschool children by government if the woman chooses to remain at home. The consequences—social, psychological, economic, and political—of this course of action may be determined by examining outcomes of previous similar efforts. Insofar as this level of information is available, possible consequences can be made manifest to the planner.

Thus, this class of design tools provides the means whereby the planner can outline the strengths and weaknesses of a given course of action. Studies may have demonstrated, for example, that a given course of action may be quite unacceptable for one social class segment of working women but acceptable to a different social class segment of working women. In recommending a mode (or several modes) of intervention, the planner can be secure in the knowledge that a differential outcome prediction has been attempted.

Two dimensions of intervention are suggested without elaboration: intervention with the client system and with the service system. Intervention with the client system aims to deal with the conditions of the client system that accommodate or block actions aimed at improvement. Intervention with the service system aims to deal with bureaucratic and interorganizational conditions in the community that accommodate or block actions aimed at improvement. Both dimensions are necessary for the innovating planning professional.

A brief note on intervention theories seems in order. Intervention theories are vitually nonexistent as explicit frameworks.[6] Implicit theories of intervention hover around various scales of human systems. Psychosocial therapy and psychotherapy are implict intervention theories aimed at personality systems. "Institutional change" is aimed at community subsystems and their vertical counterparts at the national level. Nonviolent protest is implicitly aimed at modifying the national system. Revolution is an attempt to replace an existing national or social system with a substitute. While the explication of interventive theories is primitive, the planner must constantly check himself in selecting an intervention mode for an underlying implicit theory of intervention, attributed by himself or by others.

Information About Target Populations

The fourth class of design tools falls under the heading "Information About Target Populations." Without discussing this aspect in detail, this class would appear to include the following subclasses: (1) knowledge of population, for example, culture and life styles, race, religion, income characteristics, shape and trends of movement and growth, households and their formations, density, housing and neighborhood characteristics, and so on; (2) analysis of resources, for example, state of the economy, industrial development and investment phenomena, manpower utilization trends, public expenditure patterns, private consumption patterns, land-use patterns, and so on; (3) knowledge of social standards, for example, minimal health and welfare standards formulated by the community, forms of organization for enhancing or policing standards, and so on. In one sense, this class of design tools might be termed "tempering items." That is, with respect to the three classes of design tools discussed above, information about target populations provides an important correction factor. These "tempering items" closet the design guide at the appropriate point with information about reality, thus relieving it of an entirely utopian character.

Value Considerations

Value considerations constitute the fifth and final class of design tools. Evaluative biases will always be expressed by the planner, by the reviewers of the plan, and by the community that will be asked to accept it. Such underlying values as are not expressed in preceding classes should be expressed in this class. This is the final tempering item, and should provide a guide to the possible as well as the desirable. In a way, it is the transitional zone between plan-making and plan-carrying out. That is, it constitutes the last analytical category of a plan and it also is the first order of information input into a strategy of implementation. The context of this category largely holds promise of answering the questions, "Is the plan appropriate?" and "Will it go?"

Social-Planning Design Guide

Beginning with a statement of the problem and moving through the subsequent classes of design tools has the function of expanding the basis for the concrete conclusions that constitute the social plan. The test of the design guide is the degree to which a unitary problem statement can be built up into multiple explanations and interventions. The design guide, then, possesses a built-in "branching mechanism" which can be schematically presented.

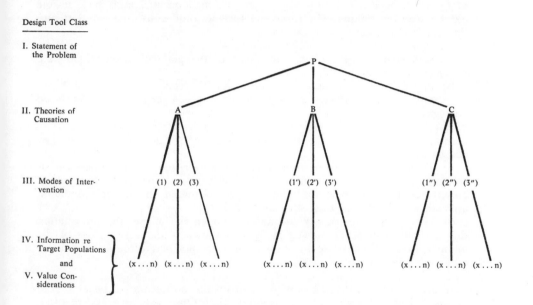

The general value of the branching characteristic is this: A unitary, initial problem item is developed by the planner to yield multiple solutions. And the primary characteristic is this: The planner is constrained from taking anything for granted and is impelled to employ the limits of exploration.

Beyond its service as a guide for ordering activities by the practitioner, the design guide can be viewed as an entity, a technical-mechanical aid to the professional planner. It is, in this sense, a plan-making instrument.

As a plan-making instrument, the guide consists of three components:

1. *An input component* consisting of all available written information pertinent to each class of design tools. For example, the problem statement class would include an encyclopedia of problem situations set forth as prob-

lem statements, alphabetically arranged and justified in terms of meeting the model criteria for designation as a problem; the theories of causation class would include a compilation of existing theories of causation keyed to the compendium of problem statements and containing the history, basic premises, and empirical basis for each theory; the modes of intervention class would be comprised of a compilation of intervention approaches and experiences appropriately keyed to both problem and theories of causation. The final two classes, target population information and value elements, are self-explanatory, empirically collected data.[7]

2. *A storage-retrieval component.* Employment of an electronic device for storing and obtaining classes and items of information is essential, given the geometric progression of possibilities once the statement of the problem has been formulated. The technical problems pertaining to this component, it will suffice to say, would require the full-time attention of computer technicians and programing experts.[8]

3. *An output component.* Because the design guide is a utilitarian instrument geared to assist the social planner, the final product must be a usable aid for decision-making. The following format could constitute a report outline capable of meeting that criterion:

a) Statement of the problem and goals of the planner encompassed in a statement of the antiproblem.

b) Propositions of a causal nature: Given the statement of the problem, if *such and such holds* true then it occurs or reacts *in such a way* due to *such and such* factors.

c. Propositions of an interventive nature: Given the causal proposition, then approaches to intervene in *such and such* ways will have *such and such* consequences.

d) Tempering items of a realistic nature: Given the above, differences or similarities between theory and practice or between previous tests and an anticipated test based on this plan are, by virtue of the target population and other ecological factors, *such and such.*

e) Tempering items of a value nature: Given the above, the information thus far refined must be viewed in light of the *such and such* values of the planner, of the client or service system as were not heretofore stated and of other relevant persons or groups.

In order to gauge the utility of the instrument, an evaluative system could be applied as a further aid to decision-making. One evaluative system often referred to but rarely utilized is cost-benefit analysis. This approach, recently and experimentally adapted from economic and physical planning techniques, provides a more quantitative basis for judging the relative merits of the many possible alternatives generated in the design process. Were a truly useful version of this approach operational, it could constitute an excellent supportive component for the basic instrument.

It is envisaged that the social-planning design guide, as an instrument, would be available to planners working on several scales of problem-solving, from neighborhood scale to the national scale. How this can be done realistically—through a university, foundation, or governmental agency—warrants the concerted attention of the social work profession.

A major problem not addressed in the preceding text concerns the decision-making tasks facing the planner who utilizes either process or instrument without aids such as cost-benefit analysis. The major unanswered question is this: How is the practitioner to choose from among the many alternatives yielded by the branching mechanism? This question can be addressed in terms of the notion of priorities, in the value sphere, and in terms of the notion of feasibility, in the reality sphere. Answers to this question, as they evolve from subsequent work, are necessary to adequately provide plan-making capacities among social workers.

It must suffice to say that the design guide can provide parameters for judgment. It constitutes a mechanism against which the planner can pit his judgment and experience, a means for checking his own professional diagnosis.

The guide is *not* a substitute for professional expertise. It is a superrational, systematic means for quickly refining the content and delineating the boundaries of a pressing problem. Used at the outset of the task, the guide offers a group of directions for possible pursuit. Used after considerable cultivation of the problem, the guide provides a means whereby the planner may check his judgment for gaps or needed supplementation.

The social-planning design guide provides a challenge to social work. It is the projection of one means to enhance the plan-making capacities of those members of the profession who seek to move boldly ahead in the solution of broad-scale social problems.

NOTES

[1] Alfred J. Kahn, "Social Science and the Conceptual Framework for Community Organization Research," in Leonard S. Kogan (ed.), *Social Science Theory and Social Work Research* (New York: National Association of Social Workers, 1960), pp. 64–80; Jack Rothman, "An Analysis of Goals and Roles in Community Organization Practice," *Social Work,* Vol. 9, No. 2 (April 1964); Thomas D. Sherrard, "Planned Community Change," *The Social Welfare Forum, 1964* (New York: Columbia University Press, 1964); and Charles F. Grosser, "Community Development Programs Serving the Urban Poor," *Social Work,* Vol. 10, No. 3 (July 1965).

[2] A special definition of the term "social problem" is used throughout this discussion: "A social problem is a situation which threatens an established societal value with the concomitant realization by some sub-group of that society of the need for taking collective action with respect to the threatening situation." Paraphrased from Robert Merrill, "The Analysis of Social Problems," *American Journal of Sociology,* Vol. 30 (April 1924).

[3] A different, complementary approach to social problems is contained in Herman Stein and Irving Sarnoff, "A Framework for Analyzing Social Work's Contribution to the Identification and Resolution of Social Problems," in *The Social Welfare Forum, 1964* (New York: Columbia University Press, 1964).

[4] The terms "vertical" and "horizontal" are used here and later in his discussion in the sense developed by Roland A. Warren, in *The Community in America* (Chicago: Rand McNally, 1963), especially Chaps. 8 and 9.

[5] *Ibid.*

[6] The beginnings of an explicit theory of intervention is provided in the elaborated concept of "institutional change" developed by Richard Cloward and Lloyd Ohlin, in *Delinquency and Opportunity* (New York: The Free Press, 1961). See also Ohlin and Martin Rein, "Social Planning for Institutional Change," in *The Social Welfare Forum, 1964* (New York: Columbia University Press, 1964).

[7] Some of these have already been evolved in at least primitive form. Bernard

Berelson and Gary Steiner, in *Human Behavior* (New York: The Free Press, 1964), have assembled much data regarding causation and intervention; the Bureau of Census reports more data about populations than are commonly used, and even more are available for analysis, but not published.

[8] A start has already been made to store and retrieve complex data about human problems. The MEDLARS Program for quick retrieval of vast stores of medical data and the Yale Studies Program dealing with human cultures are two examples.

5. Comprehensive Criminal-Justice Planning *

DANIEL L. SKOLER

ALL INDICATIONS ARE THAT 1968 will be the year in which federal aid to law enforcement and criminal justice will join federal aid to education, health, highway safety, public welfare, and similar subjects of social concern as a major program in support of services administered at state and local levels.

National interest in the crime and delinquency problem has reached new peaks, pilot programs have probed approaches of federal aid in this area,[1] and a searching President's Commission study has identified major avenues for improving crime control and criminal administration capabilities.

Legislative blueprints for the new federal program were introduced in 1967 and are now in the final stages of congressional consideration.[2] Briefly, they provide funds for development of comprehensive improvement plans; offer annual matching grants to help implement the programs, projects, and goals established in such plans; and permit special support for education and training and for research, development, and demonstration programs designed to produce or test new knowledge and techniques for the criminal administration community.

A basic principle and mandate under all versions of the anticrime legislation now pending is that state and local governments ʼmust develop and maintain *comprehensive* improvement plans—that is, the plans must consider all aspects of criminal administration: law enforcement, correction, courts and prosecution, citizen action, crime prevention. They must also integrate, to the greatest extent possible, the work of all agencies and levels of government carrying law enforcement and criminal justice responsibilities in the planning jurisdictions.

When the new federal aid partnership becomes law, the states and communities of the nation will be obliged to undertake a collective planning effort of a scope and depth unknown to our institutions of criminal-justice administration. The impact of this will be felt by correctional administrators, police commissioners, judicial structures, state budget agencies, and others as they are asked to work on plan components, analyses, and data-gathering efforts. The perspectives and understanding by all concerned must be sufficient to produce the most useful and effective programs possible. This

* Daniel L. Skoler, "Comprehensive Criminal Justice Planning—A New Challenge," *Crime and Delinquency*, Vol. 14, No. 3 (July, 1968), pp. 197–206. Reprinted by permission of the author.

article will seek to explore the role of comprehensive planning, its current status in the federal aid and criminal-justice contexts, and possible issues and requirements likely to be considered as the concept is defined under the coming grant-in-aid program. The precise standards and formats to be developed will depend on the legislation ultimately approved. They will undoubtedly undergo evaluation and refinement as experience is accumulated under that legislation and initial planning efforts help reveal what can realistically be achieved and which approaches to planning offer most promise for the crime-reduction goals of the program.

PLANNING AS A PREREQUISITE FOR ASSISTANCE

The experience of past years has amply demonstrated that the mere infusion of even a vast amount of federal money is no assurance of success or effective action. Well-defined objectives, realistic goals, appropriate techniques, proper allocation of resources, and careful study and program design are requisites for assuring prudent use of public funds and for guaranteeing, in an increasingly complex age, that the desired results will be achieved.

Accordingly, federally financed planning has become a basic tenet of national aid policy, and virtually every important program launched in recent years has included a planning requirement as a condition of eligibility for large-scale aid.[3] The Highway Safety Act of 1966 requires approved "highway safety programs"; the Comprehensive Health Planning and Public Health Services Amendments of 1966 requires approved plans for "comprehensive state health planning"; the Demonstration Cities and Metropolitan Development Act of 1966 requires approved plans for "comprehensive city demonstration programs"; the Land and Water Conservation Fund Act of 1965 requires "comprehensive statewide outdoor recreation plans"; and even more modest efforts, such as the Technical Services Act of 1965 (programs to communicate technical and scientific data for use of commerce and industry) and the Older Americans Act of 1965 (programs for the aging) begin with planning grants as a condition of aid for action projects.

Recognizing that programs such as crime control embody at least the order of complexity that has launched a "generation of planners" in these other areas of public activity, Attorney General Ramsey Clark noted at the 1967 National Conference on Crime Control:

> Our purpose is to commit ourselves to excellence as we now see it and later refine it. This will require definitive planning coordinated with all relevant agencies. Our time, our numbers, the complexity of our lives compel planning.[4]

Similarly, the President's Crime Commission accorded priority to planning as a first step for criminal-justice improvement:

> A state or local government that undertakes to improve its criminal administration should begin by constructing, if it has not already done so, formal machinery for planning. Significant reform is not to be achieved overnight by a stroke of a pen; it is the product of thought and preparation. No experienced and responsible state or city official needs to be told that. The Commission's point is not the elementary one that each individual action against crime should be planned, but that all of a state's or a city's actions

against crime should be planned together, by a single body. The police, the courts, the correctional system and the noncriminal agencies of the community must plan their actions against crime jointly if they are to make real headway.[5]

The Commission caveat has been embraced in the pending legislative proposals for law enforcement aid and has attracted little opposition from federal legislators. However, planning in criminal justice, as in other social problem spheres, must deal with important constraints. These include the "state of the art," available resources, intergovernmental complications, and the demands of the "comprehensive planning" mandate.

CURRENT STATUS OF CRIMINAL-JUSTICE PLANNING

Today, the nation has almost no validated models of good comprehensive planning in crime control. It confronts its mission, however, with (1) a variety of personnel, operational, and performance standards, and codes of good practice, and (2) some models of good survey work in specific segments of criminal-justice activity—both largely the work of responsible professional groups supported, in varying measure and at different times, by academic and public agency competencies. Guides such as the American Correctional Association's *Manual of Correctional Standards*, the American Bar Association's new *Minimum Criminal Justice Standards*, the U.S. Children's Bureau's *Standards for Courts Dealing with Children*, and the National Council on Crime and Delinquency's model legislation and other publications are available to aid planners as they assess local needs and frame action plans. Similarly, recent state correctional system surveys by the National Council on Crime and Delinquency (in Oregon and Indiana) and a variety of metropolitan and municipal police agency studies by the International Association of Chiefs of Police (in Baltimore, Puerto Rico, Washington, D.C., and elsewhere) offer valuable models of the level of analysis, comprehensiveness, and detailed action programing that might be expected in the correctional and police components of a comprehensive criminal-justice plan.

The best of this body of accumulated professional experience, standards, and reform goals has been integrated into the report volumes of the President's Commission on Law Enforcement and Administration of Justice, which has added important new insights and improvement measures. This is all to the good. However, translating standards and precepts into well-designed and properly phased programs responsive to the conditions and circumstances of particular state and local governments is the largely uncharted course which intelligent federal assistance must nurture.

Much remains to be done to develop resources. State and local planners in criminal justice are in short supply. Organizations currently capable of providing study and survey services have inadequate capacity to meet the demands of the national planning effort contemplated by the proposed legislation. Although they are beginning to show interest in criminal-justice work, firms and organizations with general systems analysis, operations research, and organizational development capabilities have relatively little experience with and knowledge of the field. Planning and research units in correctional, police, and other criminal-justice agencies are, for the most part, in early evolution. General criminal-justice planning and coordination units, new on

the scene, offer promising potential but are still few in number and have
not had enough experience to offer the required levels of guidance and
leadership.

A further complication confronting comprehensive planning is the frac-
tionalization of responsibility for police, court, and correctional activities
on the local level. With important exceptions, states and counties remain
dominant in operation of correctional institutions, counties and municipalities
have prime responsibility for police activities, and states and counties shoulder
the major load in operation of court and prosecution systems. In a given
metropolitan area, all three levels of government may play important roles
in the police, court, and correctional services provided to residents. Planning
must therefore transcend jurisdictional boundaries and individual agency
responsibilities, a difficult task under the best of circumstances.

BUILDING PLANNING COMPETENCE

Such problems, large as they may seem, are not greatly different from
those facing intergovernmental partnerships which address other contemporary
needs. Many responses are possible. A particularly important one is the opportunity presented to the federal government to match grant funds with an
aggressive technical assistance program aimed at building planning competence. This could include national workshops for training of criminal-
justice planners, development of materials and guides for planning, provision
of consultant services to planners, and development and dissemination of
successful planning models. This kind of help has frequently been neglected
in other federally stimulated mass planning programs, often to the detriment
of program quality.[6]

Federal assistance of this type will undoubtedly have to draw on the
capabilities of universities, leading crime control agencies, professional associations, and qualified consulting organizations.[7] Federal agencies have
themselves no superior wisdom or store of resources for this purpose, although
encouraging progress is being made through such instrumentalities as the
Bureau of Prisons' new Community Services Division, which was established
expressly to provide technical assistance and consulting services to state and
local correctional agencies. However, because of its national perspective and
grant dollar stewardship, the federal government is uniquely situated to
marshal qualified resources, often in short supply, and deploy them to maximum advantage. It is important to recognize, moreover, that the "technical
assistance" role is as appropriate and proper to the federal-state-local partnership as the grant-in-aid technique. Because of its advisory nature, it is consistent with the trend toward greater local autonomy in defining problems
and mapping programs of action and yet meets a need particularly important
at the starting juncture of the crime-control planning effort.

Through other federal help, all states and major localities are today developing technologists and permanent planning agencies whose skills, blended
with those of criminal-justice specialists, can provide a valuable resource for
crime-control planning. These include the forty-four state planning agencies
and more than two hundred regional planning agencies and metropolitan
councils of government supported by urban planning grants from the Department of Housing and Urban Development (an investment aggregating

nearly $80 million over the past ten years) and, more recently, the core-city planning bodies to map comprehensive neighborhood improvement schemes under the Model Cities Program.

Within the past three years nearly thirty states, assisted by Department of Justice pilot grant funds, have established special commissions, councils, or committees to examine criminal-justice needs and map comprehensive programs for improved criminal-justice administration.[8] An increasing number of cities and other local units are taking similar action, even before the advent of federal subsidies to assist in such efforts. For the most part, the staffs of these units are too small, their resources too modest, and their origins too recent to permit substantial progress toward complete models of comprehensive plans. However, as they build strength and get their bearings, these specialized state and local criminal-justice planning agencies should be able to demonstrate increasing effectiveness and themselves assume major roles in providing technical assistance for coordinated criminal-justice planning. Thus, experienced state criminal-justice planning agencies might well assume a major part of the training, consulting, and guidance services which initially will require federal impetus.

THE SHAPE OF COMPREHENSIVE PLANNING

Despite the newness of the comprehensive planning concept in crime and delinquency control, we can discern the directions indicated by limited past experience, the lessons of planning efforts in other social problem areas, and the results the new federal aid partnership hopes to achieve.

How Much

Planning is a continuing process; any program for effective plan development must recognize that fact. Although the production of a comprehensive written plan is contemplated as a condition of aid eligibility under all versions of the anticrime legislation now under consideration, it must be recognized that planning efforts cannot stop with achievement of a jurisdiction's initially approved "comprehensive plan." Indeed, it is a virtual certainty that this first-year plan will be rudimentary in relation to the fully delineated and refined plan achievable over, say, the five-year initial operating period contemplated for the new legislation. Accordingly, all planning authorizations anticipate federal support not merely for the initial preparation of a plan, but also for its modification, revision, and expansion. Planning agencies should expect increasingly demanding standards of quality and thoroughness as time and experience provide the opportunity for the research, care, and detail which may not be possible in meeting initial plan deadlines.

How Detailed

A dominant purpose of comprehensive criminal-justice planning is to permit jurisdictions to select, adapt, and apply general measures and concepts of improvement to the context and needs of a particular state, city, or metropolitan area. This being the case, the most thorough analysis and detailed planning possible, within realistic constraints of time, money, and the need for action, would seem desirable. It will be easy enough for a jurisdiction to echo general standards, tenets, and goals of improved operation in planning documents. These abound in the report volumes of the President's Crime Commission and in the "standards of good practice" which each of the disciplines has developed through its professional and research arms. More difficult will be the tailoring of these to the resources and special problems of the jurisdiction so that maximum prospects for success will be assured and, before that, ascertainment of which measures are valid for that jurisdiction. A high level of detail will help lay bare deficiences, inadequate assumptions, faulty data, and feasibility of implementation. What must be watched in the process of detailing is the introduction of detail at the proper stage of planning. The comprehensive plan that determines a need for a new facility may not need to produce a detailed design of that facility in the long-range program, but jurisdictions should be prepared to delineate and justify in much greater detail the action program to be undertaken with their fund allocations for a program year.

How Comprehensive

A comprehensive plan must cover all aspects of criminal administration. This means that police, correction, prosecution, and court services should each receive attention, that all major phases of their operations should be examined, and that the work of all agencies carrying responsibility in a particular jurisdiction should be accounted for. It probably means further that the need for citizen action, crime prevention efforts of other governmental agencies and private groups, and reform undertakings having no significant "money" dimension (for example, criminal code revision) also be reviewed and, where appropriate, planned for. This will be a complex task and dilemmas are bound to arise. For instance, what if a significant law-enforcement agency (for example, the state police) operating in the planning jurisdiction is not under the authority of that jurisdiction; and what if the planning jurisdiction feels that intensive upgrading of a particular function (for example, police) should be pursued to the substantial exclusion of other criminal-justice operations (for example, courts and correction)? These conditions could create serious imbalances in plans which, before extension of plan approval, should carry a heavy burden of justification to show, in one case, that efforts would be integrated with those of the nonsupervised agency or, in the other, that the priority is reasonable and justified in the light of local progress and needs.

How Soon

The deadlines for comprehensive planning can have a critical effect on the quality of that planning. At present, it appears that plans will have to be produced before the end of the first year in which the new grant-in-aid program becomes operative to permit a jurisdiction to qualify for its share of action funds appropriated for that year. This is because action-fund requests must be based on previously submitted plans which have been approved as complying with statutory standards. This could create unfortunate pressures. Notwithstanding opinion that a number of jurisdictions are well advanced in developing comprehensive state and local plans, no such plans are yet on the scene and many jurisdictions will be hard pressed to develop the data and to conduct the studies they require, distill these into an accurate profile of existing resources and needs, prepare a comprehensive master plan, and reconcile opposing viewpoints along the way, all within the first fiscal year of federally supported planning operations. The experience of the existing state planning committees suggests that we may be underestimating the time needed for such work, including time to organize and properly staff a new planning operation.

Three types of remedial measures for such deadline problems have been accorded recognition in different versions of the anticrime legislation:

1. Permitting a jurisdiction's first-year action funds to be carried over to another fiscal year so that they will not be forfeited if the plan takes longer to develop than anticipated (utilized also in the Urban Mass Transportation Grant Program).[9]

2. Permitting the jurisdiction to apply for first-year action funds without first submitting a plan, thereby enabling a more deliberate pace in plan development (utilized also in the Highway Safety Aid Program).[10]

3. Accepting an "interim plan," admittedly incomplete in scope and quality, as a basis for release of first-year funds but not as a substitute for the detailed, comprehensive plan which will ultimately be required (utilized also in the Outdoor Recreation Grants-In-Aid Program).[11]

What Machinery

The machinery that a state or local jurisdiction establishes for comprehensive planning can measurably affect the success of the planning effort. It is important, first, that planning groups have strong commissions, committees, or advisory boards to help review and establish programs and priorities. This is especially critical where the planning program encompasses more than one kind of jurisdiction and addresses multiple criminal-justice fields (police, courts, and correction). Broad representation of all interests, including not only operating agencies but research and educational resources, should be welded into a structure suited to the planning jurisdiction's needs and political structure. A number of "commission-subcommittee-advisory group" mixes are possible; the determination of the mix should be left to local initiative.

Equally important are strong planning staffs with capabilities spanning all criminal-justice specialities. These will be needed even where substantial elements of planning are delegated to concerned operating agencies. Without this staff capability, the integration of plan components and the necessary attention to total system performance required by comprehensive planning may be put in jeopardy. Planning machinery must also fix ultimate responsibility in a single unit of state or local government enjoying support of the chief executive and the jurisdiction's legislative authorities. Such a unit can be effectively housed in a variety of structures—in an independent agency or in an office within an existing state department (for example, the attorney general's office or a public safety unit)—so long as the responsibility is pinpointed and the necessary staff capability provided.

The quality of planning machinery not only will have a critical effect on the planning process but also will be an important determinant of plan implementation. Appropriating necessary local funds, securing cooperation of criminal-justice agencies in carrying out the plan, and accepting plan priorities should prove as large a task for the planning agency as formulating the plan.

Steps in Planning

The planning process must itself be an orderly development. After the first steps of organization and staff, it would normally involve (1) design of the planning study, (2) collection of data and conduct of studies and surveys necessary for plan formulation, (3) formulation of the total plan, (4) delineation in detail of components for short-term or immediate implementation, and (5) review and approval of the plan and its priorities. Work on each of these phases can, to some extent, be advanced concurrently and certain studies and efforts can be assigned for future accomplishment as part of the plan scheme. Whatever the case, a well-conceived and specific, albeit flexible, work plan and time sequence should be developed. Stinting in preliminary stage work (for example, design of the planning effort, data collection and surveys, problem definition) to arrive at final results more quickly could seriously impair the quality of the final plan. To insure against omissions, some federal programs have established requirements for interim submissions that delineate such components as problem analysis, general goals, and program strategies to be used in plan formulation.[12]

Goals and Evaluation

Well-defined long- and short-range targets are, of course, essential to a meaningful improvement effort. Equally essential is a system for evaluation of progress in attaining the goals, and this should be an integral component of the plan. As with other endeavors in social measurement in our dynamic and changing society, evaluation of the crime-control effectiveness of improvement plans will be a difficult undertaking. Validation may be slow in coming until programs have a chance to take hold and we can factor out variables that obscure the picture. Federal guidance will probably be needed to define expectations and provide a common measurement base to which state and local jurisdictions can, if they desire, add refinements. Evaluation should deal with attainments of both "capability" goals (for example, achieving model casework levels in correctional treatment programs, or securing crime labs or computerized information centers in law-enforcement programs) and "performance" goals (for example, reduction of serious crime, or lowering the recidivism rate, or raising the conviction rate in prosecuted cases). The objectives should be explicitly stated in quantified terms so that measurement is possible and expectations can be tested and adjusted against the realities of actual program experience. Cost analysis should be built into evaluation efforts wherever possible because costs are important determinants not only of what can be attempted but of the comparative value of alternative solutions or techniques.

Movement in this direction can be seen in other programs. The Model Cities Program is asking planning grantees to define both one-year and five-year performance goals in quantitative terms (for example, specified percentages of reduction in personal assault rates, in infant mortality differentials, or in low-rental housing deficiencies toward levels normal for the total city) and is providing guidance on how progress toward these should be measured.[13] Something comparable should be fashioned for anticrime programs, supported by adequately defined and nationally conducted collection of statistical data.

As the criminal-justice community moves toward large-scale planning, it is important to keep in mind that the technique must serve and not dominate our crime-control efforts. Some aid programs have had their disappointments with planning efforts; some are searching for more effective applications; none appears to have developed clearly superior or error-free approaches. We hope that our commitment to planning will feed on critical examination as well as intelligent adherence to the formulas and formats which emerge and that sufficient flexibility will be maintained by those administering the program to permit the fullest expression of state and local creativity. The Attorney General cautioned a group of criminal justice planners in 1966 that "the vital purpose of reform is action, not abstraction." [14] Planning is action and should be seen in that light. Properly executed and utilized, it can prove to be one of our most effective tools in the cause of criminal-justice reform.

NOTES

[1] Under the Law Enforcement Assistance Act of 1965, P.L. 89–197, 89th Congress, the Department of Justice has provided more than $20 million in grant and contract support for over 350 training, demonstration, and study projects covering all phases of law-enforcement, correction, and criminal-justice administration. Under the Juvenile Delinquency and Youth Offenses Control Act of 1961, operative from 1961 to 1967, a comparable $47 million investment in delinquency and youth crime projects was administered by the Department of Health, Education, and Welfare.

[2] Safe Streets and Crime Control Act of 1968, S. 912, 90th Congress; Law Enforcement and Criminal Justice Assistance Act of 1967, H.R. 5037, 90th Congress. At May 1, 1968, versions of this legislation had been approved by the House of Representatives and were ready for floor action in the Senate. See also Juvenile Delinquency Prevention and Control Act, H.R. 6160 and 12120 and S. 1248, 90th Congress.

[3] In late 1966, the Bureau of the Budget tabulated eighty-two federal grant-in-aid programs (nearly 75 per cent of them enacted since 1961) which required plans or planning as a condition of assistance. See *Creative Federalism*, Hearings before Sub-committee on Intergovernmental Relations, 89th Congress, 2d Session.

[4] *First National Conference on Crime Control, Proceedings*, U.S. Department of Justice, 1967, p. 16.

[5] President's Commission on Law Enforcement and Administration of Justice, *The Challenge of Crime in a Free Society* (Washington, D.C.: Government Printing Office, 1967), pp. 279–80.

[6] One new comprehensive planning program where proper emphasis has been given to preparation for planning is the Partnership for Health Program, P.L. 89–749, 89th Congress. Here, the statute makes specific provision for training grants in comprehensive health planning, and these grants were processed as a priority item even before planning grants were awarded to eligible states and regions.

[7] Excellent examples in the correctional sphere of technical assistance provided for state and local agencies by professional associations under the Law Enforcement Assistance Act are the American Correctional Association's self-administered study guide for measuring local achievement and needs against national correctional standards (LEAA Grant No. 306) and the National Council on Crime and Delinquency's correctional training information clearing house (LEAA Grant No. 224).

[8] See state planning committee grants listed in Appendix 2, *Third Annual Report to the President and the Congress on Activities Under the Law Enforcement Assistance Act of 1965*, Department of Justice (April 1968).

[9] *Urban Mass Transportation Act of 1964*, 49 U.S.C. 1604 (b).

[10] *Highway Safety Act of 1965*, 42 U.S.C. Sec. 402.

11 *Land and Water Conservation Fund Act of 1965,* P.L. 88–578, Sec. 5.
12 See *Plan Submission Requirements,* CDA Letter No. 1, Model Cities Administration, Department of Housing and Urban Development (Oct. 1967). The "Statement of Problem Analysis, Goals, and Program Strategy" must be submitted by planning grantees midway through the planning period.
13 See "Measures of Living Quality in Model Neighborhoods," Technical Assistance Bulletin No. 2, Department of Housing and Urban Development (April 1968).
14 Address, Conference of State Planning Committees in Criminal Administration, University of Maryland, Oct. 15, 1966.

6. *Dilemmas of Social Reform* *

PETER MARRIS AND MARTIN REIN

A CONFERENCE. HOT COFFEE EXPIRES in paper cups. The project director switches restlessly from pipe to cigar to cigarette, seeking to appease at once his fear of cancer and the tension of the meeting. Soft-footed secretaries insinuate pink telephone messages and airline bookings before the foundation representatives who, even as they talk, tirelessly weave their web of influence. The tone of the discussion is bland: the city is to be congratulated on its progress, the funders on their far-sighted support. But the air is heavy with unspoken reservations. Only the foundation staff are disinterestedly committed to the project, and they are beginning to wonder what they will see for their money. Beside them is their most powerful ally in the community, who recognizes in the project a chance to extend his influence beyond the limits of his formal jurisdiction. Across the table sits the representative of a public agency, indifferent to the project's wider aims, but determined to secure from it funds for his favorite scheme. Another participant is neutral. He is there because nothing can be done without him; he has no quarrel with the project, so long as it makes no serious demands on his overburdened administration. But one is hostile; he sees in the project a fundamental threat to his authority. He is not for this reason any less genial than the rest, merely vaguer. The disagreements are marked only by a subtle pause in the meeting's unruffled urbanity. Ideas will be worked on, rather than accepted; proposals redrafted, not submitted; decisions postponed. Later in the day, the members of the meeting will exchange, in private, obliquely collusive telephone conversations, prepare memoranda to their boards, draft letters. And around midnight, after a reception and a formal dinner, the foundation representatives will gather in a hotel bedroom to analyze the springs of conflict—prizing up the platitudes of mutuality to confront the implacable face of power.[1]

From the first tentative explorations to the negotiation of a renewed grant, the reformers were continually preoccupied with the intractable rivalries

* Peter Marris and Martin Rein, *Dilemmas of Social Reform: Poverty and Community Action in the United States* (New York: Atherton Press, 1967), pp. 139–63. Reprinted by permission of Atherton Press, Inc. Copyright © 1967 Atherton Press, Inc., New York. All Rights Reserved.

which underlay the agenda of every meeting. Lacking means to coerce agreement, they sought to turn their weakness to advantage, manipulating a commitment to change more enduring and widespread for being voluntary. But unless institutions could be persuaded to subordinate their policies to a master plan, the whole strategy of reform would be abortive. Without some concession of autonomy, no project could be organized at all; and only if the concessions were made in good faith could the project promote an integrated program of innovation.

The reformers therefore had to subvert a traditional principle of American government, which holds that, since all power corrupts, it is wiser to corrupt many people somewhat than a few altogether, and contains the temptations of authority by an elaborate counteraction of many limited and often overlapping responsibilities. "The major problem of American systems," remarks the French sociologist Michael Crozier,

> concerns the strictness and arbitrariness of jurisdictional delimitations of competence. . . . This system has great advantages. It makes it possible to tap many kinds of human resources which would otherwise remain indifferent or hostile. Very diverse kinds of initiative flourish, and citizens participate at all levels of the decision-making machinery. . . . On the other hand, the detours imposed by the mere existence of all these different authorities, the difficulty of coordinating them and of harmonizing possibly conflicting decisions, call for an extremely complex strategy of procedures that is the focal point of American administrative disfunctions. Willful individuals can block the intentions of whole communities for a long time; numerous routines develop around local positions of influence; the feeble are not protected so well against the strong; and generally, a large number of vicious circles will protect and reinforce local conservatism. The American system may also be viewed as a system that cannot correct its errors easily.[2]

The reintegration of institutional functions was, then, not only a prerequisite of any other action, but a reform in its own right, designed to rescue cities from the jurisdictional conflicts which frustrated rational adaptation to changing needs. "We wanted to provide a framework," as Lloyd Ohlin, consultant to the President's Committee, explained,

> where we could concentrate a whole series of programs together in the same area. This would show greater impact. We felt that the problem was not just one of providing new services here and there, but of trying to reach a new threshold by an integrated approach.[3]

Here both the President's Committee and the [Ford] Foundation faced the problem of a community structure adequate to the purpose. Since they believed that city hall and the school system should assume the leading responsibility for an imaginative social policy, and yet were mostly poorly prepared to provide it, they wanted to create a structure that the mayor and public agencies would accept, but that could not be controlled by narrow political or bureaucratic interests. The Ford Foundation relied mostly on its promise of money to negotiate a workable structure. But the President's Committee was led, for a while, into a more ambitious attempt to secure an intellectual commitment to reform through a highly articulated planning procedure.

In Search of a Structure

At first, the cities had responded to the opportunity with a clamor of competing applications from their public and private agencies. In its first year, therefore, the Committee's staff was much preoccupied with the promotion of structures able to organize a comprehensive, innovative plan of action. William Lawrence, as the Committee's consultant to some of the cities, was concerned to bring together city hall, the school system, and the private agencies in a coalition of leading institutions. This structure was not to be so broadly representative as to inhibit challenging innovation—though it might be served by a more inclusive advisory committee. On the other hand, it would have been futile to exclude such major institutions as the schools which, however conservative, necessarily limited innovation to what they would accept.

But the Committee did not seek to impose a single organizational model. At the outset the federal staff seem to have had four possibilities in mind, suitable to differing local circumstances, which set out a range of institutional and unofficial representation:

—a government elite, comprising key officials of state and city departments;
—a power elite, where nongovernment leadership—including the Negro community—joined key agency staff in a small board;
—a larger board, responsible to the mayor, representing voluntary agencies, senior professional staff of public and private services, and community leadership; or
—a coalition of public and voluntary agencies, such as the mayor's office, the welfare department, the juvenile courts, schools, voluntary foundations, and welfare councils.

At this stage, the staff was preoccupied with marshaling established power, and the participation of those to be helped by the projects was overlooked.

By March 1962, it had become clear that any such structure would need time to establish itself as an effective instrument. The cities had not organized their social services according to any comprehensive, integrated plan, and could not immediately meet the Committee's criteria. The Committee would either have to revert to the funding of isolated projects or provide resources for extensive preliminary planning and regrouping. To rescue the integrity of a comprehensive approach, it therefore decided to institute a policy of planning grants, to precede any funding for action. Here Mobilization for Youth, which provided a model for so much of the Committee's thinking, provided a precedent. It had been pressed by NIMH to undertake two years of preliminary planning, and the Committee had been influenced from the first by this example.

A comprehensive program depended, then, on planning. But what did comprehensive mean—a program that tackled all the causes of delinquency? which involved every institution? or which simply integrated every aspect of a particular service—as a youth employment program might integrate counseling, training, and placement? "We act as if we really have something in the concept," a member of the Committee's staff confessed, "but we really do not. I talk with glib generality about these ideas, but when pressed to pin down the meaning of them specifically, I'm at a loss." But the Committee continued to assert that the concept was crucial, however vaguely defined.

> The point at which a program would qualify as comprehensive must be related to the particular set of conditions and institutions in the given community. But always proposed action will be examined in the light of federal policy of supporting these programs which have identified many sources of the problem and have proposed to seek changes in many institutions.[4]

By the end of the first year, the principles underlying the conception of a comprehensive program had become more explicit. Firstly, delinquency arose as much from social frustration as personal maladjustment, and the demonstrations should concentrate upon changes in the social environment rather than in personality. Secondly, the planning organizations must, therefore, possess the authority and community influence to bring such changes about. Thirdly, successful planning depended on advanced knowledge, and "should utilize and integrate the theoretical and research skills of . . . universities and research organizations."[5] Finally, action must be integrated with evaluative research. One other principle was not officially endorsed until a year or two later, but became increasingly influential—the participation of the residents in the demonstration communities. This was seen both as a means of legitimizing the reformist aims of the program and of repairing the distintegration of community self-help.

Taken together, these criteria placed the emphasis on social reform through rational planning. The vested interests and conservative prejudices of bureaucracy were to be overborn by an alliance of academic experts with political innovators. Since the Committee lacked power to force change against the will of established community leadership, everything depended on the persuasiveness of the planning process. If the analysis of the problems were only thorough enough, if the authority of specialists were sufficiently recognized, if the aims of the program were given a truly rational justification, the forces of enlightened understanding might prevail. The President's Committee staff conceived this as a radical departure from conventional social service planning, where tradition and conformity to upper-class interests were dominant. But to achieve it, the planning had to be protected against the contamination of expediency; it must precede action, defining its aims, and never concede the right of institutional interests to distort the logic of fact. "We have to hold this line at all costs," Lloyd Ohlin insisted,

> maintaining the integrity of planning by keeping action out of the planning phase. We couldn't get an effective coordination of effort unless we forced the planning processes, where they would be forced to dig into the facts of the situation and to justify their program together.

Ohlin and some of the Committee's planning staff were perhaps more single-mindedly committed to this conception of policy than David Hackett himself, who had to bear in mind the political needs of the Kennedy Administration: Hackett also employed political troubleshooters to negotiate on a more political level when projects ran into difficulties. In the end, Lloyd Ohlin's line proved after all untenable, under pressures within both federal and local government. But in principle, to place goals before means, thought before action, fact before program was compellingly rational.

The Foundation had taken a different line, stressing leadership and consensus rather than rational planning, but it was equally convinced of the need for a new organization to receive the grants, work out the program, oversee their performance, evaluate their success, and develop new ideas. Both funders rejected the existing public and voluntary planning structures. Welfare councils were accused of ignoring public agencies. "They have labored under an illusion of community inclusiveness that hampers their capacity to recognize and deal with problems in the public and political sphere." [6] Publicly sponsored youth commissions, as in Chicago, St. Louis, Los Angeles, New York, were passed over because of their traditional bias. The funders preferred a broadly representative structure, which would include both the major public and voluntary institutions, and established community leadership—financial, political, religious, and racial. Political government, the funders believed, must play a crucial role. Only government could command the resources to implement the demonstrations on a larger scale and coordinate functions. Social planning was becoming too important and costly to be left to the councils of voluntary agencies. Against the tradition that democracy was best protected where government was least intrusive, they put forward a new principle of political responsibility.

A variety of structures were created to adapt these criteria to local circumstances. In New Haven, Boston, Philadelphia, New York, Washington, and North Carolina a quasi-public agency was incorporated with an independent board. In Los Angeles a new district government was created under state legislation that authorized governmental bodies to develop formal relationships by a joint powers agreement. Oakland administered its project from within the city manager's office, under the guidance of an advisory committee. Cleveland created an incorporated structure comprised of city, county, schools, and courts, and community representation. Chicago and St. Louis formed unincorporated planning bodies appointed by the mayor, but administratively responsible respectively to the Youth Commission and the Welfare Department. Occasionally, the projects adopted different structures during different phases of operation. In St. Louis, for example, an unincorporated body had been created to work out plans, but they were implemented through a nongovernmental, privately incorporated organization —the Human Development Corporation.

In Search of Commitment

To invite the participation of established power in a new coalition, and win their allegiance to the need for reform, the funders relied on the inducement of money. In the recipe of social change, seed money was the crucial ingredient. Seen as a proportion of the total budget of the institutions they were attempting to reform, the grants were meager. But the scarcity of local funds made the promise of several million uncommitted dollars a worthwhile prize; and Foundation support also lent prestige. As Paul Ylvisaker remarked to a gathering of philanthropies: "You have discovered, and I have discovered, that we are usually wanted not for our money but for what we supposedly represent: society's seal of approval; the hallmark of rationality; the symbol of personal disinterest." [7] The process of bargaining for funds, the visibility of much-publicized grants, the encouragement of national sponsorship to insurgents within the established bureaucracies, all gave the seed money a power for change much greater than the services it could buy. It could show what needed to be done and stimulate a new spirit in social policy committed to cooperative innovation. But it clearly could not meet the cost of reform. The federal legislation called only for demonstrations, it was not conceived as a grant-in-aid program. The Foundation had allotted only limited funds, and did not intend to continue its support indefinitely. Sustained reform must depend, in the end, on an investment by the local community. The strategy needed to ensure that adequate local resources would be committed when the demonstration period ended.

Two interrelated principles were adopted to achieve this aim—matching funds and participation. The initial planning grants were to be matched by local contributions, and the programs were to be jointly financed. The amount and the form of the local contribution was not specified, as the funders recognized the difficulties. They did not wish to insist rigidly on criteria which could defeat the project before it was launched. But they were equally convinced that it was crucial to bargain for local matching, because a contribution had the symbolic value of a pledge. Institutions would be eager to protect the capital they had invested, and make it yield dividends.

Participation meant sharing in decisions. Lay leaders representing community interests were to join in determining final policy, while professional agency staff were to be drawn into program development. The more they were engaged in the formulation of policy, the more they would abide by the outcome, while conflicts of interest would be worked out in open discussion. At the same time, they were to design their programs within an experimental framework and submit political expediency to the test of scientific analysis. If the programs succeeded, institutions would be impelled by the logic of empirical demonstration to establish them more widely.

If the reformers' theories were right, bureaucrats were continually distracted from their true function by pressures within their organization toward a rigid, protective conformity. By laying down a challenge and some funds to meet it, the funders hoped that mere conformity would be discredited. Now the agency executive with imaginative ideas would stand to win more for his organization than his conservative colleagues, and he would find his natural allies among innovators in other agencies. The strategy assumed, then, that if you offered enough money to excite attention, by the process of self-education, shared responsibility, and growing financial commitment, you could reintegrate a divided bureaucracy and commit it to a demonstrably rational program of innovation, procuring a new reasonableness at little cost. Institutions could hardly reject a program of change that was at once based on knowledge, supported by a prestigious coalition, and in which they themselves had participated fully.

THE FRUSTRATION OF COMMITMENT

But this manipulation by the power of money suffered from the equivocal position of the funders. As we have discussed, their right to intervene depended on the tolerance of the communities with whom they were bargaining, and they could not press their criteria too forcefully. Though they held a power of veto in the negotiations, once the bargain was struck they had few sanctions to uphold its terms. And in practice, they were virtually com-

mitted even before the negotiations were concluded. The more prolonged
the discussion, the more difficult it became to repudiate expectations. The
promise became insensibly more specific and more embarrassing to withdraw, until the funders could no longer withhold their approval, though
much had still to be resolved to their satisfaction. The Committee hoped
that the preliminary planning, by sheer force of logic, would constrain the
projects from betraying its intentions, while the Foundation reserved a large
part of its grant in a development fund, to be released as acceptable programs were put forward. But the first expedient presupposed a much tighter
theory of reform than any social scientist could confidently provide, even
without politicians and administrators looking over his shoulder. And the
second merely postponed a part of the negotiations until later, when the
Foundation's bargaining position would be largely undermined by the prior
commitment of the funds.

Because of these weaknesses, the strategy succeeded most where it was
needed least. When a community had already formed a coalition committed to reform, the added funds of the President's Committee and the
Foundation could be used to best advantage and with least controversy.
Where no integrated, progressive leadership stood ready to exploit the grants,
the funders faced continual frustrations. They returned from their visits to
the cities discouraged by unresolved jurisdictional wrangles, indifferent performance, delays, and inconsistencies. And to much of this, they could only
reluctantly acquiesce. The principle of matching funds, for instance, was
relaxed until it lost its point as a community commitment. Matching in kind
was accepted, so that cities were able to meet the requirement by off-
setting a part of their current costs. The President's Committee was even
driven to accept the Ford Foundation grant as local matching, while Ford
reciprocally accepted federal money. In the end, the cities seldom made any
substantial contribution from their own resources. And after the projects
were funded, innovative ideas tended to relapse into conventional practice
or were simply ignored; undertakings were not honored; or programs that
should have reinforced each other were, for administrative convenience,
implemented without coordination.

These frustrations arose because, so often, institutions would not in
practice commit themselves either to the sacrifice of autonomy implied by
the project's structure or to its innovative spirit. The reformers supposed,
for instance, that if the school system took part in the planning of changes
in curriculum and teaching practice, it did so out of genuine interest. But
its participation seems often to have been merely defensive. To have rejected
a grant, and refused its cooperation in a progressive community venture,
would have incited a public opinion already critical of school performance.
But it did not at heart believe that shortcomings sprang from unimaginative
administration and insensitive teaching; it preferred to lay the blame on
inadequate resources. To the school system, the projects were a fund-raising
resource, whose independent views on education practice were a tiresome
impertinence, directing money into peripheral experiments.

The strategy of intervention depended on the authority of the project itself
to sustain the ideals of reform. In principle, this authority was protected by
the endorsement of community leadership, whose prior commitment was a
condition of the grant. But since the momentum of negotiation forced the
funders to release their funds before the conflicts had been truly settled,
the project itself could become a no-man's land over which more powerful

interests fought for supremacy—an executive without a constituency of its own. Even where its authority was not so wholly demoralized, it might still find that agency participation had not, after all, educated officials into any enthusiasm for self-critical innovation.

The experience of PCCA [Philadelphia Council for Community Advancement] has already shown how hard it could be to establish an effective authority behind the project and how, in its absence, endemic conflicts inhibited a coherent program. Not that the failure was necessarily final. Coalitions that seemed at the outset hopelessly divided among themselves, sometimes—as in Syracuse for instance—were once more pulled together. But though the breakdowns may be only stages in a long drawn-out process of reintegration, they demonstrate the vulnerability of the funders' strategy.

Characteristically, conflicts arose—as in Philadelphia—over the balance of authority within the planning process, the appointment of a director, or the exclusion of powerful interests. Sometimes they frustrated the project from its inception, blocking any agreement acceptable to the funding agencies; more often, it distracted attention from the development of programs, or insidiously undermined the project's ideal to save an appearance of community action. The experiences of Chicago, Cleveland, and Los Angeles illustrate the breakdown of the strategy at each of these stages. In all these cities, the issue turned essentially on the control of the project, not the nature of its proposed reforms.

CHICAGO: CITIZENS AGAINST POLITICIANS

In Chicago, an elite group, formed at first as a neighborhood advisory committee, was led to challenge the political control of the project. They were determined enough to force a stalemate, and the project was virtually abandoned at the end of the President's Committee's planning grant.

The district selected for the Chicago project adjoined the Gold Coast, and most of the members of the local community advisory board were not drawn from the slum residents, but their wealthy neighbors. The bias of the Community Board was conservative, and its attitudes towards racial segregation divided. But it was united in its hostility to overweening political control. "Politicians don't want citizens to help themselves," the chairman protested, "they want citizens to be beholden to them, especially at election time. People are taught to be beholden to precinct captains. Elected officials fear that citizen participation may grow in such a fashion so as to be competitive with their political interests." On this fundamental issue, the project eventually foundered.

At the outset, the project's planners had not intended to involve citizen's groups as a challenge to the political establishment. The neighborhood panels and the Community Board were to inform the Joint Youth Development Committee—to which the project was responsible—of their understanding and experience of the "area's youth-related problems," suggest programs, and "develop attitudes of receptivity and support for the demonstration plan." But as the planners became increasingly alienated from public agencies, they turned to the Community Board for more militant support.

The project's professional staff and its technical advisors had based their plans on school reforms. The schools were "a key focal point of entrance into community life to effect fundamental change." "If the school's goals can be restructured beyond academic achievement to induce socialization, it then offers an effective basis for social change." But the school superintendent rejected this conception of community schools, resenting the implied interference of the community in the management of education. The director of the Youth Welfare Commission, an influential member of the Youth Development Committee, also interpreted the encouragement of neighborhood organization as a threat to the mayor's control, especially as its leaders included political opponents. The project's planning director, caught between the President's Committee, which supported his conception, and the powerful public officials of Chicago who rejected it, turned to the Community Board.

The chairman of the Community Board, misled—as he later complained—by the project's staff, overestimated the authority assigned it in the planning structure. But when the Youth Development Committee and the school superintendent sought to curb it, the board came together in a determined stand against an overbearing bureaucracy. "There is some irony in the situation," as a newspaper report remarked.

YDC staff members tried hard to get the Near-North Lincoln Park residents interested and involved in planning the project. They succeeded so well that now the citizens have come to think of the project as "ours"—and want to keep it that way. They fear that recent action placing it under the control of a city agency, the Commission on Youth Welfare, means their voices will be cut down to a whisper, if not stilled altogether. . . . The issue of how citizens should participate—as doers or as mere endorsers—goes to the very heart of the federal delinquency control program.[8]

"This issue," noted a President's Committee staff report, "has become a wide open fight between the representatives of the City and the Community Board, . . ."

The Board finally repudiated the city altogether. Armed with the sympathy of the local newspaper, and a community organization of its own, it went in search of funds for an independent project. The President's Committee, unable to accept either a city program without citizen support, or a community program divorced from public agencies, extricated itself from Chicago with a token grant.

The planning of the Chicago project was also inhibited by another characteristic source of breakdown. The competition for control may be disguised under an involved organizational structure which does not resolve rivalry. Charles Livermore, director of the Commission on Youth Welfare, saw the project as falling under his jurisdiction. But the mayor assigned responsibility to his deputy commissioner of city planning, who was also cochairman of the Commission. Though the Commission became the nucleus of a new, more comprehensive planning committee, its director was bypassed. Such a compromise between jurisdictional claims within City Hall was not really viable. When the deputy planning commissioner resigned, for personal reasons, Livermore was able to secure control. But by then, the professional planning staff was already committed to a conception which Livermore mistrusted, and the conflict with the local community began to evolve.

We have seen in Philadelphia how an elaborate system of task forces was devised to reconcile conflicting interests, and how the ambiguity of the compromise left the issues unresolved. The reformers' manipulation of the power structure was most often frustrated by the instability of the coalitions they engendered. The boards of the new agencies might be broadly representative, the planning procedures drawn out. But when crucial decisions were to be made, the forms of cooperation were too vaguely delineated, and too half-heartedly endorsed, to arbitrate an agreed solution. The basis of the project's authority might thus never be clearly established.

CLEVELAND: THE MAYOR AGAINST THE SCHOOL SYSTEM

In Cleveland, a struggle between City Hall and the school system eventually destroyed the tenuous consensus on which the project had been founded. Cleveland Action for Youth was constituted under a board on which—besides the welfare federation and the juvenile courts—the county commissioners, city government, and the Board of Education were equally represented. At the end of the planning period, the board became locked in a conflict over the appointment of the director for the demonstration phase. The controversy had political overtones, pitting the mayor, who stood for the Independent Democrats, against his natural enemies, the Democratic school board and county commissioners. The chairman of the school board was seriously thinking of running against the mayor in the forthcoming elections on a white-backlash platform.

If the school system and the county welfare service were not to withdraw from the demonstration, a director acceptable to all parties had to be found. The mayor supported the director of the project's planning phase, while the schools pressed their own man. By way of compromise, the deputy superintendent of schools received the appointment, while the current director was relegated to his assistant. This division of responsibility between an experienced planner, who was politically unacceptable, and an inexperienced compromise candidate proved as unworkable in Cleveland as it had in Philadelphia. After much contention the associate director resigned.

The mayor regarded the compromise as a personal defeat, and opposed it when a formal vote was taken by the board. Local resident organizations protested that they had not been consulted in the appointment, and circulated a letter at the Board meeting expressing their sense of betrayal. Later, before a congressional subcommittee, they accused the director of being anti-Negro. The project's staff were also out of sympathy with their new chief, who had no previous experience of the project, and owed his loyalty to the school system—he retained his title of associate superintendent and saw the project essentially as a political asset in his bid to secure the superintendent's post when it fell vacant. Thus even the school system, once it had won control, continued to mistrust the project, since it recognized the disunity of the director and his staff. It refused, for instance, to supply information about its pupils, for fear that members of the project staff, actively engaged in the civil rights movement, would use the information against them. Its leadership was cautious and constraining and did not encourage a vigorous, innovative program. Finally, it threatened to abandon the project altogether, unless it diverted more of its resources to the schools' own, independent, compensatory education program.

The compromise appointment failed, then, to satisfy any interest. It alienated the mayor, the local residents, and the project's staff, leaving control to a school system that sought only to exploit it for their own ends and never trusted it. The board which should have lent their authority to the new agency remained uncommitted, and acted chiefly to protect their own interests. A federal report asked in despair: "Does anybody really feel loyalty to the project, as an entity, apart from its instrumental use in funding and in personal and institutional ambitions?"

Wherever community action bases its authority on a coalition of institutional power which is not already secure, the project seems to reach a point at which it can no longer contain the rivalries it has stimulated. At the outset, the proposal appeals to every interest frustrated by scarce resources and constricted function. But as the project takes shape, it begins to appear as a new jurisdiction in its own right, and not merely as a means to escape the limitations of the old. It threatens those who cannot control it, provoking rather than appeasing latent conflict. The project's original aims then become unrealizable. If no interest is strong enough to capture the project, the plans break down in stalemate; if one succeeds, it alienates the others. Either way, the project is no longer viable as an expression of community action. When such an outcome threatens, the project may try to save itself by abandoning its pretentions to integrated reform. So for instance, by conciliating powerful interests, the Los Angeles project survived and even grew. But it no longer fulfilled the ideals for which the President's Committee had supported it.

Los Angeles: All Against Coordination

The Los Angeles Youth Opportunities Board formally constituted a limited metropolitan government, without the power to tax, created under the joint powers agreement. It brought together five separate jurisdictions: city, county, their two school systems, and the state. The city was represented by the mayor's executive assistant, who served as chairman, the county by the probation department, and the state by the employment service. Of these, only the mayor was eager for the board to evolve a coordinated program. Since the probation, health, and welfare services of the city were controlled by county, not city, government, the mayor hoped to secure a voice in the development of the city's social services through his representation on the board. The board might also be able to implement policies that his own City Council had rejected. The council were generally conservative, and suspicious of federal or foundation grants as potentially subversive. They had voted against a community renewal program and were unsympathetic to research on the city's social problems—"We don't need to have information on how many niggers are moving into my district." The mayor's executive assistant hoped to go round their opposition by funding, through the Youth Opportunities Board, a comprehensive data-collection system. This storehouse of knowledge was to provide the basis of an integrated policy, despite the council's hostility to any systematic study of human needs.

The other jurisdictions represented on the board were, however, indifferent to these larger issues. The county treated the board as a personal interest of the county supervisor, whose constituency lay in the city's Mexican-American community. The county administrator believed the board was primarily to deal with school dropouts—which was not a concern of county government—and associated it so little with wider problems, that he made his own independent study of delinquency prevention. The county's official representative on the board, the head of the probation department, was more interested, but out of sympathy with the broadly preventive approach to delinquency which the President's Committee had promoted. Finally, the county had earlier established a Community Services Department which, though it was not highly regarded, might be revived as an alternative to the Youth Opportunities Board whenever it was politically convenient.

The city school system had its own agenda of reform. It had already established a special unit for compensatory education and had unsuccessfully approached the Ford Foundation for a grant under the great cities' schools program. It wanted to use the board as a source of funds for its own plans, without interference. The county school system was less involved, since its role in the city was not administrative; it merely ensured that state educational standards were met.

If the other members of the board were largely indifferent to its aims, the employment service was even hostile. It was solely concerned to protect its own jurisdiction and prevent a direct relationship between the federal government and the board's employment project. Not that the employment service had made up its mind to start a special program for disadvantaged youth itself. It did not want to become still further identified with jobs of low prestige; and since it was compensated by the federal government according to the number of placements, it might suffer financially by taking on difficult applicants who preoccupied the time of its staff for little reward. At the same time, it was unwilling to surrender any of its responsibilities.

In these circumstances, the parties to the coalition could not be expected to subordinate their interests to the new agency. Though the mayor was seeking an instrument of coordinated planning, his hopes derived from the very factors that made them insubstantial—the weakness of his own position and the limited jurisdiction of city government. The project never, for instance, risked antagonizing the schools by putting forward educational proposals of its own. An administrator from the city school system was co-opted as the project's director, and the programs that evolved, while acceptable to the schools, were scarcely innovative. "The city schools program will be a problem," observed the President's Committee, more concerned with reform than political accommodation, "because of the Deputy Director's lack of program skills and his rigidity about change." Its fears were confirmed: the programs were later described in a federal report as "discrete and remedial services with little emphasis on classroom or curriculum revisions."

As another concession to the self-interest of established power, the project placed its youth employment service in the Mexican-American community of East Los Angeles, where the county supervisor sought his votes, rather than in the Watts section—the project's target area. The employment service was not, however, reconciled, and once it became clear that the training programs were not to be conducted under their auspices, as their program, they raised a series of obstacles. The training program could only be approved after the employment service had surveyed the labor market to prove "a reasonable expectation of employment." By a rigid interpretation of this criterion, the employment service brought the planning of any training program to a standstill for several months, until the state governor and congressional leaders intervened. Even after half a year, the only course approved was for clerical training, which seems especially unsuited to a Spanish-speaking neighborhood where half the young jobseekers could reportedly neither read nor write.[9]

By its conciliatory tactics, the Youth Opportunities Board escaped destructive conflicts and reconciled jurisdictional rivalries more successfully than many projects. But, though it ran several programs of its own, it was essentially a broker, channeling federal funds to support institutional ambitions. The inadequacy of this bland evasion of more fundamental reform was tragically underlined when in 1965 the project's target area was overrun by five days of rioting in which thirty-four people lost their lives.

The experience of Los Angeles, Cleveland, Chicago, and Philadelphia suggests that community action projects, as the Ford Foundation and the President's Committee conceived them, could not after all master the jurisdictional rivalries which pervade city government in America. In practice, institutions remained stubbornly self-interested, and their formal endorsement of the project did not guarantee any commitment to its aims. The new agency merely provided another setting in which to deploy the struggle for power and generated, not a self-sustaining process of reform, but a self-sustaining conflict over the control of reform. This was a profound and disturbing issue which no one was in a position to resolve, but which could not be ignored so long as the project remained true to its innovative spirit. Sooner or later, it found itself forced to choose between its principles and survival.

The evidence of less conflict-ridden projects does not contradict this disappointing conclusion. Community action seems nowhere to have brought into being a more unified power structure than had already been created. It could only extend the resources of an established coalition. In New Haven, Oregon, and some of the North Carolina communities, a concerted leadership already held effective control. In New Haven, for instance, before CPI came into being the mayor had already established the Redevelopment Agency and reinvigorated the school system by appointing a progressive school board under the chairmanship of Mitchell Sviridoff, later director of CPI. Community Progress was thus one further component in an executive-centered coalition under the leadership of City Hall. CPI did not create a new consensus; its success was a reflection of consensus that had earlier been achieved. When it ventured outside the mayor's sphere of influence it succumbed to the same conflicts that the other cities encountered. Its legal program, for instance, ran against the opposition of the Bar Association. Under this attack the members of the bar co-opted on to CPI's planning committee retreated into neutrality, and the program waited upon the reconstruction of a viable consensus of legal support.[10]

Similarly, if Oakland achieved more than Los Angeles, this was partly because the city manager had previously brought county, city, and schools together in the Associated Agencies and partly because the settlement houses had been deeded to the city in the 1920's, establishing in the recreation department a tradition of cooperation between social work, recreation, and the schools. Even so, the Oakland Interagency Project nearly foundered in conflict in its first two years and recovered only by compromising the funder's intentions. The programs remained encapsulated within their departments, with little relationship to each other or even to their own administrative system; some were merely an extension of conventional practice; and the City Council never came to endorse the project's aims with any enthusiasm, or to vote any substantial financial support. In Boston, the project reflected the position of an independently minded mayor, who was not beholden to a political machine and sought a broader basis of power through the Redevelopment Authority and ABCD, whose professional administrators were influential in their own right yet owed their opportunity to him. But faced with the ethnic and religious tensions of the city, the independence and power of the voluntary agencies, and the difficulty of reconciling social and physical planning, Mayor Collins had not yet established an underlying unity. He could protect ABCD from attack upon its legitimacy as an instrument of social planning, [but] he could not ensure it the authority to realize its plans. ABCD therefore promised more than in its first few years it was able to fulfill—its reports [are] a reasoned apology for continual frustrating delays.

As a means of reintegrating community leadership about a concerted program, the strategy seems, then, to have proved ineffectual. The projects depended on whatever unity had already been achieved and could only nominally enlarge its scope. Where did the fundamental weakness of the strategy lie?

Were the grants too small? If the funding agencies had offered more, they would, of course, have given communities a greater incentive to meet the criteria of concerted action. But they would also have raised the stakes in the competition for control of the project's resources. As the experience of Philadelphia shows, once the poverty program opened a prospect of much larger grants, the conflicts became sharper. Mayors everywhere began to assert the authority of City Hall, and even state government was alerted to look to its interests. If the gray area of delinquency projects had been put forward on a larger scale, they might have been forced, from the first, to accommodate even more to institutional pressure. A marginal addition to the city's resources stood at least a chance of insinuating an influence for change without intruding a challenge to bureaucratic authority too obvious to overlook.

Were the funding agencies too impatient? If they had guaranteed support for six years, instead of three or less, the projects could have worked gradually toward a viable place in the structure of community power, secure at least in their immediate future. But the funders would then have left themselves with even fewer sanctions to protect their intentions; as it was, they were virtually helpless to insist on their principles once they committed their support. They could reject a specific program proposal or return drafts for reconsideration, but they could not ensure that the spirit of their grant was honored. If larger grants would have provoked more unmanageable conflicts, longer grants might only have enabled more projects to survive to confound their promoters' ideals, as they drifted into uncontroversial programs subservient to institutional ambitions.

The crucial flaw seems to have lain, not in the financial inducement, but in the insistence on formal coordination as a prerequisite rather than an outcome of changes in the power structure. Independent authorities were to commit themselves at the outset to the principles of a planning procedure which none of them could individually control. The plans were to evolve from an analysis that deliberately disregarded established boundaries of service, and none could know whether, if he were to allow the logic of the procedure to take its course, he would end up with greater responsibilities or less. In assuming that participation in an innovative agency would lead to a sacrifice of sectional interests, the strategy misjudged institutional motives. The project opened an opportunity to advance all manner of institutional claims; it did not follow that those who were disappointed would gracefully subordinate their ambitions to the plans that evolved. When it comes to the point, no one voluntarily surrenders power. Personal ambition apart, loyalty to the organization he serves makes any agency director honorably reluctant to compromise the responsibility entrusted to him. Where the pressure to cooperate is strong, he safeguards his autonomy by seeking to control the policy-making or, if this fails, subverts its intentions when they threaten his own. These tacit reservations and maneuvers for control undermine the cooperative endeavor.

The realignment of power and policy must, then, be achieved first, and this depends as much on new men as new ideas. No formal procedure for integrated planning can persuade independently powerful executives to abandon their prerogatives. Reform must await the opportunity to promote its own supporters to positions of authority. So, for instance, to realize his educational plans, Mayor Lee had first to get his own nominees onto the New Haven Board of Education, and they in turn had to wait for an opening to appoint a new assistant school superintendent.[11] The authority of CPI's programs rested on ten years of patient recruitment through which a group of like-minded reformers had been gradually insinuated into key positions.

The experience of community action suggests that there are no short cuts. A project board room is no magic circle, where long-standing conflicts dissolve under the spell of planning. On the contrary, it introduces new hopes and fears, new ambiguities, which can harden resistance and complicate intrigue, embittering old rivalries. In any city where the foundations of a viable coalition have not yet been laid, innovation from within the power structure can only make ground by manipulating vulnerable institutions one by one, not by confronting all at once the issue of jurisdictional autonomy. This alternative strategy has, in fact, been supported by the Ford Foundation in Kansas City, and succeeded where a gray-area project would probably have failed.

The Kansas City Association of Trusts and Foundations was formed in the 1940's to combine the resources of four local philanthropies and redirect their grants from the relief of symptoms to a concern with the roots of social problems. Under its executive director, Homer Wadsworth, the association built up a network of influence that did not depend on any formal structure. The office itself consisted only of the director, his assistant, and two secretaries. But through staff in agencies its supported, through its board members, through the committees on which Homer Wadsworth sat, the association established its own constituency for reform.

Its strategy typically exploited the weakness of a potentially valuable institution. A charity hospital, for instance, is in difficulties—out-of-date and short of funds. At this point, Wadsworth or one of the association's supporters is likely to turn up on the board of the failing agency and suggest an evaluative study. The association offers to meet the cost of the analysis, which—naturally enough—is contracted to Community Studies, a research organization founded and subsidized by the association. The evaluative report sets out a sweeping plan of reorganization, which rescues the institution from its financial embarrassment, replaces its administrative head, and adapts it to the association's conception of the city's needs. Re-established on a new footing, the agency may become a cornerstone of the association's larger plans.

Perhaps the most ambitious of the association's schemes concerned the University of Kansas City. Founded unluckily in 1933 by the Methodist Church, the university had become increasingly indebted, and its board of trustees was at a loss. Homer Wadsworth appeared on the Missouri Council of Higher Education, equipped with a plan prepared by Community Studies.

The university was to become a campus of the University of Missouri system, while the present trustees were to remain as a fund-raising body, with the task of finding one and a half million dollars every two years for faculty salaries and improvements. The plan was approved, and the trustees have already raised over a million dollars, agreed to a higher salary for a new chancellor, and encouraged new departments. The university is growing in both size and quality and appeals no less to local pride for being now a branch of the state system. At the same time, it has been drawn into the association's plans for a new medical complex to be built on one hundred acres cleared under urban renewal. The association's schemes have been, at times, as comprehensive as any gray-area project's programs; and just because it must manipulate without any formal power, the outcome seems often more radically integrative.

In 1961, encouraged by a grant of one and a quarter million from the Ford Foundation, the association began to develop a series of experimental demonstrations in the public schools—over whose board Wadsworth presided. These programs have been very similar to the gray-area projects—work study for likely dropouts, tutorials by college students, special scholarships, visiting teachers, nursery schools, curriculum changes, upgraded classes—but depended far more on the school budget and local financing. The association also helped to promote a reorganization of vocational education and, on a small scale, ways of finding jobs for high school dropouts.

As a means to institutional change, the association has engineered reforms as innovative as any gray-area project. As a means to overcome the handicaps of poverty, its educational programs have been as imaginative. As a stimulus to community concern, it has recruited local resources in support of innovation. Yet it has never sought to institutionalize a consensus of community leadership, nor to incorporate its reforming spirit in an operating agency.[12]

The association's experience in Kansas City does not prove that its strategy would work elsewhere, or with another executive. But it does suggest that— in a city that has traditionally lost most of its ablest talent, where leadership has often been lethargic, and segregationist attitudes still covertly widespread —the aims of the gray-area projects may be better realized by discrete political opportunism than by attempting to induce a coalescence of power. Such a strategy does not create leadership, but unobtrusively supplies it, manipulating the existing structure. It demands no prior commitment and threatens no jurisdiction. It does not predetermine the targets of reform or theorize its plans, but exploits its chances. This flexibility makes it less vulnerable, more resilient under attack, and surer of its goals.

But such a strategy takes time, and though the Ford Foundation could perhaps afford to work gradually, here and there, through agencies like the Kansas City Association, the President's Committee staff had to seize the moment of their political opportunity. By insisting on the creation of an instrument of comprehensive planning, they hoped to force the growth of a will to use it. Where, as in New Haven, a coalition of leadership was ready to absorb it, the new organization had scope to deploy its professional talent. But wherever the rivalries within the power structure had not been resolved, the intrusion of fresh resources to exploit only aggravated the conflicts. It seems then that very different strategies may be appropriate to different communities, and the search for a leverage for change must adapt very sensitively to time and place, without putting its trust in any one prescription.

Community action that rests upon the combined authority of elected officials and established institutions may have to be content to limit its scope to those cities whose power has already coalesced, or to that part of the power structure that had been brought under unified leadership. If neither of these alternatives is acceptable, it must turn to a less structured opportunism, patiently infiltrating positions of leadership. If this, too, cannot satisfy the urgent idealism of reform, community action must abandon the security of bureaucratic endorsement and seek a different kind of authority to legitimize its intervention.

NOTES

[1] This is not, of course, an account of any particular meeting, but a synthesis of impressions from many.

[2] Michael Crozier, *The Bureaucratic Phenomenon* (Chicago: University of Chicago Press, 1964), pp. 235–36.

[3] In an interview with the authors.

[4] "Policy Guides to the Presentation of Proposals for Funding Under Public Law 87–274" (Sept. 1963), p. 3.

[5] "The Federal Delinquency Program: Objectives and Operations Under the President's Committee on Juvenile Delinquency and Youth Crime and the Juvenile Delinquency and Youth Offenses Control Act of 1961" (Nov. 1962), p. 5.

[6] Sandford Kravitz, "The Implications of Governmental Participation in Health and Welfare Planning—Possibilities and Problems," speech to the New York State Association of Community Councils and Chests.

[7] Paul Ylvisaker, "Private Philanthropy in America," speech to the National Council of Community Foundations, May 1964.

[8] *Daily News,* Jan. 16, 1964.

[9] See Joseph L. Weinberg, "Evaluation Study of Youth Training and Employment Project, East Los Angeles" (Washington, D.C.: Department of Labor, Office of Manpower, Automation, and Training, Aug. 1964) (mimeo).

[10] The program was finally launched without the Bar Association's endorsement.

[11] See Robert Dahl, *Who Governs?* (New Haven: Yale University Press, 1961), pp. 205–14.

[12] When Kansas City came to put together a proposal to the Office of Economic Opportunity for a poverty program, this became a liability. The preparation of the proposal was bogged down in long drawn-out negotiations, which suggests that the association's work had ingeniously circumvented but not resolved the city's bureaucratic rivalries. The requirements of the poverty program may make its position altogether more difficult.

Index